AFTER PALMARES

AFTER

A BOOK IN THE SERIES RADICAL PERSPECTIVES:

A RADICAL HISTORY REVIEW BOOK SERIES

Series editors Daniel J. Walkowitz, New York University,

and Barbara Weinstein, New York University

PALMARES

DIASPORA, INHERITANCE, AND THE

AFTERLIVES OF ZUMBI · Marc A. Hertzman

DUKE UNIVERSITY PRESS

Durham and London 2024

© 2024 DUKE UNIVERSITY PRESS
All rights reserved
Printed and bound by CPI Group (UK) Ltd,
Croydon, CR0 4YY
Project Editor: Bird Williams
Designed by Matt Tauch
Typeset in MeropeBasic by Westchester Publishing Services

Library of Congress Cataloging-in-Publication Data
Names: Hertzman, Marc A., author.
Title: After Palmares : diaspora, inheritance, and the afterlives of Zumbi
    / Marc A. Hertzman.
Other titles: Radical perspectives.
Description: Durham : Duke University Press, 2024. | Series: Radical
    perspectives | Includes bibliographical references and index.
Identifiers: LCCN 2023047389 (print)
LCCN 2023047390 (ebook)
ISBN 9781478030522 (paperback)
ISBN 9781478026310 (hardcover)
ISBN 9781478059547 (ebook)
Subjects: LCSH: Zumbi, 1655–1695. | Maroons—Brazil—Palmares
    (Pernambuco) | Fugitive slaves—Brazil—Quilombo dos Palmares. |
    Fugitive slave communities—Brazil—Quilombo dos Palmares. | African
    diaspora. | Quilombo dos Palmares (Brazil)—History. | Palmares
    (Pernambuco, Brazil)—History—17th century. | BISAC: HISTORY /
    Latin America / South America | SOCIAL SCIENCE / Black Studies
    (Global)
Classification: LCC HT1129. P27 H47 2024 (print)
LCC HT1129. P27 (ebook)
DDC 981/.34—dc23/eng/20240414
LC record available at https://lccn.loc.gov/2023047389
LC ebook record available at https://lccn.loc.gov/2023047390

Cover art: Joan Blaeu, Praefecturae Paranambucae Pars Meridionalis,
1665 (detail)

For Ikuko and Kai

Perhaps the earth can teach us

as when everything seems dead

and later proves to be alive.

—PABLO NERUDA, "KEEPING QUIET"

A bird doesn't sing because it has an answer,

it sings because it has a song.

—MULTIPLE AUTHORS

CONTENTS

ACKNOWLEDGMENTS

Like anyone completing a book these days, I struggle to adequately account for, let alone fully thank, all the people who held me together and made research and writing viable and meaningful pursuits during the COVID-19 pandemic. Much of the early work and thinking about this book began before the pandemic and coincided with my time as Director of Undergraduate Studies in the history department at the University of Illinois, a position that brought me face-to-face with some of the best and also some of the most challenging aspects of higher education. Counterbalancing the financial pressures felt throughout the humanities and often intensely so at public universities were the incredible intellect, spirit, and generosity of my family, friends, colleagues, and students. Without these remarkable people, I would not have been able to complete, much less find purpose in, writing this book.

My first individual debts of gratitude are owed to those who read the entire manuscript and offered indispensable critiques and observations. Kathryn (Kate) de Luna's contributions to this project are too many to list in their entirety. Endlessly generous and insightful, she read, conversed, and critiqued, lending brilliant ideas and instruction throughout; I could not have written this book without her wisdom and insights. Yesenia Barragan provided an incredibly generous and thoughtful reading full of sharp and powerful insights that improved the manuscript immensely. Barbara Weinstein, mentor and friend, gave a close reading replete with crucial critiques that helped push the project over the finish line in much better shape than it was before she read it; I am eternally grateful. I was also very fortunate to workshop the manuscript with Marcus de Carvalho, Flávio Gomes, and Silvia Lara, scholars whose works have shaped my own for years. I benefited enormously from the different ways that they engaged my work before, during, and after the workshop. Alejandro de la Fuente encouraged this project along in ways that I cannot repay adequately, but for which I am especially thankful. Sean Mannion offered meticulous copyediting and insightful suggestions, and the team at Duke University Press was similarly phenomenal. Gisela Fosado has given me unparalleled support and encouragement for years, which made the editorial process intellectually stimulating and thoroughly enjoyable. I also thank Alejandra (Ale) Mejía, and Bird Williams for the enormous amount of time and energy they put into preparing the manuscript for publication. From England, Geoff Wallace drew expert maps that are central to the histories narrated in the book.

Other friends and colleagues gave precious time by reading chapters or writing letters of support for funding (and sometimes both): Paulina Alberto (who read the full manuscript and lent her typically brilliant insights), George Reid Andrews, Ana Lucia Araujo, Teresa Barnes, Jacob Blanc, Dain Borges, Larissa Brewer-García, Claudia Brosseder, Antoinette Burton, Jerry Dávila, Brodwyn Fischer, Maria Gillombardo, Kalle Kananoja (who not only read a chapter draft but also was incredibly generous in sharing archival notes), Craig Koslofsky, Erik McDuffie, Yuko Miki, Mauro Nobili, Cynthia Oliver, Lara Putnam, Dana Rabin, Tatiana Seijas, Carol Symes, Shelley Weinberg, and James Woodard. James Sweet has generously fielded questions and bounced ideas back and forth for years, shaping the project (as his scholarship has, too) in innumerous ways. Severino Albuquerque taught me Portuguese many years ago and continued to teach and help during this project. Jerry Dávila has been a valued colleague and coeditor. John Marquez has been an incisive interlocutor, first as a student and now as a colleague; he contributed in multiple ways to the project, including as part of an Omohundro Institute Coffee Table on Language as Archive and Method. In that seminar, led by Kate de Luna, I was fortunate to count as colleagues John Balz, Alejandra Dubcovsky, Michaela Kleber, Virginia Reinburg, and James Sidbury. I also had the good fortune to present, test out, and exchange ideas at institutions and conferences, including at Brown University, Harvard University, the Lapidus Center for the Study of Transatlantic Slavery, Pennsylvania State University, the University of California at Los Angeles, the Universidade Federal da Paraíba, the Universidade Federal do Rio Grande do Norte, the

University of Wisconsin-Madison, Wesleyan University, and the 2022 meeting of the Associação Nacional de História—Seção Pernambuco.

In Illinois, I am grateful to have such a rich intellectual environment and fantastic group of friends and colleagues. I shared drafts at many campus venues, including the Center for African Studies, the Center for Advanced Study, the Center for Latin American and Caribbean Studies, the History Department Workshop, the Lemann Center for Brazilian Studies, and the Premodern World Reading Group. I also counted on the following friends, colleagues, and interlocutors, in addition to those already mentioned: Tariq Ali, Flávia Andrade, Mary Arends-Kuenning, Eugene Avrutin, Marsha Barrett, Dave Beck, Merle Bowen, James Brennan, Adrian Burgos, Tamara Chaplin, Teri Chettiar, Amanda Ciafone, Clare Crowston, Ken Cuno, Kim Curtis, Augusto Espiritu, Peter Fritzsche, Poshek Fu, Daniel Gilbert, Matt Gilbert, Faye Harrison, Waïl Hassan, Kristin Hoganson, Rana Hogarth, Nils Jacobsen, John Karam, Diane Koenker, Rosalyn LaPier, Joe Love, Ralph Mathisen, Bob Morrissey, Kevin Mumford, Yuridia Ramírez, Leslie Reagan, Laurie Reynolds, David Sepkoski, Michael Silvers, Gisela Sin, Antonio Sotomayor, Maureen Warren, and Rod Wilson. Of all my wonderful friends in Urbana-Champaign, a special shoutout is due to John Randolph for his generosity, humor, and kindness, and soccer, chess, and beer-brewing enthusiasm and expertise. Graduate students in the history department and from other programs on campus have provided priceless insights and engagement during the research and writing, neither of which would have been possible without the staff who handled and solved logistical nightmares: Elis Artz, Tom Bedwell, Cindy Gilbert, Nate Oliveira, Kasia Szremski, and Dawn Voyles. Caroline da Rocha Birnfeld did great work as a research assistant.

Thanks also go to friends and colleagues at other institutions: Andy Apter, Rebecca Atencio, Judy Bieber, Kathryn Bishop, Alex Borucki, Victoria Broadus, Celso Castilho, Sidney Chalhoub, Amy Chazkel, Camila Cowling, Robyn Derby, Chris Dunn, Marshall Eakin, Rebecca Earle, Marcela Echeverri, Anne Eller, Roquinaldo Ferreira, Ada Ferrer, Cécile Fromont, Jessica Graham, James Green, Keila Grinberg, Frances Hagopian, Andy Kirkendall, Hendrik Kraay, Elizabeth Landers, Jane Landers, Hal Langfur, Jeff Lesser, Dan Magaziner, Bryan McCann, Teresa Meade, Alida Metcalf, Ian Read, Matthew Restall,

Gabriel de Avilez Rocha, Tom Rodgers, Anadelia Romo, Sarah Sarzynski, Kara Schultz, Kirsten Schultz, Terri Snyder, Amara Solari, Jared Staller, Elizabeth Sutton, Vikram Tamboli, John Thornton, Zeb Tortorici, Sarah J. Townsend, David Wheat, and Daryle Williams.

The research and writing could not have happened without generous institutional funding. In spite of the aforementioned challenges and demands placed on public universities, the University of Illinois offered generous resources that allowed me to complete this project. In the history department, I have received material and intellectual support. The Campus Research Board provided a subvention to support the maps and other publication costs, and the funding I received as a Conrad Humanities Scholar was pivotal, as was a semester off as Fellow at the Center for Advanced Study (CAS), which allowed me to make a crucial final push. I am ever thankful to Masumi Iriye for her support at CAS. A Summer Stipend from the National Endowment for the Humanities was also critical for the project's completion. Chapter 7 is a modified version of my article, "The 'Indians of Palmares': Conquest, Insurrection, and Land in Northeast Brazil," *Hispanic American Historical Review* 103, no. 3 (August 2023): 424–60. Copyright 2023, Duke University Press. All rights reserved. Republished by permission of the publisher.

In Brazil, as always, the generosity bestowed on me was much greater than what I feel capable of repaying. In João Pessoa, Carla Moraes has been an amazing friend and collaborator. Solange Rocha and Matheus Guimarães were similarly kind and generous, as were archivists in the city and folks throughout Paraíba, including Professors Lúcia Júlio and Waldeci Chagas; their students—Maria de Fátima de Sales Silva, Rogério Chaves da Silva, Severino Ramos Santana da Silva, and Murilo Raili—who taught me a great deal; residents of Caiana dos Crioulos; and José Avelar Freire. In Rio Grande do Norte, I thank Carmen Alveal, who has helped in innumerous ways, and Lindemberg Araújo, Daliana Cascudo, Julie Cavignac, Thiago Alves Dias, Danielle Bruna Alves Neves, Tyego Franklim da Silva, Antônio Tenório, and the residents of Zumbi, first and foremost Damiana de Oliveira Silva for her help and many interventions, and others in the community who were kind enough to sit for interviews with Damiana and me. Special thanks also go to Sérgio Marques Caetano in Sibaúma for doing the same and to Elenize Trindade Pereira and Marcelo Igor, who provided indispensable geographic information systems work. In Pernambuco, I thank George Cabral, Marcus de Carvalho, Mariana Albuquerque Dantas, Luana Ribeiro, Edson Silva, and the wonderful staffs at archives, especially the Arquivo Público Estadual Jordão Emereciano, the Instituto Arqueológico Histórico e Geográfico Pernambucano, and the Museu da Cidade de Recife. In Alagoas, Celso Brandão, Aruã Lima, Danilo Luiz Marques, Luana Teixeira, and, here too, the wonderful archivists, including Quel Lira and the staff at the Instituto Geográfico e Histórico de Alagoas, and everyone at the Arquivo Público de Alagoas and the Museu Théo Brandão. I am also grateful to many others elsewhere in Brazil, including Ana Barone, Juliana Bonomo, Rafael do Nascimento Cesar, Renato Vargas Chaves, Felipe Aguiar Damasceno, Dmitri Cerboncini Fernandes, Elisa Frühauf Garcia, Antônio Sérgio Guimarães, Nadya Guimarães, Renata Lemos, Ana Gabriella dos Santos de Lima, Estevam Martins, John Victor de Oliveira and the Instituto do Ceará, Gino Negro, Arabela Oliven, Ruben Oliven, Ian Prates, João Reis, Gustavo Rossi, Alexandra Lima da Silva, and Giovana Xavier. From Portugal via Zoom and email during the pandemic, João Paulo Salvado offered generous guidance, and Ana Maria Leitão Bandeira at the Arquivo da Universidade de Coimbra was amazingly patient and helpful.

I am especially grateful for family: Jeri and Rachel Hertzman in New Mexico; David, Emme, Jackson, Josh, and Mitchell Blasingame in St. Louis and Pittsburgh; Alex, Harrison, and Laura Hertzman in Colorado and Maryland; and Mayumi and Yukihiro Asaka, whose generosity, delicious food, and exciting travel itineraries have made Japan feel like home. This book is dedicated to my life partner, Ikuko Asaka, and our son, Kai Sydel Asaka-Hertzman. Kai, who was born as the project was taking shape, has brought unimaginable joy to our home and has grown from the most adorable baby to the most remarkable, compassionate, brilliant, and funny baseball-basketball-piano-soccer-playing young man. For the last two decades, Ikuko has buoyed me. Her incredible intellect and love as partner and parent far exceed what I am able to express here. At the dinner table, in the kitchen, in the car, and during walks and hikes in Illinois, Kansai, and national forests and parks, she listened to and shaped with her always brilliant insights and thoughts most of the ideas that form this book. Writing about afterlives, I thought and wished every day that this life—with her and Kai—could last forever.

A NOTE ON LANGUAGE

Black rebels. Fugitives. Mocambos and quilombos. These are among the many labels that have been used for four centuries to refer to the place known as Palmares and the people who lived there. Each word has a backstory. Though their multiple and changing meanings are discussed in the chapters that follow, a few words about the conventions I use are in order here. Portuguese colonial officials who wrote many of the documents used in this book often referred to the people of Palmares (or "Palmar") as *negros* or pretos. Both words may be translated into English as "Black," though racial categories in Brazil are more numerous and often different than in the United States. Today, the Brazilian census uses two primary categories to recognize people of African descent: preto and pardo. The dictionary definition of pardo is "between white and Black," and, to many, *negro* encompasses both preto and pardo.[1] In Brazil, as in the United States, racial labels have been hurled with venom toward people of African descent, who have reclaimed some terms — *negro*, for example — with pride.[2] The contested contemporary meanings of these words necessarily inform how we write about historical categories.

As Elise A. Mitchell notes, though "semantics" will not "solve" racism, it is at the same time paramount to address the fact that "racial grammars are always steeped in history and more political than they appear on the surface."[3] Historians seek to make sense of this and accurately render these terms while working with what Paulina Alberto aptly calls "the compromised, deficient, indeed toxic vocabularies bequeathed by legacies of racial slavery."[4] I strive to remain faithful to my sources and, when not quoting directly from them, attempt to reflect something approaching consensus among Brazilians who call themselves Afro-Brazilian (afro-brasileiro), African-descended or Afro-descended (afrodescendente), Black (*negro* and preto), and, in some cases, pardo. Alongside these imperfect translations into English, I generally leave pardo untranslated and do the same with *mulato*, a term that also denotes racial mixture but, appearing regularly in historical documents, is used much less today.[5] These words are also gendered, and Portuguese often defaults to masculine, generally denoted by words ending in -o. I sometimes use "*negro/a*" and similar constructions to avoid that default and its many implications.

Branco/a, "white," also appears in my sources, though with less frequency, a telling absence that indicates how whiteness became increasingly normalized at the top of the racial ladder as the history of Palmares unfolded.[6] While the sources I use almost always identify Black, Indigenous, and mixed-race people as such, they just as often leave "white" unsaid. I use "European," "of European descent," and similar terms, though these are also imperfect choices, as there were, of course, many people in Europe who were not white. But even if imperfect, explicitly signaling whiteness helps account for the documentary silences that leave white lineage unremarked and naturalized. In doing so, I hope to provide insights about how whiteness and other racial categories were constructed and maintained. I also adopt what is becoming standard practice, employing "enslaved," rather than "slave," and "enslaver," rather than "master" or "owner," to reflect the processes and violence behind the creation and naturalization of these categories.[7] Most of the history discussed here took place in what are today Brazil and Angola, though the former did not become an independent nation until 1822 and the latter only in 1974. While the maps and descriptive material found in the following pages help delimit my areas of focus, as shorthand, I nonetheless use both names along with more specific ethnic, regional, and racial labels.[8]

My approach to terminology and language is inevitably shaped by my own identity. As a white, Jewish, male professor working at a university in the United States, I am an outsider many times over to the histories that animate this book. In attempting to tell a history that accounts for the long afterlives and violences of slavery and racism, I hope that awareness of my own privilege has helped me do some justice to the book's main protagonists: Africans and their descendants in Brazil. Like the vocabulary itself, the capitalization of racial categories presents another set of imperfect options. I agonized over this and other related questions, ultimately deciding that while there are good arguments to not capitalize any racial category or to capitalize all of them, I opted to capitalize "Black," "Indigenous," and "Native" to recognize the importance and meaning that doing so can carry today. Capitalizing "white" runs the risk of negating the effect and importance of capitalizing "Black" and "Indigenous," while leaving it uncapitalized threatens to further normalize whiteness. Faced with this conundrum and mindful of my own identity, I do not capitalize "white."[9]

The capitalization and spelling of "Zumbi" are also consequential. When capitalized here, "Zumbi" refers to one of three things: Palmares's most famous leader; place-names of lakes, rivers, streams, and small towns; and, on several occasions, a saintlike deity. When left uncapitalized, the word has multivalent meanings discussed over the course of the book, most notably a flying spirit of the dead and a deserted or isolated place. In some instances, the relationship between the meanings of big-Z Zumbi and little-z zumbi is unclear, and to reflect this I often employ a hybrid: Z/zumbi. Portuguese renderings of Z/zumbi varied in terms of not only capitalization, but also spelling. In many cases, it is difficult to discern whether colonial agents meant to refer to a distinct entity—Zambi, for example—or simply misunderstood or misrepresented African and diasporic creations and ideas. As I show, when referring to the Palmares leader, colonial officials used the letter /o/ more often than /u/, making "Zombi," not "Zumbi," the stated target of their missives and military forays. This is likely the product of colonial Portuguese spelling conventions, which frequently made /o/ and /u/ interchangeable, though future research may reveal more about the origins and meanings of "Zombi" and its relationship to Zumbi and other words and figures from the diaspora (for example, the Haitian "Zombie").

After Palmares plunges into the many manifestations and renderings of Z/zumbi, intent on thinking through what they may tell us about Palmares, diaspora, slavery, colonialism, and the afterlives of each. Though I generally employ what is now the standardized form (Zumbi), when directly quoting sources, I honor the original language (Zumby, Zombj, and other variations). A large number of documents from the seventeenth century have been transcribed, and while I use many of these, as we will see, some transcription errors have distorted and invented meanings, and so, as often as possible, I consulted originals alongside the transcriptions. When there are discrepancies or when it is otherwise meaningful to do so, I cite both the transcription and original source. Otherwise, I cite whichever version I consulted most.

While attempting to think about history from the perspectives of those who lived in Palmares, I follow the current consensus to refer to those people as Palmaristas. Though the label appears in some colonial sources, it is an approximation.[10] Most often, the people who wanted to destroy Palmares called its denizens "the Blacks of Palmares" — "*os negros* [or 'os pretos'] dos Palmares" — or "os *negros* levantados [or 'alevantados'] dos Palmares," a phrase that may be loosely translated as "the rebel Blacks of Palmares" or "the Black insurgents of Palmares." The verb levantar (and alevantar), which the adjective (a)levantado comes from, means to rise or raise up, suggesting an active state of rebellion and uprising. "Black rebels" and "insurgents" seem to be the best, if not entirely adequate, options in English to represent these meanings. As noted, it can also be confounding to label the would-be destroyers of Palmares. Though I generally use "Portuguese," "Dutch," "European," or "colonial," the armies sent to attack Palmares comprised Black, Indigenous, white, and mixed-race soldiers and officers, whose relationship to the European crowns attempting to colonize the Americas varied greatly.

In the English-language scholarship, it is common to use "fugitive" and "maroon" to refer to people who escaped slavery. The word "maroon" (and the act of marronage) comes from the Spanish word "cimarrón," which, Gabriel de Avilez Rocha writes, is itself "a Castilian neologism of the early colonial era, forced into the language through the strength of Native and Black insurrection."[11] The actions and characteristics most often associated with maroon communities — namely, flight from and resistance to slavery — are addressed over the course of the book, as are the meanings of mocambo and quilombo, multifaceted words whose most common meanings are roughly synonymous with "maroon settlement," "maroon community," or "maroon society." While I use these terms (and "maroon" and "fugitive"), I do so uneasily because they have tended to lock our conversations into the structures of slavery and what is often taken for granted to be its opposite: freedom. The uncounted many who were born in Palmares, and those who escaped to Palmares, also surely harbored other thoughts and objectives. It can be difficult to balance this with the reality that European colonialism and slavery nonetheless shaped their existence in undeniable ways, and I often revert to the terms used in the documents, though I hope that my discussion of language and linguistics throughout the text adds additional views and perspectives.

To simplify without losing sight of complexities, when directly quoting sources, I preserve original spellings and elsewhere employ the following practices. Some scholars assert that the names of several Palmares leaders began with "Gana" (a West Central African word for the title "lord") and not "Ganga" (a "priest," spirit medium, or other kind of "expert"). As I show in chapter 3, this hypothesis overdraws the existing evidence and unnecessarily (if somewhat unintentionally) sidelines the religious and spiritual roles these leaders likely held. To reflect a more capacious approach that accounts for the indeterminacy of the written record and allows for the likelihood that both titles were used in Palmares, I employ a hybrid: "Gan(g)a." The relationship between "nzumbi" and "zumbi" is slightly different from that between "Ganga" and "Gana" and requires a different standard. While "Gana" and "Ganga" refer to distinct West Central African concepts—one that historians of Palmares have elevated while discounting the other—the relationship between "nzumbi" and "zumbi" derives from sound changes and spelling rules. Portuguese ears were not always attuned to all the sounds used in Bantuphone languages. For example, Europeans often heard and rendered /ng/ and /nz/ simply as /g/ or /z/, contributing to an unwieldy collection of orthographies that was complicated further by unevenness and changes in Portuguese spelling norms. In Portuguese documents, West Central African spirits of the dead called nzumbi are frequently written as "zumbi," a reflection of the way that /nz/ sounds in Bantu languages that were often heard and written down as /z/ by the Portuguese. Though "zumbi" took on new meanings over time in Africa and especially in Brazil, for the most part, the difference between "nzumbi" and "zumbi" reflects this somewhat mundane fact. (The same is true for "nzambi" and "zambi.")

Accordingly, and also because scholars have not explicitly dismissed "nzumbi" in the same way that some have dismissed "Ganga," I employ "zumbi" and "nzumbi" and only rarely use "(n)zumbi."

At various points in the text, I use comparative historical linguistics to discuss reconstructed word roots, which are depicted with an asterisk followed by a dash (*-), for example, *-dùmb, for the proto-Bantu verb root "to rain." Following the standard practice in the field, the asterisk indicates that the word or root has been reconstructed, and the dashes show that additional morphemes (prefixes, suffixes, etc.) may be added to the root. Much like in English, where "hunt" can become "hunted" or "hunter," the same is true for the Bantuphone roots discussed here, and so the verb root *-dùmb- becomes *-dùmbí, a reconstructed noun for "rain." I discuss this methodology in more depth in appendix A. Throughout the book, I use the following characters to represent the seven-vowel proto-Bantu system: i ɪ e a o ʊ u.

Portuguese orthographic conventions varied during the colonial era and have changed multiple times since. This creates multiple challenges, including the case of authors whose names appear with multiple spellings. For clarity and consistency, I adopt contemporary rules for most authors' names. For example, I spell the eighteenth-century writer Sebastião da Rocha Pita's name as it would appear today, instead of as "Rocha Pitta," as it was often written while he was alive. I use the same approach for individuals who did not leave behind writing of their own, using "Manuel," for example, instead of "Manoel." I deviate from this usage in direct quotations and when citing and referring to historical documents, whose titles I render using the spellings, accents, and capitalizations as they appear in the original—preserving, for example, the title of Rocha Pita's 1730 book *Historia da America Portugueza* (which, using today's rules would be *História da América Portuguesa*).[12]

CHRONOLOGY

evidence of a large network of mocambos named for individual leaders.

1641   The seven-year Dutch occupation of parts of Angola begins.

1645   On March 21, an unnamed Palmares woman is murdered by a Dutch bugler.

1648   The Dutch occupation in Angola ends.

1651   The first phase of the so-called War of the Barbarians (Guerra dos Bárbaros) begins in Bahia.

1654   The Dutch occupation of northeast Brazil ends.

1670s   Written sources emerge of mocambos with leadership controlled by either family lineage or political succession. Gan(g)a Zumba is Palmares's most powerful leader, and Macaco is the dominant mocambo.

1678   Gan(g)a Zumba and Pernambuco's governor, Aires de Sousa de Castro, negotiate a peace accord.

1679–80   The accord fails, the leader known as Zumbi is at large, and Gan(g)a Zumba dies, with word spreading that he has been assassinated.

ca. 1680–95   The third major era of Palmares occurs. Zumbi is the most powerful and visible leader, and Serra da Barriga is the dominant settlement in Palmares. Its destruction in 1694 and his death in 1695 signal the formal end of the Palmares wars.

ca. 1681   Pedro Soeiro and other Palmares prisoners are in Portugal.

1682   The Portuguese Crown issues a decree regarding "the freedom, slavery, and punishment of the Blacks of Palmares."

1687   Domingos Jorge Velho is contracted to lead colonial efforts to destroy Palmares.

1687	The Guerra do Açu (the second, crucial, phase of the so-called War of the Barbarians) begins.
1694	In February, colonial forces defeat Palmaristas at Serra da Barriga, effectively ending the major military campaigns of the Palmares wars.
1693–95	Major discoveries of precious metals in Minas Gerais.
1695	On November 20, colonial forces kill Zumbi.

AFTER THE DEATH OF ZUMBI

1696–97	The governor of Pernambuco forces the people of Santo Amaro to resettle further into the Palmares backlands.
1697	Pedro Dias publishes *Arte da lingua de Angola*.
1700	After being temporarily relocated, the people of Santo Amaro return to their aldeia.
1700s–1720s	A significant number of Inquisition cases in Angola reference (n)zumbi spirits.
1710–11	The Guerra dos Mascates (the Peddlers War).
1714	Colonial forces capture Mouza, believed to be the last surviving leader of a seventeenth-century Palmares mocambo.
ca. 1720	The Guerra do Açu concludes.
1727	The Portuguese Crown grants land in Palmares to an unnamed Indigenous sergeant major and other unnamed Indigenous combatants.
1728–95	During this time period, land grants mention Zumbi place-names in Paraíba.
1730s	Rumors of Indigenous uprisings circulate in Paraíba and beyond.
1730	Sebastião da Rocha Pita publishes *Historia da America Portugueza*.

1731	A major battle occurs at Cumbi, a mocambo in Paraíba believed to have included members who formerly belonged to Palmares mocambos.
1746	The town council of Penedo (Alagoas) writes to the king of Portugal, requesting assistance against the "Indians of Palmar."
1756	Witchcraft charges are leveled against a West Central African man and West African woman in Minas Gerais for worshipping Zumbi and Saint Benedict.
1775	Portugal awards the final land grant connected to military service against Palmares.
1802	The Bishop of Olinda compares rebellious Indigenous people in Pernambuco to the Black rebels of Haiti.
1822	Brazil separates from Portugal, forming an independent monarchy.
1832–35	The Cabanada uprising shakes Pernambuco and Alagoas.
1850	The licit trade of enslaved Africans to Brazil formally ends. The Brazilian Land Law is passed.
1871	The Brazilian Free Womb Law is passed.
1884	Alfredo do Vale Cabral publishes his definitions of Z/zumbi and Zambi.
1885	Pedro Paulino da Fonseca publishes his "Posthumous Baptism" story.
1888	Slavery is abolished in Brazil.
1889	Brazil transforms its monarchy into a republic.
1904	Raimundo Nina Rodrigues publishes landmark essay on Palmares.
1963	Director Carlos Diegues's film *Ganga Zumba* debuts.

1964	The military seizes control of Brazil, beginning a twenty-one-year dictatorship.
1965	Luís da Câmara Cascudo pronounces zumbi dead in Angola.
1971	Grupo Palmares begins to observe November 20 as a singular day in Black history.
1984	Director Carlos Diegues's film *Quilombo* debuts.
1985	The military relinquishes control of Brazil.
1988	Article 68 in Brazil's new constitution guarantees rights to federally recognized quilombo communities.
	Serra da Barriga is declared a national monument.
	The Fundação Cultural Palmares (FCP) is created.
1995	Commemorations are held on the tricentennial of Zumbi's death.
1996	Zumbi is included in Brazil's *Livro dos Heróis e Heroínas da Pátria* (Book of Heroes and Heroines of the Fatherland).
2007	The Parque Memorial Quilombo dos Palmares atop Serra da Barriga is created.
2011	Congress declares November 20 the National Day of Zumbi and Black Consciousness.
2013	Manuel Lopes's descendant Francisco Galvão publishes a blog describing himself as a relative of the man who killed Zumbi.
2019	President Jair Bolsonaro appoints Sérgio Camargo as director of the FCP.
2023	President Luiz Inácio Lula da Silva appoints João Jorge Rodrigues as director of the FCP.

ATLANTIC
OCEAN

PACIFIC
OCEAN

SOUTH
AMERICA

Amazon R.

São Luis

Natal

PALMARES REGION

Olinda
Recife
Alagoas do Sul

Salvador

Diamantina

Mariana

São Paulo

Paraná R.

Rio de Janeiro

N

Colônia do Sacramento

Approximate Area in South America
under Portuguese Control, circa 1700

MAP FM.1 Portuguese America and the African Coast

Ilha da
Madeira

Canary Is.

AFRICA

Cacheu

Ouidah

Elmina

São Tomé

Congo R.

Nile R.

Loango
Mpinda
Cabinda

Luanda

ATLANTIC

OCEAN

Benguela

0   250 500   1,000   1,500   2,000
                                              Miles
                                              Kilometers
0   500   1,000   2,000   3,000

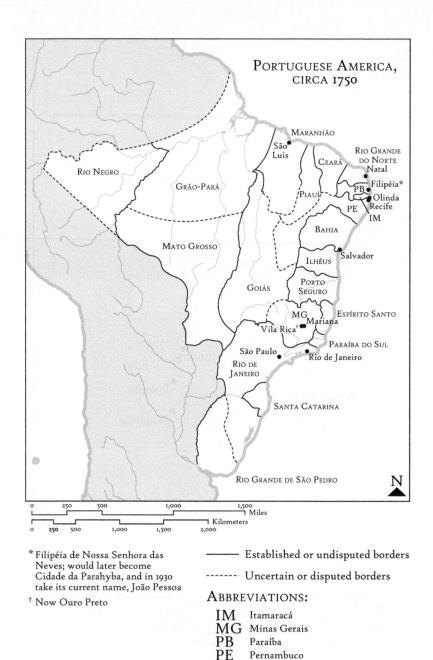

PORTUGUESE AMERICA, CIRCA 1750

MARANHÃO

São Luis

CEARÁ

RIO GRANDE DO NORTE
Natal

RIO NEGRO

GRÃO-PARÁ

PIAUÍ

PB

Filipéia*

PE

Olinda
Recife

IM

BAHIA

MATO GROSSO

ILHÉUS

Salvador

GOIÁS

PORTO SEGURO

MG
Mariana

ESPÍRITO SANTO

Vila Rica†

PARAÍBA DO SUL

São Paulo

Rio de Janeiro

RIO DE JANEIRO

SANTA CATARINA

RIO GRANDE DE SÃO PEDRO

N

| 0 | 250 | 500 | 1,000 | 1,500 | Miles |
| 0 | 250 | 500 | 1,000 | 1,500 | 2,000 | Kilometers |

* Filipéia de Nossa Senhora das
Neves; would later become
Cidade da Parahyba, and in 1930
take its current name, João Pessoa

† Now Ouro Preto

—— Established or undisputed borders

------- Uncertain or disputed borders

ABBREVIATIONS:

IM Itamaracá
MG Minas Gerais
PB Paraíba
PE Pernambuco

MAP FM.2 Portuguese America, circa 1750

INTRODUCTION   Layered Diasporas

The year 1695 holds great symbolic importance in Brazilian history. Though not quite as prominent as 1492 in Spanish and North America, or 1500, when Portugal "discovered" Brazil, 1695 represents a key turning point in the history of Portuguese America. That year, the recent discovery of precious metals in Minas Gerais reached a crescendo, launching Brazil's "Golden Age" and the promise of sparkling wealth to rival what Spain was extracting from its American colonies.[1] As the Portuguese plunged deeper inland in pursuit of riches, economic and political gravity shifted south, away from the captaincy of Pernambuco, a key slaving port in what would become northeast Brazil—and home to Palmares, one of the largest and longest-lasting maroon societies in the history of the Americas. The story of Palmares is also typically said to end in 1695—on November 20, to be precise—when colonial forces killed its most famous leader, Zumbi. Thanks to years of tireless work by Black activists, November 20 is now memorialized in Brazil as the National Day of Zumbi and Black Consciousness. Like 1492 and other iconic years, 1695 is a historical marker that is both illusory and impossible to ignore. It is impossible to ignore because a lot did change after 1695 but also illusory because while mining and the death of Zumbi facilitated important shifts, the histories behind both hallmarks did not simply or suddenly end. Enslaved and formerly enslaved people continued to arrive in, leave, and live and die in Pernambuco, and Palmares continued to play a significant role in colonial affairs. These simple facts confound neat chronologies.

Boundedness also often marks discussions of marronage. Though literature on the topic is rich, scholars tend to treat maroon communities—mocambos or quilombos in Brazil—as terminal locations, where histories of survival and defiance, however remarkable, conclude.[2] While Palmares and other such settlements are rightfully understood as spaces of diasporic refuge and resistance, unless descendants can trace their lineage directly back to them, through land possession or genealogy, scholars implicitly define them as endpoints: formerly enslaved people either lived out their days there or were recaptured or killed. Though this perspective holds many truths, it is incomplete. This book travels across 1695, narrating histories that preceded and succeeded the fateful year, and advances a new framework that highlights the literal and figurative afterlives of Africans and their kin in Brazil, and in doing so it conceptualizes maroon settlements not only as destinations but also as points of origin, capable of generating new diasporas and novel forms of inheritance.

Beginning around the turn of the seventeenth century, Africans who escaped enslavement in Pernambuco found refuge in a large wilderness that soon came to be known as Palmares (or Palmar). For the next century, they created settlements whose extent and relationships to one another are not often clear in surviving documents. The mocambos changed over time, and some moved because of environmental factors, agricultural practices, and military threats. Those who lived in Palmares (Palmaristas) numbered in the many thousands, and Palmares itself became a fixture in the landscape, an autonomous territory, and, at least to the Europeans, a polity that had to be either crushed or brought to heal through political negotiation. The mocambos were (and are) indelibly associated with palm trees; in Portuguese, "palmar" means a collection of palm trees (palmeiras) or even a "town or hut in the middle of a palm grove."[3] But though many of the mocambos were indeed hidden among the region's ubiquitous palm trees, the settlements, the terrain that surrounded them, and the trees themselves were diverse, a multiplicity indicative of the many storylines that lie behind the more well-known histories and images of Palmares—and which are the subject of this book.

Made by Africans and their children, the mocambos of Palmares were magnets for refugees and at the same time capable of propelling outcasts, survivors of war, prisoners, and spirits of the dead to new destinations. In short, Palmares was created by diaspora and also created diaspora. The fates and trajectories of the people of Palmares were entangled with those of the white, Black, Indigenous, and mixed-race soldiers who assaulted Palmares and then traveled to new places, taking war stories and in some cases prisoners with them. The human and spiritual trajectories fueled by these processes produced overlapping, layered diasporas that invite fuller examination. For all the symbolic value that Palmares and Zumbi retain, researchers know little about their legacies in the century following Zumbi's demise. Aside from a handful of now-canonical eighteenth-century histories written by white men of privilege, the century following Zumbi's death appears to be a chasm, bracketed by a comparative wealth of documentary sources from the seventeenth, nineteenth, and twentieth centuries.[4] *After Palmares* looks into and beyond the eighteenth century, bringing into view new narratives, geographies, and forms of inheritance that blur the line between worlds of the living and the dead. In African and Afro-Brazilian religious beliefs and practices, place-names, oral traditions, and colonial documents, memories of Zumbi and Palmares survived in multiple forms in the aftermath of 1695, including in toponyms for the natural landscape and through ancestor spirits that transcend human mortality.

Though there is a great deal of work on Palmares in Portuguese (if drastically less in English), many of the questions that have framed the literature are somewhat narrow: Who came to the mocambos? What were their identities? What kind of "state" or "kingdom" was Palmares?[5] These are important topics, but they are asked almost entirely in the past tense. Too few questions have been crafted about the future—about those who survived and were taken prisoner, or about what became of those whom the dead left behind, not to mention the Palmaristas who, by choice or force, themselves left Palmares behind. Now, in addition to asking who and what made Palmares, we may also ask: What did Palmares make?

Thinking about Palmares as not only a terminus but also a starting point has far-reaching implications for both the histories of Palmares, Brazil, the African Diaspora, and marronage and also contemporary debates about slavery and reparations. In 1988, Brazil adopted a new constitution as it emerged from a military dictatorship that had seized control of the nation in 1964. Article 68 guaranteed rights to Black quilombo communities, though only in vague terms. Revised and expanded in 2003, the provision recognizes communities that can prove historical land possession and trace descendance from groups who suffered and resisted racial oppression.[6] Though not explicitly conceptualized as such, the rules represent a small form of reparations for slavery— which ended later than in any other nation in the Americas, in 1888—and may serve as a reference point in conversations in the United States. But while Article 68 signaled an important victory, there exist today many communities that for any number of reasons do not meet the categories and regulations to gain official recognition, and even those that do have rarely found legal protection to be a panacea.[7] There are also millions of Brazilians whose lineage passes through enslavement and traces to Africa who do not live in quilombo communities, and the very categories "quilombo" and "quilombola" (member of a quilombo community) remain debated and contested.[8] Palmares represents both the great potential and limits to the federal quilombo project; the many creations and inheritances forged in and that passed through Palmares are collectively incongruous, fragmented, and dispersed. The numerous and expansive paths they traveled—tangled, chaotic, and uneven—demonstrate the need for a broader and fuller account of the legacies, inheritances, and debts owed for slavery that elude even the important provision codified in 1988.

To reckon with those legacies, inheritances, and debts, and to tell the history of Palmares and its afterlives, this book begins with a chapter that takes the reader into Palmares by way of an event—the death of a female Palmarista—that has received little mention. This starting point not only draws attention to archival absences and silences, but also demands that we ask new questions and seek out sources and methodologies that have been overlooked or underused. Those questions, sources, and methodologies unfold in the book's five thematic parts. The first four—"War and Conquest," "Spirits," "People," and "Places"—focus primarily on the seventeenth and eighteenth centuries with some glimpses into later moments. Death, afterlives, and rebirths are explored throughout the book and brought to the fore in the final part, "Deaths and Rebirths," which traces several of the main pathways along which Palmares and Zumbi became contested symbols of national identity during the nineteenth and twentieth centuries. Here we also see how Palmares was capable of not only generating and creating but also erasing and denying.

To write this history, I grounded my work in archival research, oral and environmental history, and comparative historical linguistics, while also availing myself of a powerful collection of digital archives.[9] In addition to a large collection of colonial records, Brazil's National Library (Biblioteca Nacional, BN) has digitized its enormous collection of newspapers, an incredible resource that can also be disorienting. For example, its search engine finds 1,668 instances of "zumbi" in a single newspaper from Manaus, thousands of miles away from where Palmares once stood.[10] Some are false hits (words that the site mistakes for "zumbi"), others refer to places named Zumbi, and many duplicate narratives about Palmares or are reprints of advertisements involving Zumbi place-names. The mountains of digital "hits," many un-moored from any direct connection to Palmares, represent a certain symme-try to the anonymous data points that count the number of enslaved people forcibly carried across the Atlantic and are now accessible at the click of a mouse. They also underscore the challenge of representing a focused history that is faithful to a seemingly endless number of plots.

Digital sources, especially the Trans-Atlantic Slave Trade database (TST, housed on the Slave Voyages website), have revolutionized our understanding of how many people enslavers had forced onto ships in Africa, and where in Africa the ships departed from before arriving in America.[11] Overwhelmingly, during the era of Palmares, those arriving in Pernambuco came from West Central Africa. For these men, women, and children, home was somewhere in what the Portuguese called the "Kingdom of Angola," or what today cov-ers more than half of Angola, the greater part of the Democratic Republic of Congo, much of the southern part of the Republic of Congo, and parts of northwest Zambia.[12] Within the region, we know a great deal about individual societies and places, ranging from Benguela in the South to Kongo (and be-yond) in the north.[13] This region was central to the formation of Pernambuco, though there are massive gaps in scholarly knowledge about connections between the two areas. Though Pernambuco received enslaved captives al-most continuously from the mid-sixteenth to mid-nineteenth centuries and became one of the most important sugar-producing regions in the world, his-torians still "know less about the slave trade to Pernambuco than about any other major branch of the traffic."[14] Data is "incomplete or nonexistent" from 1655 and 1719, years that overlap with Palmares's heyday, the life and death of Zumbi, and the immediate aftermath of 1695, but scholars have found other ways to address the absence.[15]

Numbers and demographics can anchor us and provide clarity about some aspects of the past, such as the broader points of origin that we think most Palmaristas came from. If taken as suggestion and with an awareness of how much is missing, numbers may also propel us forward by prompting us to ask what lay beyond 1695. While I use the numbers and demographic information that have been compiled by the TST creators and contributors alongside my own estimates of prisoners taken in Palmares, I do so not only to understand origins but also to think forward in time, to consider not only where Palmaristas came from, but also what became of them. The "data" for this work is more impenetrable than the already opaque material found in ship logs, which often hides names, gender, and other details. Reports about Palmares prisoners taken during battle are stingier still, often refusing even to part with numbers, offering nothing more than "many" or other hopelessly vague descriptors. The cautious estimates that I draw from this material are faceless and nameless, and important precisely because of that. One of my primary intentions in making them is to center the people who built, lived in, died in, and fled Palmares, those whose names we do not know and whose lives and deaths did not even merit register in the life-draining counts of battlefield deaths—the lives captured and hidden in lifeless adjectives such as "many."

Though stingy, the colonial archive, especially when read alongside other sources, offers insights about gender and sexuality, a topic that has received little attention in Palmares. Work by historians in other areas of the diaspora helps point the way. Discussing insurgency among the enslaved in Cuba, Aisha Finch shows "how deeply masculinity and male embodiment have structured the way in which we think about black opposition."[16] This is especially true for Palmares and Zumbi, who became almost a prototype of masculine Black rebellion, though there is now a female counterpart, Dandara, a fictionalized figure known to some as Zumbi's wife, who fought and died by his side. Though she is a literary creation, or a popular legend who gained greater notoriety through a novel, Dandara continues to hold great power and symbolism.[17] Finch also points out "that certain *actions*—as much if not more than certain *people*—became masculinized during moments of rebellion."[18] Colonial documents and latter-day accounts of Palmares highlighted the bravery of male fighters, generally only mentioning female Palmaristas as they were taken prisoner. But we know that women controlled mocambos within Palmares, and there is little doubt that some participated in combat and other tactical exercises often categorized as male. More importantly, we will see that behind iconic stories of male Palmares warriors lies a rich collection of other histories and afterlives, some made more visible through lenses trained on the post-1695 era.

War and Conquest

Warfare and the European quest to conquer Palmares help periodize its history, even while disrupting other chronologies. Chapter 1 begins on a forgotten day in 1645, an unconventional entry point into Palmares meant to beckon toward the many unknown aspects of its history. From the late sixteenth century through the Dutch occupation of northeast Brazil (1630–54), Palmares developed in spurts, with the creation of an unknown number of mocambos. In the 1660s, the kingdom of Kongo plunged into civil war, thanks in part to agitation and funding provided by Pernambuco's governor, André Vidal de Negreiros.[19] Warfare in West Central Africa helped speed the transfer of captured men, women, and children to Brazil. Meanwhile, the Portuguese trained a vicious wave of attacks on Palmares leading up to a short-lived peace treaty in 1678. During this time, details about the names of individual mocambo leaders emerge in surviving documents. The peace accord, signed by the Palmares leader Gan(g)a Zumba and Aires de Sousa de Castro, the governor of Pernambuco, did not last long. Rivals assassinated Gan(g)a Zumba and the area descended once again into violence. Over the next decade and a half, Zumbi consolidated power and held off the Portuguese until his death.

During the 1670s, Palmares was organized in a network of mocambos, each likely under the control of a single leader, whose place was secured and preserved either through lineal succession or political maneuvering. In the 1680s and 1690s, under Zumbi, Palmares was centered atop the mountain called Serra da Barriga (in colonial documents, also "Serra do Barriga" and "Outeiro da [or do] Barriga"). Though Palmares fell after Zumbi's death, which followed a bruising battle at Serra da Barriga in 1694, the defeat was incomplete, as Palmares remained a site of refuge for years to come. The post-Zumbi years saw dispersal, fragmentation, and rebirth, as surviving Palmaristas alighted to new locales and, in some cases, remained in Palmares, where, though dramatically fewer in number, colonial reports of mocambos, fugitives, and insurgents nonetheless persisted for decades. The continued cycles of attacks that the Europeans leveled against the mocambos may be understood as a series of loosely connected military conflicts waged over the course of a century: the Palmares wars.[20] The violence trained against Palmares engendered subsequent forms of violence as well as wealth and at least the dream of social ascension for Black, white, Indigenous, and mixed-race soldiers who attacked, killed, wounded, and placed their own lives at risk in exchange for material gains that some secured more easily than others, and which could generate new forms of wealth, security, and historical notoriety.

Like the Spanish conquest, Portugal's defeat of Palmares generated triumphant written accounts. Sebastião da Rocha Pita, a Brazilian-born writer of Portuguese descent who helped formalize the study of history in Brazil, penned a foundational account of Palmares and Zumbi in his famous 1730 tract *Historia da America Portugueza* (*History of Portuguese America*), a book that one observer in 1922 called "possibly the most important historical production of the colonial period in Brazil."[21] Palmares began, Rocha Pita explained, when a small group of Africans escaped bondage and founded their own society. Eventually, it took on characteristics of the world's great ancient civilizations. Unburdened by the "speculation of Aristotle and Plato in their written republics, or the laws promulgated in Athens," Palmares was both comparable to and distinct from classical societies.[22] In conjuring ancient Greece, Rocha Pita tapped into an obsession among the chroniclers of colonial America with what might be called the "savage civilization slot"—a pre-conquest people and society that was at once marvelous and barbaric.[23] Explorers and writers across the Americas searched for, wrote about, and in many senses created and imagined primitive pasts fit for admiration if not wholesale embrace.[24]

Works like Rocha Pita's often replicated and also embellished language and accounts found in petitions and other official communications that soldiers and officers used to relate battlefield exploits and seek reward, blurring the lines between fact and fiction. In no case is this clearer than the iconic, tragic moment of Zumbi's death. Beginning with Rocha Pita, some of Brazil's foundational historical texts maintained that, when the Portuguese finally cornered him, Zumbi leaped off a cliff, killing himself rather than facing capture and enslavement. This apocryphal story was based on hazy accounts of a moment on a darkened battlefield, when scores of Palmaristas, though not Zumbi, leaped or fell from a cliff. Plumbing the gaps and connections between soldiers' accounts and published texts reveals the material stakes behind the narratives, evident especially in the way that rumors of Zumbi's demise circulated years before his death, as soldiers sought monetary awards for killing him. In Gabriel García Márquez's famous novel *Chronicle of a Death Foretold*, members of an entire village learn one by one that the central character will be killed, even while he remains unaware.[25] During the final two decades of intense fighting in Palmares, colonial agents foretold death in a different way, repeatedly seeking rewards based in claims that they had killed Zumbi, who in fact continued to survive despite the immense efforts and resources dedicated to defeating and killing him.

Reading Palmares through the lens of war and conquest also raises an unusual chronological question: How did it come to pass, and what does it even mean, for Portugal to have conquered in the Americas an African society

8

whose very existence came about through the transatlantic slave trade? In the Americas, the very idea of conquest depends on a prescribed order: Europeans invade America and defeat the inhabitants. That Africans and their kin established a place large and formidable enough that Europeans set out to conquer it—and that doing so took a century to complete—speaks to the mocambos' size and strength and illustrates the need to think more fully about the unique aspects of this particular conquest. Over the last four decades, as historians dismantled previous accounts of Europeans steamrolling their way to victory over Indigenous people in the Americas, thanks to a combination of military might, disease, and Native passivity, they have come to understand conquest as a word and idea that hides and distorts a great number of subtleties and counternarratives, including the role of Indigenous alliances and divisions. Crucially, scholars have also radically revised our understanding of 1492 and the dates that mark the defeat of the Aztec, Inca, and other Indigenous people. Far from signaling erasure of what came before, scholars now take 1492, 1521, 1532, and other luminous dates to be conduits—key moments of transition, to be sure, but not endpoints.[26]

In the case of Palmares, conquest may be understood, at least in part, as a narrative tool that mainly benefited Europeans but could also be meaningful and potent for others. Like any conquest, this one required an outlay of capital to fund troops and also generated wealth for the most decorated and well-connected soldiers and officers, including nonwhite combatants, whose trajectories offer suggestive points of comparison with Black and Indigenous conquistadors from Spanish America.[27] The post-Palmares journeys of colonial combatants through Brazil and beyond reveal a complex interplay between diaspora and conquest. As soldiers journeyed beyond Palmares, they parlayed stories of their exploits, including false boasts of killing Zumbi, into monetary awards, which they passed on to heirs. While Palmares's destroyers and their descendants gained wealth and social power, the descendants of Palmares's inhabitants faded from view, at least in the documentary record.

Spirits

After killing Zumbi, colonial soldiers delivered his head to the new governor of Pernambuco, Caetano de Melo de Castro, who ordered that it be displayed "on a stake in the most public place" in Recife, an act meant "to mollify the offended and justly querulous and to terrorize the Blacks who superstitiously view Zumbi to be immortal, and to make clear that in this undertaking Palmares has been destroyed once and for all."[28] What Castro called superstition was in fact a complex set of religious beliefs organized around understandings of a relationship between the worlds of the living and the dead that were much more fluid than the terms used by the governor.

Palmaristas looked to the worlds of the living and the dead as they confronted challenges and obstacles. For most Palmaristas, religion was politics — a means for controlling spirits that determined life, death, and the environment's capacity to provide sustenance.[29] Their spiritual beliefs have received little attention for reasons similar to those that elsewhere segregate politics and spirits in historical analysis.[30] If those who considered Zumbi to be immortal understood that he took different form after 1695, many likely believed that form to be a West Central African flying spirit of the dead known as nzumbi, eventually known in Brazil as zumbi. During the nineteenth century, Black women who labored as caregivers for white children in Brazil told them stories that suggested that the man (Zumbi) and the spirit (zumbi) could be one and the same. Later, as the children became adults and established themselves as scholars, they used those stories to catalog meanings of Z/zumbi, while at the same time rejecting what the women had said earlier and disaggregating big-Z Zumbi and little-z zumbi. Alongside these later renderings, the voices of those Black women suggest a crucial way that Z/zumbi lived on after 1695.

Spiritual beliefs were shaped in the corridor connecting Brazil and Angola, which Roquinaldo Ferreira conceptualizes "not as two geographical places separated by an ocean, but as one social and cultural continuum connected by an ocean."[31] If humans, goods, and ideas traveled across the Atlantic as if on a highway, souls must have journeyed in even more complex and connected ways, further blurring distinctions between the living and the dead, and between Africa and America. While some spirits were moored in Africa, others emanated from new homelands in Brazil. For surviving Palmaristas confronting the aftermath of 1695, returning "home" might not mean (only) crossing the Atlantic, as the act is often conceptualized in literature on the diaspora, but instead (or also) involve a return to Palmares or other similarly generative American sites.

People

The afterlives of Z/zumbi and Palmares circulated not only via spirits but also through the almost entirely unexamined diaspora of those who survived the mocambos' destruction. Exploring multiple meanings of Z/zumbi at once reinforces the centrality of the leader (or leaders) who went by that name and suggests a larger universe of expression that extends far beyond any single individual. In the last century, scholars have compiled a massive archive of colonial engagement with Palmares. What began during the first half of the twentieth century, with authors such as Ernesto Ennes and Edison Carneiro publishing transcriptions of colonial communiqués, grew in the second half, as Décio Freitas and others did the same.[32] In the first decades of the twenty-first century, Flávio Gomes followed in their footsteps while blazing new trails, compiling a trove of documents along with a set of insightful, critical essays.[33] Most recently, Silvia Lara published an exhaustively researched book about Palmares, coedited a critical edition of one of the most detailed contemporaneous sources on Palmares, and built Documenta Palmares, a website featuring the fruit of years of labor — thousands of pages of documents and an interactive map, all now accessible to researchers around the world.[34]

One of the main assumptions that undergirds work on Palmares is that even these impressive archives render inaccessible the lives and voices of all but the most powerful and important members of the mocambos. My book counters this by presenting remarkable individual portraits: a young girl born in Palmares, taken by colonial forces, and presented as a "gift" to an Indigenous colonial officer and his wife; a man captured in Palmares and sent to Portugal, where he worked for daily wages in the royal tobacco plant, contracted smallpox, and sought the patronage of a white military officer before dying; a woman whose mother was Indigenous and whose grandfather was a white conqueror, and who became the matriarch of a powerful family that settled land taken from the mocambos. I combine their stories with those of larger communities, such as the Indigenous people who battled for formal rights to land in Palmares after helping defeat it. Though they suffered brutal treatment, throughout the seventeenth and eighteenth centuries these Indigenous people advocated for, and sometimes secured, property and rights by calling themselves "conquerors of Palmares."

Richard Price, a pioneer in the study of maroon societies, contrasted Palmares with settlements whose descendants live on the same land as their

ancestors and trace clear lineages across centuries.[35] It is true that few individuals or communities today trace descent from Palmares. Yet the absence of
genealogical lineage does not mean a lack of historical connectivity. For that, we
must consider those who were captured or fled, groups I discuss throughout
part III and elsewhere in the book. Veterans of all kinds also play a central role
in this story. Some embarked on far-flung journeys after 1695, carrying stories
(and most likely captives) with them. To what degree is it possible to trace the
African Diaspora through the paths traveled by those charged with enslaving or
killing its members? This question is especially complex for Black and mixed-
race officers and soldiers who fought against Palmares; they were part of the
diaspora and also destroyers of one of its most monumental creations. The
trajectories of colonial combatants demonstrate connections between the
pre- and post-1695 eras and among seemingly distant dots on the Portuguese
colonial map. They also suggest the need to expand the maps we typically use
for Palmares and the directions that memories and meanings traveled along.

Places

For new insights, I also turn to the natural world with an approach encapsu-
lated by the book's first epigraph, Pablo Neruda's poetic suggestion that the
earth can demonstrate how what once "seems dead . . . later proves to be
alive."[36] Marcus de Carvalho and Anna Laura Teixeira de França provide a useful starting point for bringing environmental history into our understanding
of Palmares. In addition to the human and political stories, they write, "When
we think about Palmares . . . we should also think about the forests, mountains, rivers, caves, caverns, rain, and sun."[37] Part IV, "Places," takes up this
call by studying landscape, geography, and place-names in Pernambuco and
also in surprising places that rarely appear in the literature on Palmares and
languish on the margins of Brazilian historiography. Building on the work in
part III about the Palmares diaspora, part IV explores in more detail some of
the unexpected points to which Palmares survivors fled. Compared with that
largely anonymous group, we know a good deal about the soldiers and officers whose names and exploits are registered in colonial archives. While some
veterans remained close by after 1695, settling on the land formerly occupied
by Palmares, others traveled to out-of-the way places such as Paraíba, Rio
Grande do Norte, and much farther still: Rio de Janeiro, Angola, and Portugal.

An indication of how the topics highlighted in each part are intertwined throughout the book, my treatment of place depends on tracing the movement of people and extending my discussion of spiritual beliefs. Before the Portuguese killed Zumbi, Palmares had withstood assaults from two European empires (Portuguese and Dutch) almost since its inception. Its longevity would later lead observers (often steeped in racial essentialism and outright racism) to compare Palmares to Haiti. But unlike the Haitian Revolution or any other revolt, Palmares was not an event—it was a place, a collection of settlements occupying an area twice the length of Rhode Island and some fifteen kilometers wider.[38] The Palmares wilderness represented many things to the different parties it touched—a colonial frontier, menacing backlands, a place of refuge and sustenance, a site of deep spiritual power, and a vast space whose coordinates shifted and which included or bordered multiple topographies and microclimates that fostered lush, dense vegetation as well as arid, barren landscapes. And, as we will see, Palmares was not simply shaped by the colonial frontier but also helped generate, delimit, and make it.

African, African-diasporic, and Indigenous toponyms are found throughout Brazil. The meanings and the messages they conveyed and convey depend on context and could change over time. Read carefully alongside more traditional archival sources, unique insights are offered by place-names, the landscape, and the built environment about how slavery and colonial power were forged, asserted, and opposed.[39] In addition to diasporic ancestor spirits, the name Zumbi survived in toponyms—lakes, rivers, small towns, and neglected neighborhoods—many of which are, or once were, imbued with spiritual meanings. Each presents a unique opportunity to sharpen our understanding of Palmares, trace its post-1695 histories, and grasp how crucial those histories are to larger struggles over land, religion, memory, wealth, and power. For groups whose histories have not been recorded in writing, understanding how and why a place-name came into being, or what it meant to them, is sometimes possible through careful inference based in other sources. For some toponyms, it is possible to deduce likely paths from Palmares, while, for others, distinct origins are more likely. A special set of challenges arise when interpreting the numerous plantations (engenhos) called Engenho Zumbi or Engenho Mocambo, seemingly oxymoronic constructions that may signal a diasporic imprint on the landscape, white appropriation, or something in between. Far from a simple tale of survival or triumph, the history of place reveals an uneven terrain that bequeathed different and unequal inheritances to those who lived and died on it.

Deaths and Rebirths

As the histories of place suggest, some of the most interesting stories emanating from Palmares pass through surprising locales. Part V, "Deaths and Rebirths," builds on this insight to also demonstrate how some histories previously associated with Palmares may, on further reflection, now direct us to think beyond Palmares—to other diasporic histories that the famous mocambos have obscured. During the nineteenth and twentieth centuries, writers inserted Palmares, especially descriptions of its destruction, into narratives to bolster nascent regional and national identities. As one of the most visible examples of African contributions to Brazil, Palmares became a go-to reference for scholars puzzling over words and ideas that were unfamiliar to them. Influential (mainly white and male) authors wrote about African words, including multiple definitions of Zumbi (and zumbi) in a way that helped preserve in print a wide range of meanings while also attempting to shape and narrow those meanings to their liking. While that process could be destructive, it also helped facilitate later waves of writing, reclamation, and activism, which elevated Palmares and Zumbi into more dynamic and unquestionably powerful symbols of Black identity and resistance. Traces of some of the memories and ideas that have been passed down orally are found in the written record, conveying a broad set of beliefs and ideas shaped by not only the circulation of written texts but also the diasporas of millions of Africans forcibly taken to Brazil during the slave era.

In some cases, the histories that emerge from this tangle of people and documents provide insights about Palmares and its uneven and unequal inheritances. For example, the final chapter describes how today in Rio Grande do Norte one man openly identifies as an heir to the colonial officer who killed Zumbi. But that officer did not, in fact, kill Zumbi, and the story, passed down over centuries, vividly illustrates the length and impact of the inheritances bequeathed by some Palmares conquerors. By contrast, the lineages of a Black community nearby do not pass through Palmares, and yet some members of the community today call themselves the "heirs of Zumbi," a deeply meaningful choice, and one of the most effective ways of gaining visibility and advocating for rights.

If these histories demonstrate the value of remaining connected to Palmares, others suggest how and why it is at the same time important to think beyond Palmares. When the celebrated nineteenth-century writer José de Alencar wrote a novel about the Guerra dos Mascates (the Peddlers War), a Pernambuco rebellion that pitted Portuguese merchants against mazombos, a pejorative term for the local plantation owners on the other side of the conflagration, he turned to Palmares in search of a definition for the word "mazombo." As I show in the final chapter, linguistic evidence points us elsewhere, indicating the presence in Pernambuco of men and women from Zombo, an area in West Central Africa whose relation to the political unrest of the early eighteenth century in Brazil invites further research. While some histories await future work, the example illustrates that while Palmares and its memorialization have created different meanings and forms of inheritances, both have at the same time marginalized or denied other lines of inquiry. This book is deeply committed both to telling new histories about Palmares and to pointing the way to other stories yet to be written.

Language, Africa, Afro-Latin American Studies, and Palmares

In terms of both what it places front and center and what it pushes into the background, Palmares has much to teach us about Brazil, its connections to Africa, and the wider histories of diaspora in the Americas. Even within the vibrant, growing field of Afro-Latin American studies, it is not always clear how Africa relates to "Afro."[40] In recent years, scholars of diaspora have placed added emphasis on centering Africa, and diaspora has been richly studied and theorized for decades.[41] But what African languages, beliefs, ideologies, and histories must scholars of Afro-Latin America learn? While there is no single answer, recent Africanist provocations highlight the need to pay greater attention to linguistics, a daunting task for most Latin Americanists, given the sheer number of African languages.[42] The Niger-Congo language phylum, the most relevant to this study, is the world's largest and includes nearly 1,500 distinct languages.[43]

This book embraces the challenge of participating in what might be called a second linguistic turn, or at least what could become that for scholars of the diaspora: a turning toward African languages in more detail and with new energy. Unlike the first linguistic turn, which mined the nuances of discourse to produce against-the-grain textual readings and deepen, complicate, or counter structuralist and materialist approaches, this one will employ historical linguistics to move beyond historians' "traditional archives and methods."[44] Related approaches have been honed for years by Africanists and scholars of Indigenous history in the Americas, most prominently in Latin America by practitioners of the New Philology.[45] But not a great deal of this kind of work bridges the Atlantic, at least not in the ambitious ways suggested recently by Kathryn de Luna and several others.[46] De Luna and other Africanists who employ comparative historical linguistics share with the pioneers of the first linguistic turn the belief "that language is the constitutive agent of human consciousness and the social production of meaning."[47] Perhaps ironically, their "documents"—words and roots—often feature a durability that bears more than a passing resemblance to the sturdy stuff at the core of materialist and structuralist history. It is no accident that comparative historical linguists liken certain words to "fossils" or "artifacts," which, with careful work, may be excavated to determine previously buried meaning(s).[48]

Africanist comparative historical linguistics sits in productive tension with Americanist scholarship on slavery. Recent years have brought innovative approaches to breaking through the archival gaps and silences that erase Black voices, especially women's. In one of the most eloquent contributions to the field, Marisa Fuentes asks, "How do we narrate the fleeting glimpses of enslaved subjects in the archives and meet the disciplinary demands of history that requires us to construct unbiased accounts from these very documents?" In posing the question, Fuentes challenges the distortions and violences of "the traditional archive," which she rereads to tell new histories.[49] Concerned with the very same problems, de Luna and other Africanists propose language as a path out of the colonial archive by tracing longue-durée meanings and changes in word roots to better get at "one of the most pressing concerns of Atlantic history—what enslaved Africans thought about their experiences—in and on the terms of the enslaved."[50] As Marjoleine Kars pithily notes, there was a "common theme" during the ages of slavery and Atlantic revolutions: "elites wanted one thing; commoners wanted another. Both called it 'freedom.'"[51] Africanist approaches and comparative historical linguistics take us even further to reveal additional vocabularies and ideas.[52] Utilizing these methods alongside others, *After Palmares* explores worlds after and beyond freedom, marronage, and other familiar and undeniably powerful terms and concepts.

While scholars of Palmares and Brazil have long been interested in African languages, we have approached them with a limited tool set. A prime example is in the overreliance on and oversimplification of Kimbundu and Kikongo, which were forged through violent and complex colonial processes and represent just a fragment of the languages spoken in West Central Africa. While a modern Kimbundu dictionary, the go-to reference for many scholars, can be revealing, it also often prevents the more nuanced accounts that comparative historical linguistics can provide. In appendix A, I lay out my approach, which I hope will be useful for other (Latin) Americanists interested in African languages. Three central points merit presentation here. First, in the context of the African Atlantic, de Luna writes, "Durable words were those that could speak from multiple perspectives simultaneously."[53] This is not as straightforward as it might appear. Wordplay, false cognates, subjective or simply erroneous translations, and a lack of evidence often make it difficult to identify, let alone make sense of, "durable words." Military, spiritual, human, and natural contexts help do this work, suggesting how and why Z/zumbi and other words and concepts came to mean and signal multiple things, sometimes at once, and how some definitions remained while others faded. Second, previous interpretations of language in Palmares are best thought of as starting points that often offer accurate but incomplete pictures. De Luna suggests that "Palmar" and "Palmares" did not just reference palm trees, which has been taken as a given, but also additional ideas with great cultural and political significance for Africans who arrived in Pernambuco and heard of or made their way to the mocambos.[54] Intriguing too is Luiz Felipe de Alencastro's observation that, as early as the sixteenth century, Portuguese sailors feared doldrums off the coast of Kongo called "Palmar," which could wreak havoc and even cause "deaths among the crew."[55] The association between "palmar(es)" and palm trees is, therefore, not incorrect, just incomplete. My own linguistic analysis, focused especially on Z/zumbi, is meant to generate new questions and fill in larger pictures. Third, while some aspects of African languages and comparative historical linguistics can be daunting, other insights are attainable through simpler means, sometimes through something as apparently bland and insignificant as a single letter—the difference between Zumbi and Zambi—or even the difference between capitalized Zumbi and lowercased zumbi. In some of these fine details dwell enormous and remarkable histories, often with reach that extends far beyond Palmares's capacious borders.

This proliferation of etymologies and ideas pushes the discussion of Palmares beyond the usual topics covered in scholarship on maroon communities. For reasons that are perhaps obvious, most of the literature on marronage centers freedom and liberty, concepts that scholars have long suggested exist only in relation to slavery.[56] Some authors push beyond this dyad. Jean Casimir describes how French colonial officials and historians have often failed to grapple with the fact that freedom and "the norms and principles of the Christian, capitalist, and racist West" were not the end goals of all enslaved people or maroons in Haiti.[57] Anthony Bogues similarly pushes beyond "normalized" understandings of freedom by highlighting "invention" and "the radical imagination."[58] Invention and the radical imagination were staples of African action, idea, and belief throughout the Americas and in the face of overwhelming violence and insufferable conditions. Maroon settlements across the hemisphere are one of the most powerful testaments of this struggle. Simply assuming that they were endpoints risks falling back into dialectical traps and teleologies that Bogues and others have warned against. Internally diverse, existing in different iterations for a century, covering a state-sized swath of land, and populated by many thousands, Palmares was a generative space capable of becoming a point of genesis even as violent struggle turned it into a graveyard. The mocambos conferred power on some and subjugated others, all under the constant threat of military assault that altered its borders and prompted regular movement. To understand those dynamics and the worldviews and experiences that extend beyond the confines of freedom, liberty, and other western liberal idioms, it is necessary to look beyond 1695, into and through the eighteenth century, when now-familiar histories of Palmares became consecrated, often at the expense of other, less well-known stories.

While the book focuses on what happened after Palmares fell, it is also *about* Palmares. Only through deeper engagement with language, place, and spirit may we begin to craft a fuller picture of the mocambos and by extension other spaces and creations of Africans and their kin in the Americas. Thinking hard about language and place together reveals new possible meanings of Zumbi's name that also unveil a larger set of spiritual practices and beliefs. The paths that these meanings, practices, and beliefs traveled into, within, and beyond Palmares illustrate how language, place, and spirituality may

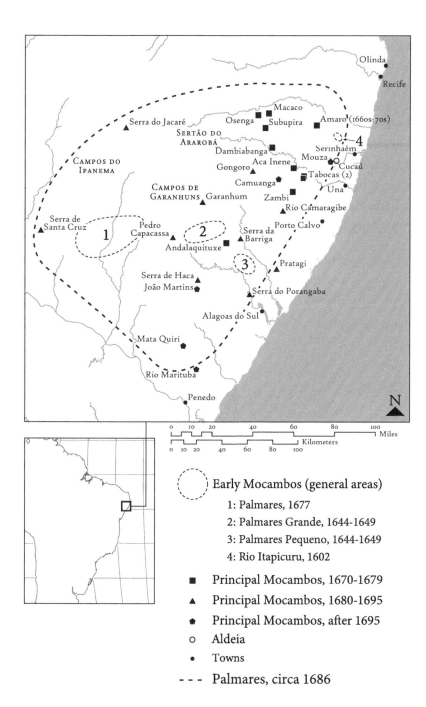

Early Mocambos (general areas)

   1: Palmares, 1677
   2: Palmares Grande, 1644-1649
   3: Palmares Pequeno, 1644-1649
   4: Rio Itapicuru, 1602

■   Principal Mocambos, 1670-1679
▲   Principal Mocambos, 1680-1695
⬟   Principal Mocambos, after 1695
○   Aldeia
●   Towns
- - -   Palmares, circa 1686

MAP I.1 The Mocambos of Palmares

help us reconsider Palmares and in the process gain a better understanding of larger diasporas. While studying those diasporas and thinking about how to best challenge old narratives while suggesting future lines of analysis, I found the book's second epigraph, which favors capacious songs over narrow answers, to be an inspiring guide. The history of Palmares and its afterlives brings us face-to-face with the tension and interplay between songs and answers. Maybe not by chance, several of the most poignant examples of this arise in the form of birds and other flying figures. These and the different human, animal, and "supernatural" beings that animate the book all have songs to sing, some easier to hear than others.

I   WAR AND CONQUEST

1. WAR AND CONQUEST

March 21, 1645

If the death of Zumbi in 1695 represents an unsatisfying conclusion to the history of Palmares, when should the story begin? Covering a vast expanse of terrain and with inhabitants whose backgrounds and reasons for being there varied, Palmares defies easy categorization and periodization. One could start in 1603 with the first written reference to "rebellious Blacks" in Pernambuco: a short description of a colonial attack against a stronghold situated in "the Palmares," where Portuguese victory resulted in "many dead and captured."[1] Or perhaps six years earlier, when the Jesuit Provincial of Brazil wrote about three "enemies" of Portuguese settlers: the "extremely barbarous" Aimoré Indians; the French; and the greatest enemies of all, "rebellious *negros de Guiné*," who occupied mountains in Bahia and "dare[d] to attack and destroy farms, as their kin on the island of São Tomé do."[2] Looking back centuries later, another Jesuit author described the statement as a "vision" of what came next: "mocambos, Palmares, and revolts."[3] Though the sixteenth-century cleric did not predict Palmares, in highlighting the danger that Africans posed, he connected them to their "kin" on São Tomé, revealing a sprawling cartography with fugitive communities at the center of the struggle for colonial dominion.[4] Because Palmares formed in waves and comprised mocambos whose relationships with each other and from one era to the next are not always clear, we might ask another question: With whose life (or death) should the history of Palmares begin? Despite his fame we know relatively little about Zumbi, but we know even less about the thousands who lived and died in the mocambos but whose names colonial scribes did not record. With their histories in mind, this chapter enters Palmares through an obscure date and with a woman whose name we do not know.

A Death in the Forest

In contrast to November 20, 1695, the date March 21, 1645, does not register now in any meaningful way. On that day, a bugler in a Dutch military expedition murdered a Black woman in Palmares. The event is hastily recorded in a diary frequently attributed to the Dutch captain Jan Blaer.[5] Other observations from the diary, one of the earliest accounts of Palmares, hold a prominent place in the historical record. The expedition found what it deemed to be a church, which historians have long cited as evidence of Christianity in the mocambos. An estimate about the number of people living in Palmares and details about food and other aspects of daily life are among the observations that have been repeated over the centuries. The unnamed woman killed by the bugler has gone unremarked.

By contrast, Blaer secured his place in history, despite falling ill several days into the expedition and returning home, leaving his men under the guidance of Jürgens Reijmbach. Though some scholars call the text the Blaer-Reijmbach diary, most just use Blaer's name when referring to the source, his absence for most of the journey notwithstanding. The woman's presence in a diary named for a man who did not write it represents an apt metaphor for the mythmaking and silences that for centuries have shaped and limited our understanding of Palmares and its afterlives. Before the bugler-assassin killed the woman, the convoy traipsed through the wilderness for days, suffering harsh conditions and searching in vain for people to capture and enslave. They had heard legendary stories about Palmares before finally arriving at its gates. The massive complex struck the group with awe. "Great trees" that Palmaristas had felled and then "cross[ed] and intertwine[ed]" to form defense structures were among the impressive aspects that the diary describes with a reverence reminiscent of the journals of Spanish conquistadors encountering cities of the Aztec and Inca empires.[6] After such grand buildup—the tales they had heard and their harrowing journey—there remained the formidable task of breaking through two massive doors surrounded by stakes. The group broke through this line of defense, but the bugler fell into the next obstacle, a spike-filled moat. After the other men rescued him, they made their way inside. The complex was abandoned. Residents had left five or six days earlier to tend to their plots and hunting traps before receding farther into the woods; they had received warning about the expedition from their network of lookouts, allies, and spies.[7] Only a few Palmaristas remained, and the expedition captured some of them. Having failed yet again to engage the enemy, the injured bugler's frustration boiled over. "Enraged for having fallen into the moat," the diary reads, he "cut off the head of a Black woman."[8]

The woman disappears from the historical record as quickly as she enters it, passed over by generations of scholars interested in other stories. Hers became part of written history in the briefest, most violent, and dismissive way possible, a bloody prop on the stage of European conquest. We know nothing about her life, and her death garnered not even a full line in the diary. In short, she resembles the many millions more ensnared in slavery and colonialism, who gained archival presence "only in the moment of their disappearance."[9] To seek details about a person whose life comes to us only in death, as a fragment in an archive meant to marginalize and erase her, is to engage in a hopeless, though still meaningful, pursuit.[10] And yet there is even more to consider. What became of the woman after she was killed? What did death mean under these circumstances, and who remembered her? We will have the opportunity to return to these questions in part II, but for now we will focus on the other aftermaths that followed the woman's death.

After the bugler killed the woman, the expedition captured "another *negra*" and stayed two nights in the settlement, gathering information and generally continuing along the downward spiral of frustration and injury that had marked their journey to that point. They found "a lot of palm oil . . . but nothing else."[11] The remaining Palmaristas told the expedition that "five hundred men, plus women and children," once lived in the mocambo, and Reijmbach "presumed that together there were fifteen hundred inhabitants." He sent a team to "beat the forest" in search of prisoners, but they "only were able to catch one Black woman without one leg named Lucrécia." They let her go because, with so many of their own men wounded, there was no way to travel with her as a captive. On the way home, they captured "a *negro* with his wife and a child" and encountered "a Black man full of tumors in the company of an old Indigenous woman, slave of the [Palmares] king's daughter," who told them that the woods were still full of Blacks. Not surprisingly by this point, a group sent to search for them was unsuccessful. Though they found the "king's daughter's" house, it was empty, and they set it on fire.

Even in this short span of time, the expedition encountered and chased a wide range of women, whose rank and privilege ranged from royalty to those apparently discarded or left behind. That range highlights the way that unnamed Palmaristas challenge conventional categories, a point rendered vividly in Gayl Jones's epic novel, *Palmares*. When asked if she is "a slave woman or a free woman," a Palmarista character responds, "I am neither kind."[12]

Jones's character belonged to the Palmares elite; the woman from the Blaer-Reijmbach diary did not. Hers was instead among the unknown number of untold histories and unremarked-upon deaths. In this sense, her death directs us not only beyond the history of Blaer and the expedition, but also beyond Zumbi, whose life and death dominate narratives about Palmares, and perhaps even beyond Palmares itself. Why was the woman at the abandoned settlement when the Dutch arrived? Had she momentarily returned? Had those who left ostracized her? If answers are elusive, the questions help us think about divisions and hierarchies within Palmares and also the different trajectories and paths traveled by Palmaristas in moments of struggle, change, and upheaval.[13] Prisoner capture was just one way that military assaults displaced the people of Palmares. An untold number more were uprooted by battle, as colonial forces often burned the empty mocambos they found, razing the landscape and ensuring that its inhabitants would have to once again seek refuge elsewhere.[14]

If the motley cast that the expedition encountered illustrates Palmares's capacity to leave behind and exclude, the many more who eluded the Dutch contingent draw our attention to the fact that Palmares could move. One of the mocambos' most successful strategies was to decamp into the wilderness when enemy forces approached, reconstituting later in new locations. Doing so entailed massive coordination and mobilization and could also mean severance from community. From the perspective of vulnerable individuals left behind, mobility could be disastrous. For those who moved, though, such abandonment might also be protective and even generative. We still know little about this, but it is likely that the most successful and longest-lasting communities in Palmares were able to let fields lie fallow to regenerate. Movement in such cases would mean not flight but instead intentional relocation followed by an eventual return to once again plant and reap harvests.[15] Those who moved to evade the Dutch and Portuguese remade settlements or founded new ones along and beyond what seemed to be an endless colonial frontier, what João Capistrano de Abreu called the northeast's "outer backlands" (sertões de fora), marked by war but also trade routes and burgeoning economies.[16] The state of those whom the expedition encountered—old, hobbled, apparently left behind—suggests different stations and relationships among diverse groups within the Palmares wilderness, a vast space that beckons deeper exploration.

Placing Palmares and the People Who Lived There

Though we now associate Palmares with those who escaped slavery, Europeans at the time rarely referred to its inhabitants as fugitives, more often calling them "the Blacks of Palmares," "rebels," or "insurgents." These labels, Silvia Lara notes, carried "clear political connotation."[17] Even to contemporaries, the identities of individuals living in Palmares were not always clear.[18] In 1671, authorities arrested and ordered the demonstrative punishment of Antonio, an enslaved man believed to be the leader of a group of rebel Blacks based in Ipojuca, about fifty kilometers south of Recife. Though there is no indication that these insurgents were formally aligned with the mocambos of Palmares, they clearly threatened the colonial project, given that the judge ordered a punishment cruel enough to spread "terror among all the other rebel Blacks in all of these captaincies."[19] Sizable as it was, Palmares belonged to a larger insurgent landscape.

At first glance, Palmares would seem to occupy a marginal place in the Atlantic world, backlands buried in the interior of a South Atlantic colony. But those backlands and the mocambos they hid were connected in important ways to seemingly distant global forces and events. During the early seventeenth century, the high price of sugar on global markets made Pernambuco the wealthiest captaincy in Portuguese America and an attractive target for the Dutch.[20] When sugar prices fell in the 1640s, Pernambuco suffered more than Bahia, a captaincy that repelled the Dutch and emerged in the 1650s as the new colonial center of power and finance. The Dutch invasion and ensuing fighting (coupled with the rise of Caribbean competitors) hampered Pernambuco's prodigious sugar industry.[21] Beset with epidemics, failing and destroyed plantations, and a seemingly unconquerable enemy in Palmares, Pernambuco declined over the second half of the seventeenth century.[22] Even as Pernambuco declined, Palmares became an increasing source of concern for colonial officials on both sides of the Atlantic, including during the Dutch occupation of Angola (1641–48), which fortified the region's connection to Pernambuco.[23] The Dutch sent forces from Recife to Luanda and Benguela, and the Portuguese, who alternately allied with and fought against local groups in West Central Africa, also deployed troops from Brazil to Angola.[24] Many Portuguese soldiers who returned from West Central Africa landed in the Brazilian northeast, and were now employed to attack Native and fugitive Black settlements, including Palmares.[25] As Lara argues, the Palmares that the Dutch encountered was different from the Palmares that the Portuguese re-engaged with in the 1650s. West Central Africa also changed during the same time. After 1648, when the Dutch left Angola, the region entered a period of relative stability after the constant warfare and upheaval of the first half of the century.[26] Even then, the Portuguese continued to "recruit" troops in Brazil to fight in Angola.[27]

The way that Palmares was intertwined with events across the Atlantic is seen in events narrated by Lara and José Lingna Nafafé.[28] In 1671, the Portuguese secured a military victory in West Central Africa that resulted in the capture of members of the Ndongo royal family.[29] The Crown designated them as political prisoners and puzzled over where to imprison them. Leaving them in Angola would run the risk of escape and the reconstitution of Ndongo forces, and so they were sent to Brazil. But concerns persisted: one official feared that if they remained in Brazil "they could flee [back] to Angola or join up with the Blacks of Palmares."[30] Finally, the Portuguese Overseas Council (Conselho Ultramarino) determined that the prisoners should be transferred back across the ocean to Portugal.[31]

Yet Palmares was also deeply intertwined with its more immediate environs in Portuguese America. The mocambos and their relationships with the surrounding areas blur old categories that scholars once used to categorize slave flight: gran marronage (the creation of large permanent settlements like Palmares) and petit marronage (smaller acts such as leaving a plantation for a day or two). While the mocambos that formed in Pernambuco clearly belong to the first category, there was significant communication, trade, and even fluid lines of belonging between Portuguese and Palmarista settlements. One example is found in the case of an enslaved man who the Portuguese hoped would speak with his father, who lived in Palmares, to gain intel about Palmarista military plans.[32] This family and the potential for communication across Palmares's borders provided evidence of relationships and identities that go beyond older categories. This points to internal diversity and change over time, which concepts such as gran marronage and other labels used by scholars to classify Palmares—"kingdom," "neo-African kingdom," "Little Angola," "Black Troy," "fully-fledged state," "African state in Brazil," "republic," and others—tend to bely, with their suggestion of a singular history.[33]

However much Palmares varied or changed across eras, there is little doubt that West Central Africa shaped it more than any other African region did. War in West Central Africa led to an increased number of enslaved people sent to Brazil. Beginning in the 1610s, an "Angolan wave" ushered what John K. Thornton calls a "notably homogeneous" period of the trade of enslaved people across the Atlantic. Many enslaved West Central Africans arrived in Pernambuco on Portuguese ships, making the captaincy for a time, in Thornton's estimation, "probably the most Angolan captaincy in all of Brazil."[34] Estimates about how many people lived in Palmares vary, ranging from several thousand to thirty thousand.[35] The Europeans who recorded descriptions of Palmares probably often exaggerated to make their encounters seem more impressive, but whether numbering ten thousand or thirty thousand, there is no doubt that Palmares was enormous and likely home not only to a large Black majority but also to Indigenous, mixed-race, and perhaps even white members. In this diverse setting, men and women from West Central Africa dominated. Belying the diversity of West Central Africa, colonial documents gloss the men, women, and children captured there and sent into bondage as "Angolan," a phrase that some contemporaries applied to the people of Palmares.[36]

Though the numbers from the Trans-Atlantic Slave Trade database (TST) illustrate the importance of the "Angolan wave" to Palmares, four factors qualify this picture. First, enslaved Africans also arrived in Pernambuco from other parts of the continent, thousands through 1670 and at least several hundred more through 1695. Second, following the death of Zumbi, new waves of ships arrived from West Africa, carrying tens of thousands of people.[37] Third, like similar umbrella terms, "Angola" hides internal complexities, symptomatic of the conceptual assumptions by scholars that Palmares was made by a "homogeneous" wave of Africans.[38] Fourth, even among those immersed in the languages and cultures created and passed down by West Central African parents, anyone born or raised in Palmares would have had unique understandings of many things, including what "home" meant—and where it was located.

The Landscape

Palmaristas made their homes on a seemingly boundless frontier. In the Caribbean, Africans mastered island terrain and its "condensed exaggeration of [African] homelands, with familiar features jammed into a miniature surrounding."[39] Palmares's landscape would have likewise been familiar, though hardly in "condensed" or "miniature" form. The vastness of Palmares helped make it a formidable refuge and allowed Palmaristas to resettle and evade the Europeans. While Jamaican maroons used the island's mountains to their advantage, the island was finite, circumscribed by colonial settlements and the ocean. Palmares, situated within and along an immense interior, had no such territorial limitation.[40] And while the vast landscape may have contained some familiar aspects, the kind of "landscape literacy," to borrow Rosalyn LaPier's eloquent phrase, that would allow them to not only utilize the terrain but also find in it the capacity to record and tell history would not simply come overnight.[41] If it took time to recognize and cultivate the land's intimate and powerful forms of inheritance, the Portuguese utilized land grants to foster different relationships and forms of possession, awarding massive territories to individuals meant to populate and turn profit from the land. Dozens (and even hundreds) of kilometers long from north to south, the donatory grants stretched inland to the line of Tordesilhas (or Tordesillas), the vertical demarcation between Portuguese and Spanish America. In practice, though, Portuguese settlements clung to the coast, the prominent exception being in São Paulo, where colonial expeditions probed the interior in search of precious metals, Indigenous people to enslave, and fugitives from slavery. These marauders, also called paulistas, would eventually be called north to lead assaults on Palmares. In Pernambuco, mountains, dense forest, and dry, forbidding terrain formed an immense sertão, or backlands. Though Europeans sought to encroach on that haven, sometimes the opposite took place: Dutch officials described would-be settlers fleeing *from* inland areas to live closer to military outposts in fear of the Blacks of Palmares.[42]

It was not always clear where Africans and their kin fled to within the vast interior. The Dutch identified the location of one fugitive community simply as in the "Forest of Brazil" (Mata do Brasil).[43] As new encampments formed, a collection of loosely aligned or disconnected, and perhaps even antagonistic, mocambos emerged, often understood from the outside as a single entity. Europeans' inability to ascertain exact locations made destroying the mocambos all the more difficult, and the vastness of the forest of Brazil gestures toward a broad horizon to which Palmaristas traveled during and long after the Dutch occupation. While the verified locations of the mocambos of Palmares are in an area that today traverses the states Alagoas and Pernambuco, the Dutch seemed to place some settlements farther north, in Paraíba, though many references are ambiguous.

Palm trees featured prominently across the lush landscape. What the Portuguese referred to as "palmeiras" were, in fact, different plant species, some indigenous to Brazil and others whose seeds arrived on ships from West and West Central Africa. Scholars previously believed that the pindoba palm (*Attalea* spp.), a species native to Brazil, grew in Palmares, but Case Watkins observes that the tree is rarely found in climates comparable to Serra da Barriga's.[44] He suggests, therefore, that Palmaristas went to great lengths to cultivate the pindoba on the mountaintop settlement. There is little evidence to go by here, but it is also possible that previous scholars were incorrect and that the denizens of Serra da Barriga did not grow pindobas and instead grew or otherwise lived among another kind (or kinds) of palm tree. This would not preclude the possibility that the pindoba was instead found in other mocambos with more propitious climates. Whatever the case, as Watkins shows, what the Portuguese called "palmeira" belies a large, varied collection of palms in the area.[45]

Often too dense to penetrate, the lush vegetation that the different species of palms grew amongst could yield birds, lumber, and other commodities. The Dutch provided special axes, hoes, machetes, and other tools to Indigenous men, who "were promised rewards" to clear paths and attack the mocambos.[46] European expeditions also took advantage of the knowledge and skill of Indigenous (and Black) guides in order to sustain themselves on fish, wild pigs, and an array of plants. One Portuguese account described the landscape as "naturally rugged, mountainous and rustic, seeded with all kinds of trees, known and unknown, with such density and chaos of branches that in many places no light penetrates; the diversity of thorns, bushes, and poisonous plants [are] enough to prevent passage." According to the account, the combination of impenetrable woods and "the most fertile lands" made Palmares a "natural couto," or hideout, for fugitives.[47]

Pernambuco's coast, with access to Atlantic ports, vegetation, and plentiful rain, became grounds for sugar plantations, which by the early seventeenth century extended as far as fifty kilometers inland.[48] Many observers commented on the seemingly endless expanse of the zona da mata (forest zone) and its seemingly infinite number of trees to be razed and land to be turned into engenhos. The Portuguese eventually carved the region into captaincies. For long periods of time, Alagoas, Paraíba, Rio Grande do Norte, and Ceará were administratively subordinate to Pernambuco, represented in what became a common phrase: "Pernambuco e anexos" (Pernambuco and appendages [or subdivisions]).[49]

The Pernambuco wilderness served multiple functions and held diverse meanings. Mountaintop settlements such as Serra da Barriga, which Zumbi controlled in the 1680s and 1690s, leveraged the landscape for protection.[50] Elevated above the surrounding area, the stronghold offered both vistas to help spot enemies and steep inclines to deter attacks (see figures 1.1 and 1.2). For Africans sprinting away from a plantation, the dash to the forest was terrifying. The dense woods to which they fled, full of menacing animals and insects, made their journey all the more harrowing. In West Central Africa, the dead were often buried in forests, which many associated with an Other World populated by ancestor and territorial spirits.[51] While this could scare anyone, some Africans who came to Palmares would have also looked hopefully to the woods for signs of spiritual potency and protection. Some elements of the Palmares landscape likely possessed strength, akin to the "places of power" that Elizabeth Colson describes in Central and Southern Africa: rocks, mountains, rivers, and lakes inhabited by spirits.[52] Some who came from Africa had already seen densely wooded areas serve as physical barriers against rivals or as havens from enemies.[53] Europeans projected their own ideas onto the forest. While the Portuguese imagined "civilized" settlers conquering "savage" people and lands, they depended heavily on both the settlers and the so-called savage groups not only to defeat Palmares and Indigenous people in the region but also to then occupy and harvest the land.[54]

Many understood Palmares as a universe unto itself. According to one hyperbolic estimation, the rebel Blacks controlled "a forest of such excessive grandeur that its circumference is larger than all of Portugal."[55] As Carvalho and França point out, the matas of Palmares were considered sertão, but not always because they were far away. Some areas "right nearby" were still considered backlands "because it was impossible to cross them easily."[56] That did not prevent observers from envisioning a lucrative landscape dedicated to agriculture. A Portuguese communiqué written near the end of the Palmares wars envisioned that the "total destruction" of Palmares and the taming of

FIGURE 1.1 Serra da Barriga, viewed from below (undated photograph). Courtesy of the Arquivo Público de Alagoas.

FIGURE 1.2 Serra da Barriga, viewed from above (in 2021). *Source*: https://www.gov.br /palmares/pt-br, accessed May 23, 2023.

Pernambuco's "many other deserts" would pave the way for "abundant pastures for livestock, useful lumber, land for plantations, and the capacity for all kinds of farming."[57] Between the 1580s and the turn of the eighteenth century, the number of engenhos in Pernambuco increased from sixty-six to around five hundred.[58] But even the growth of sugar and the spread of other forms of agriculture could not dent the dense surroundings, at least not until long after Palmares's heyday. And even then, the zona da mata remained vibrant and extensive. Writing in the 1810s, more than a century after Zumbi's death, a French visitor marveled at the "eternal verdure" of the forest.[59]

Multiple Meanings

The groups, communities, and societies that occupied the Palmares wilderness are today often rendered with a single term, quilombo, which scholars have interpreted as a colonial or American version of kilombo, the name of the mobile military unit utilized by roving groups of Imbangala in seventeenth-century Angola.[60] During the twentieth century, Black Brazilian activists such as Abdias do Nascimento placed quilombo (and Palmares) at the center of their political projects. Popular culture cemented the association further, a classic example being *Quilombo*, Carlos Diegues's (second) acclaimed film about Palmares, which showed at the 1984 Cannes Film Festival.[61] (We will return to the film and Diegues's first Palmares film, *Ganga Zumba* [1963], in the conclusion.) Though Palmares is now inextricably tied to "quilombo," colonial officials who wrote about Palmares rarely used the word, and not until the late seventeenth century.[62] They instead preferred "mocambo," a word that scholars have used Kimbundu dictionaries to translate as "hideout" or "fugitive camp." De Luna's forthcoming work uses more sophisticated linguistic analysis to deepen our understanding of the origins and meanings of "mocambo," which are more complex than previously thought.[63]

That the word "mocambo" was already in wide circulation before it appears in documents about Palmares is evident from four examples: a 1580 report by a Portuguese priest that describes a mountain on São Tomé called the Pico de Mocambo, home to "many Black rebels"; a 1625 Portuguese nautical manual that refers to a river and a place on the coast in Mozambique, both named "mocambo"; a famous manuscript about Portuguese America from the same decade that describes "a mocambo, or group of fugitive Blacks from Guinea, [in] the Palmares of the Rio Ytapucurú"; and a dictionary published by Rafael Bluteau in the 1710s and 1720s that contains two definitions of mocambo — "rustic villages" of Blacks in Brazil and "the name of one of the neighborhoods of Lisbon. . . . In earlier days there was in this spot a quantity of fishermen's huts, and negros."[64] Just within a small handful of Portuguese records, we find references to "mocambo" for areas stretching from Mozambique to São Tomé to Bahia to Lisbon, all by the early seventeenth century. Atlantic slavery would link Mozambique and Brazil in the 1640s, but the flow of enslaved people between the two areas remained sporadic until the second half of the eighteenth century.[65] In Lisbon, an area of the town was called Mocambo; it was home to Black communities, known for African spiritual practices, and was a destination for fugitives escaping slavery. The neighborhood's main street was Rua do Poço dos Negros (Street of the Blacks' Pit), named for a burial site where people communed with spirits and the dead.[66]

For most of the eighteenth century, Bluteau's readers would associate mocambo with not only Lisbon and "rustic" Black villages in Brazil, but also Palmares. The entry following mocambo is for "mocamaos," a word of uncertain origin, which Bluteau defined as follows: "In the sertão of Brazil, there are some rebel Blacks, who are called Negros dos Palmares; they give this name to the aldeias they inhabit."[67] In 1789, when another author revised the dictionary, these meanings had shifted somewhat. Mocambos were now "Quilombos, or dwelling made in the forest by Black runaway slaves in Brazil," and "Mocama'os" referred not to settlements but people: "Black runaways in Brazil, who live in Quilombos in the forest, also calhambolas." The later edition also includes an entry for quilombo: "(used in Brazil): a dwelling situated in the forest, or deserted place, where calhambolas, or fugitive slaves live."[68] The different versions of the dictionary convey important change. While adding "quilombo," the later edition dropped the references to Palmares and the neighborhood in Lisbon, suggesting that, at least for many Portuguese speakers, over the course of the eighteenth century, memory of Palmares had faded, even while other runaway settlements proliferated, now often called quilombos.

Though mocambos were the foundational unit of Palmares, even within Palmares they could take different forms. Writing in 1689, a Portuguese official highlighted this multiplicity within Palmares, "whose mocambos are so diverse."[69] Thirty years earlier, the Dutch artist Franz Post painted a landscape of rural Pernambuco titled Mocambos (see figure 1.3), populated with

FIGURE 1.3 *Mocambos*, Franz Post (ca. 1659). *Source*: https://commons.wikimedia.org /wiki/File:Frans_Post_-_Mocambos,_c._1659.jpg, accessed May 10, 2023.

characters, at least several of whom appear to be Indigenous.[70] Post's serene painting contrasts with the descriptions of Portuguese colonial officials, who viewed mocambos as emblematic of the forest and sertão, where the savage and wicked wreaked havoc on white colonists. The existence of such Indigenous mocambos in Palmares is plausible. Authorities in the Amazon called hidden settlements created by Indigenous people "Indian mocambos" (mocambos de índios). This was not a "semantic error," writes Marcus de Carvalho; instead, it reflected a "social reality," that mocambos were homes for any group "of similar, though not necessarily equal, origins and disposed to fight."[71]

Some mocambos in Palmares were named for leaders, while others alluded to nature or topography. The most powerful mocambo during the 1670s, what the Portuguese understood to be a "Royal City," was named Macaco. It was ruled by Gan(g)a Zumba, likely Zumbi's uncle, whom the Portuguese understood to be Palmares's "king." "Macaco" means monkey in Portuguese, and Europeans believed that the mocambo was named for a primate that died in the place where the settlement was made, but as we will see in chapter 8, the landscapes of Pernambuco and other areas retain Macaco place-names that suggest definitions far beyond the singular Portuguese translation.

Angola Janga and Tapera d'Angola

One of the phrases most associated with Palmares is "Angola janga," which appears in a document written after Zumbi's assassination on behalf of Domingos Jorge Velho, Palmares's most vaunted "conqueror," by Bento Surrel Camilio, who represented Jorge Velho's legal interests in Portugal.[72] According to Jorge Velho and Camilio, "Angola janga" meant "little Angola." Scholars repeated the translation until Robert Anderson proposed instead that the phrase came "from KiMbundu *ngola iadianga*, 'first Angola.'"[73] Africanists have since rejected Anderson's translation, and its definition remains open.[74]

There is no doubt what Jorge Velho understood the phrase to mean, which, even while likely distorting African meanings, is instructive. Unless the Crown awarded his men land there, Palmares would be left vacant, a point punctuated with the often-forgotten wording that precedes the now-famous phrase: *"there could be another* Angola Janga, Little Angola, as they call it."[75] West Central Africa was still a key source of enslaved laborers for the Portuguese and a site of ongoing conflict. So was São Tomé, where Portugal had recently defeated a group of Black rebels.[76] The last thing the king wanted to see in Brazil was the persistence, revival, or creation of a new "Angola." Proffered by Jorge Velho, "Little Angola" was an idea to convince the king to accede to his demands, an illustration of the power of what had come before—nearly a century of war that left the Crown constantly grasping for answers as the mocambos defied repeated waves of attack.

A lesser-known reference to Angola appears on a Dutch map of Pernambuco from 1665, which some scholars believe includes the only contemporaneous visual depiction of Palmares: of Black men pulling a fishing net from the water below a wooden structure (see figure 1.4). The structure, which appears to be a lookout, may have been a kind of stock image, as it resembles other illustrations of African military lookouts created and circulated by European artists.[77] In some versions of the map, the lookout is empty, but in the one pictured here a man is stationed on top, perhaps a mocambo member scanning the horizon for enemies. "S. Amaro" (labeled #1 in figure 1.4) was the Indigenous aldeia Santo Amaro, discussed in detail in chapter 7. (Aldeias

FIGURE 1.4 Southern Part of the Prefecture of Paranambuca (1665). *Source*: https://archive.org/details/dr_praefecturae-paranambucae-pars-meridionalis-108521259, accessed May 23, 2023.

were settlements created to concentrate Indigenous people on fixed plots of land, generally under the watch of Native leaders, though, as in the quotation from Bluteau, aldeias could also be used to refer to Black settlements.) Positioned along one of the main access points to Palmares, the community was utilized by the Portuguese and Dutch as a human shield against the mocambos and a staging ground for launching attacks on them. In the bottom righthand corner of the map (#2 in figure 1.4) is another interesting place: Tapera d'Angola. The name appears to bring sounds from three continents together, as "tapera" is a Tupi word for a village or aldeia that has been "destroyed" or is "in ruins."[78] The full phrase may be translated as something like "abandoned Angola" or "ruins of Angola."

Tapera d'Angola must have held different meanings to those who heard or voiced the name. For some, the phrase suggested a deserted, isolated place, or perhaps a remnant of Africa. Tapera d'Angola likely also conveyed change over time, and while decline and loss seem intrinsic, what was lost and at what point is unclear. The possibility that by the mid-seventeenth century a once-vibrant place named Angola existed in Pernambuco long enough to rise, fall, and see its ruins memorialized illustrates the overlapping waves of diaspora that flowed into and shaped the area. In Palmares, colonial forces regularly reported encountering abandoned mocambos. While in many cases this was the product of military engagement and evasion, there were likely other reasons to pick up and move. In West Central Africa, the BaKongo had a practice of abandoning a village when its chief died and building a new one at a different site. "The old chief's household fence," writes Wyatt MacGaffey, "became the stockade about its gate. Each village of the living then had its counterpart of the previous generation, the village of the dead in the forest."[79] The second edition of Bluteau's dictionary defines tapera a bit differently: "a rural property or farm that previously was cultivated, then abandoned, and allowed to become forest."[80] As the definition suggests, if tapera indicated decay to some, abandoned land could also signal rejuvenation and regeneration: cultivated land left unplanted could regenerate into forest, just as fields left fallow could later produce rich harvests. From this abandoned place, new forms of life might grow.

The possibility for such new forms of life is illustrated further on the Dutch map itself. The 1665 map that scholars often refer to was in fact a reproduction of just one panel of a massive wall hanging that became part of the Klencke Atlas, given by the Dutchman Joannes Klencke to the British king to curry favor in 1660 and drawn in 1647 by the Dutch cartographer Joan Blaeu (see figures 1.5 and 1.6). The size of the Atlas and its forty enormous maps, each more than three feet tall and five feet wide, were meant to show that it contained "all the knowledge in the world."[81] The illustrations in the 1647 original contain additional details that expand the scene of the Black men on the lookout and in the water, condensed for the smaller version. When the scene is viewed in its entirety, we can see that the men are traveling in boats along a river that winds provocatively inland but without a clear destination. Such men would have found spiritual meanings in the water that bore their boats, but the indeterminacy of the river's endpoint is also instructive. Whether by land or water, Africans and their kin who escaped slavery in Pernambuco charted paths that Europeans often had difficulty following, some of which have remained invisible even to historians.

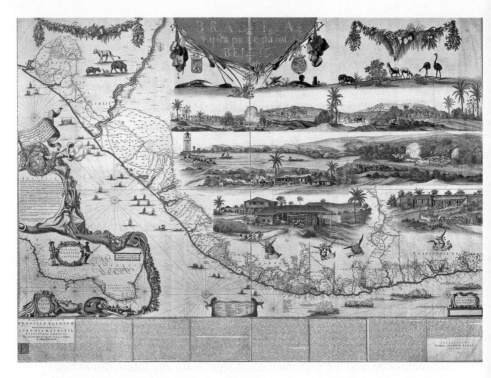

FIGURE 1.5 The Klencke Atlas (1660; original, 1647). Courtesy of Barry Lawrence Ruderman Antique Maps Inc.

FIGURE 1.6 Detail of the Klencke Atlas.

The Early Wars (1640s to ca. 1680)

Embodying loss and subsequent life, "abandoned Angola" defies the assumed timeline and geography of conquest and disrupts paradigmatic chronologies. The classic Palmares historiography, based in accounts such as the Blaer-Reijmbach diary, depicts the mocambos' history unfurling in linear fashion, from the rise of small groups of fugitives in the early seventeenth century to the formidable network of communities in the second half of the seventeenth century and the Portuguese victory in 1695. But "abandoned Angola" reminds us that the basic chronology is limited, occluding meaningful details and stories such as the woman killed on March 21, 1645, and the countless others like her ignored in the standard historical narrative. Knowing the contours of this chronology, though, better allows us to keep an eye on otherwise forgotten histories.

The basic history of Palmares can be divided into three eras: first, the early seventeenth century, which we know little about. Second, the 1640s to about 1680, when Dutch and Portuguese forces assaulted Palmares, a period that culminated with mocambos controlled by individuals who drew and passed power through either family lineage or political succession and, in the 1670s, the most detailed written accounts in colonial documents of that structure. In 1678, Palmares's powerful leader, Gan(g)a Zumba, signed a peace treaty with the governor of Pernambuco. The treaty was short-lived, and as Gan(g) a Zumba died, apparently poisoned by rivals, Zumbi was already on the rise, solidifying power and ushering in a third era from the early 1680s to his death in 1695, a period also marked by war between the Portuguese and an alliance of Indigenous groups in the northeast that became entangled with the Palmares wars.

We have inherited this chronology from colonial and nineteenth-century authors who were biased and motivated to emphasize an inevitable, absolute victory. A more circular history emerges as we reread with new eyes colonial documents that detail the military campaigns to destroy Palmares, which lasted decades and evoke the "endless" or "forever wars" of the twentieth and twenty-first centuries. In contrast to the steady, inevitable march of European might conveyed in published narratives of Palmares, military reports show an unending quagmire: complaints about assaults by the rebel Blacks, followed by orders to wipe them from the face of the earth, and then premature declarations of victory.[82]

Early histories written in Portuguese suggest that much of the mocambos' growth in Palmares occurred during the Dutch occupation.[83] Though there is truth to this, enslaved people fled captivity at different times, for different reasons, and headed toward different destinations. In response, Europeans employed gruesome, demonstrative punishments. The 1654 expulsion of the Dutch was promptly followed by a Portuguese order to quarter and hang in public the corpses of Palmaristas killed in battle.[84] Throughout

Brazil, those who escaped slavery posed an intractable, even existential threat to the colonial project, and Palmares became the dominant symbol of that threat. The flip side of the mocambos' strength and success was the violence used against them. While the Portuguese hoped to capture and imprison "*negros* levantados," they also deemed it acceptable to kill and display Palmarista corpses at sites where they had escaped slavery or carried out an assault.[85]

Such demonstrations of violence were part of a continuous cycle. In 1663, a priest sent to Palmares to negotiate was dismissed with "contempt and scandalous words" by mocambo leaders who also beheaded two Palmaristas in favor of accepting the offer.[86] The failure inspired Portuguese calls for more force and to hang any Black fugitive over the age of fifteen. In 1671, the Overseas Council determined that all male Palmares prisoners older than seven should be branded on the face with a hot iron and sent to Portugal.[87] Living with the constant threat of such brutality, Palmaristas knew that even the landscape around them was at risk when expeditions approached. One governor of Pernambuco ordered the construction of new paths to penetrate thick woods that gave cover to Palmares and its seemingly ever-growing collection of mocambos, which were "fortified by nature" and the "roughness" of the forest. The new paths, he hoped, would help "demolish" and "extinguish" the communities.[88]

Stymied by the mocambos, colonial officials conjured an array of measures to strengthen their hand. In addition to orders to sell prisoners to distant lands and the gruesome directives to mark, maim, and kill, the Portuguese provided exemptions for almost any crime committed by men participating in attacks on Palmares.[89] During the 1670s, men who would become some of Brazil's most famous conquerors began to emerge from the colonial military ranks in starring roles in the Palmares war enterprise. Pernambuco governor Pedro de Almeida (1674–78) assigned the task of destroying Palmares to a Portuguese officer named Manuel Lopes Galvão. Lopes would petition the Crown for recompense based on repeated, but dubious, claims that he killed Zumbi. In late 1675, he set off from Porto Calvo with 280 "whites, *mulatos* and Indians" to attack the mocambos. Lopes's men encountered a "great city of more than 2,000 dwellings," where they "killed many, wounded more than a few, and captured seventy."[90] After the battle, the soldiers set up a makeshift fort and remained in the area for five months. Word arrived that some Palmaristas had escaped "twenty leagues beyond Palmares." Penetrating a set of "craggy trails so prickly and savage" that they seemed impassable, colonial forces killed "many" and set others fleeing once again.[91] The wounded included "Zambi," which, according to a Catholic priest, Padre Antônio da Silva, meant "God of War" or "God of Arms."[92] Zambi survived the battle "but was maimed in one leg."[93] He was likely the leader of a mocambo named Zambi and probably not the man who later came to be known as Zumbi, though Lopes and later histories would fold these figures into one.

Though Lopes inflicted serious damage on Palmares, Almeida chose another man of European descent, capitão-mor (captain major) Fernão Carrilho, "to put a final end to those enemies."[94] Carrilho had already made a name for himself in Bahia and Sergipe, where he had "extinguished" settlements of "rebel Blacks."[95] He was celebrated in one of the earliest texts about Palmares, the *Relação das guerras feitas aos Palmares de Pernambuco no tempo do Governador D. Pedro de Almeida de 1675 a 1678* (*Account of the Wars Waged against Palmares in Pernambuco during the Time of Governor D. Pedro de Almeida from 1675 to 1678*). For centuries, the text's author and date were unknown, until Lara and Phablo Fachin's sleuth work revealed it to be Padre Antônio da Silva. In 1678, he penned the text, which he later revised, and it was subsequently edited and changed by other hands centuries later.[96] The *Relação* celebrated Carrilho for "destroying mocambos and Tapuia aldeias that infested [the Bahian backlands]."[97]

According to the *Relação*, Carrilho led a 1677 expedition in late September that targeted the "cerca de Aca Inene" (Aca Inene Fort), named for "the mother of the king."[98] Most of the Palmaristas fled, including Aca Inene, whose name different versions of the *Relação* also rendered as Arotireve, Aqualtune, and Acatirene.[99] Several days after driving Aca Inene from her stronghold, Carrilho's men found the corpse of a female member of her court. Though we know little about her and other female Palmares leaders, Aca Inene was likely just one of a larger female contingent that held powerful positions in the mocambos. Carrilho's forces took prisoners, who told them that Gan(g)a Zumba, his brother Gan(g)a Zona, and "all of the most important and powerful leaders" were in Subupira, a "great, strongly fortified city," gathering an army to confront Carrilho. When Carrilho arrived, the city had been burned to the ground, "only its ashes left to demonstrate its grandeur." Carrilho ordered a fort built on the site, which he renamed Bom Jesus e a Cruz (Good Jesus and the Cross), and called for reinforcements.

From the fort, Carrilho sent his men on forays to "unveil the secrets of those woods." In one encounter, they captured more than fifty Palmaristas, including Gan(g)amuisa (also Gan[g]a-Muiça), "field general of the people of Angola." If he was not a military leader in Africa before coming to Palmares, certainly others were. The prisoners also included "the most well-known captains" of Palmares: Gaspar (also Gpar), a member of the king's guard; the "infamous captains" João Tapuya and Ambrosio; and others whose anonymity consigned them to be buried in "perpetual oblivion." Gan(g)a Zumba had fled and remained at large. In the months that followed, colonial envoys battled with Palmares forces at multiple sites. The next target was the Mocambo de Amaro, with an estimated one thousand dwellings and whose namesake "is celebrated in those Palmares and feared in our towns." During the battle, one of Gan(g)a Zumba's sons, Tuculo, died along with another important leader, whom the *Relação* identifies as "Pacassa."[100] Carrilho's men took forty-seven prisoners, including "two free Black women [duas *negras* forras] and a little *mulata* girl, the daughter of a noble resident of Serinhaém, who had been robbed by those same Blacks." By taking the two "free women" as prisoners, Carrilho illustrated not only the precarity of freedom but also the limits of colonial legal categories and of the very concept of freedom. Did the women travel to Palmares of their own accord? If so, what drew them there? The fact that the women identified (or were identified) as free suggests that the designation might help them even after being captured. Others may have claimed similar status, though like the character in Jones's novel, they almost certainly understood themselves in terms that surpassed the boundaries of "slave" and "free."

The *Relação* also recounts the capture of multiple grandchildren and nephews—and, one presumes, nieces, though the default masculinity of many Portuguese nouns (in this case, sobrinhos) leaves that somewhat open. Two of Gan(g)a Zumba's sons, including "a macho named Zambi," apparently a different man than the leader wounded previously, were among those taken prisoner.[101] Gan(g)a Zumba, wounded by an arrow, survived, "fleeing in such a hurry that he left behind a gold-plated firearm and sword."[102] Additional battles resulted in more casualties, including another "potentate" (named Gone) and prisoners.[103] Carrilho returned to Porto Calvo in early 1678 to a hero's welcome. He brought more prisoners, including an elderly couple related to Gan(g)a Zumba by marriage named Matheos Zambi (or Matheos Dambi) and Madalena, "a Black Angolan woman."[104] Convinced that the war against Palmares was finally all but over, Almeida undertook final preparations to end it.

Though clearly written to glorify Almeida, the *Relação* is instructive for what it both includes and overlooks. Carrilho and a handful of other Euro-descended officers who directed attacks on Palmares are the central figures; Black and Native soldiers and officers are all but absent. The text also preserved the names of select Palmaristas. Though not all the names in the *Relação* line up with those in official communiqués, they are nonetheless suggestive. João Tapuya may have been Indigenous; "Tapuia" was an umbrella term that the Portuguese used to refer to non-allied Indigenous people. Not surprisingly, there is little discussion of those whom the Europeans deemed unimportant, like the unnamed woman killed on March 21, 1645, those whose memories the *Relação* describes as destined for "perpetual oblivion."

The specific details that are included in the text about Palmaristas, though, cannot all be taken at face value. Whether claiming to be free by Portuguese law or other means, those imprisoned in Palmares hoped to leverage anything at their disposal to shield against what was to come: enslavement, prison, or death. Precedent in Africa would suggest to the prisoners that being part of a royal Palmares family might yield benefit in much the same way that similar standing kept the royal Ndongo prisoners alive. Whether any of the Palmares prisoners embellished their identities by inventing or exaggerating kinship ties, some of those whom the Portuguese considered to be Palmares royalty would, indeed, soon receive favored status.

Riding Carrilho's successes and certain that Palmares was on the verge of defeat, Almeida prepared a treaty to incorporate surviving Palmaristas as loyal vassals to the king. In a report written in February 1678, Almeida retold successes of the last year, highlighting a group of prisoners that included three women believed to be wives of Gan(g)a Zumba and ten of his grandchildren. Almeida also claimed that Gan(g)a Zumba was dead.[105] This was untrue. Gan(g)a Zumba was still alive and Almeida was preparing a separate message, which he sent to Palmares via a lieutenant: Carrilho was about to launch another offensive that would not spare a single life "in that entire sertão." The only alternative was to "live in peace" and "union" with the Portuguese, who would guarantee fair treatment, cede land, and hand over the women and children they had taken prisoner. Almeida's messenger returned to Recife with a Palmarista entourage that included three of Gan(g)a Zumba's sons. "Prostrate at the feet of Dom Pedro de Almeida," they requested an end to the war and to be recognized as Portuguese vassals.[106] Almeida's successor, Aires de Sousa de Castro, participated in deliberations and was present at an elaborate ceremony at a church decorated and adorned with candles for the occasion. Perhaps exaggerating, the *Relação* recounts that "old, young, whites, Blacks, and everyone" celebrated.[107] The next day, the Portuguese agreed to send a Black officer "who knew how to read and write" to present the terms of the treaty to Gan(g)a Zumba. That, the *Relação* concluded, was how "the ruin [of] Palmares, so feared in these captaincies, came to pass."[108]

The *Relação's* triumphant narrative excludes and distorts key dynamics and events, including the treaty, which Lara has studied in depth. When Almeida's term as governor ended, he returned to Portugal, where he hoped to secure a new post, but colonial officials were nonplussed with his achievements and he faded into obscurity. The earliest surviving document regarding the treaty, dated June 22, 1678, is a letter laying out the proposed terms, which Aires de Sousa de Castro sent to Gan(g)a Zumba.[109] Gan(g)a Zumba would guarantee that he and Palmares's other "potentates" would cease hostilities and hand over anyone who fled to the mocambos. In return, he would be pardoned "for living for so many years outside of our obedience," as would anyone born in Palmares and a group including Gan(g)a Zumba's wife, his children, and two leaders, Amaro and João Mulato (both of whom the Portuguese had captured). The Palmaristas would move to a place called Cucaú, where they would live semiautonomously, in a settlement resembling Indigenous aldeias.[110]

From the governor's perspective, the chance to finally end the wars with Palmares was tantalizing, as was the prospect of having its leader stationed in a permanent, accessible location and responsible for preventing the creation of new mocambos and further uprisings. Once its sworn enemy, Gan(g)a Zumba would become the Crown's loyal vassal. To Gan(g)a Zumba, there was also much to gain. He would maintain control over Palmares, enter into a formal relationship with the Portuguese, and see the return of his family members and trusted lieutenants. Cucaú represented another attractive part of the deal. The land, rich and full of palm trees, would provide sustenance, and the Palmaristas were guaranteed the same rights as any other vassal to the crops they would grow. While notable for showing the relative power that Palmares wielded even in apparent defeat, the proposed treaty also left no doubt about who had the upper hand. In becoming a Portuguese vassal, Gan(g)a Zumba agreed to submit to a strict military, economic, and political order. Catholic baptisms would formally seal religious conversion.[111]

Negotiations were aided by convoys representing both parties: Palmares leadership and members of the all-Black Henrique Dias regiment. The two sides exchanged gifts: black woolen cloth and another offering, most likely an axe, for Gan(g)a Zumba, and an unnamed object for Castro, who expressed great appreciation and sent flour to aid the resettlement in Cucaú.[112] In the months ahead, Castro sent three more letters, two to Gan(g)a Zumba (whom he addressed as "Ganazumba") and one to Gan(g)a Zona ("Ganasona"), continuing to convey enthusiasm and confidence in the process. In July, he reaffirmed his commitment to the treaty and assured Gan(g)a Zumba that his family members were in good health, including a son who had been wounded before being captured. The governor closed by asserting that he would provide Gan(g)a Zumba, Gan(g)a Zona, and Zumbi everything they needed, as long as they remained peaceful. Leaving the identity of Zumbi still in doubt, Castro refers to "Zumbim" in one letter and to "Zambim" in another.[113]

It is possible that Castro had two different people in mind but more likely that he simply slipped between "Zumbi" and "Zambi," unsure of the actual name. There is no record of direct communication between Castro and Zumbi (or Zambi) at this juncture, though by mentioning him (or them) alongside Gan(g)a Zumba and Gan(g)a Zona the governor highlighted his (or their) rising influence. In a separate communication, Castro emphasized that the resettlement process depended on "those who they [the Palmaristas] call kings" to corral groups and individuals who were scattered across the region.[114] Castro also confirmed his understanding that Gan(g)a Zona and "Zambim" would ensure that all Palmaristas settled in Cucaú, leaving the area free of all fugitives and mocambos.

In November, Castro wrote to Gan(g)a Zona and then to Gan(g)a Zumba.[115] He once again expressed his confidence in the process, but the governor informed Gan(g)a Zumba that his son had died, reassuring him, "[Your son] had a death that every white person would envy." Noting that he had already sent priests to educate the Palmaristas, Castro explained that because the son "died as a child of the church," his father could take comfort in knowing "that he is in heaven."[116] It is possible that Gan(g)a Zumba took solace in the governor's explanation, but even if not, his son's death did not derail the treaty. Gan(g)a Zumba and Gan(g)a Zona moved to Cucaú with three hundred Palmaristas.[117] The war, at long last, was over.

Except that there was a catch (two, in fact). A few months earlier, an official had written that "another potentate who they call Zomby" was still in the forest with an untold number of Palmaristas who viewed with "repugnance" the prospect of returning to slavery.[118] In March 1680, on behalf of the governor, Manuel Lopes issued a proclamation (bando) informing "Zumby" that the governor had again "pardoned" him and imploring him to join "Ganazona" and "to live in . . . liberty with his entire family."[119] Whether at this time there was also a leader or leaders named Zambi, by now the man whom the Portuguese knew as Zumbi (or Zombi) was the focal point of colonial military and diplomatic strategy. Lopes gave Zumbi four months to accept the offer, though once again betraying the Portuguese inability to pin him down, the proclamation itself was addressed to "any person, whatever their standing," who could locate him and deliver the message. It is unclear if Zumbi ever received Lopes's message.

The second catch was that, by the time that Lopes issued his bando, Gan(g)a Zumba was now truly dead. The Portuguese had arrested a group that included João Mulato, Amaro, and Gaspar, whom they accused of poisoning Gan(g)a Zumba.[120] We do not know how Zumbi made his decision to reject the treaty, or who else participated in making it. Nor is it definite that he was involved in Gan(g)a Zumba's assassination. Nonetheless, the results were clear: Gan(g)a Zumba was dead, the treaty had collapsed, and the man the Portuguese were coming to know as Zumbi was somewhere in Palmares, apparently unwilling to negotiate and girding for more war.

In the wake of the failed treaty, colonial officials increasingly employed the word "war" (guerra) to refer to the struggle against Palmares, a rhetorical device that laid bare what had been obvious for many years. Even as Gan(g)a Zumba led hundreds of Palmaristas to Cucaú, the Portuguese drew up plans to attack those who chose not to be part of the accord. The next year, confounded by Zumbi, they issued the proclamation to pardon him but also sent men to destroy him. Authorities also placed new emphasis on sending prisoners far away, to either Rio de Janeiro or Lisbon. In March, an important Palmares leader, Moioio, was captured and then jailed in Recife.[121] With the death of Gan(g)a Zumba, Portuguese officials backed out of the agreement made with him and insisted that everyone who had resettled in Cucaú be treated as runaways.[122] Less than two years after signing the treaty, the Portuguese invaded Cucaú, killing many and imprisoning between two hundred and six hundred people who had resettled there with the promise of freedom.[123]

The repeated cycles of violence that marked the pre-treaty years resumed. A report written in 1680 suggested that Manuel Lopes had brought the Portuguese once again close to victory. Lopes claimed to have killed and imprisoned more than eight hundred Palmaristas, leaving a "great quantity" of others to starve to death. The "principal leaders" had all perished, except for "Zombi . . . who governs them today, though there are very few of them."[124] This was another false diagnosis. In 1682, the Crown issued a lengthy order that announced the continuation of the war and that regulated the terms of "freedom, slavery, and punishment of the Blacks of Palmares."[125] The order preserved a key clause from the Cucaú treaty about prisoners: those born in Palmares, or who were free before coming to Palmares, would retain their status. But whether enslaved or free, all prisoners over the age of seven would be exiled from Brazil, and those who were free and did not leave would face whipping and the galleys. Prisoners who tried to escape would be hung "because flight is always an indication of guilt."[126] The order also instructed that the individuals suspected of killing Gan(g)a Zumba should be tried and that those found guilty would be executed and decapitated, their heads displayed on tall posts.

In 1684, Carrilho was accused of undermining the Portuguese by attempting to negotiate with the Palmaristas on his own accord, in violation of the agreed-upon strategy of "cruel war." As early as 1654, the Portuguese called explicitly for "cruel war" against Palmares. The category was constructed in opposition to the more well-known "just war," which colonial agents often used in Africa and America as legal window dressing to legitimize abuses.[127] He was exiled to Ceará and replaced by an officer who spent "the entire winter" in Palmares with his troops, with little to show for it.[128] The following year, the Portuguese king, Pedro II, directly appealed to "Captain Zumbi of Palmares" with an offer reminiscent of the accord with Gan(g)a Zumba. Stating that he understood Zumbi's "defiance," the king offered Zumbi "whichever dwelling place" he desired and the opportunity to live "with your wife and children, and all of your captains, free of any form of slavery or subjugation, as my faithful and loyal vassals, under my royal protection."[129] It is not known whether Zumbi received the letter. Peace, in any case, was not on the horizon. Carrilho had been released from prison and sent back to Palmares, where he apparently abandoned any thought of brokering peace. Debates in Lisbon about whether to approach Palmares through negotiation or military force ended in favor of the more hawkish arguments.[130] Bent on war, some members of the Conselho Ultramarino dismissed negotiations with Palmares as "always a deception," a feeling that, especially after the invasion of Cucaú, was surely mutual.[131]

Cruel and Entangled Wars

In the years following Gan(g)a Zumba's death, three important developments shaped what would be remembered as Zumbi's heyday. First, with many mocambos now destroyed or abandoned, the center of power shifted south, with Serra da Barriga emerging as the most important settlement. Though colonial attacks drove Palmaristas from the stronghold on several occasions, this was the nucleus of Zumbi's Palmares. Second, as the post-treaty Palmares took shape, officials in Pernambuco and Portugal contracted soldiers from São Paulo to battle Palmares. Third, in 1687 a massive uprising of Indigenous people in Rio Grande do Norte drew attention and resources away from Palmares and ultimately entangled Black, white, Indigenous, and mixed-race combatants and officers fighting for the Portuguese into two expansive war fronts. While for obvious reasons Palmares has been understood in relation to Atlantic slavery, the campaign to destroy it was also entwined with the Portuguese design to rid the continent of Native people or confine them to aldeias. The Native uprising in 1687 was part of a prolonged, multifront war, the so-called Guerra dos Bárbaros (War of the Barbarians), which was fought in two main phases. The first took place in Bahia between 1651 and 1679.[132] The second, also known as the Guerra do Açu, began in the late 1680s and ended in the early eighteenth century.[133] Fighting spanned across the northeastern sertão, but beginning in the 1680s the focus shifted to the Pernambucan hinterlands and Açu, in Rio Grande do Norte.[134] Wars against Native people and Palmares had been connected by varying degrees for some time. In 1655, soon after expelling the Dutch, the governor-general of Brazil expressed his satisfaction with reports of a successful battle in Palmares and "the pacification of the Tapuias of Rio Grande." He hoped "that neither the Blacks energize themselves to flee again, nor the Indians to rebel."[135] Neither wish would come to pass.

During the Guerra do Açu, the Portuguese realized early on that they needed reinforcements, the first waves of which would come from Pernambuco. When even those forces proved insufficient, fighters from São Paulo were called north. Many had participated in bandeiras, expeditions into the interior named for the banners that the men carried. Later glorified as national symbols and trailblazers of a unique white São Paulo identity, the paulistas, also known as bandeirantes, would play a determining role in the Palmares wars.[136] The governor-general of Brazil who appealed personally to the paulista military leader Jorge Velho used bloodlust and the promise to keep captives to help lure him to fight in Rio Grande, but in Palmares Jorge Velho's 1687 contract directed him to bring all prisoners to Recife, where they would be loaded onto ships destined for distant ports. He and his men would be allowed to keep for themselves children between the ages of seven and twelve who were born in Palmares (filhos dos Palmares, or "children of Palmares"), though that was later revised.[137] Jorge Velho and his fellow conquerors would also have the opportunity to secure land "to populate and cultivate as their own."[138] Local plantation owners would pay a fee for fugitives Jorge Velho captured, but anyone born in Palmares would belong to Jorge Velho "as if he enslaved them in war."[139] The terms of the contract projected a precise operation with a clean end: the mocambos would be destroyed, the prisoners would be enslaved or sent far away, and the conquerors would settle the land. But before any of that could happen, the governor-general pulled Jorge Velho back from Palmares and sent him to Rio Grande do Norte. Jorge Velho would return to Palmares, but only after laying waste to parts of Rio Grande do Norte, where even Portuguese victories were so destructive that colonial settlers fled the captaincy in their wake.[140]

When Jorge Velho returned to Palmares, a new governor-general, Antonio Luis Gonçalves da Câmara Coutinho, suggested he take with him a group of Indigenous soldiers, who would be motivated, Coutinho reasoned, by "the hate that all types of Indians have for Blacks."[141] The practice of employing Black and Indigenous regiments in Palmares and Rio Grande illustrates dueling processes that shaped both wars. Each struggle was meant to obliterate nonwhite people, even while the forces used to do so depended on Black, Indigenous, and mixed-race soldiers. Most early twentieth-century writers described the paulistas as mamelucos (a term for offspring of white and Indigenous parents, meant in this case as an epithet: "half-breeds"), but over time they became exalted as white.[142] In reality, paulista ranks were full of nonwhites. In one regiment, more than half of the members were Indigenous; nearly a quarter Black or mixed-race.[143] Like many other regiments, this one had a high desertion rate: 82 of its 213 men fled.[144] While some escaped to join different regiments, others left the military altogether, some likely join-ing Black and Indigenous settlements.

During this time, Zumbi consolidated power and continued to fend off Portuguese attacks. In the second half of the 1680s, the Portuguese launched fewer attacks on Palmares than they had (and would), perhaps because of the attention and resources drawn to Rio Grande do Norte.[145] In Pernambuco, talk of Palmares's demise was replaced with a recognition of facts on the ground. An attack led by Carrilho was foiled when word arrived well ahead of the sol-diers, who were caught in ambushes; Carrilho's forces determined that the Palmarista fortifications were "impenetrable" and "invincible."[146] Other lead-ers and mocambos emerged in the 1680s, including Miguel Cacunda (also Caconda), the "leader of many insurgents" who resided in the Mocambo do Sertão.[147] We know little about what, if any, relationship he had to Zumbi and other Palmares leaders. Rebel Black strongholds extended deep into the inte-rior. One Portuguese expedition took soldiers ninety leagues into the sertão to confront "heathens from Guinea." The attack sent the insurgents fleeing even further into the backlands.[148]

When the Guerra do Açu wound down in the early eighteenth century, a member of the clergy denounced the war for abandoning the principles of "just war." The enslavement of Indigenous people in Açu, he wrote, was "not just unjust but fraudulent."[149] No such defense would be proffered on behalf of Palmares. In 1691, the powerful priest António Vieira wrote a demonstra-tive letter that would help set the tone for what was to come.[150] Vieira wrote striking denunciations of Indigenous slavery, but in the case of Palmares, he was unflinchingly brutal.[151] Vieira rejected a proposal to send priests into Palmares, which, he explained, would be "impossible and useless for many reasons." Palmaristas, he argued, would only trust people "of their nation and language," but even clergy from Africa would not be able to convince them that they were not colonial spies, and the slightest misgiving would lead the Palmaristas to poison the priests, "as they do in occult and darkly secret ways to one another."[152] In the unlikely event that the Palmaristas could be convinced to stop their "assaults" against the "Portuguese people," they still would never stop welcoming "those from their nation who flee to them." As "rebels and slaves," Vieira intoned, Palmaristas lived in "continuous sin" and could not be absolved or receive "the grace of God" without submitting to slavery, which they would never do. Without even more dramatic measures against it, Palmares would beckon "the total destruction of Brazil" as Blacks everywhere would continue to flee "to the forest with all of their property, which is nothing more than their own body." Soon, "every city, every village, every small settlement, every plantation would become so many other Palmares."[153] Pedro II concurred. No mission would be sent to Palmares. Instead, the Portuguese would continue to assault the mocambos with what the king described as "the means necessitated by its obstinance."[154]

Conclusion

Rather than proceed straight through from this ominous declaration to the rest of the 1690s and Zumbi's death and the final years of warfare, a brief pause is in order. Both the linear European triumphalism of traditional historiography and the unending cycles of assault and premature declarations of victory found in colonial documents are correct, at least in part. Different versions of Palmares did rise and eventually fall, and the campaigns to destroy it were long, repetitive, and often ended empty-handed, much like the Blaer-Reijmbach expedition. Viewed either through the traditional historiography or the primary sources, Vieira's missive and Pedro II's pronouncement signal the beginning of the end for the mocambos. But though this conventional interpretation is not without merit, it leaves little space for the kind of open-endedness suggested by Tapera d'Angola, where decay could also beckon rebirth, or the woman whose death in 1645 may be understood not only as coarse and violent but also as a piercing reminder of the immense number of lives, deaths, and histories overshadowed by Palmares's most famous protagonists. Signaling the potential for life after death and growth after loss, the unnamed woman and Tapera d'Angola therefore complicate and allow us to push beyond conventional chronologies, which also founder in the case of Palmares's most famous leader, Zumbi, whom, we will see in the next chapter, colonial forces claimed to have killed many times before he died.

Before He Died, I Killed Zumbi

In 1694, Padre Antônio da Silva, the author of *Relação das guerras feitas aos Palmares*, delivered an ecstatic sermon in Recife. The address celebrated the conclusion of a debilitating siege and devastating assault at Serra da Barriga in early February of that year.[1] By that point, soldiers, officers, and officials had written scores of reports about the seemingly invincible leader of Palmares, a man they referred to as (among other names and spellings) Zambi, Zombi, and Zumbi. Convinced that Zumbi was finally dead, Silva used confusion about his name to explain the significance of the victory. "If the name of the Governor of the Blacks was Zumbi, this was the greatest victory we have seen. If [the governor's name] was Zambi this is the greatest victory that we have ever seen and that we could ever see. Zumbi means demon. To defeat an armed demon on the battlefield is a triumph of God. Zambi means God. We have never seen nor ever could see a God defeated." In either case, the priest reasoned, "the victory" was one "that only a God could achieve."[2]

Once again, the Portuguese had gotten ahead of themselves; the invincible leader was not dead. For a year and a half after the battle at Serra da Barriga, colonial forces sought in vain to disprove the rumor that continued to circulate: that Zumbi was not dead and could never be killed. Finally, in late November 1695, they tracked him down with the help of an informant. After killing Zumbi on November 20, soldiers cut off his head, which two men carried one hundred leagues to Recife. There they delivered it to the governor, Caetano de Melo de Castro, who displayed it on a pike—the gruesome apparent conclusion to an endless war.[3]

While the Portuguese used the occasion to once again mark the end of the wars, for years colonial combatants had been claiming that they had killed Zumbi as they sought wealth and promotion through military and administrative ranks. Their ability to make these claims owed in part to confusion about who Zumbi was. Now taken for granted, Zumbi's rise was shrouded in mystery, at least to the Portuguese. The first written reference to him may appear in a 1676 Overseas Council discussion of candidates for a notary position. The council lauded the winner, Manuel Lopes, for fighting "against the rebel Blacks of Palmares" and "killing and wounding a quantity of Blacks, among them the brother of their King [known] by the name Zamby."[4] The mundane nature of the document is striking. Buried in the dry deliberations about an administrative position appears to lie the first written record of Brazil's most revered maroon leader.

But typical of other communiqués, this one is vague on crucial matters: Did Lopes wound or kill Zamby? And was Zamby actually the same man whom the Portuguese killed in 1695, whom we now know as Zumbi? The wording even leaves open the possibility that Zamby is the king, and that Lopes has killed (or wounded) his brother. It is likely that the man whom Lopes claimed to have wounded or slain was the same "Zambi" the *Relação* describes Lopes wounding but not capturing. And though this man was, in fact, almost certainly not the man called Zumbi who was killed on November 20, 1695, over time Lopes would suggest without hesitation that it was—a tale that, we will see at the end of this book, has been passed down to his descendants today. In the seventeenth and eighteenth centuries, others joined Lopes in making apocryphal claims about the great leader's death, in the process helping consolidate a single figure known as Zumbi. But the confusion and misdirection that mark the colonial documents also suggest other paths and trajectories cut short—additional lives and narratives left behind or otherwise marginalized by the now-singular icon. The wealth that Lopes and other colonial combatants secured from stories of Zumbi's death illustrates one of Palmares's most palpable inheritances, while the false claims expose cracks in the foundations on which that wealth—and often, by extension, white masculinity—was constructed. And while Lopes profited from Zumbi's death, others found different uses and meanings for it: transformation rather than conclusion or disappearance. Competing understandings and uses of Zumbi's death carried him across 1695, alternately viewed as an immortal (or slain) warrior, an everlasting spirit, or a war trophy.

Death and Mercê

Claims that Lopes and other soldiers made about Zumbi's death owed to a basic fact. Just as the Crown and those who traded and enslaved people assigned monetary values to Black people and their labor, so too did they monetize their deaths. This occurred in many forms, ranging from insurance policies to compensate plantation owners for "lost labor" (i.e., enslaved people who escaped captivity or died) to financial rewards for surgeons who kept mortality rates on slave ships under a designated level.[5] Fearful of the creation "of many new Palmares," authorities institutionalized the position of "forest captain" (capitão-do-mato), a state-sponsored man charged with apprehending fugitives from slavery.[6] Plantation owners asked colonial authorities to help capture and return the formerly enslaved alive and able to labor once again under their control, but while the armed bands that ventured into Palmares often returned with prisoners, they also killed many of the people they encountered.

The quest to destroy Palmares depended on the orders, financial backing, and physical labor of a diverse group of actors with different interests and stakes, including Black, Indigenous, white, and mixed-race men forced or enticed into battle; mainly white or Euro-descendant landowners and city councils; and also mainly white or Euro-descendant colonial authorities ranging from low-level administrators to royalty. The commodification of Black life and death shaped the economics of war and provided opportunities for upward-striving combatants to seek payment from the Crown, which taxed the human prizes that combatants claimed as their own through an obligation known as the "royal fifth" (quinto real). Soldiers and officers of the Portuguese empire owed the Crown one-fifth of any bounty, human and precious metals alike, that they seized in conquest expeditions. Many went to great lengths to hide or obscure the number or value of captives and other prizes in order to avoid or lessen their obligation to pay the Crown.[7] In early 1680, a town council in Alagoas made known a bounty list: 2$000 (two milréis) for those who escaped slavery in the town and its surroundings, 4$000 for those who escaped from elsewhere in Alagoas, 8$000 from Pernambuco, 10$000 from Bahia, and 12$000 for those "from the forest of Palmares."[8] In addition to illustrating another way that colonial society commodified Black people, the list highlights the diverse origins of those who fled to Palmares and the significance of those born in the mocambos.

As they killed and bled on behalf of the Crown, soldiers and officers had rewards on their minds. To earn royal compensation, they enumerated their military achievements, often via written petitions. Many claimants sought mercê, which meant awards, gifts, and privileges granted by the royal throne. The Portuguese used mercê to secure loyalty across its empire. More than a simple payment, mercê indicated that the monarch had magnanimously bestowed divine "grace" (also "favor" or "mercy") on the recipient in return for a service or favor previously rendered.[9] The Overseas Council considered mercê petitions and forwarded recommendations to the monarch, who made the final decision. Most combatants asked for soldos (salaries), tenças (pensions), promotions, and reimbursement for personal expenditures made in support of a military campaign.[10] Some received sesmarias (land grants) or hábitos, "insignias" that bestowed membership in elite religious and knightly orders. To receive mercê, petitioners often highlighted the number of enemies they killed or took prisoner, compiling grisly résumés for material reward. Petitions often quantified, and no doubt exaggerated, death tolls; except in the case of well-known leaders, they often left the dead nameless. Officials complained for years that to secure rewards soldiers and officers falsely claimed to have participated in battles that they did not appear in and otherwise invented exploits. In 1689, Recife's municipal council registered a forceful denunciation of such practices, and in 1690, additional levels of review were added to the mercê system, though the problem persisted, among not only veterans but also their descendants.[11]

Portugal cultivated violence in the colonies by rewarding brutal acts. This is made clear in deliberations for prestigious and lucrative military and administrative positions, which highlighted the number of people each candidate claimed to have killed and captured on the battlefield. Take the case of one colonial commander, who petitioned to replace his recently deceased uncle as alcaide-mor (constable) of Porto Calvo. In the long list of accomplishments he submitted to buttress his case, he highlighted, in addition to battlefield exploits and the fact that he had provided enslaved people and other resources to the war effort, how he had organized a convoy to kill one enslaved man who had fled to Palmares. The group tracked the man down and returned with his head, "intimidating" Palmaristas so greatly that, at least according to the report, "many" returned to slavery. The commander rewarded the men who captured and killed the fugitive, and he too would soon profit. Enslavers often complained when soldiers killed fugitives whom they claimed as property, but in this case the commander ordered the assassination himself. By sanctioning the murder, he made a blood-drenched career investment, turning the violent act into an achievement to bolster his case for promotion. The Crown granted him mercê and made him constable of Porto Calvo.[12] The same documents that detail the blood-for-reward exchanges intrinsic to Portugal's colonial machinery also reveal other stories. The same commander who became constable reportedly had "many slaves in Palmar," including one man, named Felipe, who had become a well-known commander in his own right, leading troops of "filhos do palmar" in "repeated assaults" on area residents.[13] That Felipe linked up with Palmaristas who were born in the mocambos and had grown old enough to carry out brazen attacks illustrates the depth and power of the communities created in Palmares. His leadership role there, in addition to suggesting that family lineage was not the only way to claim authority in Palmares, also demonstrates how some evaded death even amid the brutal wars against Palmares.

Manuel Lopes Kills Zumbi

No Palmarista leader seemed to escape death longer than Zumbi. Some false claims about his demise were, like the one apparently made in Lopes's 1676 notary application, ambiguous, leaving Zumbi's identity in doubt or suggesting that he was dead via wording that left open the possibility that he was only wounded. Other soldiers unequivocally stated that they had killed him. Most, but not all, of the claims came from men of European descent. Some who pursued Zumbi viewed him in mystical terms, a warrior who might be impossible to kill. In defying death, Zumbi helped keep Palmares alive while propelling a familiar cycle: colonial officials cursing the mocambos, mobilizing against them, and reporting another almost-victory only to begin again as war's end once more lay just out of reach.

Even accounting for ambiguity surrounding Zumbi's identity and the possibility that more than one Palmares leader carried the same name or title, in many cases it is clear that soldiers and officers exaggerated or intentionally obfuscated in hopes of securing rewards, and perhaps none did so more than Lopes. Though he did not achieve the renown of the most famous Palmares conquerors, he was no marginal figure. A member of the Overseas Council called him "one of the great living soldiers and officers from the wars of Pernambuco."[14] But while the *Relação* hails Lopes for his "experience, zeal, and valor," he rarely appears elsewhere in the text, in contrast to Pedro de Almeida, the manuscript's principal hero, and Carrilho, Almeida's right-hand man.[15] Lopes's relatively marginal place in Palmares lore may be due in part to the fact that he was born in Portugal: paulistas and soldiers born in the Brazilian northeast fit more easily into later narratives that wrapped the Palmares wars into triumphant national history. Lopes, though, fought against Palmares and served the Crown for more than half a century. In 1667, he was named "Tenente Geral (lieutenant general) of the War against Palmares," an impressive title, given later to Domingos Jorge Velho, that, at least in theory, assigned power over the entire war operation (in Lopes's case, though, it functioned more as a prop label, with the governor left in charge of the war).[16] During the 1670s, Lopes became sargento-mor (sergeant major), a prestigious position with a high salary.[17] In 1673, he asked for a hábito de Cristo—a highly sought-after conferral of status—for himself and for one of his children. He also requested a large pension, two alvarás de lembrança (guarantees for preferable consideration in future petitions) for his children, and a governorship in Rio de Janeiro, to be followed by another governorship or other high office in Paraíba or Pernambuco.[18] Though the length of his record was long, this was an enormous ask.

The Overseas Council responded that they would award him a hábito de Cristo (not one for his children), a pension (smaller than what he asked for), and one alvará de lembrança—no small reward, but much less than what Lopes had requested.[19] Lopes appealed the decision, asking that his hábito and pension be awarded to whomever his young daughter would eventually marry.[20] He also asked to be guaranteed a position as sergeant major. The council agreed to defer the hábito and the pension but would not promise to make him sergeant major.[21] However, Lopes won an ostensibly open competition for the position soon after the council declined to guarantee it outright.[22] His son Francisco secured administrative positions and promotions almost entirely because of his name.[23]

In 1679, Manuel received a sesmaria in Pernambuco for his service fighting against Palmares, though he would continue to fight for years to come.[24] As sergeant major, he directed multiple attacks against Palmares and served in auxiliary roles in others. In March 1680, he issued the proclamation asking "any person" who could locate Zumbi to advise the Palmares leader that amnesty was on the table if he would agree to a treaty.[25] The announcement leaves no doubt that in 1680, four years after applying to become notary based on claims of "killing and wounding a quantity of Blacks, among them the brother of their King [known] by the name Zamby," Lopes knew that Zumbi was alive and well. Nonetheless, on four other occasions over the next decade Lopes claimed to have killed the Palmares leader. Lopes's folha de serviço (service report, or summary of service), written in 1681 or 1682, described his successes against Palmares. In addition to reporting that in 1679 he had "killed and imprisoned more than eight hundred peças," Lopes also claimed that in 1681 he "killed and imprisoned" many more Palmaristas, including "Zombi," the "governor of their war."[26] Lopes repeated both claims and used the same spelling for the leader's name in 1684, when he applied (unsuccessfully) for another administrative position.[27] In 1689, he became field master (mestre-de-campo) of Pernambuco. The carta patente (letters patent) announcing the appointment commended Lopes for his long years of service and highlighted his exploits against Palmares. The Crown also noted, this time with no ambiguity, that Lopes and his men had killed the "governor Zombim."[28] If Lopes's original claim referred to another man or reflected honest confusion, by now the story had become one that even Lopes knew was false.

Others Do Too

Lopes was hardly the only one who leveraged false or ambiguous claims about killing Zumbi (see table 2.1). Another powerful Portuguese-born man, Manuel de Inojosa, did so at least three times, securing power and wealth for himself and for a nephew in the process.[29] In 1677, Inojosa, who earlier fought against Indigenous groups in Bahia, proposed to the Overseas Council a plan to defeat the mocambos of Palmares and to "populate and conquer" the area.[30] Inojosa based his plan, which was ultimately rejected, on information he claimed was provided by an enslaved man he sent to Palmares as a spy with the promise of freedom upon his return.[31] That someone would journey to Palmares and return to a plantation in order to secure freedom once again suggests the complex and shifting alliances that Palmares engendered, not to mention the paradoxical nature of Portuguese-sanctioned liberty.

Some petitioners created ambiguity by simply placing Zumbi among the dead and wounded, but Inojosa hedged no bets, directly stating that he killed him. According to a story Inojosa offered multiple times, in 1680 he had

TABLE 2.1 Soldiers Who Claimed They Killed or Vanquished Zumbi before He Died (1676–1694)

YEAR OF PETITION	COMBATANT	KILLED ZUMBI IN ... (alternate name/ spelling in parentheses)	"VANQUISHED"[Δ] ZUMBI IN ... (alternate name/ spelling in parentheses)
1676	Manuel Lopes	No year given (Zamby)	—
1680	Manuel Lopes	—	No year given (Zombi)
1682[ΔΔ]	João de Mota and Manuel de Inojosa	No year given (Zombi)	—
1682	Manuel Lopes	1681 (Zomby)	—
1683	Manuel de Inojosa	1681	—
1684	Manuel Lopes	1681 (Zomby)	—
1684	Manuel de Inojosa	1682 (Zonbî)	—
1685	Manuel de Inojosa	1681? (Zombi)	—
1685	Manuel Lopes	—	No year given (Zomby)
1687	João da Fonseca	—	1679 (Zomby)

(Continued)

TABLE 2.1 *(Continued)*

YEAR OF PETITION	COMBATANT	KILLED ZUMBI IN . . . (alternate name/ spelling in parentheses)	"VANQUISHED"[Δ] ZUMBI IN . . . (alternate name/ spelling in parentheses)
1688 (three petitions in the same year)	Domingos Rodrigues Carneiro	—	1681 (Zomby)
1688	Sebastião Pinheiro Camarão	1681 (Zamby and Zumby)	—
1689?	Manuel Lopes	No year given	—
1689	Manuel Lopes	No year given (Zombim)	—
1693	Domingos Rodrigues Carneiro	1681 (Zomby)	—
1693[ΔΔ]	João da Mota and Manuel de Inojosa	No year given (Zombi)	—
1694	Domingos Rodrigues Carneiro	—	1681? (Zombi)

[Δ] Also "ousted," and so on. This column also includes ambiguous mentions, where Zumbi is among the "dead and wounded."

[ΔΔ] In 1682, Inojosa vouched for Mota, saying he had helped Inojosa kill Zumbi. The document is reproduced in 1693.

SOURCES: See appendix B.

captured the "captain named Majojo" and destroyed Zumbi's hideout, causing him to flee. The following year, Inojosa located Zumbi again, in a new settlement. This time the Portuguese-born would-be conqueror burned to the ground 170 dwellings, "kill[ed] the aforementioned zonbi," and captured his family, including "his white wife and son who had been taken to Palmares by force."[32] This last claim deserves further scrutiny. Palmaristas did regularly raid farms and plantations and return to their mocambos with individuals whom, depending on the account, they liberated or took prisoner. While there is more work to be done about the relationship between Palmaristas and those whom they took to the mocambos, there is no evidence that Zumbi kidnapped a white woman, a story that would nonetheless be repeated many times. The claim, suspiciously similar to panicked reports from other slave societies, highlights the way that white masculinity (in this case, Inojosa's) depended on and was constructed in relationship to fantasies and fears about Black masculinity, white femininity, and other racialized and gendered foils.[33]

In 1685, Inojosa became captain major in Benguela, the highest authority there; he held the position for several years before passing away.[34] His successor was also a Palmares veteran, an illustration of how stories about Zumbi and Palmares traveled back along the route taken by ships transporting enslaved Africans from Angola to Brazil.[35] Inojosa's petitions also show how inaccurate reports of Zumbi's death transformed into wealth that multiplied across generations. In addition to being appointed captain major, he secured an enormous 50$000 pension for his nephew, who also inherited an insignia. Little is known about the nephew, though he appears briefly in the written record as a godfather at a wedding in 1695 in Almodôvar, Portugal.[36] Did Inojosa tell his nephew that he killed "Zomby," and did the nephew regale the wedding party with stories about his uncle? If these questions are unanswerable, the nephew's presence in Portugal illuminates another pathway along which the material inheritance connected to Zumbi's apocryphal death, and perhaps spoken memories of it, flowed.

Like Inojosa and Lopes, two prominent officers in the Black and Indigenous militias claimed they had killed Zumbi before he was actually dead. The Portuguese created what became known as the Henrique Dias regiment (also known as the Black regiment, or Terço da Gente Preta), which was deployed in a number of settings, including Angola and Palmares.[37] The regiment's namesake, Henrique Dias, gained a title of nobility in 1638 for his service fighting the Dutch and then greater acclaim and reward after helping drive them out of Brazil years later.[38] Portuguese officials called him "Governor of the Blacks," and his troops were often called henriques, a term that became synonymous with Black soldiers.[39]

Though they rewarded Dias for his service, the Portuguese were divided about where and when it was acceptable to arm Black men.[40] Palmares brought the question to the fore. While some authorities feared that doing so represented a threat to the colony, others considered the Henrique Dias regiment a mechanism for keeping Palmares in check. Over vocal dissent, the Overseas Council devised a plan to send "the most exemplary religious figures" to Palmares to convince its members to leave and join the Dias regiment.[41] Another scheme was concocted by a viceroy who sought to send Dias and a priest to Palmares, but these plans were not carried out.[42] After Dias's death in 1662, the regiment remained intact, and the henriques would play a central role fighting against and negotiating with Palmares.

One of the most successful officers of the Henrique Dias regiment, Domingos Rodrigues Carneiro, effectively leveraged claims about killing Zumbi before running up against limits not imposed on white counterparts. In 1688, he traveled to Lisbon and secured the position of sergeant major of the regiment and a pension of 18$000, a significant sum but just a fraction of what the Crown gave to Inojosa's nephew, who did not even fight in Palmares.[43] In 1688 and again in 1693, when he successfully applied to become field master, Carneiro reported that an attack he led in 1681 on the Serra da Barriga left "many dead and wounded, among them their leader Zomby."[44] While claiming to have killed (or wounded) Zumbi helped Carneiro secure the coveted positions in 1688 and 1693, it did not work in all instances. While he secured the position of sergeant major in 1688, Portuguese officials denied him the prize he coveted most as recognition and recompense for his service from the Crown—knighthood.

Little known today, in seventeenth- and eighteenth-century Pernambuco, Carneiro was a man of renown, and parts of his story, including his link to Zumbi, made their way into one of the now-consecrated eighteenth-century texts that mentions Palmares, *Desagravos do Brasil e glorias de Pernambuco (Requitals of Brazil and Glories of Pernambuco)*, written by Domingos do Loreto Couto in 1757 (though not published until 1903).[45] Loreto Couto called Carneiro a "decorated crioulo [Brazilian-born Black man] of admirable qualities: bravery, loyalty, and knowledge."[46] Apparently referring to the 1681 assault (though he gives the date as 1680), Loreto Couto reproduced the wording from Carneiro's petitions almost verbatim: "There were many deaths and wounded, among them Zumby, their Prince." He also described Carneiro's continued engagement with Palmares, highlighting an eight-and-a-half-month campaign in 1686 and an offensive launched in 1700, "even after the final victory," in which Carneiro "destroyed many Mocambos, imprisoned one hundred Blacks and the oldest son of Camoanga [more often spelled Camuanga], the dead Zumby's brother."[47] It is unclear what led Loreto Couto to suggest that Zumbi was the brother of Camuanga, a Palmares leader who emerges in documents after Zumbi's death.

When writing about Carneiro, Loreto Couto retained the ambiguous language found in most of the official documents: "There were many deaths and wounded, among them Zumby." Two centuries later, another writer, Francisco Augusto Pereira da Costa, removed the ambiguity by taking out the phrase "and wounded." Loreto Couto, he wrote, "says that [Carneiro] took part with his people [the henriques] in the attack on the rebel Blacks of Palmares in which there were many killed, among them their prince, Zumbi."[48] It is possible that in 1681 Carneiro killed a different leader named Zumbi or Zombi, or a leader whom Carneiro and others thought went by that name. It is also possible that Carneiro, well aware of the value assigned to killing the most important Palmares leader, honed his narrative over time to best match what he thought colonial administrators wanted to hear. He hardly would have been alone. Repeatedly across the centuries, military men like Carneiro and authors writing about Palmares sharpened blurry lines into clear, but misleading, narratives.

In 1693, when he applied to become field master of the Henrique Dias regiment, Carneiro was competing against another Black officer, Manuel Barbalho de Lira.[49] Carneiro's claim to have killed Zumbi may have made the difference. Both Carneiro and Lira boasted of more than twelve years of military service, and both referenced Palmares—Lira highlighting how he had "fought in the war against the rebel Blacks." While the Overseas Council praised Lira for having always faithfully "fulfilled his obligations," Carneiro's record was more detailed: he had fought directly against Zumbi.[50] But while the claim to have killed Zumbi helped Carneiro secure the coveted position in the all-Black regiment, it was his Blackness that was explicitly invoked in denying his earlier request for knighthood. The Mesa de Consciência e Ordens (Table [or Council] of Conscience and Orders) venomously wrote that "it does not seem right" that "the habit of São Bento de Avis be seen on a person so despicable in the esteem of people as that of a Black."[51] Carneiro's parents were from Angola, where they had been captured and enslaved, and he was born into slavery in Brazil before securing his freedom. Having worked his way from slavery to field master, he occupied a privileged space that also had clear limitations.[52]

Indigenous service in the Palmares wars generated additional claims of Zumbi's death. Indigenous soldiers were crucial to Portuguese military successes in Palmares and other wars. During the seventeenth century, Indigenous regiments similar to the Henrique Dias regiment were formed. Named for Dom Antônio Filipe Camarão (1580–1648), the camarões fought against the Dutch, battled Indigenous armies not aligned with the Crown, and helped defeat Palmares.[53] He had changed his name to Antônio Filipe Camarão in 1612, when he was baptized. The word "camarão," which means "shrimp" in Portuguese, was a label for "Potiguar," one of the principal Indigenous groups in the northeast. Despite being a pejorative, the name was nonetheless passed down to subsequent generations.[54] Dom Filipe became captain major and governor of the Indians of Pernambuco and attached captaincies, the latter a position that the Portuguese Crown created to reward loyal Indigenous leaders by allowing them to direct armed militias and function as semiautonomous rulers. Both positions would be held by Dom Filipe's heirs, including Dom Sebastião Pinheiro Camarão (1650s?–1720s?), who played an important role in the fight against Palmares and would invoke Zumbi's death in advertising this role.[55]

In 1688, the same year that Carneiro became sergeant major and received a pension of 18$000, Sebastião received a mercê of 48$000. In his successful petition, he highlighted his service seven years earlier, when he helped "punish" the Blacks of Palmares for kidnapping women and taking them to the sertão. Sebastião had marched "against the marauder Zamby, their governor and captain," and, after "ousting the enemy" from their fortification, had pursued them further into the backlands, "imprisoning some and killing many, among them the same Marauder Zumby."[56] Like others, Sebastião named Zumbi among the captured or dead, though his petition placed "killing" after "imprisoning," perhaps an unintentional reversal of order that nonetheless seemed to suggest that Zumbi was dead. That the slippage in spelling between Zamby and Zumby appears just a few lines apart in Sebastião's petition, and apparently in reference to the man called "Zombi" in Lopes's documents, illustrates the ongoing confusion regarding the leader outside Palmares. For Sebastião Pinheiro Camarão, the key thing was that he had killed, or at least thought or could convincingly claim that he had killed, an important Palmarista.

Lopes, Inojosa, Carneiro, and Pinheiro Camarão built careers during the 1680s and 1690s based in part on the assertion that they had killed Zumbi, and all four claimed that they had participated in a battle in 1681 during which Zumbi died. The fact that four men made the same claim suggests a shared belief that they had killed Zumbi, or at least wounded him. It is possible that their men killed a Palmares leader named Zumbi, Zombi, or Zambi in 1681 and that another leader with the same name or title rose in his place. The ambiguities may instead simply reflect confusion and obfuscation. The documents make clear that the Portuguese did not always have a firm grasp on who Zumbi was and that at least some of the claims made about his death were mistakes, but in many cases soldiers and officers no doubt intentionally overstated their case. While Lopes may have initially believed that he had killed Zumbi or that there was more than one man with that name or title, his petitions conveyed little such subtlety and over time became more pointed, eventually declaring without equivocation that he had killed "Zombi," the "governor" of Palmares. In the eighteenth century and beyond, such claims would find new lives and continue to generate wealth, power, and prestige for descendants of the soldiers and officers who fought against Palmares, especially those of European descent.

Zumbi Kills Himself

Colonial attacks on Palmares ebbed and flowed during the 1680s and 1690s, culminating with the consequential battle at Serra da Barriga in February 1694. Laying waste to Palmares's fortified mountaintop settlement and resulting in high casualties, numerous prisoners, and an untold number of others fleeing for their lives, the battle also gave rise to a new narrative about Zumbi's death. After arriving from Rio Grande do Norte in the early 1690s, Jorge Velho had directed a ferocious campaign that culminated in the assault. Under the field command of Bernardo Vieira de Melo, Portuguese forces lay siege to the encampment and pummeled Serra da Barriga with artillery fire. The most detailed account of the battle is found in *Rellação Verdadeyra da Guerra que se fez aos Negros Levantados do Palmar* (*True Account of the War against the Rebel Blacks of Palmar*).[57] Like Padre Silva's *Relação das guerras feitas aos Palmares*, which paid homage to Pedro de Almeida, the anonymously authored *Rellação Verdadeyra* glorifies a single figure, Vieira de Melo, cast as the hero who finally ended the war. According to historian Maria Lêda Oliveira, the *Rellação Verdadeyra* was written either soon after the battle or in the 1710s, while Vieira de Melo languished in prison after participating in the Guerra dos Mascates (Peddlers' War, 1710–11), a failed anti-Portuguese rebellion (if the latter, the text's author was unsuccessful, Vieira de Melo eventually dying in prison).[58]

According to the *Rellação Verdadeyra*, the battle at Serra da Barriga ended when hundreds of Palmaristas leaped to their deaths. On February 6, at around one o'clock in the morning, Vieira de Melo's men attacked, forcing the Palmaristas toward paths that dead-ended at the edge of a cliff: "They did not have any other option other than to begin throwing themselves off the [precipice]. Already wounded, it was their leader, named 'Zombj,' who incited them to do this. He released a son, who carried him on his back [because he was wounded], and seven concubines, tied to one another at the waist and with one tied to his waist. And right there he [Zombj] let go of this entire cargo."[59] The passage is suggestive but not definitive about what happened when Zumbi "let go." The manuscript makes no mention of his capture or escape and therefore seems to suggest that he jumped to his death. The next lines describe the fate of those who plunged from the peak: "they were greeted at sword point, which was often unnecessary because they were already dead when they [hit the ground]. This drudgery continued until dawn."[60] Finality was undermined only by the fact that "a few Blacks escaped, what with the darkness and multitude of those falling it was not possible to behead them all."[61] Not naming Zumbi as among those who escaped or were taken prisoner, the *Rellação Verdadeyra* all but says outright that he died in the battle at Serra da Barriga.

During the seventeenth and eighteenth centuries, unpublished manuscripts such as the *Rellação Verdadeyra* circulated among the empire's "lettered elite."[62] Though read by a smaller circle of men, the letters that colonial officials in Brazil sent to each other and to Portugal also facilitated the often-rapid spread of news and rumor. Less than three weeks after the battle at Serra da Barriga, hundreds of kilometers to the south, the municipal council of Salvador (in Bahia) authorized expenditures for a public celebration of "our victorious Forces against the Blacks of Palmares."[63] Two days after the battle, Jorge Velho sent a letter to the king, reporting that the Portuguese had repelled a Palmarista attack "in a way that forced them to leap off a ledge that was so high that most of them perished."[64] Ten days later, Castro sent a more detailed report, announcing the "glorious restoration of Palmares" and embellishing Jorge Velho's account.[65] Castro described the impenetrable defenses of Palmares and, positioning himself as the hero, wrote, "I resolved to go myself to those Palmares."[66] In his telling, news of his impending arrival struck fear in the Palmaristas, who "determined to flee," but before they could escape (and before Castro could journey to the battlefield), a Palmares scout described the imposing ring of Portuguese forces surrounding the stronghold, which caused panic to set in. "In the confusion, that same night the Blacks flung themselves desperately onto our fortification." The Portuguese greeted them with gunfire. "So many were killed and so many wounded that their spilled blood served as a guide for our troops to follow. We imprisoned many and others retreated but [in the confusion] took the wrong path and a large number of them crashed headlong [despenhar-se] off a high peak, their bodies smashing to pieces below."[67] The language is ambiguous. Castro uses "despenhar-se," the same verb used in the *Rellação Verdadeyra* and other accounts that depict the deaths as intentional. While the most common meaning of despenhar-se refers to an intentional act—to fling or hurl oneself—the verb can also be translated as "to fall (or crash) headlong," which may be the meaning here, given the description of Palmaristas taking the wrong turn on the darkened mountain paths.[68] In either case, the result was the same. As daylight arrived, the Portuguese entered the Palmares fortification, "where all was surrendered." In total, "deaths numbered greater than 500, among them a valorous Black who was their general and all the other important captains."[69] This moment in battle is today memorialized in the park that now sits atop Serra da Barriga with liquid clarity in the form of a plaque that asserts that the Palmaristas intentionally jumped, choosing death over slavery (see figure 2.1).

Significantly, in his battle report, Castro does not name Zumbi among the dead. It is possible that Zumbi was the "valorous Black" general, but then why not name him? More likely, the Portuguese could not identify many of those who died and were either unsure if Zumbi was among the dead or certain that he was not. Though the *Rellação Verdadeyra* suggests but does not say outright that Zumbi died at Serra da Barriga, Vieira de Melo's own documents make no reference to Zumbi. In December 1694, he sought and won the position of captain major of Rio Grande do Norte, highlighting his actions against Palmares to secure the post. The letter awarding him the position notes that Vieira de Melo captured "four principal leaders" before the battle at Serra da

Barriga, where he was credited with killing some two hundred Palmaristas and imprisoning four hundred more.[70] If Vieira de Melo thought that Zumbi was among those killed, he surely would have highlighted the fact. Instead, he rode the massive number of casualties and captives to become captain major in June 1695.[71]

Aside from the *Rellação Verdadeyra*, which does so ambiguously, no other contemporaneous account states that Zumbi died at the Serra da Barriga. But that did not prevent others from crafting fanciful tales. In 1730, Sebastião da Rocha Pita published his landmark *Historia da America Portugueza* and helped embed an unambiguous narrative of Zumbi committing suicide into the bedrock of national history. "Zombî," Rocha Pita wrote, whose name "in their language is the same as the devil," led his followers to their death. "Wanting to avoid becoming our slaves, and despising death by our swords, they climbed to the peak and voluntarily threw themselves off it, and with that form of death demonstrated to not love the life of slavery and to not want to die by our blows."[72] With just a few lines of text, Rocha Pita declared that Palmaristas

FIGURE 2.1 View from the top of Serra da Barriga (in 2022). Today, a plaque marks this spot as the place where "many [Palmaristas] threw themselves off the cliffs, preferring death to captivity." *Source*: Author.

chose death "voluntarily" and asserted with authority that Zumbi died then and there — and by suicide. By having Zumbi kill himself, Rocha Pita removed blood from Portuguese hands, even while making clear that Zumbi feared those hands and the bloody swords they held. In doing so, Rocha Pita put in place a template that would be used time and again, one that cast Zumbi's death as product of a noble choice: death instead of slavery. Seizing on the ambiguity of the *Rellação Verdadeyra* to allow himself creative license, Rocha Pita helped craft a legend for the ages, putting order to chaos and erasing confusion about Zumbi, a fearsome Black male foil whose name meant "demon" or "devil" and who died a noble death at the hands of heroic conquerors.[73]

Serra da Barriga: Legends Grow

Rocha Pita's account overlooked the fact that months after the battle at Serra da Barriga, colonial officials seemed to agree that the war was not, in fact, over. In August, João de Lencastre, the recently appointed governor-general of Brazil, suggested that Jorge Velho stay in Palmares until all mocambo "remnants" were "extinguished."[74] In November, even while pronouncing victory, the Overseas Council acknowledged that "the final end of this war" would not come until every last "rebel" was gone "because experience has shown that even just a few are sufficient to drag others into flight."[75] Castro reported that Jorge Velho had "diverted a great number" of prisoners taken at Serra da Barriga and recommended that the paulistas remain in Pernambuco only temporarily, in order to pursue the "many" who fled and "scattered through these backlands." However, the paulistas would not be allowed to settle permanently in the area because they diverted prisoners and terrorized residents even more "than those rebel Blacks."[76] Reliant on Jorge Velho and the paulistas to track down survivors, the council also disapproved of their behavior. Tensions between paulistas and others in Pernambuco would simmer for years.

In January 1696, Lencastre wrote to Castro thanking him for a recent letter informing him that Zumbi was dead. "With his death and the destruction of the Blacks," Lencastre wrote, "I consider nearly finished the Palmares war."[77] Castro's original letter has not been located by historians, but we do have subsequent communications, including a second letter sent by Castro in March 1696 on a ship bound for Ilha da Madeira, where it was transferred to another vessel destined for Lisbon.[78] An Overseas Council report, which conveyed to the king the contents of the letter, resurfaced in the early twentieth century.[79] It is tempting to speculate about the stories that might have been told as the letter wound its way from Pernambuco to Portugal. In it, Castro describes how in the final months of 1695, Zumbi had separated from "the little family that [remained] with him" and dug into a position along with twenty companions. He stationed fourteen of them at traps set for the Portuguese and retreated to a tiny hideaway with the other six. Castro obtained this information from a man imprisoned by locals in Rio de São Francisco, a *mulato* who had committed "grave crimes."[80] Castro agreed to spare his life in return for guiding troops led by André Furtado de Mendonça to Zumbi's hideout. The fight there was bloody; the soldiers killed Zumbi and all but one of the Palmaristas who were with him.

The *Rellação Verdadeyra* was not the only document to circulate news of the deaths at Serra da Barriga. The letters that Vieira de Melo himself submitted in 1694 to become captain major of Rio Grande do Norte, while they did not mention Zumbi, describe the incident at the peak in the same terms as those used by Jorge Velho in the days following the battle: Vieira de Melo had secured a "felicitous victory" over the Palmaristas, thanks largely to the counterattack that "forced them to leap off a ledge that was so high that most of them perished and were smashed to pieces."[81] Similar wording appears in additional documents that officials wrote, read, and signed in Lisbon, Recife, and Natal.[82]

Though the *Rellação Verdadeyra* sealed Vieira de Melo's association with the deaths at Serra da Barriga, lesser-known actors who participated in the battle also sought credit on less public stages. In 1699, Gabriel de Góes and João de Montes competed for an infantry position in the paulista regiment.[83] The new governor of Pernambuco called Montes "one of the best sertanejos [backlanders] and most valorous soldiers who fought in the Conquest [of Palmares]," and Góes one of "the good paulista soldiers."[84] Montes, who won the position, had served for decades, at one point marching forty leagues in search of a mocambo, sustaining himself on roots to survive. Tracing the same path that many other Palmares veterans followed, he fought in the Guerra do Açu and then returned to Pernambuco (in the early 1690s) to once again take up arms against Palmares. Montes also pursued Palmaristas fleeing Serra da Barriga and attacked the Mocambo das Catingas, taking forty-five prisoners there, and another unnamed mocambo, where he took an additional twenty-three captives.[85]

Perhaps because he had served in so many battles over so many years, Montes did not go into detail about what happened at Serra da Barriga, other than to boast of the large quantity of casualties and prisoners. By contrast, Góes had served for fewer than five years, beginning with a march of "almost 250 leagues." His crowning achievement came at Serra da Barriga, "where the Black Zomby was."[86] When the Palmaristas attacked, he helped drive them back with force that "frightened the Blacks, who by [our] luck leaped from a precipice, more than 350 of them dying and [this] being the cause of their total ruin and [our] beautiful Victory."[87] The document, written five years after the battle, lays bare some of the main ambiguities found in declarations about Zumbi's death and the war's conclusion. Though Góes highlights the fact that Zumbi was at Serra da Barriga, he does not say that he died there. By the time Góes applied for the infantry position, Furtado de Mendonça had received credit for killing Zumbi in 1695. While not directly challenging Furtado de Mendonça's role, Góes mentioned Zumbi in a way that bolstered his own record and left the relationship between Zumbi and the deaths at the precipice ambiguous. Though Góes described the battle there as the end of the war, in the same account he also enumerated his later efforts in Palmares: defeating "a quilombo" and taking forty-five prisoners, among them "the principal leaders"; capturing another eighteen elsewhere; and serving at a fort, all part of his service fighting "in this war."[88]

Other folhas de serviço relayed similar stories and illustrate how "this war" continued after 1695. In 1703, Cristovão de Mendonça, a paulista sergeant major not related to André Furtado de Mendonça, competed for the position of field master. After journeying from São Paulo to Pernambuco in the late 1680s to fight against Palmares, he traveled to Rio Grande to fight in the Guerra do Açu. In the early 1690s, he returned to Pernambuco and in 1694 participated in the siege and battle at Serra da Barriga, where he claimed to have had a hand in five hundred casualties and "many others" taken prisoner, "in addition to all those who fled and leaped."[89] Mendonça provided no further detail, as if the Overseas Council would already understand the reference. Nor did he mention Zumbi. Mendonça also detailed his post-1694 service, which included the promotion to sergeant major in 1695 and a brief encounter with Camuanga, while he was reportedly attempting to kidnap an enslaved woman from an engenho. Mendonça's men captured eighteen people, including the woman, though not Camuanga.[90] Though Mendonça likely believed that Camuanga was attempting to take the woman by force, it is, of course, also possible that she was attempting to escape. It is also plausible that she wanted to escape and was at the same time fearful of the men who had come for her.

Even though others who were present at Serra da Barriga referenced the Palmaristas who leaped or fell from the precipice in their own reports, the *Rellação Verdadeyra* helped link the event most closely to Vieira de Melo, who returned to Pernambuco after his term as governor of Rio Grande do Norte ended in 1701. While competing for new positions, he continued to highlight his role at Serra da Barriga.[91] The association survived and continued to generate wealth for his heirs even after he died in 1719. Vieira de Melo left behind an enormous extended family that retained wealth and power in Pernambuco, often drawing on his military record and highlighting the deaths at Serra da Barriga to do so. In the late 1720s, exactly when Rocha Pita was completing *Historia da America Portugueza*, Vieira de Melo's son Bernardo appended his father's papers to his own documents, repeating the story of hundreds of Palmaristas falling to their deaths.[92]

Domingos Simões Jordão included the same story in documents he submitted to the Crown. In 1718, he became the captain of a fort in Salvador, the latest stop on a winding trajectory that passed through Palmares and then Angola, Portugal, Ceará, and Rio Grande do Norte. The letter announcing his appointment described how he joined "the battle against the *negro* Zambi, occupying on this occasion the position of great risk, imprisoning more than 600 peças [and] killing many in the assault in addition to those who leaped from a precipice."[93] He made the same claim while competing for another position nine years later, and in 1730 he referenced his efforts against the "*negro* Zonbi," changing the spelling from his 1718 claim and omitting its mention of Serra da Barriga.[94] In 1734, when Jordão became captain major of Ceará, he once again restated the description of his exploits fighting the "*negro* Zomby," now reinserting the description of the many who died when they leaped from the Serra da Barriga peak.[95] Through Jordão and others, the deaths at Serra da Barriga grew into a legend about the fall of Palmares that was flexible enough to include or exclude Zumbi and to reward the claims made by multiple soldiers and officers. At least in written accounts, the best-preserved narrative placed Zumbi at the center and packaged his and the others' demise to fit romanticized accounts of Portuguese conquest and Black submission. As we will see in the chapters ahead, competing and complementary memories of Zumbi and Palmares were also preserved by other means.

Post-1695 Claims about the "Famous Black Zomby"

Almost immediately after delivering Zumbi's head, Furtado de Mendonça profited, establishing a farm on land whose title he would formally secure years later.[96] In late 1697, he sought to become captain of the Terço dos Palmares (Palmares regiment) and, claiming that he was "very poor" and unable to pay his soldiers, asked the Crown for financial support.[97] Many petitioners used similar language, which, even if often performative, betrays the fragility of their social standing and dependence on the Crown to grant mercê. It also indicates what these petitioners were seeking: social ascension and a tighter grip on publicly recognized and celebrated forms of masculinity. If whiteness was not always an explicitly stated goal, there is no doubt that these men were also seizing hold of the immense privileges already attached to it.

There was also a mutual dependence between soldier and empire that helps explain the unending loop of premature pronouncements of Palmares's defeat. With its positions in Africa and Brazil still often tenuous, the Crown needed men like Furtado de Mendonça to do its bidding. But while many combatants called themselves conquerors of Palmares, and others claimed to have helped wound or even kill Zumbi, Furtado de Mendonça's apparently singular act would seem to trump them all. Recommending a subvention to him of 50$000 to be used in service of "the defense of the Conquests," the Overseas Council tacitly recognized the ongoing threat posed by fugitive Blacks, even while lauding the "major role" that Mendonça had played in bringing the "conclusion of the Palmares war, for it was he who cut the head of the Black Zombi."[98] In granting his request to become captain, the council noted that even though he was well short of the twelve years of experience that the position required, he deserved the title because of his success in the "Palmares Campaign," in which he had slayed "the greatest scourge" to plague Pernambuco, "the Black Zomby, so famous for the hostile acts he perpetrated."[99]

While leading the Palmares regiment, Furtado de Mendonça took charge of the Arraial de Nossa Senhora das Brotas, an encampment that Jorge Velho built in 1697 with the hope of maintaining control over land formerly occupied by the mocambos. The Palmares regiment was first composed of paulistas but eventually incorporated Indigenous soldiers. Though Furtado de Mendonça's achievements and rewards were impressive, it is somewhat surprising that he did not prosper even more. In 1708, he competed for the position of sergeant major of the Terço dos Palmares, which instead went to Bernardo Vieira de Melo.[100] Two years later, Furtado de Mendonça asked the Crown to intervene against Cristovão de Mendonça, who had imprisoned him for two weeks "without a sentence, without a crime."[101] Furtado de Mendonça learned later that Cristovão, whom we have seen earlier encounter Camuanga, had implicated him in the death of "a wicked *negro*," who "wandered freely" in the area and had been responsible for "several deaths and robberies." Under Furtado de Mendonça's order, a group of Tapuia men stationed at the Arraial de Nossa Senhora das Brotas had pursued the man and, when he attempted to flee, killed him. As he asked the Crown for assistance against Cristovão de Mendonça, Furtado de Mendonça highlighted his lineage in one of São Paulo's "most important families," his service fighting under Jorge Velho (who had died in 1705), and his role in the "conquest" and "destruction" of Palmares, which, however singular, did not secure invincibility against a rival colonial power broker. Nor did that victory prevent a Black man from roaming freely in the area and wreaking havoc.

Others followed Furtado de Mendonça after 1695 in invoking Zumbi's death to bolster their reputation with the Crown. In 1698, in a lengthy treatise that was part of an extended dispute with the Crown about renumeration for his service (the same document that includes the famous reference to "Angola janga"), Jorge Velho twice noted that his forces had killed "their little king [seu régulo], the famous Zumbi."[102] The next year, while competing to be captain major of Ceará, an officer who had fought against the Dutch negotiated with Gan(g)a Zumba and Gan(g)a Zona and participated in the final assault on Serra da Barriga and recalled accompanying Fernão Carrilho (who won the competition) on an earlier expedition "to drive off Zomby"; the name appears as "Zamby" in a subsequent confirmation of mercê for the officer.[103] Other reports include similarly vague, and sometimes simply incorrect, assertions. A 1709 account dated Zumbi's death to 1694, crediting an officer with "destroying the *negro* Zomby with all of his captains, soldiers, and army at the Outeiro da Barriga."[104] King Dom João V nominated another man for a lofty military position, crediting him for "a large part of the victory against the aforementioned *negro* [Zombi]"; no additional details about this victory are provided.[105] Another petition for promotion, filed in 1708, stated that a soldier was present ". . . where Black Zombi was killed."[106] The tantalizing ellipsis reflects how at some point, the letter was torn, erasing the crucial first part of the sentence.

Vague, false, and misleading accounts written before Zumbi's death gained new life after it. In 1710, two decades after the Crown denied his first petition for knighthood, Domingos Rodrigues Carneiro reapplied. Included in the thick file he submitted was a copy of one of the 1688 documents that described his participation in the 1681 attack that left "many dead and wounded, among them their leader Zomby."[107] The recirculation of old papers in new petitions helped preserve war stories, an almost incidental process joined by more intentional retellings of the past. In 1724, when Carneiro petitioned the Crown for higher salary, he abandoned an ambiguity in his earlier accounts: without providing a date, place, or any additional details, he now simply stated that he had "killed their leader, named zunby."[108]

And those who claimed to kill Zumbi before Zumbi's death continued to generate wealth for their families well after 1695. Manuel Lopes's success in transforming his service into a legacy of patronage, prestige, and material wealth is further evident three-quarters of a century after he first mentioned "Zamby." In 1748, his great-grandson Inácio de Sousa Magalhães highlighted Lopes's exploits to secure the position of infantry captain of Rio Grande do Norte.[109] Five years later, another great-grandson, Antônio de Sousa Magalhães, petitioned successfully to inherit the mercê and pension that Lopes had won decades earlier.[110] Throughout the seventy-five-page-long petition, which was ultimately granted, Magalhães referred to himself as Lopes's descendant and included a hand-copied transcription of Lopes's 1689 petition to become field master. The eighteenth-century copy reproduces the story that Lopes killed Zumbi in 1681, though with a small twist. In 1748, the scribe apparently misread the 1689 document, which describes the death of "governor Zombim," and wrote instead that Lopes and his men killed "the Governor Zombo."[111] As he re-copied the original, the scribe carried forward an apocryphal story about Zumbi from the seventeenth century into the eighteenth. In changing the spelling, he also revealed both the ever-changing orthography of Zumbi in Portuguese and the mystery that still surrounded him.

Lopes and Zumbi journeyed forward in time, linked together through petitions made not only by Lopes and his family but also via other soldiers, who evoked the two in ways that morphed, sometimes contradicted, and continued to sprout new branches that extended into and across the eighteenth century. One soldier described how while serving in Lopes's company he helped cause Zumbi to flee and then burned his mocambo to the ground. He retold those exploits in 1691 when applying for a military position and again the next year, when he requested (and received) a mercê.[112] A decade later, a small group of men vied for membership in an infantry company in Pernambuco. Several counted combat against Zumbi and Palmares among their qualifications, including one who described serving under Lopes and fighting in a battle that "resulted in removing Zomby, head of those Blacks, and other marauders."[113] The reference is indicative of how Palmares veterans continued to call on the destruction of Palmares and the death of Zumbi, even as they continued to fight in the region. The competition itself also illustrates how well Lopes had done for his family. In this case, the winner was not one of the men who had actually fought in Palmares but instead Lopes's son Francisco.

Conclusion

Long before it happened, Zumbi's death generated wealth and power for colonial soldiers and officers, and even after he died, their fabulations could yield rich compensation. Those riches represent one of the most palpable forms of inheritance that Palmares generated. The written documents of those who claimed they killed Zumbi also provide an initial set of clues about one way that memories of Palmares circulated beyond Padre Silva's *Relação* and the small handful of consecrated eighteenth-century texts. As they journeyed through the Brazilian northeast and beyond, the men who fought against Palmares carried stories and in some cases wealth and decorated titles with them.

Retold later as a story of inevitable triumph engineered by manly white heroes, the war was in fact an unending slog, often funded locally and fought by a mixed-race fighting force. Conquest, masculinity, whiteness, and European dominance could be fragile, despite the massive resources spent and blood spilled in pursuit of them. The fact that that pursuit generated false rumors about Zumbi's death also represents an interesting counterpoint to the suggestion that Blacks "superstitiously" believed him to be immortal. These were not simply distinct European and African belief systems at play but instead (or also) competing, overlapping, and intertwined rumors and war stories. The way that apocryphal news of Zumbi's demise circulated not only by word of mouth but also in written form illustrates how rumor can travel and take shape both in whispers and in writing. It may even be said that a backbone of Palmares historiography comprised rumors recorded and circulated on paper.[114] While many accounts of Zumbi's death may be characterized as rumor, mistaken identity—or rather confusion outside Palmares about who Zumbi was—also clearly shaped colonial narratives. That confusion about Zumbi's identity once again draws our attention to the many people who shaped Palmares and whose names and lives we do not know. While the historiography consecrated a singular Zumbi figure, it is possible—even likely—that there were others with the same name or title in Palmares.

The process that helped consolidate a singular Zumbi was intertwined with the formation of racial and gendered categories. While most of the documents pertaining to Black and Indigenous soldiers clearly and conspicuously note their color, the whiteness of Manuel Lopes and other conquerors is announced through absence and silence, embedded in their claims for recompense and accompanying assertions of masculine valor. The material wealth that Lopes and other colonial combatants amassed stands in stark contrast to what the Palmares survivors took with them as they fled. Unable to pause even to bury their dead, they faced a "dual crisis" in some ways reminiscent of the experience of the Middle Passage, where, Stephanie Smallwood writes, victims "were enslaved and commodified" in such a way that the living had to confront "the trauma of death and the inability to respond appropriately to death."[115] The Portuguese commodified Palmaristas in a different form, each dead body a coin amassed by colonial fighters in pursuit of personal gain. But though vast, the disparity between the forms of inheritance that Palmares bequeathed to those who destroyed it and to those who built it does not signal an absence of the latter. Severed from their kin, cut off from their home, and deprived of its resources as they fled, surviving Palmaristas carried and were accompanied by memories, spirits, and other forms of inheritance as they struck out in search of new places to dwell.

II SPIRITS

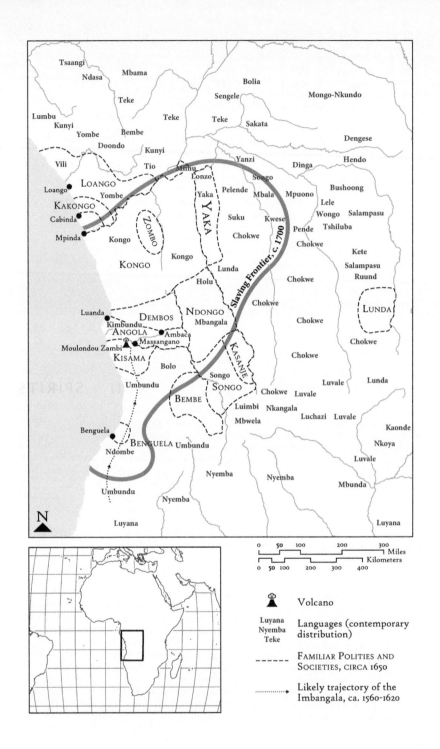

MAP 3.1 West Central Africa

Whose Confusion?

By ordering Zumbi's head displayed in public, Pernambuco's governor tacitly acknowledged that just as false rumors and stories of Zumbi's death spread among colonial soldiers and bureaucrats, so did knowledge of his immortality circulate far and wide in other circles. He believed that enslaved and free Blacks knew who Zumbi was and that news of his death could sound an ominous note in the same "common wind" that made Palmares a powerful symbol and that spread news of rebellion in slave societies across the Americas.[1] One official hoped that the governor's act would put an end to the "confusion that [people] had that it was impossible to kill [Zumbi]."[2] To the Portuguese, "confusion" and "superstitious" belief in immortality were signs of Black difference and inferiority. To Palmaristas and many others in Pernambuco, the relationship between the living and the dead extended far beyond the narrow terms applied by colonial officials. Though Caetano de Melo de Castro, his contemporaries, and future authors would use singular labels to describe Zumbi and his death, others understood his name and passing in multivalent terms that convey a rich cosmology of ancestor and territorial spirits, an indication of the various ways that Palmaristas engaged with not only the dead but also the natural world. Some details are accessible by way of seventeenth- and eighteenth-century missionary reports and Inquisition documents from Angola and Pernambuco. Others come into view through linguistic work that reveals previously overlooked meanings of Z/zumbi. By exploring religious beliefs and practices alongside several reconstructed proto-Bantu roots, part II provides a fuller picture of Palmarista spiritual beliefs and practices than previously available, while also highlighting important connections between Palmares and West Central Africa.

Zumbi's followers likely believed that he possessed supernatural or superhuman strengths, and it is fair to surmise that many who wanted to kill him did too. Zumbi had evaded the Portuguese for the better part of two decades, and Castro's missive makes clear that the demonstrative act of placing his head on a pike was intended not only for would-be Black rebels but also for whites. By severing Zumbi's head, Castro inflicted spiritual terror in much the same way that colonial authorities and enslavers did elsewhere. Seizing control of Zumbi's immortality, if only temporarily, and bending it to his will, Castro sent a gruesome message to would-be fugitives and rebels also intended to bolster his own standing with the king and the "justly querulous" local landowners. In addition to "mollifying whites and terrorizing Blacks," Castro's order helped lay the groundwork for Zumbi's transformation into a martyr much like other Black rebels in the Americas who in death "became transatlantic spirits."[3] It is also likely that some enslaved and free Blacks, and likely some Palmaristas, also feared Zumbi. Far from just signaling closure, his death and decapitation also inspired and added momentum to conflicting storylines and vectors of power. While Castro used spectacular violence to announce his power, other forces far beyond his control would continue to emanate from Palmares long after Zumbi, Castro, and other contemporaries had left the world of the living.

The "Orthographic Error"

An entry point into these spiritual lives and afterlives of Zumbi can be found in the Brazilian scholar Raimundo Nina Rodrigues's landmark 1904 essay that cast Palmares as a "Black Troy."[4] Rodrigues intended to correct long-standing "errors" and "lacunae," among them the fact that "the great majority of our historians write *Zumbi* for *Zambi*."[5] Zambi—but not Zumbi—Rodrigues explained, was the Palmarista leader's title. "It is well known," he wrote, that "Zambi . . . is the word that Bantu peoples use for their principal deity." Palmaristas "called their king the [same] name," and Zambi was therefore a leadership title and the word for Supreme Being or God. In Palmares, Rodrigues reasoned, Zambi likely also meant something akin to "god of war, a terrible warrior spirit." An "orthographic error"—replacing an /a/ with a /u/—had been repeated for ages by writers and also "in the popular tradition," eventually metastasizing into something more serious: the obscuring of historical fact.

Rodrigues's argument is significant not only for what it got right or wrong but also for whom he was attempting to correct. "Even today," Rodrigues wrote, "especially in the states of Brazil's North, [Zumbi] retains the meaning of divinity or saint for Blacks from the Coast."[6] Rodrigues's knowledge of "popular tradition" was informed by his amas, Black female caregivers—almost certainly enslaved and likely wet nurses, all anonymous in his account— whom he recalled telling him stories as a child about "a mysterious being, a kind of witchdoctor (feiticeiro), clandestine and withdrawn" named "zumbi." Three decades later, in his landmark 1933 book *Casa grande e senzala* (*The Masters and the Slaves*), Gilberto Freyre traced what he famously cast as Brazil's uniquely benevolent race relations (what scholars now call the "myth of racial democracy") to the Black women who, Freyre wrote, were "to suckle the master's son, rock him to sleep, prepare his food and his warm bath for him, take care of his clothing, tell him stories, and at times take the place of his own mother."[7] These were the same women who told stories about Z/zumbi to Rodrigues. Citing the white geographer-statesman-folklorist Henrique de Beaurepaire-Rohan, Rodrigues essentially overruled the women, insisting that parts of their stories were mistaken and that, contrary to what they said, the "mysterious" little-z zumbi they spoke of had nothing to do with Zumbi dos Palmares, whose real name, after all, was Zambi.[8]

To Rodrigues, there existed four distinct entities: (1) Zambi, the real name and title held by Palmares leaders; (2) Zumbi dos Palmares, or capital-Z Zumbi, which was, in fact, simply a misnomer for Zambi; (3) little-z zumbi, the ominous spirits that Rodrigues's amas spoke of; and (4) the Zumbi "divinity or saint" revered by Blacks in northeast Brazil. Rodrigues presented each as "tidy, singular" entities, cleanly separating human and nonhuman beings.[9] For others, the lines dividing them could be much less pronounced. Today, more than a century after Rodrigues wrote, and with new documents and technologies at our disposal, it is possible to examine some of his arguments more closely.[10] In doing so it is also important to note that Rodrigues, who had outsized influence on Brazilian thought, advanced racist ideas, even while helping bring African history and culture into intellectual debate. As his brusque dismissal of the Black women who cared for him as a child indicates, the inheritance, preservation, transmission, and modification of histories,

stories, and religious traditions in Brazil involved many of the same power dynamics that governed ownership of material things.[11] Like the unnamed Black woman in the Blaer-Reijmbach diary, Rodrigues's amas remain anonymous, conjured and then discarded after he all but accuses them of being ignorant of their own history. But what if our starting point is that the women were not confused and that the "orthographic error" was nothing of the sort?

Language and Religion in West Central Africa

Any attempt to address this question necessarily passes through the languages and history of West Central Africa. Over the course of the sixteenth century, slavery and conflict in the region gave shape to two large "contrasting 'Kongo' and 'Mbundu' communities," roughly divided by the Kwanza River.[12] Brazilianists and other Americanists frequently use two broad linguistic labels to refer to these communities, a practice that often implies a false uniformity and stasis to what was in fact a much larger collection of people and languages. Many of the region's languages, especially to the east and south of the mouth of the Kwanza, belong to the Njila group, itself a subset of Bantu languages, comprising four subunits and dozens of individual languages, including Kimbundu but not Kikongo.[13] The shape and internal dynamics of Kikongo, Kimbundu, and the many other languages in the area changed along with population density, agricultural and subsistence patterns, Atlantic slavery, and war and were then interpreted and labeled in new ways by Europeans.[14]

Over time, "Kikongo" came to refer to a language cluster, thanks mainly to ethnographers. The label hides a complex subgroup of dozens of languages, and modern Kikongo is the result of centuries of often violent cultural, commercial, military, and colonial interactions.[15] Kimbundu, which refers to languages spoken to the south of the Kongo political system, has a similarly complex history. Portuguese priests published catechisms that helped standardize Kimbundu and turn it into a written language.[16] Kongo people likely used -*mbundu* to designate certain groups as outsiders, but the label "Kimbundu" did not acquire wide use until ethnographers began to use it, and today it can refer to either a group of languages (Kimbundu, Sama, Bolo, Songo, and, in some designations, also Shinji and Mbangala) or a more narrowly defined language, which some linguists suggest might in fact be its own language cluster with constituent "dialects" that are not always mutually intelligible.[17]

The linguistic labels that these processes created are useful constructs that also hide other histories. Categories such as Kimbundu and Kikongo, writes Marcos Abreu Leitão de Almeida, are "the byproduct of late ethnic imaginations and linguistic standardization, not ethnolinguistic categories of great time-depth."[18] It is also worth noting how labels for European languages also evolved over time, often from regional variants, as in the case of modern Italian, for example, which descends largely from a Tuscan dialect.[19] The languages and dialects eventually grouped as Kikongo and Kimbundu also changed during the Middle Passage and in the Americas, but even in Africa variances between and within each are significant. Scholars have debated the expanse and significance of the slaving frontier in West Central Africa, some suggesting that it moved steadily inland and others arguing that the coast remained central even as European domain expanded.[20] Even if subscribing to the school that emphasizes the importance of the coast, where Kikongo and Kimbundu were most prominent, the variation between and within both labels is enormous. By some measures, Kikongo languages are less alike than English and German, and the difference between Kimbundu and most Kikongo languages is even larger.[21]

It is therefore often inadequate to assume that a Kikongo or Kimbundu dictionary from the twentieth (or even nineteenth) century will reveal all the definitions and meanings that Palmaristas and other Africans and their kin shared and made, though that has been the standard practice of historians of Palmares (and much of Brazil).[22] While Kimbundu and Kikongo may provide windows into the meanings and ideas that circulated in Palmares, historical linguistics and attention to a larger and deeper set of Bantuphone roots open more expansive and likely more accurate vistas. Palmaristas who understood standardized Kimbundu also spoke and could comprehend other languages and certainly developed language and vocabulary unique to the mocambos.[23]

The challenges and allure of Kimbundu are evident in Brazilian-born Jesuit Pedro Dias's 1697 linguistic primer, *Arte da lingua de Angola*.[24] Some scholars have interpreted the text as evidence that Kimbundu was the principal language of enslaved people not only in Bahia but also in Palmares, but several linguists characterize that idea as a "historically groundless hypothesis."[25] The problem derives from the internal complexity and diversity of Kimbundu and is exacerbated further by the distortionary effects of missionary projects in Angola and Brazil. That Bahian Jesuits chose Kimbundu as the language of instruction for enslaved people is less indicative of the native languages of the enslaved than of the practice of missionaries in Angola, whose own choices about which dialect to use for catechism had important consequences.[26] Dias, who never traveled to Angola, based his work on observations from Jesuits in Angola and, most importantly, what he heard spoken in Bahia, Pernambuco, Rio de Janeiro, and several other places in Portuguese America.[27] The Kimbundu that he recorded was hardly a "pure" African rendering and instead a product filtered through multiple layers of transcription, selection, and consolidation in Angola shaped further in Bahia, where West Central Africans formed the majority but by no means the totality of enslaved people who arrived during the seventeenth century.[28] While many Palmaristas likely understood what Padre Dias (and historians today) called Kimbundu, most, if not all, were polyglots who heard additional meanings and ideas in the words and sounds catalogued by the priest.

Language and culture were shaped not only by the powerful and destructive forces that uprooted people in Africa and shipped them west across the Atlantic, but also by currents flowing in the opposite direction. By the mid-1600s in Benguela, brasileiros (Brazilians), a collection of convicts, soldiers, traders, and others born in Portuguese America, had become "the face of Portuguese imperialism."[29] Political developments in Brazil could reverberate across the Atlantic, and social and cultural influences did as well. In the nineteenth century, some wealthy Luanda residents spoke Portuguese with Brazilian accents acquired during travel in America.[30] Priests also brought news of Brazil—and Palmares. When an Italian priest adapted a Portuguese-Kikongo catechism to include Latin and what we now know as Italian, he counted on the help of José de Pernambuco, a Black cleric born in Olinda, who traveled to Kongo in 1648 before dying there four years later.[31] In 1667, an Italian Capuchin destined for West Central Africa first traveled to Pernambuco, where he learned of the "Neri dos Palmares" (Blacks of Palmares), who had fled slavery and numbered near twenty thousand.[32] These crosscurrents help situate Rodrigues's amas not as individuals who forgot or somehow misapprehended their history but instead as latter-day interlocutors in a long, dynamic exchange of beliefs, ideas, and vocabularies that for centuries flowed both ways across the Atlantic.

The analytical challenges that these complex processes pose are compounded further by religion. Widely used in West Central Africa, Zambi, which Rodrigues maintained was the real name of the Palmares leader, is often translated as "God" or "Supreme Being," though, Wyatt MacGaffey writes, "It is impossible to say how much the idea . . . owes to missionary teaching."[33] John Thornton traces use of "Nzambi a Mpungu" in Kongo as far back as the fifteenth century. Building on the work of MacGaffey and Anne Hilton, he suggests that Kongolese used the phrase to refer to the king of Portugal, a place that some believed "was actually in the Other, spiritual, World."[34] By the sixteenth century, Nzambi a Mpungu referred to a "creator deity," and a 1624 Portuguese catechism used to teach Christianity in Kongo used Nzambi a Mpungu as a direct translation for the Catholic God. The congruence does not capture what James Sweet calls the "volatility in the nature of the supreme being" in Africa, where cosmologies "were not constructed around a [single] supreme being in the way that Christianity was," and instead consisted of "a variety of separate and distinct ancestral spirits and deities [who] were the spiritual arbiters of the temporal world."[35]

Nonetheless, European priests and missionaries in Iberia, Africa, and the Americas treated Nzambi a Mpungu, and Nzambi or Zambi, as shorthand for a singular all-powerful god, similar to Christian references to God.[36] When Jesuits in Buenos Aires adapted the 1624 catechism, they preserved the Zambi-God equivalence while acknowledging, "It has been doubted whether [Zambi] really means the true God, or some other idol of that people."[37] Though Dias also equated Zambi and God, like the Jesuit in Buenos Aires, he seemed to understand the complexity beyond that comparison. To illustrate the formation of plural nouns, he used: "Nzambi, God. Gimzambi [or Jinzambi], Gods."[38] But Christian clerics most often employed singular comparisons to spread the gospel. Their work informed Padre Silva's delineation of Zambi as God and Zumbi as a demon during his sermon celebrating the battle at Serra da Barriga, which also belonged to a long tradition of Europeans assigning a "Manichean quality of spirits, good and evil, God and the devil" to African religious beliefs.[39] Centuries later, Rodrigues and other writers of his generation divided human and spirit in similar fashion.

Palmaristas would have understood the individual(s) known as Zumbi to wield a different set of religious and political capacities than the leader(s) called Zambi. In West Central Africa (and, indeed, much of the continent), religious worship revolved around two separate forms of "Otherworldly beings."[40] Powerful, distant spirits such as Zambi were distinct from the more ubiquitous souls of the deceased, which in West Central Africa could take the form of jinzumbi, the plural form of (n)zumbi.[41] Especially in western Angola, religious and political beliefs privileged "positional succession, which placed strong emphasis on communication between the living incumbent in a name or title and the spirits of his predecessors."[42] Harm and power could be passed down to heirs. Nzumbi was an "ancestor spirit; by extension, the spirits of deceased occupants of permanent position." By the same token, because "*jinzumbi* harmed only their own relatives, an offending spirit always belonged to the same lineage as the person afflicted."[43] António de Oliveira de Cadornega, a Portuguese soldier who arrived in Angola in 1639 and remained there for some fifty years, maintained that Blacks believed that "dreaming of their dead" was a kind of disorder that could be passed down "like leprosy among Spanish Royalty," but he also seemed to suggest a wider circulation, noting that the (n)zumbi spirit could be "a relative, *or any other* who has died."[44] The Italian Capuchin Jerom Merolla da Sorento wrote, "The word Zumbi . . . signifies an apparition of the deceased person, they being of opinion, that to whomever it shall appear, that person will presently die."[45] There was also the precedent of West Central African leaders incorporating (n)zumbi into their name: (B)ushi wa Nzumbi, for example.[46] When one Imbangala (also "Mbangala" and "Imbangola") leader became king in the early seventeenth century, the (n)zumbi from his predecessor's corpse entered his body.[47]

Jinzumbi appear in the colonial record in relation to the widespread but persecuted practice of contacting, placating, or expelling spirits to heal ailments or seek guidance and protection. One Angolan jailer wrote to the Inquisition after a free Black woman and an enslaved Black man were turned over to him for their alleged role in a ceremony to cure the woman's son of a zumbi that afflicted him. The flummoxed official complained that he did not know what to do with the two or "so many other Blacks, who have been arrested during recent years for the same reason."[48] Among those filling the jails in Angola were individuals known as nganga a nzumbi, priests or spirit mediums who alleviated suffering wrought by the spirits of kin who had passed away and who were skilled in communicating with jinzumbi.

The nganga a nzumbi was just one of seventeen ngangas — priests or skilled specialists or experts — that the Italian Capuchin Cavazzi da Montecuccolo registered during the seventeenth century. Throughout West Central Africa, in parts of Brazil, and elsewhere in the diaspora, men and women sought the guidance and help of ngangas to banish, soothe, or connect with spirits of the dead, and for any other number of matters.[49] Thornton suggests that the word "nganga" likely "derives from a Kikongo root that means 'knowledge' or 'skill,' but specifically the kind of skill that applies to religious matters."[50] Though the term is sometimes translated as "medicine-man," linguists show that it could encompass an even larger set of meanings and refer "more generally to an expert" of various kinds.[51] Different forms of ngangas were found in West Central Africa, and some of our earliest sources about them come from European clerics such as Cavazzi.[52] The seventeen different kinds of ngangas described by Cavazzi reflect a multivalence that is seen further in the fact that Africans also used the term to refer to Cavazzi and other European priests.[53]

Indeed, there is suggestive evidence of this conflation between priests and ngangas in Palmares. The lesser-known first version of *Relação das guerras feitas aos Palmares*—after registering several Christian symbols, including a "chapel" with "a very perfect image of the Baby Jesus, another of *Nossa Senhora da Conceição* [the patron saint of the Portuguese empire], and another of *Saint Blaise* [São Brás]"—notes that one of Palmares's "most cultured" (ladino) members served as priest (pároco) and oversaw baptisms and marriages (though not always according to Church dictates), and that the Palmaristas "call [them] Ganga."[54] In Angola, "acculturated" or "Latinized" Africans called ladinos spoke Portuguese or Spanish, were baptized, practiced Christianity, and often occupied favored positions relative to other enslaved peoples.[55] While the similarities between pároco, a generic term for Catholic parish priests, and nganga may have not have been self-evident to all, many would have understood the two to share much in common, as did the Africans who encountered Cavazzi.[56]

According to the *Relação*, Gan(g)a Zumba was the "Great Master" (Senhor Grande) and "King and Master to everyone, as much to those born in Palmares as those from outside."[57] The names of at least two other prominent Palmaristas—Gan(g)a Zumba's brother, Gan(g)a Zona, and the military leader Gan(g)a-Muiça—likely also included "ganga."[58] Thornton argues that Ganga Zumba was in fact "Gana Zumba," derived not from nganga and instead from the Kimbundu word ngana, or "lord," and Lara adopts the same conclusion.[59] Jan Vansina details how the word "ngána" was associated with wisdom and used as a "term of address" for leaders, and perhaps this is why Pernambuco's governor, Aires de Sousa de Castro, addressed Gan(g)a Zumba as "Gana" in their communications.[60] But the terms that colonial officials used to address Palmares leaders during negotiations may well have differed from what Palmaristas called them or knew them by, and the evidentiary basis to eliminate nganga from the story, as Thornton and Lara have, is unclear. In fact, another prominent colonial source, the *Relação*, uses "Ganga" to refer to the same leaders.

Beyond the fact that, in writing, the Portuguese used "Gana" and "Ganga" to refer to Palmarista leaders, there are other good reasons to believe that "Ganga" held great currency in Palmares, likely in addition to "Gana." Ngangas were widespread in Bantuphone Africa, where, according to Vansina, the proto-Bantu root *-ganga* had "practically universal distribution."[61] In 1672, Kakulu ka Kahenda, an Mbundu ruler in Dembos, purportedly confessed to a Portuguese Jesuit that "their Gangazumba, or healer, instructed them in doctrine that did not work."[62] While Mbundu kings did not possess the same supernatural powers as Imbangala counterparts or perform religious functions themselves, they relied on priests and war leaders to channel "magic" against rivals. In Pernambuco, a leader similarly capable of harnessing spirits to damage enemies and heal followers would hold great value.[63] Scholars' insistence that the leader's name was not Ganga Zumba is indicative of how religion and spirituality are often sidelined in histories of Palmares. While keeping both Gana and Ganga in view—Gan(g)a—we may say with confidence that Palmaristas believed that their leaders possessed great powers, including superhuman or supernatural, or had access to them through intermediaries.

If Gan(g)a Zumba was vested with the spiritual powers of a nganga, Palmaristas likely saw Zumbi in a similarly supernatural or superhuman light. Echoing other descriptions, Cavazzi described the nganga a nzumbi as a "priest of spirits," especially those seen in dreams, and dismissed them as hucksters who tricked gullible victims "every day."[64] Palmaristas who followed or knew followers of (n)zumbi mediums in Africa would have understood a man named Zumbi to be a powerful force. If he possessed the gifts of persuasion that Cavazzi saw in African nganga a nzumbi, his power would have been all the clearer.

It is also likely that many Palmaristas and others in Pernambuco believed that the dead took the form of (n)zumbi and that the man named Zumbi possessed powers connected to them. Cavazzi associated (n)zumbi spirits with the Imbangala, whom he (and others) called jaga.[65] "If a jaga dreams of one of his dead kin or feels that they have not sufficiently remembered that spirit, they turn to the *nganga-ia-zumbi*, or 'priest of spirits.'"[66] Cadornega spoke in broader terms, describing beliefs about (n)zumbi among the "Ambundo," while Jerom da Sorrento Merolla described rituals involving (n)zumbi in "the kingdoms of Cacongo and Angoij."[67] Cacongo (or Kakongo) lay north of the Kongo kingdom; nearby "Angoij" was "a kingdom rather in name than in dominions, being but a very small territory" and included the port of Cabinda, where Portuguese and Dutch traded with Africans.[68] It is significant that people north of Kongo used (n)zumbi to reference ancestor spirits, considering that the same word was used by the Imbangala, whose incursions into Mbundu territory were concentrated to the south.[69] This raises the likelihood that the term was recognizable and attached to spirits that crossed the Kongo-Mbundu divide.[70] Inquisition cases from the first half of the eighteenth century suggest general use of the term, at least in the Angolan hinterlands.[71] In 1721, a priest testifying before the Inquisition in Lisbon in a case from the Portuguese fort in Massangano described beliefs about jinzumbi circulating in Angola. Another case from around the same time places jinzumbi inland from Benguela, and another case (from 1750) does the same in two locales (Icolo and Golungo) east of Luanda.[72]

One of the most interesting Inquisition denunciations regarding jinzumbi was leveled in 1716 against a Portuguese lieutenant in Luanda, who sought out the help of a Black feiticeiro to help cure his godfather, who lived in Massangano.[73] "Invoking the devil," the feiticeiro declared that the godfather was afflicted by the "Zumbi of his children's amas."[74] The prospect of wet nurses in Angola taking the form of (n)zumbi spirits to haunt the people who enslaved them lends additional insight to the stories that Rodrigues's amas told him a century later—(n)zumbi (or Zumbi) was a powerful force from beyond the grave that could be channeled in multiple ways against the living. Imagining a conversation between enslaved Black caregiver and white child in Brazil, it is easy to see how "Zumbi" could refer to both the Palmarista leader and the frightening spirit of the dead, just as Rodrigues's amas apparently told him.

Years later, Rodrigues was on to something important when he distinguished Zumbi and Zambi, even if the conclusions he derived were overly narrow. Moving beyond the answers that he found, we may ask new questions with an ear keyed to a fuller song: Who in seventeenth-century Pernambuco distinguished between Z/zumbi and Zambi, who might have confused them, and who might have found it meaningful to combine them? If Z/zumbi was not "demon" or "devil" to most Palmaristas, what, aside from ancestor spirit, did the word mean to them? Some crucial insights are found, through lexical reconstruction, in linguistic "fossils" and the revelatory processes of linguistic change.

Reading Linguistic "Fossils"

If Padre Dias's Kimbundu primer funneled and filtered, lexical reconstructions provide access to a wider range of meanings recognized, shared, and exchanged by Africans speaking an array of Bantu languages. A key to understanding the relevant linguistic evidence lies in the fact that Bantu languages are agglutinating. This means that the prefixes, suffixes, and other morphemes (basic grammatical units that make up a word) fit together in ways that make the boundaries between them "clear and easy to recognize . . . as if the bits of the language were simply 'glued' together to make up larger words."[75] These individual elements can provide a great deal of insight. For example, Bantuphone words ending in -i often indicate the transformation of a verb into an "agent noun": -lob̲-a, "to fish," becomes mu-lob̲-i, "fisherman," with the prefix mu- referring to human beings and the suffix -i imbuing the noun with action. Many Bantuphone words ending in -i and formed in this way have notable durability and are of great interest to linguists, who liken them to "the fossils of a no longer active process from an earlier stage of the language."[76] "Zumbi" likely falls into this category. What, then, can this linguistic fossil tell us?

Crucial elements lie in sound change. As they took shape, many Bantu languages merged seven vowel sounds into five. In some cases, the transition also changed the pronunciation of certain consonants, a process known as Bantu spirantization.[77] By reconstructing the patterns and rules accompanying such transitions, linguists trace change over time. The beauty of this kind of linguistic excavation is that it can help identify specific locales where a root or word evolved while also indicating sounds and ideas that individuals from different places would have found mutually recognizable. One pattern of Bantu spirantization turned a *d* sound preceding a high closed *u* sound into a *z*, precisely the situation that we seem to have in the word "zumbi."[78] This suggests that "zumbi" came from the verb root *-dùmb-, "to rain," or the noun root *-dùmbí, "continuous rain" or "rain mist," meanings that would have been intelligible to people from a wide swath of Bantuphone Africa. (The asterisk followed by a dash [*-] signals that a root has been reconstructed using comparative historical linguistics. See "A Note on Language" and appendix A.) Both *-dùmb- and *-dùmbí were found in Bantuphone languages spread across a large expanse of West Central Africa, Central Africa, and beyond. A key delimiting factor is the fact that not all Bantuphone languages follow this spirantization rule. Even accounting for that, spirantization patterns suggest

FIGURE 3.1 "Conjuring Rain in Angola" (1687). *Source*: Cavazzi da Montecuccolo, *Descrição histórica*, 1:197.

that *-dùmb(i)* became zumbi in nearly two dozen languages spread across seven distinct linguistic zones, including Kimbundu, Mbundu, Hungu, and Chokwe (present-day Angola); Yaka and Lega-Mwenga (present-day Democratic Republic of Congo); and Kerewe and Shambala (present-day Tanzania). Speakers of each language would have understood this durable word and likely connected it to rain.[79] Rain made crops grow and gave life (see figure 3.1). It could also neutralize European firearms.[80] It is likely not incidental that, as one nineteenth-century traveler observed, Serra da Barriga "is subject to frequent thunder-storms."[81]

The connection to water takes on even greater meaning given a rich collection of lakes and rivers named Zumbi in northeast Brazil, discussed in more detail in part IV. Sebastião da Rocha Pita emphasized the importance of water to Palmares. According to his 1730 *Historia da America Portugueza*, Zumbi's Palmares "had a lake, that provided them [the Palmaristas] copious fish, many streams, and wells, which they call Cacimbas, from which they drew abundant water."[82] There is also little doubt that Palmares's inhabitants, like kin and counterparts in West Central Africa, understood lakes, rivers, and other bodies of water to possess spiritual power, often as home to the deceased or as a dividing line between worlds of the living and the dead.[83] There are even hints in the colonial record that "zumbi" was understood in Palmares as referring to water. In the 1630s and 1640s, the German naturalist Georg Marggraf (also Marcgrave) traveled in Brazil to collect observations about its flora, fauna, and people, published posthumously (in Latin) as *Historia naturalis brasiliae*.[84] Marggraf reported that that there were two encampments in the Palmares wilderness where Blacks sought refuge, the smaller of which had a stream called Gungohubî.[85] Historical changes and misapprehensions between languages suggest what this name might have meant. An aspirated /z/ is often heard as an /h/, and nasal sounds, such as /n/ or /m/, often disappeared when Europeans heard and attempted to render African words. For these reasons, "nzumbi" became "zumbi" in Portuguese, and in the case of Marggraf's manuscript it may have been written down as "humbi" or "hubi."[86] Puzzling out the meaning of "gungo" would require further research, but if this stream's name indeed included "zumbi," it could represent an early manifestation of or point of genesis for what became the name for Palmares's most famous leader.

These associations diverge significantly from the meaning of "Zambi," which lexical reconstruction suggests descended from the proto-Bantu form *-jàmbé* ("God") with attestations stretching up Africa's west coast and inland from central Kongo.[87] While the audible difference between Zumbi and Zambi may have seemed trivial or confusing to Portuguese or English speakers unfamiliar with Bantu languages, for people who spoke those languages, the words' sounds would have ranged from moderately to radically distinct. On an acoustic scale of Bantu languages divided into "high," "low," and "middle," /u/ is a high sound and /a/ is low; the two letters, or rather, the multiple /u/ and /a/ sounds of different Bantu languages, cluster at opposite ends of the acoustic spectrum.[88] Zumbi and Zambi, then, sounded nothing alike to Bantu-language speakers, and there is little chance that they confused the two.

The Portuguese were slightly more likely to mistake a /u/ for an /a/, though that is probably not what happened. More likely, as Padre Silva's sermon and the multiple spellings in colonial communiqués suggest, lack of clarity about the Palmares leader's name fed into multiple renderings of it, which authors interchanged and mistook over time. Portuguese speakers heard and represented African words differently because of not only the intricacies and complexities of African languages but also similar dynamics within Portuguese, where variable spelling and regional and continental differences lent their own forms of internal diversity.

Documenta Palmares facilitates a systematic appraisal of these variations. In nearly two hundred documents that the site tags with the keyword "Zumbi" (and a few additional sources), several patterns emerge (see table 3.1). While the Portuguese regularly referred to "Zambi" during the 1670s, the name appears less frequently thereafter, at which point "Zumbi" and especially "Zombi" dominate. This would support a hypothesis that the two men called "Zambi" in the *Relação* possessed a name or title—or belonged to a lineage— whose meaning or valence diminished as Zumbi rose to power. During Zumbi's reign in the 1680s and 1690s, the Portuguese refer most often to either Zumbi or Zombi. Scattered references to Zambi during this time may mean that another leader with that name wielded power (the figure whom the *Relação* mentions as escaping Manuel Lopes Galvão's late 1675 attacks on the mocambos with an injured leg?), or they could reflect confusion or misunderstanding. Miscommunications were legion not only between Portuguese and African actors, but also between Portugal and Brazil and even within Brazil, due in part to the way that language evolved in different ways in America.[89]

One of the most striking aspects of the colonial documents is the sheer dominance of "Zombi," which may indicate a unique Palmares name or title or, more likely, reflect Portuguese spelling conventions. During the seventeenth century, Portuguese speakers began to pronounce the letter /o/ more like /u/, especially in pretonic syllables: unstressed syllables that fall before a word's stressed syllable. For example, dormir (to sleep) was increasingly pronounced durmir. Colonial documents reflect this process, often interchanging the two letters, just as they do with /i/, /j/, and /y/, which explains the multiple endings: Zumbi, Zumby, Zumbj.[90] While the difference between Zumbi, Zumby, and Zumbj was likely insignificant, the relationship of Zumbi and Zombi is slightly less clear. Stress operates differently in African tonal languages than in Portuguese, and the /o/ and /u/ in "Zombi" and "Zumbi" are not pretonic in Portuguese; both nouns fall naturally in the stressed syllable. This suggests that while the prevalence of Zombi in the colonial documents is likely due to the vagaries of seventeenth-century Portuguese pronunciation and orthography, it is possible that colonial officials understood Zombi and Zumbi as distinct names or titles, and that reflected a reality in Palmares.[91]

While more research is needed to determine the significance of "Zombi," other conclusions are possible now. As verbs turn into agent-noun "fossils,"

TABLE 3.1 Occurrences of "Zumbi," "Zambi," and "Zombi" in Portuguese
Colonial Documents

	ZAMBI[Δ]	ZUMBI[ΔΔ]	ZOMBI[ΔΔΔ]	OTHER	TOTAL
1676–1679	5 (63%)	1 (13%)	2 (25%)	0	8
1680–1695	10 (15%)	15 (22%)	41 (61%)	1? (1%)	67
1696–1757	1 (1%)	11 (11%)	89 (88%)	0	101
Total	16 (9%)	27 (15%)	132 (75%)	1? (1%)	176

[Δ] Variations of "Zambi": Zamby, Zambim, Zambj, Sambi

[ΔΔ] Variations of "Zumbi": Zumby, Zumbby, Zumbohy, zumbim, Zumbj, Zumbuy, zunby

[ΔΔΔ] Variations of "Zombi": Zombj, Zomboy, Zomby, Zombij, Zombim, Zonbi, sombj, xombj, Zombî

SOURCES: My research assistant, Caroline da Rocha Birnfeld, helped me compile and organize the data for this table using documents culled from Documenta Palmares.

they can "become increasingly independent of their verbs of origin and may start to acquire a more specialized or fixed meaning."[92] This process took additional twists and turns in war-torn Pernambuco. At least in the colonial imagination, Zumbi and Zambi became ethereal warrior figures. Zambi was "God" and also "God of War" or "God of Arms," the man who was wounded but eluded the Portuguese, and the "macho" of the same name, whom they captured. Zumbi was "demon," "devil," and evil spirit, and also "governor," "potentate," "king," "little king," and "scoundrel." But Palmaristas preserved and created other meanings. Especially during Zumbi's reign, his name carried special and specific potency, even as the Portuguese pronounced and spelled it in multiple ways and filtered Zumbi and Zambi through their own lenses.

"Evil" and Its Uses

Linguistic changes and manipulation (purposeful or not) could have significant consequences, especially in the case of spirits that could cause serious harm to the living and that often became imbricated in colonial military conflict. Cadornega, who in 1680 completed a three-volume manuscript about his time in Angola, associated Zambi with nearly invincible might in the course of describing an "impenetrable Fortress of the Stones of Mapungo, whose very name in the Ambunda language of Angola, means [a] thing of admiration and fear." The name "Mapungo," he wrote, came from "pungo," or "Heaven," and when people in the area "name their God, they call it Zambi Apungo." "Má," he maintained, "is the same" as what it means in Portuguese: "evil."[93] This is a fantastic example of colonial invention. The deity in question was Nzambi a Mpungu (or Nzambi Mpungu), the Kongolese deity that Europeans often equated with "God."

In the Bantu prefix ma-, Cadornega heard—or, rather, created—the sound as a Portuguese word, turning Nzambi (a) Mpungu into Zambi Mapungo and imbuing the being with an evil aggression that most Africans would not have recognized.[94] Kongolese people, Thornton writes, were more engaged with ancestor and territorial spirits and did not view Nzambi a Mpungu "as being particularly active in the world."[95]

Cadornega's inventive insertion of "evil" may help redirect one long-standing etymological debate connected to Palmares. In an influential essay, Stuart Schwartz wrote, "There is, I believe, a deeper story in Palmares and one with broad implications for the subsequent history of slave resistance in Brazil. A key to the problem lies in the etymology of the word *quilombo*."[96] Schwartz links Brazilian quilombos to the mobile war camps in West Central Africa called kilombos that were utilized by Imbangala fighters as they invaded Mbundu territory in the late sixteenth century and the first half of the seventeenth. The Imbangala divided their camps into "distinct sections, each under the leadership of its own 'captain,'" a structure similar to Palmares, at least during the 1670s.[97]

Other scholars have refined Schwartz's hypothesis, emphasizing, as I mentioned in chapter 1, that the word "quilombo" does not appear in primary sources about Palmares until the end of the seventeenth century (though it entered Portuguese lexicon by 1615).[98] Others have questioned the assertion of intentionality underlying his hypothesis: in contrast to Schwartz's claim that "if the founders of Palmares had used the Imbangala *ki-lombo* as the basis for their society their version of it was incomplete or at least a variation on the basic model," Lara suggests that careful historicization of Palmares defies the possibility of gleaning the intentions of Palmares's "founders" in documents from the 1680s and 1690s.[99] Nevertheless, Schwartz's hypothesis raises the question of what more may be said about the relationship between Imbangala kilombos and the mocambos of Palmares, particularly in light of Cadornega's invocation of "evil." During the sixteenth and early seventeenth centuries, roving bands of Imbangala warriors reshaped key dynamics in West Central Africa.[100] The Portuguese allied with Imbangala armies, who wreaked havoc on Mbundu states and attacked the Kongo kingdom. Imbangala leaders fought alongside and against powers across the region and partnered with the Portuguese, who sought to sow chaos and incite civil wars to speed the capture of prisoners to enslave. The arrangement made the Imbangala "the ambivalent keystone" of both the illegal and legal traffic in humans.[101]

Stories about Imbangala cannibalism, most of them fantastical, fed into their renown as fearsome, and no doubt to some people as "evil," warriors. The Imbangala "internalized" this renown, Jared Staller argues, strategically utilizing ritual acts of cannibalism in order to gain superhuman strength on the battlefield and strike fear in enemies and even new recruits. They "strutted through their cannibal displays, as much performance as practice, in a terrorizing tactic meant equally to control their own novices and to overawe outsiders."[102] In the early seventeenth century, an English sailor named Andrew Battel published a memoir of his time in Angola, where he lived among the Imbangala for a year. His widely cited account emphasizes cannibalism.[103] Though Palmaristas may not have "modeled" their society on African kilombos, and while there is no indication that Palmaristas even engaged in performative or ritualistic acts of cannibalism, there is no doubt that they knew about Imbangala armies, who may have helped deliver many of them into bondage. At least a small number of Palmaristas were likely themselves Imbangala. Joseph C. Miller suggests the possibility that "in the besieged circumstances in which the escaped slaves of Palmares lived, [Palmaristas] would have turned to even a few trained Imbangala warriors among them for effective techniques of integrating young male recruits into disciplined fighting bands capable of defending the settlement."[104] The Imbangala's "aggressively masculine" culture would not have appealed to all female mocambo leaders, and Imbangala practices would have been of little use in Palmares, while others would have been of great value.

Part of the kilombo's appeal derived from its novel approach to lineage and power. The Mbundu structured leadership around matrilineal descent, which also determined who belonged—and who did not. Doing so fostered unity but limited the ability to grow and raise armies. The kilombo solved that problem, using initiation ceremonies to conscript and incorporate new members with no previous kinship ties to the group.[105] By helping mobilize large armies, the kilombo allowed the Imbangala, allied with the Portuguese, to "revolutionize" politics in the region, Miller writes, helping erect "a completely new set of European and African states founded on the export of slaves from Africa to the Americas."[106] Strict discipline gave kilombo members physical and superhuman strength. Members gained entrance to a kilombo through battlefield exploits and rites and practices that kept them in peak physical condition, impervious to enemy weapons, and "in a state of perpetual supernatural readiness."[107] Similar methods would have been useful in Palmares, whose existence depended on assembling and maintaining fighting forces out of individuals from all kinds of backgrounds and preparing them for intense warfare.

Thornton rejects the Imbangala-Palmares link, arguing that the Imbangala's ephemeral military and political success prevented them from having a significant impact across the Atlantic. Though convincing and instructive on so many other points, Thornton is unnecessarily dismissive of the possibility that Palmaristas borrowed and modified from the Imbangala. He claims that "Imbangala bands were unlikely to become the model for runaway settlements, like Palmares in Brazil" because the "Imbangala were regarded by most people in Angola as evil and their radical model of forced recruitment was not favored by any state system."[108] But for those who fled to Palmares, borrowing select strategies from "evil" raiders, whose practices they otherwise feared and abhorred, might not have seemed like such a bad idea. As Thornton himself explains, the Ndongo Queen Njinga did just that. Though she would later convert (for a second time) to Christianity, "in the heat of war" she became wife to an Imbangala leader to secure an alliance.[109] Banished by the Portuguese, Linda Heywood writes, Njinga thus refashioned herself by "making a life-changing transformation from exiled Mbundu queen to Imbangala captain in her own right." The appeal lay mainly in the fact that the Imbangala "reputation for carnage, cruelty, and cannibalism made enemies and allies alike quake with terror."[110] Or, as Staller puts it, Njinga strategically employed and deployed "calculated cruelty."[111] There is no reason to think that Palmaristas did not make similar strategic decisions.

The fear that the Imbangala could inspire was profound. In 1619, the Bishop of Kongo reported that even the mention of the Imbangala would cause opposing armies to flee in disarray.[112] Some Imbangala "actively assumed the role of witches, whose fundamental characteristic was that they killed and ate their victims."[113] One story that circulated during the second half of the seventeenth century, after the Imbangala heyday, maintained that even some deities "were so terrified by the Imbangala that they went and hid in the lakes and rivers, only to reemerge when time had caused the Imbangala to soften their ways."[114] The ability to vanquish not only powerful human enemies but also rival spirits would have had obvious appeal in Palmares.

The fact that memories of Imbangala spiritual terror survived in West Central Africa into the second half of the seventeenth century increases the likelihood that similar stories circulated in Pernambuco, which remained closely tied to Angola. In 1656, when Njinga entered into a peace treaty with the Portuguese, she provided ninety-nine enslaved people in exchange for the release of her sister. The Portuguese shortly sent them to Pernambuco, where references to Njinga circulated among the enslaved in religious and popular celebrations.[115] When Njinga confirmed the treaty, Palmares was entering a new, post-Dutch occupation era, and the Imbangala's power in West Central Africa was waning. While discarding lineage practices helped the Imbangala grow in number, it left them disconnected from and without access to ancestor spirits. Faced with this challenge, the Imbangala adapted again, assimilating Mbundu rites for venerating dead kin through none other than nganga a nzumbi priests who communed with jinzumbi.[116] The same Cadornega who added "evil" to Zambi, as we will recall, was likely informed by encounters with such priests in Angola when he described the (n)zumbi spirits.

While the Imbangala enjoyed short-term success, their way of life did not meld easily with the Mbundu: "the Imbangala ideology of non-humanness and the rigorous conditions of life in the *kilombo* differed too dramatically from the backgrounds of the people they incorporated."[117] By the middle of the seventeenth century, the kilombo had become obsolete, and the Imbangala, once wandering warriors, had settled into villages. But even while the kilombo faded, individual Imbangala kings continued to prosper by adapting to Mbundu lineage practices and allying with the Portuguese. By first rejecting and later embracing Mbundu lineage practices, the Imbangala skillfully adapted during tumultuous times.

Such tumult might suggest explanations as to why the Portuguese did not use "quilombo" in reference to Palmares until the 1680s, decades after the Imbangala kilombo faded from view in West Central Africa. We know that Gan(g)a Zumba's death and Zumbi's rise ushered great change and eventually made the Serra da Barriga into Palmares's main settlement. Did the new era also include an increase of smaller, mobile military camps that Africans and Europeans might think resembled Imbangala kilombos? In other words, were Imbangala ideas and practices more present in Zumbi's Palmares than Gan(g)a Zumba's? A latter-day resurrection of the Imbangala kilombo would not have been without precedent: Njinga had previously "rekindl[ed] the energy of Imbangala kilombos" to secure power, even as most Imbangala groups were settling into agricultural societies.[118]

If Imbangala was not a widespread identity or societal "model" in Palmares, African-born Palmaristas and enslaved peoples in Pernambuco had multiple memories of, relationships to, and ideas about the group. Many surely feared the belief in nonhumanness or had bitter memories of becoming enslaved at the hands of the Imbangala. While Cadornega invoked "evil" to disparage African beliefs, perhaps Palmaristas advertised or cultivated it as a potential source of power to counter the gruesome violence of the Europeans. Just as the Imbangala adapted to Mbundu practices, the leaders of Palmares would have had every reason to incorporate ideas and practices not only from their diverse followers but perhaps even from enemies renowned for their "evil" ways.

Fleeing Palmares

The Blaer-Reijmbach diary provides a rare glimpse of how some Palmaristas understood Z/zumbi and the spirit world, particularly in light of encounters with Christianity and colonial violence. The Imbangala were hardly the only experts at adaptation, which was also a central feature of Christianity in West Central Africa.[119] In Luanda, even those who had been "extensively exposed to Christianity" still sought aid from all kinds of ngangas.[120] Similar flexibility likely existed in Palmares. The Blaer-Reijmbach expedition reported that there one could find "every kind of man, and their king govern[ed] them with harsh justice, not allowing witchdoctors [feiticeiros] among their people."[121] The flexibility is further emphasized by the fact that when the Palmarista informant(s) told the Blaer-Reijmbach expedition about this, the conversation likely occurred in the vicinity of a large structure at the center of the Palmares settlement, which the expedition described as a church. But while the Dutch understood "witchcraft" in relation to European Christianity, their informant(s) may have meant something quite different: not communion with the devil, but rather the misuse or selfish utilization of powers that could otherwise be put to good.

The "harsh justice" meted out by the Palmares ruler to feiticeiros recalls Afonso I, Kongo's sixteenth-century king, who embraced Catholicism and labeled those who did not as witches, whom he targeted with brutal punishments, including enslavement.[122] In Europe, Christian authorities defined any contact with spiritual forces made outside the direction of the Church as diabolic "witchcraft," while many African societies also looked down on "witchcraft," but without associating it with the devil.[123] The "harsh justice" also highlights divisions and differences in the mocambos. According to the diary, "When any Blacks fled, they would send Brazilian-born Blacks after them, and once caught they were killed in a way that struck fear in them, especially the Blacks from Angola."[124] The presence and apparent primacy of Brazilian-born Blacks indicate a diverse, internally differentiated Palmares and resonate with events across the Atlantic. Just a few years before the Blaer-Reijmbach expedition, the Portuguese confronted a revolt in West Central Africa led by a Mbundu noble named Gregorio, whose soldiers reportedly fought under the influence of a "witch." After negotiations led by priests failed, the Portuguese attacked, capturing Gregorio, whom they beat and dismembered before feeding his remains to dogs.[125] In addition to instilling fear, the gruesome spectacle deprived Gregorio of a proper burial and treatment of his corpse, acts that would have affected the destiny of his soul and the ability of the living to commune with it.

Events in Spanish America help further contextualize the punishments for those who fled from Palmares. Kathryn Joy McKnight analyzes a nearly one-thousand-page manuscript detailing two ritual executions that took place in 1633, in what is today Colombia.[126] The first was carried out by leaders of the Palenque de Limón, a maroon community outside Cartagena de las Indias, against white and Indigenous residents from a nearby farm, and the second by Spanish colonial officials against the community. Drawing on Miller's work, McKnight believes that the first executions, during which a female leader drank the blood of the victims, whose corpses "the Angolas" prohibited from being buried, share "important kernels" of meaning with Imbangala practices of human sacrifice, which imbued leaders with power and invincibility to the group. The European response struck at the heart of that invincibility, as Spaniards killed the accused and chopped their bodies into pieces, which they displayed in public, completing a "gruesome symmetry of violence" that denied the executed the burials that would facilitate peaceful afterlives and served as gory warnings against others who harbored thoughts of challenging colonial power.[127]

The Palmares leader, in an important difference from the ritual executions occurring a decade earlier, exacted violent punishment not on Europeans or Indigenous people but instead on African former members of the mocambos, "Angolans" who were distinguished from Brazilian-born Blacks—rather than someone from the same group—or, rather, people assigned the same ethnonym as in Palenque de Limón. Several dynamics evident in the well-documented incidents in what is now Colombia provide helpful entry points for understanding what happened in Palmares, for which we lack such detailed accounts. Locked in a state of war, and with slavery looming as an ever-present threat, Africans and their descendants in the Americas preserved what they could, while also adapting and borrowing. The "Angolas" in Colombia might have been Imbangala or borrowed from the Imbangala's repertoire of spiritual terror. Similarly, the "harsh justice" of the Palmares leader—who may or may not have been Imbangala—might have emulated their violent practices. But if he was not Imbangala and eschewed their ways altogether, his successors—or perhaps the forbidden feiticeiros—could have employed some of the methods that gave the Imbangala renown as merciless warriors. The fact that individuals not only fled to Palmares but also from it illustrates a key point worth highlighting here: as formidable as they were, the mocambos were not always or only endpoints. At least for those who ran away and were violently punished for doing so, Palmares was not a hospitable destination.

Conclusion

Beginning with the earliest European accounts of Z/zumbi and Zambi in West Central Africa and Palmares, confusion and, in some cases, intentional obfuscation reigned. While Cadornega may have sincerely believed that Nzambi a Mpungu was an "evil" Zambi Mapungo, colonial translations of "Zumbi" as "devil" and "demon" clearly owed to the deeply held religious beliefs of Padre Silva and other church officials and followers. While it is not surprising that Silva's translation of Zumbi and Zambi was an expression of his own ideas, alternative renderings have been hard to come by, perhaps due in part to the long-term effect of Rodrigues's dismissal of his amas' stories. But the fact that those stories made their way into his work had its own long-term impact, preserving important ideas, however much filtered, in writing. Returning to those ideas now, we find that, far from "orthographic errors," manifestations and memories of Z/zumbi in Brazil convey new sight lines through which to view Palmares.

One of the most important sight lines emerges through the multifaceted meanings of Z/zumbi. In the late 1960s, when Miller did ethnographic work in Angola, an Imbangala informant explained to him how, in Miller's paraphrase, history could function "like an ancestor spirit (*nzumbi* [. . .]) in relation to the ancestor when he was alive."[128] The past could journey into and accompany the present. During the slave era, zumbi spirits were a likely vehicle for this kind of time travel. Many of those forcibly taken from Africa to America did not understand their journey across the Atlantic to mean that Africa was in an isolated past but instead that they had traveled into a hellish new world. Some believed the Atlantic to be controlled by cannibalistic white monsters.[129] In this vicious realm that was dominated by enslavers and the daily warfare of slavery, Africans found use in tools, weapons, and alliances that might not otherwise have appealed to them. If Cadornega inventively inserted "evil" into his definition of "Zambi Mapungo," others found different applications for and meanings in the concept, ranging from the Imbangala's spiritual warfare to the "harsh justice" described in the Blaer-Reijmbach diary. As he secured power in Palmares, Zumbi may have projected similarly fearsome ideas, but his name also evoked spirits of the dead and life-giving water. In a leader named Zumbi and in spirits called (n)zumbi, Palmaristas found and forged connection, continuity, and signifiers that linked them to familiar spiritual grammar and helped them make community and resist slavery and continuous military assaults. In both its durability and capaciousness, Z/zumbi would continue to generate new meanings, symbols, and legacies that proliferated even after colonial forces killed and dismembered Zumbi, and under the continuous deadly violence of warfare and slavery.

Flying Home?

The spiritual nexus traced in Palmares invites a tragic question: For those nameless masses who perished at Serra da Barriga, what did their deaths mean to them and to those they left behind? Rocha Pita projected crystal clarity on this point in his romantic and paradigm-setting retelling of Zumbi's death: leaping was a deliberate decision to die free rather than live in slavery. But such certainty neglects how the actual calculations must have been made in the moment with lightning speed and under duress, and that is to say nothing of long-held beliefs, fears, and aspirations of the men and women who died in Palmares. The *Rellação Verdadeyra* describes how, while fleeing battle, Palmaristas would say "in their language '*olenga, olenga*, Barriga is no more.'"[1] Silvia Lara translates "olenga" as a form of the Kimbundu verb "lenga," "to flee," and interprets the quotation to mean that Palmaristas called the mountain simply "Barriga." "Serra" (mountain or ridge) was a colonial addition, she reasons, as was the other name sometimes used for the mountain: Outeiro da Barriga, "outeiro" being the Portuguese word for "hill or knoll."[2] The Portuguese-Kimbundu dictionary that Lara uses renders "lenga" as "to flee," but this is just one of many possibilities. Another dictionary provides different compelling meanings, including "to wail" or "lament."[3]

Yet, in Portuguese, "barriga" means "stomach" or "belly," and in West Central Africa, the belly is often associated with power and life force. Objects called nkisi are imbued with cosmic powers and often depict figures with holes in their stomachs that are filled with herbs, gunpowder, grave dirt, and other materials that animate the spirit.[4] Pedro Dias's compendium of Kimbundu grammar translates "oteiro" as "malundo." Perhaps some Palmaristas called the elevated settlement Malundo Barriga and understood it similarly to Moulondou

Zambi (Zambi Mountain), a spiritually potent volcano in Angola. In the 1820s, when a French traveler desired to climb to the top, locals refused to take him, explaining that it was "the entrance of spirits into the other world."[5] In Kongo, mountains were similarly potent spaces, where ancestor spirits and other powerful forces dwelled.[6] Whatever name(s) they assigned their own mountain in Pernambuco, it is likely that in addition to offering crucial tactical advantages, the Serra da Barriga similarly possessed spiritual power. Though not literally a volcano, the mountaintop mocambo was nonetheless quite capable of unleashing military and spiritual might on its enemies, a "place of power" in both military and religious terms.[7] Driven from this powerful stronghold, Palmares refugees likely had the impulse to flee and mourn at once, a nearly impossible and almost mutually exclusive pair of objectives, especially amid the violence of war.

The spiritual issues raised in chapter 3 make even more complex this dual impulse to flee and mourn: there was still the potential for continuity and connection, even though contact between the living and the dead could be treacherous for survivors. It was also possible that flight continued in a new form posthumously. In North America and the Caribbean, the act of dying and "flying home" is most often associated with West Africans, especially Igbo (also Ibo, Ebo, and Ebos) people, thanks in part to the lasting cultural significance of Igbo Landing, a site off the coast of Georgia where in 1803 a group of Africans perished in what is remembered as a coordinated, collective suicide carried out as a means for spiritual journey back home across the Atlantic.[8] Similar references are found throughout the circum-Caribbean. In 1733, for instance, enslaved Akan people revolted and seized the Danish-controlled island of St. John. When colonial forces wrested back the island, dozens of the insurrection's leaders reportedly killed themselves to avoid capture. A Danish–West Indian governor wrote that the Akan "believe that at their death they return to their fatherland, or as they express it . . . 'when I die, I shall return to my own land.'"[9] In considering such stories, we must also keep in mind the long-lasting myths about supposed natural proclivities among certain enslaved people to take their own lives, which reflect the fantasies and fears of those who enslaved and traded humans, not reality.[10] Additionally, as I will discuss further shortly, such references to flight via suicide are notably scarce in Brazil, especially before the nineteenth century. But such stories do raise an intriguing question about the many from Palmares who died at Serra da Barriga and elsewhere, their names never recorded in the archive. If fallen

Palmaristas did not fly home, what became of them? And if they did fly home, where was home, anyway? As Walter C. Rucker points out, for Blacks born in the Caribbean "my own land" might not necessarily (or only) mean Africa.[11] This point resonates deeply in the case of Palmares, itself a formidable site of birth and death, and a starting point for a larger cosmology of flight. Thinking about Palmares as home also opens a wider vista into cosmic worlds that included water and territorial spirits, and that helped Africans and Brazilian-born Palmaristas not only process the death of kin but also nurture crops and confront all sorts of challenges in the world of the living.

Multiple Celestial Paths

Esteban Montejo, whose life history and account of escaping slavery in Cuba remains one of Latin America's only recorded life stories of a formerly enslaved person—a sharp contrast to the rich corpus of slave narratives in North America—drew a provocative distinction between suicide and transmigratory flight, explaining, "The Blacks didn't do that [commit suicide] because they went flying, flying in the sky, and headed off for their homeland. The Musundi Congolese were the ones who flew the most. They disappeared through witchcraft. They did the same as the [island] witches, but without a sound."[12] Though recorded in the 1960s and mediated by a prominent author, who transcribed and edited Montejo's first-person account, the description is nonetheless suggestive in its geography, identifying supernatural flight not with the Igbo, who were from West Africa, but instead with West Central Africa (Kongo).[13]

Part of the challenge to understanding where the Palmarista dead would have flown to and what their death signified to them is the striking absence of references to posthumous flight in colonial Brazil, especially before the nineteenth century. The fact that relatively few Igbos arrived in Brazil might explain this in part, but not entirely.[14] One such reference occurred during 1835 parliamentary debates about a proposal that eventually passed to enforce death sentences on any enslaved person who killed or injured their enslaver, overseer, or member of the enslaver's family. The legislator Antônio Pereira Rebouças, whose mother had been enslaved before gaining her freedom, argued against the law on the grounds that enslaved people found in death an escape from misery: "They believe in transmigration [and] . . . that in dying they pass from this land to their own."[15] Where he learned that, and how many others shared the belief, is unclear, but in the 1800s European travelers in Brazil described similar examples and also noted cases of whites who mutilated and decapitated corpses of enslaved people, believing that doing so would prevent transmigration or convince the living that it would and thereby deter suicide.[16]

Though belief in transmigration may have been somewhat common among enslaved Brazilians during the nineteenth century, we know little about local beliefs concerning the afterlife and spirituality in seventeenth- and eighteenth-century Pernambuco.[17] While Padre Silva and others suggested, given that Zumbi was a demon, that the souls of the rebel Blacks of Palmares were destined for Hell, Palmares survivors, their descendants, and others in Pernambuco had different beliefs. Like their kin in Africa, Palmaristas understood the worlds of the living and the dead to be closely related and often in contact. The means for traversing the threshold dividing the two worlds varied, but belief that souls or spirits transmigrated in some form was widespread in West and West Central Africa, as was the "widely held consensus . . . that the dead went to an afterlife where they might influence the living."[18] Spirits emanated from and animated the dead, taking the form of birds, goats, and other animals, and often prompting the living to seek protection from healers and religious leaders. Many living in Pernambuco may have believed that Zumbi was literally immortal and could not be killed. But for many Africans and their kin, Zumbi's "immortality" was likely closer to the "invincibility" that Imbangala combatants could achieve in battle, what Jared Staller describes as not "momentary triumph over physical death but rather eternal victory through it."[19]

Palmares survivors must have gone to great lengths to honor the dead. Joseph Miller suggests that the atrocities of slavery left enslaved people "resolved, if not obsessed, with converting continuing deaths . . . into affirmation of a community who would recognize, and memorialize them."[20] In West Central Africa, individuals who suffered violent deaths (in war and otherwise) or were not buried belonged to a special category "of ghosts and other wicked spirits" that the living went to great lengths to avoid.[21] One can imagine the anguish as those who survived the battle at Serra da Barriga grasped for solid ground and safe harbor, conscious all the while that the departed could inflict illness and worse not only then but on future generations. As they fled or were enslaved, some survivors may have taken comfort knowing that their dead kin or comrades had passed to the spirit world, a journey that may have returned them to Africa or perhaps meant lingering closer to Serra da Barriga or following surviving kin.

The mobility and expansive distances that zumbi spirits could cross suggest how posthumous journeys could take multiple forms and move in multiple directions, sometimes in opposition to, or otherwise beyond, the more familiar west-to-east journey from America to Africa. Selma Pantoja describes jinzumbi as "souls [that] . . . walk around in the air, lost."[22] Though "wandering" may be more apt than "lost," a zumbi spirit would not necessarily or only gravitate from Brazil toward Africa. In the 1820s, a woman in Benguela accused her servant of using a zumbi to kill her husband, no small feat given that he was living in Rio de Janeiro, slain, according to his widow, by a spell cast across the Atlantic via a deceased soul.[23] Wherever their earthly moorings, spirits of the dead could travel in multiple directions, as likely to fly across the Atlantic as to travel to and within Brazil. Flight was also central in Kongo, where nature spirits were closely associated with birds, suggesting a layered spiritual matrix in which various forms of flight featured prominently.[24]

The ability of spirits to not only fly to Africa but also pursue the living in America must have had a profound effect on Palmares survivors. The carnage at Serra da Barriga left many kinless, and for those who survived, the inability to bury their relatives could have catastrophic results. "Virtually all Africans," Staller writes, "believed that people had to be buried in their ancestors' lands."[25] Funerals in West Central Africa often involved elaborate, weeklong feasts and rites.[26] Rituals to purge malevolent zumbi could include the exhumation of corpses believed to be responsible for earthly afflictions.[27] Unable to tend to the dead, Palmaristas fleeing battle faced the prospect of being haunted with no remedy.[28] The remarkable way that spirits could transcend the line between human beings and nature illustrates the significant role that the fallen could play in the lives of the living. In both Kongo and Mbundu belief systems, John Thornton writes, "The great territorial deities shared religious space with the ancestors, whose sphere of activity was their descendants rather than whole regions and territories."[29] Once again, Imbangala adaptations are instructive. They "brazenly postured as man-eaters," Staller writes, not only to strike fear in their enemies but also to establish familylike attachments and ensure that spirits "deprived brutally of ancestral burial lands, would remain secure in the afterlife." Doing so led orphaned Imbangala combatants to "consider their brother-in-arms as their family, not the deceased ancestors of their murdered parents."[30] As mentioned in chapter 3, there is no indication that Palmaristas engaged even in performative acts of cannibalism, but surely other strategies were employed. One way to ensure security in the afterlife may have involved the mountain-sized "belly" on which Zumbi's stronghold sat. Like the Zambi volcano in Angola, the fortified city on Serra da Barriga may have been understood to consume and protect dead Palmaristas. A sacred space, Serra da Barriga was also a home capable of anchoring the living and the dead.

Hunting (and Marketing) "Witchcraft"

The idea of Serra da Barriga as a space of sacred protection raises another intriguing question. In what ways did Palmaristas engage the spirit world for protection in their everyday lives, both before and after the devastating battle of 1694, and for connection with those whom they lost?

Inquisition records provide an avenue for understanding such questions of spirituality in Palmares and Pernambuco. In Brazil, the Inquisition relied on local prosecutors, who recorded denunciations in cadernos do promotor (prosecutor's books). The Pernambuco cadernos, which also included denunciations from Paraíba, Rio Grande do Norte, and Ceará, make clear that suspicion of "witchcraft" permeated coastal towns, the sertão, and seemingly every space between. Divinations and other forbidden acts often took place in isolated, wooded areas, and some feiticeiro/as were born in the vaguely described forested regions associated with Palmares and other fugitive spaces: the mata (or mato).[31] The power of sorcery in Pernambuco was so widespread and intense that in 1714 a local judge charged with opening an investigation about witchcraft refused the assignment, fearing that if he accepted he would be "killed with spells."[32]

Within the Pernambuco cadernos, I identified 109 accusations involving illicit religious practices, most of which were leveled during the eighteenth century.[33] The cases provide filtered glimpses of some of the religious beliefs that Palmaristas likely held. Registered mainly in the decades after 1695, they are particularly insightful about the religious milieu that awaited Palmares survivors. The 109 cases leveled charges against nearly two hundred individuals, half of whom the prosecutors identified as Black or mixed-race and just under 10 percent as Indigenous. Officials attached no racial category to most of the remaining 40 percent. Most of these individuals were likely understood as white, another indication of how whiteness could function as an unspoken norm. Four in ten were women. About half of the Black and mixed-race suspects were enslaved, and the other half was evenly split between free people and those whose legal status was impossible to determine. At least twelve were African: six from West Africa (identified as Arda, Coyrana, Mina, and Cabo Verde), five from West Central Africa (Angola, Kongo, and Dongo), and one man, likely white, from Ilha da Madeira.

This diverse group utilized various methods to connect with, honor, and appease the dead. What they themselves called those methods is difficult to glean. For two-thirds of the denunciations, the practices in question were either left unnamed by officials or labeled as feitiçaria (witchcraft). About a quarter of the cases involved pouches called bolsas de mandinga, containing stones, roots, powders, papers with prayers written on them, and other objects.

The remaining handful were a combination of quibando, calundu, and lesser-known traditions. Quibando involves a medium employing shears and a sieve to divine any number of things. The practice originated in Europe but over time became "Africanized" and therefore treated as exotic and diabolical. Because it resonated with many African divination practices, quibando became a popular ceremony, though the Portuguese and their descendants remained its main practitioners.[34] Calundu was also popular, a spirit-possession ritual that emerged through a complex process shaped by slavery and involving myriad people and traditions from West Central Africa, Europe, and Brazil. During the seventeenth and eighteenth centuries, church officials in Bahia, Minas Gerais, and Pernambuco regularly denounced its practitioners.[35] While church officials sought to purge or exorcise "malign spirits," the people they persecuted took a different approach, using powders, potions, and elaborate rituals to repair relationships with kin who had not been properly put to rest or who were otherwise angered. The intention behind curing through calundu, writes Alexandre A. Marcussi, "was the reestablishing of a situation of normalcy and respect in the relationship between an individual and their ancestors."[36]

The search for divine protection was invoked by those charged with destroying Palmares as much as by those who lived in the mocambos. An anonymous 1687 letter likely written by Fernão Carrilho, the captain major at the center of the Relação das guerras feitas aos Palmares for his violent efforts against the mocambos, claimed that the people of Palmares feared him so greatly that they believed he was a feiticeiro.[37] Whether or not the letter was composed by Carrilho, the fact that the idea was believable illustrates the intertwined nature of spiritual and physical warfare. Colonial clerics, landholders, and officials dreaded but also courted the potent religious forces wielded by Africans and their descendants. In 1692, one of the soldiers of Manuel Lopes, whom we have seen was among the boldest in claiming to have killed Zumbi, confessed to paying an enslaved man from West Africa to use feitiçaria to help him seduce a woman he hoped to marry.[38] In 1716, a captain recounted hearing how Dionizio, a *mulato* man enslaved by Joaquim de Almeida, used orations to pass through the walls and doors of houses.[39] Almeida, who had a pension and hábito and belonged to a distinguished family, was a veteran who served with great "zeal" in the Palmares wars.[40]

The use of bolsas de mandinga, which could render wearers impervious to attacks, was widespread among soldiers, who confronted spiritual and supernatural powers on the home front as well as the battlefield. About a quarter of the accusations in the Pernambuco cadernos involved bolsas de mandinga. Worn or carried, the bolsas provided many forms of protection, including from physical harm and even slavery. By the turn of the eighteenth century, the Portuguese Atlantic was awash with pouches that the Inquisition determined to be diabolic.[41] Though the cadernos make few explicit references to Palmares, there is no doubt that Palmaristas and their enemies used bolsas de mandinga and other protective devices. The confrontations recorded in the cadernos involved soldiers who traversed lines of alliance and affiliation. A soldier's son denounced two enslaved men for casting spells for the wife of Andre Dias, a former captain major who fought against Palmares. Another man denounced a member of his own company for carrying a bolsa.[42] The accused and the accuser served under Manuel da Rocha Lima, a Palmares veteran who had fought against Zumbi. In 1712, another Palmares veteran, João da Mota, who had earlier claimed falsely that he killed Zumbi, raised the ire of the Church when he captured a reputed feiticeira and then promptly set her free.[43]

As they sought ways to honor and commune with the dead, Palmarista survivors who remained in Pernambuco would benefit from a rich collection of religious and curing techniques shaped by the flow of people through the captaincy. In 1692, several witnesses denounced "a freed Black man from the Mina nation named Matheus," who lived near the salt mines outside of Recife and whose "fame" for "curing feitiços [spells]" spread widely. To ascertain whether a given affliction was caused by a spell, he used powders, a wash-basin, and a piece of bread.[44] Perhaps a form of quibando, the ceremony goes unnamed in the Inquisition notes. But the case suggests that, even before the conclusion of the Palmares wars, the spiritual landscape of Pernambuco was shaped by not only West Central Africans but also West Africans, a shaping that became even more pronounced during the eighteenth century.[45] Though West Central Africa continued to serve as the largest place of origin for enslaved people arriving in Pernambuco, West Africa gained prominence during the eighteenth century, even exceeding West Central Africa during the 1720s and 1730s.[46]

This meant that those seeking spiritual guidance or intervention had a veritable marketplace of options. A man in Pernambuco accused a Portuguese-born feiticeira of making him and his wife (both white) sick. The feiticeira (also likely white) had been exiled to Pernambuco, where she promptly became a local fixture, known for her powerful spells and for reportedly mentoring local feiticeiras. She agreed to reverse the feitiços in return for payment, but the couple was cured only after contracting an enslaved Black man named Domingos João, who lived on a plantation and "cured and divined in the houses of many white men," acting with the open consent of his enslaver, who took a share of the proceeds from his practice.[47] Though Palmaristas captured in battle and then enslaved might not have had the means to contract healers, they would likely build connections in religious networks that offered multiple options for confronting fallout from war, death, and loss. Some may have embraced a version of what a Black couple described to investigators in Paraíba, where Indigenous people believed that they had "two souls" and that "what they cannot obtain through God they obtain through the devil."[48] Removing the rigid Christian titles, it is not difficult to imagine Palmaristas embracing strategies that would provide multiple options for reestablishing or maintaining equilibrium.

Zumbi, Gangazumba, and Sacred Goats

While the Pernambuco cadernos obscure the names of most of the rituals under investigation, they leave no doubt that communing with ancestors and using powerful spiritual tools to divine and heal were common practices in the captaincy. Many of the ceremonies resemble calundu, and at least in some parts of Angola zumbi spirits were all but synonymous with those spirits conjured through this ritual.[49] In one illustrative case, Inquisition officials called the place where individuals were accused of conducting ceremonies involving jinzumbi the "sítio do Calundo," or "place of the Calundu."[50] Goats, which helped connect the living and the dead throughout West Africa, West Central Africa, and the diaspora, also feature prominently in the cadernos and were thus likely a key conduit in Palmares, where livestock was common. West Central Africans worshipped goats to bring rain, rid themselves of poisonous insects, venerate the dead, and cure physical ailments caused by the spirits of deceased relatives.[51] An Inquisition list of "Pagan Rites from Angola" maintained that Blacks there "worship the Devil in the figure of a goat they call caçuto, many of them gathering at night with great noise from Atabaques [drums] in their Senzallas [slave quarters]."[52] Caçuto (or Caçûtû) was just one of several forms of devotion in which an "oracle" would manifest itself as or through a goat.[53]

Two other names linked to devotion and goats indicate their likely prominence in Palmares: gangazumba and (n)zumbi. In Angola, Cavazzi described "an idol called Ganga-n-zumba, which in the end is nothing but a live goat, very large, covered with very black fur, with a very long beard, and deformed so that it looks like a devil: husband and wife care equally for this beast and therefore are known by the name of Ganga-n-zumbi."[54] Followers would position the goat on an altar, as shown in an illustration in Cavazzi's 1687 account of Angola (see figure 4.1). Cavazzi took the image from a set of watercolors painted sometime between 1663 and 1687. In the original, whose artist is unknown, a caption describes the goat as "adored by all the Jaga people as a god with the name of zumbi."[55] The convergence (or confusion) here is remarkable. What the anonymous author described as zumbi, Cavazzi called both zumbi and zumba, previewing (or conveying) the titles of Palmares's two most famous leaders.[56] Equally provocative is Cavazzi's observation that a man-and-wife pair tended to the sacred goat, as it suggests the possibility that there existed an eponymous female counterpart to Zumbi or Gan(g)a Zumba, gesturing to a deeper and more varied set of individuals and relationships behind the iconic male leaders of Palmares.[57]

Goats played central roles in some of the best-known cases involving jinzumbi in West Central Africa. In 1750, the Inquisition charged the captain major of Ambaca, João Pereira da Cunha, with being a feiticeiro.[58] According to one witness in Ambaca, "There are neither Blacks nor whites who do not

FIGURE 4.1 "Sacred Goat" (1687). *Source:* Cavazzi da Montecuccolo, *Descrição histórica,* 1:209.

know of his evil doings." Cunha had a shack behind his house where he kept three idols—Quibuco, Muta, and Gangazumba—tended to by a Black woman whom Cunha had enslaved and later freed. Gangazumba was a "goat with black whiskers," which Cunha used to harm and even kill others; one witness called the animal a "demon."[59] In another case, brought decades earlier in Benguela, a Black military captain sought help to alleviate a persistent hernia that tormented him.[60] To rid himself of the affliction, he hosted a large gathering at the advice of a Black feiticeiro from Dombe, who diagnosed the problem as being caused by the zumbi of the captain's wife. Enslaved women who lived with the captain organized the rituals, which included the sacrifice of a cow and the adoration of a goat.[61] Intriguingly, one witness who testified against the captain hailed from Pernambuco.[62]

Goats also figured centrally in rituals and practices persecuted by the Church in Pernambuco. A priest in Recife reported that Luzia de Barros, a free *mulata* woman, and an unnamed, enslaved Black woman had danced naked with a goat, an act that the priest "understood to be a diabolical thing."[63] A *mulata* woman named Susanna described seeing Paschoa Maria, a parda woman, "in dishonest acts with a man that were offensive to God." Shortly after they had finished, Susanna saw a goat levitate above Paschoa Maria. Others also saw the levitating goat and reported that Paschoa Maria had had sex with the animal, who breathed smoke from its nostrils.[64] A Tapuia man who confessed "spontaneously and voluntarily" to having made a pact with the devil as a child, told a priest that "the Devil sometimes takes the form of a Black man and other times a goat."[65] Another Indigenous man, the captain major of the same aldeia, made a similar confession, admitting to "vile, wicked, and sodomitical acts" with the devil, who appeared "sometimes in the figure of a Black man or Black woman and other times as a large goat."[66]

Long-standing European associations between goats and the devil were clearly at play here, though other dynamics were as well. It is hard to determine details because in contrast to the reports from Angola, which explicitly name (n)zumbi (or gangazumba) as well as other entities and practices, most denunciations from Pernambuco do not. Among the most prominent exceptions to this, though, besides the already-discussed quibando and calundu, are what the Inquisition glossed as Jurema, a number of rituals first practiced by Indigenous people catalyzed by the consumption of a hallucinogenic plant of the same name. Use of the plant was widespread across the northeast and likely predates the arrival of the Portuguese, though the religious rituals seem to have first drawn the attention of church authorities in Paraíba and Pernambuco during the eighteenth century.[67] Particularly vexing to the region's colonial administrators was the habit of some Indigenous people to flee aldeias for days at a time to gather in the forest for Jurema rituals.[68] Many such rituals involved goats and, James Sweet writes, "just as with Caçûtû, the goat sometimes served as the oracle."[69] Like rituals involving (n)zumbi, Jurema could also be used to contact souls of the dead, a practice reportedly exercised by not only Indigenous people but also Blacks and whites at multiple locales in the northeast.[70] It is unclear whether a companion "cult of (n)zumbi" or "cult of gangazumba" coexisted with or fed into the cult of Jurema, but there likely was ample room for such adaptation and correlation. The prevalence of goats in Inquisition denunciations from Pernambuco and the links that the witnesses and priests involved in these denunciations made between goats, the devil, and Blacks all suggest again that what many knew in Angola as (n)zumbi played a central role in the spiritual worlds of seventeenth- and eighteenth-century Pernambuco.

Forbidden ceremonies involving goats persisted in Pernambuco for quite some time. A 1780 report described two kinds of dances performed in Pernambuco. "Those that the Blacks dance, divided in Nations and with [their] own Instruments," were not "the most innocent" but were still considered relatively harmless by religious authorities. Of greater concern were "those that the Blacks from the Mina Coast perform in secret, whether in homes or fields." These dances featured a "Black Female Leader, with [an] Altar of Idols worshipping live Goats, and others made of Clay."[71] The altar, goat idols, and female leader all seem to suggest continuity with earlier manifestations in Pernambuco and Angola, though the prominence of West Africa here is once again compelling.

It is tempting to read these repeated appearances of goats in the Inquisition records in light of the animal's multivalent meaning in African, European, and American beliefs and ideas about enslavement. In 1728, the Portuguese king ordered that any enslaved person who "found themselves without owners" anywhere in the empire should be treated like stray livestock (gados do vento), which, when captured, were to be sold with profits going to the Crown. The order drew on Portuguese law, which likened enslaved people whose masters could not be identified to wandering animals.[72] The galling comparison takes on additional meaning by considering innovations that took place during the eighteenth and nineteenth centuries along the Kongo-Angola borderlands. Villagers in the area called individuals who escaped slavery nkombo, or goats. The Kikongo word was adapted by Kimbundu speakers and was imbued with spiritual meaning. In this area of West Central Africa, enslaved people had a degree of mobility. With luck and skill, some could change enslavers, a process consummated by killing a goat, which the enslaved and their new enslaver ate together.[73] In other words, while the Inquisition associated goats with devils and Portuguese law associated livestock, in general, with chattel slavery, goats could also represent spiritual power or mobility, both of which would once again have obvious appeal in Palmares.

Zumbi and Saint Benedict

If goats provide insights about spiritual beliefs in Pernambuco before and after 1695, a remarkable case decades later in Minas Gerais testifies to Z/zumbi's surprising persistence and scattered presence, as well as the rich multivalence it could assume as European, Palmarista, and African associations collided and migrated in Brazil. The discovery of mineral wealth in Minas Gerais at the end of the seventeenth century quickly siphoned power and labor away from the northeast—around the time, as noted earlier, of Zumbi's assassination—and during the first half of the eighteenth century, traffickers brought tens of thousands of enslaved people into Minas Gerais, some 4,400 to 5,000 arriving each year between 1715 and 1735.[74] As Minas Gerais rose, Pernambuco's economy faltered under the pressure of plummeting prices for sugar and the skyrocketing prices paid to purchase enslaved people.[75] While Pernambuco's relative proximity to Africa kept it entrenched in the slave trade, the captaincy came to function as a way station on the path from Africa to the mines, where the demand for enslaved laborers was nearly insatiable.[76] Eighteenth-century Minas Gerais was home to men, women, and children who were born, lived in, and traveled through a wide array of places and brought with them a similarly large collection of languages and religious beliefs.[77] Though a great majority came from Africa, thousands were born in or had already lived in Brazil, and even those whose journeys began across the Atlantic passed through Recife and other Brazilian ports before embarking on long overland treks to Minas Gerais.[78]

Many of the enslaved people taken to the mines came from or passed through Pernambuco, which surely contributed to the especially pronounced anxiety about "another Palmares" in Minas Gerais. In 1718, the governor of the captaincy, the Count of Assumar, wrote to the king that the behavior and "inclinations" of Blacks in Minas Gerais were similar to those in Palmares.[79] Nearly three decades later, a colonial official charged with destroying mocambos in Minas Gerais warned that "without doubt" the area would soon have its own Palmares.[80] Between 1710 and 1798, officials documented the destruction of 160 fugitive communities in the captaincy.[81] Some were isolated, but many were close to urban or mining centers, farms, and colonial villages, a proximity that, one historian writes, "guaranteed that the quilombos were never far from the minds" of those living in the many towns and settlements of Minas Gerais. In 1711, 1719, 1728, and 1756, colonial forces violently suppressed uprisings of enslaved people.[82] Another historian suggests that colonial officials in Minas Gerais were so fearful and spoke so frequently of the prospect of a new Palmares taking root close to home that they unwittingly helped turn it into a popular symbol of "anti-slavery resistance."[83]

The vigorous flow of people into Minas Gerais brought individuals from West and West Central Africa into close contact, including a free Black Mina woman named Francisca Correa and an enslaved Black man named Manuel, "from the Benguella nation." The two lived together, worshipped, and administered cures, which brought accusations of illicit behavior in 1756. An investigation was launched in Curral del Rei, a parish in southern Minas Gerais, and testimonies were recorded in the town of Mariana.[84] By this time, Manuel and Francisca were already long entangled in the violent flow of people, ideas, and objects pouring across the Atlantic, as well as the smaller streams within Brazil that connected Pernambuco's sugar plantations with the mines. The case notes suggest that Manuel had boarded a slave ship in Benguela.[85] What little else we know of him comes from accounts provided by witnesses who denounced the couple.

The two shared Francisca's house, where they allegedly kept a variety of dolls and pots used by Manuel, according to one witness, to "worship" the "god of his land." The same witness said that Manuel and Francisca regularly held calundus and that Francisca owned a young girl from the Mina Coast whom Manuel had cured by using a hot iron he submerged in water.[86] Another witness claimed that it was "public" knowledge and widely known that "Manoel is a feiticeiro and has a Zumby, which he worships as his God . . . and he puts his God Zumby on top of a table and places food and meat [on the table] and later asks [Zumby] permission to eat."[87] A third witness concurred that Manuel and Francisca lived together and carried out acts "against our holy faith" but did not mention Zumby; instead, the witness said that Manuel and Francisca kept "a saint called Sam Benidy, who they put various stews in front of and ask to eat, and when he does not they ask permission to eat [the stews themselves]."[88] The final witness, an enslaved woman "of the Mina nation," stated that she had heard from Francisca's slave that Manuel "took from a pot a Zumby, which in the language of Angola is a Saint, and places before it various meats, tobacco, and pipes, and tells [the Zumby] to eat, and then asks permission to eat, and shares with the other Blacks."[89]

There is the possibility that Manuel's Zumbi evoked Palmares or a mocambo in Minas Gerais, where fugitive settlements flourished. During the 1740s, colonial officials were locked in a state of war against mocambos not far from Curral del Rei, where Manuel and Francisca lived.[90] In a captaincy whose landscape was dotted with mocambos and where Palmares was a regular point of reference, it would be hard to imagine that Zumbi did not also wield a presence. As surviving Palmaristas and other enslaved and free people dispersed from or passed through Pernambuco, they carried memories and spiritual belief systems. Within this context, the most famous leader of Palmares, a man regarded as both godlike and demonlike and whom many believed to be immortal, would have carried great meaning and power. Wrenched from his homeland, forced onto a slave ship, and taken to Minas Gerais, Manuel could have very reasonably derived inspiration and even spiritual power from Palmares's Zumbi. And if their Zumbi had any link to Palmares, Manuel and Francisca would have had good reason to keep the connection a secret: in 1717, the governor signed an order stipulating that anyone who knew of a mocambo and did not report it would be whipped and then exiled across the Atlantic.[91]

Though Manuel and Francisca's Zumbi may have had a connection to Palmares, the case need not lead us down a path whose only end is discovery of an uninterrupted epistemic chain originating in Pernambuco. The two deities named by the witnesses—the "God" or "saint known as Zumby" and "Saint Benidy"—themselves merit further consideration. That a man from southern Angola would worship a "God" called Zumbi in eighteenth-century Minas Gerais suggests how different meanings and practices were forming in the diaspora. Though one witness described Zumby as a "Saint" in "the language of Angola," the presence and influence of Francisca, who was from West Africa, raise the question of whether she brought or ascribed her own meanings of Zumbi. Whatever the case, a durable word that was becoming recognizable and meaningful to individuals from different regions in Africa was taking shape.

The third witness's suggestion that Manuel and Francisca worshipped "Saint Benidy"—certainly a reference to Saint Benedict—adds additional layers of richness and complexity. In Africa, Europe, and throughout the diaspora, Blacks venerated Catholic saints, often assimilating them into non-Christian spiritual matrices.[92] Preceding the Church's 1743 beatification of Benedict by well over a century, Blacks in Portugal, Angola, and the Americas chose him as their patron saint. A Black brotherhood dedicated to Benedict was established in Lisbon in 1609, and his image circulated around the same time in Latin America.[93] Devotions to Benedict were widespread in Brazil, where his curative powers and sympathy for the enslaved were renowned. A brotherhood in Rio de Janeiro began in the seventeenth century, and when church officials testified to beatify Benedict, they also highlighted followings in Recife and Olinda.[94] In Minas Gerais, he had followers by at least the early eighteenth century, and likely before that.[95] An especially evocative, if somewhat cryptic, reference comes from northern Minas Gerais, where during the nineteenth century, and possibly earlier, revelers held religious festivals in honor of Benedict every August that included music some reportedly called "zumbi."[96] Evocative nineteenth-century iterations of the saint are also found in Maranhão, where Blacks created the quilombo Saint Benedict in Heaven, a community sufficiently fortified and emboldened to launch a brazen rebellion during which a force that was four hundred strong attacked plantations and a village demanding freedom for all the enslaved.[97]

In Angola, Blacks revered Benedict by the end of the seventeenth century, if not earlier. In Massangano and surrounding areas, rumors circulated that he was born not in Palermo, as others believed, but in Angola: Saint Benedict of Kissama.[98] The Portuguese military fort in Massangano had a church dedicated to Benedict for Blacks to worship, and, according to Cadornega, crowds of 20,000 people would gather each year to commemorate St. Benedict's Day in Luanda.[99] While the "Angolan wave" shaped Benedict's reception in Brazil, so too did other diasporic routes. At the turn of the eighteenth century, and likely much earlier, a Black brotherhood up the coast from Recife observed Saint Benedict's Day every year, as ordained by the society's 1706 code of regulations. Written just a decade after Zumbi's death and referencing a longer history, the regulations point to a diverse set of diasporas. The society welcomed as members "all Black people, crioulos and crioulas of this land and [those from] Angola, Cape Verde, São Tomé, Mozambique, and from any land as long as they are Black."[100] At the time that witnesses denounced Manuel and Francisca in Mariana, a brotherhood dedicated to Benedict had existed there for at least three decades; among its membership West Africans outnumbered West Central Africans.[101]

The appearance of Benedict alongside Zumbi in Francisca and Manuel's house evokes three important aspects of saint veneration. First, by the mid-eighteenth century, Christianity had already taken shape for hundreds of years in Portuguese Africa.[102] Any saints and beliefs that Manuel and Francisca brought with them to Minas Gerais were shaped by long histories of interaction, exchange, and negotiation in Africa. Second, many Africans and their descendants venerated saints for the access they provided to dead kin, making the juxtaposition of Benedict and Zumbi especially interesting. Roger Bastide observes that West Central Africans viewed Benedict as one of several Catholic "'intermediaries' compatible with their own" and "identified the notion of the saints as intercessors between man and god with their own belief that the ancestors presented their requests to Zumbi or Zambi."[103] Bastide also suggests that Kongolese and Angolans in Brazil "often copied the *candomblés* [sic] of the West African Negroes, merely changing the names of the divinities (replacing Oxalá with Zumbi . . . etc.)."[104] Bastide does not home in on when such processes began, though Candomblé, which took shape mainly during the nineteenth century, would suggest that what Bastide refers to occurred after the case in Minas Gerais. Third, the name changes that Bastide references are an example of how difficult it can be to trace the relationships between saints and deities over time. In contrast to Bastide, Luís Camara de Cascudo (who will be discussed in more detail in chapters 9 and 10) argues that, unlike other Catholic saints, Benedict never gained a following in Candomblé or other Brazilian–West African religions that grew during the nineteenth and twentieth centuries.[105] If he is correct, then the appearance of Benedict alongside Zumbi in the home of a woman from the Mina coast during the eighteenth century is all the more significant.

The Massangano fort, where Benedict had a particularly strong following, and other military outposts in Angola were prime sites of adaptation and invention that brought together ideas from not only Europe and Africa but also Brazil. Military officers and soldiers stationed at Massangano were among those accused of seeking out healers to help purge themselves or loved ones of the malevolent spirits called zumbi.[106] Soldiers who traveled to Brazil after serving in Angola brought beliefs and stories about Benedict and zumbi with them, but this was a two-way flow of people and ideas, shaped also by soldiers traveling from Pernambuco (and other points in Brazil) to Angola.

Palmares figured directly into these transatlantic processes, especially via soldiers who journeyed to Angola after fighting in Pernambuco. One veteran who participated in expeditions sent to locate and destroy Zumbi later became a captain in Recife and in the 1720s went to Angola.[107] Domingos Simões Jordão, who in petitions to the Crown highlighted his battles against Zumbi and repeated the story that hundreds at Serra da Barriga killed themselves, journeyed to Angola after fighting in Palmares.[108] Others unnamed likely ended up journeying there too, given the special warning issued by Governor Aires de Sousa de Castro in late 1679, as he prepared to attack Zumbi: anyone who deserted or otherwise resisted aiding the attack against the "mocambo where the Black Zambj is quartered," even the enslaved men charged with carrying supplies for the soldiers, would be consigned to "infamy for withdrawing from such an important occasion" and, more concretely, would be whipped and then exiled to Angola.[109]

We will never know how many times Zumbi dos Palmares's name was uttered or whispered among enslaved people, fugitives, and others in the aftermath of his death, but it is well established that even a brief stay at port was enough for news and rumors of rebellion to circulate to and from ships.[110] Whether directly connected to Palmares or not, Manuel and Francisca's Zumbi and Benedict were products of multiple and likely new forms and meanings taking shape and taking root on both sides of the Atlantic. Whether as a spiritual conduit between the living and their deceased brethren, a means for conjuring rain, a name that evoked Black resistance and defiance, a saintlike deity, or some combination of all these things, zumbi—and perhaps Zumbi— was very much alive in 1750s Minas Gerais, now the object of additional diasporic reinvention.

Conclusion

Almost two decades after the accusations were made against Manuel and Francisca in Mariana, a Black man in the same town confessed his sins. A "true Catholic," Domingos from "the Angola nation" recounted how "in his land he saw other Blacks perform various superstitious things." When someone was seriously ill, a voice that Domingos said he thought was the devil's would sound, offering to spare the infected person in exchange for the performance of unnamed ceremonies and acts. Domingos admitted that in Minas Gerais, he had attempted "a few cures" in "the style of his land," but that the cures did not work. "Imagining that the souls of other Blacks" had infected acquaintances in Mariana, he asked "a few questions to the Blacks who were ill . . . but that never in this land did a single voice speak as they do in his land."[111] In at least parts of Angola and Kongo, those voices were called (n)zumbi. That Domingos did not use the name, or that it was not recorded by the scribe, underscores the significance that Manuel and Francisca (or at least the witnesses who accused them) did, and it illustrates the multiple layers of violence that slavery wrought on the living and the dead. It is possible that Domingos said that he could not hear the dead in Brazil to demonstrate his innocence. Even so, and though he did not elucidate why the spirits never spoke in Minas Gerais, their silence and the apparent impotence of the cures he knew from home illustrate profound loss.[112]

Despite such enormous obstacles, enslaved and free people of color were able to connect with dead kin in the eighteenth century. A *mulata* woman in Recife told a nun that a man named Perdigão "came to speak with me after he died."[113] Similar statements were made about a Black enslaver from São Tomé named Gaspar de Andrade, who faced a litany of charges in Bahia. A witness who encountered Andrade and his captives on the road to a gold mine relayed a story that one of the enslaved men told him: sometimes Andrade would levitate for an entire night so that "the souls of his relatives" could "advise and speak with him."[114]

The travel of spirits from Africa to Brazil suggests one way that Palmares survivors coped with loss. Whether haunting survivors or channeled to harm enemies, the spirits of the dead that took to the air and wandered about did not simply or only return to Africa. They also remained closely connected to the physical spaces that surviving Palmaristas now called home. Spirits of the dead in Brazil held great importance, and those living in America also called ancestors across the Atlantic *from* Africa. In 1716, a priest witnessed a ceremony in Recife carried out by Blacks playing drums and "singing in their language." Men and women formed a roda (circle or ring) with a calabash in the center. A free Black woman, whose name the priest could not remember, walked around the gourd before "falling to the ground in a trance" and then moving "like those who carnally cohabit," at which point the calabash began to speak. The priest could not understand what it said, but a participant explained to him that the "festival was to gather alms for masses [dedicated] to some of their dead relatives."[115] The rituals (described by the priest as "masses") being performed incorporated some kind of offering ("alms") to the dead, in which they would receive healing, protection, and strength. The woman at the center of the roda likely projected one of the spirit's voices through the calabash.[116] The priest provided no further details about the people or their deceased kin. Perhaps some were Palmares survivors — children taken prisoner years earlier. Certainly, most in attendance had heard of Palmares, and many likely called the ancestor spirits (n)zumbi. The relatives being honored may have died in the Middle Passage, Palmares, or elsewhere in Brazil, just as their spirits' posthumous journeys could have headed in many directions. Even if these spirits had first traveled to Africa, and even if they were known by multiple names of diverse origins in Brazil, these zumbi or zumbi-like spirits were now being summoned to Pernambuco.

III   PEOPLE

Pedro, Paula, and the Refugees

While spirits traced multidirectional paths through Pernambuco, what happened to the humans who lived in Palmares and survived the repeated colonial assaults? Where did those who escaped or were taken prisoner go, and what became of them? Suggestive fragments reveal compelling portraits of life after Palmares—and raise additional questions. Several years after Zumbi's assassination, the Henriques Dias regiment officer Domingos Rodrigues Carneiro discussed in chapter 2 marched with 270 men on a journey of fifty leagues from Recife into Paraíba to destroy a mocambo "in the mountains called Cumbê," believed to be home to Palmaristas who had fled north.[1] When the army arrived, the stronghold was deserted; the inhabitants had learned of the attack ahead of time and dispersed into the wilderness. This cat-and-mouse game, which had been going on for the better part of a century, generated new diasporic paths even after 1695. In 1712, the governor of Pernambuco charged Carneiro and his regiment with reining in the captaincy's "many fugitive Blacks" and pursuing them "wherever [they] are found, be it in mocambos or outside of them."[2] The king issued a similar order in 1736.[3] As armed bands continued to pursue Black insurgents, where and when Palmares began and ended became even more unclear. Which mocambos had connections to seventeenth-century settlements, and which were entirely new?

We know exceptionally little of the thousands of men, women, and children who were taken captive in Palmares during the seventeenth and early eighteenth centuries. Even their names elude us. Immediately following the battle at Serra da Barriga, soldiers on the Portuguese side demanded that they share the bounty from selling their prisoners, threatening to behead the captives if their demands were not met. The carnage was averted, but nearly a third of the prisoners did not arrive in Recife. They must have died, escaped, or been surreptitiously sold or enslaved by the soldiers.[4] Mercê petitions help illuminate some of the routes that fugitives traveled during and after the wars. Two survivors whose stories remain in the archives bring into focus divergent paths possibly followed by others: Pedro Soeiro, who was captured in the 1680s and exiled to Portugal, and Paula da Silva, who remained in Pernambuco after being kidnapped as a child. Together with a dramatic case of Palmares refugees who apparently sought shelter in a Portuguese military fort, these stories animate dry quantitative data and provide a fuller picture of what happened to Palmares and its people after 1695.

Toward a Palmares Diaspora

Almost as soon as Blacks began to occupy the forest and backlands of northeast Brazil, the Portuguese sent forces to attack them, and these forces sometimes returned to the coast with prisoners, who likely ended up back on area plantations. During the Dutch occupation, authorities ordered some "Blacks of the forest" to be hanged or burned alive and set monetary rewards for capturing others.[5] Some fugitives captured during the Dutch occupation may have been among the Africans and Brazilian-born Black people who were taken by the Dutch to distant shores, including Suriname, Angola, New York, and Europe.[6] Tantalizingly, the language spoken by Saramaka maroons in Suriname is what Richard Price calls a "Portuguese-based creole," and some scholars believe that many of the community's first members escaped slavery from Dutch colonists who had resettled in Suriname from Pernambuco.[7]

War kept Palmares and its members regularly in motion. Colonial military expeditions and assaults were the most common reason for dispersal, as Palmaristas either resettled elsewhere in the sertão or fell captive. A 1644 expedition against a mocambo that the Dutch estimated was home to six thousand residents returned with only thirty-one adult prisoners (as well as "some mulatto youths").[8] The captives included six Native Brazilians, an indication of the diverse relationships shared by Black and Native people, which could be collaborative or adversarial. On one occasion, the Dutch related that a small group of Indigenous men (whose ethnic identities the account describes as Carapató and Vaipeba) attacked Palmares.[9] Prisoners taken in such a raid would have been sold to Europeans or taken to Native settlements.

Though fragmentary and sparse, documentation of slave ships leaving Recife during the seventeenth century offers suggestive clues about the shape and extent of the early Palmares diaspora. The Inter-American Slave Trade Database (IASTD), an offshoot of the Trans-Atlantic Slave Trade database, has a massive gap in records from Pernambuco, with no data about slave ships leaving the captaincy between 1630 and 1778. Between 1601 and 1630, the IASTD records ten ships leaving Pernambuco with enslaved people purchased there. The vessels, which each carried up to 125 captives, were all destined for Buenos Aires, except for one ship that took fifty captives to New York.[10] The database also registers a Dutch ship, the *Tamandare*, which set out from Brazil in 1650 with thirty-one enslaved people, thirty of whom disembarked in Virginia.[11] Surviving documents do not specify the Brazilian port it left from, but it was likely Pernambuco, the center of the Dutch occupation and home to Tamandaré Fort, constructed in 1645 and taken by the Dutch in 1646.[12]

While the scarcity of ship records limits our understanding of where Palmarista prisoners were sent, Portuguese communiqués allow for rudimentary estimates of the number of people taken from Palmares during the seventeenth and early eighteenth centuries. I used more than one hundred battle reports and administrative communiqués to make my estimates, data that I interpret mindful both of critiques of quantitative analysis of slavery and the slave trade and of the need to look beyond what Jennifer L. Morgan calls "the incompleteness of statistical reckoning."[13] Beyond providing a low baseline estimate of how many Palmaristas were imprisoned by colonial forces during the seventeenth and eighteenth centuries, the documents reveal people in almost constant motion, even leading up to and during the 1670s, when mocambos organized by political or lineal succession emerge in the written documents.

The constant movement is evident in reports from the 1660s, which describe raids that yielded dozens of prisoners at a time. Colonial soldiers enslaved some prisoners, handed over others to local enslavers, and sold others outside the captaincy. Some may have been conscripted into military service and forced to fight against the same mocambos from which they were taken. In 1663, Francisco de Brito Freire, the governor of Pernambuco from 1661 to

1664, launched a five-month campaign to destroy Palmares. He described the mocambos as home to "such a quantity of Blacks," who lived "in numerous towns, bolstered by many children." The soldiers returned with almost one hundred captives, a disappointing number given that Brito Freire had estimated that Palmares was home to thirty thousand people.[14] The previous year, Palmares spies helped foil three Portuguese attacks. Warned ahead of time by their informants, the Palmaristas "left their mocambos and scattered through the woods in such a way that they could not be found."[15] On the third attempt, the Portuguese returned with forty-eight prisoners. Brito Freire also filed a report describing how Palmaristas had recently raided local plantations, taking with them sixteen enslaved people who were yet to be found. The contrast between the lightning raids launched from Palmares against plantations and the lengthy, often fruitless slogs mounted in response left Brito Freire pessimistic, and he ordered a group of "twenty-five Indians with women and children" to settle in Serinhaém, where their presence, he hoped, would "put a brake on the insolence of the Blacks."[16]

All told, during the 1660s, records tell that several hundred Palmaristas were taken prisoner. Repeated assaults during the 1670s resulted in more captives, between 1,000 and 1,700. Similar numbers emerge from the 1680s, when colonial forces took between 1,000 and 1,500 prisoners. In the early 1690s, the Portuguese captured at least two hundred Palmaristas before the fateful battle at Serra do Barriga, where as many as six hundred fell into enemy hands. In the five decades following Zumbi's death, colonial forces imprisoned hundreds more. In all, between the 1660s and the early 1740s, colonial forces likely took at least 3,300 and as many as 5,100 or more Palmarista prisoners (see table 5.1 and appendix B).

Considered within the incomprehensible vastness of Atlantic slavery, these numbers are reduced to a statistical margin of error; for much of the seventeenth and eighteenth centuries, three thousand enslaved people arrived each year in Pernambuco. But whether the equivalent of one, two, or more years of slave ships arriving packed with human captives, the recorded number of Palmares prisoners is most meaningful when divided by itself into one: a single universe of meaning, complexity, sorrow, desire, and joy. Accordingly, these estimates are presented not simply to count but also to offer a starting point for exploring the lives and stories attached to each number.

TABLE 5.1 Estimated Number of Prisoners Taken
in Palmares (1660–1741)

YEARS	NUMBER OF PRISONERS
1660–1669	168 ≤ 338
1670–1679	1,049 ≤ 1,693
1680–1689	1,033 ≤ 1,438
1690–1694	591 ≤ 902
1695–1741	522 ≤ 816
Total	3,363 ≤ 5,187

SOURCES: See appendix B.

"Always at Least Thirty Times Greater"

In 1698, while negotiating with the Crown for compensation, Domingos Jorge Velho elaborated his own math while scoffing at the notion that the mocambos had been annihilated. Though he and his men had "conquered" the "rebel Black slaves of Guiné," the paulistas remained in Palmares to "continue to extinguish what remains of those Blacks, diffuse and scattered in various little mocambos in the vastness of these very extensive woods." In response to a suggestion that there remained no more than thirty "of those Blacks" in Palmares, he retorted that the actual number "will always be at least thirty times greater" than official reports.[17] Trying to demonstrate both the absoluteness and incompleteness of his victory, Jorge Velho exaggerated, but he was not entirely wrong. Palmares's "very extensive woods" would remain home to rebel and fugitive Blacks—and others—for a long time to come.

The year before Jorge Velho made his pronouncement, twenty-five soldiers journeyed forty leagues to attack a mocambo, where, according to one account, they imprisoned eighteen people, including the wife and a child "of the Black Camuanga, Zomby's successor."[18] One soldier, whose career began in 1694, spent the better part of the next eight years traipsing around the backlands, traveling dozens of leagues on missions that could last months.[19] In April 1695, Bernardo Vieira de Melo reported hearing that after the battle at Serra da Barriga some survivors had fled sixty leagues into the Ararobá sertão.[20] Ararobá comprised a large section of Pernambuco's southwest frontier, where some mocambos already existed and others newly arose. Further inland were the Campos do Ipanema and to the south the Campos de Garanhuns, whose outer edges concealed Zumbi's final hideout.[21]

The persistence and creation of new mocambos were bolstered by the flow of enslaved people into and out of Pernambuco and by continuous flight by the enslaved.[22] At the turn of the eighteenth century, the Portuguese Crown attempted to prohibit plantation owners from selling the enslaved outside the captaincy. The law proved untenable and was revoked in 1709.[23] But local officials in Olinda and elsewhere pleaded for strict measures to keep enslaved people in Pernambuco, where labor shortages were threatening production and wealth.[24] Some individuals posed as allies for fugitives, only to then sell them into slavery.[25] Traders in Pernambuco also trafficked captives to Rio de Janeiro and elsewhere. And those taken to Minas did not always arrive enslaved. Some fled there. Created by multiple forces and toward different ends, a multilayered "second" diaspora from Pernambuco had become a major issue for colonial officials and plantation owners, even while rebel Blacks represented an ongoing threat. In 1704, the residents of Porto Calvo complained that they no longer had enough enslaved laborers to produce sugar because "the insurgent Blacks [had] taken so many" people away from the plantations.[26]

It was often impossible to untangle new fugitives from old, as flight and community formation continued after 1695. A 1714 communiqué noted that "many fugitive Blacks" operated unimpeded, "some joining with others, already with mucambos," which they used to launch attacks on farms and travelers.[27] Eight years later, the town council of Olinda complained that the enslaved were regularly escaping to find "the greatest security in the most expansive sertões, where they enjoy complete tranquility."[28] Between 1739 and 1742, one soldier helped capture ten "escravos filhos do matto" along with two "Black women from the coast" before marching another eighty leagues in search of others.[29] Escravos filhos do matto (or "mato"), or "children-of-the-forest slaves" is a seemingly contradictory label, signaling enslavement and at the same time indicating that they were born free in the forest. Were these people Serra da Barriga survivors, or were they born in new mocambos that had formed after 1695? Were the two "women from the coast" related by blood to the group, or did they link up with them another way? Though there was no precise parallel to an "underground railroad" in Brazil, fugitives there clearly forged their own remarkable networks, which survived and were made anew after 1695.

In the twenty years following Zumbi's assassination, those networks produced and maintained potent mocambos led by individuals such as Camuanga. The mocambos of Garanhum, Pedro Capacassa (or Papacaça), and Gongoro were destroyed in 1693, 1694, and 1695, respectively, while mocambos of Camuanga (1699–1704), João Martins (ca. 1702–5), and Mouza (1714) rose and fell later. These mocambos occupied territory that was significantly smaller than that held by the rebel Blacks during the 1680s and early 1690s.[30] But there was also significant activity on the ever-shifting margins, in the far-flung settlements that survivors journeyed to after 1695, such as Mata Quiri (1670s–1713) and Rio Marituba (1704–37).[31] While we know little about these and other smaller encampments, the accounts left by soldiers offer some indication of the scattered nature of the post-1695 world. Domingos João de Carvalho financed a "campaign" in the early 1710s in the "Campos de Matta de Guiri," where there was "word that a mocambo of rebel Blacks was forming." He and his men spent thirty-four days in the wilderness, experiencing "excessive thirst and troubles." Though he took "all diligence" to find "the mocambos," he was unsuccessful and returned with no prisoners.[32]

Closer to colonial centers of power, officials attempted to both negotiate with and kill mocambo leaders. Exasperated with the dueling imperatives, Pernambuco's governor reported that attempts by a bishop to meet with Camuanga "at a set time and specific location" had been rendered impossible by constant attacks from the paulistas, which prevented Camuanga from "lingering in one place."[33] In 1704, having already captured his wife and one child, colonial forces seized another son, whom they delivered to Recife and imprisoned in a fort. Before the Portuguese could send him to Lisbon, the son escaped. Five years later, another son (or perhaps the one who escaped) died in Lisbon shortly after arriving on a ship from Pernambuco.[34] The escape of such a high-level prisoner drew the attention of Catarina de Bragança, the king's daughter, then serving as regent of Portugal. She ordered an investigation into the matter, though it is unclear what became of it.[35] The last known leader who historians believe had a direct connection to seventeenth-century

Palmares was Mouza, captured in 1714. According to a contemporaneous report, "the barbarous Black Mouza" had terrorized the area, directing assaults from his mocambo "in the Palmares forest." After they caught up to him, troops lay siege to his stronghold, eventually taking him prisoner along with "a Black comrade," two women, and a young girl, believed to be Mouza's daughter.[36] The last archival trace of Mouza is a March 1715 report stating that "the Black Mouza of Palmar" was in prison in Serinhaém with a serious injury that prevented him from walking, much less being transported to Lisbon, where officials had hoped to present him as a war trophy.[37]

Pedro Soeiro and the Terrible Deaths in Lisbon

Though Mouza likely perished in Brazil, colonial agents forced other Palmares captives onto ships and sent them to Portugal and other locations. In 1678, when Pedro Almeida wrote to the Crown, claiming (mistakenly) that Fernão Carrilho and his men had killed Gan(g)a Zumba, he promised to send three of Gan(g)a Zumba's wives and ten grandchildren, all taken prisoner. Sixteen years later, after the battle at Serra da Barriga, officials in Recife sent Maria Moreira, a "parda woman" they believed to be Zumbi's wife, along with four of their children, to Lisbon.[38] In 1697, the king wrote to Governor Castro to reiterate that capturing prisoners and paying taxes on them was an act "of the greatest piety" that those engaged in "the conquests" had a special responsibility to carry out. He also explained that he was aware that the distribution of prisoners and payment of taxes had not been handled with the "care" that it deserved.[39] An untold number of Palmares survivors were sold (or kept) on the sly by the paulistas.[40] The Portuguese approach to handling and classifying prisoners also changed over time. In the late 1670s and early 1680s, before Gan(g)a Zumba signed the treaty promising to return fugitives to enslavers and then in the aftermath of the treaty's dissolution, the Crown incentivized soldiers to attack Palmares by granting them the right to enslave those they captured in the forest. That posture would oscillate in the coming years.[41]

Silvia Lara has pieced together sources to estimate the price that Palmares prisoners yielded for those who turned them over to the Crown. She shows that the wealth reaped in exchange for prisoners varied widely by the social standing of the soldiers, officers, and colonial power brokers involved.[42]

Officially, in addition to Lisbon, Palmares prisoners could be sent to Maranhão, Rio de Janeiro, or Buenos Aires. We know almost nothing about those sent to these destinations, though there are intriguing clues about each place. Maranhão, an enormous territory eventually divided into five captaincies, is especially suggestive.[43] A 1702 communiqué complained of a group of "slave aldeias" that had existed there "for many years." The king appointed none other than Fernão Carrilho, who had resettled in Maranhão, to destroy the settlements. His expedition returned with 120 captives.[44] The large region, home to Indigenous people and the target of multiple European colonial designs, was also full of waterways and impenetrable jungle. If the Crown sent Palmares prisoners to Maranhão, or if Carrilho and other veterans took captives on their own, the landscape and battles between competing powers presented plentiful opportunities for flight.[45]

Prisoners sent to Rio de Janeiro found a bustling port city, which became the colonial capital in 1763 (it had previously been in Salvador). Surrounded by tree-covered hills and mountains, Rio offered numerous opportunities for escape. Though in smaller number and size than Palmares, as early as the seventeenth century, mocambos in the larger captaincy (also named Rio de Janeiro) were, Flávio Gomes writes, an "endemic" and "chronic problem" for authorities.[46] And as they did in Minas Gerais, officials in Rio expressed fear that Blacks would "do in this captaincy what they did in Palmares."[47] In addition to being connected to other ports, the city was a hub for overland slave routes, including to Minas Gerais. While we have little means with which to trace Palmares prisoners in Rio de Janeiro, in chapter 11 we will return to the city to explore other afterlives.

Portuguese officials also identified Buenos Aires as a suitable destination for prisoners. The IASTD registers a steady stream of ships arriving in Buenos Aires from Brazil throughout the colonial period, though once again there is an unfortunate gap in the material (between 1680 and 1726), precisely when Palmares prisoners would have been sent.[48] Nor is there much data for that time in Colônia do Sacramento, the Portuguese outpost fifty kilometers away from Buenos Aires. Founded in 1680 and ceded to the Spanish in 1777, the colony was dominated by merchants from Rio de Janeiro and was a hub for the licit and illicit trade in humans.[49]

The lack of direct references to Palmares prisoners in Maranhão, Rio, and Buenos Aires makes it difficult to go much further with stories there, but there is slightly more to go on in Lisbon. Pedro Soeiro, one of the few individual

Palmares prisoners whose trajectory we can trace, surfaced in Portugal in 1681, just as Zumbi was consolidating his power in Palmares. Officials deemed most of the prisoners sent to Portugal to be of high value, and royal orders provided that upon arrival they stay in private homes. In 1680, twenty Palmares prisoners, Soeiro likely among them, arrived in Lisbon and were delivered to Roque Garcia, a royal functionary. While under Garcia's charge, all the prisoners contracted smallpox, and at least ten died of the disease.[50] Smallpox, which ravages the skin with blisters, wreaks "a truly torturous death" on its victims.[51] Garcia would nonetheless claim that he and his family cared for the prisoners "day and night," and he pleaded to be compensated for the great cost he had incurred.[52] A doctor claimed to have attended to the "Blacks of Palmares" for more than a month, a job that continued into early 1682 and moved the medic to repeatedly seek compensation from the Crown.[53] He was not the only one to profit as the prisoners died. Twelve years later, the council recommended that the king reward Garcia for his many years of service in the empire's "conquests."[54]

Soeiro was the subject of a remarkable petition that Fernão Carrilho submitted in 1681. Carrilho referred to Soeiro simply as a "preto do palmar," though his position in the mocambos was likely significant given that he had been taken to Portugal after capture. He was now sick, starving, and unable to work. Illness, Carrilho wrote, had rendered Soeiro incapable of the labor "from which he sustained himself" and facing "many miseries without being able to buy bread."[55] In Lisbon, Soeiro likely worked at the fábrica de tabaco, Portugal's imperial hub for tobacco production and where Palmares captives were meant to work as day laborers. During the 1680s, the fábrica employed more than 150 workers to break down tobacco leaves grown in Brazil into consumable products for market.[56] Carrilho requested that Soeiro be released "not with title of his slave" and instead simply so that Carrilho, who was in Portugal to request mercês, could provide sustenance to him. The Overseas Council rejected the petition, observing that while working at the fábrica "these Blacks from Palmares" were kept under close surveillance and that Soeiro should simply be remanded to a hospital for care.[57] There, he would await a ruling from Pernambuco, where officials were determining whether he and the others should be considered free or enslaved. Whatever close surveillance looked like in person, the fábrica de tabaco's daily worker logs, which run intermittently from 1679 through 1681, do not preserve traces of Soeiro or any other Palmares prisoner.[58]

Pedro's fate is unknown, though it is clear that he and the others occupied a liminal place, their legal status hanging in the balance as they battled a deadly disease and labored (while able) at the fábrica, where shifts ran from five and six in the morning until the night.[59] Though the prisoners likely slept under lock and key, staying at private residences may have afforded them the mobility to visit the area of town called Mocambo, or at least they had heard others speak of it. Lisbon and its large Black population had also long provided cover for people fleeing slavery in the Portuguese countryside.[60] What Pedro and the other prisoners thought about these fugitives or Lisbon's Mocambo is difficult to know. Whatever thoughts he and the others had, their time in the city was short and likely ended in incredible pain.

Shelter in a Surprising Place?

Some post-Palmares trajectories covered much smaller distances than the long overseas journey that Soeiro and his companions endured. On March 31, 1713, Pernambuco's governor instructed Recife's jailkeeper to turn over "all the Black men and women from Palmar held in [your] prison" to André Furtado de Mendonça and to provide information about how many prisoners had been released to local enslavers or sent into exile.[61] Rather than the pro forma (and often assumed to be male) "negros do Palmar," the governor specifically mentioned *negros* and *negras*, a rare direct acknowledgment of female rebels. On April 18, he again referred explicitly to *negros* and *negras*, now while ordering Mendonça to disburse payments for prisoners taken in Palmares.[62] In a separate order the same day, he emphasized the need to prevent the "smuggling" of captives taken "in the Conquest of Palmar" and insisted that all prisoners be sent away to Rio de Janeiro, despite protests by plantation owners who were angry to see people they claimed belonged to them sent outside the captaincy.[63] The simmering anger of plantation owners derived in part from an intractable problem: how to distinguish Palmares Blacks from other fugitives.[64] Years earlier, in 1698, the governor had issued two orders stating that enslaved people "moving from one plantation to another [and] captured within a few days" should simply be returned to their enslavers and treated differently than those who fled permanently to mocambos.[65] While clear in theory, the rule did not address cases of individuals captured after "a few days" in the forest, or those who traveled between sertão and plantation.

In 1706, word spread about an even more enigmatic group—Black fugitive-refugees seeking shelter at a fort established to prevent the creation of new mocambos in Palmares. At the fort, Blacks had been turning themselves in and declaring their fealty to the Crown.[66] They also insisted that they should not be sold into slavery because they had not been "taken in war." A junta was convened to determine their status, and the presiding judge agreed that they should be considered free (forros) but obligated to remain at the fort and serve as guides "in the forest," a decision that the king approved.[67]

There are no other indications about where the refugees, referred to only as *negros* and then forros, came from or whether there were women among them. The king may have intentionally avoided descriptors such as "rebels," "fugitives," or "palmar," which would have placed his decision to allow them to remain at the fort in conflict with his own previous orders. There is a slim possibility that these people were already determined by law to be free, but it is more likely that they came from a mocambo (or mocambos), displaced by the violence that continued after 1695 and now desperate enough to cast their lot with the paulistas. It is possible that the paulistas captured them and fabricated the claims so that they would not be obligated to turn them over to the Crown, but this is unlikely. The group's claim that they were not "taken in war" suggests intimate knowledge with Portuguese law. As war captives, they could be sold or kept as slaves, a fate they were clearly determined to avoid. It is possible that the refugees thought of themselves in terms similar to Gan(g)a Zumba's followers, Palmaristas who strategically decided to make peace with the Portuguese. Though it is unclear whether drought, disease, hostile groups in the sertão, or some other figurative storm brought them to the fort, the refugees' knowledge of the forest likely saved them, rewarding their bold gamble and allowing them to secure their status as forros and forge a path to survival.

Their story takes on even greater meaning when considered alongside an account from a 1737 colonial attack against one of the post-1695 mocambos, during which a Black man reportedly "resolved to die" before falling into Portuguese hands. An "agile Indian" soldier "leaped and fought with" him until others came to his aid, subduing and "saving" the man.[68] It is possible that, like the fabricated pronouncements about Zumbi's self-immolation, this report was untrue, and there is no way to parse the internal thoughts of the combatant. The encounter nonetheless seems more believable than the romanticized depictions of group suicide at the Serra da Barriga or Zumbi's "noble" decision to die free rather than live as a slave. The most telling element here is the violent struggle to prevent the man from taking his own life. As the soldiers knew well, a living prisoner could bring immediate financial return that a corpse would not. The incident also underscores the significance of the decision of the refugees who turned themselves in at the fort and highlights the collection of agonizingly awful choices that most rebel and fugitive Blacks faced.

Declared free but forced to labor in danger as forest guides for the colonial military, the refugees do not fall easily into the primary categories and vocabularies associated with Palmares, but Africanist scholarship on pawnship and other relationships that blurred the boundaries of slave and free may be instructive.[69] While the Palmarista refugees did not enter a relationship that replicated how pawnship generally functioned in West and West Central Africa, where individuals become collateral to guarantee debt payment, neither did they become slaves. It is also unlikely that they became indentured laborers, who might eventually be allowed to leave after they had worked long enough as guides at the fort. The fact that the Palmaristas secured legal freedom as forros indicates that they found at the fort a relationship that protected them from slavery and famine, drought, or whatever it was that drove them into the enemies' hands. This resembles the way in which pawnship in Atlantic Africa, as Paul E. Lovejoy argues, could be exploitative even though it was "not part of the process of enslavement" and in fact could "entail protection against enslavement."[70] Interestingly, while pawnship was common in West Africa, some scholars argue that it was less prevalent in West Central Africa and did not develop there until the eighteenth century.[71] The case of the Palmares refugees suggests how the Pernambuco frontier functioned as a space where unequal partners forged relationships that were at once tethered to and distinct from more formal practices and legal mores. This made Palmares, even after 1695, part of a larger Atlantic world, where new forms of oppressive labor regimes were developed, negotiated, and challenged in Africa and America.[72]

Soldiers on the Move

Fleeting archival references to the refugees and Pedro Soeiro provide some glimpses of where Palmaristas ended up after the defeat at Serra da Barriga. But we might also be able to infer the movements of the Palmarista diaspora by using the fuller, more readily accessible details about soldiers who settled on land formerly controlled by the mocambos or who traveled after the wars, particularly given the likelihood that some of these soldiers took prisoners with them. To take just one example, Jorge Velho's men reportedly stole a "large number" of prisoners, whom they kept for themselves or sold.[73]

In 1699, confident that he had vanquished the rebel Blacks and "restored" Palmares, Caetano de Melo de Castro concluded his post as governor of Pernambuco. He soon traveled to Lisbon and eventually Goa, where he would serve as governor from 1702 to 1707.[74] Though few journeyed that far, he was hardly the only one with deep connections to Palmares who later traveled the world. The Palmares wars and the so-called Guerra dos Bárbaros propelled soldiers in all directions, dragging them into conflict from as far away as São Paulo and Angola before pushing and pulling them across the northeast and beyond, a messy process exacerbated by conscription and frequent desertions. After fighting in Pernambuco during the early 1680s, one officer went to Bahia, Angola, Montevideo, and Rio de Janeiro, also serving aboard ships that crossed the globe.[75]

The military sojourns of some combatants concluded in Pernambuco, where they secured land or new positions. For many others, Palmares represented a single stop in careers that would take them to all corners of Brazil and beyond.[76] Two typical post-1695 destinations for soldiers were Paraíba and Rio Grande do Norte, locales discussed in depth in part IV. Another was Ceará.[77] Carrilho's son also fought in Palmares and then went to Ceará and Maranhão. At some point after Palmares, he helped "with great risk to his life" to suppress an uprising orchestrated by "slaves . . . fugitives and criminals."[78] Other destinations of Palmares combatants included Minas Gerais, Piauí, Pará, Rio de Janeiro, and the Colônia do Sacramento.[79] Pedro Lelou was born in Brussels and served the Portuguese Crown in Europe and Ceará before joining Manuel Lopes's regiment in Pernambuco during the Palmares wars.[80] He later settled in Ceará, where he raised livestock. Lelou passed inheritance to his son, who also participated in the Palmares wars. Both men highlighted their participation fighting Zumbi at Serra da Barriga in petitions to the Crown. Soon after the battle, the son settled near Recife with four enslaved people.[81] Another soldier described fighting at Serra da Barriga, in the battle "where the Blacks leaped."[82] Prior to 1694, he had traipsed through the Pernambuco interior in search of mocambos, capturing individuals he described (without naming) as important Palmares leaders. He also traveled to Rio de Janeiro and

Angola, fought against pirates off the Brazilian coast, and served in Maranhão, Ilha da Madeira, and Pará.[83]

Many soldiers were on the move before they journeyed to Pernambuco. One officer served in Ceará, then Portugal and Angola, stopping in the Azores on his way to Pernambuco, where he "found himself in the Palmares wars, and in an assault on a mocambo [where] he killed and imprisoned many Blacks, making others flee through the forests."[84] Another veteran participated in Portuguese naval forays before landing in Angola, where he had "good success" against "the Jaga Caconda and Gola engimbo."[85] "Gola engimbo" (Ngola Jimbo) was a ruler who eventually pledged vassalage to the Portuguese.[86] The Jaga Kakonda warred and negotiated with the Portuguese and occupied an area east of Benguela also inhabited by Imbangala "bands."[87] The insurgent Black Miguel Cacunda (also Caconda), who established a mocambo in the Pernambuco sertão, likely came from the same area. After fighting against Ngola Jimbo and the Jaga Kakonda in Angola, the soldier spent time in Pernambuco, in Bahia, and on the seas fighting pirates, before participating in the battle at Serra da Barriga and then helping convey Palmares prisoners to the Crown. Another soldier claimed to have helped kill a Kongolese king and destroy his army before slaying another African "potentate" and bringing another eighteen "potentates under [his] Majesty's obedience," all precursors to his service in Palmares.[88] Careers like that of Manuel de Inojosa, who turned false boasts of killing Zumbi into generational wealth, before spending the last years of his life in Angola, are equally suggestive. He overlapped in Africa with Cadornega, the Portuguese soldier who invented the "evil" rendering of Zambi.

Among the few surviving records of the ships that traveled from Recife to Lisbon during the early eighteenth century, a small set of documents from 1720 shows that among those arriving in Lisbon from Recife that year were Manuel Marques, who brought with him an enslaved woman, and Manuel Gomes da Silva, who arrived with two male captives.[89] Men by these names fought in the Palmares wars. If the two Manuels who journeyed to Portugal were war veterans, their captives might have been from Palmares, though it is impossible to know for sure, a frustrating but common conclusion to the documentary trail. But even given the limitations imposed by sources, the expansive travels of Palmares veterans illustrate the many paths that at least word of the mocambos, and in some cases prisoners taken from them, traveled.

Kidnapped

The trajectories of Palmares veterans and the stories of Pedro Soeiro and the Palmares refugees suggestively animate data about how many prisoners were taken in battle. The story of a Black woman named Paula da Silva, kidnapped in Palmares as a child by colonial forces, illuminates another harrowing post-Palmares path. Sometime between 1695 and 1697, a group of paulista and Indigenous combatants delivered 130 prisoners to Recife. Authorities boarded eighty onto a ship bound for Rio, and the others, young children who did not "exceed the age at which Your Majesty allows them to be banished," remained in the captaincy.[90] In addition to those children and others who remained captive in jails, on plantations, and in homes, an untold number of adult Palmares prisoners destined for exile lingered in Pernambuco through at least the 1710s.

Paula's story provides perhaps the only direct account of the children who remained in Pernambuco, under the sanction of law, after being taken by soldiers. Our window into her life, like so many others about Palmares, comes to us by way of a military record, this one for a Black-Indigenous officer named Lázaro Coelho de Eça—Paula's son. While the bulk of the record details his achievements and those of his father, who was a decorated Indigenous officer, small glimpses into Paula's life are narrated on a single page of testimony given by Luís Mendes da Silva (no relation to Paula). At the time a soldier (and later a captain), Luís served as a colonial administrator of several Indigenous aldeias and vouched for Lázaro's father, Manuel Cubas Frazão, a captain who had fought under Domingos Jorge Velho.[91] Manuel participated in multiple battles and pursued Blacks who fled before "making [new] mocambos in various quilombos" ("se amucambarão em varios quilombos"), a fascinating linguistic construction that turns "mocambo" into a verb, suggesting something more than just "making mocambos," closer to an act of "mocambo-izing themselves" within a quilombo. Manuel, one veteran gushed, had confronted such threats and pursued his enemies "through every cranny in the land."[92]

Manuel's brother, Sergeant Major Lourenço da Silva, also fought under Jorge Velho. "After the Restauration [of Palmares]," Manuel married Paula, a crioula filha do mato, or "Brazilian-born Black daughter of the forest."[93] During one of the attacks "against the Black children of Palmar," Jorge Velho had "captured that crioula at a very tender age." He gave the child to Lourenço and his wife, an Indigenous woman named Maria Antiga. The couple "raised that lass among them and with the love of a child because they had neither son nor daughter." After Paula "became a woman" she "lived in Freedom" and married Manuel, "with the approval" of Lourenço and Maria. Paula and Manuel lived for a time on an Indigenous aldeia created in Palmares to aid against the formation of new mocambos. There they had Lázaro, whose trajectory is discussed in chapter 6.

It says a great deal that a short description on a single page in a forgotten document represents one of the only accounts of those who were taken from Palmares. Paula must have harbored complex feelings about Lourenço and Maria. The narrative presented by Luís implies that the couple granted her freedom when she came of age, suggesting that however much love Lourenço and Maria had toward her, Paula grew up enslaved. The chain of possessions and relationships that first made Paula the property of Jorge Velho, then a "gift" for Lourenço and Maria, and finally delivered her into marriage with Manuel vividly illustrates the brute nature of patronage and reward embodied through the theft of a young child. It is therefore reasonable to read her odyssey through the lens of power and powerlessness. Kidnapped and then shuttled from one military man to the next, even in freedom she never escaped a small network of men determined to destroy Palmares, her birthplace. It is at the same time true that she secured legal freedom and formed a marital partnership with a powerful man. Both narratives may be correct, even if we do not know what combination of empowerment and helplessness—not to mention anger, sadness, love, joy, desire, and hate—Paula had harbored.

It is unclear what "tender age" Paula was when she was taken, or the exact year she was kidnapped. In addition to distinguishing Palmares-born prisoners (the filhas and filhos do mato) from those who fled to the mocambos, the Portuguese often differentiated adult male prisoners from women and children. An order issued in 1681 gave men participating in expeditions against Palmares the right to keep children and women prisoners for themselves.[94] But in 1682, the lengthy order regulating the terms of slavery and freedom for Palmarista prisoners left no doubt that any prisoner over the age of seven must be banished from the colony. Children had to be deported "because in anyone older [than seven] we must fear the same repetition of flight, and with this the damages that come." Even a young child, the order explained, would develop traits "inherited through blood and derived by nature."[95] In 1737, Luís Mendes da Silva attested that Paula and Manuel had been married for "more than thirty years."[96] If Paula was married in 1705, for example, at the age of sixteen, she would have been born sometime in the early 1690s, the same time as Jorge Velho's expeditions against Palmares.

Her fate was tied to not only Jorge Velho's physical actions—wrenching her from her family—but also his entrance into debates about the fate of prisoners. Jorge Velho's first contract with the Crown (1687) mandated that the only prisoners who could remain "in these captaincies" were "the Black children of Palmares age seven to twelve."[97] The contract also stipulated that in addition to receiving a portion of the money paid for fugitives from slavery whom he captured, Jorge Velho would also maintain total control over the fate of imprisoned filho/as do mato.[98] While these clauses explain the official mechanisms that paved the way for stealing Palmares children from their families, a 1694 request to readjust the terms of his service sheds light on another important aspect of the debates. Among the points raised was the fate of female prisoners. "Whether captives from the coast or children of the forest, whatever age," Jorge Velho insisted that they not be sold "across the sea."[99] Women were not a threat to "make war," he assured the Crown, and the only African-born women in Palmares had themselves been kidnapped by the mocambos' "Black pirates" who took them from plantations to the forest. Folding women from Africa and Palmares into a single, unthreatening mass that also negated the existence of female Palmaristas born elsewhere in Brazil, Jorge Velho struck an apparent tone of lenience, however contrived, that he would repeat in the future.

For African-born women who had children, he maintained, it was a "great cruelty to tear the babies from their breasts." Of course, the "cruelty" was not really about the separation of mother and child; he was more concerned with the "unjust" denial of "property" to his soldiers, to whom the women rightfully "belonged." Being forced to sell the mothers overseas put the paulistas in an additional bind when it came to children, whom they had no interest in providing for. That made the rule obligating paulistas to sell female prisoners "away from the land" an "injustice" that left his men "greatly damaged." The rule, Jorge Velho implored, was "more obstinacy than necessity" that "scandalized" the people of Pernambuco. Pleading for "justice and humanity" to be served, he asked that the sale of female prisoners overseas be halted once and for all.[100]

If there was any doubt about Jorge Velho's intentions, his actions elsewhere left no question: He was infamous for assaulting Indigenous communities, killing the adults and taking children captive.[101] It is also important to note that children taken captive could be at risk of enslavement and also being pressed into the horrors of military service, perhaps sent overseas to fight in West Central Africa, where child soldiers regularly filled gaps in the colonial army.[102] Even if he took Jorge Velho's argument at face value, Governor Castro did not agree with it. After consulting with religious and administrative officials, he determined that the new rule should stay in place. Women would be treated the same as men and sent far away.[103] "Experience has shown," the governor wrote, that "Black women and male slaves [as *negras* e os escravos] who gain their freedom" were the most prone to run away again. The threat was such that "all the Blacks of Palmares" must be permanently removed because if not they would continue to "disperse throughout these sertões."[104] Castro was so concerned with the ongoing threat posed by Palmares that he wanted any fugitive Black, male or female, captured anywhere in Pernambuco to be expelled. Once again, there was a subtext. While the governor happily reported that "shortly we will be done with all those rebels" in Palmares, he worried about the prospect of paulistas remaining in the area after the war. "Like wild, barbarous people," the paulistas "live from what they steal," causing more damage to the captaincy than even the Palmares rebels."[105] Propelled by simmering tensions with the paulistas, Castro's vision of a post-Palmares world would include few remnants of the war. All fugitives would be killed or sent as far away as possible, and even the paulistas would be sent packing.

Debates about women and children taken captive in Palmares continued after the most intense fighting wound down but amid the unceasing specter of sexual violence against Black women. While such violence often went unremarked, whites voiced panic about Palmaristas stealing white women from plantations. From outposts that "infest[ed] all the land," they attacked engenhos at will, "taking with them the wives and virgin daughters [filhas donzelas] and killing the fathers and husbands."[106] This kind of discourse shaped discussions about what to do with female prisoners, which peaked in 1695. In March, the king rejected Jorge Velho's request that female prisoners remain in Pernambuco.[107] In doing so he concurred with the Overseas Council. "With the love that they have for freedom," the council wrote, women would "induce" Black men to seek the same.[108] The king also ordered that "the Black men and women of Palmares may not be sold or given to any parts of Brazil, except Maranhão, where they cannot cause harm and will be put to good service."[109] Echoing Jorge Velho, one official advocated for an exception. "It seems just," the official wrote, that Black women who were still nursing be allowed to remain in Brazil at least until the child turned three, "at which point they can live without their mother's milk."[110] While recognizing the financial damage that separating mother from child could inflict on the paulistas, the king rejected even this exception while confirming the Overseas Council's decision: "The Black men and Black women of Palmares" would all be sold to distant lands.[111]

At its core, this debate was little more than a disagreement among powerful white men squabbling over who had the right to enslave Black women and children. Jorge Velho's own language betrayed the fact that protecting his and his men's monetary interests was the real motivation. And the official who sided with him was also simply concerned with the value of enslaved children, evident in his suggestion that mothers be kept in Brazil only until their children reached the age of three. Lara shows that such determinations also must be understood in a longer historical context, demonstrating how, during the second half of the nineteenth century, jurists, abolitionists, and enslaved people referenced these discussions as they advocated for individual freedom and the end of slavery.[112] The relationship between an enslaved mother and her child would continue to be the subject of debate until the passage of Brazil's Free Womb Law in 1871 and abolition in 1888.

It is also worth considering Paula da Silva and Jorge Velho as central actors in this trajectory. Taxes paid on enslaved people from Luanda were different for children who were old enough to walk and considered taxable property (crias de pé) and for children who were still nursing (crias de peito).[113] The latter were understood to form "a single property [cabeça] with their respective mother."[114] As Jorge Velho's "gift" to Lourenço and Maria—a human war trophy delivered as patronage—Paula grew up in a household in which she was likely enslaved and may also have felt tenderness, if not "love," for the couple. Paula's story would seem to represent both a confirmation of and challenge to colonial order. In Luís Mendes da Silva's estimation, she was as much child as slave to Lourenço and Maria. Raised by one Palmares veteran and married to another, Paula might also be seen as a product of the Portuguese victory, the filha da mata transformed into loyal vassal. There is no way to know what lay beneath the veneer of Luís's narrative, but it is worth noting again the fact that the debate about prisoners concluded with an open declaration that women, like men, were threats that had to be banished from the land. Alarmist or not, colonial officials saw the children of Palmares as a universal, unending menace that had to be destroyed, not reformed. In other words, Paula and others like her had a profound impact on colonial policy and the fears and psyches of colonial officials.

Surely there were others like her. Not only have their stories not been recounted, but it is also likely that many children such as Paula did not figure into colonial prisoner counts. Paula's story, remarkable as it is, therefore helps us look beyond numbers and to rarely discussed post-1695 histories. Some surviving children of Palmares fled to live, while others were forced into slavery or war. Paula's unnamed mother, whose fate is unknown, must also be understood as crucial to the fundamental change at the end of the debate about prisoners. Almost without exception, when colonial officials wrote about the "Blacks of Palmares," masculinity was the default. But when determining the fate of captured Palmaristas, officials left no doubt that Black women had to be expelled along with Black men. So often rendered invisible, children and women like Paula and her mother had forced colonial authorities to do something they rarely did: account for and utter the collective name of the women of Palmares.

Conclusion

Palmaristas who traveled to new lands illustrate how the mocambos could function as starting points or stopovers in a longer diasporic sojourn. Those who left as prisoners also exposed a fundamental tension in the colonial project. Determined too dangerous to remain in Pernambuco, by leaving the captaincy prisoners represented another threat to its enslavers: the drain of forced labor. Paula's story, in light of the order banishing women as well as men from Pernambuco, captures this duality: she was a child taken from her home and a woman whose very presence in Pernambuco was threatening. Within and between these dual aspects of Paula's life story are vast, complex spaces, inhabited by truly countless others. For two days after the battle at Serra da Barriga, Bernardo Vieira de Melo hunted for survivors, eventually returning with two more prisoners, Black women whose names and identities he did not bother to record. In a report vouching for Vieira de Melo's service, Jorge Velho noted without any additional detail that Vieira de Melo "pardoned [both] on account of being women," a compelling if cryptic account of two lives that had endured incredible violence and now survived to live another day.[115]

Though most Palmares prisoners were either sent far away or imprisoned in Pernambuco, there is also a great deal of distance between Paula, the refugees, and Pedro, whose post-Palmares trajectory took him across the Atlantic. While the individuals considered in this chapter experienced an array of different fates, whether they found refuge in surprising places, were enslaved in Pernambuco, or were forced onto ships to cross the Atlantic or bound for other points in America, Palmares prisoners shared a forced dislocation from home. For Paula and other "children of the forest," that meant leaving behind their birthplace. For Palmaristas born in Africa, imprisonment in Palmares might lead to another journey akin to a second Middle Passage. For these and other Palmaristas who endured the wars but fell into colonial hands, being captured meant two seemingly contradictory things: the triumph of survival and the torture of enslavement. At least for some, the post-1695 years also brought an existence that fell somewhere between, and perhaps beyond, slavery and freedom.

CHAPTER SIX

The Powerful and
Almost Powerful

As Paula da Silva's path out of Palmares shows, violence and intimacy
could take multiple forms and shape allegiances and identities in
complex ways. Her story may also help us understand the pressures
on and calculations of others, such as the man who led colonial soldiers to Zumbi in 1695, or two of Gan(g)a Zumba's sons, Dom Pedro
de Sousa Castro Ganasona and Bras de Sousa Castro, who, according
to the eighteenth-century memorialist Domingos do Loreto Couto,
were baptized and fought for colonial forces.[1] A 1696 communiqué
mentions a "Captain of Palmares" named Francisco Gandû, who left
the mocambos and provided a "great service" to the Crown, "fighting
in all of the encounters . . . against his kind," including the attack
that killed Zumbi.[2] He received a garment, commissioned by the Portuguese in recognition of his service, a unique, physical reward for
a former Palmarista. Additional information about these individuals is, frustratingly, nonexistent. The stories of others, ranging from
Black, Indigenous, and mixed-race officers tasked with annihilating
Palmares to white landowners bent on the same, are somewhat more
accessible.

The playing field between white and nonwhite was never level as
individuals made claims on the mocambos' ruins, even as old settlements persisted and new ones arose. The success of Black, Indigenous,
and mixed-race veterans was often delimited by structures favoring
white veterans and powerful landowners, who accumulated wealth and
exercised power and violence with impunity. This chapter discusses
some of the nonwhite veterans who sought recompense after 1695 as
well as powerful white men who exerted dominance on plantations

and the Palmares frontier. Especially in the latter setting, nonwhites and two women (one white; one with a mother who was Indigenous and with a paternal grandfather who was one of the most famous white Palmares conquerors) also carved spaces, some more tenuous than others. In addition to demonstrating the challenges and limited successes of nonwhite veterans, the examples considered here illustrate the broader power dynamics taking shape in Pernambuco after Palmares's fall. While the focus is on powerful white men and almost powerful others such as Black and mixed-race veterans who gained some rewards but ultimately fell short of attaining the wealth and authority of the most successful white veterans, accusations against some of the white men also provide insights about the fates that awaited Palmares prisoners who remained in the captaincy after being captured.

Black and "Almost Black"

The post-1695 landscape left most Black soldiers destitute and many heading to distant places, such as Rio Grande do Norte, where they sought to carve out existences on the colonial frontier.[3] In 1726, the Black soldier Manuel Barbalho de Lira was promoted from sergeant major to field master of the Henrique Dias regiment. He succeeded Domingos Rodrigues Carneiro and had served as an officer for decades. The promotion made him part of the most elite lineage of Black officers in Brazil. After Henrique Dias and Carneiro, only three other men had held the title.[4] Though he did not secure great renown or wealth, his daughter would later secure a mercê and pension in his name, an indication of his success not only on the battlefield, but also in the fraught game of seeking favor as a Black man in an empire dominated by and organized around slavery.[5]

Though Lira's record was less distinguished than Carneiro's, he too had a long, successful career, aided in part by privileged lineage; his father was also a decorated soldier.[6] The chains of succession from one Black military leader to the next indicate another way that memory and military engagement traversed 1695. Lira became an officer in 1694, and the three men who would compete to fill his place in the Henrique Dias regiment when he was promoted to field master all began their careers after Zumbi's assassination. Each had logged long distances in their years of service. The Crown treated money paid to Black and Indigenous soldiers as mercês, not regular salaries, a distinction that differentiated soldiers of color from white counterparts and made it easier to withhold or limit the amount and frequency of payments.[7] While a small circle of men could secure monetary rewards, they did not gain access to the large plots of land awarded directly by the Crown to white veterans. After the battle at Serra da Barriga, Lira and a group of henriques petitioned the Crown to occupy and cultivate land hundreds of kilometers away, in Rio Grande do Norte. Though not granted a sesmaria, the Black settlers were authorized to maintain a colonial presence in the area and ward off Indigenous uprisings.[8] In Palmares, Henrique Dias regiment veterans were generally denied even this kind of tacit granting of land, though in chapter 7 we will see a telling exception: a case where land was provided to Black veterans to pit them against an Indigenous aldeia.

If only a small number of Black veterans successfully transformed service against Palmares into concrete rewards, compensation was even scarcer for Indigenous soldiers and officers. Few Indigenous combatants received mercês for fighting against Palmares: Paula da Silva's husband, Manuel Cubas Frazão; Antônio Pessoa Arco Verde, a soldier, infantry captain, and eventual Governor of Indians; an unnamed sergeant major (likely Frazão), who received a sesmaria in 1727 to share with his soldiers for helping "conquer" the area; and Dom Sebastião Pinheiro Camarão, the renowned Governor of Indians who claimed that he killed (or wounded) Zumbi.[9] Over his long career, Pinheiro Camarão logged many achievements. He entered the Order of Santiago in 1672, an honor due at least in part to a broader strategy by the Crown to cultivate Indigenous allies.[10] He traveled to Portugal on at least two occasions to request mercê.[11] But even while compensating Pinheiro Camarão, royal officials expressed misgivings similar to those expressed while considering Black petitions for knighthood: rewarding Pinheiro Camarão might inspire other Indigenous soldiers to seek the same.[12]

The bars that Blackness and Indigeneity could pose to veterans and their families receiving rewards for service in the Palmares wars from the Portuguese colonial state are revealed in the travails of Paula da Silva's son, Lázaro Coelho de Eça. Lázaro's military record provided the only glimpse possible into Paula's life, as we saw in chapter 5. It also provides the only known record of his Indigenous father's mercê. The file includes testimony from a host of white soldiers and officers, who all attested that Manuel Cubas Frazão had faithfully served the Crown in multiple campaigns and along the colonial frontier, "since the time of the Restoration [against] the rebel Blacks of

Palmares."[13] While Frazão had white allies, his son's network was decidedly less robust. Though Lázaro was a field master, the eleven men who vouched for him spoke almost exclusively about his father; only two mentioned Lázaro's accomplishments.[14] Lázaro asked to be appointed "Governor of All the Missions and Aldeias of the People commonly known as Straight Haired," a request that one official found preposterous, framing his rejection of the request with an utterly damning description of Lázaro: a "Black man, or almost Black, not an Indian of this Country."[15] In less than a sentence, the judge previewed the argument that he would outline to the Crown. With an Indigenous father and Black mother (who was born in Palmares, no less), Lázaro was neither Black nor Indigenous, could not be trusted, and would not be respected by anyone outside of the aldeia where he was born. His Blackness, inherited from his mother, Paula, trumped his Indigeneity, all but erasing the capital accumulated by his father. But his Blackness was also incomplete. He was both too Black and not actually Black. The brusque dismissal of his petition highlights the challenges faced by even elite people of color, limits that stand in stark contrast to many white Palmares veterans, who were able to secure benefits not only for themselves but often for generations to come. While Frazão's service alongside Jorge Velho helped him secure significant rewards, his ability to pass them on was severely circumscribed. Other Indigenous officers had varied results as they curried favor with Portugal. Antônio Pessoa Arco Verde, who preceded Pinheiro Camarão as Governor of Indians, was unsuccessful in his own attempts to secure a hábito.[16] While the Crown acknowledged his service battling "Tapuia Indians and the Blacks of Palmares," it agreed only to pay him a salary and as long as he was willing to remain in Palmares to protect colonial interests.[17]

Pinheiro Camarão had more luck, though it came at a steep cost to others. In 1702, he sent eighty families living on his aldeia to work in salt mines, an act the Crown gleefully acknowledged.[18] This came on the heels of a report that life on the aldeia was so brutal that residents were fleeing into the forest, defeating the Crown's intention to create tightly regulated Indigenous villages.[19] But Pinheiro Camarão's loyalty and willingness to furnish forced labor to the mines were quite valuable to the Crown. In 1710, rivalry between plantation owners near Olinda and royalist merchants in Recife, many of them Portuguese, turned into the conflict known as the Guerra dos Mascates. The rebel plantation owners sought to expel Portuguese traders in Recife and maintain Olinda's previously favored position over Recife.[20] Pinheiro Camarão remained loyal to Portugal, a stinging rejection of the separatists, whose leadership included Bernardo Vieira de Melo and other white Palmares veterans. Pinheiro Camarão's decision, which likely derived at least in part from long-simmering resentment over abuses committed by white soldiers, was met with brute force.[21] In retaliation for siding with Portuguese interests, rebels burned his aldeia (São Miguel de Una) and its fields of crops to the ground.[22]

White Soldier-Settlers

The Crown promised (though did not always deliver) land to paulista soldiers who fought in Palmares, implicitly (and effectively) excluding all but the most fortunate Black and Indigenous combatants from formal landownership. During the wars, officials hoped that distributing land to white soldiers would help encroach on and delimit mocambo territory. As fighting waned, settlers would provide a buffer separating towns and plantations from mocambos, unallied Indigenous people, and the forest and sertão. Jorge Velho imagined the settlements in grandiose terms, forming a barrier "stronger and more permanent" than the "famed" Great Wall of China that would "liberate" the area by blocking attacks from the "savage Tapuia" and "the runaway slave."[23]

Much of the land awarded during the late seventeenth century had gone unused, often because fear of the rebel Blacks dissuaded would-be settlers from planting roots near areas controlled by mocambos.[24] Jorge Velho's representative, Bento Surrel Camilio, wrote that the Crown had promised the "lands occupied by the Blacks of Palmares" to too many parties; the territory once controlled by Palmares now had "many intended owners."[25] Indigenous aldeias added another layer of complexity, as some of the lands awarded to or sought by the paulistas had also been reserved for Indigenous settlements. Despite regular complaints against paulistas, in the decade following Zumbi's death, royal orders nonetheless favored paulista settlers and put in place a framework that would allow the white conquerors of Palmares and their descendants to claim land. Eager to put an end to the massive areas that wealthy colonists owned and left uncultivated, the Crown allowed for the seizure of unused land, which would be parceled into smaller plots and redistributed to settlers who would occupy and develop it.[26] The practice helped put in place pieces of the "wall" that Jorge Velho and royal officials envisioned, while also setting the stage for generations of land disputes.

The process of carving the land into sesmarias began during the wars. In 1678, Belchior Álvares Camelo received a grant of forty square leagues in southern Alagoas, possibly on land that he seized from the mocambos.[27] A landowner born in Portugal, Camelo entered the military in 1620, fought against Palmares and the Dutch, and belonged to one of the most powerful families in Pernambuco.[28] The sesmaria was one of several that he and his family acquired in the area.[29] Camelo's kin would follow in his footsteps by fighting against mocambos. His son received a hábito in the Ordem de Cristo. So did his grandson, whom the Crown lauded for traipsing hundreds of leagues across the backlands and for demonstrating "outstanding bravery destroying many mocambos and killing many Black warriors, taking more than three hundred prisoners."[30] By the early eighteenth century, the grandson had amassed so much land that the Crown authorized him to establish his own town.[31] Land, wealth, and power circulated not only through lineal inheritance, but also in larger networks of relatives, friends, and patronage. Some women inherited property from a father or brother, while others directly received sesmarias. Jorge Velho's widow, Jerônima Cardim Fróes, petitioned for land, as did other women.[32] In 1698, Governor Castro noted that before the paulistas could take full control of the land they needed their wives to move from São Paulo, but most did not have the resources to pay for their passage to the northeast. The Overseas Council agreed to send a ship for them, noting the "great convenience" it would be for the men "to have with them their wives because that is the path to start populating the sertões."[33]

The settlement project progressed unevenly. In the 1710s and 1720s, large landowners abandoned their fields to escape the ongoing threats posed by fugitive communities and to pursue lucrative mining ventures.[34] But though mocambos continued to loom, power tilted toward colonists, and over time, Felipe Aguiar Damasceno writes, small landholders, who raised livestock and grew tobacco, fruit, and other crops, had helped create the "long desired barrier between [mocambos] in the Pernambucan forests and the 'world of sugar' on the coast."[35] Zumbi's assassin, André Furtado de Mendonça, was one such landholder. In 1717, he received a sesmaria for property that he and his family had already occupied for almost twenty years. The plot was situated some fifty kilometers from the coast and near sesmarias given to other Palmares veterans. In the years following Zumbi's death, Mendonça occupied the land, a portion of which had been awarded in the early 1680s to another group of soldiers. Mendonça and his family grew tobacco, maintained fruit trees, and raised livestock on three square leagues, a significant area in line with what other Palmares veterans received but that paled in comparison to some of the massive sesmarias and de facto holdings of the era.[36]

Miguel Godói de Vasconcelos, who also participated in the attack that killed Zumbi, received a sesmaria north of Mendonça's.[37] Battles against mocambos were the central part of his military record. In 1708, when he competed (unsuccessfully) to become sergeant major of the Terço dos Palmares, a regiment established to control the land occupied by the mocambos, Vasconcelos boasted of time fighting under Jorge Velho. That included a confrontation against "Zomby," the "governor of the Blacks," in which forty prisoners were taken, among them Zomby's "primary wife" (mulher principal). Vasconcelos also highlighted a separate expedition, which targeted an unnamed "quilombo of rebel Blacks," all of whose "principal leaders" were captured.[38] His service in Palmares continued after Zumbi's death. In 1699, he led an attack against Camuanga, taking prisoners, including the mocambo leader's son and wife.[39]

Many of those who received sesmarias had careers that began near the end of the Palmares wars. Agostinho Moreira Guterres entered the military in 1694 and received a sesmaria in Palmares in 1724.[40] A resident of Porto Calvo, Guterres was among the wealthy local colonists who spent their own money to fund military forays on behalf of the Crown. In 1695, he went in search of an unnamed mocambo, where he "imprisoned forty-two Blacks and killed many of those who resisted," before spending more than two months searching for others.[41]

Domingos João de Carvalho, who fought with Mendonça, was awarded a sesmaria in 1724 that he shared with Luís Mendes da Silva. The two adjacent plots were bordered by land owned by Mendonça.[42] This kind of proximity was typical and also indicative of deeper relationships (and rivalries). In 1739, Silva vouched for Jerônimo Martins dos Santos, who had received a sesmaria in the area in 1724, attesting to Santos's having fought against Palmares.[43] In 1752, Silva testified again for Santos, this time describing Santos's efforts "enquadrinhando forests, taming backlands [rompendo sertões], [and] leveling [or cutting] mountains [cortando serras]."[44] The language evokes both an enormous, unconquered landscape and the Portuguese vision of what it should become. "Enquadrinhando," from "enquadrar," "to make square," or "to frame," illustrates the perpetual goal of creating borders around the seemingly endless forest, complemented by "taming," "cutting," and razing other features of the landscape. Carvalho also provided testimony for Santos, who had traveled across many "sertões and dry lands, scaling numerous mountains," crossing many rivers, and nearly starving to death. At one unnamed settlement, Santos took thirteen prisoners, eleven of whom were filhos do mato.[45]

Through the 1770s, the Crown continued to award land in Palmares. In 1758 and 1760, two brothers secured a land grant by citing the actions of their father, who helped conquer the land of the "Blacks of the mocambos" (negros amocambados).[46] Luiz Ferreira de Moraes, who won a sesmaria in 1775, is the last-known Palmares sesmeiro (recipient of a sesmaria). Moraes claimed, and was taken at his word, to be the "legitimate son" of Luis da Silveira Pimentel, a paulista who had fought against Palmares in the late seventeenth century and in the Guerra do Açu in the late seventeenth and early eighteenth. If a son being alive so many decades after his father fought in a war seemed suspect, there is no indication that officials contested the assertion. When Pimentel petitioned the Crown for compensation decades earlier, his long list of exploits included two battles against Zumbi.[47] Though Moraes did not mention those battles, he described his forebear as a "conqueror" of Palmares, a title that still held significant value.

Power (Almost) Unbound

Though land grants pushed the frontier further inland, the territorial line of colonial domination was marked by large gaps and pockets of resistance. So too was Pernambucan society simultaneously characterized by ostentatious markers of white male dominance and cracks in those otherwise imposing pillars of domination. Both the exercise of and resistance to colonial power contain portraits of what life was like for those who were captured in Palmares and remained in Pernambuco. The rise of mines to the south, violent struggles with mocambos and Indigenous people, and the rivalries and tensions among warring elites left eighteenth-century Pernambuco a society on edge. Prohibitions were issued against offensive speech, and nonwhites were barred from carrying weapons or sharp tools.[48] In 1740, "to remedy the insolences of Blacks," the governor unleashed a flurry of regulations, barring Blacks from selling goods or being on the street at night. Loitering on corners, playing music, and carrying knives were forbidden or strictly regulated, and men speaking with Black women at night could be sentenced to hard labor, and the women jailed for a month.[49] These orders reflect the intensity of colonial surveillance and power, though the strict rules themselves also belie the effect and perceived threat of Black "insolences," a catch-all term that encompassed actions ranging from violence to profane speech.

The attempts to control and punish resonated with similar projects in colonial societies organized around what Vincent Brown calls "garrison government," exemplified by Jamaica, "a fortified commercial outpost, run by military veterans focused on order and security."[50] Pernambuco shared much in common with Jamaica. Both were colonial centers built around slave-based sugar economies, where military men and "martial sentiments" dominated.[51] In Pernambuco, Portuguese and Dutch authorities carved out spaces on the coast and amid forest and hills to create fortified cities and military encampments. On plantations and in urban centers, a "martial masculinity" similar to the one in Jamaica, which "valorized violent self-assertion, absolute control over black subordinates, and sexual dominance of women," prevailed.[52]

Colonial records from Pernambuco also reveal another side of "martial masculinity": sexual violence leveled by white men against Black men. In 1702, Vicente Crioulo accused his enslaver, Luís de Mendonça Cabral, of repeated sexual assault. Cabral "often committed and persuaded" Vicente to engage in sexual acts against his will. The abuse caused Vicente to frequently run away, and Cabral placed him in irons "to force him to submit to his depraved appetite." Though clearly disgusted with Cabral and even admitting that he was a "renowned" sexual predator, the Church gave him a free pass. Other enslaved people had also denounced Cabral, but no additional witnesses — that is, no white witnesses — stepped forward, and officials chose to look the other way.[53]

Cabral, a prominent military officer and fixture in local governance and church leadership, was no doubt aided by his large donations to Catholic institutions in Recife.[54] He was also the proprietor of the storied Engenho de Apipucos and had contributed significantly to Portuguese military offensives against Palmares.[55] Three years after Vicente registered his accusations, Cabral submitted a thick bundle of files to the Crown, petitioning for compensation for his service and that of a deceased uncle who fought against the Dutch. Though Cabral served in the military, his case for mercê was based mainly on his lineage, the success of his plantation, his role in local government, and the material support he provided for the war against Palmares. While still governor, Castro had written that Cabral's "nobility" and the success of Apipucos, which, he noted, was among the captaincy's "best" engenhos, made him one of Pernambuco's "most important" residents.[56]

While most mercês involving Palmares centered around battlefield exploits, Cabral's featured his financial backing. Governor Castro attested that Cabral "personally" offered to accompany him to Palmares on the visit he had planned to make in 1694 before receiving word of the victory at Serra da Barriga.[57] Cabral had contributed "a lot" to the military campaign, which had a multiplier effect, inspiring (or forcing) other planters to do the same.[58] He also functioned as a creditor, floating large loans to the local tax collector and another officer responsible for collecting separate royal tithes. Cabral's largesse and the financial support he provided to the military campaign against Palmares positioned him as well as anyone in Pernambuco to receive Palmaristas captured in battle. Whether Vicente Crioulo himself was born in Palmares or spent time there during his frequent escapes, his experience suggests one harrowing reality for those captured in Palmares. The utter impunity with which Cabral operated allowed him to prey on an untold number of victims. Despite the many accusations against him, in 1706, the king granted Cabral a pension and hábito.[59]

Cabral was hardly the only powerful man to inflict sexual violence. Antônio Curado Vidal possessed a hábito and large pension and was the nephew of André Vidal de Negreiros, one of the principal leaders in the war against the Dutch in Brazil and twice the governor of Pernambuco, as well as of Maranhão, Grão-Pará, and Angola.[60] The sexual violence inflicted by Curado Vidal came under scrutiny in the 1670s, years after Negreiros had entrusted him to carry the Kongolese king Mani Mulaza's crown and scepter, a gift the Pope had given his father, across the Atlantic. After making their way to Pernambuco, the objects soon disappeared, rumored to have been stolen by Curado Vidal.[61]

In 1675, Recife's town council wrote to Lisbon to ask for an investigation into Curado Vidal's actions in Pernambuco. The complaint enumerated eleven instances of him killing, ordering killed, brutally attacking, or otherwise terrorizing others.[62] It was widely known that he ordered the castration of a man he enslaved and had carried out the same violent act himself against a *mulato* man. Among those willing to testify against Curado Vidal was Zenóbio Acioli, a Palmares veteran who fought against Zumbi. Despite the preponderance of evidence, the Overseas Council described the accusations to be "born more of hate than [honest] zeal" and, as they did with Cabral, looked the other way.[63] Despite and likely also because of Curado Vidal's gruesomely violent behavior, he was able to generate and pass wealth on to heirs, even as the crown and scepter gifted to the Congolese king from the Pope vanished into thin air.[64]

The impunity with which powerful white men unleashed sexual violence leaves little doubt about the hellish lives that awaited Palmares prisoners on plantations. Some forms of physical violence were inscribed in laws such as one issued in 1741 that codified the act of violently marking the bodies of those who escaped enslavement. Authorities were to burn the letter "F" (for fugido, or runaway) into the flesh of captured fugitives. If they apprehended an individual already bearing the scar, they were to cut off an ear.[65] In the far reaches of the sertão, impunity could take multiple forms. In 1787, a justice of the peace reported that in Pernambuco's vast backlands it was "difficult and almost impossible to punish and avoid crimes."[66] Though he did not identify who was to blame for the brazen crimes taking place, it would be reasonable to presume that he had in mind Blacks, Indigenous people, or poor whites—the usual suspects when colonial officials discussed violence and disorder. But in other instances, white men were the source of fear among authorities and landowners. This was the case for several decades in Garanhuns, deep in the interior and not far from where colonial forces killed Zumbi. "Garanhum" was the name of a seventeenth-century mocambo, situated in a larger area, the Campos de Garanhuns, which eventually became home to the town of Garanhuns. While the eighteenth century witnessed an increase in the number of stable, occupied fazendas, Garanhuns remained densely wooded and home to rebels and fugitives. In the forest, colonial officials identified trees with medicinal qualities and wood suitable for naval ships, but even in the early nineteenth century, previously awarded land remained lush and unoccupied.[67] In this faraway place, power cultivated during the Palmares wars surged forward in time violently and almost without restraint.

This can be seen in the 1764 report written by the governor of Pernambuco to detail a dramatic case against Antônio Vieira de Melo, who had inherited land in Garanhuns from his father, Bernardo, the famed Palmares conqueror and a leader of the separatist faction in the Guerra dos Mascates.[68] The complaint noted that Antônio had a massive amount of land—thirty square leagues, 50 percent more than what his father had inherited decades earlier and most of which he had either taken extralegally or left uncultivated. While land use was the official justification for the case, the more than a dozen witnesses who testified against Antônio described a litany of offenses.[69] For "many years," Antônio and his now-estranged son-in-law had overseen a "despotic" reign of terror, committing offenses with abandon.[70] Maria Paes Cabral, a wealthy white landowner, had registered one accusation in 1750. The previous May, while she was traveling to Recife, Antônio sent a band of men to her properties, which they raided, burning crops, uprooting trees, killing and stealing livestock, and making away with household valuables and twenty enslaved people.[71] The pretense was to serve a warrant for her son, though no evidence of a warrant was produced. Maria's testimony was just one of many against Antônio and his son-in-law, who were notorious for all manners of violence, including turning their homes "into a jail" and forcing a rival into stocks for three days.[72] Despite the widespread anger toward them, an official inquiry was launched only nine years after Cabral filed her complaint. With land, financial resources, and political connections that stretched to Recife, he could do almost anything he pleased in the sizable fiefdom he built on the edges of the Pernambuco frontier.[73]

Luís Mendes da Silva, the military man and colonial administrator who provided testimony on behalf of Manuel Cubas Frazão, settled in Garanhuns and, in 1741, remembered how Antônio "always" provided "all the necessary supplies" and accompanied Silva's men "on the occasion of the siege and battle against Zumbi in which he acted with absolute valor and conduct and suffered a wounded leg."[74] During the first half of the eighteenth century, Antônio amassed a fortune in Garanhuns, while establishing new farms and forging roads to connect the area to the coast and other settlements.[75] To do so, he destroyed Indigenous and Black settlements, sometimes by "thinning the dense forests with repeated fires," one approving observer recalled.[76] By attacking and transforming the landscape, he expanded his domain, some of which he gave to his daughter and her husband along with livestock and five enslaved Black people as dowry when they married.[77] The dowry and Antônio's empire are lucid examples of how decorated, well-connected white soldiers and officers leveraged military service into generations of affluence and power. His violence toward Blacks was especially pronounced. Witnesses recalled him shooting an enslaved woman, whipping a free woman named Ignes, and driving a nail through the tongue of an enslaved man. It was also well known that he and his son-in-law hunted people who escaped slavery and then meted out atrocious violence on those they captured.

Eventually, Antônio's excesses became too much, and colonial authorities intervened, finally acting on Cabral's complaint and the widespread and long-standing resentment toward him. Local anger toward Antônio elicited testimony from a multiracial set of witnesses that included four pardo men, among them Felipe Neri da Cruz Teixeira, a forty-two-year-old who lived on the suggestively named Sítio Mucambo, where he raised cattle.[78] ("Sítio" means "place" or "dwelling" and generally implies the presence of crops or some other form of subsistence.) Beneath the simmering anger that residents harbored against Antônio lay a complex set of relationships. Though Antônio targeted Black people and inspired a large, multiracial group of witnesses to testify against him, he also clearly understood the power of selectively undermining white property and authority. Multiple witnesses reported that he arbitrarily granted freedom to the enslaved man of a rival and counted on an Indigenous "gang" (quadrilha) to impose his will.[79] Some witnesses testified that a group of Indigenous men indeed lived on his land but had not committed any misdeeds. Others complained that the men devoured their cows and committed all kinds of crime. The governor concluded that testimony "uniformly proved" that the men, who were meant to live at a nearby mission, had been "incited" to leave by Melo.[80] Another witness insisted that Melo sought to "drag [the Indigenous men] from that obedience and subjugation that they should have for . . . Missionaries and established officials" and therefore "interrupted" the "tranquility" of life at the mission.[81]

The most obvious storyline to emerge from the documents is Antônio's impunity and cruelty, which eventually caught up to him. There is no indication how the case ended, other than that Antônio was now considered a "fugitive" of the law. He eventually made his way to Recife, where he died, in 1764.[82] Whether he did so in custody or on the lam, Antônio spent some time on the run, a surprising and almost poignant fate for a man who built a dynasty largely from his father's and his own violence against Black fugitives. Years earlier, Bernardo Vieira de Melo had transformed his military service into wealth and legacy that decades later Antônio turned into a personal fiefdom of terror. Antônio's cruelty may therefore be understood, at least in part, as a predictable extension and inheritance of the cruelty and viciousness of the Palmares wars. For the Indigenous men who lived on his land, doing Antônio's bidding may have been preferable to mission life. Carmen Alveal suggests that the Native men considered themselves Antônio's "vassals," clearly subordinate but also benefiting from "the shield of his dominion."[83] While the accusation that they devoured livestock smacks of racial sensationalism, the opportunity to take sustenance from settlers who may have invaded their own land would be appealing, and their situation bears a certain resemblance to the Palmares refugees who became forest guides at the Paulista fort.

The testimonies against Antônio also illustrate some of the ways that others challenged white masculine power. For example, Teixeira, a free man of color, had lived on the Sítio Mucambo and joined other residents in a formal complaint against Bernardo Vieira de Melo's powerful heir. Though he occupied a space that was palpably distant from that of the rebel Blacks of Palmares, his testimony and the very land that he lived on suggest different legacies of the wars. Maria Paes Cabral suggests an additional vector of power. Clearly a victim of Antônio's violence, she was also an enslaver with multiple plots of land. Despite the long delay in the case being heard, Antônio's assault on her property was likely the offense that sealed his fate. A power broker in her own right, she was, like Teixeira and the Indigenous men who lived on Antônio's land, both subject and opposition to a virulent white masculine force.

The power that women exercised against male tyrants in the Pernambuco countryside is illustrated further, and with fascinating twists, in the history of another woman from Garanhuns, Simôa Gomes de Azevedo, whose biography improbably combines aspects of both Paes Cabral's and Paula da Silva's. Born in 1693, Simôa was the granddaughter of Domingos Jorge Velho. Her father, Miguel Coelho Gomes, married an Indigenous woman in Garanhuns, and the couple had Simôa in the waning years of the Palmares wars.[84] She married Manuel Ferreira de Azevedo, a colonial military officer with whom she eventually shared a sprawling collection of properties. Local lore remembers her as a matriarch born from the kind of romanticized sexual encounters that would become fixtures of Brazilian racial mythology. A representative account, published in 1987, suggests that the Indigenous people of Garanhuns greeted Jorge Velho and his men in a "cordial and fraternal manner," exemplified by the eventual "union" of Gomes and the unnamed "Indian woman," who produced "a girl named 'SIMÔA GOMES' — MATRIARCH OF THE MOUNTAIN CITY [Garanhuns]."[85] Near the end of her life, Simôa donated a large amount of land to a local church.[86] In 1950, a glossy magazine remembered her as a "rich and powerful senhora."[87]

Her legacy is evident not only in fantastical tales of racial harmony, but also in something as simple as a family tree, reproduced in a 1987 book along with other genealogies of the town's most important families. Spanning twenty pages and beginning with Jorge Velho and his wife, Simôa's family tree encompasses eleven generations.[88] The land that she and her family acquired included places such as Sítio Mocambo (likely the same land that Teixeira lived on) and Sítio Quilombo.[89] Gomes and her descendants owned not only a great deal of land, but also many enslaved people, whom they passed on to descendants along with land and other property. Simôa and her husband also freed an Indigenous woman named Domingas, who had been given to their daughter as a present, and, according to two authors, she also liberated Blacks whom her family had enslaved.[90]

Surviving notary records do, in fact, show that Simôa authorized the freedom of an enslaved man named João in 1729. The records contain freedom letters (cartas de alforria) for thirty-one men, women, and children, who gained formal liberty in Garanhuns during the early eighteenth century.[91] On one hand, the letters are somewhat unremarkable in how much they resemble countless other papers that enslaved people secured throughout the Americas. On the other hand, the small, fragmented collection illustrates how even while veterans struggled for riches, others set different courses, some of which challenge and expand our understanding of Palmares and what came after it. One letter, signed in Recife on November 23, 1695, granted legal freedom to a woman named Domingas Francisca. Three days after Zumbi's death and entering a period when Pernambucan enslavers complained repeatedly of being unable to secure enough enslaved laborers, Domingas (identified in the document as crioula, or Brazilian-born Black woman) gained new life.[92] That the granddaughter of a white Palmares conqueror, who was also the daughter of an Indigenous woman, granted similar accessions further illustrates the many entangled legacies taking shape in and after 1695. Colonial domination was expressed, secured, and challenged through violence, property rights, legalized freedom, curfews and limitations on Black mobility, and sexual assault—a toxic, dangerous, and varied collection of obstacles and opportunities strewn across the postwar landscape.

Conclusion

As the example of Simôa Gomes de Azevedo illustrates, in Garanhuns the path to wealth and privilege could pass through unexpected places. The dual storylines found in the case of Antônio Vieira de Melo—one about the power that he wielded, the other about the leverage and spaces that the Indigenous men and others made for themselves—also illustrate larger trends. While some Black and Indigenous military men successfully petitioned the Crown for recognition and reward for their service, there was a clear limit to how much room Lisbon would make for them in elite royal spaces. After spending decades risking their lives to conquer the sertão, not even battling against Zumbi could put decorated Black and Indigenous veterans on equal footing with white counterparts. Meanwhile, sodomy, a crime for most, was a privilege for select white men, who, of course, also routinely raped and exploited enslaved women, acts that colonial and church officials rarely even considered an abomination.

Like Antônio Vieira de Melo and other powerful white men who fought in or helped bankroll the Palmares wars, the Indigenous power broker Dom Sebastião Pinheiro Camarão terrorized those under his dominion, though he had little defense when the white insurrectionists he spurned during the Guerra dos Mascates burned his aldeia. The Indigenous men who lived on Antônio's land in Garanhuns occupied a parallel, though not equal, position, subject to and beneficiaries of local power structures. The life and career of Paula da Silva's son Lázaro is even more layered—his mother was from Palmares, which his father and grandfather were charged with destroying. His own trajectory exemplifies the hall of mirrors that colonial military and political institutions could become for upwardly mobile nonwhite men. Borne of Palmares and its enemies, he was Black but not quite Black, stuck in a similar purgatory as other nonwhite officers, though also shaped by seemingly contradictory lineages.

Many white veterans never attained the rewards and trappings of masculine honor that military service could bring, nor were they able to exercise the brazen impunity of Antônio and other powerful white men. Poor, blind, and old, one colonial officer regretted wasting "his youth" battling "savage Tapuyas" and conquering "all of palmar."[93] For another veteran, war and transatlantic travel preceded a violent death. After fighting at Serra da Barriga, he participated in the assault on another mocambo, helped construct a fort, marched through the sertão, and then traveled to Angola to aid Portuguese forces.[94] He eventually returned to Pernambuco and one day in 1712 drew his sword to attack an enslaved man named Agostinho, who, authorities were concerned to learn, had directed "injurious" words at him.[95] Thirteen years later, the veteran was killed by a Black woman whom he had enslaved and another soldier. We do not know what motivated the murder, or much of anything about the relationship between the accused soldier and enslaved woman, but the man's death allowed her to escape bondage and flee to the sertão with the soldier.[96] The incident underscores the fact that one of Palmares's most powerful legacies was the violence that the wars against it engendered. Frontier spaces like the one that Antônio turned into his own violent playground were shaped by those wars, and moving the frontier inland also, paradoxically, created new spheres beyond colonial control. Though some nonwhites carved out spaces in those settings, for most, wealth and even just reprieve from multiple forms of colonial violence remained elusive. As we will see in chapter 7, that elusiveness did not prevent a surprising group from playing a significant role in the ongoing struggle to control the land formerly occupied by Palmares.

CHAPTER SEVEN   The "Indians of
Palmares"

As the lives of Paula da Silva, Simôa Gomes de Azevedo, and Lázaro
Coelho de Eça show, the histories and trajectories of Indigenous
people in Pernambuco were intertwined in complex ways with
Palmares. There is still little scholarship on Indigenous people and
Palmares, and what work does exist tends to focus on the types of
narrower questions surrounding identities and ethnogenesis in
Palmares. Looking across 1695 reveals other histories and opens new
questions.[1] Before 1695, some autonomous Indigenous people in the
region likely negotiated and sparred with mocambos, while others
maintained friendlier relationships. Many fought in colonial armies
against the mocambos. Some of the most fascinating dynamics took
shape after 1695, as multiple parties vied to control the lands once occupied by Palmares. Glimpses of this little-known history come into
view through the lives and experiences of Simôa, Lázaro, and the Indigenous power broker Sebastião Pinheiro Camarão. Additional insights are provided by an urgent letter that the town council of Penedo
wrote to King Dom João V in 1746. The missive bore all the hallmarks
of countless earlier communiqués about Palmares.

Writing a half-century after the assassination of Zumbi, the
Penedo council complained that plantation owners in the area were
losing enslaved people, who either ran away to join others in Palmares
or were being taken in raids by enemies stationed deep in the woods,
where they lived "licentiously" and grew in number. If the king did
not act soon, the council warned, war would bring "great loss of life
of Your Majesty's most loyal vassals and to our fazendas."[2] The Penedo
letter is remarkable for several reasons, not least being its timing.

What could explain the crisis that enveloped Penedo fifty years after Zumbi's death? Had new mocambos formed in place of the old ones? Answers lie in a crucial aspect of the council's complaints: unlike the countless earlier communications that decried the brazen acts of the Black rebels, this one identified a new enemy: the "Indians of Palmar," who, like their predecessors, were wreaking havoc on the colonial project.

Before and well after 1695, Palmares functioned in two main ways for Indigenous people. As a physical space, the area could provide refuge and a place to settle, though rarely without violent challenges. Over time, Indigenous participation in the mocambos' defeat also made Palmares a historical reference and an important source of leverage in struggles for land—an opportunity to position themselves as conquerors of Palmares and the Crown's true "loyal vassals." Few Indigenous people who survived the wars against Palmares claimed the lands they occupied as their first homes. Most came instead as military conscripts and postwar settlers, occupying land awarded for service in the Palmares wars or being forcibly placed on aldeias by colonial officials and missionaries, making them a mix of "ethnic soldiers" and (often involuntary) settler colonists.[3] The postwar years brought little respite, as Indigenous people faced new challenges while occupying and being assigned stations and categories that ran the gamut from war veterans to the fugitive scourges derided by the Penedo council.

As Indigenous conquerors of a Black polity in the New World, the "Indians of Palmares" therefore put conquest on the table in a way that it has rarely been in Brazil. Centering Indigenous people in the post-1695 history of Palmares also brings into focus Indigenous-led rebellions (or threats of such).[4] Revolting multiple times during the eighteenth and nineteenth centuries, siding alternately with liberal and conservative factions after Brazil secured independence from Portugal in 1822, and all the while staking claims to land by highlighting historic fealty to the Portuguese and then Brazilian crowns, the "Indians of Palmares" defy easy categorization.[5] And while the nineteenth-century rebellions in the land formerly occupied by Palmares have been studied, the eighteenth century contains suggestive bridges between 1695 and the later rebellions, as the Penedo town council's letter suggests. Embracing the mantle of conquerors and insurgents, the "Indians of Palmares" drew comparison to the revolutionaries of Saint-Domingue. At the turn of the twentieth century, Raimundo Nina Rodrigues and others would liken the rebel Blacks of Palmares to Haiti, but the contemporaneous comparison between Indigenous Brazilians and the revolutionaries in Saint-Domingue introduces other connections and lineages into the conversation and reveals an expansive landscape of violence and unrest that took shape in northeast Brazil during the century after Zumbi's death, galvanized not only by the continuous waves of insurgent and fugitive Blacks in the area but also by Indigenous rebels, who crafted their own legacies and relationships to Palmares.

The Making of the "Greatest Asylum and Seminary of Vagrants"

When the Penedo councilmen wrote to the king in 1746, a half-century had passed since Zumbi's death, yet they were concerned with the continued loss of enslaved laborers, who, they argued, had found physical harbor in the Palmares backlands and legal cover in royal law. Though Indigenous slavery had been illegal for more than a century, the practice endured thanks in part to the doctrine of Just War, which allowed for the enslavement of certain war captives. In practice, slavery and near-slave conditions persisted for Brazil's Indigenous people for centuries.[6] Nonetheless, individuals accused of waging illegal war could be brought to heel by the state.[7] This provided an important opening that Indigenous people—and, if the Penedo town council is to be believed, others—sought to use to their advantage.

During the colonial era, the proliferation and entrenchment of regional and local interests—and the particularities of war and negotiation across Portuguese America—created a varied legal terrain, which Indigenous people engaged in manifold ways. And even the law could not determine on-the-ground realities: in 1730, the governor of Pernambuco complained to the Overseas Council that local military leaders flouted royal orders by "taking male and female Indians from the aldeias" and exploiting them "for their conveniences."[8] According to the Penedo town council, the law was also abused in the opposite way, as enslaved people who were "very far from Indian" or "merely mestiço" had been claiming protection under the provision and thereby "abusing" it. Other enslaved people were simply fleeing. The council named ten residents whose enslaved people, the councilmen claimed, had escaped to a fort in the woods, some stealing "whatever they could" as they fled. If lawlessness and prohibitions against Indigenous slavery were pushing enslaved people to the fort, another force was pulling them there. According to the council, an untold number had been "violently stolen by the

Indians of Palmar." The problem was so severe that Palmares had become a destination for individuals from as far away as Bahia. "All of these slaves," the council fumed, "are stolen and protected by the Indians and Soldiers of Palmar, where they claim to be Indians."[9]

While slavery and freedom were clearly important elements here, the situation was also shaped by other factors and categories, and the prospect of Black and Indigenous people finding harbor in a colonial fort resonates strongly with the case of the Palmares refugees discussed in chapter 5. The situation also clearly illustrates how violence was engrained in colonialism and the processes that entangled Indigenous and Black combatants into wars of conquest. The colonial army remained dependent on Indigenous soldiers long after the main fighting subsided in Palmares. As late as 1775, forty-five of fifty-eight soldiers stationed at forts in the area were "Indian."[10] Even as Indigenous people continued to serve in the military and help settle the frontier, colonial officials labeled them, often along with Blacks, mixed-race individuals, and poor whites, as violent threats. That contradiction is embodied in the very fort lamented by Penedo's councilmen, one of several military outposts that had been created at the end of the Palmares wars. The Penedo council thought that forts, ostensibly symbols of colonial dominion, had the potential to be just the opposite, beckoning a Palmares redux primarily driven by Indigenous people. Drawing a direct connection between the seventeenth-century mocambos and the new danger brewing, the council described the fort in question as "situated in the deepest woods . . . of Alagoas, that long ago was a quilombo of Black runaways." The stronghold had since become "the greatest asylum and seminary of vagrants and bad actors of every caste . . . Indians, Blacks, and even some whites," who committed brazen acts that threatened safety and "other insolences improper of such a Catholic Kingdom." That kingdom, the council made clear, was not protecting the faithful, and as a result dangerous antagonists now filled the void once occupied by the mocambos. Though the town council identified individuals of "every caste" occupying and launching attacks from the fort, they feared an even greater threat to come. "We are certain," the council pronounced, "that united with a few Indian Aldeias," the fugitives would wage a war that they were capable of winning.[11] Some aldeias had already attacked missionaries and raided fazendas. Something had to be done.

The council hoped that colonial forces would bring the situation under control by rounding up offenders "in a single group and mov[ing] them to another place."[12] The councilmen also raised another concern. In 1700, the Crown had decreed that Indigenous groups of one hundred families or more would receive a square league of land on which to live. In typical fashion, additional rulings limited which groups were eligible and attached severe punishments for subjects who "fled" these aldeias.[13] Though the land it granted was paltry compared with the much larger parcels given to white settlers, in theory the law would provide a degree of autonomy and protection to Indigenous people. The Penedo town council fumed that defenseless landowners had seen their property damaged by Indigenous raids and taken away through aldeia grants. To make matters worse, the councilmen claimed, Indigenous communities with fewer than the required one hundred families were benefiting from the law. The rub, of course, was that the aldeias, the very communities that the council feared were poised to unite and overrun the countryside, were also crucial to the colonial "wall" that Domingos Jorge Velho and others desired.[14]

Santo Amaro and the Struggle for Land

Several aldeias were created as the Palmares wars wound down; they were located close to colonial forts. Others had been in existence for much longer. All were shaped by colonial violence and other elements of the seventeenth century that informed the eighteenth and nineteenth. For instance, the Indigenous aldeia known as "the S[aint] Caetano Fort of Jacuype, district of the old Palmar," was close to a fort dedicated to a Catholic saint in the land once occupied by the Palmares mocambos.[15] At this and other forts in the northeast, the Portuguese stationed Indigenous soldiers who came from all over the region and beyond.[16] While pairing aldeias and forts in an area formerly controlled by the mocambos was in line with the Crown's larger strategy to shield villages and plantations, the combination could be volatile and, as the Penedo town council's letter suggests, threaten colonial settlements. Of course, these settlements were hardly the only ones in danger. Indigenous groups, refugees from the destroyed Palmares mocambos, and others who stood in the way of colonial expansion faced constant attacks, and the forts and companion missions were themselves toxic sites, where abuse and exploitation of Indigenous people, often by the clergy, were common.[17] The aldeias in Palmares were also shaped by land distribution.[18] Though the Penedo town council complained of the Crown recklessly awarding aldeia grants, there is written record of just one Palmares sesmaria given to Indigenous combatants: in 1727, the governor of Pernambuco granted a four-square-league plot to "the sergeant major of the Indians of Palmares and his soldiers and those from the other nations who helped restore . . . Palmar."[19] Though the amount of land granted was relatively small, the sesmaria's wording and the grant itself are noteworthy—Indigenous people were the conquerors, not the conquered.

The unnamed officer—likely Paula da Silva's husband, Manuel Cubas Frazão—and the other recipients of the 1727 sesmaria created the aldeia Urucu.[20] While scholars note that the 1727 sesmaria was the only one given to Indigenous people for service against Palmares, aldeias throughout Alagoas and Pernambuco took shape before and after the end of the Palmares wars. Though some gained formal recognition via other means (for example, the 1700 law promising land to Indigenous communities), most called on their history of fighting against the mocambos to assert their rights. A case in point is the aldeia of Santo Amaro, an Indigenous community that formed around the same time that the first Africans were creating settlements in the area, and whose peripatetic existence traverses and extends well beyond the seventeenth century.

In 1602, a Portuguese colonist arrived near the edge of what would become Palmares. He brought with him an unknown number of Indigenous people, whom he had marched from the coast.[21] The captives may have been entangled in French-Portuguese confrontations and may have been first transported to the coast from elsewhere in Brazil. More likely, they lived near the coast and were Caeté, an Indigenous people that one author describes hyperbolically as having suffered "total decimation" during the colonial encounter.[22] By 1640, there were as many as two hundred Indigenous people living in the community, which came to be called Santo Amaro.[23] Portuguese and Dutch colonists treated it as a source of labor and soldiers and as a human buffer against Palmares. (The aldeia appears on the mid-seventeenth-century Dutch map along with Tapera d'Angola, discussed in chapter 1.)

In the early 1640s, a Dutch captain assigned to oversee the community moved at least ten families north to work on plantations under his command. One Dutchman reported that colonial settlers near Palmares soon demanded that they "return to reside in Santo Amaro because they know the land and all the paths and always provided great service against bandits."[24] A second report left no doubt about who the "bandits" were: "the Blacks of

Palmares," who terrorized the countryside and caused the Indigenous people to refuse to move back to Santo Amaro without the assurance of military protection.[25] Taken from the coast and then shuttled between Santo Amaro and plantations, the people of Santo Amaro suffered multiple displacements and brutal conditions. Alternately valorized for their prowess defending the area against Palmares and derided for their request for protection, they were in a no-win situation. Stationed strategically along the main passage into Palmares, they were also in constant peril.[26] Nonetheless, and despite repeated contestations of their land rights, the community persisted for a remarkably long time.

The colonist who forced the community to move from the coast acted on behalf of Diogo Soares, a Portuguese nobleman who had won donatory rights to the land; still in Lisbon, Soares later entrusted the land to his son Gabriel, who set up "farms and plantations." The transported community served as "obstacles to the rebel Blacks of Palmares" and battled coastal pirates and other Indigenous groups. Around 1624, "lacking Blacks" to work on his properties, Gabriel sold a half-league of land to the community in exchange for their labor and an annual supply of firewood.[27] Though confirmed in writing, the arrangement fell apart after Gabriel died. New landowners moved in, greased the palms of local officials, and usurped the community's property. In 1684, the aldeia became the ward of a group of priests.[28] The arrangement offered little protection. Two years later, a white colonist secured the property through a deal that the community denounced as illegal.[29] He built a ranch with livestock that ruined soil vital to the community's survival. At one point, six or seven members of the community made an agreement to withdraw the aldeia's claim, an agreement that others resisted. In 1696 and 1697, just as the Palmares wars seemed to conclude, Caetano de Melo de Castro forced the aldeia's residents from their land and ordered them "to resituate in Palmar" on a new aldeia called Nossa Senhora da Victoria, seven leagues "deeper into the serra," where their presence would "further confine" the nearly vanquished rebel Blacks.[30]

Displaced once again, the community was now accompanied by a priest, Manuel de Encarnação, who in 1699 petitioned the king to intervene on their behalf. In a lengthy memorial, Encarnação presented the community's case, stating that Santo Amaro had been founded "around 1614" and had taken formal possession of the land ten years later, living there for an additional "73 years, until 1696 and 1697." Across those decades, the people of Santo

Amaro remained "on the front line of Palmar, going on every expedition . . . to fight, leaving many dead and wounded."[31] Now they were vulnerable to powerful landholders, local officials who ignored their property rights, and paulista war veterans who terrorized the area. Having battled Palmares, pirates, and Indigenous armies, and after living for the better part of a century in the cross fire between mocambos and colonial settlements, the people of Santo Amaro now found themselves cast adrift and vulnerable. Pushed deeper into the interior, the community did not possess "a spit of land on which to plant [crops], not even the very plot that they purchased with their sweat."[32] Without intervention, an already dire situation would spiral even further out of control. Isolated from their home and unable to plant crops, in 1699 thirty Santo Amaro children starved to death, a staggering indicator of the calamity that Indigenous people faced after the Palmares wars concluded.

Encarnação noted that the community did not want to live as "subjects to the dominion" of the paulistas, but their situation had also been dire under the charge of Sebastião Pinheiro Camarão.[33] After his term as governor of Pernambuco ended in 1699, Castro recommended that the community remain in the new aldeia and also have their rights to the original parcel of land restored. Encarnação and the community, he explained, were loyal to the Crown and trustworthy, in stark contrast to the paulistas, who were stealing property in the area and living "like Turks."[34] In 1700, Pernambuco's new governor, Fernando Martins Mascarenhas de Lencastro, returned the community to its former lands. Later that year the Crown issued the order granting land to communities with one hundred families. But as the community returned to their aldeia, they once again found their ownership tenuous. The colonist who had built the ranch that encroached on their land died, but his widow and son, Catarina de Araújo and Antônio Correia Pais, continued to interlope on the community's land and filed petitions to gain legal right to it through at least the 1720s.

Encarnação continued to petition on the community's behalf, as did another advocate, a high-ranking military official whose account of the community's history of service and suffering echoed Encarnação's. In a long petition written in 1726, he stated that the Indigenous community "and their ancestors" had conserved the aldeia for "more than 120 years"; he also noted that two enslaved men who lived on the ranch had recently been seen cutting wood on the community's land.[35] In response, Araújo and Pais insisted that they had always treated the community well and, based on local rulings overturned by Lencastro, were the land's rightful owners. While appealing through official channels the decision to restore the land to the community, Araújo and Pais also exerted pressure through other means. In addition to raising livestock and cutting wood on the aldeia's lands, they either invited or tacitly allowed a group of Black veterans to settle there. Appended to a petition filed by Pais was a letter signed by eighteen veterans who attested to having lived on the aldeia for five years under the benevolent care of Pais, a priest who provided spiritual guidance without charging rent. The men lived with their families, raising tobacco and other crops, paying taxes, and remaining ready to serve the king. In exchange for living rent free, the new tenants acted as an instant source of credibility for Araújo and Pais, willing to vouch for their kindness. The Black veterans also attested that Araújo and Pais's land, crops, and livestock did not cause "any kind of harm."[36] It is unclear what became of Araújo, Pais, and the veterans, but Santo Amaro persisted for well over another century; references to the aldeia appear in official documents and newspapers until at least 1878, six years after Alagoas's provincial president officially dissolved aldeias. Targeted to disappear, enrolled in countless battles, and subject to displacement and continuous encroachment, the community nonetheless survived for far longer than many hoped or expected.

Intertwined Forms of Violence

Forced to exist on the border between Palmares and Portuguese America, the people of Santo Amaro became conquerors — soldiers and settler colonists, if not by choice — but were also the targets of unremitting abuse. Their complex relationship with colonial violence was shared by other aldeias in the area, whose trajectories also help place within a longer historical context the Penedo town council's complaints about the rampaging "Indians of Palmares." The council was likely exaggerating; at least in theory, greater threats to a colonial village would yield greater resources to protect it. However, the violence and disruption that was emanating from the Palmares fort was a byproduct of the Indigenous soldiers on whom colonists depended to conquer Palmares and of the forts and aldeias eagerly established near one another on the colonial frontier: violence begat violence. Additional evidence also leaves no doubt that Indigenous people throughout the area repeatedly planned and threatened to rebel during not only the nineteenth century but also the eighteenth.

In many ways, Santo Amaro was not unique. Diaspora and displacement mark the histories of aldeias throughout Alagoas and Pernambuco, whose inhabitants came from as far away as Ceará and even São Paulo. For example, the aldeia Atalaia, whose name means "sentinel" in Portuguese, grew around one of the forts established in Palmares. According to Alagoas's 1891 almanac, "inhabitants from other places" flocked to the outpost after 1695, "not only to sell basic supplies . . . sugar . . . honey, tobacco, and rum, but also to establish residence there, protected and sheltered by [the soldiers] against the depredations of the quilombolas."[37] Such a description differs markedly from the perspective of Penedo's residents in 1746, who thought that the ruins of Palmares had given rise to a lawless space occupied by new villains, the "Indians of Palmares." From the vantage of the late nineteenth century, the area became just the opposite — safe harbor for those seeking refuge from the still-menacing threat of fugitive Blacks. Indigenous people are highlighted in the Penedo letter — they are the enemy — and sidelined in the almanac's account, in which Atalaia is a military outpost, not an Indigenous settlement. In reality, Atalaia was both a fort and an aldeia, a combination that gave rise to a larger population center and made the aldeia a destination for multiple groups, including war veterans.[38]

Located near the Pernambuco-Alagoas border, the aldeia Jacuípe also took shape around a fort constructed at the end of the Palmares wars. In 1702, the fort's commander, Cristovão de Mendonça, the decorated white veteran and rival of André Furtado de Mendonça, received four square leagues of land.[39] A government report from 1862 provides a vague account of the aldeia's subsequent formation: "In this area, the fort was set up. Later, the Indians left, planting crops far away without encountering any kind of resistance."[40] The area had become so populous by 1761 that the fort, established "to prevent the quilombos that fugitive Blacks used to make," was no longer deemed necessary and thus relocated to the farthest western reaches of the frontier, where it would instead fend off "invasion from the wild savages" of the interior.[41]

Both sources and targets of colonial violence, aldeias in and around Palmares also became sites of resistance and insurrection. In 1730, Pernambuco's governor wrote to the king to describe "insolences" committed by Sebastião Pinheiro Camarão's son, Dom Antônio Domingos Camarão, who had inherited the position of Governor of the Indians of Pernambuco and attached captaincies at his father's behest in 1728.[42] Antônio's offenses included allegedly planning an uprising.[43] Years earlier, as we have seen, Sebastião had taken the opposite side of Pernambuco's sugar barons during the Guerra dos Mascates. His allegiance with the Portuguese traders, writes Gefferson Rodrigues, "marked a large fissure in the relationships between Indians and local elites," namely the powerful planters who rebelled and with whom the Camarão family had previously allied.[44] Though the community of Santo Amaro was among those who complained about oppressive treatment under his command, Sebastião took refuge there after the rebel forces destroyed his aldeia.[45] Like Sebastião, Antônio was also accused of exploiting the Indigenous people whom he represented, including illicitly renting aldeia members to plantation owners seeking cheap labor.[46] A conflict with Pernambuco's governor led to Antônio's imprisonment. According to subsequent allegations, after he was released he traveled from aldeia to aldeia, gathering forces for an insurrection. Before he could execute the revolt, though, he was arrested and imprisoned.

The descriptions from these subsequent allegations are revealing. Antônio had supposedly planned to "assemble a corpus of people to make assaults, gathering in some of the mountains as the Blacks with whom they have some kinship [parentesco] once did and also adding to their forces others and *mulatos*."[47] That Black people who lived in Palmares before 1695 or descended from those who had were now engaged in an uprising with Indigenous forces—and that the two groups shared "some kinship"—suggests a fascinating bridge between the seventeenth and eighteenth centuries and indicates intertwined trajectories of Black, Indigenous, and mixed-race rebels after 1695. The prospect that newly arrived Black people and *mulato/as* would join the rebellion is equally suggestive and recalls the "Indians of Palmares" and their Black, white, and mixed-race accomplices whom the Penedo town council would decry sixteen years later.[48]

The prevented uprising in 1730 was just one of several planned in the area. Reports circulated about another apparently unrealized revolt in 1730 by Indigenous people, who would kill "as many" white people as possible on Christmas Eve. Officials believed that a wider conspiracy linked rebels in Paraíba and Ceará. One cleric claimed that the conspiracy might reach as far as Minas Gerais and involve plans to create a "republic" in "this Americas."[49] Such conspiratorial fears would persist in the long shadow of Palmares. In the 1780s, officials in the town of Pombal pleaded for royal support. Located deep in the interior of Paraíba, Pombal had been built soon after Palmares's defeat, as part of the drive to advance the frontier further inland. Echoing earlier complaints of officials from Penedo, Pombal's officials now claimed that they were "surrounded by five Indian villages, allied with the pardos [and] pretos," all poised to attack.[50] Much like the earlier cleric who, in worrying about a Paraíba-Ceará conspiracy, evoked concerns about an Americas-wide republican revolt, Pombal's officials expressed fears of Indigenous, Black, and mixed-race people overthrowing the colonial order.[51]

When Raimundo Nina Rodrigues wrote about Palmares at the turn of the twentieth century, he famously likened the mocambos to a Haiti that never was, lauding Palmares's conquerors for destroying the would-be Black republic and paving the way for the future Brazil.[52] A century earlier, in 1802, the Bishop of Olinda similarly invoked Haiti, claiming that the "barbarous Indians of the backlands of Pernambuco," "though small in number," represented an existential threat. "The Blacks on the island of Saint-Domingue," the bishop wrote in his missive, "just gave the world a terrible example of these surprises." But his specific concern—that Indigenous people in Pernambuco "could be at the point of gathering [with] the support of fugitive Blacks and even discontent whites"—suggests that by the turn of the nineteenth century officials in Pernambuco feared a reconstitution of Black mocambos less than they did an uprising of Indigenous people, a reprise or continuation of threats posed during the previous century by the "Indians of Palmares" and their various potential allies.[53]

"Sacrifices and Blood" Bear Limited Results

While few of the planned uprisings of the eighteenth century materialized, during the nineteenth century, multiple rebellions shook Alagoas and Pernambuco. During these mobilizations Indigenous people took up arms, sometimes in concert with Black, white, and mixed-race allies, and at other times on their own.[54] Eventually, rebellion gave way to land expropriation and the dismantling of aldeias. In 1815, in the wake of a rumored uprising of Black people in Alagoas, a local official wrote that the Indigenous people of Atalaia required "no less vigilance than the Blacks, for the danger" they represented.[55] Some of the nineteenth-century unrest involved liberal, conservative, and royalist factions struggling for political control after Brazilian independence was declared in 1822, and some derived from internecine disputes among the area's landed elite, who often prioritized land and personal rivalries over political ideology. Indigenous entanglement with this "complex and contradictory process" produced changing and sometimes surprising alliances with the colonial and imperial states and even with the same planters who threatened and usurped their land.[56]

Indigenous people employed two primary strategies to fend off land invasions. First, they fought back. In October 1837, more than one hundred armed Indigenous men raided property near Atalaia. As fearsome as the attack itself was, an official anticipated worse to come, using language that indicates that this was not an isolated event: "Generally when the Indians attempt to destroy all the properties," he wrote, even "more horrific things" followed, creating "a state of total anarchy."[57] Second, Indigenous people and their representatives defended land, now more than a century after the fall of Palmares, by regularly referring to their role in its conquest.[58] In this strategy, service against Palmares became a potential solution to a seemingly unsolvable problem: how to stake land claims amid constant encroachment and shifting laws, all in a nation that enthusiastically pursued and pronounced the disappearance of Indigenous people.[59]

The strategies that they employed are illustrated in a petition made by the aldeia Palmeira dos Índios to the provincial government just before Brazil declared independence. They had lived "calm and peacefully" on the land for "more than 80 years" but now saw their fields "looted" by usurpers who seized the land and forged "fictitious titles." As a result, the community was unable to plant crops "for its sustenance and that of its children." The letter called the aldeia's members "citizens and His Majesty's subjects" and cited seventeenth-century laws that guaranteed their protection.[60] Though in the long run, the community lost its land, the petition elicited a positive response: official recognition of their property rights.[61]

Independence changed some dynamics and left others the same. In the decades that followed, Palmeira dos Índios and other aldeias alternately participated in and helped put down armed resistance against the new nation.[62] An 1831 law once again prohibited Indigenous slavery, illustrating the continued precariousness of Indigenous autonomy. Even long after that law was passed, Indigenous people were still vulnerable to forced labor. Additionally, when Brazil declared independence, the colonial system of awarding land grants had already been abolished, and for the next three decades "an anarchical situation" reigned, as squatters with financial means and access to guns and force took land for themselves.[63] Brazil's 1850 Land Law permanently did away with colonial laws, and after this aldeia residents often found land titles that had been awarded earlier to carry little weight, especially when the arbiters of land disputes were friendly with powerful whites.[64] By leaving so many questions about Indigenous land rights vague, the Land Law facilitated subsequent interpretations and rulings that were part of a larger "radicalization" of "land usurpation" that fractured and destroyed aldeias throughout Brazil.[65] In Alagoas and Pernambuco, communities waited decades to have their land demarcated, and even demarcation rarely prevented encroachment and theft by powerful whites. Despite these obstacles, deep into the second half of the nineteenth century Indigenous communities and their advocates asserted rights and appealed for protection, often referencing their ancestors' role in the Palmares wars and grants that the Land Law had ostensibly made obsolete.

Brazil's unique trajectory—breaking with Portugal but preserving a monarchy that descended from the Portuguese Crown—created opportunity and also quandaries for Indigenous people. In 1850, Alagoas's diretor geral dos índios (the administrator responsible for managing and representing Indigenous affairs in the province) noted how "these original Brazilians . . . during the time of the conquest of Palmares fought like lions to destroy the Blacks in great number for the king of Portugal." In return, he continued, they had received land that they cultivated, but this land was now being usurped despite their "always having been the Brazilians most ready [to serve] and most faithful to the throne."[66] These men and women rebelled while simultaneously displaying fealty to two crowns split by independence that they projected as one—Portugal's king and Brazil's emperor.[67] Their role in defeating Palmares was central to demonstrating their historic loyalty and laying the groundwork for their claims.

The way that multiple forces and actors thwarted such Indigenous claims—and more evidence of Palmares's enduring presence—is on display in a bundle of papers held at Alagoas's state archive. The cover page, written at some point in the nineteenth century, describes the bundle as containing "documents about the history [of] Indians from the province of Alagoas: of the Paulistas and Palmares."[68] The pairing of paulistas and Palmares is telling. While Indigenous people would repeatedly reference their service in fighting against Palmares, the subsequent battles over land would overwhelmingly favor white settlers, many of whom claimed descendance from the paulistas. The next page in the collection is a brief, handwritten account of the final battles of Palmares that hews closely to paradigmatic histories written during the nineteenth century, which celebrated white conquerors who placed themselves in great danger to achieve *"glory!"* (to quote the handwritten account).[69] This framing further illustrates what Indigenous people were up against. While the blood they had spilled against Palmares provided an apparent opening to shore up their land claims, their white counterparts regularly trumped these claims by successfully leveraging their own connection to the conquest of Palmares in order to secure—and often steal—land.

At least part of the problem for Indigenous communities was that the narrative of the Palmares wars, like any conquest narrative, was susceptible to erasure and change. The way that dynamic shaped land claims is seen in another set of forgotten documents. Brazil's Biblioteca Nacional holds the papers of Arthur Ramos, one of twentieth-century Brazil's most influential scholars. His large archive includes documents given to him by Bonifácio Silveira, a politician and patron of popular culture in Alagoas.[70] Silveira gave one small collection, which he told Ramos he had found among "decaying papers" (where, he did not specify), a name: "Precious Documents about Palmares."[71] The impressive title likely struck Ramos as exaggerated. The papers themselves detail an early nineteenth-century land dispute among descendants of white soldiers and contain few details about Palmares or the questions of its racial and ethnic origins that fascinated Ramos (and many others). Yet despite the documents' mundaneness, they vividly illustrate the challenges facing the "Indians of Palmares."

The land dispute involved two dynastic white legacies: the heirs of the Portuguese-born Belchior Álvares Camelo, one of the landowners mentioned in chapter 6 who accumulated massive tracts of land and wealth, and the descendants of paulista soldiers who received land grants decades later. The narratives and evidence presented by both parties sidelined Indigenous people discursively and materially. The Camelo clan thought their rights were indisputable, given that their forebear had received a royal grant in 1634. To the paulista families, this same point invalidated the Camelos' claims. The paulistas' own predecessors had received titles to the same land at the turn of the eighteenth century for their service against Palmares. Camelo's original title was no longer valid because the Dutch occupation had left the area in chaos and precipitated the rise of Palmares, which meant that land formerly belonging to Portugal had to be reconquered by the paulistas. The land in question, the paulista families argued, had been taken when "the slaves rebelled against the power and dominion of their masters [and settled] in these lands and forests of Palmares . . . united with the savage Indian gentiles of the time and some rebellious freed Blacks."[72] The argument conveniently ignored any land possession that predated the Portuguese, the fact that Camelo was also a Palmares veteran, and the large role that Indigenous (and Black) soldiers played in the paulistas' military successes. The land under dispute included areas also claimed by Indigenous people, cast now not as soldiers fighting against Palmares but as members of the mocambos; the arguments of these Indigenous people were not heard in the dispute. The case is indicative of larger patterns. In 1830, a judge rejected Indigenous claims to land in Jacuípe, finding instead that the land belonged to the family of another white conqueror. "This place," the judge declared, "was never an aldeia but rather a royal Paulista Palmares fort."[73]

In response to this kind of attack, Indigenous people (and those who petitioned on their behalf) called on their long history of service to the Crown, especially in the Palmares wars. In 1851, the diretor geral dos índios of Alagoas reported that the forced appropriation of Indigenous land was accelerating. A handful of powerful men had established "many" engenhos on Indigenous lands and "even prohibit[ed] the Indians (the true owners)" from cultivating their land, which had been "donated [by the Crown] since the restoration of Palmares." The Indigenous people, whom the diretor geral dos índios called "original Brazilians," had "provided loyal services during the conquest of Palmares, destroying the Blacks in large number, for which the king of Portugal remunerated them by providing land to cultivate and on which to form aldeias and become civilized." Urgent assistance was needed as "men without conscience" had stolen land titles from local archives and destroyed other records of Indigenous ownership.[74] The diretor, who also exploited the aldeias for labor, would sound similar alarms on other occasions, repeatedly explaining how he had searched every repository possible but could not find the land titles. Local landowners took advantage of this, he explained, by forging "fraudulent titles" and invading Indigenous land.[75]

For the most part, there was little interest in enforcing colonial legal vestiges, not only because the 1850 Land Law made them obsolete but also because doing so would often mean protecting Indigenous people at the expense of powerful whites. An 1861 survey noted that "tradition" maintained that the Atalaia aldeia was three square leagues. Those coordinates were confirmed in a land demarcation but were subsequently nullified for lack of written documents. The official who wrote the survey report had no doubt that the area, which had twenty engenhos, was first "settled by the field master Domingos Jorge Velho."[76] Urucu, the aldeia formed on land awarded in 1727 to the unnamed "sergeant major of the Indians of Palmares" and his soldiers, retained its association with Palmares, even while Indigenous property claims were disregarded. In 1862, a group of "Paulistas" from Murici claimed to hold land titles to Urucu that were older than those described by the current residents. The same year, an official report on Indigenous lands acknowledged the role of Indigenous conquerors along with unnamed others but claimed that there was an "absolute lack of knowledge" about the original parceling of Urucu and, consequently, what property belonged to whom.[77] The contingent from Murici did not present their documents before the deadline set by the official adjudicating the dispute, but the adjudicator left little doubt that, after clearing the necessary bureaucratic obstacles, the paulistas would once again triumph.[78]

Work, Pain, and Extinction

As land battles played out, directors of so-called public works initiatives and large landowners conscripted Indigenous people into backbreaking labor. The experience of Santo Amaro is once again instructive. The community flits in and out of nineteenth-century government documents, sometimes included in lists of aldeias, at other times not. One report noted that its members were regularly drawn away from their land in order to work "wherever they are called to."[79] For the aldeia, much like for Indigenous communities elsewhere in Brazil, the nineteenth century was marked by two well-known vestiges of the colonial period described by historian Maria Hilda Baqueiro Paraíso: "work and pain."[80]

Brutal conditions and land seizures prompted some Indigenous people to leave their aldeias. In 1854, authorities marched residents of Cocal to the coast for hard labor. The aldeia was formed largely by people originally from Jacuípe seeking shelter from postindependence violence. For those who came from Jacuípe, conscription to work on the coast represented another leg in an itinerant journey.[81] Years later, residents of Cocal fled to Riacho do Mato, on the Alagoas-Pernambuco border, after authorities attempted to force them to resettle elsewhere. In Riacho do Mato, they joined refugees from Jacuípe, who had also gathered there.[82] The chains of violence and flight almost seemed to have no beginning or end; Riacho do Mato also received refugees from Escada, an aldeia farther north in Pernambuco formed by Indigenous combatants who had fought against Palmares.[83] The resettlement materialized when Indigenous representatives from Escada traveled to the royal court, in Rio de Janeiro, where they negotiated the community's move to Riacho do Mato. Later on, in the 1870s, one of these representatives described in a petition to the provincial president (roughly the equivalent of governor) how he and others had been forced to wage "12 years" of "civil war" in defense of their land.[84]

Even when state-appointed bureaucrats petitioned on behalf of Indigenous communities, the decks remained stacked against them. A priest who sought to take land from Jacuípe marshaled written documents, including a sesmaria given to a paulista officer at the turn of the eighteenth century and documents from the sale of the land a century later by the paulista's heirs.[85] Despite legal mobilizations and violent resistance, there was no way to forestall the creep of "agricultural capitalism" in Alagoas and Pernambuco.[86] In 1870, a disastrous drought pummeled the area. Others followed. The provincial president dissolved Alagoas's aldeias in 1872 and made the land public property, dealing yet another staggering blow.[87] The harsh times, reminiscent of earlier periods, transpired as others accumulated wealth.

The state-led process to liquidate the aldeias lasted for decades.[88] In Pernambuco and Alagoas, aldeias were disbanded and then slashed into tiny parcels for some of the individuals and families who had been part of the aldeia; these parcels, which paled in comparison to the properties of surrounding landowners, were over time subject to invasions and theft. Nevertheless, the plots that some Indigenous people secured when the government liquidated their communities also represented small yet hard-won victories, however Pyrrhic and ephemeral. In a map depicting what became of Riacho do Mato, crowded boxes delineate individual plots given to former aldeia members, squeezed between large swaths of territory possessed by individuals outside the community.[89] Though small and subject to subsequent attacks, these boxes represented for those who received the land a significant conquest: property rights recognized on paper by the state. Yet there were clear limits to this triumph. Less than a third of the lots went to Indigenous people, which created division within the community, and within a few short years white landowners had moved in and taken most of the land assigned to Indigenous families.[90]

Throughout, Palmares loomed large. Even as administrators declared them extinct, Indigenous people continued to draw on their long-standing identity as conquerors of Palmares. In 1865, Joze Lopes da Silva—a military officer and representative of the aldeias, identified in government communiqués as "Citizen Indian"—appealed directly to the emperor after years of abuse leveled against him and the communities he represented. The aldeias, he attested, occupied "the vast territory once dominated by the fugitives of Palmares, [who] were expelled by the force and sacrifices of the Indians." Those sacrifices secured a "sacred legacy" that now belonged to their descendants. Even if they could no longer provide written proof of the grants, the fact that they had continuously and productively occupied the land was itself a legitimate claim to possession.[91]

In at least some cases, officials recognized the uniqueness of such claims. In 1874, Brazil's minister of agriculture wrote to the president of Alagoas in order to clarify lingering questions about the disbandment of aldeias, including Urucu, formed on the sesmaria issued in 1727 to Indigenous Palmares veterans. Nineteenth-century law notwithstanding, the minister wrote, the sesmaria must be honored, because it "was issued not purely and simply, as most concessions of that nature [were], but . . . in remuneration for relevant military services rendered during the Palmares war." The residents of Urucu, he continued, "objecting now in no small number, as they have always objected [to having their land taken]," must have their property rights recognized and protected.[92] While the order shows how Indigenous people doggedly preserved memory of their service and deftly negotiated the legal system, it also lacked teeth. The minister directed the provincial president to demarcate the land, echoing countless edicts before his and doing little to stave off the steady dismantling of Indigenous property.

Conclusion

In 1851, *O Constitucional*, a newspaper based in Maceió, the capital of Alagoas, published a short history of Palmares, along with a list of popular "traditions" that had kept its memory alive.[93] Of special note was the "rustic pastime called the Quilombos," in which participants throughout the province reenacted "the assault of the Indians against the Blacks" of Palmares. After defeating them, the Indians "sell" them as captives to the spectators. According to the paper, "the people" (o povo) had preserved the tradition "from that distant epoch to the present (158 years after it happened!)." Like most surviving accounts of the quilombo dance, this one left the identities of the performers unclear. We know little about the tradition's origins, other than that it traces to at least the first half of the nineteenth century and was practiced in areas around Serra da Barriga, including those near Indigenous settlements.[94] Though rarely practiced today, it remains one of the few visible memories of the Indigenous conquest of Palmares. Authors have dismissed the historical veracity of the spectacle's narrative, even suggesting that the portrayal of conflict between Indigenous and Black groups was the product of "white machination"—a myth created by landowners to pit nonwhites against one another.[95] While that may be true, there is also more to consider here, including the possibility that Indigenous people, as they did elsewhere in the Americas, commemorated their role as conquest soldiers.[96] Once again, the violence of the Palmares wars was seen to generate new developments and processes long after 1695.

Performative celebrations of the Indigenous conquest of Palmares accompanied concrete dispossession. O Constitucional also noted that it had "consulted" land titles held by "descendants of the warriors of that time," a group it called "Paulista[s], etc." O Constitucional even possessed "a copy of the Urucu sesmaria, awarded to Major Alexandre de Brito and C. Maximiano Pereira in 1727." Such documents, they concluded, would ensure "that the families of those whose many services built [our] country continue to enjoy the benefits that they deserve."[97] Of course, the original 1727 sesmaria for Urucu does not name Brito or Pereira, and while it is possible that they were Indigenous, it is much more likely, considering the paper's description of the "warriors" who conquered Palmares as "Paulista[s], etc.," that the "copy" was in fact a falsified document used to take Indigenous land—particularly given the long patterns of dispossession and fraudulent titles.

Viewed longitudinally, the histories of Palmares's Indigenous people provide a window into the allegiances and strategies that the mocambos and the violence unleashed on them engendered after 1695. The concomitant rise of aldeias and forts on the Palmares frontier generated subsequent waves of violence, often directed at Indigenous people and also propelling some to take up arms against their tormenters, be they large landowners or the colonial and imperial state. The suggestion that would-be Indigenous rebels had built a multiracial allied force, and shared "some kinship" with fugitive or insurgent Blacks in Palmares, highlights the almost dizzying, changing array of allies and enemies forged in the backlands. If that is somewhat unsurprising for a frontier setting, the implications for our understanding of Palmares and maroon settlements elsewhere are more significant. The destruction of the mocambos did not simply erase them and instead ushered in a new era, informed by the previous one and in which land and power were not only contested within (or beyond) the boundaries of colonial law and control but also shaped by the unique relationships and arrangements that continued to flow from and through Palmares.

This dynamic influenced and, in some ways, bound the potential that Indigenous people found by calling on their service against Palmares to hold the Portuguese Crown to its word, even long after it fractured in two. Doing so provided toeholds on a steep and slippery slope that delivered far more setbacks than victories, a fact that illustrates the force and extent of discursive and physical anti-Indigenous violence. Though the label "Indians of Palmares" hides a complex and internally differentiated set of peoples and was constructed at least in part by white elites, it became an important tool for many of the area's Indigenous people. It also reminds us of how much has been erased and marginalized in narratives that have elevated familiar icons and rivalries—Palmaristas versus Paulistas—and left behind others. That the label could function as reductive shorthand and as leverage for asserting land rights, and could signal fealty or trigger fear of Haiti-like, earth-shaking rebellion, points to the label's power and capaciousness. Similar openness—and richness—is found in legacies etched into the landscape and place-names of Palmares and neighboring regions, the focus of part IV.

IV   PLACES

Greater Palmares

CHAPTER EIGHT

As the trajectories of the "Indians of Palmares" make clear, violent land contestations were one of the enduring legacies of Palmares and the wars to destroy it. The natural landscape and human-made structures were also sites of contestation. If enslaved people compiled what John Marquez calls a "counter-archive" of legal knowledge and strategies collected and passed down over generations and across the Atlantic, the landscape could function as a separate site for asserting and preserving other words, ideas, and traditions, sometimes in ways that outlasted even the deepest and most violent acts.[1] In this part of the book, having paid attention most closely to spiritual and human afterlives thus far, we now turn more fully to place. The plantations, aldeias, forts, and settlements erected during the seventeenth and eighteenth centuries etched colonial dominion into the landscape, marking the wilderness with symbols of colonial power (see figure 8.1). In urban centers such as Recife, the construction of churches created similarly imposing symbols.[2] Each arose alongside signs of Palmares's durability and longevity, traces of which are still evident today, especially in place-names and other aspects of the natural environment. Some traces illustrate Palmares's lasting imprint, while others take us further back in time and revise our understanding of the mocambos and the spaces they inhabited in Pernambuco and Alagoas, discussed in this chapter as "Greater Palmares." Yet others push the story through and beyond Palmares to histories situated farther north, in Paraíba and Rio Grande do Norte, the subject of chapter 9.

Studying place provides a helpful path around some of the archival silences and illusions that often make it difficult to access the histories of Palmares, challenges vividly embodied in a single, miscopied word: "Hainam." The word appeared in a transcription of a 1707 letter

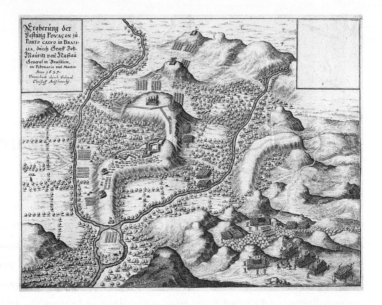

FIGURE 8.1 Porto Calvo (1637). Note the hills, varied terrain, and wooded areas in the landscape surrounding Porto Calvo and nearby fortifications. *Source*: Matthaeus Merian, *Eroberung der Vestung Pavaçon zu Porto Calvo in Brasilia, Durch Groff Joh. Mauritz von Nassau General in Brasilien, Im Februario und Martio Anno 1637*, Biblioteca Nacional, Acervo Digital, Cartografia, accessed May 25, 2023, http://objdigital.bn.br/objdigital2 /acervo_digital/div_cartografia/cart354227/cart354227.jpg.

awarding a mercê and pension to Páscoa dos Santos. In 1943, Brazil's National Library (Biblioteca Nacional) published the transcription of the letter in *Documentos Históricos*, a 112-volume set of colonial records printed between 1928 and 1955, willed into existence by Mario Behring, the library's director, who years earlier played a key role uncovering documents that helped refute the Zumbi suicide myth.[3]

Santos was receiving this recompense as the daughter of Manuel Barbalho de Lira, the former field master of the Henrique Dias regiment. The transcribed letter describes how in 1700, before becoming field master, Lira journeyed with 150 men to "take the battle to the rebel Blacks escaped from Palmares in Hainam and put an end to their hostile acts." To reach this place called Hainam, Lira and his men traversed "many rivers and scal[ed] mountains across 56 leagues and 25 days," laboring "to enter the distant sertões and agrestes [areas characterized by dryness]." Even as guides led the men astray or deserted, Lira "always acted with honor."[4] The fact that the Portuguese sent a large contingent into battle five years after Zumbi's death highlights the mocambos' stubborn refusal to disappear. Lira's journey across daunting terrain, and the fact that the guides led him off track (apparently with intention), echoes the trials of the 1645 Blaer-Reijmbach campaign and so many other previous expeditions. Now five years after Zumbi's death, a familiar scene had played out once again, the wilderness almost swallowing a colonial contingent seeking to kill or capture Palmaristas.

But if the document illuminates an expansive map and timeline for Palmares, it also presents a confounding question: Where was Hainam? The place appears on no known maps, which led some scholars to speculate about its location.[5] The answer lies in the ragged, deteriorating original letter, housed at the Arquivo Nacional Torre do Tombo in Lisbon.[6] During the transcription in 1943, a blurry "que" (that) was mistaken for "em" (in), an error that cascades into the next word, which is "havião" (or haviam: "they had"), not "Hainam."[7] The original sentence does not read "Take the battle to the rebel Blacks escaped from Palmares **in Hainam**" (fazer guerra aos negros levantados **em Hainam** escapados dos Palmares), as it appears in *Documentos Históricos*; instead, it reads, "Take the battle to the rebel Blacks **that [who] had escaped** from Palmares" (fazer guerra aos negros levantados **que haviam** escapados dos Palmares). Hainam, it turns out, is no place at all. A place created by mistake and read casually for years to signify somewhere in the vast northeastern backlands, Hainam is an apt cipher for the main subjects of this section of the book: places that Palmaristas and other fugitives lived in, fled to, and otherwise shaped before and long after Zumbi died. Though often difficult to spot in the historical record, unlike mythical Hainam, these places were quite real, persisting despite multiple forms of violence trained against them.

Forts and Frontier in the "Continent of Palmares"

As the Palmares wars wound down, the neighboring coastal centers Olinda and Recife tracked nearly opposite paths. Olinda, which some observers once compared admiringly to Lisbon, was in decay, while Recife's power grew. Connected by a thin isthmus, the towns were framed by the Atlantic, a series of rivers, and dense forest. Both towns were entrepôts of Atlantic slavery and functioned as command centers and recruiting grounds for inland military campaigns; convoys also departed from the coast with captives destined for places that stretched the colonial frontier.[8] The coastal centers were also home to powerful elites and large, multiracial poor and middling classes. Even during the seventeenth century, colonial officials in these urban nucleuses complained of uprisings of the enslaved, a compelling illustration of the wider, multifaceted matrix of Black actions and expressions of which Palmares was a part.[9]

Inland, the Portuguese continued to string together outposts, in a perpetual quest to realize the great "wall" envisioned by Domingos Jorge Velho. In 1705, Jorge Velho died and was replaced by Cristovão de Mendonça as the ranking officer at the Nossa Senhora das Brotas military encampment. Mendonça was tasked with policing the "Palmares frontier" against "the Blacks who are still there" and who continued to "assault" area farms.[10] Wary of ongoing threats but also financially stretched, the next year Pernambuco's governor proposed a reorganization of the Palmares regiment that would save expenses while protecting "the residents of these captaincies [that] neighbor Palmar" from "the continued raids that the Blacks carry out."[11] Fewer in number, they were now even more "difficult to find."[12] The "great distance" between forts exacerbated the problem, and so the governor proposed the creation of a new fort in Cucaú, where Gan(g)a Zumba and his followers had temporarily settled after the peace accord in 1679. The Palmares regiment itself would be diminished in number and divided into six companies, with two each assigned to Cucaú and the other two forts.

As the town council of Penedo would attest, forts were no panacea for the Portuguese and in some cases hardly even functioned within the colonial sphere of control, much less stood as sentinels to defend the vast frontier that stretched from the São Francisco River in the south to Recife in the north. While the military structures could project an imposing appearance, they faced stiff tests from the elements. In 1711, enslaved men, who likely had to carry special permits for the sharp tools they would use, were called on to cut back "very thick" vegetation that had engulfed the Tamandaré Fort, near the coast (see figure 8.2).[13] The challenge was endemic to the captaincy, where the line between town and landscape often blurred. The city limits of Recife and Olinda crept inland unevenly, making the difference between rural and urban often difficult to ascertain.[14] The Palmares forts, built in the rough landscape of the interior, faced similar challenges from nature and no shortage

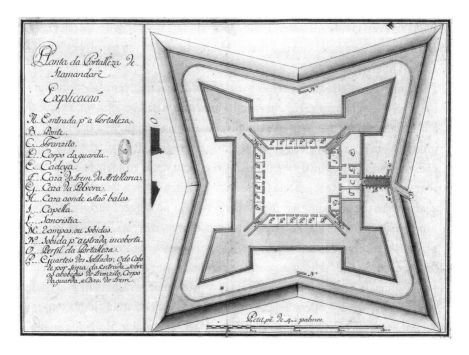

FIGURE 8.2 Tamandaré Fort (1740s). Like most forts, this one had a chapel and jail. Even the best-designed forts could be overcome by vegetation and climate. *Source:* "Descrição de Pernambuco," 1743, Manuscritos do Brasil preceding folio 605, Arquivo Nacional Torre do Tombo.

of others caused by humans and spirits. In 1718, a girl reported being "very horrified" after seeing a Black man beheading a saint. The accused, whose name no one could remember, was a "famed feiticeiro" with an "eaten away" nose, who lived in the paulistas' Nossa Senhora das Brotas encampment. He practiced feitiçarias with another man who lived there too.[15]

Soldiers feared meeting the same fate as the saint, especially while on patrol, where they might confront fugitive Blacks or Indigenous groups not allied with the Portuguese. In 1705, officials ordered rough punishment to address widespread insubordination in the forts among "even brancos and *mulatos*, along with *negros* and Tapuyas."[16] Six years later, amid the tumult of the Guerra dos Mascates, concern was raised at a colonial fort about the "unrest of the caboclos," a term for mixed-race individuals of European and Indigenous parentage that was also employed to emphasize Indigeneity and nonwhiteness. Authorities hoped that "prudence" would be applied to avoid an even greater disaster: Indigenous soldiers uniting with "Black fugitives," whose land had been conquered but remained driven to recover "their ancient liberty."[17]

Though they effectively lay in place foundations for eventual control of the area, the Palmares regiment and the area's forts had serious weaknesses and were often unable to prevent fugitive Blacks and unaligned Indigenous groups from continuing to occupy the frontier region. In 1730, the king approved a request to whittle the Palmares regiment down to a single company that would also be responsible for servicing Tamandaré and another fort. A year earlier, the governor wrote that the regiment no longer "performed any function because the Blacks have been extinct for many years." Only in "some places" were there "refugees," separated from society by a "great distance" and "ensconced" in the "thick woods of the sertões."[18] Not everyone was so sure. Other officials deplored the "miserable" condition of residents in Alagoas, who faced a barrage of challenges, including the reduction of the Palmares regiment, while Blacks continued to occupy "the mountains of the continent of Palmares."[19] That enormous space continued to loom large and at times could still seem to overwhelm the resources that colonial authorities were able or willing to muster. A 1741 communiqué reveals that the king's earlier order was not carried out; there were still two Palmares companies, though both were in bad shape. One was captained by a man now eighty years old, deaf, and "completely unable" to participate in forays against the "Blacks of the Mocambos."[20] Despite pleas to provide a new captain, he would not be replaced for another three years.[21]

In 1761, another proposal was made to keep just one company in the region, but in 1775, there were still two Palmares companies, each comprising fifteen white and forty-three Indigenous soldiers. They had little support. In both companies, the last captains on record were already "deceased," and the next in line were fifty-six and sixty-three years old. A lack of adequate replacements had left the forces in a "decadent state."[22] The forts themselves met a similar fate, eventually falling into disrepair.[23] Meanwhile, the "continent of Palmares" continued to cast a long shadow. Into the late 1750s and beyond, troops in the area described the ongoing challenge posed by the area's "fugitive slaves and those fortified in mocambos" (amocambados).[24] A map commissioned in the 1760s by the secretary of the navy features a noteworthy label nestled among the inland mountains: "Os Palmares," a place that, now more than a half-century after it ceased to exist, still existed (see figure 8.3).

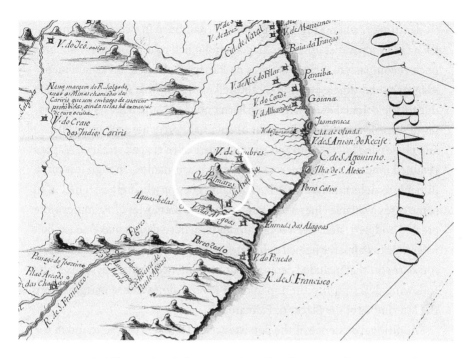

FIGURE 8.3 Os Palmares (1766). *Source*: José Gonçalves da Fonseca, "Carta topografica, a onde se compreendem as capitanías de que se compoem ao prezente o governo de Pernambuco," 1766, 10438-2A-27A-102, Biblioteca Digital do Exército (Portugal).

Giving Name to Place

Though no other surviving map from the colonial era names Palmares, the mocambos' legacies are inscribed in other toponyms across Alagoas, Pernambuco, and beyond. While some mocambos flourished, thanks to their invisibility, others became topographical reference points, much like rivers, mountains, or farms, that even colonial and imperial officials would use to demarcate land. Some references, registered in writing during the nineteenth century, seem to suggest direct links to Palmares, while others indicate new waves of flight, fugitivity, and diasporic creation. Portuguese officials, and surely Africans, saw similarities and resonances in the climates and landscapes of West Central Africa and Brazil. During the eighteenth century, soldiers and settlers from Brazil traveled to Angola to help "populate" and control the area. In some cases, officials specifically requested that they come from the sertões of Pernambuco (and also Bahia and Portugal) to ensure that they would be accustomed to what they would confront in Africa.[25]

Until 1817, when King João VI split Pernambuco in two as punishment for a failed separatist uprising, Alagoas and much of the land that Palmares once encompassed, including Serra da Barriga, belonged to Pernambuco.[26] Alagoas's subordinate position is captured in the way that some referred to it during the colonial era: "Alagoas de Pernambuco." Named for its many bodies of water ("alagoa" is a remnant of colonial Portuguese meaning "lake") and possessing hilly terrain and an abundance of rivers and streams, Alagoas retained (and retains) numerous evocative place-names. Though it is often difficult to determine how far back a name goes or who first assigned it, in some cases available clues show how and where memories of Palmares were created and persisted. Even some toponyms whose names make no explicit reference to Palmares helped delineate its borders and preserve its memory. A 1749 report that included details about Pernambuco's waterways affixed the following descriptor to the Tapamondé River: "along whose margins were the Mucambos of the Blacks of Palmares."[27]

Additional evidence of the persistence of Palmares can be found in the cluster of places named Macaco—which, as we saw in chapter 1, was the name of the most powerful mocambo during the 1670s. Silvia Lara has critiqued other authors for mistakenly referring to Serra da Barriga, the de facto capital under Zumbi, as Macaco, which was the seat of Palmares under Gan(g)a Zumba.[28] While it is true that some scholars were simply mistaken, there is no doubt that there was historically a place called Macaco near Serra da Barriga—in fact, multiple places: a mountain, stream, and settlement. They merit further attention.

In the 1670s, before the rise of Zumbi's Serra da Barriga, the Portuguese confronted a "troop of Blacks hidden among the cliffs and woods" near the Rio Mundaú, "which bathes the bases of two very tall and rugged mountains."[29] Lara and coauthor Phablo Fachin show that this expedition traveled near Serra da Barriga, and later maps show a mountain named Macaco right nearby.[30] This indicates that Palmaristas inhabited the area before Zumbi's rise, though it is unclear what names they gave the land at this time. Evidence from the 1680s and 1750s is more definitive. In addition to a stream, mountain, and settlement, there was also a large area (campo) called Macaco near Serra da Barriga. While the settlement arose during the eighteenth century—and was known as Macacos—the mountain, campo, and likely the stream date to the seventeenth century. A fifteen-league sesmaria adjacent to

Serra da Barriga, granted to three soldiers in 1682, used the "Serra do Macaco" as a reference point.[31] Another sesmaria granted four years later was in "the place called campo do Macaco."[32] This second sesmaria was further north, in Pernambuco, but a third sesmaria, secured in 1755 by another Palmares veteran, was framed by the "Stream [Riacho] called Macaquo, at the foot of the Serra do Barriga, where the main war against the Rebel Blacks took place."[33] The land grants show that the mountain close to Serra da Barriga was called Macaco by the 1680s and that the nearby stream carried the same name by the mid-eighteenth century and was closely associated with Palmares. Even more suggestive in relation to Palmares is the connection elsewhere in Brazil beyond Pernambuco and Alagoas between mocambos and Macaco place-names.[34] One particularly evocative example is a river in Rio de Janeiro state that changes names from Rio Simão Pereira to Rio Macacos when it passes by a place named Quilombo, a fascinating transition that highlights the human hands and active processes behind place-names—what, in this case, seems to be a fugitive settlement (or area associated with one) changing the name of a river as it flows past, imbricating human and aquatic movement into one.[35]

The cluster of Macaco place-names in Pernambuco and Alagoas—and the compelling example from Rio de Janeiro—suggests a deeper meaning to the name than usually assumed. In Portuguese, "macaco" means "monkey," and the *Relação* provides a seemingly straightforward explanation of how Gan(g)a Zumba's mocambo got its name: "They [the Palmaristas] call the royal city Macaco, a name that comes from the death of one of those animals [monkeys] in that place."[36] Kathryn de Luna's forthcoming work shows that, though Portuguese speakers understood macaco to mean monkey, many Africans would not have, or at least, many would have also or instead heard in the word deep political and cultural meaning—and communal bonds.[37] While we await her findings to understand the full significance of the word, the prevalence of places in Palmares called Macaco indicates diasporic pathways flowing through and outliving the mocambos. When Zumbi settled in Serra da Barriga, he and those who came with him must have preserved or adapted some aspects of previous mocambos, possibly including Macaco.

The Macaco stream ("the Stream called Macacquo") is just one of a collection of richly referential waterways in the area. Another stream, the Riacho do João Mulato, must have been named after João Mulato, one of the Palmarista leaders accused of killing Gan(g)a Zumba.[38] Palmaristas also undoubtedly found great meaning in the Rio Mundaú, which snakes its way from Garanhuns through Alagoas, past Serra da Barriga, and finally to a lagoon near Maceió, on the Atlantic coast. This crucial aquatic artery feeds the lush Mundaú River basin and extends for 150 kilometers.[39] Combined with the dense foliage and steep mountains, it must have been one of the primary reasons that Zumbi settled atop Serra da Barriga.[40] Some colonial sources, including the seventeenth-century Dutch map on which Tapera d'Angola appears, call the Mundaú River Rio Mondaí, and there is some consensus that that name is Tupi for "thieves' water."[41] One easily imagines reasons why Indigenous people would call European colonizers or Black maroons usurping their land (or water) "thieves."[42] Nor does it require a great deal of imagination to see the potential for shared understandings and misunderstandings: what Indigenous people might call stolen water, Black fugitive settlers would have considered to be life-giving.

Similarly evocative are the names, still present today, in Alagoas's "sea of hills," an area that includes Serra da Barriga and Serra do Macaco, and that stretches to the border with Pernambuco. Among the most interesting names of the serras and peaks in the area are Andalaquituche, Lunga, and Mocambo.[43] Andalaquituche (or Andalaquituxe) was the name of an important Palmares leader during the 1670s, identified in the *Relação* as the "brother of Zambi," and his mocambo was, as the *Relação* referred to it, "the palmar of Andalaquituxe."[44] The survival of his name in the landscape is one of the most specific retentions from Palmares, but others are no less suggestive. The peak and stream named Lunga conveyed their own formidable ideas.[45] To men and women from West Central Africa, "lunga" could refer to a U-shaped, clapperless iron bell that was "a sacred object" used in battle and an "announcement of danger; rebellion, war, uprising."[46] According to Cadornega, "all the Jaga quilombos" possessed a lunga bell.[47] But this bell was just one form of lunga, a larger category of sacred objects from which leaders derived their authority. Lunga objects were central to the consolidation of political power and, Jan Vansina writes, "accompanied the rise" of the "major principalities" of West Central Africa.[48] The word "lunga" likely comes from kalunga (or calunga), a multidimensional word often translated as "great water" or "Land of the Dead," a place that could carry complex and ominous meanings—an inverted spirit world marking the line between the living and the dead, which was the Middle Passage for some.[49] Lunga objects could also function as "lineage emblem[s]," were often associated with water spirits, and could be used to conjure rain.[50] The lunga place-names in areas formerly occupied by mocambos therefore may have evoked not only the bellicose meanings described by Cadornega but also a wider range of significance: politicking, mocambo formation, lineal succession, and spiritual and practical meanings of water.

Other names are provocative by raising challenging questions. Mocambo and Zumbi, for example, surprisingly also appear as the names of farms and plantations, properties that depended on enslaved labor.[51] In some cases—Cucaú, for example—a mocambo's name was preserved by the white settlers who moved onto the conquered land.[52] Naming a plantation after Zumbi might also have been a form of trophy-making, a boast staked into the land, though this was not the only meaning that such labels could convey.[53]

Like Alagoas, Pernambuco has a large collection of intriguing place-names, including the municipality called Palmares (officially designated as such in 1862).[54] Pernambuco also has at least four Mocambo (or Mucambo) toponyms. Another likely reference to Palmares is contained in at least thirteen places named Cumbe or Cumbi (including one of the peaks in Alagoas's "sea of hills"), though the fact that both spellings appear in historical documents complicates our ability to exactly decipher the reference.[55] As was briefly mentioned in chapter 5 and will be discussed in more detail in chapter 9, Cumbi (or Cumbe) was the name of a mocambo in Paraíba that received Palmaristas leaving Alagoas and Pernambuco. In some parts of Spanish South America, maroon communities were called cumbes.[56] A dance "of extremely sensual character" called Cumbé was popular in Portugal during the eighteenth century and is described by one source (without additional details) as being "of African origin."[57] Some have suggested Tupi origins for the word, and further research may substantiate that hypothesis.[58] While the apparent similarity between Cumbi and Zumbi has also been alluring to scholars, a closer look at Bantuphone roots points toward more likely provenances. The noun root *-kùmbí* could refer to two kinds of birds, while *-kùmbì* meant sun as well as cloud.[59] The verb root *-kúmb*, "to bend," presents interesting possibilities, especially for individuals from Central Kongo, where it became *-kúmby-*.[60]

One of the richest collections of Palmares-related place-names in Pernambuco is found in Garanhuns. Though on the far western fringe of Palmares, the area was connected to Serra da Barriga and the Atlantic coast by the Rio Mundaú; as mentioned in chapter 6, it was not far from where colonial forces killed Zumbi. The Cariri, a Tapuia people, first lived in the area, including, some evidence suggests, a group known as the Garanhus (or Gara-nhun or Unhanhú)—hence the area's name.[61] An alternative genealogy traces Tupi origins of the word Garanhuns, which has been translated as "Black indi-vidual" and "black bird."[62] By 1660, and perhaps earlier, the area was entangled with Palmares. A sesmaria granted that year defined one edge of the property as formed by the "Mocambo [o]f fugitive Blacks of Palmares."[63] During the second half of the seventeenth century, white colonists had limited success securing land in Garanhuns and the larger surrounding area, the Sertão do Ararobá. One of the first sesmeiros in the area was Bernardo Vieira de Melo. In 1671, he was awarded a twenty-league grant, which he initially shared with two other men but later came to possess on his own and then passed down through the family, including Antônio, his evildoer son.[64]

During the Palmares wars, Bernardo and other white colonists rarely suc-ceeded at establishing stable fazendas in Garanhuns. In the late 1670s or early 1680s, Fernão Carrilho led an attack that destroyed the Mocambo Garanhum in the area.[65] Oral histories attest to other mocambos in the area—Congo, Magano, Negra Maria, and Timbó—not mentioned in the documentary rec-ord.[66] This might reflect the local memory of Palmares mocambos passed down over time that Vieira de Melo and other colonial combatants did not know or otherwise failed to record. It is also possible that these mocambos developed during the eighteenth century and became associated later with Palmares, an illustration of how the idea of Palmares continued to grow over time.[67] Even after claiming possession of land, Bernardo saw control of it slip beyond his grasp. According to testimony recorded in 1721, he left behind a vaqueiro (cowboy) and an enslaved man to care for his property, the Fazenda Jupi, which was subsequently attacked by members of a nearby mocambo, who killed both caretakers and attempted (unsuccessfully) to take the cattle. The fazenda remained vacant for years.[68] As the war wound down, Antônio took control of the land—the results of which were recounted in chapter 6.

Alfredo Leite Cavalcanti, who published a history of Garanhuns, con-sulted eighteenth-century documents that provide further insight into how the area's place-names developed. Some area toponyms, such as the Fazenda Lagoa (Lake Farm), referred directly to the landscape. Farms named with In-digenous words and phrases were also legion, and European words figured prominently too. But traces of Palmares's legacy can also be gleaned from many of the names. According to Cavalcanti, the Sítio Flamengo was tribute to the role the Dutch played "hunting the rebel Blacks of Palmares"; Flamengo means "Flemish" in Portuguese.[69] To its north was the Sítio Paulista, named for a fort whose construction owed largely to the efforts of Luís Mendes da Silva, the soldier and colonial administrator, whose testimony serves as the only surviving documentary record about the kidnapped Black daughter of the forest, Paula da Silva.[70] Garanhuns and the Sertão do Ararobá were also dotted with sítios and fazendas with African and African diasporic names. Several sesmeiros called their land Sítio do Quilombo, inspired, Cavalcanti writes, "for having known that the site had once been a fort built by the rebel Blacks of Palmares."[71] Part of the original Vieira de Melo sesmaria, inherited by Antônio's sister, Arcângela Bezerra, was called Sítio Mucambo.[72] Another sítio was called Tigre (Tiger), also the name of a Palmares mocambo in the area.[73] The Fazenda do Papacaça took its name from Pedro Papacaça's mocambo, located not far from where colonial soldiers killed Zumbi. When the owners sold it in 1712, one of the property's boundaries was formed by "the lands of Father Pedro Fernandes Aranha and the Recollect Priests, which they call the Mocambo da Negra Maria," or "Black Maria's Mocambo."[74] A sesmaria awarded to an officer who led attacks on Palmares in the 1670s described the property's southern border as formed in part by a mocambo.[75] Similar references are found in sesmarias and colonial communiqués across the northeast, a clear indication of the durable presence of mocambos, which helped delineate property boundaries as would a farm or any other permanent or semipermanent built structure of part of the landscape.

This durable presence was likely due in part to how mocambo attacks on fazendas in Garanhuns were intense enough to drive away would-be settlers. The Negra Maria and Papacaça mocambos were on or near land that the Crown assigned to sesmeiros.[76] Other sesmarias were simply abandoned due to this landscape of mocambos. Mocambo attacks left the Fazenda Garcia unoccupied for so long that by 1705, when it was sold to Simôa Gomes de Azevedo's husband, its name had changed to "Tapera do Garcia": "Garcia's Abandoned (or Ruined) Farm," an echo of Tapera d'Angola.[77]

The presence of mocambos and abandoned land in Garanhuns provides context for the places named after Zumbi in the area. In what is today the town of Arcoverde, about ninety kilometers northwest of the town of Garanhuns, there is a small river named Zumbi, suggestive of the name's spiritual and aquatic meanings.[78] But one especially compelling place with this name was a farm called the Sítio do Zumbi. Though it is uncertain when these two places acquired their name, there is no doubt that the Sítio do Zumbi was named before 1754, when the farm's owner died.[79] In all likelihood, the name evoked the fallen Palmares leader, though that may not have been the only association. This out-of-the-way farm may be an early example of how another meaning of zumbi emerged. At some point, among Portuguese speakers, the word also came to mean "deserted" or "haunted." Located in Garanhuns, on the margins of Palmares and amid an abundance of abandoned property, the Sítio do Zumbi may well have evoked two things at once: a deserted place made so by combatants in Zumbi's army.

The association between the word "zumbi" and deserted places took root in some of the earliest writings about Palmares. Describing the Portuguese assault against Maioio, Domingos do Loreto Couto wrote, "After tracking through deserted lands . . . they found a hideaway, where fear had hidden three-hundred Blacks."[80] Loreto Couto then explains how colonial soldiers were unable to "destroy the Empire of Zumby, Prince of Palmares," who retreated with his forces "to remote places."[81] Almost by definition colonial forces had to locate and penetrate "remote places" every time they battled Zumbi, or most any Palmares settlement. By the late eighteenth century, that obvious point was officially registered in the second edition of Bluteau's dictionary, which included "deserted place" in its definition of quilombo.[82] All of this suggests how zumbi could mean more than one thing at once. In places like the Tapera do Garcia, where mocambo attacks led colonists to flee, Z/zumbi could be a river as well as an "abandoned" or "uninhabited" place, and it could also conjure memories of the Palmares leader.

Disappearance and Persistence

Over time, two apparently contradictory processes shaped the Alagoas-Pernambuco landscape. First, the expansion of agriculture, settlements, and urban areas—and the arrival of the railroad—pushed the frontier deeper into the interior. Second, while urban and agricultural growth continued, Black and Indigenous people continued to preserve or create places of autonomous or semiautonomous existence. Four maps vividly illustrate the results. The first, hand-drawn by a Portuguese military engineer at some point around the turn of the nineteenth century, plots major points of reference along Brazil's northeast coast. Among the few inland places denoted is the

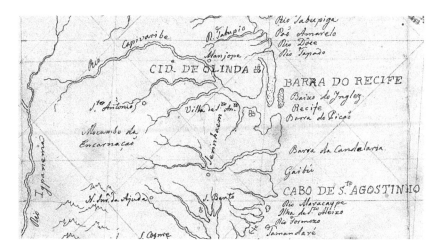

FIGURE 8.4 Mocambo da Encarnação (in the late eighteenth or early nineteenth century). *Source: Litoral do Rio Grande do Norte e Pernambuco, 1794–1823, 5230-1A-9A-99,* Biblioteca Digital do Exército (Portugal).

Mocambo da Encarnação, west of Recife (see figure 8.4). There is little additional record of this mocambo. Its prominence on the engineer's sketch suggests the importance of fugitive settlements that either left no written record or appear only fleetingly in surviving documents.

A second map, from 1853, plots the first leg of a rail line connecting Recife and the Rio de São Francisco and illustrates that however many settlements arose or persisted after 1695, urban sprawl and agricultural growth could be inexorable forces. This map portrays a landscape dotted with towns, farms, and descriptive labels such as one area "entirely occupied by Sugar Estates" (see figure 8.5). If the military engineer's sketch portrays an open inland domain, at least part of which was mocambo territory, and the railroad map illustrates the encroachment of towns and plantations, two other maps further illustrate how these processes could be intertwined. The first, an 1813 map of Indigenous and missionary lands near the Alagoas-Pernambuco border, records multiple, perhaps competing, labels and definitions applied to the land. One segment of the map includes Quilombo Mountain (Serra do Quilombo) located between lands belonging to two landowners and adjacent to Indigenous territory. Just to the southwest of the mountain was a place known as Olho d'Agoa da Ganga, or Ganga Spring.[83]

FIGURE 8.5 Recife–São Francisco rail line (1853). *Source:* Alfred de Mornay, *Map Shewing the First Section of the Railroad between Recife & the River São Francisco . . .* (London: C. F. Cheffins, Lith., 1853), Biblioteca Nacional, Acervo Digital, Cartografia, accessed May 26, 2023, http://objdigital.bn.br/objdigital2/acervo_digital/div_cartografia /cart172333/cart172333.jpg.

The second, another military engineer's map, this one from 1843, provides a compelling apotheosis of the overlapping processes evident in the others. Like the railroad map, this one includes descriptive labels for the swaths of land found between and beyond the many towns of Pernambuco and Alagoas. On the western and southern margins were "Lands entirely uncultivated for lack of water" and "Catinga [dry terrain with brush] with many Cotton plantations." Interspersed among the inland mountains and hills where Palmares once stood, "Virgin Forests" remained alongside those being harvested for lumber. Toward the bottom of the map in the heart of Alagoas, affixed to a prominent peak, was another label, wedged poetically next to the towns of Macaco and Bernardo Vieira, the first a remnant of Palmares, the second of one of its conquerors. Written nearly 150 years after Palmares's defeat and now weathered to the point of being almost inscrutable, it is still possible to make out the words: "Serra da Barriga, where the famous Palmares habitation was" (see figure 8.6).

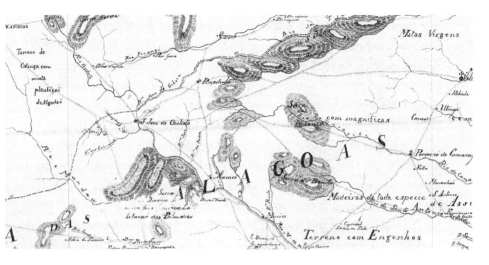

FIGURE 8.6 "Serra da Barriga, where the famous Palmares habitation was" (1843). Source: *Mappa topographico da parte da Província de Pernambuco*, 1843, Biblioteca Nacional, Acervo Digital, Cartografia, accessed May 26, 2023, http://objdigital.bn.br/objdigital2 /acervo_digital/div_cartografia/cart525821/cart525821.jpg.

Drowned

While the worn reference to Serra da Barriga names a place whose presence can be traced continuously from the seventeenth century to today, toponyms whose earliest known written references are from the nineteenth century provide a different kind of clue—provocative but not definitive evidence of connection to Palmares that prompts us to also think through and beyond Palmares. A case in point is a collection of Zumbi place-names, including at least two rural engenhos, one due north of Recife, close to Paraíba, and another in Cimbres (today Pesqueira), northwest of Garanhuns.[84] There were also a cluster of places named Zumbi in a semiurban area outside of Recife, which may be traced at least as far back as the 1830s. These Zumbi place-names may have originated in Palmares or by way of West Central Africa and in either case must have evoked multiple things for the people who lived in or near them. By the time the references appear in writing, Zumbi and Palmares were nationally—indeed, internationally—known. In the time that transpired between the battle at Serra da Barriga and the 1830s, well over a half a million enslaved Africans arrived in or passed through Pernambuco and Alagoas. Seven in ten boarded slave ships in West Central Africa, and tens of thousands in all came from different areas of the continent or sea islands.[85] Though many simply passed through Recife, the waves of arrivals indelibly shaped the city. An 1828 census counted nearly 8,000 enslaved people in a population of just over 25,000. The study did not enumerate race among the sizable "free" population, but there is no doubt that a large, diverse set of Black and mixed-race communities made up a significant portion of the city.[86]

Many lived in Afogados, a peripheral neighborhood whose name means "drowned" (or "the drowned") and was "inhabited," Marcus de Carvalho writes, "by *negros*, pardos, and all kinds of dispossessed people."[87] According to one seventeenth-century observer, the name came from the effects of the Capibaribe River, which could be "violent and furious with the tide, and in which many people drowned, especially Black slaves."[88] South of Recife, wedged between the Capibaribe and Tigipió Rivers, and touching the sea, the area also featured numerous swamps (see figure 8.7).[89] Those swamps could provide shelter, however unhospitable and dangerous, for fugitives, and the area itself functioned as the border between the city and its plantations.[90] The area drew the watchful eye of authorities and also was an important component of Recife's "Black cartography."[91] During a series of violent uprisings in the 1840s, the minister of foreign relations called the residents of Afogados "out-of-control rabble."[92] By the end of the nineteenth century, the area had grown into a sprawling district with a Black brotherhood and 23,000 inhabitants, a large number of whom lived in straw-roofed dwellings.[93]

With a largely nonwhite, "dispossessed" population, and situated near flowing water and amid swamps, Afogados was home to a number of places named Zumbi. (The area also had a hill named Cumbe.[94]) Though the earliest written references to such places that I have located date to the 1830s, the content of the references suggests longer histories, and the proximity of the places to swamp, city, waterways, plantations, and the sertão beyond made for dramatic juxtapositions. In 1835, a young boy named João, from the "Cassange nation," escaped bondage while out selling sugarcane one afternoon. His enslaver published an advertisement instructing would-be captors to "bring him to the sítio do Zumbi, next to the Engenho do Torre."[95] A year later, another advertisement asked that the eighteen-year-old Maria Benguella be returned to the same place.[96] Ripped away from Angola and brought to Recife, these youth now set out on their own by escaping from Zumbi. Both likely brought West Central African meanings with them. Laboring on the Engenho do Torre, one of Pernambuco's oldest sugar plantations, they surely also heard

FIGURE 8.7 Afogados (ca. 1858). *Source*: Augusto Stahl, "Afogados." Instituto Moreira Salles, accessed May 29, 2023, https://acervos.ims.com.br/portals/#/detailpage/16656.

new stories from other enslaved people, illustrating how multiple meanings of Z/zumbi likely evolved together in Brazil.[97]

In addition to the sítio, Afogados had a sizable forested area called Mata Zumbi where landowners disputed property lines. This forest was likely full of palm trees; the people who lived in Afogados produced oil from the seeds of dendê palms, native to West Africa and spread throughout Brazil and much of West and Central Africa.[98] Mata Zumbi in Afogados also included small bodies of water resonant with zumbi's proto-Bantu associations with rain and water—a stream (the Riacho do Zumbi) and "a lake named Zumbi"—and hills called the "outeiros do Zumby."[99] During the second half of the nineteenth century, the Mata Zumbi disappeared as Afogados became increasingly urban and as slavery slowly declined, but, as it has elsewhere, the name Zumbi demonstrated a knack for survival, here in the form of a train station in Afogados named Zumby.[100]

The multiple ways that Z/zumbi could serve as backdrop to new struggles and meaning making in Afogados are also demonstrated in an 1830s land dispute between the powerful proprietors of the Engenho Bulhões and the Engenho Suassuna, which hinged largely around an area bordering the Riacho do Zumbi.[101] The Suassuna proprietor was an influential military officer, later elevated to Baron of Suassuna. The owner of Bulhões, himself a "legendary Pernambucan," helped lead the separatist revolt that resulted in the king severing Alagoas from Pernambuco in 1817.[102] The land dispute involved property that belonged to Suassuna but which enslaved people from the Engenho Bulhões used, possibly unbeknownst to the landowner, to plant subsistence crops. In this out-of-the-way space near the Riacho do Zumbi, conflict between two of Recife's most powerful families passed through territory that enslaved people used to nourish themselves.

Long Afterlives

Through the better part of the nineteenth century, mocambos (now often called quilombos) occupied a prominent place in the Pernambucan and Alagoan landscapes. The most famous one, Catucá, in Pernambuco, elicited specters of Palmares. In 1829, for instance, an official urged the province to take "energetic and decisive" actions "to once and for all exterminate the Quilombo of the Blacks of Palmares of Catucá."[103] Another official suggested that Catucá members sought "to imitate the example" of Palmares.[104] Catucá was located in the forest of the same name, which connected the outskirts of Recife to the dense interior and encompassed swamps, rivers, engenhos, and an area known as Cova da Onça, or Jaguar's Hollow.[105]

Names with potentially charged memories persisted into the nineteenth century in Alagoas as well. In 1884, a Maceió newspaper published a short story about "Devil's Cave," at "the base of Serra da Barriga" in a "place called Jurema," which reputedly had images of a "corpulent black Lucifer" on its walls. The fear associated with it made the cavern an ideal "point of refuge for fugitive Blacks," the only ones who would dare enter it.[106] Another legend, which, a nineteenth-century author wrote, "the old folks swear is true," held that an image of Our Lady of Piety repeatedly went missing from a local church, only to be found "by caboclos" in a deserted site "where one of the descendants of the Palmares fugitives died." The writer would not hazard whether the story was "superstitious." "What is certain," he concluded, was that the area was still home to "descendants of the old inhabitants of Palmares, original types of their race: they settled there after the destruction of the Quilombo da Serra do Barriga."[107] Related stories abounded. "Among old illiterates in Viçosa," Alfredo Brandão wrote in the twentieth century, there was a story from long ago in which an armed contingent passed through the Dois Irmãos (Two Brothers) Mountain, located near Viçosa, with a group of captives. Brandão was born in Viçosa and sought to secure for his hometown a place in national lore, a vivid display of what Lara aptly calls "ufanismo regional" (extreme regional patriotism).[108] He claimed that the pivotal battle at Serra da Barriga had in fact taken place at Dois Irmãos, not far from Viçosa. The story he retold proved his point. Under the cover of darkness, the contingent's prisoners fled, "but as the night was very dark, they didn't see the cliff's edge and plunged into the abyss. Couldn't this case be a remnant of the much talked about suicide of Zumbi and his comrades?"[109]

During the 1830s and 1840s, uprisings rocked Alagoas and Pernambuco, and the interior continued to be both a home to violent rebellion and the target of agricultural expansion. By the end of the century, the town of Atalaia, which began life as a military outpost and an Indigenous aldeia formed in intimate response and relation to the Palmares wars, was at the center of a lucrative agricultural hub.[110] But running parallel to the seemingly unstoppable concentration of wealth, rebels and fugitives continued to abscond to the interior, often to aldeias or their remnants.[111] Maps again provide a bird's-eye view of these processes. One, apparently drawn in the 1830s and now wrinkled and faded, identifies a ring of land on the border between Alagoas and Pernambuco as "the woods that Vicente Ferreira de Paula inhabits." Paula was the famed leader of the Cabanada, an insurrection in the 1830s that included significant participation from Indigenous and fugitive Black groups.[112] Within the territory he and his troops occupied, the map shows a settlement named Macaco Frio, not far from a place called Macuca. Just at the edge of the territory was Cova da Negra, near Serra da Barriga and Serra do Macaco, with the Rio Mundaú running between the two peaks. On the other side of the rebel territory was a town whose name conveyed another diasporic pathway: São Benedito (Saint Benedict). If the meaning of that settlement's name is self-evident, Macuca's is less so. According to one dictionary, "macuca" was the name of a "coin used among the natives of Angola," though the etymology the dictionary proposes seems suspect.[113] In Tupi, macuca may mean a bird or a tasty meal.[114] One compelling proto-Bantu root is *-kúk-, "to cover," and another is *-kuka, which Marcos Abreu Leitão de Almeida finds derives from nineteenth-century Kisikongo and was employed by raiders who "drew from

[a] broad semantic domain . . . to specifically refer to their practice of 'raid upon a town and carry people away into slavery.'"[115] The ma- prefix turns verbs into two categories (or "classes") of Bantu nouns: class five, which includes "natural phenomena, animals, body parts, collective nouns, and undesirable people," and class fourteen, "nouns of abstraction that similarly [reference] collectivities."[116] However Alagoas's Macuca acquired its name, the proximity to places that reference Saint Benedict and Macaco suggests that multiple waves of diaspora left traces in a relatively small section of the landscape.

In 1823, descendants of one of the first European families to secure a sesmaria in Garanhuns sold a large parcel of their land. More than a century after the family had claimed the territory for themselves, vivid remnants of Palmares and diasporic creations built on top of it remained. A map delineating the property shows the Rio Mundaú winding its way to Serra da Barriga fed by two forks: one bringing water from Garanhuns and another stretching toward "Mucambo da Negra," likely the Mocambo da Negra Maria whose origins trace to the early eighteenth century. Papacaça Stream, Palmeira dos Índios, and a serra and stream named Lunga suggest additional continuity from the Palmares era.[117]

Conclusion

One of the most enduring legacies of Palmares and Z/zumbi may be their capacity to appear, disappear, reappear, and take new shape. In 1871, an author grudgingly included a small settlement in Alagoas named Mocambo in a geographic dictionary of the province. The place was "so insignificant that it [wasn't] even worth mentioning," he wrote, if not "for the notability of its valhacoutos [hideaways] in these recent times."[118] Other nineteenth- and twentieth-century maps of Pernambuco and Alagoas reveal more Zumbi place-names, perhaps an indication of toponyms created long after the fall of Palmares, or perhaps simply the first written reference to a much older name. Take, for example, a settlement named Zumbi in the Campos de Ipanema and a small Zumbi Lake not far from the Tamandaré Fort.[119] It is unclear when these toponyms came into existence or who gave either its name.

Whether remembered with reverence, fear, or triumph, or understood simply as parts of the landscape, the names of fugitive settlements along with African terms and ideas persisted and appeared in Alagoas and Pernambuco long after Zumbi died. The traces that the mocambos of Palmares left behind ranged in size from the "continent of Palmares" to tiny, out-of-the-way places called Zumbi. These markers and others that lingered long after Palmares's fall tell intertwined stories of domination, resistance, persistence, and creation. Colonial forts conveyed an imposing sense of power, but the fact that vegetation could easily swallow them—and that they could also became sites of insurrection—suggests the presence of other forces that challenged the captaincy's garrison culture.

The fact that most of the places and place-names discussed in this chapter have rarely made their way into discussions of Palmares, even while Hainam—a place that never existed—was embedded into the written record that scholars have consulted for decades, is instructive for what it tells us about sources, archives, and the writing of history, and how certain stories and places are favored over others. But the preservation and creation of Z/zumbi and other African and diasporic place-names were not simple or straightforward, "bottom-up" processes. In 1881, Pernambuco's director of public works, a French man named Victor Fournié, claimed that a string of shoals off the coast of Recife had been anointed by a decorated naval officer, Manuel Antônio Vital de Oliveira, with "the Black name Zumbi."[120] Born in Recife, Oliveira studied in Rio de Janeiro and traveled in northeast Brazil and France. He died during the War of the Triple Alliance (1864–70), and at least two ships were named for him, including the first Brazilian vessel to circumnavigate the globe.[121] In a description of the northeast coast, Vital de Oliveira also mentioned rocks jutting out of the water near Olinda: the largest one, he wrote, "they call Zumbi."[122] There is no way to know for sure who "they" were, but the pronoun indicates that Oliveira was repeating, not just creating, names. To consider the possibility that he carried descriptions of Zumbi shoals across the Atlantic, or to imagine the tales that sailors in the ship bearing his name took with them around the globe, is to envision the many paths that stories of Palmares and Zumbi traveled, even while their memories were being simultaneously contested, erased from, and embedded in the landscapes of Alagoas and Pernambuco.

CHAPTER NINE   Farther North

While Alagoas and Pernambuco provided shelter for some Palmaristas after 1695, other survivors, as we saw in chapter 5, arrived in more distant places. Directly north of Pernambuco, what are today the states of Paraíba and Rio Grande do Norte retain often unexpected echoes of Palmares. Some of these echoes can be traced through written sources documenting the movement of people, but a fuller story of what happened after 1695 is, once again, accessible through the natural world. As they did in Alagoas and Pernambuco, Palmares survivors and other people of African descent left indelible marks on the landscapes of Paraíba and Rio Grande that suggest how, as people continued to flow into and out of Alagoas and Pernambuco, symbols, icons, and ideas from the seventeenth century were preserved, altered, and replaced, often in surprising places. Paraíba and Rio Grande do Norte expand the spatial horizons for understanding Palmares's enduring legacies, while at the same time underscoring the importance and value of also thinking through and beyond Palmares. Both places also beckon deeper study by scholars of the African Diaspora. Though slavery was widespread in both states, the Trans-Atlantic Slave Trade (TST) and Inter-American Slave Trade (IASTD) databases contain little information about either, but, as scholars and activists are showing with increasing force and volume, both are home to rich diasporic histories.

Two Paths to Paraíba

Paraíba became a captaincy in the late sixteenth century, but its economy developed slowly, and at the turn of the eighteenth century the area was still sparsely populated.[1] The captaincy, its government located in Cidade da Parahyba (known officially as Parahyba do Norte and renamed João Pessoa in the twentieth century), had little political power within the Portuguese empire.[2] During the late eighteenth and early nineteenth centuries, colonization advanced unevenly there. Forests extended inland from the Atlantic coast, eventually giving way to the Brejo, which linked the lush coastal woods with the dry sertão that dominates western and much of southern Paraíba.[3] In the 1640s, a Dutch expedition that attempted to penetrate the Paraíba interior returned empty-handed. During the slog, the group encountered an abandoned settlement where they found items such as "caps and boots," suggesting to the entourage that "Negroes who were forest-dwellers" once lived there.[4] During the eighteenth century, towns and settlements in the region clung to the coast, and even Paraíba's dry, imposing sertão drew Portuguese colonizers before the Brejo did.[5] The Brejo, which can mean "wasteland," was dotted with underbrush, swamps, bogs, and marshes. Frequent rains provided fertile soil but also dense, wild vegetation, which, combined with uneven terrain, delayed attempts to colonize the land. The combination of humid climate and few colonists made it an ideal place for refugees and fugitive settlements. Fugitivity was endemic in Paraíba, especially along the border with Pernambuco. In 1722, the king called for something to be done about the main road that led from Pernambuco to Paraíba, where a whopping 571 arrests had been made that year.[6] Forty years later, "bands of wicked men, composed of Mamelucos, Pretos, and other mixtiços" around Goiana "infested" the border area and troubled authorities who categorized their brazen acts as an uprising.[7]

The population of enslaved people in Paraíba remained lower than neighboring Pernambuco and represents a tiny fraction of Brazil's African Diaspora.[8] Some enslaved people arrived unaccounted for in official records, smuggled to Paraíba to evade taxes, while others were brought from Recife and other ports. There is some evidence to suggest that the enslaved population in Paraíba grew through natural birth, something not thought to have often occurred in Brazil.[9] Ships carrying enslaved people also arrived surreptitiously.[10] Whether born in Paraíba or arriving by ship or by land, the captaincy's enslaved and free Black populations remained smaller than most in Brazil but still outnumbered whites.[11]

Though Paraíba appears infrequently in discussions of Palmares, local lore has both retained connections and invented some. Some histories of Paraíba depict Domingos Jorge Velho as a founding colonist who conquered

Black and Indigenous people, killing some and putting others to work on farms that would give rise to the region's agricultural economy. A late nineteenth-century work of historical fiction (that some might have read as nonfiction) described how, after defeating Palmares, Jorge Velho traveled to Piancó, in western Paraíba, with "many Palmares Blacks," including Zumbi's son, a "Black prince" named "Zombi," who quickly escaped to establish a new quilombo that wreaked violent havoc in the area for years.[12] Though the story is fictional and traffics in racial fantasy and stereotype, Jorge Velho likely did take Palmarista captives to Paraíba, and he was hardly the only Palmares veteran to travel to the captaincy.[13]

While some Palmares survivors arrived in Paraíba as prisoners, others came as refugees, including some who settled in the mocambo named Cumbi (or Cumbe, as it also appears in records), the same word that appears as a toponym in Pernambuco. Scholars have located Paraíba's Cumbi mocambo in different places within Paraíba, but Maria da Vitória Barbosa Lima's research, the most thorough on the topic, points to the municipality of Pilar on the bank of the Rio Paraíba in an area once dominated by Cariri people.[14] The area includes the Serra da Copaoba and is part of the Borborema Plateau, a string of elevated land that stretches from Pernambuco to Rio Grande do Norte and includes Garanhuns.

What we know about Paraíba's Cumbi suggests how the processes of flight and conflict in Palmares could repeat and generate additional permutations of flight and conflict elsewhere. A petition submitted in 1700 by a soldier who accompanied Domingos Rodrigues Carneiro into "the mountains called Cumbê" describes a "powerful" mocambo there populated with "escaped Blacks from Palmar."[15] In 1731, royal officials reported a battle against a force of more than seventy from the mocambo "Cumbi," where colonial soldiers killed four Native people and captured fifty-six Indigenous and seven Black prisoners, leaving the fates (and identities) of ten or so others unknown.[16] Though individuals fleeing Palmares likely helped to found or maintain at least one iteration of Cumbi, the 1731 report suggests the prominent role of Cariris, some of whom had escaped a nearby aldeia, members of one fractured community joining forces with another.

A Constellation of Zumbi Places

Fascinating bits of evidence about the people who journeyed through and dwelled in the Paraíba backlands are also found in Zumbi toponyms. Some of these toponyms have been erased over time, while some of those that exist today have had their origins obscured. The latter is the case for the Distrito de Zumbi, deep in the Paraíban Brejo. Distrito, or District, is an administrative category that usually comprises several neighborhoods in a city, but the District of Zumbi is miles away from the nearest population center. Though officially part of Alagoa Grande, a city with 26,000 residents, Zumbi is for all intents and purposes its own very small, out-of-the-way town.[17] In 2005, under the government of Luiz Inácio Lula da Silva (popularly known as Lula), funds were provided to pave the road connecting Zumbi to the nearest major highway. A concrete post, now stained and weathered, marks the turnoff (see figure 9.1).

There is no consensus among locals about the name's origin. I visited Zumbi in 2018 and met a small group of young men and women who were collaborating to write the first history of their hometown (see figure 9.2). Solange Pereira da Rocha, a university professor and activist in João Pessoa, Paraíba's capital, introduced me to two teachers who were working with their former pupils, among the first in the community to attend college and the founding members of the Comissão História Zumbi (Zumbi History Commission). I met the group at their old high school, named for a large property owner who, one member of the commission told me, worked his grandfather to death. This member would soon become a lawyer; three others have history degrees. A friend who tagged along told me that she was there because "nobody cares about this place. Nobody cares about Zumbi." It is unclear when the Distrito de Zumbi acquired its name. When shown a map from 1868 with Zumbi on it, one of the earliest written references to the town, one member exclaimed approvingly, "Zumbi existed!"

The history and meaning of the Distrito de Zumbi is entwined with Caiana dos Crioulos, a nearby community legally constituted as a quilombo since 1999.[18] At least among those I spoke with in Caiana, Zumbi dos Palmares did not figure significantly in their historical pantheons, which highlight instead women, family lineage, and more general, encompassing memories of slavery. The community retains several origin stories, though, and one of these, recorded by anthropologists in 1998 as part of the process through which the

FIGURE 9.1 Road sign marking the turnoff to Zumbi, Paraíba (2018). *Source*: Author.

FIGURE 9.2 Countryside near Zumbi, Paraíba (2018). *Source*: Author.

community gained legal status, highlights Palmares. According to this version, the community began with "the arrival of Blacks in Alagoa Grande fleeing the massacre of the Quilombo dos Palmares, which explains the existence of the place called Zumbi in the area."[19] When this story is put in conversation with a handful of colonial-era documents, it becomes clear that at least some in the area indeed called features of the surrounding landscape Zumbi since at least the turn of the eighteenth century. Whether named for the Palmares leader or not, the area was home to places that shared his name soon after the mocambos' defeat.

One of these documents comes from 1728, when a man (likely white) named Manuel Correia Pinto secured royal permission to take possession of a "parcel of lands in the Lake named Zumby," which was large enough to contain sizable islands.[20] This parcel was in an area of the Brejo known as the Sertão do Paó. Pinto claimed it was "empty and abandoned"; to gain possession, he promised to make it productive. Thirty years later, two other men (also likely white) requested and were awarded a sesmaria to the east of Pinto's parcel; the sesmarias' borders were marked by several rivers, including one called Zumbi.[21] In all, during the eighteenth century at least six Paraíba sesmarias mention a place or body of water called Zumbi: in addition to the lake and river, a stream, three sítios, and another lake, together forming a remarkable constellation of sites stretching some sixty kilometers east to west, and about fifteen kilometers north to south (see map 9.1).[22]

Fugitives fleeing slavery and on the run for other reasons passed through and settled in the land dotted by the sesmarias, all located in the Brejo or other sparsely inhabited areas.[23] It is possible that the Zumby Lake islands were neither "empty" nor "abandoned," though the suggestion that they were provides another indication about how the definitions of zumbi as "deserted" or "empty" likely evolved. It is interesting to note that spiritually potent fixtures of African landscapes are often located in "isolated or otherwise marginal areas," due in part to their might.[24] A landscape with too many "power points" could be "fraught with danger."[25] While the cluster of Zumbi places may have carried a similar risk, it also might have signaled solace or hope, much as natural places imbued with power in Africa could become "meeting places for diverse groups, like immigrant communities, passing pilgrims or just local seekers for help."[26] If African-born Palmares refugees named the places Zumbi, their thinking may have been informed not only by the traditions and beliefs of their native lands, but also by ideas shared with other groups on the

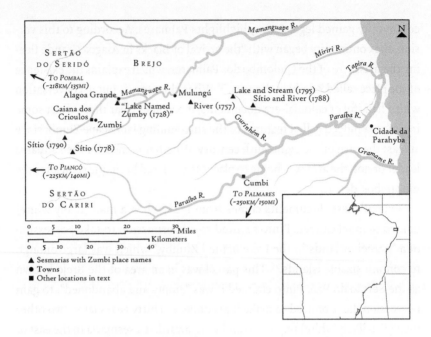

MAP 9.1 Zumbi Place-Names in Paraíba

move, who found naming their new land a crucial part of adapting to it.[27] It is also possible that the Zumbi names in Paraíba predate the arrival of Palmares refugees. As the Dutch expedition to Paraíba's interior leaves no doubt, by the 1640s the area was home to formerly enslaved Africans. If the Zumbi place-names arose before Palmares refugees arrived in the area, their meanings would have had special effect on those fleeing violence in the south, lending familiarity in a new land.

Whether or not they passed through Palmares before arriving in Paraíba, many Africans would have understood that nature spirits could fortify those who, like Palmares refugees unable to properly bury their kin, lacked other forms of protection. Such spirits, writes Ras Michael Brown, "allowed those who lacked ties with named ancestors or who may have come to a region as strangers to still have access to agents of otherworldly powers and to feel attached to the land where they lived."[28] Once again, water would have been especially powerful. Spirits linked with ancestors and death could dwell in water, sometimes by way of powerful leaders who met their end or were laid to rest in, and then dwelled at the bottom of, rivers and lakes.[29] The Kongolese considered rivers to be sacred places dividing the spirit and everyday worlds.[30] It is also significant that, as Monica Schuler points out, posthumous journeys in the diaspora could travel along both "astral and aquatic" paths.[31] In Paraíba, perhaps flight and water merged. It is also possible that water's form shaped its meanings. Waterfalls, currents, and other aquatic elements that were relatively fixed in place, not unlike mountains and other permanent aspects of the landscape, were especially likely to possess spiritual power. The "Lake named Zumby" may have fallen into this category, and it is also possible that the rushing water of rivers and streams held special meaning for refugees and others fleeing slavery and violence, or otherwise on the move.

After the sesmarias, the next written reference to Zumbi in rural Paraíba that I found appears in an 1864 government report that references an arrest order near Alagoa Grande.[32] An 1868 atlas of Brazil (the map I showed the members of the Comissão) contains a dot in the Brejo that identifies "Zumby" as a small town.[33] In the following decades, Zumbi—as a place, a lake, a river, and a stream—flits in and out of official documents. Zumby Lake would eventually disappear from the written record, while the sítios, river, and stream appear occasionally on maps and in newspapers and official documents.

The 1868 atlas locates Zumbi northeast of Alagoa Grande, a possible indication that the small settlement mentioned in the 1864 report moved; most likely though, the atlas was mistaken. The 1914 *Diccionario chorographico do Estado da Parahyba* (*Chorographic Dictionary of the State of Paraíba*) describes Zumby as a river "of certain importance" northeast of Alagoa Grande that empties into the Mamanguape, just above the town of Mulungú, a fascinating word that can refer to a range of trees and holds spiritual meaning in multiple Native Brazilian and African languages.[34] Such multiplicity once again highlights the way that words and spiritual symbols could multiply and engender new markers capable of carrying meanings ranging from hallowed to empty, describing a lake that is home to a powerful spirit or a desolate place to be colonized. Excluded, overlooked, and forgotten, the Zumbi places in Paraíba's Brejo provide a trail that suggests multiple routes and pathways along which surviving Palmaristas and other people, ideas, and figures traveled across time and space, traversing the northeast and surviving into the nineteenth century and beyond.

The way that Z/zumbi continues to inhabit the landscape of the Paraíban interior, often hidden in plain sight, is seen today in Alagoa Grande, a city built around a lake that still figures prominently in its identity. The city's hymn celebrates the lake, said to reflect "the image of the cross."[35] Residents call it Lagoa do Paó, a reference to the colonial designation for the larger

FIGURE 9.3 Alagoa Grande, formerly the "Lake named Zumby" (2018). *Source*: Author.

Sertão do Paó, or simply Big Lake (Alagoa Grande). But though significantly smaller now than it was in 1728, satellite imaging confirms that it is the same body of water once referred to as the "Lake named Zumby." Today, about half of a kilometer across, the lake may have once been nearly six times that size (see figure 9.3). But though diminished by the harsh dryness of the northeastern backlands and the ravages of the earth's warming climate—and with its eighteenth-century name erased from memory—the body of water still stands, silent testament to the state's overlooked diaspora and another marker of Z/zumbi's travels.

On the Margins of a City on the Margins

As they did in Pernambuco and Alagoas, Zumbi place-names emerged not only in rural but also urban areas of Paraíba. Founded in the late sixteenth century, Cidade da Parahyba had a population of eight thousand in 1746 and around 21,000 inhabitants by the 1840s.[36] At the turn of the nineteenth century, a third or more of the city's residents were preto/a, a percentage that is all the more notable considering the likelihood that mixed-race individuals did not figure into that count.[37] There was also a significant presence of Indigenous people, in theory confined to rural aldeias but in reality often moving fluidly across the captaincy and, as we have seen, periodically plotting rebellions.[38]

From the seventeenth through the nineteenth century, Cidade da Parahyba evolved from colonial outpost into provincial capital.[39] The city sits near the mouth of the Rio Paraíba, which winds its way more than three hundred kilometers inland. Nested inside a long inlet, the site, as Portuguese and Spanish explorers found, was ideal both for the access it provided to the ocean and the Rio Paraíba and for the protection the inlet provided against invaders. A smaller river, the Rio Sanhauá, connects the city to the Rio Paraíba and the Atlantic, and it passes in front of Varadouro, Cidade da Parahyba's original port area. Located in the Cidade Baixa (Lower City), the port area had muddy streets, commerce, and the city's jail and pelourinho, a public whipping post often used to punish fugitives and the enslaved; the Cidade Alta (Upper City) was home to most of the city's wealthy residents.[40]

Both areas of the city had vibrant Black communities, including a chapter of the Black Catholic brotherhood, the Irmandade de Nossa Senhora do Rosário dos Homens Pretos, founded in 1711 in the Cidade Alta.[41] Throughout the eighteenth and nineteenth centuries, Blacks circulated within and through the capital. A man named Francisco Gangá gained his freedom and amassed connections and properties in Cidade da Parahyba, probably arriving in Brazil in the late eighteenth century. His last name seems to illustrate the wide circulation of some of the same spiritual and cultural matrices that shaped Palmares but may also or instead be an example of the way that durable words and concepts took hold and became recognizable to a broad array of people. Matheus Guimarães plausibly suggests that the name evoked West Central African nganga, though it is also possible that Gangá (which accents the second /a/, as opposed to nganga, which, in Portuguese and Bantu languages, accents the first /a/) denotes West African origins.[42] In either case, Francisco Gangá was one of many Africans to arrive in or pass through Paraíba. In the 1860s, an enslaved man named Pedro was imprisoned in Cidade da Parahyba. He had run away and been captured four months earlier, having fled from a "place named Zumbi" in Pernambuco, north of Recife, apparently a different location than the ones in Afogados, which lies in Recife, toward the southern end of the city.[43] While we do not know if Pedro also ended up in any of the places named Zumbi in Paraíba, the possibility alone suggests the many diasporic circuits that Blacks created and traced, as well as the potential for those circuits to keep alive and create new meanings of Z/zumbi.

Enslaved people on the run also carved paths into the swamps and dense forest that surrounded Paraíba's capital. Henry Koster, the Portuguese-born son of a British sugar baron who moved to Brazil and became a plantation owner, described the landscape as he looked out at it from the Upper City: "extensive and evergreen woods, bounded by a range of hills, and watered by several branches of the river, with here and there a white washed cottage . . . and these, though they were situated on higher spots of land, were still half concealed by the lofty trees. The cultivated specks were so small, as to be scarcely perceptible."[44] Vegetation thick enough to hide dwellings also provided excellent hiding spots. Well into the second half of the nineteenth century, fugitives sought refuge in the city's outskirts.[45] Night was propitious for clandestine movement of all kinds, and the swamps that skirted the Lower City provided especially effective cover.[46] The city's river-banks, Koster wrote, "are covered with mangroves . . . and they are so close and thick, that there seems to be no outlet."[47] The seemingly impenetrable swamps could provide refuge and formed a central piece of a larger area that by the early nineteenth century, and likely well before, was known as Zumbi. The area is visible on an 1855 map, which shows a "Rua do Zumby" (Zumby Road) in the port area, running to the edge of town toward the swamp. A second, undated nineteenth-century map also places the "Rua de Zumbi" near the docks at the edge of town and adjacent to a large swampy area (mangue), another compelling juxtaposition suggesting how Z/zumbi became associated with deserted places that harbored fugitives—and once again with water as a central feature (see figure 9.4).

The city's Zumbi places were marginalized in visceral ways. In 1862, confronted with a growing trash problem, the Câmara Municipal designated four sites to dump waste, including "Zumbi in Varadouro."[48] Though there is no nineteenth-century demographic data available for the area, it is clear that many people of color worked and lived in Varadouro. An auction in 1864 for a massive estate included property running along the Rua do Zumbi and "twenty-five slaves of all ages."[49] The Rua do Zumbi extended through a larger, vaguely defined area, roughly synonymous with Varadouro and referred to as "Zumbi," "the place called Zumbi," and even the "Port of Zumbi."[50] That place was at once self-evident and shifting, an area that residents knew well,

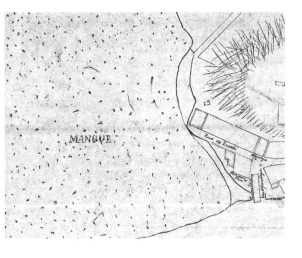

FIGURE 9.4 Detail of *Planta da Cidade da Parahyba do Norte* (18??). Rua de Zumbi runs to the edge of town, right next to the large swamp (Mangue). *Source*: Biblioteca Nacional, Acervo Digital, Cartografia, accessed May 27, 2023, http://objdigital.bn.br/objdigital2 /acervo_digital/div_cartografia /cart539223/cart539223.jpg.

FIGURE 9.5 Cidade da Parahyba's port area, once known as Zumbi (1922). Courtesy of the Acervo da Comissão Permanente de Desenvolvimento do Centro Histórico de João Pessoa.

but whose borders could move and transform. In 1866, an order regulating "the traffic at the port" referenced multiple "Zumbi places" for the unloading of wood, sugarcane, and bricks.[51] In 1869, officials marked the city's outer boundaries by stringing lights around the periphery, including on the Rua do Zumbi. Meant in part to deter deviant behavior, the lights also distinguished the "civilized" capital from the swamp and wild landscape beyond.[52] Like the Zumbi toponyms in rural Paraíba, those in the capital were both powerful and neglected. Once a bustling area, eventually the port fell into disrepair (see figure 9.5).

A Mythical Absence

If Paraíba is a surprising place to find histories of Palmares and Zumbi, Rio Grande do Norte represents an even more unlikely setting. Histories of Palmares rarely mention the state, and its own dominant historical narratives have all but erased people of African descent. The erasure of Blackness is at odds with not only the large proportion of norte-rio-grandenses (people from Rio Grande do Norte) who today self-identify as pardo/a, but also the fact that Rio Grande do Norte is home to more than thirty federally recognized quilombos.[53] Of its three million people, nearly 60 percent of the population identifies as nonwhite, though most of that population call themselves pardo/a—less than 5 percent of the state identify as preto/a.[54] After the Portuguese established colonial rule in the late sixteenth century, the area passed through Dutch hands and for much of the colonial period was administratively subordinate to Pernambuco, Paraíba, or Bahia.[55] As a subordinate region with a relatively small sugar economy and no precious metals, Rio Grande do Norte acquired few enslaved people and, the story goes, consequently never saw Black communities of any import materialize. In fact, the area was and is home to a diaspora that is audacious in its very being—its existence shattering Rio Grande do Norte's mythical whiteness—and also its expanse, which stretches from coast to sertão, and slashes north, south, east, and west across the backlands.[56]

In 1650, a Danish soldier took four Black fugitives who had lived in the Paraíba interior "for many years" to Rio Grande do Norte, where he sold them into slavery.[57] They may have arrived in Brazil through Recife; though more than one hundred and fifty kilometers away from Pernambuco, Rio

Grande do Norte (known simply as Rio Grande until 1737) was the destination of enslaved people who escaped bondage in Recife and other parts of the captaincy.[58] Portuguese colonization into the Rio Grande sertão generally followed the paths of rivers that connected the coast to the interior and helped shape the captaincy's borders.[59] These backlands became war theaters and sites of colonial incursion—and eventually home to enslaved people and those fleeing slavery, groups whose existence scholars would deny centuries later. Many of the first colonizers of the backlands came from Pernambuco or Paraíba, likely often bringing enslaved people with them.[60] There are reports of mocambos in Seridó, a region in the southern part of the state, dating to the early eighteenth century.[61] During the second half of the century, the Portuguese viewed the backlands with growing interest, seeking to colonize it with cattle farms, whose owners would dislocate Indigenous people and function as bulwarks against encroachment from other Europeans.[62] Salt deposits along the Açu and Apodi Rivers provided additional motive and, eventually, lucrative business. At the turn of the nineteenth century, enslaved people composed a full quarter of the captaincy's population, and free and enslaved pardo/as and preto/as outnumbered branco/as.[63] Nonetheless, the foregoing wisdom, passed down to the present day, was summarized by the nineteenth-century priest and author Manuel Aires do Casal, who stated simply, "Blacks are few in this province."[64]

Names of the Land

It is difficult to overstate the influence that Luís Câmara de Cascudo (1898–1986) had in shaping this and other narratives about Rio Grande do Norte. He was one of the state's most famous and widely read writers, a white historian and folklorist who published dozens of books over a long, decorated career. In the capital, Natal, he is memorialized with street names, statues, and other dignities often reserved for military or political heroes. While, on the one hand, a pioneer in writing about Black and Indigenous culture and folklore in Brazil, on the other, Cascudo was also adamant that in Rio Grande do Norte slavery had been inconsequential and, as a result, the captaincy received few Africans.[65] Other dismissive assertions flowed from this belief. He wrote, for example, "We did not have quilombos or Black rebellions in Rio Grande do Norte."[66] Nonetheless, Cascudo catalogued a rich collection of toponyms in the book *Nomes da terra* (*Names of the Land,* 1968), many of which seem to counter his own thesis about the nonexistence of Blacks in Rio Grande and, more importantly for our purposes, provide glimpses of Palmares far from its original home.[67]

Among the numerous toponyms that reference African and diasporic elements, in Seridó, an area called Mulungú sits near a quilombo community, suggestively echoing the convergence of Mulungú and Zumbi in Paraíba.[68] Mulungú also graces other streams and mountains across Rio Grande do Norte.[69] Quilombo, in Pau dos Ferros, suggests an additional path and likely destination for people fleeing slavery.[70] Cascudo also identifies multiple places called Cumbe: a lake in Assú, a place in Ceará-Mirim, a stream and two small mountain ridges in Caraúbas and Martins, a location at the headwaters of the Apodi River that dates to at least 1754.[71] Echoing the processes of appropriation in Alagoas and Pernambuco, at least one engenho owner named their plantation Zumbi.[72]

Sesmarias reveal an even broader landscape of names associated with those who lived outside of slavery's grasp and provide some of the clearest glimpses of Palmares afterlives, many bunched in southwest Rio Grande, on the border with Ceará (see map 9.2). In 1733, Francisco Teixeira de Seixas received a sesmaria for land in "the place called Mocambo" that also included a stream with the same name.[73] Twenty years later, Colonel Bento Fernandes de Lima received a land grant in an area called Cumbe.[74] He had already secured a separate tract of land, which referenced a small stream named Couto.[75] Some seventeenth- and eighteenth-century observers called Palmares and other fugitive settlements "couto," which Antonio Vieyra's 1773 Portuguese-English dictionary translates as "a place of refuge or security, a shelter."[76] Rafael Bluteau defined it as a "refuge" and also "a settlement whose distance from villages and cities, has its own judges and lands . . . and is a place . . . where debtors and miscreants gather."[77] Cascudo also noted a "place" (lugar) and mountain a bit north of the sesmarias named Couto.[78] Other documents from the eighteenth and early nineteenth centuries reference sítios named Mocambo (and Mucambo) and Couto (and Coito) in the Rio Grande–Ceará borderlands, and Cascudo describes a 1737 sesmaria in the same area, with land occupied by "fugitive Blacks who plant[ed] banana trees" and manioc.[79] These place-names are important for their location—in Rio Grande do Norte's western frontier, deep in the backlands of a captaincy where people of African descent are said to have hardly stepped foot, we find places named Cumbe,

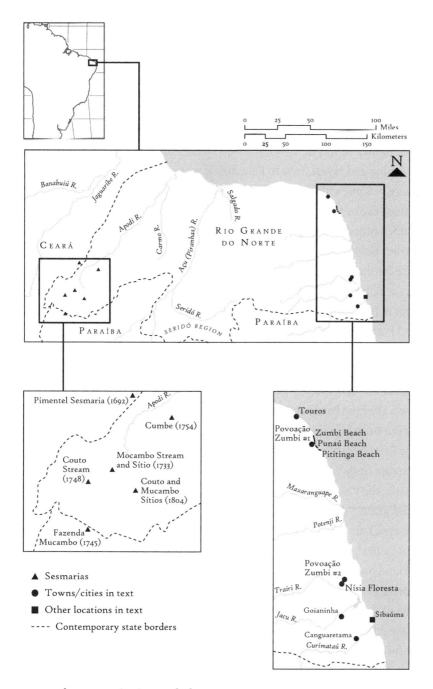

MAP 9.2 Place-Names in Rio Grande do Norte

Mocambo, and Couto, marking the presence of fugitive communities and, at least in some cases, memories of Palmares.

The Wealth They Carried

The names found in Rio Grande do Norte's landscape take on additional meaning and reveal links to Palmares if we consider the people who settled there.[80] Some military men gained ownership of land in areas whose place-names evoke fugitive slave settlements. Seixas's 1733 sesmaria in "the place named Mocambo" also references a riacho named "Mocambo" as well as an earlier petition by his relatives, who were descendants of Antônio da Rocha Pita for the "sítio called Mocambo."[81] There were several Rocha Pita families in the northeast, but it is almost certain that Sebastião da Rocha Pita, the author of *Historia da America Portugueza*, was part of the same branch as Antônio and Francisco.[82]

Other connections to Palmares are more direct. Manuel Barbalho de Lira, as reward for his effort to "take the battle to the rebel Blacks escaped from Palmares," successfully petitioned along with twenty-four other henriques soon after the battle at Serra da Barriga to be transferred from Pernambuco to Rio Grande, where they settled on "fertile" land. Other Black veterans of the Palmares wars came, as did many white veterans, who helped administer the captaincy.[83] In 1692, just to the north of what would become Seixas's sesmaria, the Palmares war veteran Luis da Silveira Pimentel received a massive land grant.[84] Decades later, as we saw in chapter 6, the man claiming to be his son, Luiz Ferreira de Moraes, would receive the last sesmaria in Palmares, but in 1692, Pimentel leveraged his extensive service to secure a large tract of land on the Rio Grande–Ceará border. The long list of exploits that he reported to the Crown included two battles against Zumbi.[85] Pimentel was just one of many decorated officers who battled the rebel Blacks of Palmares and traveled far and wide—Bahia, Pernambuco, Angola, Portugal, Mecca, Goa— before settling in Rio Grande do Norte.[86] As officers and soldiers moved to Rio Grande do Norte, the Palmares wars provided a model for conquering and "populating" the area.[87] These military men would also carry spiritual practices that the Church deemed to be witchcraft, including bolsas de mandingas, calundu, and divination.[88]

Bernardo Vieira de Melo was among those who traveled between Pernambuco and Rio Grande do Norte. After fighting against Palmares, he became captain major of Rio Grande, a position that he held for six years (1695–1701). Eight years later, he retraced his steps, becoming sargento-mor of the Terço dos Palmares.[89] He owned land in Assú, where he also built a military outpost, supported by the henriques who moved to the area.[90] Vieira de Melo's connections to the Rio Grande sertão were fortified by familial bonds. He married twice, the second time to the daughter of one of the first sesmeiros to claim land west of the Rio Açu.[91] Vieira de Melo and members of his family also served as godparents to two children of Teodósio da Rocha, one of his most trusted officers, whom, according to Vieira de Melo, the Indigenous people of Assú "respect and love very much."[92] Rocha, described in one colonial document as "trigueiro" (wheat-colored), attained the rank of captain in Assú, where he enslaved Indigenous and Black people and established a small family dynasty.[93] Vieira de Melo gave much of the land he conquered in Rio Grande to family members and other elites, whose support he depended on to consolidate and wield power.[94]

Other Palmares veterans also secured positions in Rio Grande.[95] Manuel da Rocha Lima's application to become infantry captain attests that before serving in Rio Grande, he fought against "the negro Zomby."[96] The record presented on behalf of Gabriel de Góes in 1699 for a similar position recounted how he fought against Zumbi and his forces at Serra da Barriga, also highlighting the hundreds of Palmaristas who plunged to their death during the battle.[97] Though, as we saw in chapter 2, João de Montes won the position, Góes would become the "patriarch of an important family in the northeast, where he left numerous descendants."[98]

One of Rio Grande do Norte's most prominent family lineages descend from none other than Manuel Lopes Galvão, whose boasts and distortions about killing Zumbi exceeded perhaps all other veterans. Branches of the Lopes Galvão family settled all over Rio Grande do Norte. Lopes's brother Cipriano, who received a hábito, served in military efforts across the captaincy.[99] Other branches of the family owned plantations. Cipriano Lopes Pimentel, possibly Manuel's nephew, owned land in Goianinha. In 1720, he left behind an estate there along with fifteen enslaved people, including several born in Brazil, four from Africa, and one Indigenous woman.[100] Some members of the Lopes Galvão clan owned land and enslaved people nearby. Cipriano Lopes Galvão, also likely Manuel's nephew, settled in Seridó, founding the town Currais-Novos.[101] When his wife died there in 1793, she left behind twenty-four enslaved people.[102]

Devils in the Water

While Palmares veterans settled or journeyed throughout Rio Grande do Norte, and while Couto and Mocambo place-names are concentrated in the western interior, a number of Zumbi toponyms hug the coast. In *Nomes da terra*, Cascudo lists four places named Zumbi in Rio Grande do Norte, including a beach and "settlement" connected to a small community of Black fishers and farmers about sixty kilometers up the coast from Natal. There was also a Zumbi settlement in Nísia Floresta, forty kilometers south of Natal, and a Zumbi Lake in Goianinha, twenty kilometers further south (see map 9.2).[103] There are few historical traces or evidence today of the lake, whose ethereal nature may be due to nature itself. One author described it as one of "many" lakes in the state that were "by rule, really just simple ponds, whose waters rise in the winter [but] do not resist prolonged droughts."[104] In the dry northeast, this small body of water may have disappeared over time, ravaged by an already harsh climate whose effects have been accelerated by an increasingly hot planet. Slightly more information is available about the town and beach called Zumbi. Like the Distrito de Zumbi in rural Paraíba, Rio Grande do Norte's Zumbi town is largely unknown outside (and even within) the state, though its proximity to the coast and the nearby Praia Zumbi (Zumbi Beach), a beautiful vacation spot, makes it more outwardly visible than Paraíba's landlocked Distrito (see figures 9.6 and 9.7).[105] Once part of nearby Touros, today the town belongs to the municipality of Rio do Fogo (River of Fire). A local census taken in 1832 counted 32 dwellings and 148 people.[106] For centuries, the area has generated stories about magical, otherworldly, or otherwise mysterious forces, which may contain clues about the origins of its name. Cascudo provides a frustratingly fleeting glimpse into the town's origins when he writes that "in 1777, Manuel Gomes Tição possessed [possuía] the sítio Zumbi in PUNAHU beach."[107]

Beginning near Touros and running south parallel to the coast almost halfway to Natal, a shelf of reefs and sandbars forms the eastern edge of the São Roque Canal. Manuel Antônio Vital de Oliveira, the naval officer who

FIGURE 9.6 The main road into Zumbi, Rio Grande do Norte (2019). *Source*: Author.

FIGURE 9.7 Praia Zumbi, Rio Grande do Norte (2019). *Source*: Author.

wrote about the Zumbi rock and shoals off the coast of Pernambuco, described Zumbi Point, with "low, red-colored reefs, covered in vegetation and close to the beach" and not far from Petitinga (also Pititinga) Point.[108] For centuries, the treacherous currents, and the reefs and sandbars themselves, felled ships and sent the fear of God and the devil into sailors, who spoke in awe of the "small, vigorous reefs" named "Zumbi or Hell."[109] Manuel Lopes's brother Cipriano was involved in a shipwreck in the São Roque Canal.[110] A nineteenth-century Spanish guide to the coast of Brazil described "a small reddish gully" off the coast of Zumbi "called Reefs of Hell."[111]

In May 1694, the slave ship *Nossa Senhora dos Remédios e Almas, e Santo Antônio* appeared off the shore of Pititinga Beach. The vessel had departed nearly a year earlier from the Azores, stopping in Cacheu, on the Upper Guinea Coast, where it loaded captives into the hold and departed for Brazil.[112] The crew intended to deliver the enslaved people to Maranhão, but the vessel took on water and had to change course. Strong currents foiled attempts to land in Paraíba and carried the ship north to Pititinga, where it settled, bobbing perilously in the waves. While the sailors used a small launch to shuttle the captives and cargo to shore, the task of fixing the ship was assigned to the boatswain, who was later accused not only of failing to save the boat but of intentionally trying to sink it. He told others that "there were evil things" onboard and that he had heard and seen voices "that spoke and told hideous things." After asking one sailor "to come see the devils that crept" in the hold, he ordered the crew to destroy the ship.[113] Though the sailors refused, that night, as they slept, he smashed holes in the side of the vessel. Only with help from some residents who pitched in to help was the crew able to save clothes, supplies, and several Black women who were onboard.[114] The boatswain was imprisoned, but nearly two months passed before the ship's captain secured a new ship and departed for Maranhão, human cargo once again in tow. During that time, the crew and captives of the *Nossa Senhora* shuttled between land and sea, and between Natal and Pititinga. It is unclear exactly how many enslaved people were sent to Natal or whether any escaped, but the long, chaotic ordeal almost surely presented opportunities to do so. Though the ship's West African captives may not have called the spirits that haunted the vessel "zumbi," at some point, the nearby treacherous waters, shoals, and the land itself acquired that name.

Conclusion

Inscribed into bodies of water, rural landscapes, and urban spaces, Z/zumbi arrived and lived on in Paraíba and Rio Grande do Norte long after the man of the same name was killed far to the south. Short of the most explicit renderings, rarely can we be certain of exactly what the word evoked. But we do know—beyond doubt—that Z/zumbi appeared in Paraíba within years of Palmares's fall and throughout the eighteenth and nineteenth centuries. Knowing that Palmaristas fled and were taken to Paraíba, we can be certain that they carried the memory of Zumbi dos Palmares with them, likely imbuing the landscape with that memory as they fled. The multiple meanings of Z/zumbi complicate linear narratives, especially when taking a long historical view. Even if first named after Zumbi dos Palmares, each place also came to embody other definitions—a deserted, eerie place; a swamp at the edge of the capital; a lake and river deep in the Brejo: all places that fugitive slaves inhabited. Zumbi dos Palmares, then, may have become, or also helped give rise to, other forms of zumbi, dark areas on the edge of, or far beyond, "civilization," watery swamps, deadly currents, and other aquatic bodies and forces. The prevalence of water is especially noteworthy, suggesting the transfer and adaptation of meanings passed down from proto-Bantu origins and intelligible to a large number of people.

Similar histories mark the land and water of Rio Grande do Norte. From Luís da Silveira Pimentel on the far western border to Bernardo Vieira de Melo in Natal and the descendants of Manuel Lopes Galvão, who settled throughout the captaincy, those who fought against Zumbi or knew someone who did could be found all over. They were not the only ones whose paths traversed Rio Grande do Norte. Enslaved people, fugitives, shipwrecks, and free people arrived and passed through as well, some surely carrying memories and stories of Palmares and Zumbi. This diverse set of individuals underscores the way that the meanings of Z/zumbi, and of diaspora itself, were shaped from inside and out. The fact that nonwhite soldiers and officers fought in Palmares and Assú and then, like any veteran, carried stories, memories, wealth, and rumors into their postwar lives also blurs the very categories of "inside" and "out."

But blurred lines of affiliation do not preclude broader clarity. Archival documentation about Black lives in Rio Grande do Norte are available only in bits and pieces, a great contrast to the stacks of documents that Manuel Lopes and other white men compiled as they fought for and secured wealth and prestige for themselves and their heirs. So too does the property that Lopes left his descendants contrast with the way that Black and Indigenous inheritances of all kinds have been systematically erased over time in Rio Grande do Norte. Given the long histories of physical violence and discursive erasure, the preponderance of Zumbi place-names in Paraíba and Rio Grande do Norte is especially significant. But while the land may speak, in these places it tells stories that rarely have a complete arc or satisfying ending.[115] Nonetheless, histories of Paraíba's and Rio Grande do Norte's audacious African diasporas also reveal Z/zumbi in surprising locales and indicate larger Black worlds found in out-of-the-way places, testament that the land does not just speak but also remembers and carries its own forms of inheritances.

V   DEATHS AND REBIRTHS

Killing Zumbi
(Again)

If spirits, people, and the natural world carried memories of Palmares and Zumbi into and across the eighteenth century, entrenching them not only in Pernambuco and Alagoas but also in more distant and surprising locales, the overarching story of Palmares's dissemination from the nineteenth century forward seems, at least at first sight, to be more conventional. In broad outline, the story is already known: via the written word, authors spurred a kind of revival, drawing especially on Rocha Pita's *Historia da America Portugueza*, to conjure Palmares and big-Z Zumbi with increasing frequency. The trend picked up speed after independence, thanks to regional elites who sought to insert their own local histories into nascent narratives about national history, and reached an inflection point around 1888, when slavery was abolished, and 1889, when Brazil replaced its monarchy with a republic.[1] Upon closer examination, this apparently linear process was, in fact, more complicated: these writers with access and influence within Brazilian and transatlantic print cultures—possessing an insatiable urge to winnow, narrow, and define—were conducting their research while popular meanings of Zumbi and zumbi proliferated (glimpses of which we have already seen in the previous chapters). As a result, the histories of Palmares and Z/zumbi simultaneously grew and shrank. This chapter describes these processes, focusing especially on the 1800s but also examining how ideas from that century spilled into the next.

Writing from privileged positions, the mainly white, mainly male authors actively curated information and material that passed through their hands. Their views indelibly shaped knowledge of Palmares and Z/zumbi, but they were also informed by what had come before and were undeniably influenced by the stories of anonymous informants, such as the enslaved Black caregivers whom Raimundo Nina Rodrigues mentioned and summarily dismissed. The myth that Zumbi died by suicide featured prominently in nineteenth-century discourse. Near the end of the century and then more forcefully during the twentieth century, authors such as Rodrigues, Mario Behring, and Edison Carneiro showed the story to be false, but it nonetheless persisted long after their refutations.[2] Part of the suicide story's appeal for writers intent on conveying cohesive and forward-moving historical narratives lay in the finality that it provided. However strained the logic, the idea that Zumbi took his own life also functioned to absolve the Portuguese of killing him.

The suicide narrative also enjoyed rebirths outside Brazil. In 1918, a University of California history professor, Charles E. Chapman, likened Palmares to Numantia, the ancient Iberian civilization whose inhabitants were said to have committed suicide en masse in the face of a Roman siege.[3] Melville Herskovits used Chapman in his field-shifting 1941 book, *The Myth of the Negro Past*. "Most of [Palmares's] warriors committed suicide," Herskovits wrote, citing Chapman, "and those who were captured, being deemed too dangerous to be reenslaved, were killed." Herskovits was well acquainted with the work of Edison Carneiro, a trailblazing Afro-Brazilian intellectual who demonstratively rejected the suicide narrative a few years later, but the same passage remained in subsequent printings of Herskovits's influential text.[4] Passed down from Rocha Pita through regional elites, the mythical story of Palmares's heroic finality continued to grow.

The suicide story emphasized Palmares's and Zumbi's conclusion and absolute destruction. Other nineteenth-century accounts delimited the boundaries around Palmares and Z/zumbi by cataloguing definitions of little-z zumbi in the course of extricating Zumbi dos Palmares from religious, spiritual, and folkloric meanings. This process, marked by secularization and division, represents another act of violence: the discursive separation of a complex web of meanings into isolated parts. The published authors were not, of course, somehow incapable of subtle or complex thought, nor did their informants never think or say anything simplistic. The fact that the words of Rodrigues's amas found their way into his writing illustrates how the lines separating scholars and their oral sources were permeable, a point reinforced by individuals such as Carneiro, who traveled in multiple circles. But broadly speaking, different epistemologies guided published writers and many of the people whose ideas, histories, memories, and beliefs they wrote about. Rodrigues and other authors knew what they wrote about Palmares and Z/zumbi to be true because their evidence came from privileged access to informants (whose knowledge they valued but were also prone to overrule) and because they themselves carried prestigious positions and titles, with access to libraries of written work published by other scholars on both sides of the Atlantic. Those who inherited and learned about Palmares and Z/zumbi from family, healers, friends, and personal experience based their knowledge on different forms of evidence.

The processes of representing Palmares and Zumbi are also stories of literacy, a key flashpoint in Brazil. The republic, founded in 1889, was putatively a democracy, but literacy was a requirement to be eligible to vote all the way until 1985; as late as 1950, fewer than half of all Brazilians knew how to read and write.[5] For much of Brazil's history, the majority of the population, blocked from formal political participation, created, preserved, and altered traditions and histories orally. Authors who wrote about Z/zumbi (and other diasporic figures and histories) kept some of those traditions and histories in view via the written word but, by doing so, sought to control them, silencing some and repackaging others.

One of the most prominent aspects of the texts shaped by the interplay of these different systems of knowing and conveying knowledge is the reduction of dense meanings into smaller bits, and the stripping of manifold meanings into spare, disconnected parts.[6] It is therefore all the more notable that Z/zumbi nonetheless remained remarkably polysemic, even in the hands of writers otherwise intent on separating and isolating different meanings. Also significant is how some meanings disappeared or were marginalized while others arose or persisted. While the processes that preserved Zumbi as an iconic male warrior figure involved the silencing of other figures and definitions, his enduring meaning and power leave no doubt about the significance that his singularity held—and continues to hold—for Africans and people of African descent during and long after his heyday. The predominant histories and definitions of Palmares and Zumbi that survive today were created collaboratively, even if the parties involved often operated with different forms of evidence and understandings and regularly found themselves in disagreement or conflict.

"Often Confused in the Brazilian Tradition"

The way that the meanings of Z/zumbi could seem to grow and shrink at once in nineteenth-century writing is seen in a note that appeared in the *Diário de Pernambuco* in 1857. The author regularly used "quilombo" and "Zumbi" to lampoon political rivals, a practice that others employed elsewhere. Now "everyone," he wrote, "wants to know what Zumbi means. Some say that it is a kind of monkey from the Coast of Africa, others that it is the name of a God among the heathens, others that it is the name of an evil spirit, and others, at last, that it is the devil in the general language of Congo. Very well, but it is none of these things, or it is all of that at the same time."[7] After recounting a short chronology of Palmares, which concluded with Zumbi and the other Palmaristas killing themselves, the author wrote, "Even today, the Blacks from the Coast of Africa call ghosts and the possessed—that is, those who say they are possessed by the devil—or the devil in person, Zumbi."[8] Though other writers would similarly enumerate definitions, few would glide as easily between declaring Z/zumbi to be "none of these things" or "all of that at the same time." Instead, most nineteenth-century writers would winnow Palmares and remove it from the multifaceted Z/zumbi, insisting in strong terms what Z/zumbi was and was not.

In 1888, the year that slavery was abolished, Sílvio Romero lamented that Brazilian scholars had not paid more attention to African languages and religion, and the same year João Ribeiro published a short entry on "the Black element" in his *Diccionario grammatical*. With these two contributions, writes linguist Yeda Pessoa de Castro, "timidly began the [first] chapter of the history [of systematically studying] the African roots of Brazil's Portuguese language."[9] Though the year was, indeed, a watershed, there had been some interest in African language prior to 1888. Before and after abolition, some of the authors who pioneered this field of study homed in on Z/zumbi, often intent on completing two tasks that would seem to be at cross-purposes— listing as many definitions as possible and then rejecting a number of them by explaining faults and flaws in the work of other scholars. Doing so allowed writers to demonstrate vast knowledge—they had read the work of their peers and also had special access to historical texts and popular meanings and expressions—that was deep and precise enough to allow them to correct those peers, who were, of course, at the same time, competitors.

One scholar who sought to collate and reject meanings of Zumbi with the end of providing an authoritative definition was Alfredo do Vale Cabral, a functionary at the National Library in Rio who actively collected definitions for a compendium on folklore and "supernatural beings." Cabral's collection, first published in 1884 in the *Gazeta Litteraria*, included an eight-point definition of Z/zumbi with entries from Angola and Brazil—spirits, religious beings, and supernatural monsters—as well as an additional twelve inches of text about Zambi. "Zumbi," Cabral wrote, "is a very popular being in Brazil, inherited from Africans."[10] He then laid out nine definitions of the word, enumerated with the letters A through I.[11] The first definition could have been taken directly from a seventeenth- or eighteenth-century Inquisition or missionary account:

a. Among the Angolans, people who die, soul from the other world.

The second and third entries added a more recent wrinkle: supernatural beings that haunt city streets:

b. In the oral tradition of other African nations, ghost, Devil, who wanders the streets at night. . . . [Blacks say] . . . *Zumbi walks with him*, that is, the Devil travels inside his body.
c. In Rio de Janeiro, "*Zumbi da Meia Noite* [Midnight Zumbi]" was a "phantom that wanders late at night through the streets."

Cabral's fourth definition, which quotes a well-known song, illustrates how deeply Z/zumbi had become engrained in popular culture:

d. Zumbi, werewolf
And other goblins,
Have rosaries
For sale.

The next entry, drawn from an informant, returned the reader to the other side of the Atlantic: *e.* "African term (Benguella) that means soul." The next drew them once again back to Brazil, this time with a poignant account of a bird provided by a pharmacist from Minas Gerais:

f. [The] soul of the Black transformed into a bird that lingers at dusk at the edge of farms, pastures or in deserted places, wailing and calling passers-by by name, and sometimes at mid-day it sings and laments the life it lived as a slave and says: *Zumbi . . . biri . . . ri . . . poor thing! . . . Zumbi . . . biri . . . ri . . . poor thing! . . .* [12]

For the eighth entry, Cabral crossed the Atlantic again twice, first via an 1881 account by Portuguese naval officers Hermenegildo Capelo and Roberto Ivens of their expedition in Angola, a source frequently used by contemporaries in Brazil and still regularly consulted today, and then through unnamed informants in Brazil:

> g. Capello and Ivens, referring to the Blacks in the region of Dombe Grande [near Benguela], report that Blacks pour alcohol on the ground, "'in order to sate . . . the *zumbi* or *n'zumbi* (soul from the other world) . . .' In Brazil, when African women eat or drink water or alcohol, they place the first portions on the ground and when asked why they do this, they respond *it is for the saint*, who is close to them. Some Brazilian-born Black women do the same and say *it is for S[ão] Cosme and S[ão] Damião*, two saints for whom Black slaves have a predilection and whom they ask to intervene to secure their liberty."[13]

Though once again mediated, here we gain another glimpse at Z/zumbi's sacred meanings and another potential connection to saints, revered this time in Angola and by Black women born in Brazil.

For the final two entries, Cabral drew from (and critiqued) no fewer than six authors, first quoting a study published in 1880 by the philologist Antonio Joaquim de Macedo Soares, who defined zumbi as follows:

> h. "Word that the amas use to frighten children who cry: 'Look, the Zumbi!' Others say: 'Look, the Bicho [creature]!' Are they synonyms? Could this be the same as the Portuguese Papão [monster]? It seems so."

Like Rodrigues, Soares used unnamed Black female caregivers as his source. Where Rodrigues explicitly corrected the women by asserting that Zumbi dos Palmares's real name was Zambi and thus had no connection to any monstrous being named zumbi, Soares simply noted that Zumbi was the "title of the leader of the famous mucambo dos Palmares" and then described how the Black caregivers used the word to scare children.[14] Determined to distinguish Zumbi from zumbi, Cabral excised Soares's first sentence, severing the two definitions. Cabral also maintained that while zumbi could "serve to intimidate children," it was not synonymous with other terms. There was another figure, "*Tutú-Zambê* (or *Cambê*?)," in Bahia that might be similar, Cabral offered, but he did not know enough about it to suggest a firm link.[15] Still in the same entry (for *h*), Cabral continued:

In Africa, there is a mount called *Mulundú Zumbi*, which may be translated . . . as *Monte das Almas* [Mount of Souls, or Souls' Mount]. And it is said that this name comes from the laments and wails heard there from the Souls of the Other World.[16]

Here, Cabral relies on three authors for his translation of "Mulundú": Henrique de Beaurepaire-Rohan, whom Rodrigues also cited in dismissing the stories he heard from his amas; José Zephyrino de Menezes Brum, who worked with Cabral at the National Library; and Bernardo Maria de Cannecattim, a Capuchin monk who published two Mbundu primers in the early nineteenth century.[17] What Cabral called Mulundú Zumbi, European sources called Mulundú (and Maloundou) Zambi, or Zambi Mountain, the dormant volcano in Angola that residents considered an entrance for spirits into the other world.[18] Though all of his sources called the mountain "Zambi," Cabral uses "Zumbi," offering no explanation for the switch. In the final entry (*i*) for zumbi, Cabral disputed a definition offered by Silvio Romero, another prominent scholar, who, citing the same popular song that Cabral reproduced, translated zumbi as "werewolf." This was incorrect, Cabral contended. Though the song, which struck Cabral as "pretty old," linked the two, "The significance [of Zumbi as rendered by Romero] is not exact and neither are [zumbi and werewolf] synonyms."[19]

After enumerating his definitions of zumbi, Cabral turned to Zambi. "It is the word that Blacks from Angola use for the supreme being, God . . . and if they are asked about impossible or mysterious things, they say: Zambi knows."[20] He first cites two authors, whose works bracket the eighteenth century: Pedro Dias, the author of the 1697 Kimbundu primer *Arte da lingua de Angola*, and Cannecattim.[21] Cabral then jumps to Capelo and Ivens, quoting an encounter they had in Tchiboco, seven hundred kilometers inland from Benguela, with a local man who showed them a wooden object of "a small figure representing a man with outstretched arms, and above another that looked like a small bird, said to be the *N'gana N'Zambi* (*Senhor Deus* [God Almighty])."[22]

Several details about the figure that did not make their way into Cabral's account are worth recounting. The man's outstretched arms were likely meant to evoke the Christian cross (see figure 10.1). To some, the bird may have represented the Catholic Holy Spirit, while to others it was a "protector" against evil spirits.[23] When Capelo and Ivens asked their informant about the object's

N'GANA N'ZAMBI

FIGURE 10.1 Drawing of the figure given to Capelo and Ivens (1881). *Source*: Capelo and Ivens, *De Benguella*, 1:104.

provenance, he answered, "An ambaquista had brought it from the *calunga*."[24] Ambaquistas were lettered and worldly Africans, who considered themselves "staunch Christians" and served as crucial intermediaries for European explorers.[25] Many trafficked in enslaved humans.[26] Calunga, as we have seen, has multiple meanings. Capelo and Ivens translated the word into Portuguese as "mar," or "sea," which may suggest that the informant was referring to the Atlantic Ocean, though it is also possible that he instead spoke of a "great water" in West Central Africa.[27] The object bears close resemblance to another Zambi figure from northern Angola, which suggests that the figure presented to Capelo and Ivens originated in Africa.[28] Nonetheless, the references to the ambaquista and calunga raise the fascinating question of whether this object or other manifestations of Zambi in West Central Africa were shaped by ideas and people in Brazil.

The flow of people, objects, and information from Brazil to Africa was of less interest to Cabral and his colleagues than what traveled in the other direction. Cabral reproduced another anecdote from Capelo and Ivens's travels. At a farm near where they were given the wooden object, residents called Capelo, on account of his white beard, by the same name assigned to the bird: "N'gana N'Zambi."[29] Cabral supplemented this information with his own informal ethnographic work in Brazil. He asked a "Black man born in Angola how to say God in his language, and he responded, *Zambi*." When Cabral asked what N'gana N'Zambi meant, the man pointed to the sky and said, "Senhor Deus" (God Almighty).[30] These examples helped Cabral set the record straight. "Zumbi and Zambi," he wrote, "are often confused in the Brazilian tradition, but as we can see, they reflect different things."[31] Zambi was a singular higher power, while Z/zumbi referred to the panoply of smaller ghostlike beings. Drawing a final example from Brazil to seal his point, he asserted, "When a slave master or overseer, someone they should respect, approaches, Blacks say frightened and quickly: Zambi's coming!" This fact, along with the anecdote about the Angolans calling Capelo N'Gana N'Zambi "proved" the same point that Rodrigues would later make: that Zumbi dos Palmares's real name was, in fact, Zambi.[32]

Cabral's collection of definitions and assertions epitomizes the power and challenge of works from his era. He was correct to distinguish Z/zumbi and Zambi, as West Central Africans and Black Brazilians clearly also did, though the way he excluded Zumbi and zumbi from the history of Palmares is indicative of the rigid lines drawn during the era. Cabral and his peers recorded ideas and definitions shared with them by Black people in Brazil, such as the women who cared for Soares and Rodrigues and the unnamed "Black man born in Angola" who defined N'gana N'Zambi for Cabral, while also censoring them, as Rodrigues did. The list Cabral compiled also illustrates how many meanings had been attached to Z/zumbi and Zambi by the second half of the nineteenth century—even if, in his final declaration on the words' definitive definitions, he attempts to wield such multitude both to establish his authority and then to set aside such multitude. Of course, though, he did not have the last word.

"And What Is the Zumbi?"

Cabral's report was followed two months later in the *Gazeta* by a response from a reader who called himself M. S., undoubtedly Antonio Joaquim de Macedo Soares, who provided several of his own lengthy additions and corrections. Of Zambi, he wrote, "[It] is the spirit that no one sees. It is the thing from the other world, the soul separated from the body or that never had a body. It is the magical, the *quid incognitam*, the voice of thunder, the brilliance of lightning, potent force of nature, of which the poor Blacks have an understanding as perfect as ours of our God, the trinity, unified, equally mysterious and unknowable."[33] Soares also suggested that animals and God could be "synonyms," before asking, "And what is the Zumbi?" His answer included another suggestive reference to birds: "It is the devil or the evil god. It is the soul of the other world, ghost, werewolf, the soul of the Black transformed into a caburê, or acauran, or other birds that sing, or whistle, or shout through the night."[34] Though this description resonates provocatively with the zumbi bird related to Cabral by the pharmacist from Minas Gerais, the rest of Soares's definition was almost a direct rebuttal of what Cabral had written: "In Angola there could be some subtle synonymic difference between zambi and zumbi; among us [in Brazil], the two words are perfect synonyms, with just a slight vocal alteration between a and u. The leader of Palmares was Zumbi or Zambi; both forms are found in [texts] from the era. In popular language, zumbi is also the rain-maker [manda-chuva], the political force in the local district."[35] Though the distinction seemed small to Soares, for Bantu-language speakers, as we have seen, the difference between /a/ and /u/ was hardly a "slight vocal alteration." Like Cabral, Soares was both insightful ("Zumbi" and "Zambi" do both appear in colonial documents) and dismissive (treating the two as inter-changeable parts of a larger jumble of African concepts).

Soares's response, as did the essay to which he was responding, also il-lustrates the expansive set of concepts, figures, and ideas that Z/zumbi and Zambi had taken on by the late nineteenth century. If they did not agree on every matter, Cabral and Soares certainly concurred that Z/zumbi and Zambi had come to mean many things in Brazil. What each author did with that con-clusion indicates the two poles around which future debates would revolve: on one end was Cabral and the insistence on drawing impermeable lines around Zumbi, zumbi, and Zambi, and on the other Soares, and the tendency to treat the terms as indistinguishable elements in an inscrutable alphabet soup. The second pole is further demonstrated at the end of Soares's response, which references two "bilingual" terms, zumbi-assú and zumbi-mirim, both with a "bundu noun qualified by [a] tupi adjective." Soares notes that the combina-tion "indicates interesting considerations," but he does not expand on them further.[36]

The combination of winnowing and jumbling found in the observations made by authors such as Cabral and Soares indicates how definitions of Pal-mares and Z/zumbi narrowed in writing, even as the meanings of these words seemed to grow in popular memory. This was a long process that passed through the seventeenth century, with António de Oliveira de Cadornega, who in 1680 inventively inserted "evil" into his rendering of the Angolan cosmos, and Padre Silva's 1694 sermon calling Zambi "God" and Zumbi a demon. The Capuchin monk Cannecatim, writing in the early nineteenth century, served as a bridge between those seventeenth-century writers and Cabral and fellow writers in the late nineteenth century. Cannecatim's 1804 *Diccionario da lingua bunda ou angolense* defined "Zámbi" as "God" and "Zámbi iá Macútu" as "Goddess," an interesting dual-gender rendering that com-pletely fell from view among Brazilian writers, who wrote about Zambi and Z/zumbi and either ignored gender or assumed a male identity. In an 1805 grammar guide, Cannecatim more explicitly equated Zambi with a Christian conceptualization of God.[37] Cannecatim's work, published in Lisbon, became an important reference for Brazilian scholars, including the pioneering Fran-cisco Adolpho de Varnhagen, whose writings are often cited as the beginning of modern Brazilian historiography.[38] Varnhagen's *Historia geral do Brazil*, first published in the 1850s under the patronage of Brazilian emperor Dom Pedro II, received enthusiastic reviews by Alexander von Humboldt, among others, and became a foundational national text.[39] Citing Cannecatim and previewing Soares, Varnhagen wrote that "Zombi" was the "equivalent of what in the Congolese language means God," noting that "Zambi" could mean the same thing.[40] Cabral, Rodrigues, and others would soon correct that kind of equivalence, but only in the context of a debate shaped by a drive to establish authority and correct peers. In that context, the answer to the question that Soares posed in response to Cabral—"What is the Zumbi?"—was almost predetermined to say more about writers such as Soares and Cabral than about Z/zumbi, even in spite of the important insights and evidence that they preserved and conveyed.

Reducing Meanings and Excising Palmares

Some Brazilian scholars also consulted English-language texts, especially British travel writing and translations of missionary accounts from Angola and Kongo.[41] The work of the Swiss missionary Héli Chatelain was also influential.[42] The engagement with Chatelain and British travel writing is indicative of how, at the time that Brazilian scholars were delimiting and defining Palmares and Z/zumbi, European ethnographies of Africa were shaping written knowledge in Brazil. For instance, Capelo and Ivens's trip to Africa, so important to Cabral and his contemporary writers, was part of a renewed "awareness of the empire" among Portuguese adventurers and intellectuals, who during the late nineteenth century traveled to Africa and South Asia to collect and create maps, ethnographies, and local and colonial folktales around which to build a new nationalism and sense of imperial grandeur.[43] Their works appeared alongside the publications of European missionaries who traveled to and wrote about Portuguese Africa and thus created a new web of outsider knowledge about African culture and language.

The shaping influence of this knowledge in Brazil is illustrated in the work of José Francisco da Rocha Pombo, another eminent white historian, who was born in Paraná and, like many of his contemporaries, moved to Rio de Janeiro, where he eventually became a member of the Brazilian Academy of Letters.[44] His ten-volume *Historia do Brazil* (1905) remains one of the nation's foundational historical texts.[45] In *Historia*, Rocha Pombo wrote about Palmares in grandiose terms, reproducing lengthy passages from yet another lettered white man, J. P. Oliveira Martins, who called Palmares "the most beautiful, most heroic of all the example of slave protest. It is a Black Troy, and its history an *Iliad*."[46] Rocha Pombo also noted that Palmares had individual quilombos, ruled by a "supreme chief (zumbi)," and, quoting Martins again, reproduced an elaborate story about mass suicide, catalyzed by "Zumbi" and that extended even to Palmares prisoners.[47] While Rocha Pombo faithfully reproduced Martins's tale of the Palmaristas' total self-annihilation, he changed one detail without explanation: Martins called the mocambo leader "zambi," not "Zumbi." The edit (or oversight) was not the only one that Rocha Pombo would make.

These subsequent edits demonstrate the influence of European ethnographies of Africa. For instance, when expounding on other meanings of little-z zumbi, Rocha Pombo drew from a text written by the Portuguese author Alfredo de Sarmento, who in 1880 published an account of his travels in Africa.[48] The expedition set out from Luanda in 1856 to take control of a malachite mine.[49] Among "the people of the African backlands," Sarmento wrote, the *"chinguilador"* inspired incredible "veneration and respect." The chinguilador, which he translated as "witchdoctor or soothsayer," possessed "supernatural" powers and "exercises the profession of n'ganga, or surgeon." The people he encountered "believe that the *zumbis*, or spirits, of those who die enter the chinguilador's head, and reveal crimes perpetrated, adulteries committed, thefts, deceits, vengeances, and, above all, the secrets of the future." Believers would form a circle around the chinguilador, invariably a preto ladino, an "educated" or "acculturated" Black man, who would shout, signaling "that the zumbi had entered his head," and then convulse wildly as it possessed him. The great reverence for chinguiladores reflected their status as "master[s] of reading the past and predicting the future."[50]

Rocha Pombo drew from this description and also quoted most of a story that Sarmento recounted about an eighteen-year-old named Záu, whom he met during his travels. "Tall, robust, athletic in form," Záu was "the perfect model of the African race."[51] Záu's uncle had loaned him as credit in order to borrow land, and he was now far from home, toiling for the creditor. An excellent shooter, Záu accompanied Sarmento on hunting expeditions. One day, Záu appeared morose. Sarmento asked him what was wrong, and he replied, "The zumbis (spirits) of my plantation call me. For the last two moons they are with me, surrounding me. . . . I have to reunite myself with them." Shortly, he cried, "There they are! . . . there is the *N'gana-Zambe* (Deos) [God]! . . . *muene-tata!* . . . *muene-tata!* (meu pai! meu pai!) [my father! my father!]," and then placed the end of a rifle in his mouth and shot himself. "The sorrow," Sarmento wrote, "led him to take his life."[52] While Sarmento took the death to be exceptional, Rocha Pombo cast it as representative, writing, "Similar facts of Blacks committing suicide for longing of home or family fill the annals of slavery in all of America."[53] In Záu and Zumbi, readers of *História do Brazil* therefore encountered two versions of "robust" Black men who valiantly took their own lives, a recurring fantasy about the limits of Black male potency.

In their drive to enumerate and isolate, Rocha Pombo and other authors overlooked or omitted many of the details from the sources they consulted and these omissions tell fascinating stories. Rocha Pombo skipped over elements of Sarmento's account, such as the chinguilador's ability to utilize zumbi spirits to read the past and the future, an act that resonates with the observation from Joseph Miller's 1960s ethnographic account of nzumbi ancestor spirits similarly bridging time.[54] Other authors who drew on Sarmento did the same as Rocha Pombo, extricating noteworthy elements. Alfredo Brandão, the Alagoan author who wrote the account of Palmares discussed in chapter 8 that centered his hometown, Viçosa, presented his ideas at the First and Second Afro-Brazilian Congresses, landmark events in the study of Black history and culture in Brazil, and in other published materials.[55] He narrowed Sarmento's descriptions even further: "Alfredo Sarmento, cited by the historian Rocha Pombo, says that **zumbis** were plantation spirits."[56] Filtered through Rocha Pombo and reduced down even further, Sarmento's definition of zumbi had been condensed to a singular element: a supernatural plantation spirit.

Sarmento described zumbi spirits occupying much larger terrain, though especially after the sun set. According to him, Africans "never travel at night, so great is the[ir] fear of the dark, and the[ir] superstitious terror of meeting zumbi, the spirits, which, according to belief, wander at that night through the forests and deserted places, carrying out their vengeance and spells."[57] When Z/zumbi's association with deserted places emerged, and whether it appeared first in Brazil, Africa, or in tandem, is uncertain, though Sarmento and other writers clearly had a hand in cultivating the "fear of the dark" element attached to zumbi. But this was certainly not their invention alone. At least some learned to link nighttime, supernatural creatures, and Z/zumbi at a young age from enslaved caregivers, and popular culture spread similar definitions, as evident in the popular song cited by Cabral linking zumbi to the "werewolf and other goblins."

The multiple waves of reduction and delineation that mark late nineteenth-century and early twentieth-century publications extended into Brazil's postslavery republic a practice that dated back to the time of Padre Silva and Cadornega, who similarly cut and invented as they translated Z/zumbi, Zambi, and other terms. When he wrote about Palmares in the early twentieth century, Rodrigues chided his peers for "almost lament[ing]" the quilombo's destruction. Brazilians, he explained, needed to shed their new-found "unconditional idolatry for liberty" and give thanks to history's real heroes—the colonial forces who defeated Zumbi and destroyed "the greatest of threats to the civilization of the future Brazilian people, this new Haiti, resistant to progress and inaccessible to civilization."[58] Palmares had to be excised in order to create (or preserve) space for stories about its utter annihilation. The idea resonated with the even more openly racist rhetoric of early twentieth-century historians who wrote about Domingos Jorge Velho and other paulistas. The bandeirologistas, as these scholars were known, described Palmares as an "African cyst," a frighteningly ugly phrase that not only revealed the racist nature of the writing but also conveyed the questionable but pervasive idea of Palmares as a bounded entity.[59] Showing Palmares to have been cleanly removed from the colonial landscape left fertile soil in which to plant other narratives about Brazil that confined Black history to the past, or worse.

Speaking into the Wind

The way that works from the nineteenth and twentieth centuries may be both limiting and illuminating is seen vividly in the writing of Rio Grande do Norte's favorite son, Luís da Câmara Cascudo. His *Dicionário do folclore brasileiro* (now in its twelfth edition) includes a long entry for Z/zumbi, reminiscent of (and drawing on) Cabral's. Cascudo chastened his peers for what he considered to be obvious mistakes, including one scholar who "fooled himself" by confusing Zambi and Zumbi.[60] In *Geografia dos mitos brasileiros*, he made further distinctions, this time pertaining to Z/zumbi's many manifestations. In addition to regional difference, he emphasized a distinction between forms of Z/zumbi. "The Alagoan Zumbi," he stressed, was not the same as the one found in Bahia or Sergipe, but neither did it "refer to the title of the leader gloriously defeated in the 'quilombo' of Palmares, the Black Troy of the seventeenth century. The Zumbi that became popular [in Alagoas], in addition to the heroic one [Zumbi dos Palmares], was a being that took an entirely new form in Brazilian Folklore: a *zumbi* that represents the materialization of the spirit of dead animals."[61] By enumerating different variations of Z/zumbi, Cascudo showed how multiple meanings and definitions of the word had taken shape locally and nationally, while at the same time drawing a firm line of separation between zumbi spirits and "the gloriously defeated" Zumbi dos Palmares.

Among the many cultural forms he catalogued was a little-z zumbi that took the form of "a little Black boy, easy to confuse with Saci, who appears on the roads of Sergipe and is the companion of Caapora (Caipora) in Sergipe." Cascudo continued, "[Like Saci], he also asks for a smoke and ferociously beats those who don't satisfy the request. He is tiny, agile, naked," and haunts children.[62] "Saci" was Saci-Pererê, a demon trickster often depicted as a small Black boy with one leg, who smokes a pipe and terrorizes children. In the 1910s, the writer José Bento Monteiro Lobato collected firsthand accounts of Saci from newspaper readers in São Paulo and Minas Gerais, which he then published and annotated, helping ensconce Saci in national print culture.[63]

Cascudo's reference to Caapora (also Caipora), an Indigenous demon trickster figure similar to Saci, in proximity to zumbi suggests another intriguing meeting of African diasporic and Indigenous figures.[64] Saci, with whom zumbi was "easy to confuse," also seemed to have parallels with or connections to Indigenous traditions not only in Brazil, but in Uruguay, Argentina, and, elsewhere, almost always in the form of a bird.[65] In Brazil, Cascudo linked Saci and Z/zumbi in Sergipe, the nation's smallest state, sandwiched between Bahia and Alagoas. In Espírito Santo (between Bahia and Rio de Janeiro), he wrote, "the Black Zumbi" — the name now capitalized — appeared in forms that resembled those in Rio de Janeiro, but not Bahia. Along with Saci, this Zumbi "emigrated [to Sergipe] from the south to the north."[66] Enslaved people from Rio, he surmised, catalyzed the migration. Cascudo emphasized the south-to-north route to illustrate that this convergence had not come from Pernambuco or Alagoas, once again forcefully rejecting any connection between zumbi and Zumbi dos Palmares.

While foreclosing that connection, Cascudo suggested yet one more link between zumbi and other African spiritual manifestations. Saci is the conduit for this connection, which, according to Cascudo, originated from two "constitutive elements": zumbi and what he called "the Bantus' *Gunôco*."[67] Though Cascudo labeled "Gunôco" (also Gunocô or Gunocôu) as Bantu, other sources (including Cascudo's other writings) trace the little-known figure to Nigeria, where Nupe (or Tapa) people considered it a spirit of the dead.[68] In Bahia, Blacks also associated Gunocô with spirits of the dead and incorporated it into Candomblé.[69] In addition to its association with the dead, Gunocô is linked to forests, another indication of how and why it could overlap and even combine with zumbi. One chronicler called it "the divinity of the forests . . . *ghost.*"[70]

If Gunocô's presence in Brazil highlights transatlantic connectivity, its trajectory also suggests how loss accompanied connection and invention. In the 1930s, Brazilian informants told the German scholar Günther Protasius Frikel, "Gunocôu has left. . . . [He] has gone back to the Coast. . . . He spoke into the wind, but no one understood him anymore. . . . He went back to Africa."[71] The heartrending description of spiritual loss is reminiscent of that described by Domingos, the Angolan man encountered in chapter 4 who, while confessing to church officials in Minas Gerais, said that in Brazil, spirits did not "speak as they do in his land."[72] That the West African Gunocô linked up with West Central African zumbi, both of which Brazilians also associated with forests (and other "deserted" places) and often translated as "ghost," illustrates the dynamic way that layered diasporas could meet in Brazil. That together the two beings might have given rise to a third figure, Saci-Pererê, further illustrates the elaborate forms of diasporic creation that drew from an expansive range of elements, ideas, and traditions.[73] Early twentieth-century descriptions of Saci illustrate this point further and suggest how some of the same memories embedded in Z/zumbi took new shape and form in other, differently named figures. While the iconography and imagery attached to Saci is large and varied, a central feature is his whistle and association with birds, whose form he is often said to take—an association also noted by the pharmacist in Minas Gerais who described the zumbi bird to Cabral. One informant told Monteiro Lobato, "When [Saci] was sad, he would transform into a bird, and sing in the dark corners of chicken coops . . . a nostalgic song, repeated every five minutes: 'Sa . . . ci!'"[74] Another declared that Saci "was nothing less than the runaway slave" (escravo fujão).[75]

A "Posthumous Baptism" and One More Death

In 1885, a year after Cabral published his catalog of supernatural beings, a paper in Minas Gerais printed an "Alagoan Legend" penned by Pedro Paulino da Fonseca, who was born in Alagoas and would become governor and later a national senator. In 1891, he signed the republic's first constitution. His brother, Marechal Manuel Deodoro da Fonseca (also born in Alagoas), was the nation's first president. Before all that, in 1885, Pedro's mind was on Palmares. Nine years earlier, he had published his own version of the *Relação das guerras feitas aos Palmares de Pernambuco*, taking the liberty to change important details from the original text.[76] In "Alagoan Legend," Fonseca told a story about Sebastião Dias Maneli, a sergeant major in the colonial army. Fonseca preceded his tale with a quote from the Book of John: "Quis non renatus fuerit ex aqua et Spiritu Sancto non potest introire in regno coeli" (He who would not be born of water and the Spirit cannot enter into the Kingdom of the Holy One).[77]

Fonseca described Maneli as a virtuous officer, who took part in the battle at Serra da Barriga and was as adept with "the harquebus and dagger as with religion's inimical arms." Maneli "was one of those soldiers who, in the infidel's final breaths, never forgot to give him, in exchange for the life he was taking, the sacred formula of the baptism." In battle, after delivering "the mortal blows to his enemies," he would "pass his arms from left to right" and say, "I baptize you *In nomine Patris, Filii et Spiritu Sancti, amen.*" But at Serra da Barriga, he was unable to deliver salvation to those he slayed. Barreling past the Palmares defenses, Maneli "s[aw] in front of him the very chief of the Black republic, who ran . . . [and] sought a terrible death, throwing himself from the peak. Zumbi and most of his compatriots were crioulos, of the second generation of Palmares, where they knew no other religion than the most grotesque fetishism." Severed from Africa, uninstructed in Christianity, and dying at the bottom of the cliff, Zumbi was never baptized.

Years passed, and when Maneli died he was interred at the Convento de São Francisco, a seventeenth-century church in the town of Vila Madalena, renamed Marechal Deodoro, after Fonseca's brother, in the 1930s. Soon after burying Maneli, a monk at the convent saw apparitions. A "combat" ensued "between his conscience and fear. The thing was supernatural." The monk consulted with others at the convent and on the third night spoke to the spirit:

— Who are you, brother, and what do you want?
— I am Sebastiãa [*sic*] Dias Maneli, who erred and suffers for letting Zumbi die without rescuing his soul from eternal sin.

After the exchange, the monks and others from the community decided to "perform the solemn baptismal act" on Maneli's grave, "hoping to extinguish the sins of the chief of Palmares and rescue his spirit for heaven. What is certain, says the legend, is that the following day, the community . . . heard a prolonged sigh" emitting from the grave, "patent proof that the spirit of Maneli would remain in peace and free of remorse. And from then on, the convent's peace was never again disturbed." Putting aside its factual distortions, the story is ripe with symbolism. After death, the colonial conquistador all but possesses Zumbi's body and spirit, necessitating the baptism, which was done ostensibly to save Zumbi's soul but really so that Maneli (and the community) could rest in peace.

If Fonseca hoped to exorcise Zumbi's unbaptized ghost from the national psyche, decades later Cascudo simply declared little-z zumbi to be dead, at least in Angola. In 1963, Cascudo traveled to Africa, later publishing a series of essays about the trip called *Made in Africa*.[78] In Angola, his main interlocutor was the writer-folklorist Oscar Ribas, the son of a Portuguese father and Angolan mother.[79] First published in 1965, Cascudo's *Made in Africa* was an American bookend to Capelo and Ivens's trek through Angola decades earlier but also shaped, in turn, by Ribas, who met Cascudo at the airport and served as his guide. The two had corresponded regularly by mail and would stay in touch for years to come.[80] Ribas shared with Cascudo a desire to catalog and define "folkloric" practices and "authentic" cultural expressions. In 1960, Ribas had sent to Cascudo his book *Ilundo*, a collection of Angolan "divinities and rites" that he dedicated to, among others, Cascudo and three other "Illustrious Brazilian Intellectuals."[81] As he traveled in Africa, Cascudo set out to change what he understood to be a lack of proper knowledge of the continent in Brazil. He drew from *Ilundo* and other works by Ribas, along with Brazilian authors, and what he saw during the trip.

In a chapter titled "News of Zumbi," he reproduced Cabral's nine-point definition of Z/zumbi along with Ribas's entry in *Ilundo*. Also called "dele," Cascudo wrote (quoting Ribas), in Angola zumbi was "the soul of a recently deceased person." The word zumbi derived from the Kimbundu verb kuzumbika, which Ribas translated as "perseguir," to pursue or hunt, "the command of the feiticeiro." In Luanda people used "dele" more, while those in the interior said "zumbi," a distinction that apparently persisted even as the two words (and a third, quilulo, "afflicted soul") blended. Once "specific terms," over time "the people, with their linguistic dynamism, came to employ them indistinctly," each coming to mean "soul of the dead."[82]

Though the word zumbi still circulated inland, Cascudo was struck by what he perceived to be its disappearance, at least in Luanda, a stark contrast to its ever-multiplying meanings he was familiar with at home. "In Brazil, especially in the north," he wrote, "ZUMBI is a terrifying and complex force. . . . Brought by slaves from Angola, Zumbi abandons the somatic limits of its African representation and in Brazil gives flesh and form, enlarged many frightening figures in the collective imagination," including "an agile Black boy . . . competing with Saci-Pererê. He whistled like him." In Brazil, Cascudo continued, zumbi became "the soul of the melancholy slave" and took on the "function" of "fantastic animals" in a way that replaced and was "significantly more impressive" than similar beings in Native Brazilian traditions.[83] The collection of zumbi figures in Brazil was "incredibly larger than that available in the Angolan Zumbi."

Referencing the German philologist Max Müller, he suggested that in Brazil zumbi "grew through one of these *myths of verbal confusion*," a convergence of "*nzámbi*, divinity, divine power; and, by transference, vocative of the social leaders, *m'ganga Zumbi*; and *nzumbi*, specter, ghost, goblin, visage of a shadow."[84] Struck by the fact that no one he encountered in Angola mentioned zumbi, and basing himself in Ribas's observations, Cascudo declared zumbi to be "semi-exiled from Luanda," where dele had taken its place and was free of "the hallucinatory materializations" in Brazil, where, he noted, the word was also a toponym for beaches, rivers, lakes, and settlements in Bahia, Paraíba, Pernambuco, Sergipe, and Rio Grande do Norte, as well as a force that inhabited forests and spread a "formless terror, unjustified but real," throughout most of the country, "from Minas Gerais to Pernambuco."[85] In addition to Ribas, Cabral, and Müller, Cascudo drew from Rodrigues and Capelo and Ivens, whose account from Tchiboco he also reproduced. Cascudo concluded the essay with a kind of epitaph. Still flourishing in Brazil, in Angola, "The immortal Zumbi is condemned to death by Time. . . . But, the quimbundos say: *Mukuanhi kafuê*? Who doesn't die?"[86]

Conclusion

Pronouncing zumbi dead in Angola, Cascudo elevated Brazil as a place of dynamic, though also "terrifying" and "hallucinatory," diasporic creation—the site of a veritable zumbi empire, no incidental echo of Governor Castro's fear of the widespread "superstitious" beliefs about Zumbi in seventeenth-century

Pernambuco. Notably, Cascudo also observed that Saint Benedict had met a similar fate as zumbi, gaining greater notoriety in Brazil (and Portugal) than Africa.[87] Though in some instances, Cascudo acknowledged that the Zumbi suicide myth was untrue, in others he preserved it. In a collection of "Brazilian legends" that ostensibly reflected popular tradition and thought, Cascudo recounted the story of "The Death of Zumbi," basically a recapitulation of Rocha Pita's eighteenth-century tale, concluding with Zumbi leaping "into the abyss" along with the other Palmaristas.[88] It is possible, even likely, that the story endured in part because it was meaningful among some Black Brazilians and in communities in which history was recorded, passed down, and adapted orally. That probability does not obscure the straight line between Rocha Pita's and Cascudo's accounts. At least conveyed in writing, this was simply a colonial fantasy retold across the centuries.

From the chaotic rubble to which Cascudo and other writers reduced definitions they deemed incorrect, important meanings and storylines emerge, most prominently the rise of an airborne cosmology formed by new expressions layered on top of one another, which preserved and also remade Zumbi, zumbi, and Zambi. Even while writers divided, narrowed, and erased, elsewhere meanings and memories of Z/zumbi and Palmares multiplied. These dual processes helped consolidate singular figures and histories above ground—that is, in the most famous texts written about Palmares—while other histories swirled beneath. While the standard telling of how Palmares reemerged in regional and national consciousnesses via the written word and in linear fashion is, therefore, not incorrect, it is incomplete.

A more sprawling, uneven landscape is glimpsed by rereading the sources highlighted in this chapter and in other, less conventional places. In 1824, an international court in Cuba liberated a twelve-year-old girl named Zumbi, who boarded a slave vessel on the Windward Coast before it was intercepted at sea.[89] In subsequent decades, men and boys from West Central Africa and West Africa with names like Zamby, Zambie, and Zambee were found aboard other intercepted ships.[90] The array of meanings that these names and words accumulated over time and space is the product of not only colonial encounters in Africa and America, but also local and regional variations of African linguistic and cultural matrices. Expansive alternative paths are also evident in Brazil, as demonstrated on the pages of a 1931 Brazilian postal guide, which included scores of places called Mocambo and Quilombo, and more than a dozen places named Zumbi, not only in Alagoas, Pernambuco,

Paraíba, and Rio Grande do Norte, but also in Ceará, Minas Gerais, and Rio de Janeiro.[91]

In the processes that made and shaped the meanings attached to these places—and to Z/zumbi and Palmares—creation often accompanied destruction. By the time that the pharmacist described the zumbi bird to Cabral, the Zumbi neighborhood in Cidade da Parahyba had been consigned to receive much of the city's waste. Nationally, abolition was just a few years away and thousands of enslaved people had been displaced from the northeast to and through Minas. There, in isolated places and perched just outside the gates of fazendas, a bird could be heard calling out, "*Zumbi . . . biri . . . ri . . . poor thing!*" To some enslaved and free people of color, the sound may have provided comfort. To others it felt plaintive, possibly representing a lost loved one haunting them or sending strength and even imploring them to leave the plantation. The bird's song may have also carried a story about, and perhaps even a message from, the immortal mocambo leader of the same name.

Connected and

Beyond

Accounts of how the reemergence in writing of Palmares and Zumbi during the nineteenth century played out across the twentieth and twenty-first centuries are, like those of the nineteenth, relatively straightforward. The elevation of Palmares and Zumbi into national historical narratives was followed by the emergence of counternarratives pioneered by Edison Carneiro and other leftists, who incorporated Palmares and Zumbi dos Palmares into larger racial and political discourses and mobilizations that eventually culminated in the 1988 constitution with Article 68, which guaranteed recognition and protection to quilombo communities.[1] A book about Palmares and its afterlives could very well conclude with a detailed narration of this arc, but though I touch on these important histories here and in the conclusion, my focus is instead on one of the nineteenth century's less-understood legacies, addressed briefly in previous chapters: the fact that Palmares's remarkable ability to generate new diasporas and afterlives was joined by a similarly powerful capacity to erase or deny.

This chapter engages that legacy by pushing beyond Palmares while also exploring its centrifugal force and ability to swallow other historical narratives and lines of inquiry. As Palmares and Zumbi became embedded in national historical lore, their capacity to obscure other histories grew and, in some cases, entangled discursive meaning making with material forms of erasure, inheritance, and dispossession. The scholars who winnowed little-z zumbi away from big-Z Zumbi and hailed the mocambos' "glorious defeat" helped turn Palmares into a would-be Rosetta stone that might help them decipher unfamiliar African words. Doing so often resulted in a kind of laser focus or tunnel vision that could sideline other histories, symbols, and ideas, though, as we have seen, destruction and creation often merged, and even as Palmares obscured histories and meanings, it served at the same time as a foundation for others.

Drawing more often from oral history than I have until now, the chapter demonstrates these dynamics with examples that revisit the main themes of the book—language, places, spirits, and war and conquest (and the material rewards and inheritances they generated)—reordered here to preserve the chronological order of these examples. As they have throughout the book, here the themes are also often intertwined. It is no accident that the theme highlighted in part III, "People," emerges most vividly in the twenty-first century, not through a connection to a living descendant of Palmares but instead via a living descendant of one of its conquerors. That difference illustrates the gaping disparity between the traceable lineages and material inheritances of those who belonged to Palmares and those who fought to destroy it. Far from providing a comprehensive or tidy wrap-up, the cases discussed here further illustrate the unfinished and open-ended nature of Palmares and Z/zumbi while also bringing to the fore additional questions and provocations, some of which root us in Palmares and others that direct us away from the famous mocambos and toward diasporic histories and inheritances that tend to get lost in Palmares's long shadow. Rather than suggesting the need for an absolute abandonment of Palmares, these examples demonstrate the importance of remaining connected to the mocambos while at the same time looking beyond them.

Language: Mozambos and Muzambi

As Palmares became a regular feature in Brazilian historiography, some observers looked to it for clues about words they vaguely associated with Africa, a practice that could yield helpful insights but also foreclose other lines of inquiry. While some studied Africa in order to better understand and define Palmares, other authors did the inverse, employing Palmares to understand Africa. Treating Palmares as an African Rosetta stone also contributed to the mocambos' growing stature as an African sine qua non—the essential illustration of Africa in Brazil. A prime example comes by way of a famous account of the Guerra dos Mascates, the failed early eighteenth-century separatist uprising in Pernambuco. During the conflict, the rebel Olinda faction counted among their leaders Bernardo Vieira de Melo, transformed now from conqueror to agitator. In a speech that became part of historical lore, he called for a fight to the end. According to some accounts, Vieira de Melo suggested that the rebels form an independent republic modeled after Venice and that they draw inspiration for their fight from none other than Zumbi. The invocation illustrates the malleability that came to define Zumbi, who in this case slid easily from Vieira de Melo's mortal enemy to a model.

But did Vieira de Melo truly utter Zumbi's name? One of the earliest accounts of the Guerra dos Mascates was written by a Portuguese priest, Luís Correia. Correia's manuscript eventually came into the possession of Henry Koster, who passed the document to Robert Southey, a British author whose three-volume *History of Brazil* (1810–19) laid important groundwork for nineteenth-century Brazilian historiography and includes iconic descriptions of Palmares (with yet another reprisal of the suicide myth) and the Guerra dos Mascates. Southey's account of the Peddlers War was based mainly on Correia's manuscript, but when Southey died in 1844, his library was sold and Correia's manuscript disappeared.[2] Though Southey does not mention Vieira de Melo speaking about Zumbi, he writes that the veteran officer launched the rebellion after abandoning his post in the Palmares regiment to travel to his engenho near Recife "under pretext of an expedition against a Mocambo, which he said had been formed in that part of the country [Palmares]."[3]

The earliest surviving account of the Peddlers War that mentions Zumbi is *Os martires pernambucanos* (*Pernambucan Martyrs*), a collection of short biographies of Pernambucans who fought in the conflict or participated in a separatist movement a century later.[4] Written by the priest Joaquim Dias Martins a year after Brazil declared independence from Portugal (but published in 1853), *Os martires* maintains that when Vieira de Melo addressed his fellow landowners, he "did not neglect to mention even Palmares of the recent Zumbi," whose actions they might soon follow.[5] It is unclear what source or evidence Martins used to write his account, and there is no conclusive evidence that Zumbi's name actually crossed Vieira de Melo's lips. What is interesting is that authors wanted to believe that it did. Slain, Zumbi was not only a demon but also a potential source of inspiration.

In addition to generating malleable images of Zumbi, accounts of the Guerra dos Mascates also generated new ideas about African words, and this is where we see how Brazilian scholars turned to Palmares to translate unfamiliar terms. In 1873 and 1874, the decorated author José de Alencar published a novel about the Peddlers War in which he ventured a definition of the term "mazombo," a pejorative label applied to Vieira de Melo and his fellow insurgents. In Recife, Portuguese merchants derisively called Pernambucan-born nobles mazombos, using the term with "contempt" and likening their American rivals to Black "chieftains." Over time, Pernambucans, "especially people of color," turned the slur into a badge of honor, "transforming the title of *mazombo* into an emblem of the highest glory that a nobleman could aspire to in the land of his birth."[6] When Alencar wrote his novel, the term's origins had eluded even the studious members of Recife's literati, but he thought he knew the answer: "The destruction of Palmares helped spread a collection of African names used by Blacks in their republic. They called the supreme leader, who everyone obeyed, *Zambi*; and *Muzambi* were the great officers, who served the chief and his ministers."[7] This, he concluded, was the source of the mysterious word.

Seventeenth- and eighteenth-century Portuguese sources define mazombos as American-born offspring of European parents.[8] The word is, as Alencar suspected, African, and in appropriating a term meant to be an insult, individuals in Recife seemed to have strategically embraced an imagined "Black" or "African" martial persona, perhaps specialized in leadership. That Alencar forged his definition through Palmares speaks to the mocambos' enduring impact on the psyche and imaginations of the lettered elite. But there are other likely definitions and other stories to be told. Taking the words apart is a good place to begin. Returning to the example of mu-lob-i, which illustrates how the prefix **mu-* can be paired with the suffix **-i* to turn verbs into human agents (chapter 3), we may speculate that in some contexts muzambi may have, indeed, represented a personified version of Zambi, perhaps along the lines of what the word means in parts of Southeast Africa, where it can refer to a "spiritual bodyguard" whose power derives from their medicinal knowledge.[9] Nonetheless, there is no indication that Palmaristas called their "officers" (or anyone) "Muzambi," and while Mazombo and Muzambi may have sounded or appeared similar to Alencar and other Brazilians, few Africans would confuse the terms. Yet again, the distinct sonic registers of /a/ and /u/ in Bantu languages is key. Nor is there a likely path through which one word would have derived from the other.

Mazombo may be analyzed in similar fashion. The prefix ma-, we have seen, is found in nouns in class five ("natural phenomena, animals, body parts, collective nouns, and undesirable people") and fourteen ("nouns of abstraction that similarly [reference] collectivities").[10] It was also used to designate a "land of -x," Marcos Abreu Leitão de Almeida explains, as in mabengo, "land of Bengo (Angola)."[11] During the second half of the eighteenth century, traders in Zombo, in northern Kongo, delivered up to five thousand enslaved people each year to the Loango coast, most bound for America.[12] In addition to the meaning that circulated among Portuguese speakers, "Mazombo" very likely also referred to individuals from the region in Kongo.

With these possible meanings in hand, several lines of analysis emerge. One would be to take Alencar literally and consider more deeply the possibility that Palmaristas came not only through West Central Africa, but much further afield, as far away as Mozambique. The trafficking of enslaved people from Mozambique to Brazil dates to the seventeenth century but only became substantial during the eighteenth and nineteenth centuries.[13] Nonetheless, it is also worth recalling that as early as 1706 the Saint Benedict brotherhood near Recife specifically mentioned welcoming Blacks from Mozambique (and "any land"). Provocative as that possibility is, absent more evidence a sounder approach builds from what historical linguistics tell us: that the relationship between Muzambi and Mazombo is unlikely, at least for Bantu-language speakers. From there, we may home in on other stories that arise as we retune our ears and listen more intently to revolutionary soundings of the African Atlantic.[14] To comprehend their depth and breadth, it is necessary to at least partially unmoor ourselves from Palmares. What can we hear when we approach Palmares mythology by listening for other stories, beyond Palmares?

The ma- prefix found in Mazombo is the same one found in Macuca, one of the toponyms in Alagoas. It is also the same morpheme that Kathryn de Luna shows contains previously misunderstood meanings of the name Makandal, one of the luminary figures of the Haitian Revolution. For Africans who spoke Bantu languages, Mazombo evoked not only a specific place but, much as it did in the case of Makandal, the collectivity and a shared understanding that certain challenges must be "addressed as a community."[15] Alencar's instinct was to connect Mazombo with Palmares—and to use Palmares to decipher what to him was a strange word—understandable given the word's significance in Recife and the fact that the Guerra dos Mascates took place shortly after the mocambos' defeat. But that instinct was also shaped by the fact that, like most Brazilian elites, his knowledge of Africa was limited as well as that Palmares had become a stand-in for the continent.

It is now possible to study additional stories and see how the impulse to connect every African reference to Palmares may occlude other histories. Doing so suggests ways to reimagine and pose new questions about Brazilian history. Was there a revolutionary current in Recife that emanated or was otherwise connected to people from Zombo? Did Africans and Afro-Brazilians play a larger leadership role in the Guerra dos Mascates, long understood as a struggle between white power brokers, than previously thought? In light of these questions, it is also worth reconsidering the fact that, in 1748, a scribe replaced the name "Zombim" that appeared in one of Manuel Lopes's seventeenth-century documents with "Zombo," perhaps not just a mistake but also an indication of the word's growing purchase.[16] Whatever answers are to come of these questions, Alencar's use of Palmares to translate Mazombo exemplifies Palmares's centrifugal power and the way that other African and Brazilian histories emerge as we retrace the steps of earlier writers, now equipped with new methods, tools, and questions.

Places and Spirits: Zumbi on Distant Shores

Palmares's capacity to draw attention away from other diasporic routes and histories is also evident in one of the distant places that likely received Palmares prisoners during the seventeenth century, Rio de Janeiro (often referred to simply as "Rio"). Though there are brief mentions of captured Palmaristas sent to Rio, the documentary trail runs dry in the city, even while other enticing bits of evidence present themselves. By the nineteenth century, Rio had become a locus for national intellectual and cultural production, where Alencar, Cabral, and others worked, conversed, and published. Surrounded by mountains and dense tropical forest, the city was shaped by terrain propitious for fugitives.

During the early nineteenth century, as Palmares became a fixture in regional and national histories, the city's growing cultural and intellectual infrastructure made it a dominant force in national conversations and collective meaning-making. By the time of independence, a significant portion of Rio's elite knew the story of Palmares, at least the version advanced by Sebastião da Rocha Pita. In 1823, as Brazilians considered what the newly independent nation would look like, a publication in Rio used Zumbi's reign in Palmares as a didactic illustration of the difference between "lifelong" political positions such as Zumbi's with elected ones.[17] Alongside this kind of direct reference to Palmares, other meanings proliferated.

A factory on Ilha do Governador, an island in the bay that Rio overlooks, made Zumbi Soap, which it produced in large-enough quantities to sell locally and, at least on occasion, ship to Pernambuco.[18] The soap took its name from the area on Ilha do Governador that also included Zumbi Beach and commercial developments and residences. In addition to the beach and neighborhood, a 1922 map shows a large Zumby Hill (Morro do Zumby) nearby.[19] Builders came to prize the lime mortar that enslaved laborers on the island produced by crushing and heating mollusk shells that they gathered on beaches that stretched from Zumbi to the Praia Quilombo (Quilombo Beach) on the opposite end of Ilha do Governador.[20] Alongside plantations, wild vegetation dominated much of the island.[21] The thick flora provided shelter for people on the run, such as a Mozambican man who fled the Zumbi Soap factory in 1841, and another from the Mina Coast, who escaped from a sítio next to the factory several years later.[22]

In such stories, we hear undeniable echoes of the northeast, and yet the meanings of Z/zumbi may have been quite different in Rio. East across the bay from Ilha do Governador was another Zumbi place, located in an area outside the town of Niterói. There, plantations abutted dense forest. Fugitives sought refuge in Niterói's Zumbi, an area that also had a stream named Zumby and was home to a renowned curandeiro (folk healer or witch doctor), whom police arrested repeatedly during the second half of the nineteenth century.[23] In Rio proper, the association between Z/zumbi and witchcraft mapped onto each other in interesting ways. A poem paired the word with the Catumbi neighborhood, home to a prominent cemetery: "Friend, I'm not going again to Catumbi / Because there I ran into the zumbi."[24] An 1870 advertisement made zumbi a practitioner of witchcraft, broadcasting the sale of a forthcoming "portrait" of the "great zumby or feiticeiro," Juca Rosa, a well-known (and controversial) Black faith healer.[25] Arthur Ramos also observed, somewhat cryptically, "In Rio, Blacks know Ganga Zumba (influence of Zumbi)."[26]

In a city that likely received Palmares prisoners, had a lettered elite versed in written accounts of the mocambos' history, and was visited by ships that, between the sixteenth and nineteenth centuries, carried more than a million enslaved Africans to its port, these references might also evoke Palmares — or not. Gazing beyond the northeast, the possible connections to Palmares seem fainter, even less concrete than in Rio Grande do Norte, where the best evidence of Palmares's presence in the aftermath of 1695 comes by way of the veterans who traveled there after the wars and by the traces left by place-names. Though some Palmares veterans traveled to Rio de Janeiro, they did so in small numbers and their presence was less felt there than in Rio Grande do Norte.[27] It is possible that a Palmares veteran, Palmarista prisoner, or group of prisoners ended up on Ilha do Governador and gave the beach its name, and perhaps future research will be able to link specific veterans to sesmarias and place-names in Rio as I was able to do in Rio Grande do Norte. Absent that kind of evidence, it seems more likely that the Zumbi places in Rio de Janeiro's bay came by way of other diasporic routes.

Rio's richly diverse population, which included enslaved and free people from West Central, West, and Southeast Africa, provided plentiful opportunities for the elaboration of new ideas and meanings. This dynamic is evident in a popular performance from Rio's Carnival. During the nineteenth century, groups of Black men and women, some dressed as Indigenous people, paraded during Carnival, performing scenes through choreographed dances. The groups, known as Cucumbis, performed dances that, Eric Brasil writes, functioned as a "memory site, where [Black men and women] retold African histories and amplified [African] identities."[28] One popular performance invoked two figures that would have been familiar, at least in name, to the man named Manuel and his companion, Francisca Correa, in eighteenth-century Minas Gerais: Zumbi and Saint Benedict.[29] The plot revolves around a queen who seeks the help of a feiticeiro to resuscitate her recently killed son. At one moment, the feiticeiro sings, "Zumbi, Zumbi, Oh! Zumbi, 'Our Muxikongo mother, Oh our Father.'"[30] As the child begins to come back to life, the revelers rejoice: "Zumbi, Zumbi, oh Zumbi!" The feiticeiro asks, "[Who is] the greatest Saint?," and the chorus responds, "Saint Benedict!" Linda Heywood explains that the line evokes "Kongo origins"—Muxikongo is "a term for inhabitants of the heartland of the kingdom surrounding Mbanza Kongo"—and also employs a Kimbundu term, "*Zumbi* (from *nzumbi*)."[31]

As with the word Mazombo, this example presents challenging analytical questions about potential connections to Palmares and other diasporic manifestations. Is this the same Zumbi worshipped by Francisca and Manuel in eighteenth-century Minas Gerais? Does this pairing with Saint Benedict link up with the one suggested by witnesses who testified against the couple and with close encounters of Saint Benedict and Zumbi in Angola? What, if any, shared meaning does this Zumbi have with Zumbi dos Palmares? The first two questions deserve further attention elsewhere, but at least a partial answer is accessible for the third.[32] Revelers born in Kongo or Angola would have likely brought ideas about zumbi with them, and it is almost certain that, whether by word of mouth or the circulation of printed materials, many who participated in or witnessed the performance also knew of Zumbi dos Palmares. The consequent layering effect of diaspora and the power of durable words are both impressive here: Africans in Rio who brought meanings of Z/zumbi across the Atlantic were now in contact with not only other Africans but also American-born revelers, who brought their own memories and ideas about Z/zumbi: some forged in Rio, others emanating from northeast Brazil and likely elsewhere.

Spirits and Places: The Friar against Zumbi

Though Z/zumbi turned into and linked up with multiple forms, the singular connection that Padre Silva made in 1694 between Zumbi and the devil endured for ages, as did the associations that the Inquisition made between little-z zumbi and diabolical practices. These enduring characterizations shaped treatments of zumbi as it took the form of animal spirits, which were especially common in the northeast. In Pernambuco, zumbi was "the ghost of an animal," and some people believed that the spirit could be "exorcized by means of a ceremony in which a fire is built . . . an incantation is sung . . . , and the ashes from the fire are scattered on the grave [of a beloved animal] the following morning."[33] There was a similar association in Paraíba, where some believed that "it is not just a man who has a soul. The horse does, too. Take any person from the countryside and they will tell you categorically. There is no doubt. Just that the horse's soul isn't called a soul. It's called Zumbi."[34] Stories about how "zumbi did this, zumbi did that" were legion and caused "terror," especially for those who worked with horses and knew how zumbi could frighten their steeds. Once the spirit took hold of an animal "things are altered quite a bit. Colors change, water turning into wine, and milk into coffee." Invariably, the possessed horse would flee to the woods.

Powerful forces fought back against this kind of belief, in some cases seeking to eradicate zumbi and setting the stage for battles over meaning and place. In the early 1930s, the Capuchin friar Pio Giannotti, popularly known as Frei Damião, moved from Italy to Brazil, where he would make a name as a missionary to the "popular classes" of the northeastern sertão. Ministering to small towns and large crowds across the region, he often explained suffering, drought, and poverty as God's punishment for sins.[35] In the 1970s, Frei Damião passed through the Distrito de Zumbi, in Paraíba, and delivered a sermon imploring the town to change its name. The Comissão História Zumbi (the group of young residents writing a history of the town) interviewed a community member, who said, "It is commonly discussed that . . . [Frei Damião] said that Zumbi should change its name to Nova Aliança [New Alliance] because as long as we used [Zumbi] there would not be progress or prosperity for the community. I think that Frei Damião associated the name Zumbi [with] the superstitious belief of animal spirits."[36]

The priest's directive did not come to pass, but this was not the only Zumbi town whose name he tried to change. As in Paraíba, residents of Zumbi in Rio Grande do Norte recall Frei Damião visiting and attempting to change their town's name. According to Antonio de Paiva Fagundes, the white patriarch of one of the area's most powerful families, attempts to rename Zumbi predate Frei Damião. Before the friar arrived, there was a movement to change the name to Nova Olinda. "That name didn't stick," Fagundes said. Later, at Frei Damião's urging, some in the town "tried to make it São Sebastião [Saint Sebastian], but that didn't work either . . . because the name [Zumbi] was already consecrated."[37] When I asked Valdete Gomes da Silva Ferreira, a white woman and devout Catholic born in Zumbi in 1951, about Frei Damião, she exclaimed, "Ave Maria!" and proudly produced a picture of him having coffee with congregants of the town's church. When the topic turned to the meanings of the town's name, she said, "Look, the origins of the name Zumbi, I don't really know that, okay. But earlier, it was São Sebastião. . . . [The people] wanted this Black warrior, who was very bold, and so the name Zumbi stuck." In her recollection, Z/zumbi had interrupted a Catholic tradition, rather than the other way around. She also recalled how, as a child, she frequently saw apparitions she associated with Z/zumbi. "I saw them many times," Dona Valdete said. "Every Friday, something would appear. There would be a long procession from the church. . . . It came by [my house] all lit up. Everyone with a candle. . . . I got tired, I really got tired of seeing them. . . . They were ghosts . . . people who had died."[38]

While the towns in Paraíba and Rio Grande do Norte preserve the name Zumbi, in other places, popular memory persisted despite the imposition of new official titles. A 1943 *Guia da Paraíba* (*Guide to Paraíba*) states, "The streets of the capital are always changing names, but the people [o povo] preserve the old designations," among them "Zumbi" and "Mata-negro," named for a Black man killed in plain sight.³⁹ In Alagoas, near the base of Serra da Barriga, the settlement named Macacos was also informally known as Santa Maria for a local chapel with an image of Mary. After Brazilian independence, the village changed its name twice. In 1831, it became Vila Nova da Imperatriz (New Town of the Empress) and in 1890 changed its name again, this time to União (Union).⁴⁰ A popular refrain from the era suggests how some felt about the transformations:

> "Macacos" was my name
> I adopted Santa Maria
> I was never Imperatriz
> And União I'll never be.⁴¹

In addition to Macacos, some Alagoas place-names, including Matta Escura (Dark Forest), were either erased by urban and agricultural sprawl or replaced by new ones.⁴² But even official erasure could be partially reversed or at least altered. In 1944, Macacos changed its name for a final time, from União to União dos Palmares.

War and Conquest: Different Heirs

The transition from Macacos to União and then União dos Palmares encapsulates Palmares's capacity to deny meaning as well as to generate it: while the town is now indelibly tied to the mocambos, the more specific meaning that Macacos may have once held is erased. Similar processes have played out in the claiming and assigning of lineages descending from Palmares and its conquerors. In October 2019, the anthropologist Julie Cavignac sent me a WhatsApp message with a clip from an interview she had conducted with Francisco Galvão, a white local historian and dedicated Galvão family genealogist from Canguaretama, a town in southeast Rio Grande do Norte. During the conversation, he offered an admission about his family: "Manuel Lopes Galvão, who is one of my ancestors, here in Brazil, right?, was the one who wounded Zumbi. Zumbi dies because of this wound, right? So, he was my ancestor. . . . So, I still carry this weight. It's not easy. First that you wounded a Zumbi, no? That's difficult [quick laugh]. And this Zumbi that today is the greatest symbol of *negritude* of Brazil, well, I can't really say much."[43] Francisco's declaration, a version of which he had made publicly on a blog in 2013, is remarkable on several levels. Though somewhat sheepish, he hardly shuns the title of being a descendant of the man who killed Zumbi. Of course, even if we take the man whom Manuel Lopes claimed in 1676 to have wounded—and whom he at that time called Zamby—to be the man now known as Zumbi, the wound that Lopes inflicted two decades earlier clearly did not account for his assassination in 1695.

Equally important is where Francisco spoke with Cavignac and wrote his blog—Canguaretama. Just down the road from Canguaretama is Sibaúma, a Black community made famous in 1969, when a journalist from *Realidade*, a popular magazine from São Paulo, published a lengthy article about it.[44] In a *National Geographic*-like spread, the writer described Sibaúma as a quilombo that had remained isolated from civilization for ages. The article's title dubbed the inhabitants "the heirs of Zumbi" (os herdeiros de Zumbi), a designation less indicative of anything that the community members said to the journalist than of his own vocabulary and reference points. None of the people he interviewed seem to have mentioned Zumbi or Palmares, and while the community was founded by people escaping slavery, none of the origin stories it has passed down mention the famous mocambos. Today, some residents of Sibaúma do, in fact, call themselves "heirdeiros de Zumbi," but like many other people of African descent across Brazil, they identify as Zumbi's heirs to signal a connection to broader, shared histories of oppression and resistance, though not literal or direct genealogical descendance.

How do we square what has happened in this corner of Rio Grande do Norte? What historical processes explain the proximity of a quilombo whose members do not claim a direct connection to Palmares, and who only recently came to embrace even a symbolic link with Zumbi, and a white man who openly identifies as the descendant of the man who killed him? Some answers are found in the long histories traced in the previous chapters—on the one hand, death, dispossession, and loss; on the other, the accumulation and transfer of wealth and power. Others are found via a winding journey that connects Palmares to Canguaretama and passes through Portugal, Rio de Janeiro, Pernambuco, and Ceará.

Among the many brags, mistakes, and outright falsifications about Zumbi's death that colonial soldiers made, those proffered by Francisco's ancestor Manuel Lopes stand out. Many times Lopes stated that he killed Zumbi, and though some claims may reflect honest confusion or the existence of multiple Palmarista leaders named or titled Zumbi, others were simply false. That did not prevent latter-day writers from reproducing Lopes's declarations, even while removing important subtleties. In 1906, the Instituto do Ceará published a dossier of nineteen documents related to Palmares.[45] Founded in 1887, the institute remains one of the most hallowed intellectual societies in Ceará. The documents it published in 1906 were in the possession of Baron Guilherme Studart, a white doctor, historian, and one of the institute's founding members. In a preface, Studart framed "the battle of Palmares" as an important chapter of national history that was understudied and "still full of lacunae." He had had "the fortune to collect" the documents at the National Library in Lisbon, a "precious archive" that retained hidden treasures such as the ones he now shared. Their publication gave new life and visibility to the narratives that Manuel Lopes presented to colonial officials on mercê petitions two centuries earlier and had been preserved in Portugal's National Archive, also in Lisbon, which Studart likened to an untapped mine.

Among the documents in Studart's collection was the announcement Lopes issued in 1680 as he sought to locate and negotiate with Zumbi. Though the document itself does not associate Lopes with Zumbi's death, its inclusion in the Studart collection helped him maintain a toehold in the evolving pantheon of Palmares heroes, lacking the renown of Domingos Jorge Velho and Bernardo Vieira de Melo, but nonetheless visible, especially in the northeast. Lopes's standing and his link to Zumbi's death were bolstered further in 1941, when the Instituto do Ceará published a study of important families in the northeast.[46] The report began with the Lopes Galvão family tree, which extended throughout the region and beyond, bequeathing many "famous figures" to the nation, including Marechal Deodoro da Fonseca, the first president of the Brazilian republic, and Hermes da Rodrigues Fonseca, the eighth.[47] (This would also connect Lopes to Pedro Paulino da Fonseca, the author of the tale that described a postmortem baptism for Zumbi.) The article noted how Lopes's descendants carried on his tradition of serving in the military and cited Ernesto Ennes, a Portuguese researcher who had recently brought a vast trove of documents related to Palmares to light.[48] Lopes's "value and the service he gave to Brazil" was manifest in "official documents from the era."[49] Among these documents was a transcription of the 1689 letters patent, previously published in 1858 by the Pernambucan author Antonio

Joaquim de Mello, which included the fateful assertion that Lopes and his men killed Zumbi.[50] Whatever mystery or honest misunderstandings were to be found in other statements, this one left no room for interpretation: Lopes was responsible for Zumbi's death. Both Mello and the instituto also replaced the original spelling, "Zombim," with "Zumbi," an indication of how the rendering of Zumbi's name continued to crystallize over time.

When the instituto reprinted Manuel Lopes's letters patent, it brought clarity through two tidy assertions, at least one of which was clearly false: Zumbi was Zumbi, and Lopes killed him. But other colonial documents, and no shortage of hallowed texts, depicted other narratives of Zumbi's death, from the apocryphal suicide legend to the grisly beheading. These contrasting narratives are indicative of how memories spread in the aftermath of 1695, as Palmares survivors and veterans carried disparate stories and aims as they journeyed across the northeast and beyond. If Lopes's original petitions and claims about killing Zumbi helped bequeath wealth directly to his descendants, the narratives established during the colonial era and pushed forward in the nineteenth and twentieth centuries made Lopes's story accessible generations later to Francisco Galvão, who could publicly claim to be his heir. When Cavignac interviewed him, she asked how the information had been passed down, and he explained that he had discovered it while doing research for the family's celebration of their 350-year presence in Brazil, itself a remarkable statement about the range of family lineages and inheritances that passed through Palmares. Cavignac also asked Galvão about one of the *other* Zumbis in Rio Grande do Norte—the state's Zumbi town, which I had been discussing with her recently:

> Francisco Galvão (FG): Yeah . . . that, that . . . Zumbi. I think it's likely. That [place], I'm not familiar with it. Sometimes, I—well, geography tells us a lot, doesn't it? I don't know if the Zumbi from there or here—
>
> Julie Cavignac (JC): Or from here [Canguaretama]? Natal? Or Rio Grande do Norte?
>
> FG: Yeah, from Rio Grande do Norte. But the north coast, a bit far from here. I don't know if the name is from the wind there because it's an area with a lot of wind, you know? And I don't know [. . .] if there's a direct relationship with Zumbi de Palmares, or if it's a zumbi that appears there as a Black being [entidade *negra*], you know? . . . Anyway, you could make that link with Zumbi de Palmares.

Cavignac then asked, "Are there any histories of zumbi here [in Canguaretama]?" "No," he replied, "Not that I know of. We don't have that here in Canguaretama, and there's not an area [around here] with many Blacks. This I am not aware of." Identifying multiple possible meanings of Z/zumbi — the wind, the Palmarista leader, a "Black being" — Galvão also associated these things with the town named Zumbi, which he described as a distant, almost foreign place. The nearby presence of Sibaúma, a Black community with members who today call themselves Zumbi's heirs, did not register in his comments.[51]

Though in 2019 Galvão clearly indicated to Cavignac that his ancestor had fatally wounded Zumbi, in the 2013 blog he was more circumspect. The post, titled "The Galvão Family Presence in the History of Zumbi dos Palmares," states, "In 1676, in a battle with troops led by Manuel Lopes Galvão, Zumbi was shot in the leg, which may have left him crippled." The text then says that Zumbi was shot again in 1694, escaping death one more time, before being killed after he was betrayed by a fellow Palmarista.[52] The different meanings of Z/zumbi and the changing story about his death all reflect how multiple, shifting narratives and ideas continue to percolate below the seemingly fixed and stable narratives consecrated in writing. However one interprets Galvão's narratives, he could never have cultivated them, much less been part of one of the state's most storied families, were it not for the efforts of his ancestor Manuel, who strived to wring rewards and recognition from the Crown and in doing so left behind a trail of documents and blood that would preserve his name in regional lore and help set the terms in which the stories of Zumbi and his death were told to subsequent generations.

Of course, residents of Sibaúma have their own genealogies and histories. The community shared and cultivated land together until the 1980s, when outside investors began to purchase property, driving wedges between members and leading to developments such as the Kilombo Hotel.[53] The exploitative nature of tourism and land development in the area is "unacceptable," as stated by Sérgio Marques Caetano, a community leader and artist-musician who plays in the musical ensemble Herdeiros de Zumbi.[54] Though these processes divided the community — and while there are plenty more voices to be heard — there is general agreement about shared origins, which descend from the trunks of three family trees: the Leandros, the Caetanos, and the Camilos.[55] The first residents arrived in Sibaúma along various paths, including a shipwreck, from nearby plantations, and from Paraíba. Their arrivals likely date to the early nineteenth century, perhaps earlier. The histories that community members passed down over generations were flattened out in the 1969 article in *Realidade*, which presented them all as "heirs of Zumbi."[56] If an accurate reflection of the symbolism that Zumbi had come to encompass, the label obscured the more detailed and varied histories preserved by the community. At the same time—as the name of Caetano's group suggests—the name is meaningful for at least some members of Sibaúma.

For all its flaws, the *Realidade* article did make an important intervention, using Sibaúma to counter the dominant narratives of Rio Grande do Norte, epitomized by Câmara Cascudo's assertion, which the article quoted: "We did not have quilombos or Black rebellions in Rio Grande do Norte."[57] Sibaúma proved this to be false, and a few scraps of archival evidence provide additional context about the area surrounding Sibaúma and Canguaretama. Through at least 1860, reports suggest that the area was inhabited largely by Blacks and Indigenous people.[58] In 1855 in Tamatandubá, not far from Canguaretama, an armed "mob" stormed into New Year's Mass, demanding to "hear the letter of manumission read." The group threatened "specific people," "pronounced themselves in general to be against the engenho owners," and promised to return in a week if "that paper had not been read."[59] It is unclear exactly who belonged to this "mob," or what their fates were, but the brazen act sent a clear message to the plantation owners while also registering another example to disprove Rio Grande's mythical whiteness.

By making the residents of Sibaúma Zumbi's heirs, the *Realidade* article provided visibility, though not without drawbacks. The article inspired a reader from Minas Gerais to write to the magazine and express her desire to travel to Sibaúma so that she could help its residents learn to read and fend for themselves.[60] Along with the paternalistic offer came complaints and corrections. The original article included a box of text with information about Zumbi and Palmares, which inspired confusion and indignation among some readers. The text box, titled "Zumbi Died Fighting," described him as "the principal leader of the Quilombo of Palmares, Pernambuco."[61] A man from Branquinha, Alagoas, was thrown off by the location. "Isn't there a mistake here? Almost every day I walk along the road that connects União dos Palmares with Branquinha, where I reside. I've heard various times some say, pointing to the now famous Serra da Barriga: 'It was there . . . that Zumbi sought refuge.' . . . Is there or is there not a small confusion in relation to the states and city [in the article]?"[62] Another man from Recife congratulated the magazine for the article while also "taking the liberty to rectify certain distortions about the history of Quilombos, so little researched in our country, and always imprecise." Zumbi's Palmares, he attested, was not in the city of the same name in Pernambuco and was instead in União dos Palmares in Alagoas. Also, he continued, Zumbi was not assassinated, as *Realidade* suggested, and instead had killed himself by leaping off a cliff.[63] The magazine's editors printed a lengthy rebuttal, clarifying that they were referring not to the city named Palmares in Pernambuco, which, like União dos Palmares in Alagoas, acquired its official name long after the mocambos fell, but instead to the colonial captaincy that was called Pernambuco but also included Alagoas. Quoting Edison Carneiro, the editors also reasserted that Zumbi had not, in fact, killed himself.[64]

The responses to the article illustrate a great deal about the consolidation and erasure of historical narratives surrounding Palmares and Zumbi. Though the essay was about Sibaúma, at least for the two readers from Alagoas and Pernambuco, the most important parts were about Palmares. Even in shifting focus to their own places of residence, their letters illustrate multiple points of erasure and ongoing questions. Where, exactly, was Palmares? The man who lived closest to Serra da Barriga did not claim the mocambos as his own and instead said that he had heard others talk about them on the road to União dos Palmares. Together with the disagreement about how Zumbi died, the confusions and clarifications about location also had the combined effect of removing Sibaúma from the conversation. Palmares and Zumbi were everywhere and nowhere, signifiers that could be all-encompassing or, just as easily, empty. Sibaúma and its own histories fell out of the conversation, quickly dominated by Palmares and questions that had been and would continue to be asked for years.

Oral history can be a useful tool for grappling with histories that lay beyond, and are often hidden by, Palmares, and there is much more to be done in this regard. Some oral histories of Palmares resemble elements of what Cavignac describes as "surprising interpretations" or renderings of historical events, which "at first glance" may even appear "fantastical" but, on closer consideration, reveal complex and revelatory forms of historical memory.[65] This came through forcefully in interviews I conducted in Zumbi, Rio Grande do Norte; most were facilitated and, in many ways, shaped by Damiana de Oliveira Silva, a university student who lives in Zumbi and identifies (though only when asked) as parda. When a professor at the Universidade Federal do Rio Grande do Norte introduced us, I hoped that Silva could introduce me to members of the community, whom I would then interview, but Silva ended up also participating in the interviews, helpfully jumping in to clarify my questions and often also asking her own, for all of which I am indebted to her. During one conversation, when a resident told me that Zumbi had "founded Palmares," she interjected, saying that that was a misconception, and that a woman had founded it. Later, I asked Silva about the comment, and she told me she did not remember the woman's name but had learned about her in school.

By displacing Zumbi with a nameless woman, Silva put forth a powerful counterpoint to the history of the nameless woman who died at the hands of the Dutch bugler on March 21, 1645. The fact that Silva found it meaningful to evoke that history in a place named Zumbi makes her intervention all the more poignant. Several weeks later, she messaged me on WhatsApp, sending a link to an article about the Parque Memorial Quilombo dos Palmares (Quilombo dos Palmares Memorial Park), created atop the Serra da Barriga in 2007. The piece, which one of Silva's high school instructors sent after visiting the park, names Aqualtune as the founder of the Grande Federação Negra Palmarina (Great Black Federation of Palmares).[66] Though there was nothing called the Grande Federação Negra Palmarina, it is no more "fantastical" to suggest that Aqualtune, described in one version of the *Relação* as the "king's mother," founded Palmares than it is to say that Zumbi did.[67]

In Silva's interjection and the comment that spurred it, we find a powerful account of the historical marginalization of Palmares women and a meaningful counternarrative. Silva's intervention also dialogues in interesting ways with ongoing debates about Dandara, the fictional Palmares character who has become a deeply meaningful symbol of Black female empowerment and political mobilization despite objections, which range from racist dismissals to earnest and thoughtful calls to do more work not only to honor fictional lives but also to study the overlooked histories of Black women who existed.[68] Silva's intervention certainly illustrates the need to continue to develop new ways to bring more sharply into focus the histories of women from Palmares and other mocambos, ranging from powerful leaders, such as the one history knows as Aqualtune or Aca Inene, to those whose names were not recorded.[69]

Conclusion

That work may continue to build on the mobilizations that galvanized around the time that the *Realidade* article was published, most notably in Brazil's "other" Rio Grande: Rio Grande do Sul, the nation's southernmost state, which, like Rio Grande do Norte, often projects a white identity, a characterization that also belies vibrant Black histories. Beginning in 1971, the Black activist organization Grupo Palmares (the Palmares Group) recognized November 20—the date of Zumbi's assassination—as a day of singular importance. By the end of the decade, November 20 was observed by people across the country and would eventually become Brazil's National Day of Zumbi and Black Consciousness.[70]

The group's hard-won victories, and subsequent mobilizations, which continue to this day, harness and also respond to the fact that the histories of Palmares and Z/zumbi have been marked by proliferation, consolidation, and erasure. Just as the colonial frontier seemed like an infinite expanse, memories and meanings of Palmares and Zumbi have forged their own seemingly endless spaces, even while passing by (or trampling) other stories. When one explores the legacies and many uses and meanings of Palmares and Z/zumbi that swirled around and just below the surface of the paradigmatic narratives and figures that congealed during the nineteenth and early twentieth centuries, one will visit discomfiting, racist places. Southey named his pet cat Zombi. He first intended to name the animal, "a fine, full-grown black cat," after Henrique Dias, "in reference to both his complexion and his sex," but settled on the "title of the chief of the Palmares negroes [*sic*]."[71] Even more forcefully than Zumbi Soap from Rio de Janeiro, the nickname debases a revered figure and profound religious force. Both examples also illustrate a durable and multivalent word, which, depending on whose hands it was in, had come to mean devil, saint, hero, scourge, commodity, and many more things between and beyond. One of the ironies and challenges that scholars must continue to grapple with is the way that Palmares can simultaneously erase and make visible. Sibaúma first gained national attention when a journalist linked it to Palmares, and José de Alencar's attempt to trace Mazombo through Palmares is similarly both misleading and important. In each example and others beside them, we find Palmares to be both central and peripheral to Brazil's African Diasporas—a place and creation large and dynamic enough to both create its own diasporas and obscure others.

CONCLUSION   Tapera dos Palmares

Today, the location where Governor Caetano de Melo de Castro ordered Zumbi's head displayed on a pike — what he called "the most public place" in Recife — is marked at the Pátio de Nossa Senhora do Carmo, a bustling plaza in front of one of the city's oldest churches. The church was not completed until the second half of the eighteenth century, and it is unlikely that the Pátio was where the vicious act was actually consummated.[1] Nonetheless, in 2006, a statue of Zumbi was placed in the plaza with a plaque, now weathered and difficult to read, that makes no mention of his death or why the monument is in the Pátio do Carmo (see figures C.1 and C.2). The disjuncture is emblematic of others. Offering few historical details, likely divorced from place, and memorializing a single, masculine figure, the statue of Zumbi mirrors many of the limitations of historical writing and memorialization of Palmares and Z/zumbi. And yet as public shrines to white supremacists in the United States and Europe have fallen in recent years, causing no small amount of backlash, this statue of Zumbi, one of several in Brazil, holds great meaning.

Standing in a place where enslaved people were trafficked, its significance is undeniable, and the site has become not just meaningful but sacred for some, including practitioners of the Afro-Brazilian religions Candomblé and Umbanda, as well as Jurema, a descendant of the Cult of Jurema that the Inquisition persecuted during the colonial era. With a diverse following and incorporating Afro-Brazilian (and some Euro-Brazilian) elements, Jurema remains widely associated with Indigeneity.[2] Beginning in 2007, practitioners of Jurema, Candomblé, and Umbanda began an annual pilgrimage through the streets of downtown Recife. The procession ends in the Pátio do Carmo, chosen for its association with Zumbi.[3] In light of that choice,

FIGURE C.1 The Pátio do Carmo, Recife (1868). While by the nineteenth century, the plaza could be credibly called "the most public place" in Recife, in 1695 the church (pictured in the background) was still not complete, and the area was likely less trafficked than it is depicted as here. *Source*: Luis Schlappriz, *Vista do Pateo do Carmo, Casa de Banhos e Convento do Carmo*, Courtesy of the Museu da Cidade do Recife.

FIGURE C.2 Zumbi statue in the Pátio do Carmo, Recife (2022). *Source*: Author.

the worn plaque on the plaza's Zumbi monument takes on new meaning, portraying not only neglect, but also power and open-endedness—and provides an invitation to think once more about the many histories and paths that lead into, out of, and beyond Palmares.

Layered Diasporas and Unequal Inheritances

We might conceptualize such histories and paths under the name Tapera dos Palmares. Just as Tapera d'Angola, a little-known place on the margins of a seventeenth-century Dutch map, calls attention to surprising histories of transition and regeneration emerging from abandonment, Pernambuco's post-1695 landscape, ravaged by war, contained the potential to give new life. By focusing our attention on the simultaneous capacity to generate and erase, Tapera dos Palmares provides a necessary readjustment to how we think about Palmares, other maroon communities, and diaspora in Brazil and beyond.

In contrasting Palmares with the Saramaka people he worked with in Suriname, Richard Price highlights the difference between his own ethnographic work and what is possible in Palmares. In contrast to Palmares, which ceased to exist, in Suriname he could access "precious and precise memories" of the colonial era preserved and retold by direct descendants of early Saramaka maroons.[4] Price's intention was to encourage new and more comparative thinking about Palmares, and in many respects this book is an embrace of that challenge. At the same time, one of my basic premises has been that even in the absence of the kind of direct descendance that Price worked with, Palmares afterlives may be found through a combination of familiar and less-familiar historical methodologies: reading and rereading written documents, paying close attention to spirituality, studying the landscape, tracing the movement of people, and using comparative historical linguistics to complement and help move beyond stingy colonial archives.

Though unique in many ways, some elements of this story are generalizable. As Price and many others have demonstrated, flight and the creation of settlements large and small were daring, meaningful acts. Palmares makes clear that the story rarely ends with those acts or even with the destruction of a community. Though the sheer size of Palmares means that it generated more dispersals than most such communities, general principles may be applied to even the smallest mocambo: any fugitive settlement could be a generative starting point capable of creating and reshaping diaspora, giving it new life, and becoming an anchor for the living and the dead. Freedom, resistance, rebellion, and fugitivity—all rightfully central concepts in the study of maroon communities—only represent a portion of the ideas, beliefs, desires, concepts, and challenges that come into sharper focus by treating those communities not only as conclusions but also as starting points. Among the topics that emerge in greater light by looking across 1695 are spirituality, forging home, the passing and receiving of different kinds of inheritances, and the creation and negotiation of relationships and statuses that fell between or outside of the categories of "free" and "slave." In other settings, close attention to place, language, and spirituality will draw forth complementary, and surely also conflictual and divergent, histories.

A separate, somewhat dissonant set of lessons may also be gleaned by an awareness of the histories and designs that did not pass through Palmares. Today, there are thousands of officially recognized quilombo communities in Brazil, less than 10 percent of which are in Pernambuco and Alagoas.[5] Many others await certification, and an unknown number of other afrodescendente communities in Brazil, for multiple reasons, do not seek to be certified. As large and influential as it was, Palmares only touched a small fragment of Brazil's African Diaspora, and even while it wields incredible symbolic power and meaning, there exist countless other histories and trajectories.[6]

The stories that emerge from Tapera dos Palmares reveal diaspora to be not only about the different ways that people, beliefs, symbols, and goods were transformed, lost, and preserved in the New World and back and forth across the Atlantic, but also about how those processes renewed and repeated, and in some cases were erased or replaced, as Africans and their descendants assembled and dispersed again and again in fugitive communities, via the domestic trade, and through other routes and temporary stations. In other words, Z/zumbi, in all of its meanings, encourages us not only to think of a single or even multiple African diasporas, but also to consider a seemingly incalculable number of ancillary dispersals that emanated from internal flows of people enslaved and free, and from so many other mocambos that were destroyed but whose members survived in new fugitive or free settings, were forced back into slavery, or were killed.[7]

This process continues long after slavery ended. During the second half of the twentieth century, poverty drove groups from Caiana dos Crioulos, the quilombo community near Zumbi, Paraíba, to move to Rio de Janeiro, some settling in a community that became known as Novo Quilombo (New Quilombo).[8] As the examples of Gunocô, Cumbi, and even Z/zumbi illustrate, Brazil's and Palmares's African diasporas also brought together individuals, communities, and ideas and symbols from multiple regions, suggesting why the "Angolan wave," much like a Kimbundu dictionary, is a starting point but not nearly the whole story.

Rereading colonial documents, adding new ones, and moving beyond the written word reveals a range of meanings that Z/zumbi must have carried in the mocambos that is much broader and more vivid than what we find in more familiar archival sources. Doing so also shows good reason to simultaneously move closer to and farther away from Palmares and Zumbi. During the seventeenth century, access to and control of rain and water were almost certainly central to Zumbi's authority, as was his connection to ancestor spirits. The overlapping waves of people who arrived and were born in Palmares came into violent contact with different versions of Dutch and Portuguese colonial societies seeking to destroy it. On the margins, there were places such as Tapera d'Angola, which, whether directly connected to the mocambos of Palmares, suggests a dynamic movement linked to but also clearly apart from Africa—the ruins of, or a deserted, Angola in America. By centering fugitivity alongside colonial power (exemplified in the repeated military assaults and the awarding of land grants) on a frontier defined in large part by the mocambos, we find that Palmares represents not only a remarkable chapter in history but also a generative site that shaped the meanings of slavery, freedom, and a panoply of other relationships and categories long after colonial forces destroyed it. Palmares was not simply a product of the frontier. Rather, this frontier was also a product of Palmares, which even after its fall shaped and generated life and death in the area.

As the Palmares wars dragged on, Portuguese confusion reigned about who Zumbi was, though that did not preclude soldiers and officers from seeking to make money off his death, even years before it happened. Less directly, future authors would capitalize by sculpting tales that emphasized different forms of singularity. For Sebastião da Rocha Pita, this took the form of the suicide narrative, which held sway for ages. Later, Raimundo Nina Rodrigues insisted that Zumbi was an "error" and had nothing to do with zumbi. Similar processes occurred across the Atlantic, as António de Oliveira de Cadornega inventively attached "evil" to Zambi, and other Europeans took similar steps to shape the meanings of African ideas, concepts, and beliefs. Later, the disaggregation and stripping of dense meanings into smaller, compartmentalized parts accompanied visceral decay. The Zumbi neighborhood in Paraíba's capital, once a thoroughfare, became a place to dump trash; the distrito in the Paraíban Brejo is often left off maps and feels otherwise forgotten; and the nearby lake that was renamed generations ago and whose association with Z/zumbi and the Africans and their kin who likely gave the body of water its name have been all but erased. Yet the very out-of-wayness that marked seemingly desolate places as disposable also imbued those places with spiritual meaning.

If these forms of physical and written violence illustrate how some meanings were preserved over time while others were marginalized, they do not foreclose deeper consideration, research, or new questions. Stories of flying Africans from elsewhere in the diaspora invite further discussion about death by suicide, the meaning and place of home, and the multiple forms of posthumous flight that do not fit into the more familiar US and Caribbean examples. The deities that Manuel and Francisca worshipped in eighteenth-century Minas Gerais also suggest how multiple diasporic streams shaped the meanings of Z/zumbi, not to mention Saint Benedict, both of whom, at least in the minds of those who testified against the couple, resided in the dwelling shared by this West Central African man and West African woman. The way that zumbi, Saci, and Gunôco came together in Brazil further illustrates the geographical and spiritual expansiveness of the post-1695 world.

That world was marked by unequal fates and inheritances for groups and individuals with varied relationships to Palmares, including the stark disparity in life and death between Zumbi and the unnamed woman killed on March 21, 1645. While Manuel and Francisca likely had no direct connection to the mocambos, Pedro Soeiro and Paula da Silva did. Though both belonged to Palmares, they traveled different paths out, marked by physical and figurative distance. Silva's son, Lázaro Coelho de Eça, and Simôa Gomes show additional permutations. Neither was born in Palmares, though both were directly tied to it. Lázaro's connection came by not only his mother, who was stolen from Palmares, but also his father, who was employed to destroy the very place that Paula came from. We know nothing of Simôa's mother, other than that she was Indigenous, but have no doubt about her grandfather, the famed white conqueror Domingos Jorge Velho. The wealth that she and her family built in Garanhuns lasted for generations. As both Lázaro and Simôa illustrate, the differing fates of individuals born into the post-1695 world raise still unanswered questions: How do we account for, address, and provide redress for these dramatically different legacies and inheritances? What is owed to whom? The fact that the Palmares wars destroyed and generated Indigenous land also merits deeper consideration, not only among historians but in contemporary conversations about land distribution and the legacies of slavery—and what, we may ask, are the debts owed to heirs of Páscoa dos Santos, the daughter of Manuel Barbalho de Lira, and other descendants of Black and Indigenous combatants who fought against Palmares?

These questions underline the many ways that the Palmares wars spewed violence while generating and confiscating wealth: the murder of Black Palmaristas, the starvation of Indigenous children, the land theft, the daily violence on plantations, the unending pursuit of fugitives and refugees, the relentless attacks against non-Christian religions. The Palmares wars created wealth and material inheritances for some, much less for others, and actively destroyed physical, familial, and spiritual possessions and ties for still others. All parties—Black and Indigenous—deserve redress.

Questions also propel us beyond where most narratives take place, to locales such as Paraíba and Rio Grande do Norte, where layered diasporas have met repeated and multiple forms of marginalization. In the songs that history sings about these places, the people who lived there, and the many acts of violence unleashed on them, we find new maps of Palmares and a fuller accounting for slavery and Palmares's many disparate forms of inheritance. It is also worth recalling that the Bishop of Olinda's apocalyptic comparison of the region's Indigenous people to the Black revolutionaries of Haiti preceded by a century Rodrigues's more well-known comparison of Palmares and Haiti. In the bishop's warning, we find reason to reconsider larger paradigms, timelines, and geographies of Atlantic revolution.[9]

After and Beyond

One of the more notable moments during my time in Paraíba was when I finally understood that, just miles from a place called Zumbi, members of Caiana dos Crioulos did not want to talk about Zumbi dos Palmares. Their historical pantheon was different, and the way that federal recognition of quilombos has created or exacerbated divisions and brought little aid to the community provided additional reasons to push our conversation beyond Palmares. A slightly different dynamic is at play in Rio Grande do Norte. With nearby beaches as an attraction for tourists, this Zumbi town has more commercial infrastructure than Paraíba's Zumbi. Just down the street from the town's church is the Panificadora Zumbi (Zumbi Bakery [or Bread Factory]; see figure C.3), which offers "the best bread on the beach," an echo of the Zumbi Soap produced in Rio de Janeiro a century ago.

Some of the stories and meanings that the town's residents shared with me evoke what Christine M. DeLucia calls "memoryscapes," though, as the bakery suggests, the most prominent outcomes have trended toward erasure, or at least decontextualization. In contrast to the "seemingly blank or neutral spaces" in New England that have been transformed by oral history into "emotionally infused, politically potent places," many of Rio Grande do Norte's memoryscapes seem to track along almost an inverted path.[10] A politically freighted name to start with, Zumbi becomes less meaningful—or at least decontextualized—when it is simply the name of a town or an adjective for a commodity. And yet, as the narratives and contestations in New England are capable of "reopening history," so do Rio Grande's Zumbi place-names contain the potential to write and suggest new histories, of not only Palmares but also the state's marginalized and overlooked African-descendant population.[11]

Another insight gleaned from thinking about what happened after Palmares is that stories and meanings traveled not only by spirits and Palmarista survivors but also via soldiers of various backgrounds. Though they did multiple forms of violence to Palmares, their presence in the story does not automatically or only signal destruction. Black soldiers were, of course, as much a part of the African Diaspora as Palmaristas were. In a very different way, white veterans who settled on the far western border of Rio Grande do Norte, dotted with place-names such as Mocambo and Couto, participated in shaping and perhaps unwittingly helping propel expressions of diaspora forward. A similar dynamic is seen in the engenhos called Zumbi or Mocambo. None of these examples suggest that non-Blacks wrested control of diaspora from people of African descent. One might read them to suggest instead that even as military victors, in pinning African names to their properties, whites functioned in the service of diaspora. This was clearly no charity mission, and rather an indication of the power and sometimes unlikely pathways of diasporic afterlives and inheritances. Presenting Z/zumbi and other African

FIGURE C.3 Zumbi Bakery (Zumbi, Rio Grande do Norte, 2019), "The Best Bread on the Beach." *Source*: Author.

words, symbols, and ideas as trophies, the conquerors also left open ground to cultivate connections with old forms and nurse new ones.

A related point may be made about the treatment of 1695 as a transformational historical moment. Scholars tend to highlight the pull factors behind Pernambuco's decline and the exodus of enslaved laborers, treating the discovery of metals and diamonds in Minas Gerais as a magnetic force that drew Africans and their kin into the brutal mining that powered Brazil's Golden Age. We might also consider the cumulative impact of a century of battling rebel Blacks in Pernambuco, not to mention the long warfare against Indigenous people across the northeast, as a push factor. Of course, there were rebel Black and Indigenous people in Minas Gerais too, but perhaps the near simultaneity of the discoveries in Minas Gerais, the colonial victory at Serra da Barriga, and the assassination of Zumbi combined to push and pull Portuguese interests away from Pernambuco, lured, no doubt, by the glimmering riches on the horizon in Minas Gerais, but also bruised from the decades of entanglements with Palmares.

Using "tapera," a Tupi word, to describe the afterlives of 1695 brings to the fore the role and plight of the region's Indigenous people, a collective that confounds familiar categories and definitions. The trajectories of Santo Amaro and other aldeias highlight how a large part of the story of Palmares after 1695 is about at least three waves of land dispossession: first, the displacement of Indigenous people by Europeans and possibly the mocambos themselves; next, the "conquest" of Palmares and destruction of Black land and settlements; finally, the continued, long-term assault against Indigenous land. It was on these ruins too that Pernambuco and Alagoas eventually rebuilt their plantation economies and in which diasporas old and new emerged.

Conquest is a useful, if imperfect, lens for understanding Palmares's multiple layers of ruins and also draws attention to some of the ways that gender and race functioned during the Palmares wars and in their long aftermath. Whiteness and masculinity emerged as simultaneously powerful and fragile, prizes elusive to many and more accessible to some. Memorializations of Palmares quickly codified the once-ferocious, now-defeated Black Zumbi of "singular valor," a man who ultimately capitulated to a superior army. The durability of Rocha Pita's romantic tale is notable not only for its role in propagating the myth of Zumbi's suicide but also for how it facilitated the elevation of Zumbi above all else. Even as other meanings of Z/zumbi multiplied and circulated, in historical literature the defeated warrior rose to the top, an icon to encapsulate a heroic tale of white European conquest of rebel Blacks.

While Zumbi has become one of Brazil's most well-known historical figures, we know very little about him, and much of the history and historiography of Palmares are also clearly about erasure, marginalization, and disaggregation. We know even less about the masses of Palmaristas whose names are today unknown, not only followers of leaders such as Zumbi, but also those who left Palmares or, as in the case of the unnamed woman killed by the Dutch bugler, whom Palmares left behind. The elevation of Zumbi has also limited deeper reflection by historians about the many meanings attached to his name. As a result, the line between human and spirit became fixed, and the multiple significances of zumbi came to be thought of—at least among many scholars—as entirely and obviously distinct from the icon. But what were the intentions of the amas who evoked Z/zumbi? Some surely sought to frighten children as a means of demonstrating a modicum of control and power over their young white charges. Whatever the women's intentions, it is safe to say that some of their stories achieved an element of success in bringing unruly children to heel, even if as adults those same children would publicly put their own stamp on the same stories and, in the process, also enter them into the written record.

Back to Palmares . . .

However far history takes us beyond them, the mocambos tend to draw us back. One way this happens is through the myths codified in early histories of Brazil, which, like disappearing and reappearing ink, seem to vanish only to be reactivated later. One powerful engine for this process is the issuing of new editions or reprints of "classic" works. Many of the histories written in the eighteenth and nineteenth centuries were republished during the mid-twentieth century, and some continue to gain new lives in print, along with them old legends that die hard. In *Jubiabá*, a Marxist coming-of-age story published in 1935 by Jorge Amado, the main character communicates with Zumbi's spirit and learns that Zumbi died by suicide to avoid being enslaved.[12] The book has been reprinted dozens of times in multiple languages and depicted in film and on stage. A 2009 graphic novel retells the apocryphal suicide story and shows Zumbi diving to his death. Seemingly intent on striking one more blow against the Portuguese along the way, this living, human Zumbi, not yet a spirit, almost appears to fly (see figure C.4).[13]

For all the counternarratives, misuses, and abuses that mark the histories of Palmares and Zumbi, the places of both within national narratives are hard-won, still fiercely contested, and often flexible. In 1963, the director Carlos Diegues released the film *Ganga Zumba: Rei dos Palmares* (*Ganga Zumba: King of Palmares*), the prequel to Diegues's *Quilombo*, which debuted in 1984.[14] With a nearly all-Black cast and including depictions of enslaved people murdering white enslavers, *Ganga Zumba* was in some respects radical for its time, even though it included several tired racial and gendered stereotypes.[15] Produced and released the year before Brazil's military seized control of the country, *Ganga Zumba* was, according to Diegues, "a film about the use of freedom, how to fight and use your freedom."[16] The movie, which was filmed in black-and-white, belonged to the early Cinema Novo movement, and, in the words of the famed actor-filmmaker Glauber Rocha, was a "slow, sad anti-epic."[17] *Quilombo*, released as the military's power waned, had a different intention and feel. With bright colors and fantastical developments,

FIGURE C.4 Zumbi, Falling or Flying. *Source:* Spacca and Amado, *Jubiabá*, 18.

Quilombo was made with what would come after the dictatorship in mind; the film, Diegues, said, was "about the building of utopia."[18] Notably, both films portray Palmares as Yoruba and with Candomblé as its religion, obvious projections of the African symbols that carried the most purchase and legibility in Brazil during the second half of the twentieth century. The African sine qua non was now West African.

In addition to illustrating the flexible nature of representations of Palmares and Africa in popular culture and the different political uses to which

Palmares was put during the second half of the twentieth century, Diegues's films also provide an interesting echo of Rodrigues's amas. Diegues, who is from Alagoas, recounted doing exhaustive research for *Quilombo*, whose original inspiration he traced to his youth: "I had been thinking about the film's story since I was a child. I was born in the region where the Quilombo [Palmares] was founded. I had heard the legends. I remember an old Black woman who told me that Zumbi could fly, and I believed that. This was very important to me because I was much more interested in the myth, the legend, than in the details of history."[19] Though he does not portray Zumbi flying in the film, Diegues does show him to be defiant even in death. In the final scene, after being struck by a hail of gunfire, and with blood streaming from his body, Zumbi remains upright, unleashing a final scream and hurling his spear skyward.[20] At least on film, the weapon does not come down.

During the same era that Diegues made his films, Décio Freitas published several influential texts about Palmares. Freitas was a white dissident who was exiled during the dictatorship and collaborated with the Grupo Palmares in Rio Grande do Sul. His work also shaped Diegues's *Quilombo*. In one book, Diegues asserted that he had found new sources that revealed that Zumbi was born in 1655 in Palmares, captured by colonial forces, and then baptized and raised by a Catholic priest before fleeing back to Palmares.[21] Freitas did not cite any documents to substantiate the claims, and no one has been able to verify them since. Around the bicentennial of 1695, Luiz Mott, a historian of colonial Brazil, incorporated these biographical details into an argument that Zumbi was homosexual, a suggestion that set off a furor and resulted in attacks on Mott's house and threats against his life, a forceful reminder of the narrowly defined masculinity that Zumbi has come to embody.[22]

The late twentieth and early twenty-first centuries brought important victories and withering attacks. In 1988, along with Article 68 of the new constitution and the promise of rights for quilombo communities, the federal government created the Fundação Cultural Palmares (FCP; Palmares Cultural Foundation) to defend and promote Black culture. In 1995, Brazilians marked the three-hundred-year anniversary of Zumbi's death with demonstrations and scholarly publications. The conversations marked a turning point in mobilizations for land and rights, giving new meaning to 1695, three centuries later.[23] In 2007, the Parque Memorial Quilombo dos Palmares was created atop Serra da Barriga, and four years later congress declared November 20 to be the National Day of Zumbi and Black Consciousness.[24]

These triumphs came into being alongside other, contradictory, developments. The process of memorializing Serra da Barriga involved struggles against large landowners and twentieth-century sugar barons but also displaced rural laborers whose families had resided on the mountain since the 1950s, who clashed with activists seeking protection and recognition for a monumental symbol of Black history.[25] Elsewhere, vandals have defaced statues of Zumbi, and one prominent judge declared that he was an "invented myth."[26] In 2019, President Jair Bolsonaro appointed Sérgio Camargo as director of the FCP. As many feared, the move was comparable to Donald Trump's appointment of Scott Pruitt as the administrator of the Environmental Protection Agency; Camargo, who is Black, openly disavowed the intention of the agency he was entrusted to steward. He promptly removed from the agency's websites biographies of key Black leaders, including Marielle Franco, the politician and activist slain in Rio de Janeiro in 2018—and Zumbi.[27] In 2023, after defeating Bolsonaro in the presidential election and securing a third term in office, Lula replaced Camargo with the Black activist and lawyer João Jorge Rodrigues, whose appointment was described by the new minister of culture as "a response to what happened in the previous administration, [a response] to the disrespect of the legacy of the Afro-Brazilian community."[28] The relationship between Palmares and quilombo communities today remains complex, full of possibility and also challenges. Many struggle against "the Palmares effect," a term coined by Elizabeth Farfán-Santos to describe the challenges faced by groups that seek visibility and resources but whose histories and identities do not match the images and ideals ensconced in dominant historical narratives.[29]

Though many current quilombo communities trace their histories elsewhere, in others Palmares looms large, often challenging conventional chronologies and cartographies. Angico de Cima, a community located in the area where the mocambo of Pedro Papacaça stood centuries ago, traces its origins to an enslaved couple who fled bondage in Paraíba, passing through Palmares before settling on its margins in Papacaça, an interesting inversion of the Palmares-to-Paraíba trajectory traced in chapter 9.[30] Another federally recognized quilombo, Castainho, traces two origin stories. One maintains that the community, which is near Garanhuns, was founded by a free man who inherited land from his former enslaver. The other recalls a group of men and women who fled the Palmares wars to found the settlement. In each case, according to the report that helped establish the community's case for recognition, "the War of Palmares" is an "indisputable" axis around which "Castainho constructs its identity."[31] In 2016, a sixty-eight-year-old resident of Castainho told a researcher about the origins of his community. "Look," he said, "I was raised on this history: It all started when they killed Zumbi, there in Alagoas, and the people went crazy [saying] he didn't die. And some people went into the mountains [and arrived] here [and made] the quilombos, and others went to other places."[32] Passed down and shaped over generations, the story may rightfully be called a "precious" memory, and its larger message, if not "precise," is nonetheless instructive: for many, the death of Zumbi was and is not just an end but also a beginning.[33]

From the 1970s through the 1990s, Black activists mobilized across Brazil not only to memorialize November 20 but also to secure official recognition and protection for Serra da Barriga, which during those decades came to be seen as a place of singular importance. Much of the battle to do so took place under the gaze of the military dictatorship.[34] For the activists who journeyed to Serra da Barriga and plotted and executed plans to protect and elevate it to a place of national (indeed, international) renown, the experience transcended politics, at least as they are often conceived. As word spread, Serra da Barriga became a destination that could represent return—a place of origin and inspiration for Blacks across Brazil and beyond. Visits to the site attracted the famous and not famous from all over. Stokely Carmichael came. So did the Indigenous activist Aílton Krenak.

"In a certain sense," recalled the scholar-activist Joel Rufino dos Santos, "Palmares, the Serra da Barriga, became the Mecca of Black and democratic movements in Brazil."[35] Annual trips, what Santos described as "pilgrimages," also included Candomblé priests, once again facilitating symbolism and ideas that drew from different African traditions. A group of organizers called Zumbi the "Afro-Brazilian orixá," referencing the Yoruba deity central to Candomblé.[36] Some who traveled to Serra da Barriga had visions. Others felt possessed by orixás. It all gave the movement a greater strength and reach than if it had been "limited to the political-ideological plane," Santos wrote. "It was as if [the movement] had been anointed, from the very beginning, by this dense Brazilian religiosity as its *axé* [energy or life force]."[37]

Density. Energy. Spirits. Palmares once again provided each. In grainy footage now easily available on YouTube, renowned activist-intellectuals Abdias do Nascimento and Lélia Gonzalez delivered stirring remarks about the meanings of Palmares. From Maceió, González called Serra da Barriga

FIGURE C.5 Marker for Abdias do Nascimento atop Serra da Barriga (2022). *Source*: Author.

FIGURE C.6 Convento São Francisco (Marechal Deodoro, Alagoas, 2022). *Source*: Author.

the "first and greatest monument in the history of popular struggle in this country—of the struggle of the oppressed." Atop the mountain, Nascimento raised his hands and shouted to the heavens: "We rise from bended knee to your land, Zumbi! We rise from bended knee to this land drenched in your blood!"[38] After Nascimento died, in 2011, some of his ashes were scattered on the mountain, marked now with a beaten plaque and small fence (see figure C.5). As for so many others before him, Palmares was both destination and place of origin.

. . . and One More Time Beyond

Other histories reside in unexpected places and manifest in surprising ways. In 2022, I made the thirty-kilometer drive from Maceió to Marechal Deodoro, a town that traces its history to the late sixteenth century and was renamed in 1939 for its most famous resident, the first president of the republic, whose brother, Pedro Paulino da Fonseca, authored the fantastical tale about the

FIGURE C.7 Saint Benedict in the Convento São Francisco (2022). *Source:* Author.

posthumous baptism of Zumbi and subsequent salvation of the war veteran Sebastião Dias Maneli.[39] The road from Maceió to Marechal Deodoro is less than two hours from Serra da Barriga and passes along the coast, away from Zumbi International Airport. Marechal Deodoro is home to some of Brazil's oldest churches, including the Convento São Francisco, the site of Fonseca's story (see figure C.6).

When I arrived at the church, I learned that there remains no marker of Maneli's grave, not a huge surprise given his relative obscurity and the fact that the building, restored in 1975, retains few indications of anyone buried in it centuries earlier.[40] But while I did not find Maneli, another figure greeted me as I wandered through the chapel. This one made me think that if priests had actually resuscitated Maneli to baptize Zumbi, they might have also unleashed unexpected forces. High above the pews, alongside Jesus, Mary, and other Christian icons, is a likeness whose presence invites further reflection about what additional stories of Palmares and Z/zumbi may inhabit the church. Among a white Catholic pantheon stands a now more familiar figure: Black Saint Benedict, surveying his surroundings and suggesting many other stories untold (see figure C.7).

APPENDIX A

A Latin Americanist Introduction to Africanist Comparative Historical Linguistics

Comparative historical linguistics can offer a deeper and more expansive understanding of history, language, and meanings—a fuller song—than dictionaries and other sources more familiar to historians. In addition to defining terms and detailing the linguistic methodologies used in *After Palmares*, this appendix is meant to be a resource for Latin Americanist historians with no prior knowledge of African languages or Africanist comparative historical linguistic methodologies. In an ideal world, I would have had the opportunity to complete formal linguistic training during graduate school or to take time off from teaching to do the same. For those earlier in their career, these options may be available, but many (Latin) Americanists who study the African Diaspora find themselves more in the spot that I was in—wanting to think about, understand, and analyze language more fully but feeling unequipped to do so. This appendix will help, especially for those working with Bantu languages.

Guideposts and the Importance of Further Inquiry

As noted in the introduction, and developed more fully here, three guideposts may shape the acquisition and use of the knowledge and skills needed to become conversant in comparative historical linguistics. First is Kathryn de Luna's assertion that "durable words were those that could speak from multiple perspectives simultaneously."[1] Here too the work of Marcos Abreu Leitão de Almeida is useful, especially his suggestion that enslaved people forged "unequal speech communit[ies] sustained by participants through the use of different languages."[2] As I show in chapter 4, this could happen even between two individuals, such as a West African woman, Francisca, and a West Central African man, Manuel, who lived together in Minas Gerais and possessed in their home religious objects used to worship a deity called Zumby. In their home, Francisca and Manuel must have negotiated the meaning of the figure and its name, in the process lending new life and added "durability" to the polysemic Z/zumbi.

Second, a great deal of historical work on African languages in the Americas offers an incomplete picture that comparative historical linguistics can help fill in, though here an interesting tension arises. As historians, we are drawn toward verifiable facts, and as a result, our approach to language often channels us into narrow tunnels and lines of questioning: What did a word mean in 1702? There is plenty of utility in that approach, and when dictionaries and other sources allow us to pinpoint answers, we learn a great deal. But that kind of absolute clarity often escapes us.[3] Rather than abandon the idea of historical veracity, comparative historical linguistics helps provide it, though the answers we find are often hypothetical and multiple. The example of "olenga" (chapter 3) illustrates this. One dictionary translates the word as "to flee," which made its way into Silvia Lara's authoritative work on Palmares. But another dictionary lists multiple other possible definitions. Confronted with this kind of multiplicity, we may simply acknowledge the lack of certainty and signal the need for deeper linguistic work, as I have with olenga, or press forward into more of that work ourselves, as I did with other words and roots.

Third, at least in some cases, linguistic work may be easier than we imagine. Gleaning the different meanings of zumbi, zambi, and zombi can involve a deep dive into the world of lexical reconstructions. But other insights are available with tools that historians already have at our disposal: cataloguing the appearances and spellings used and noting change over time (or lack thereof), using other primary and secondary sources to contextualize those iterations, and, above all, asking questions: Why did the Portuguese use different spellings? What did each mean to the various parties who heard, uttered, and recorded the words? Though these kinds of questions are accessible to historians and should be asked more often, comparative historical linguistics allows us to go even further. If the Italian Capuchin Cavazzi and the anonymous painter of the watercolors on which he drew (chapter 4) confused or interchanged "Zumbi" and "Zumba," what would Palmaristas have understood the relationship between the two to be and how would that have compared to people from different areas of West Central Africa? These questions indicate how comparative historical linguistics can function as a springboard for asking new questions and charting lines of inquiry for future scholars, even—perhaps especially—when we acknowledge the limits of our own work.[4]

Key Terms, Symbols, Tools, and Concepts

In order to see those limits clearly, there is a requisite familiarity with certain terms, symbols, tools, and concepts beginning with a brief response to a basic question: What, exactly, is comparative historical linguistics? By using knowledge about sound changes and the ways that languages evolve, it is possible to work backward or "upstream" from written evidence (or firsthand ethnographic work) to make informed suggestions about earlier forms that were never recorded. This is what practitioners of **comparative historical linguistics** do. (I bold this and other key terms and concepts.) Scholars use comparative historical methodology to derive or reconstruct likely words and roots for languages "never actually seen or heard by anybody who is around now." This method "is not a hard and fast 'algorithm' for working out what's happened, but there are a series of heuristics or guidelines for making the hypotheses." At the core of the process lies the comparison of **cognate** forms in two or more "daughter languages" that descend from a single **protolanguage**, in the case of this book, **proto-Bantu**.[5] Proto-Bantu and other protolanguages are not "actual historical languages" and instead "a label or container for a body of linguistic attributes proposed to have been inherited by a group of related languages, and, therefore, to have characterized the common ancestral language from which extant languages developed."[6] Linguists use a star or **asterisk (*)** to indicate that a word was reconstructed using the comparative method. Though not carrying the stigma of a steroids-tainted home-run record, the * indicates that a word was not recorded and is therefore a hypothesis. An asterisk followed by a dash (*-) indicates the same for a root.[7]

Over time, as languages are built and revised, it is possible to comprehend larger systems of meaning. Much of the analysis of Bantu languages derives from the fact that they are **agglutinating**, which means that words are compositions of smaller parts, each with meaning(s) that remain recognizable even as they are strung together (see chapter 4). Those smaller parts—prefixes, suffixes, and other small bits of sound— are called **morphemes**, "the smallest meaningful units of language."[8] Rich repositories of morphemes, Bantu languages contain invaluable insights that were not recorded in writing. A great example of such units are Bantu **noun classes**, twenty-three umbrella categories that carry connotations ranging from human beings (class 1) to location terms (class 23).[9] Studying morphemes, noun classes, and other linguistic units makes it possible to track "historical patterns of inheritance, innovation, and contact through time."[10] **Phonology** (how consonants, vowels, and other elements are pronounced) and **morphology** (how small "meaningful units" such as noun-class prefixes construct and give meaning to words) similarly contribute to sketching a larger picture of linguistic meaning by helping us understand what a word meant when it was invented and how its meaning(s) changed over time.

Case Study: Z/zumbi

Comparative historical linguistics' potential to provide broader landscapes than the smaller, if still crucial, snapshots offered by a single dictionary is seen in the word Z/zumbi. *After Palmares* uses a wide array of sources that reveal a multidimensional set of definitions, most of which involve spirits and isolated or seemingly vacant places. But my research also revealed a significant number of aquatic references: zumbi currents, lakes, streams, and rivers (see especially chapter 9). Dictionaries provided few leads, but digging into the roots was more instructive. As I describe in chapter 3, one likely proto-Bantu root of the word was **-dùmb-*, "to rain" (and its noun form **-dùmbí*, "rain"). But to get from **-dùmb(í)* to zumbi requires a few more steps, and this is where established rules about sound change come into play. **Bantu spirantization** is linguists' name for sound changes, including the letter /d/ changing to /z/, though only in front of certain vowels, that occurred as many Bantu languages merged from a seven-vowel system into five.[11] Linguists represent sound changes using conventions that resemble a math equation: In this case, $*d\_u > /z/\_u$ means that a reconstructed d sound (*d) became a z sound, which was recorded in writing as the letter /z/. This change, the "equation" shows, happened when a *d* sound preceded a *u* sound: _u. Linguists might also use *d > /z/_u to represent this change, which I simplify further in the table and map below as du > zu. Using these established rules, it is possible to suggest with reasonable confidence that the zumbi place-names not only reflect dictionary and missionary meanings associated with spirits, but, especially in the cases of aquatic toponyms, also evoke water and rain. This, in turn, provides a deeper understanding of the powers and meanings associated with the Palmares leader(s) named Zumbi, while also suggesting the origins that helped Z/zumbi become multi-valent and durable.

Because it depends on multiple examples, the comparative method often offers useful insights about place, and here Malcolm Guthrie's work is crucial. Guthrie divided Bantuphone Africa into sixteen **zones**, assigning each a letter, tacking on numbers and additional letters to identify dialects and chart change over time.[12] In the case of zumbi, Guthrie and the Bantu Lexical Reconstructions 3 (BLR 3) database indicate that *-dùmb* and *-dùmbí* were used in twelve zones (C, D, E, F, H, J, L, M, N, P, R, and S).[13] While the Palmarista name or title of Zumbi may have come from Angola, Africans from a much wider expanse of territory would have recognized it. Many would have understood a spiritual component, but an even larger contingent would have specifically associated the word with rain or water. The rules of spirantization help narrow things within the twelve zones identified by Guthrie and the BLR 3, ultimately revealing a still-sprawling collection of nineteen languages in six zones (see map A.1 and table A.1). This insight provides crucial context for interpreting the rich collection of zumbi place-names found in the northeast and illuminates some of the worlds and meanings that Africans and their kin made in and after Palmares. In other cases, comparative historical linguistics directs us to new questions, which may be the methodology's richest and most accessible aspect. By tracing linguistic meanings across time and space, historians learn, see, and hear more than we previously thought was possible, potentially changing the parameters of what we deem to be knowable about the diasporic histories of marronage, slavery, life, death, and much more.

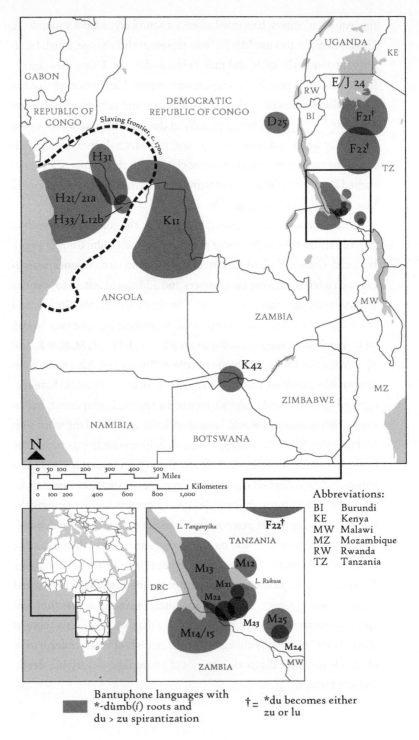

MAP A.1 Bantuphone Languages with *-dùmb(ì)* Roots and du > zu Spirantization.
Source: Janson, "Bantu," appendix A.1.

TABLE A.1 Bantuphone Languages with *-dùmb(i)
Roots and du > zu Spirantization

LANGUAGE	ZONE
Lega-Mwenga	D25
Kerewe	E/J24
Sukuma[Δ]	F21
Nyamwezi[Δ]	F22
Kimbundu	H21
Mbundu	H21a
Yaka	H31
Hungu	H33
Chokwe	K11
Ikuhane, Subia	K42
Rungwa	M12
Fipa	M13
Rungu	M14
Mambwe	M15
Wanda	M21
Mwanga	M22
Nyiha	M23
Malila	M24
Safwa	M25

Δ = /du/ becomes either /zu/ or /lu/.

SOURCE: Janson, "Bantu," appendix 1.

To complete the linguistic work for the book, I read a lot, sought and received generous instruction from Africanist colleagues, steadily familiarized myself with online resources, and enrolled in an eight-week online Omohundro Institute "coffee table," "Language as Archive and Method," directed by de Luna, and which included scholars of Indigenous languages in North America and others whose work focuses on Latin America and the African Atlantic. While each project will demand its own set of readings, most will rely on two kinds of texts: works that explain what comparative historical linguistics does, and those about the specific language(s) in play. For the former, I found Terry Crowley and Claire Bowern's *An Introduction to Historical Linguistics* very useful.[14] For Bantu- and other Africa-specific questions, especially helpful are *The Bantu Languages* (a text known to some as the "Bantu Bible"), edited by Derek Nurse and Gérard Philippson, and *Speaking with Substance: Methods of Language and Materials in African History*, by de Luna and Jeffrey B. Fleischer.[15] In theory, the most accessible tools are online databases such as the BLR 3, but in most cases one must familiarize themselves with key concepts (and website quirks) before effectively using them.[16]

One of the central, if seemingly mundane, questions that arose during research was what difference a single letter could make—what, if anything, distinguished "zumbi," "zambi," and "zombi"? While the most interesting answers lie in African linguistics, it was also necessary to learn the difference (and lack thereof) between the sounds of the letters /a/, /u/, and /o/ in seventeenth- and eighteenth-century Portuguese. *Histórica concisa da língua portuguesa*, *História da língua portuguesa*, and *The Handbook of Portuguese Linguistics* are useful for answering such questions.[17] Helpful guides for Indigenous languages most relevant to this study include two edited collections—*Línguas e culturas Tupí* and *Novos estudos sobre línguas indígenas*—and two texts by Eduardo de Almeida Navarro: *Dicionário tupi antigo* and *Método moderno de Tupi antigo*.[18]

APPENDIX B <span></span> Supplemental List

of Sources

This appendix includes citations for the primary sources used to create table 2.1 and table 5.1 as well as descriptive material for the methodology that was used for the estimates in table 5.1.

Table 2.1: Soldiers Who Claimed They Killed or Vanquished Zumbi before He Died (1676–1694)

Sources: "Carta de padrão [. . .]," April 23, 1688, Registo Geral de Mercês do reinado de D. Pedro II, liv. 5, fols. 189r–189v, ANTT; Carta patente de Manoel Lopes, March 15, 1689, Chancelaria de D. Pedro II, liv. 20, fols. 27v–28v, ANTT; "Consulta [. . .]," February 22, 1676, AHU, Pernambuco, caixa 11, doc. 1049, fols. 1r–2r, AHU; "Consulta [. . .]," August 8, 1684, Pernambuco, caixa 13, doc. 1297, fol. 5r, AHU; "Consulta [. . .]," March 15, 1687, Pernambuco, caixa 14, doc. 1411, fol. 2v, AHU; "Consulta [. . .]," January 26, 1688, Pernambuco, caixa 14, doc. 1433, AHU; "Consulta [. . .]," February 7, 1688, Consultas de Partes, cod. 49, fols. 331v–332r, AHU; "Consulta [. . .]," December 24, 1693, Pernambuco, caixa 16, doc. 1626, fol. 1r, AHU; "Informação [. . .]," July 30, 1682, Pernambuco, caixa 12, doc. 1230, fol. 1r, AHU; "Informação [. . .]," after March 24, 1683, Pernambuco, caixa 13, doc. 1248, AHU; "Informação [. . .]," after 1688, Serviço de Partes, caixa 3, doc. 446, AHU; "Nomeação [. . .]," June 15, 1684, Consultas Mistas, Cod. 17, fol. 421v, AHU; "Registo geral de mercê de (D.) Sebastião Pinheiro Camarão," March 13, 1688, Registo Geral de Mercês, Mercês de D. Pedro II, liv. 4, fol. 247r, ANTT; "Registo Geral de Mercês, Domingos Rodrigues Carneiro," January 12, 1694, Registo Geral de Mercês do reinado de D. Pedro II, liv. 5, fol. 145v, ANTT; "Registo Geral de Mercê, Manuel de Inojosa," March 14,

1685, Registo Geral de Mercês, Mercês de D. Pedro II, liv. 2, fol. 363r, ANTT; "Requerimento [. . .]," before July 5, 1693, Pernambuco, caixa 16, doc. 1601, anexo 12 (March 10, 1685) and anexo 14 (January[?] 19, 1682), AHU; "Sobre [. . .]," August 8, 1680, Consultas de Pernambuco, códice 265, fol. 29v, AHU.

Table 5.1: Estimated Number of Prisoners Taken in Palmares (1660–1741)

I read more than one hundred reports and petitions, and a smaller handful of other primary and secondary sources, to estimate how many Palmaristas were taken prisoner by colonial forces. Future work might build on and refine these estimates with more sophisticated modeling than what I used: the somewhat simple but painstaking work of counting, which itself depends on locating, organizing, and culling scores of reports in colonial sources that document prisoners taken by colonial forces. My estimates are, therefore, meant as a baseline and to illustrate the many lives that began or passed through Palmares and then went elsewhere.

Except for a group captured in Cumbi (Paraíba), the majority of whom are identified as Indigenous in the surviving documentation, almost all the prisoners captured by colonial forces are described as Black, African, or simply as being from or belonging to Palmares. Some of the reports likely exaggerated the total number of prisoners captured, which I have accounted for in two ways. First, whenever possible, I cross-checked multiple reports to verify (or cast doubt) on individual claims. Second, I used two poles ("high" and "low") to determine the highest figures suggested by the material as well as a lower, more conservative estimate. In cases where I found a single report referring to ten prisoners, for example, and had reason to doubt the claim's veracity, I would incorporate the report in two ways, once by counting ten prisoners in my "high" estimate and a second time discounting the report and not counting any prisoners in my "low" estimate. In some cases, it was impossible to determine whether multiple reports of prisoners around the same time refer to the same group. Here, again, I used two numbers: in this case one that would count each report separately and another that would count only one report. For example, for two documents that register thirty prisoners and could be duplicates, I counted thirty in the "low" estimate and sixty in the "high" estimate. If reports named different numbers for what appeared to be the same battle or attack, I used the lowest figure for the "low" estimate and the highest for the "high."

It is possible that even my "high" estimates may undercount the total number of Palmares prisoners. Just as some accounts no doubt exaggerated the number of prisoners taken, others certainly undercounted; that was how soldiers paid lower tribute taxes on the sale of captives or surreptitiously kept prisoners in their possession. My estimates also exclude the frequent reports that say that "many" prisoners were taken but do not provide any further details, and I only begin my count in the 1660s. Between the turn of the seventeenth century and 1660, we might surmise that hundreds, perhaps more, people were captured in the Pernambuco wilderness, once again underscoring the incalculable violence that colonial agents wrought and the unseen aftermaths and trajectories that followed—and which I have described and accounted for as best as possible throughout the book.

The sources that I used to calculate the estimates are listed below, organized using the periods that appear in table 5.1. In instances where it was impossible to pinpoint the date when prisoners were taken, I used contextual information to approximate the timing. The list below includes some "repeats" (documents that state the same quantity of prisoners and together helped me verify a given number), but for most such cases, I include here only one or two of the sources consulted. Dozens of other documents, which I ultimately determined would be redundant for this appendix, are not included below.

1660–1669 (168 ≤ 338 prisoners)

Sources: "Das tropas q mandei [. . .]," April 18, 1662, CCA, Disposições, VI-III-I-I-31, doc. 106, fol. 81r, AUC; "Escreveo aos mesmo [. . .]," 1668, Disposições, VI-III-I-I-31, doc. 16, fol. 49r, AUC; "Informação [. . .]," after 1668, Pernambuco, caixa 9, doc. 862, fol. 1r, AHU; Francisco de Brito Freire, "Relatório da administração [. . .]," 1661–1664, Manuscritos Reservados, Caixa 236, n. 51, fol. 2r, Biblioteca Nacional de Portugal (BNP); Lara, "Diferentes ou iguais?," 3; "Requerimento do capitão [. . .]," before January 21, 1695, Pernambuco, caixa 17, doc. 1673, fol. 51r, AHU.

1670–1679 (1,049 ≤ 1,693)

Sources: "Carta [. . .]," August 19, 1673, Pernambuco, caixa 10, doc. 988, fol. IV, AHU; carta de padrão, António Álvares Bezerra, October 18, 1700, Registo Geral de Mercês, Mercês de D. Pedro II, liv. 13, fol. 395v, ANTT; "Consulta [. . .]," May 6, 1681, in Gomes, *Mocambos,* 248, 249; "Consulta [. . .]," March 4, 1687, Pernambuco, caixa 14, doc. 1405, fol. 4v, AHU; "Consulta [. . .]," December 16, 1690, Pernambuco, caixa 15, doc. 1518, fol. 5r, AHU; "Consulta [. . .]," December 20, 1697, Pernambuco, caixa 17, doc. 1741, fol. 4v, AHU; "Consulta [. . .]," February 12, 1701, Pernambuco, caixa 19, doc. 1867, fol. 5r, AHU; "Consulta [. . .]," May 16, 1703, Pernambuco, caixa 20, doc. 1923, fol. IV, AHU; "Escreveo [. . .]," September 22, 1672, Disposições, VI-III-I-I-31, doc. 91, fol. 278r, AUC; "Informação [. . .]," after 1681, Pernambuco, caixa 12, doc. 1212, fol. 1r, AHU; "Informação [. . .]," after July 17, 1687, Pernambuco, caixa 14, doc. 1420, fol. 1r, AHU; Lara and Fachin, *Guerra,* 26, 36, 37, 38, 39, 42; "Ordenou [. . .]," June 22, 1671, Disposições, VI-III-I-I-31, doc. 18, fol. 254v, AUC; "Registro [. . .]," February 7, 1687, in Gomes, *Mocambos,* 297; "Registro [. . .]," October 27, 1688, in Gomes, *Mocambos,* 303; "Registro [. . .]," October 23, 1689, in Gomes, *Mocambos,* 308; "Requerimento [. . .]," before January 21, 1695, Pernambuco, caixa 17, doc. 1673, anexo 7, AHU.

1680–1689 (1,033 ≤ 1,438)

Sources: "Carta Patente [. . .]," November 17, 1691, Pernambuco, caixa 15, doc. 1556, fol. 1r, AHU; "Consulta [. . .]," December 23, 1689, Pernambuco, caixa 15, doc. 1496, fol. 4r, AHU; "Consulta [. . .]," December 16, 1690, caixa 15, doc. 1518, fol. 2v, AHU; "Consulta [. . .]," December 20, 1697, Pernambuco, caixa 17, doc. 1741, fol. 4v, AHU; "Consulta [. . .]," February 12, 1701, Pernambuco, caixa 19, doc. 1867, fol. 6v, AHU; "Consulta [. . .]," February 12, 1707, Pernambuco, caixa 22, doc. 2034, fol. 3r, AHU; "Informação [. . .]," July 20, 1683, Pernambuco, caixa 13, doc. 1255, fol. 1r; "Informação [. . .]," ca. 1726, Pernambuco, caixa 34, doc. 3179, fol. 1r, AHU; Lara, "Diferentes ou iguais?," 11; Lara, *Palmares,* 260; "Requerimento [. . .]," before July 5, 1693, Pernambuco, caixa 16, doc. 1601, anexo 9, AHU; "Requerimento [. . .]," before March 12, 1724, Pernambuco, caixa 30, doc. 2723, fol. 1r, AHU.

1690 through 1694 (591 ≤ 902)

Sources: "Carta [. . .]," October 11, 1718, Registo Geral de Mercês, Registo Geral de Mercês do reinado de D. João V, liv. 10, fol. 213r, ANTT; "Consulta [. . .]," December 20, 1697, Pernambuco, caixa 17, doc. 1741, fol. 3v, AHU; "Consulta [. . .]," May 16, 1703, Pernambuco, caixa 20, doc. 1923, fols. 4r–4v, AHU; "Consulta [. . .]," February 12, 1707, Pernambuco, caixa 22, doc. 2035, fol. 4r, AHU; "Informação [. . .]," after August 25, 1705, Pernambuco, caixa 21, doc. 1998, fol. 1r, AHU; "Informação [. . .]," after July 23, 1715, Pernambuco, caixa 27, doc. 2447, fol. 1v, AHU; "Nomeio [. . .]," March 14, 1709, Consultas Mistas, cod. 20, fols. 152r–153r, AHU; "Informação [. . .]," after February 28, 1729, Pernambuco, caixa 38, doc. 3398, anexos 2 and 44, AHU.

1695 to 1741 (522 ≤ 816)

Sources: "Auto [. . .]," July 23, 1715, Pernambuco, caixa 27, doc. 2442, anexo 3, AHU; carta de Agostinho Moreira Guterres, November 19, 1709, Registo Geral de Mercês, Registo Geral de Mercês do reinado de D. João V, liv. 3, fol. 175v, ANTT; Carta de Simão Vieira Lindo, March 28, 1719, Registo Geral de Mercês, D. João V, liv. 10, fol. 418v, ANTT; "Carta [. . .]," January 10, 1749, caixa 68, doc. 5782, anexo 13, AHU; "Certidão [. . .]," May 7, 1742, Pernambuco, caixa 57, doc. 4940, fol. 1r, AHU; "Consulta [. . .]," January 13, 1698, in Gomes, *Mocambos*, 400; "Consulta [. . .]," December 11, 1699, in Gomes, *Mocambos*, 444–45; "Consulta [. . .]," May 10, 1703, Pernambuco, caixa 20, doc. 1921, fol. 7r, AHU; "Consulta [. . .]," May 16, 1703, Pernambuco, caixa 20, doc. 1927, AHU; "Consulta[. . .]," January 18, 1708, Pernambuco, caixa 22, doc. 2061, fol. 4r, AHU; "Informação [. . .]," after February 28, 1729, Pernambuco, caixa 38, doc. 3398, anexo 3, AHU; "Nomeio [. . .]," March 14, 1709, Consultas Mistas, cod. 20, fols. 152v–153v, AHU; "Ordenou [. . .]," February 21, 1716, CCA, Disposições, VI-III-I-I-32, doc. 95, fol. 237r, AUC; Porto, *Paraíba*, 91; Registo de cartas régias (1698–1713), July 23, 1704, Cod. 257, fol. 143r, AHU; "Requerimento de Lázaro Coelho de Eça [. . .]," before October 26, 1754, Alagoas, caixa 2, doc. 145, fols. 13r, 17r, 23r, AHU; Vidal, "Tres seculos," 109.

NOTES

A NOTE ON LANGUAGE

1   Unless otherwise noted, all translations are my own. Michaelis, s.v. "pardo," accessed October 16, 2022, https://michaelis.uol.com.br/palavra/pox3M /pardo%3CEi%3E1%3C/Ei%3E/.

2   I leave *negro* italicized throughout so as not to confuse it with the English word "Negro."

3   Mitchell, "Black and African American," 85.

4   Alberto, *Black Legend*, xii.

5   Again, to avoid confusion with English, I also leave *mulato* in italics throughout.

6   On the normalization of "white," see Stewart, "White/white."

7   A useful guide for language and slavery is Foreman et al., "Writing."

8   The term "Brasileiro," what we now translate as "Brazilian," was first used largely in reference to brazilwood traders and only assumed its modern meaning beginning around the turn of the eighteenth century. As this meaning took shape, Indigenous people were often called Brasilienses, and those born in America to Portuguese parents were Brasílicos. See Alencastro, *The Trade*, 20, 370–71.

9   To maintain consistency, I extend this capitalization practice to primary source quotations, the one exception to my rule to honor the original wording. For a persuasive argument in favor of capitalizing "white," see Perlman, "Black and White."

10 See Lara, *Palmares*, 177.

11 G. Rocha, "Maroons," 17.

12 I hew as closely as possible to the 2013 *Acordo ortográfico da língua portuguesa*, but also cede to *The Chicago Manual of Style* and in-house editorial styles and preferences (such as capitalizing the first word in a book's subtitle, which is not always standard practice in Brazil). *Acordo*; *The Chicago Manual*.

INTRODUCTION

1   Boxer, *The Golden Age*.

2   Though by no means an exhaustive list, useful points of entry into the English-language literature on maroon societies include Diouf, *Slavery's Exiles*; Florentino and Amantino, "Runaways"; Helg, *Slave No More*, 43–63; Landers,

"Leadership"; Lockley, "Runaway Slave"; Miki, *Frontiers*, esp. 171–215; Price, *Maroon Societies*; N. Roberts, *Freedom*; Sweeney, "Market Marronage"; Thompson, *Flight*; and Wright, "The Morphology." Additional works, especially the rich Portuguese-language literature, are discussed over the course of the book.

3 Antonio Silva and Bluteau, *Diccionario*, s.v. "palmar."

4 Eighteenth-century Brazil itself remains understudied. A recent edited collection on slave revolts dedicates eleven of fourteen chapters to the nineteenth century. Reis and Gomes, *Revoltas escravas*.

5 For overviews of the literature, see, Gomes, "Review"; and Lara, *Palmares*, 9–28. Additional representative works by Gomes and Lara include Gomes, *De olho*; Gomes, *Palmares*; Gomes, *Mocambos*; and Lara, "Quem eram." Other works on Palmares in English include Anderson, "The Quilombo"; Cheney, *Quilombo*; Hoogbergen, "Palmares"; Kent, "An African State"; Schwartz, *Slaves*, 103–36; and L. Silva, "Palmares." Debates about origins and identity also emerged from archaeological digs in Palmares during the 1990s. See Allen, "'A Cultural Mosaic'"; Allen, "Os desafios"; Allen, "'Zumbi'"; Funari, "A arqueologia"; Funari and Carvalho, "Interações"; Hertzman, "The 'Indians,'" 424, 429–30; Orser and Funari, "Archaeology"; and Thornton, "Angola," 51.

6 Decree No. 4.887, November 20, 2003, https://www.jusbrasil.com.br/legislacao /98186/decreto-4887-03.

7 For example, see Farfán-Santos, *Black Bodies*.

8 English-language treatments of reparations in the context of quilombos and contestations over the categories "quilombo" and "quilombola" include Araujo, *Reparations*, 1, 154–55, 168–69; Bowen, *For Land*, 216–22, Hoffman French, *Legalizing*, 92–100; Paschel, *Becoming Black*, 97–102; and Perry, *Black Women*, 10–11.

9 My approach to digital sources owes much to Putnam, "The Transnational."

10 I conducted the searches using the BN's Hemeroteca Digital at http://memoria .bn.br/hdb/periodico.aspx.

11 Slave Voyages website, https://www.slavevoyages.org/. I discuss the limitations of this database in chapter 5.

12 I follow the delineation in Thornton, *A History*, 1.

13 Thornton, *A History*, provides a great overview. Other entry points include M. Almeida, "Speaking"; Candido, *An African*; R. Ferreira, *Cross-Cultural*; Heywood and Thornton, *Central Africans*; Miller, *Kings*; Miller, *Way of Death*; and Thornton, *The Kingdom*. Following common practice, I use "Kongo" to distinguish the precolonial area and kingdom from the contemporary nation-states. For an argument in favor of "Congo," see Alencastro, "Os africanos," 24.

14 D. Silva and Eltis, "The Slave Trade," 95.

15 D. Silva and Eltis, "The Slave Trade," 96. Also see S. Almeida, "Rotas atlânticas"; G. Lopes, "Negócio"; and A. Marques, "A travessia."

16 Finch, *Rethinking*, 142. Also see Camp, *Closer*; Holden, *Surviving*; and Morgan, *Laboring Women*, 166–95.

17 Araujo, "Dandara e Luísa Mahin"; Hertzman, "Fake News."

18   Emphasis in the original. Finch, *Rethinking*, 149. On the diverse ways that Black women rebelled, also see Kars, "Dodging Rebellion"; Sweeney, "Market Marronage"; and Thompson, "Gender."

19   Thornton, "Angola," 51.

20   I build on the work of scholars such as Mariana Candido, who examines the intertwined "threat of warfare, raids, and enslavers' activities," and Vincent Brown, who treats slavery as a constant state of warfare. V. Brown, *Tacky's Revolt*; Candido, *An African*, 15. Also see Alencastro, "História"; Barcia, *West African*; and R. Ferreira, "O Brasil."

21   Rocha Pita, *Historia*. Quote from Robertson, *History*, 147. Also see Janiga, "Sebastião da Rocha Pita's," 36; Lara, "Do singular," 82–83; Maria da Glória de Oliveira, "Fazer história," 43; and A. Reis, "Zumbi," 34.

22   Rocha Pita, *Historia*, 474.

23   I adopt "savage civilization slot" from Michel-Rolph Trouillot's "savage slot." Trouillot, "Anthropology."

24   See, for example, Earle, *The Return*.

25   García Márquez, *Chronicle*.

26   See, among others, Stern, "Paradigms." I discuss conquest at more length (and with additional citations) in Hertzman, "The 'Indians.'" For a recent take on conquest in Brazil, see, Schultz, *From Conquest*.

27   See, for example, Matthew, *Memories*; Restall, *Maya Conquistador*; and Restall, "Black Conquistadors."

28   "Carta [. . .]," March 14, 1696, Conselho Ultramarino: Brasil–Pernambuco (hereafter, Pernambuco), caixa 17, doc. 1697, fols. 3r–3v, Arquivo Histórico Ultramarino (hereafter, AHU). I consulted the AHU documents online through the Projeto Resgate, a BN website, at http://resgate.bn.br/docreader/docmulti.aspx ?bib=resgate.

29   Though studying East Africa, Neil Kodesh provides a useful and largely generalizable synthesis about how colonial Europeans (and subsequent generations of scholars) understood diverse political and spiritual elements and practices through a more singular lens of religion. Kodesh, *Beyond*, 17–20.

30   Historians, writes David M. Gordon, often struggle "to appreciate invisible worlds where spirits mobilize bodies to action in a fashion comparable to the invisible forces of their society, such as the state and its laws. Unfortunately, since the burden of the truth about the past weighs heavily on historians, they have had an especially difficult time dealing with worlds invisible and implausible to them." Gordon, *Invisible Agents*, 8.

31   R. Ferreira, *Cross-Cultural*, 245. Also see, among others, Alencastro, *The Trade*; Green, "Beyond," 111–18; and Miller, *Way of Death*. Walter Hawthorne employs a similar framework to the Amazon and West Africa in *From Africa to Brazil*.

32   E. Carneiro, *O Quilombo*; Ennes, *As guerras*; D. Freitas, *República*.

33   Gomes, *Mocambos*.

34 Lara's and Gomes's scholarship has been incredibly influential to my own work. I engage individual arguments over the course of the book. See Documenta Palmares; Lara, *Palmares*; Lara and Fachin, *Guerra*.

35 Price, "Refiguring," 212. Also see Price, "Reinventando."

36 Neruda, "Keeping Quiet," 28.

37 M. Carvalho and França, "Palmares," 132–33. Historians of slavery have not always shown the same interest in nature and place as scholars in other fields. See R. Brown, "'Walk,'" 291; R. Brown, *African-Atlantic*; Dawson, *Undercurrents*; McKittrick, *Demonic Grounds*; and Offen, "Environment." Notable recent exceptions from Latin America include de la Torre, *The People*; C. Leal, *Landscapes*; and G. Rocha, "Maroons." In the United States, see the foundational work of Camp, *Closer*.

38 Lara and Felipe Aguiar Damasceno have meticulously reconstructed maps of Palmares. See Damasceno, "A ocupação"; Lara, *Palmares*; and Lara, "O território."

39 In thinking about place, I have also been influenced by, among others, K. Basso, *Wisdom Sits*; Colson, "Place"; Cronon, "A Place"; DeLucia, *Memory*; Holden, *Surviving*; LaPier, "Land"; McKittrick, *Demonic*; and Watkins, *Palm Oil*.

40 For introductions to the field, see Andrews, *Afro-Latin America*; de la Fuente and Andrews, *Afro-Latin*; Reiter and Sánchez, *Routledge Handbook*.

41 Recent works that argue (in different ways) for the need to center Africa more fully include M. Almeida, "Speaking"; Bennett, *African Kings*; V. Brown, *Tacky's Revolt*; de Luna, "Sounding"; J. Johnson, *Wicked Flesh*; Lara, *Palmares*; Nafafé, *Lourenço da Silva Mendonça*; and Sweet, *Domingos Álvares*. The larger literature on the African Diaspora is vast. Of many entry points to choose from, see Ball, Pappademos, and Stephens, "Reconceptualizations"; Butler, "Defining"; Butler, "Multilayered"; Edwards, *The Practice*; Edwards, "The Uses"; Hertzman, "A Brazilian"; Lovejoy, "The African"; O'Toole, "As Historical"; Palmer, "Defining"; Vinson, "Introduction"; and Zeleza, "Rewriting."

42 De Luna, "Sounding"; Sweet, "Research."

43 Williamson et al., "Niger-Congo," 11.

44 De Luna, "Sounding," 584. A useful overview of the "linguistic turn" (largely from a Europeanist perspective) is found in Spiegel, "The Task."

45 For an appraisal, see Restall, "A History."

46 In addition to de Luna, "Sounding," see M. Almeida, "African"; Berry, "Poisoned"; Mobley, "The Kongolese"; and Sweet, "Research."

47 Spiegel, "The Task," 1.

48 Bostoen, "Bantu," 316; Klieman, *The Pygmies*, xxvi.

49 Fuentes, *Dispossessed Lives*, 1. Also see the enormously influential work of Saidiya Hartman (including "Venus" and *Wayward Lives*) and, among others, Alberto, *Black Legend*, esp. 10–11; Helton et al., "The Question"; Holden, *Surviving*; and Miles, *Ties*, 207–13.

50 De Luna, "Sounding," 583.

51 Kars, *Blood*, 5.

52 Also useful here is the way that Africanists have reevaluated oral history as a tool for studying precolonial history. See, for example, Kodesh, "History."

53 De Luna, "Sounding," 589–90.

54 De Luna, *The Long*, chapter 1.

55 Alencastro, *The Trade*, 254. Doldrums at sea are "The condition of a ship in which, either from calms, or from baffling winds, she makes no headway; a becalmed state." *Oxford English Dictionary*, s.v. "doldrum (*n.*)," July 2023, https://doi.org/10.1093/OED/8865412137.

56 A classic elaboration of this point is found in Patterson, *Freedom*, 27.

57 Casimir, *The Haitians*, 147.

58 Bogues, *Empire*, 37. For additional perspectives that decenter old definitions of freedom and even seek to move past the term altogether, see M. Almeida, "Speaking"; de Luna, "Sounding"; Freeburg, *Counterlife*; J. Johnson, *Wicked Flesh*; and N. Roberts, *Freedom*. Also provocative and especially relevant for the importance of nature and place is Yesenia Barragan's delineation of how Blacks in nineteenth-century Colombia "exercised vernacular freedoms as guardians" of their land's "intricate rivers" and natural wealth. Barragan, *Freedom's Captives*, 281.

1. MARCH 21, 1645

1 "Carta [. . .]," June 29, 1603, in Gomes, *Mocambos*, 157. Also see Lara, *Palmares*, 167; and Gomes, *Palmares*, 50–52.

2 P. Rodrigues, "Copia," 255. The *"negros de Guiné"* might have been enslaved people from the Upper Guinea Coast, but because Guiné was also used more generically, it is possible that the group came from the sea island referenced in the account or from another African region. See Marcus Carvalho, "Negros da terra"; Lara, *Palmares*, 181; M. Oliveira, "Quem eram"; Soares, "Descobrindo"; Soares, "Mina"; Vainfas, *Dicionário*, 424–27.

3 S. Leite, *História*, 2:358.

4 After settling São Tomé around 1470, the Portuguese created a sugar regime dependent on enslaved Blacks, who established fugitive communities and periodically rebelled. The island also became a way station for enslaved people transported from the mainland to the Americas. See Alencastro, *The Trade*, 63; Dias and Diniz, "Os Angolares"; Lorenzino, "Linguistic," 205–8; Miller, "Central Africa," 23–24; Sweet, "African Identity," 233–37; Vansina, "Quilombos"; and Wheat, *Atlantic Africa*, 74–77.

5 "Diário da viagem [. . .]," 1645, in Gomes, *Mocambos*, 167–72. On Palmares during the Dutch occupation, see E. Carneiro, *O Quilombo*, 53–63; Gomes, *Palmares*, 61–68; R. Nascimento, "Palmares"; R. Nascimento, *Palmares*, 74–77; and Nieuhof, *Memorável*, 18–19.

6 "Diário da viagem [. . .]," 170.

7 Palmares benefited from an extensive external network of contacts, who sent word of military attacks well before they arrived. Though the mocambos raided

neighboring towns and farms, they also engaged in trade and negotiated with others, much in line with how fugitive settlements throughout Brazil developed economic relationships with surrounding towns that ranged from symbiotic to antagonistic. See, for example, Mariana L.R. Dantas, "'For the Benefit'"; and Gomes, *A hidra*.

8   "Diário da viagem [. . .]," 170.

9   Hartman, "Venus," 12. Also see Fuentes, *Dispossessed Lives*, 5.

10 In addition to Fuentes and Hartman, see, among others, Helton et al., "The Question."

11 This and the remaining quotations in this paragraph are in "Diário da viagem [. . .]," 170–71.

12 Jones, *Palmares*, 55.

13 Useful here too is Kars's prescient observation that in order "to remain masterless and alive," in times of rebellion, Black women often strategically chose to be "neither purposeful rebels nor committed collaborators." Kars, "Dodging Rebellion," 41.

14 On occasion, Palmaristas may have burned their own dwellings as they deserted them. E. Carneiro, *O Quilombo*, 81. The Portuguese cautioned their soldiers not to drink from wells in abandoned mocambos for fear that the inhabitants had poisoned them before leaving. Francisco Barreto, "Regimento [. . .]," Recife, September 4, 1654, Coleção Conde dos Arcos (hereafter, CCA) *Disposições dos Governadores de Pernambuco, 1661–1713* (hereafter, *Disposições*), VI-III-I-I-31, doc. 33, fol. 16v, Arquivo da Universidade de Coimbra (hereafter, AUC).

15 See de Luna, *The Long African Atlantic*, chapter 3. In some cases, oil-producing palm trees would have been spared in this process while crops and growth closer to the ground were cleared. See Watkins, *Palm Oil*, loc. 50–55, 59 of 348.

16 Abreu, *Capítulos*, 118. On the colonial frontier, also see C. Cruz, *A escola*, 61–62; and Langfur, *The Forbidden Lands*, 290–99. On the frontier in postcolonial Brazil, see Miki, *Frontiers*, 5–9.

17 Lara, "Quem eram," 70.

18 For example, R. Nascimento, "Palmares," 44.

19 "Ordenou [. . .]," December 21, 1671, CCA, *Disposições*, VI-III-I-I-31, doc. 185, fol. 309v, AUC.

20 Boxer, *The Dutch*; Groesen, *The Legacy*; E. Mello, *Olinda*; J. Mello, *Tempo*.

21 D. Silva and Eltis, "The Slave Trade," 108.

22 Schwartz, "Looking," 43.

23 Alencastro, "História geral"; Alencastro, "Palmares"; Alencastro, *The Trade*; Candido, *An African Slaving Port*, 67–70; R. Ferreira, "O Brasil"; Lara, "Depois"; J. Mello, *Tempo*, 194; Nafafé, *da Silva Mendonça*, 256–70; R. Nascimento, "'E agora Nassau?'"

24 R. Ferreira, "O Brasil"; R. Ferreira, *Cross-Cultural*, 9; Green, "Beyond," 114.

25 See Alencastro, "História geral."

26 Thornton, *A History*, 195.

27 R. Ferreira, "O Brasil," 7–9.

28 Lara, "Depois"; Nafafé, *Lourenço da Silva Mendonça*. Nafafé's book came out shortly before I finished my own. He makes some claims about Palmares that I was unable to immediately verify, but the work is provocative and deserves more extended discussion elsewhere.

29 Ndongo, which lay to the south of Kongo, rose during the early sixteenth century and fell under attack decades later by the Portuguese and allied Africans. See R. Ferreira, "Central Africa."

30 Quoted in Lara, "Depois," 220.

31 Lara, "Depois," 210.

32 "Regimento [. . .]," September 5, 1654, CCA, *Disposições*, VI-III-1-1-31, doc. 39, fols. 20v–21r, AUC.

33 On this point, see Lara, "Quem eram," 82. The quotations are from E. Carneiro, *O Quilombo*, 39; M. Freitas, *Reino*; Kent, "Palmares"; Joaquim Pedro Oliveira Martins, *O Brasil*, 64; Schwartz, *Slaves*, 122; and Thornton, "Les États," 771. I am grateful to Liz Matsushita for translating Thornton's "Les États" into English.

34 Thornton, "Angola," 51. "Angolan wave" is from Heywood and Thornton, *Central Africans*, ix.

35 See Lara, *Palmares*, 178–79; J. Reis, "Quilombos," 16; Schwartz, *Slaves*, 123; and Thornton, "Les États," 772–74.

36 See, for example, Lara, "Palmares," 9.

37 Slave Voyages website, http://www.slavevoyages.org/estimates/7gKFkHYG, accessed June 22, 2023.

38 Instructive here is Kim Butler's discussion of the elaborate interplay of "particularity and commonality" and "the complexity of overlapping waves of diaspora arrivals or remigrations." Butler, "Multilayered," 22, 23. Also see Hawthorne, *From Africa*, 7. It is worth noting that the TST numbers, especially from West Central Africa during the early seventeenth century, may be low by at least several thousand per year. Green, "Beyond," 110–12.

39 V. Brown, *Tacky's Revolt*, 102–3.

40 A Dutch report observed, "In Brazil it is not the custom to mark borders on the sertão side [of the land]." (Sertão may also be read to mean "interior.") "Relatório [. . .]," November 26, 1643, in Gomes, *Mocambos*, 160.

41 LaPier, "Land as Text," 41.

42 "Relatório [. . .]," 162.

43 J. Mello, *Tempo*, 186.

44 Watkins, *Palm Oil*, loc. 90 of 348.

45 See Watkins, *Palm Oil*, loc. 84–85 of 348.

46 Baerle, *The History*, 237.

47 Lara and Fachin, *Guerra*, 18. In chapter 9, we will see that the word "couto" also provides suggestive clues about the post-1695 terrain.

48 Rogers, *The Deepest*, 31.

49 K. Silva, *Nas solidões*, 256–57.

50 The provenance of Serra da Barriga's name is unclear, nor is there clarity about why early documents use the masculine article "o" (the) with a feminine noun

(barriga)—Serra (or Outeiro) do Barriga—or when or why the article became feminine: Serra da Barriga. Lara poses this question and suspects that the name came from a local landowner known as "o Barriga," while Damasceno wonders whether the name comes from a word that the German naturalist Georg Marggraf recorded in the 1640s. According to Marggraf, the largest Palmares encampment sat atop a mountain called Behe. In Portuguese, the /rr/ in barriga is pronounced like an /h/, and it is possible that Portuguese colonists heard "barriga," or something close to it, instead of "behe." In the 1930s, Alfredo Brandão, whose work on other aspects of Palmares is discussed in more detail later, proposed that "behe" meant "red person" (or "Indian") in Kiriří (also, among other spellings, Karirí and Cariry), one of the principal Indigenous languages in the northeast. While the late seventeenth-century author he cites defines "be" as "red," the basis for his suggesting "red person" is unclear. More recently, linguist Aryon Dall'Igna Rodrigues translates "behè" into Portuguese as "chaga": "open wound," figuratively "affliction" or "calamity." Brandão, "Os negros," 65; Damasceno, "A ocupação," 40; Fonseca, *Nobiliarchia*, 1:164; Lara, *Palmares*, 282; Mamiani della Rovere, *Arte*, 55; Marcgrave (Marggraf), *História*, 261; Marggraf and Piso, *Guilielmi*, 261; Aryon Rodrigues, "O artigo," 209.

51 R. Brown, "'Walk,'" 306–7; Laman, *The Kongo*, 15; Lienhard, "Milonga," 98–101; MacGaffey, *Religion*, 56; Thornton, *The Kongolese*, 56.

52 Colson, "Places." For similar references from other areas, see Ehret, *The Civilizations*, 50; Gordon, *Invisible*, 47; and A. Roberts, *A History*, 70–71.

53 Palmaristas would also associate the forests of Pernambuco with hunting. We do not know if hunting remained a "male pursuit" in Palmares, as it did in the West Central African Diaspora in South Carolina and Georgia. R. Brown, "'Walk,'" 306, 308, 314.

54 K. Silva, *Nas solidões*, 185–214.

55 "Pareceres [. . .]," n.d., in Gomes, *Mocambos*, 348.

56 Marcus Carvalho and França, "Palmares," 133–34.

57 "Pareceres [. . .]," November 25, 1694, in Gomes, *Mocambos*, 347.

58 Rogers, *The Deepest*, 35–36.

59 Translated in Rogers, *The Deepest*, 21.

60 See Lara, *Palmares*, 21, 131–33, 146–48; Munanga, "Origem"; Neto, "Kilombo."

61 C. Diegues, *Quilombo*; Festival de Cannes, https://www.festival-cannes.com/en/f/quilombo/, accessed August 3, 2023; A. Nascimento, *O quilombismo*.

62 One of the first appearances of the word in relation to Palmares comes in a report from around 1685. "Informação [. . .]," after 1685, Pernambuco, caixa 13, doc. 1350, fol. 1r, AHU.

63 Nei Lopes suggests Kikongo as well as Kimbundu origins. De Luna, *The Long*; Kent, "Palmares," 164; Lara, *Palmares*, 361–62; N. Lopes, *Novo dicionário*, 173; R. Mendonça, *A influência*, 243; Thornton, "Les États," 769.

64 Bluteau, *Vocabulario*, s.v. "mocambo"; "Carta [. . .]," March 4, 1580, in Brásio, *Monumenta*, 3:188; Figueiredo, *Hidrographia*, 5; Maria Lêda Oliveira, *A "Historia,"*

fol. 145v. Bluteau's *Vocabulario* was revised and republished in 1789 as A. Silva and Bluteau, *Diccionario*. Damasceno and Lara identify the "Rio Ytapucurú" as the "Rio Itapicuru" in Pernambuco. Damasceno, "A ocupação," 31; Lara, *Palmares*, 404.

65 TST does not register any slave ships from Southeast Africa to Pernambuco before 1801 but some ten thousand to Bahia and several thousand more to other regions during the seventeenth and eighteenth centuries. See http://www.slavevoyages.org/estimates/8rP1se9z, accessed June 22, 2023. Also see Alpers, "'Mozambiques,'" 44; Capela, "Mozambique and Brazil," 243–44; and A. Rocha, "Contribuição," 200–204.

66 Bluteau, *Vocabulario*, s.v. "mocambo"; Lahon, "Inquisição," 31–33; Sweet, "The Hidden Histories," 237.

67 Bluteau, *Vocabulario*, s.v. "mocamaos."

68 The definition for calhambolas is somewhat circular: "The slave man or slave woman who fled and lives wandering around, in quilombos; the term is used in Brazil." A. Silva and Bluteau, *Diccionario*, s.v. "calhambolas," "mocama'os," "mocambo," "quilombo."

69 "Carta [. . .]," May 14, 1689, in Gomes, *Mocambos*, 306.

70 For further discussion of Post's painting, see K. Silva, *Nas solidões*, 52–54.

71 Marcus Carvalho, "Negros da terra," 331. Also see Bezerra Neto, "Fugindo."

72 Freehafer, "Domingos Jorge Velho," 172; "Requerimento [. . .]," n.d., in Gomes, *Mocambos*, 412. The term's cachet is seen, for example, in the title of Marcelo D'Salete's graphic novel: *Angola Janga*.

73 Anderson, "The Quilombo," 559.

74 For a summary of the debate, see Lara, *Palmares*, 357–59.

75 Emphasis mine. "Requerimento [. . .]," 412.

76 Garfield, *A History*, 122; Mantero, *Manual Labour*, 6.

77 For example, Hooghe, *Les Indes*, plate 65. On Dutch maps and artists' renderings of African and Brazilian subjects, see Blakely, *Blacks*; Brienen, *Visions*; Sutton, *Early Modern*; Sutton, "Possessing"; and Zandvliet, "Mapping."

78 Navarro, *Dicionário*, 462.

79 MacGaffey, *Religion*, 56.

80 Antonio Silva and Bluteau, *Diccionario*, s.v. "tapera."

81 See the Klencke Atlas, https://www.bl.uk/collection-items/klencke-atlas, accessed May 6, 2023. The British Library, where it is now housed, has called the atlas "the largest book in the world." Mark Brown, "Largest Book in the World Goes on Show for the First Time," *Guardian*, January 26, 2010, https://www.theguardian.com/books/2010/jan/26/klencke-atlas-british-library-exhibition.

82 Lara uses a slightly different periodization while also challenging the notion that the history of Palmares evolved in a linear fashion. Lara, *Palmares*, 379.

83 For example, Rocha Pita, *Historia*, 471–72.

84 Lara, "Diferentes," 4–5.

85 "Ordem [. . .]," September 19, 1661, in D. Freitas, *República*, 280.

86 Lara, *Palmares*, 63.

87 Lara, "Diferentes," 7.

88 "Carta [. . .]," June 1671, in Gomes, *Mocambos*, 186.

89 "Bando [. . .]," September 4, 1672, in Gomes, *Mocambos*, 190–91; "Bando [. . .]," October 20, 1672, in Gomes, *Mocambos*, 191–92.

90 Lara and Fachin, *Guerra*, 26.

91 Lara and Fachin, *Guerra*, 27. In colonial Brazil, a league was typically equivalent to between 6 and 6.5 kilometers but in this case was likely closer to between 2.5 and 3.5 kilometers. Damasceno, "A ocupação," 113–14; Lara, *Palmares*, 404.

92 Lara and Fachin, *Guerra*, 27, 126.

93 Lara and Fachin, *Guerra*, 27.

94 Lara and Fachin, *Guerra*, 28.

95 "Carta [. . .]," July 1, 1676, in Gomes, *Mocambos*, 217.

96 See Lara, *Palmares*, 386–92; and Lara and Fachin, *Guerra*. When citing the *Relação*, I use Lara and Fachin, *Guerra*, which includes transcriptions of the two earliest versions of the manuscript.

97 Lara and Fachin, *Guerra*, 28.

98 This quotation and those in the following two pages are drawn from Lara and Fachin, *Guerra*, 34–37. "Cerca" may also be translated as "stockade" or "fortified city."

99 Lara and Fachin, *Guerra*, 79.

100 Lara and Fachin, *Guerra*, 37.

101 "Macho" could refer to a male animal and a "robust, powerful" man. A. Silva and Bluteau, *Diccionario*, s.v. "macho."

102 Lara and Fachin, *Guerra*, 37.

103 Lara and Fachin, *Guerra*, 38.

104 Lara and Fachin, *Guerra*, 40, 140. At some point during the negotiations, the couple traveled back to Palmares as part of the negotiations between colonial forces and Gan(g)a Zumba. Lara, *Palmares*, 49.

105 "Carta [. . .]," February 4, 1678, Pernambuco, caixa 11, doc. 1103, fol. 1r, AHU. Transcribed in Lara and Fachin, *Guerra*, 166–67.

106 Lara and Fachin, *Guerra*, 43.

107 Lara and Fachin, *Guerra*, 45.

108 Lara and Fachin, *Guerra*, 47.

109 In one version of the letter, Castro also informs Gan(g)a Zumba that his sons have been baptized and that the same treatment would be extended to others. "Carta do [governador] [. . .]," June 22, 1678, Pernambuco, caixa 11, doc. 1116, AHU; "Escreveo [. . .]," June 22, 1678, CCA, *Disposições*, VI-III-I-1-31, doc. 6, fols. 334r–334v, AUC. Also see Lara, *Palmares*, 73–75, 410–12.

110 Lara, *Palmares*, 79–80.

111 Lara, *Palmares*, 80, 84.

112 Lara, *Palmares*, 239–40.

113 "Escreveo [. . .]," July 24, 1678, CCA, *Disposições*, VI-III-I-1-31, doc. 13, fol. 336v, AUC; "Escreveo [. . .]," November 12, 1678, CCA, *Disposições*, VI-III-I-1-31, doc. 16, fol. 337v, AUC.

114 Lara, *Palmares*, 85.

115 Transcribed in Lara, *Palmares*, 413–14.

116 Lara, *Palmares*, 413.

117 "Sobre [. . .]," January 26, 1680, Conselho Ultramarino: Brasil–Consultas de Pernambuco (hereafter, Consultas de Pernambuco), códice 265, fols. 26r–27v, AHU.

118 "Sobre o que [. . .]," January 26, 1680, Consultas de Pernambuco, códice 265, fol. 27r, AHU.

119 Studart, "Dezenove documentos," 268.

120 For years, the historiography cast Gan(g)a Zumba's death in personal terms, pitting Zumbi, the hero, against Gan(g)a Zumba, the villain who sold out his people and suffered the consequences. Gomes and Lara provide more nuanced terms with which to understand the two. Gomes, *Palmares*, 123–44; Lara, *Palmares*. The accusation that Gan(g)a Zumba was poisoned suggests interesting points of comparison elsewhere. See Berry, "Poisoned."

121 "Ordenou [. . .]," March 18, 1680, CCA, *Disposições*, VI-III-I-I-31, doc. 30, fol. 341v, AUC.

122 Lara, *Palmares*, 256.

123 "Consulta [. . .]," December 20, 1697, Pernambuco, caixa 17, doc. 1741, fol. 4v, AHU.

124 "Sobre [. . .]," August 8, 1680, Consultas de Pernambuco, códice 265, fol. 29v, AHU.

125 "Carta [. . .]," March 18, 1682, in Gomes, *Mocambos*, 251. The order is discussed in Lara, *Palmares*, 273–75.

126 "Carta [. . .]," March 18, 1682, 253.

127 "Regimento [. . .]," December 5, 1654, CCA, *Disposições*, VI-III-I-I-31, doc. 39, fol. 21r, AUC. On "cruel war," see Candido, *An African*, 56; Herzog, *Frontiers*, 109–15; Monteiro, *Blacks*, 27–28; and Staller, *Converging*, 67–68.

128 "Carta [. . .]," August 10, 1684, Pernambuco, caixa 13, doc. 1298, anexo 2 (November 29, 1684), AHU.

129 "Do rei [. . .]," February 26, 1685, in D. Freitas, *República*, 183. As Lara notes, this and several other documents cited by Décio Freitas seem to have disappeared. Lara, *Palmares*, 288.

130 Lara, *Palmares*, 288–97.

131 "Consulta [. . .]," August 8, 1685 (but quote from note dated February 7, 1686), in Gomes, *Mocambos*, 266.

132 Pires, *Guerra*; Puntoni, *A guerra*.

133 Scholars have chosen different dates to mark its conclusion, but armed conflict extended to at least 1720, when an Indigenous army attacked a prominent plantation. T. Silva, "A ribeira," 17.

134 Puntoni, *A guerra*, 124.

135 "Carta [. . .]," March 20, 1655, in Gomes, *Mocambos*, 178.

136 On the mythical white identity channeled through the paulista soldiers during the twentieth century, see Weinstein, *The Color*, 32–46.

137 "Condições [. . .]," March 3, 1687, in Gomes, *Mocambos*, 277, 279.

138 "Condições [. . .]," 277.

139   "Condições [. . .]," 278.
140   Puntoni, *A guerra*, 146.
141   "Carta [. . .]," April 2, 1691, in *Documentos históricos* (hereafter, DH), vol. 10 (Rio de Janeiro: Augusto Porto & C, 1929), 409; Puntoni, *A guerra*, 154. *Documentos históricos* is accessible online at https://bndigital.bn.gov.br/artigos/documentos -historicos/, accessed March 6, 2020. I cite individual volumes, which have distinct publishers, in the notes.
142   Weinstein, *The Color*, 37.
143   Puntoni, *A guerra*, 205–6.
144   Puntoni, *A guerra*, 209.
145   Dimas Marques, "Pelo bem," 63–64.
146   "Consulta [. . .]," October 29, 1686, in Gomes, *Mocambos*, 275.
147   "Consulta [. . .]," December 16, 1690, Pernambuco, caixa 15, doc. 1518, fol. 2v, AHU.
148   "Consulta [. . .]," December 23, 1689, Pernambuco, caixa 15, doc. 1496, fol. 5r, AHU.
149   Puntoni, *A guerra*, 283.
150   "Carta de Padre Vieira [. . .]," July 2, 1691, in Gomes, *Mocambos*, 319–21.
151   On Vieira's denunciations of Indigenous slavery, see Monteiro, *Blacks*, 140–41.
152   He used the word "peçonha," which may also be translated as "wickedness" or "malice," but in this case is likely "poison"; though Gan(g)a Zumba is not mentioned explicitly, the accusation seems to evoke his death. Vainfas, "Deus," 77.
153   "Carta de Padre Vieira [. . .]," 321.
154   "Carta [. . .]," February 6, 1692, in Gomes, *Mocambos*, 322.

2. BEFORE HE DIED, I KILLED ZUMBI

1   Silva, "Sermão."
2   Silva, "Sermão," 16v. On Silva, see Lara, *Palmares*, 390–92.
3   "Ordenou [. . .]," December 20, 1695, CCA, *Disposições*, VI-III-I-I-31, doc. 19, fols. 562r–562v, AUC.
4   "Consulta [. . .]," February 22, 1676, Pernambuco, caixa 11, doc. 1049, fols. 1r–2r, AHU.
5   Hertzman, "Fatal," 327–28; Lara, *Legislação*, 191–95, 403–8; Martin, "Slavery's"; R. Martins, "A obsessão," 4; Snyder, *The Power*, 20; Viotti, "As proposições."
6   Lara, "Do singular," 85.
7   Candido, *An African*, 180; Lara, *Palmares*, 31–54.
8   J. Cabral, "Narração," 170. In colonial Brazil, the basic unit of currency was the real (plural réis). A mil-réis, or one thousand réis, was written 1$000.
9   Mendes, "O serviço," 113–15. Also see Olival, "Mercados"; Olival, "Mercês"; and Olival, *As ordens*.
10   Mendes, "O serviço," 118; Silva and Bluteau, *Diccionario*, s.v. "soldo," "tença."
11   Albuquerque, *A remuneração*, 105–18; Olival, "Mercês," 68–69.
12   "Requerimento [. . .]," before January 21, 1695, Pernambuco, caixa 17, doc. 1673, AHU.

13   "Requerimento [. . .]," anexo 3 (June 25, 1691).

14   Mendes, "O serviço," 160.

15   Lara and Fachin, *Guerra*, 26.

16   Mendes, "O serviço," 53–54, 72.

17   Mendes, "O serviço," 71; Salgado, *Fiscais*, 166, 231, 311–13.

18   Mendes, "O serviço," 127.

19   Mendes, "O serviço," 128.

20   Mendes, "O serviço," 130.

21   Mendes, "O serviço," 130.

22   Mendes, "O serviço," 130–31.

23   "Consulta [. . .]," February 12, 1701, Pernambuco, caixa 19, doc. 1867, fol. 7v, AHU; Dimas Marques, "Pelo bem," 100; Mendes, "O serviço," 152.

24   "Relação [. . .]," in Gomes, *Mocambos*, 263. Gomes dates this document to 1685, but Lara shows that it is, in fact, from 1679. Lara, *Palmares*, 250. This was the third sesmaria given to Lopes. Existing documentation for the other two, awarded in 1678 and 1682, does not explicitly reference Palmares, though it is safe to say that his service there helped him secure these two as well. *Documentação*, 4:92, 104.

25   Studart, "Dezenove documentos," 268.

26   "Informação [. . .]," after July 30, 1682, Pernambuco, caixa 12, doc. 1230, fol. 1r, AHU. Resgate archivists date the document to 1682, while Laura Peraza Mendes estimates 1681. Mendes, "O serviço," 45. Peça, or "piece," was one of the crude categories that traders used to designate an enslaved person. See Miller, *Way of Death*, 66–69.

27   "Consulta [. . .]," August 8, 1684, Pernambuco, caixa 13, doc. 1297, fol. 5r, AHU.

28   "Carta patente de Manoel Lopes," March 15, 1689, Chanceleria de D. Pedro II, liv. 20, fol. 28r, Arquivo Nacional Torre do Tombo (hereafter, ANTT).

29   "Informação [. . .]," after March 24, 1683, Pernambuco, caixa 13, doc. 1248, AHU; "Registo Geral de Mercê, Manuel de Inojosa," March 14, 1685, Registo Geral de Mercês, Mercês de D. Pedro II, liv. 2, fols. 363r–363v, ANTT; "Requerimento [. . .]," before July 5, 1693, Pernambuco, caixa 16, doc. 1601, anexo 14 (January 19, 1692), AHU.

30   Lara, *Palmares*, 44–45.

31   "Sobre [. . .]," November 8, 1677, in D. Freitas, *República*, 141–42.

32   "Nomeação [. . .]," June 15, 1684, Conselho Ultramarino: Consultas Mistas (hereafter, Consultas Mistas), fol. 421v; "Registo Geral de Mercê, Manuel de Inojosa," fol. 363r.

33   For an overview of similar tropes in the context of marronage elsewhere in the Americas, see Thompson, "Gender."

34   Candido, *An African*, 85.

35   Alencastro, *The Trade*, 331.

36   For tracking down the nephew in Portugal, I owe a debt of gratitude to the contributors to the online Almodôvar genealogy forum, https://geneall.net/pt /forum/170163/almodovar-freguesia-indice-de-casamentos/, accessed April 17, 2020, The nephew's name is Antonio Guerreiro Boim. The documents showing

his presence at the marriage and identifying him as Inojosa's nephew are Casamentos (October 8, 1690 to December 6, 1727), January 9, 1695, Paróquia de Almodôvar, Registos de casamento, n/p, ANTT; and "Registo Geral de Mercê, Manuel de Inojosa," fol. 363r.

37 Mattos, "'Black Troops.'" In the Portuguese military, a terço typically comprised one thousand soldiers, divided evenly among ten companies, though in practice they could be dramatically smaller. Jesus, "Abrindo," 18.

38 Mattos, "'Black Troops,'" 7. Also see Mattos, "Henrique Dias."

39 Mattos, "'Black Troops,'" 8, 23; A. Mello, *Biografias*, 230; L. Silva, "Gênese."

40 Though the prospect of arming Black people in slave societies could seem anathema, in times of war it was common. Throughout the Americas, enslaved and free people of color served and died in armies and militias, sometimes fighting for European crowns and sometimes against them. Andrews, *Afro-Latin America*, 53–84; Blanchard, *Under*; Kraay, "Arming"; Kraay, *Race*; Vinson, *Bearing*.

41 Translated in Mattos, "'Black Troops,'" 12.

42 Mattos, "'Black Troops,'" 12.

43 "Carta de padrão [. . .] Domingos Rodrigues Carneiro [. . .]," April 23, 1688, Registo Geral de Mercês do reinado de D. Pedro II, liv. 5, fols. 189r–189v, ANTT; "Consulta [. . .]," February 7, 1688, Conselho Ultramarino: Consultas de Partes (hereafter, Consultas de Partes), cod. 49, fols. 331v–332r, AHU; "Consulta [. . .]," January 26, 1688, Pernambuco, caixa 14, doc. 1433, AHU.

44 "Consulta [. . .]," December 24, 1693, Pernambuco, caixa 16, doc. 1626, fol. 1r, AHU; "Registo Geral de Mercês, Domingos Rodrigues Carneiro," January 12, 1694, Registo Geral de Mercês do reinado de D. Pedro II, liv. 5, fol. 145v, ANTT.

45 Loreto Couto, *Desagravos*. Also see Raminelli, "Impedimentos," 713–14.

46 Loreto Couto, *Desagravos*, 458.

47 Loreto Couto, *Desagravos*, 458.

48 F. Costa, *Anais*, 4:420.

49 "Consulta [. . .]," December 24, 1693, Pernambuco, caixa 16, doc. 1626, AHU.

50 "Consulta [. . .]," December 24, 1693, fols. 1v, 2r. Lira would succeed Carneiro when he died. "Consulta [. . .]," February 16, 1726, Pernambuco, caixa 33, doc. 3016, fol. 2r, AHU.

51 Translated in Dutra, "Blacks," 29. Also see Dutra, "African Heritage," 125–37.

52 Like many other petitioners, Carneiro attested that he was poor. "Diligência de habilitação [. . .] Domingos Rodrigues Carneiro," 1710, Mesa da Consciência e Ordens, Habilitações para a Ordem de São Bento de Avis, letra D, maço 1, no. 1, fol. 2r, ANTT. ANTT uses 1688 as the date for this bundle of papers, though it includes material from the eighteenth century. Following others, I use 1710.

53 J. Mello, *D. Antonio*; K. Silva, *Nas solidões*, 142–54.

54 J. Lopes, "A visibilidade," 135.

55 Raminelli, "Privilegios."

56 "Registo geral de mercê de (D.) Sebastião Pinheiro Camarão," March 13, 1688, Registo Geral de Mercês, Mercês de D. Pedro II, liv. 4, fol. 247r, ANTT. The ANTT uses March 5 in its catalog, though the document says March 13.

57 The full title is *Rellação Verdadeyra da Guerra que se fez aos Negros Levantados do Palmar, governando estas Capitanias de Pernambuco o senhor Governador e Capitam-Geral Cayetano de Mello de Castro no Anno de 1694: da felliz vitoria que Contra o ditto Inimigo Se alcanssou.* I use the transcription in Maria Lêda Oliveira, "A primeira."

58 Maria Lêda Oliveira, "A primeira," 267–68.

59 Maria Lêda Oliveira, "A primeira," 318.

60 Maria Lêda Oliveira, "A primeira," 318.

61 Maria Lêda Oliveira, "A primeira," 318.

62 Maria Lêda Oliveira, "A primeira," 255.

63 Pedreira, "Os quilombos," 16.

64 "Domingos Jorge Velho [. . .]," February 8, 1694, in Gomes, *Mocambos*, 338. In the immediate aftermath of the battle, he also sent a letter vouching for the actions of Vieira de Melo and another officer. In this letter he did not go into detail about the battle, other than to highlight the large number of fatalities and prisoners. "Atestado [. . .]," February 8, 1694, in Gomes, *Mocambos*, 338–39; "Domingos Jorge Velho, [. . .]," February 9, 1694, in Gomes, *Mocambos*, 339–40.

65 "Carta [. . .]," February 18, 1694, in Gomes, *Mocambos*, 340.

66 "Carta [. . .]," February 18, 1694, 340.

67 "Carta [. . .]," February 18, 1694, 341.

68 Scott Allen makes this point too, in "'Zumbi,'" 46–47.

69 "Carta [. . .]," February 18, 1694, 341.

70 "Registo Geral de Mercês, Bernardo Vieira de Melo," January 8, 1695, Registo Geral de Mercês do reinado de D. Pedro II, liv. 9, fol. 244r, ANTT.

71 Puntoni, *A guerra*, 294.

72 Rocha Pita, *Historia*, 474.

73 This did not prevent confusion or the circulation of conflicting stories about Zumbi's death. As Luiz Felipe de Alencastro points out, Loreto Couto mentions Zumbi's death occurring on three different occasions. Alencastro, "História geral," 94.

74 "Carta [. . .]," August 14, 1694, in Gomes, *Mocambos*, 346. Lencastre was also known as Dom João de Alencastro.

75 "Consulta [. . .]," November 13, 1694, in Gomes, *Mocambos*, 346.

76 "Carta [. . .]," August 4, 1694, in Gomes, *Mocambos*, 344.

77 "Carta [. . .]," January 24, 1696, in Gomes, *Mocambos*, 366.

78 "Carta [. . .]," March 14, 1696, Pernambuco, caixa 17, doc. 1697, fols. 1r–2r, AHU.

79 Mario Behring, "A morte do Zumby," *Kosmos*, September 1906, n.p.

80 "Carta [. . .]," March 14, 1696, Pernambuco, caixa 17, doc. 1697, anexo 1 (August 18, 1696, fol. 1r), AHU. According to Loreto Couto, the man's name was Antonio Soares, and he was a crioulo born in Recife. Loreto Couto, *Desagravos*, 460; Lara, *Palmares*, 341.

81 "Consulta [. . .]," December 11, 1694, in Gomes, *Mocambos*, 354.

82 "Registo [. . .]," January 8, 1695, in *DH*, vol. 57 (Rio de Janeiro: Typ. Baptista de Souza, 1942), 177; "Registo Geral de Mercês, Bernardo Vieira de Melo," January 8, 1695, Registo Geral de Mercês do reinado de D. Pedro II, liv. 9, fol. 244r.

83   "Consulta [. . .]," December 11, 1699, doc. 70, in Ennes, *As guerras*, 408–13. Góes also appears as Goez and Goiz in colonial documents.

84   "Consulta [. . .]," December 11, 1699, 408.

85   "Consulta [. . .]," December 11, 1699, 409–11.

86   "Consulta [. . .]," December 11, 1699, 412.

87   "Consulta [. . .]," December 11, 1699, 412.

88   "Consulta [. . .]," December 11, 1699, 412.

89   "Consulta [. . .]," May 10, 1703, Pernambuco, caixa 20, doc. 1921, fol. 6v, AHU.

90   "Consulta [. . .]," May 10, 1703, fol. 7r.

91   "Nomeyo a Bernardo Vieyra de Mello," March 14, 1709, Consultas Mistas, Cod. 20, fol. 151r, AHU; "Consulta [. . .]," January 18, 1708, Pernambuco, caixa 22, doc. 2061, fol. 1v, AHU.

92   "Informação [. . .]," after February 28, 1729, Pernambuco, caixa 38, doc. 3398, AHU; "Registo Geral de Mercês, Bernardo Vieira de Melo," January 17, 1725, Registo Geral de Mercês de D. João V, liv. 2, fols. 472r–472v, ANTT.

93   "Registo Geral de Mercê, Domingos Simões Jordão," October 11, 1718, Registo Geral de Mercês, Mercês de D. João V, liv. 10, fol. 213r, ANTT.

94   "Consulta [. . .]," April 28, 1727, caixa 35, doc. 3220, fol. 2v, AHU; "Requerimento [. . .]," before July 15, 1730, Pernambuco, caixa 40, doc. 3652, fol. 1r, AHU.

95   "Consulta [. . .]," February 17, 1734, Conselho Ultramarino: Brasil-Ceará (hereafter, Ceará), caixa 3, doc. 153, fol. 2r, AHU.

96   *Documentação*, 1:230–35.

97   "Consulta [. . .]," December 30, 1697, Pernambuco, caixa 17, doc. 1744, fol. 1r, AHU.

98   "Consulta [. . .]," December 30, 1697, fol. 1r.

99   "Consulta [. . .]," December 19, 1697, Pernambuco, caixa 17, doc. 1737, fol. 2r, AHU.

100   "Consulta [. . .]," January 18, 1708, Pernambuco, caixa 22, doc. 2061, AHU.

101   This and the remaining quotations in this paragraph are from "Requerimento [. . .]," before July 30, 1710, Pernambuco, caixa 24, doc. 2176, fol. 1r, AHU.

102   "Requerimento [. . .]," n.d., in Gomes, *Mocambos*, 412, 413. "Régulo" may also be translated as "kinglet." The intention of the word is to diminish; Silva and Bluteau defined it as "reizinho" ("little king"). Silva and Bluteau, *Vocabulario*, s.v. "regulo." Original manuscript consulted at Documenta Palmares, https://palmares.ifch.unicamp.br/pf-palmares/record-files/Fontes%20(Fichas)/AHU _ACL_CU_015_Cx._18_D._1746_anexo_02_AbDjePc.pdf, accessed May 24, 2023.

103   "Consulta [. . .]," May 6, 1699, Ceará, caixa 1, doc. 42, fol. 4r, AHU; "Registo Geral de Mercês, Antônio Pinto Pereira," November 21, 1701, Registo Geral de Mercês, Mercês de D. Pedro II, liv. 14, no. 53, fol. 223r, ANTT.

104   "Registo Geral de Mercês, Cristóvão da Rocha Barbosa," February 1, 1709, Registo Geral de Mercês do reinado de D. João V, liv. 7, fol. 584r, ANTT.

105   "Carta Patente [. . .]," June 10, 1711, Pernambuco, caixa 24, doc. 2200, fol. 1r, AHU.

106   "Requerimento [. . .]," August 4, 1708, AHU, Pernambuco, caixa 23, doc. 2089, fol. 1r, AHU.

107   "Diligência de habilitação [. . .] Domingos Rodrigues Carneiro," fol. 8r.

108 "Requerimento [. . .]," before March 12, 1724, Pernambuco, caixa 30, doc. 2723, fol. 1r, AHU.

109 Augusto, "Famílias nordestinas," 193.

110 Dimas Marques, "Pelo bem," 101.

111 "Requerimento [. . .]," before September 4, 1753, Pernambuco, caixa 75, doc. 6240, fol. 36v, AHU.

112 "Para a companhia [. . .]," July 9, 1691, in DH, vol. 33 (Rio de Janeiro: Typ. Arch. de Ilist. Brasileira, 1936), 412; "Registo da patente [. . .]," November 18, 1692, in DH, vol. 30 (Rio de Janeiro: Typ. Arch. de Ilist. Brasileira, 1935), 381–82. In 1711, the soldier repeated the story again as he won another mercê, though that time he made no reference to Lopes. "Registo da patente [. . .]," October 12, 1711, in DH, vol. 59 (Rio de Janeiro: Typ. Baptista de Souza, 1943), 346.

113 "Consulta [. . .]," February 12, 1701, Pernambuco, caixa 19, doc. 1867, fol. 5r, AHU.

114 The participation of multiple parties in shaping these narratives resonates with Luise White's assertion that rumors are shaped and kept alive by "diverse social groups" with distinct memories and aims, but perhaps even more instructive is Matthew Restall's treatment of how fantastical written accounts of Spanish conquest and conquistador petitions (probanzas de mérito) informed latter-day histories and historiographies in Spanish America in much the same way that the mercê petitions shaped the historiography of Portuguese America. In both American cases, rumors circulate not only by mouth but also in writing. Restall, *Seven Myths*, 12–3; White, *Speaking*, 82. Also intriguing in this regard is the recent work of Hal Langfur. Langfur, *Adrift*.

115 Smallwood, *Saltwater Slavery*, 152.

3. WHOSE CONFUSION?

1 Scott, *The Common Wind*.

2 "Informação [. . .]," after July 23, 1715, Pernambuco, caixa 27, doc. 2447, fol. 1v, AHU.

3 V. Brown, *The Reaper's*, 152. Brown and others suggest that whites mutilated the corpses of enslaved people to send a message that they would not return to Africa in death. V. Brown, "Spiritual Terror," 26–27. Kathryn McKnight proposes that in Spanish America the brutal practice must also be understood "within a broader context of Spanish ideologies and practices," which moved authorities to target the bodies of criminals "regardless of their race or national origin." McKnight, "Confronted Rituals," n.p. Also see Kars, *Blood*, 20–21; and Staller, *Converging*, 1. The mythologies surrounding Makandal, one of the heroic figures of the Haitian Revolution, provide compelling points of comparison with Zumbi's mortality. See, for example, Allewaert, "Super Fly"; de Luna, "Sounding," 591–602; and N. Roberts, *Freedom*, 101.

4 R. Rodrigues, "A Troya." The essay, slightly edited, is reprinted in R. Rodrigues, *Os africanos*, 71–97.

5   This and the remaining quotes by Rodrigues in this and the next paragraph are from R. Rodrigues, *Os africanos*, 90–92.

6   "Coast" likely refers to Africa. Until the 1920s, "North" was often synonymous with "Northeast," comprising Bahia, Sergipe, Alagoas, Pernambuco, Paraíba, Rio Grande do Norte, Ceará, Piauí, and Maranhão. D. Albuquerque, *The Invention*, 37–38.

7   Freyre, *The Masters*, 370.

8   Beaurepaire-Rohan, *Diccionario*. On Rodrigues and Palmares, also see T. Souza, "De Nina Rodrigues"; T. Souza, "A Troya Negra."

9   "Tidy, singular" is from de Luna, "Sounding the African Atlantic," 586.

10 Scholars of Palmares generally leave the relationship between Zambi, Zumbi, and zumbi untouched or echo Rodrigues, in some cases going so far as calling "Zumbi" an "alteration" (corruptela) or "corruption" (corrupção) of "Zambi." F. Costa, *Vocabulário*, 808; E. Castro, *Ensaios*, 196. In a footnote in his influential *O negro brasileiro*, Arthur Ramos challenged Rodrigues's argument, pointing out the use of both "zambi" and "zumbi" in Bantu languages. A. Ramos, *O negro*, 105.

11 For an in-depth appraisal and analysis, see O. Cunha, *The Things*.

12 Miller, "Central Africa," 45.

13 Vansina, *How Societies*, 274, 277.

14 In addition to Miller, Thornton, Vansina, and other pioneering historians of the region, our knowledge of these processes owes much to the labor and insights of linguists such as Koen Bostoen, Simon Branford, Rebecca Grollemund, Malcolm Guthrie, Derek Nurse, and Gilles-Maurice de Schryver. In addition to the citations below and in appendix A, see Williamson et al., "Niger-Congo," for a helpful overview of the larger Niger-Congo phylum; and Nurse and Philippson, *The Bantu Languages*, for a plethora of information on Bantu languages.

15 M. Almeida, "Speaking"; Bostoen and de Schryver, "Seventeenth-Century Kikongo"; Schryver et al., "Introducing."

16 Vansina, "Portuguese," 273. Also see Vieira-Martinez, "Building," 90–98.

17 Angenot, Kempf, and Kukanda, "*Arte*"; Miller, "Central Africa," 44–45.

18 M. Almeida, "African Voices," 187.

19 See Maiden, *A Linguistic*, 10–12.

20 The debates are summarized nicely in M. Almeida, "Speaking," 249–58.

21 De Luna, "Sounding," 594–95. "Historians," Almeida writes, "have been working with Kikongo and Kimbundu as if they were two bounded entities as close to each other as Portuguese and Spanish. From a historical point of view, this [practice] is misleading. Kikongo and Kimbundu language clusters are genetically quite distant and internally diversified." M. Almeida, "African Voices," 180. Additional works that demonstrate the differences between and internal complexities within Kimbundu and Kikongo include Angenot, Kempf, and Kukanda, "*Arte*"; and Bostoen and de Schryver, "Seventeenth-Century Kikongo."

22 See, for example, Lara's recent book, which makes the very comparison (Kimbundu is to Kikongo as Spanish is to Portuguese) that Almeida (and others)

warns against. Lara, *Palmares*, 194. Even the meticulous and pioneering Jan Vansina oversimplified the relationship between Kimbundu and Palmares. He cites the priest António Vieira's 1691 letter, which insisted that no efforts be made to negotiate with Palmares, as evidence that Kimbundu was spoken in Brazil, Palmares, and other fugitive slave communities. But Vieira does not mention Kimbundu, writing simply that Palmaristas would only trust people "of their nation and language." Vansina, "Portuguese," 274; "Carta de Padre Vieira [. . .]," July 2, 1691, in Gomes, *Mocambos*, 321.

23 Almeida provides a useful way to think about that multiplicity and complexity in his revision of Robert Slenes's important argument that enslaved people in southeast Brazil developed a "Bantu *lingua franca*." Through the study of a single slave ship, Almeida identifies multiple linguistic traditions that produced "not a Tower of Babel, but an unequal speech community sustained by participants through the use of different languages." M. Almeida, "African Voices," 187; Slenes, "'*Malungu*,'" 61.

24 P. Dias, *Arte*.

25 Angenot, Kempf, and Kukanda, "*Arte*," 231. For an overview in English of Dias and *Arte da lingua*, see Zwartjes, *Portuguese*, 220–35.

26 Angenot, Kempf, and Kukanda, "*Arte*," 233, 234. Also insightful are the observations made by Larissa Brewer-García about the complex negotiations surrounding catechism and translation in other American settings. Brewer-García, *Beyond Babel*, 109–13, 175.

27 Ivana Lima, "Escravidão," 111.

28 Between 1676 and 1700, more than fifty thousand people from West Africa arrived in Bahia. Slave Voyages website, http://www.slavevoyages.org/estimates /iX9QZqcG, accessed June 26, 2023.

29 Candido, "South Atlantic," 57.

30 R. Ferreira, *Cross-Cultural*, 9.

31 Alencastro, "Os africanos," 21.

32 Lara, *Palmares*, 178; Guattini and Carli, *Viaggio*, 81. On word of Palmares in Africa, also see Nafafé, *Lourenço da Silva*, 243.

33 MacGaffey, *Religion*, 78.

34 Hilton, *Kingdom*, 50, 91–92; MacGaffey, "Dialogues," 258; Thornton, "Afro-Christian Syncretism," quote on 58.

35 Sweet, *Recreating*, 107. Relevant, too, is MacGaffey's observation about the multivalence of Nzambi a Mpungu, or "nzambi mpgungu," which, he notes, could not only refer to a Creator but also be used to refer to "any dead person." MacGaffey, "A Central African," 57.

36 In addition to the other citations in this paragraph, see, for example, Brusciotto, *Grammar*, 2.

37 Quotation translated in Brewer-García, *Beyond Babel*, 113.

38 P. Dias, *Arte*, 4.

39 Gordon, *Invisible Agents*, 12.

40 Thornton, "Religious," 75.

41 Remarkably, these spirits, which seem to share the name of Palmares's most famous leader, have warranted little attention in the literature on Palmares, though, for compelling suggestions, see Anderson, "The Quilombo," 559, 562; Palmié, "African States," 59; and Schwartz, *Slaves*, 127. At least in some cases, "nzambi" may have, indeed, resembled "nzumbi," at least to outsiders such as K. E. Laman, who wrote, "Departed close relations are often called nzambi. A dead father is spoken of as: 'Nzambi, my late father' . . . a corpse may be called nzambi . . . because when someone dies, he is transformed into another, invisible being with greater powers and possibilities of the kind that Nzambi possesses." Laman, *The Kongo*, 3:58. Linguists and anthropologists have written about (n)zumbi with emphasis on contemporary settings. For example, Bonvini, "Os vocábulos," 135–37.

42 Miller, *Kings*, 253.

43 Miller, *Kings*, 254.

44 Emphasis mine. Cadornega, *História* (1680), Azul 643, tomo 1, fol. 295; Azul 645, tomo 3, fols. 226–27. Cadornega's text illustrates the way that scholars have mixed zumbi, zambi, and zombi. On the page from tomo 3 of the original manuscript, he uses "zumbi," but an often-cited edition published in 1940 uses "ozombi," "ozambi," and "nzumbi" all on a single page. Cadornega, *História* (1940), 1:370.

45 Merolla da Sorrento, "A Voyage," 299.

46 Miller renders this as "Ushi wa Nzumbi," producing a somewhat puzzling combination; "ushi" means a "seller of honey." De Luna corrects the translation, suggesting that Miller missed an aspirated "b" sound that non-native speakers often do not hear. "Bushi" could be translated as "essence of the settlement," which makes much more sense in this case. Kathryn de Luna, personal communication, August 22, 2022; Miller, *Kings*, 73.

47 Miller, *Kings*, 188.

48 Translated in Kananoja, *Healing*, 40.

49 On Afro-Cuban ngangas, see Palmié, *Wizards*, 159–200.

50 Thornton, *The Kongolese*, 53–54. Also see Pantoja, "Inquisição," 127.

51 Bostoen, Tshiyayi, and de Schryver, "On the Origin," 61.

52 Cavazzi published two accounts of the region, the *Missione evangelica nel Regno de Congo* (1668) and *Istorica descrizione* (1687). I use Thornton's English translation of *Missione* and for *Istorica descrizione* the original as well as a Portuguese translation. Cavazzi da Montecuccolo, *Descrição*; Cavazzi da Montecuccolo, *Istorica*; Cavazzi da Montecuccolo, *Missione*. Like any colonial documents, these must be read with a grain of salt, because they are artifacts of what MacGaffey famously termed "dialogues of the deaf" and because of the particular way in which each text was compiled and written. Much of Cavazzi's ethnographic material was "fleshed out" in Europe where, Thornton suggests, he may have had access to a better collection of ecclesiastical reports than in Africa. Also of note, Cavazzi visited Bahia and Pernambuco, yet another indication of the multidirectional flow of ideas across the Atlantic. MacGaffey, "Dialogues"; Thornton, "New Light," 257.

53 Kananoja, *Central African*, 204; Pantoja, "Inquisição," 127.

54 Lara and Fachin, *Guerra*, 20, 118. Alida C. Metcalf and Ronaldo Vainfas suggest that an intriguing millenarian community in Bahia was, if not a direct precursor of Palmares, a signal of how different forms of spirituality could permeate communities established in the forests of Brazil. Metcalf, "Millenarian Slaves?," 1553–55; Vainfas, "Deus," 60–64.

55 Heywood, "Portuguese," 95; Kananoja, "Healers," 446; Wheat, *Atlantic Africa*, 216–52.

56 Bluteau's second edition defined "paroco" as "curate (cura) of souls," a description that could also be applied to ngangas. Silva and Bluteau, *Diccionario*, s.v. "paroco."

57 Lara and Fachin, *Guerra*, 19.

58 Could "Ganga-Muiça" have been nganga wisa, a "priest of power" who left behind few traces beyond a 1690 Inquisition case? Sweet, *Recreating*, 155.

59 Lara, *Palmares*, 394; Thornton, "Angola," 56, 60.

60 Vansina, *How Societies*, 165–66.

61 Vansina, *Paths*, 298.

62 The admission came during a debate about theology and the fate of souls after human death. "Carta [. . .]," January 15, 1674, in Brásio, *Monumenta*, 13:258. On the debate, see Thornton, "Religious," 74.

63 In other contexts, scholars have suggested that Gan(g)a Zumba may have been connected to "Gangazambe," though the likely roots seem to suggest different origins and meanings. The Inquisition defined Gangazambe as a form of "witchcraft" employed in Angola to "kill or give life" and noted that "many whites" born in Angola (brancos filhos da terra) believed in Gangazambes. "Ritos Gentilicos de Angolla," 1720?, Tribunal do Santo Ofício, Conselho Geral (hereafter, TSO-CG), liv. 272, fol. 123v, ANTT. Kalle Kananoja treats "Gangazambe" and "Gangazumba" interchangeably and suggests that the terms referred to ngangas who healed victims afflicted with malevolent spirits and "denote[d] various magical practices that were used both to kill and to 'give life,' i.e., to heal people, and to invoke hatred or love." Kananoja, "Healers," 447.

64 Cavazzi da Montecuccolo, *Descrição*, 1:203.

65 The Portuguese often referred to the Imbangala as jaga, but Mariana Candido shows that the word was a European "creation" clunkily applied to disparate peoples who were the same only "in the mind of the Portuguese colonialists." She synthesizes and critiques long debates about the meaning of jaga in *An African*, 40–41, 50–61 (quote from 59). Jared Staller later revisited the term, which he treats as one that became "useful to both Africans and Europeans as a sort of working misunderstanding that allowed interactions and interferences in political and economic endeavors, especially slaving." Staller, *Converging*, 12.

66 Cavazzi da Montecuccolo, *Descrição*, 1:203. In *Missione Evangelica*, Cavazzi includes a lengthy discussion of the priests and the spirits they tend to, which he now calls nzumbo. It is unclear why he refers to nzumbo here and nzumbi elsewhere. They may have been separate entities, though he more likely

misunderstood or misspelled nzumbi. Thornton suggests, "Nzumbo seem to be the recently dead, or those in the transitional process between living and dead." Cavazzi da Montecuccolo, *Missione*, book 1, chap. 8, editor's note on 37.

67 Merolla da Sorrento, "A Voyage," 299.

68 Merolla da Sorrento, "A Voyage," 270.

69 See Vansina, *How Societies*, 198.

70 Precisely what that process of recognition involved awaits further research. It is also worth noting that word (n)zumbi often crossed colonial and national lines as it circulated among European priests and travelers. See, for example, Merolla da Sorrento, "A Voyage," 299; and Uring, *A History*, 67.

71 Some of the cases discussed below are treated in R. Ferreira, *Cross-Cultural*; Kananoja, *Healing*; and Pantoja, "Inquisição."

72 Tribunal do Santo Ofício, Cadernos do Promotor (hereafter, TSO-CP), October 16, 1722, caderno 92, fols. 250r–278r, ANTT; TSO-CP, October 3, 1721, caderno 94, fols. 371r–387r, ANTT; "Auto de denúncia contra Ana Maria Antunes de Almeida," Tribunal do Santo Ofício, Inquisição de Lisboa (hereafter, TSO-IL), October 7, 1750, Processo 13834, fol. 4v, ANTT.

73 TSO-CP, August 4, 1716, caderno 86, fols. 41r–46v, ANTT. Others have written about this case, including R. Ferreira, *Cross-Cultural*, 186; and Kananoja, *Healing*, 66–67.

74 TSO-CP, caderno 86, fol. 45r.

75 Crowley and Bowern, *An Introduction*, 220. Bantu languages are the "textbook case" of agglutination in Africa. Beyer, "Morphology," 52.

76 Bostoen, "Bantu," 316. Also see Meeussen, "Bantu," 93.

77 The process occurs in word roots that contained the lost vowels. De Luna and Fleisher, *Speaking*, 104; Bostoen, "Bantu"; Janson, "Bantu."

78 Bostoen, "Bantu," 305; Janson, "Bantu," 93.

79 ID 1259 and 1261, Bantu Lexical Reconstructions 3 (hereafter, BLR 3), and see appendix A for a map, full list, and more information about Bantu language zones. Also see Janson, "Bantu," appendix 1; and Maho, *NUGL Online*. Though more work is required to understand the potential relationships at play here, it is interesting that *-dùmb-* and *-dùmbí* are found in southern and eastern Africa, including Mozambique. In parts of Malawi and Tanzania, *-dùmb-* could mean "praise," another concept that would have easily fit into an Nganga Zumbi title or position in Palmares. After Palmares's fall, during the second half of the eighteenth century, commercial routes would connect Malawi and Tanzania to Africa's west coast. Guthrie, *Comparative Bantu*, vol. 3, s.v. "*-dùmb-*" (c.s. 701); Malacco and Gonçalves, "Entre Senegâmbia," 79.

80 Even after technological innovations improved the durability and functioning of weaponry in wet conditions, belief that rain could make firearms useless continued. In 1665 an important battle in West Central Africa between Portuguese and Kongolese forces, waged in the rain, hinged in part on the mistaken appraisal by Kongolese forces that the storm would make the Portuguese weapons useless. Alencastro, *The Trade*, 290, 353–56.

81 Henderson, *A History*, 363.

82   Rocha Pita, *Historia*, 481.

83   In BaKongo society, writes Wyatt MacGaffey, the dead are "said to live 'in the water' as opposed to on dry land, 'in the forest' as opposed to in the village, and in the cemetery as opposed also to in the village." MacGaffey, *Religion*, 55.

84   I consulted a facsimile of the original and also a Portuguese translation. Marcgrave (Marggraf), *História*; Marggraf and Piso, *Guilielmi*.

85   Marcgrave (Marggraf), *História*, 261; Marggraf and Piso, *Guilielmi*, 261. The same observation (with the same spelling of Gungohubî) is repeated in a text published in 1682 that reproduced much of Marggraf's work. Nieuhof, *Joan Nieuhofs Gedekwaerdige*, 14.

86   I owe this insight to Kate de Luna.

87   Guthrie, *Comparative*, vol. 3, s.v. "*-jàmbê*" (C.S. 925); Mobley, "The Kongolese," 210–11.

88   See Maddieson, "The Sounds," 15–23.

89   See Basso and Gonçalves, *História*, 240–49.

90   Basso and Gonçalves, *História*, 231; Genealogical Department, *Basic*, 8; Teyssier, *História*, 61–62.

91   While /a/ and /u/ occupy opposite ends of the Bantuphone acoustic register, /o/ and /u/ are relatively close. But without additional research, Bantu spirantization patterns are not as helpful for Zombi as they are for Zumbi. It is likely incorrect to derive Zombi from the proto-Bantu root *-dómb- ("ask for"), for example, because the letter /d/ preceding an /o/ did not change to /z/ as in /du/ to /zu/. Future research may also reveal more about connections and differences between these words and "Zombie" in the French Atlantic. Maureen Warner-Lewis states that in the Caribbean, "*Jumbi* and *zombi* 'ghost,' derived from Kimbundu *(n)zumbi*, became incorporated into French-lexified creoles," while Robin Derby suggests a fascinating convergence between African and Indigenous ideas. ID 1112, BLR 3; de Luna, *The Long*; Derby, "Zemis," 32–33; Guthrie, *Comparative Bantu*, vol. 3, s.v. "*-dómb-*" (c.s. 653); Saillant and Araujo, "Zumbi"; Vansina, *Paths*, 282; Warner-Lewis, "The African Diaspora," 326.

92   Bostoen, "Bantu," 301.

93   Cadornega, *História* (1680), Azul 644, tomo 2, fol. 320.

94   It is possible that Cadornega was repeating "Zambem-apongo," which Thornton finds in an example from the late fifteenth century, though this too, he explains, was likely a misapprehension of Nzambi a Mpungu. Thornton, "Afro-Christian," 58.

95   Thornton, *A History*, 45.

96   Schwartz, *Slaves*, 125. Also see Neto, "Kilombo"; and Schwartz, "Mocambos."

97   By that point, the Imbangala kilombo had become all but obsolete in West Central Africa, though individual Imbangala rulers retained power through creative reinvention. Miller, *Kings*, 251–64.

98   Lara, *Palmares*, 366; Thornton, "Angola," 55; Vansina, "Quilombos," 453–54.

99   Lara, "Quem eram," 82; Schwartz, *Slaves*, 127.

100 The Imbangala are treated extensively in Miller, *Kings*, and more recently in Staller, *Converging*. Also see Birmingham, "The Date"; Miller, "The Imbangala"; Thornton, "The African Experience"; and Vansina, "The Foundation."

101 Miller, *Kings*, 198.

102 Staller, *Converging*, 83.

103 The Portuguese captured Battel in Brazil and sent him, as a prisoner, to Angola, where he lived for two decades. Battel et al., *The Strange Adventures*, 30; Birmingham, "The Date," 148; Vansina, "On Ravenstein's Edition"; Wheat, *Atlantic Africa*, 96–97. Battel describes the Imbangala taste for palm wine and refers to the palm groves he saw in Africa as "Palmares." To Schwartz, the importance of palm trees to the Imbangala and in Palmares suggests that similarities between Brazilian quilombos and Angolan kilombos were "more than coincidental." Alencastro interprets parallel examples similarly, but Thornton argues the opposite, pointing out that the Imbangala targeted local agriculture, "especially palm trees," which they cut down and used for wine before moving on once the supply dwindled—a wasteful practice that sharply contrasts with the habits of Palmaristas, who put Brazilian palms to use in all number of manners. Shaped by different circumstances and bent on different aims, Palmaristas and the Imbangala would have interacted in different ways with the natural world. For the Imbangala, wrecking the land and its resources was part of a ruthless military strategy. By contrast, Palmaristas sought to maximize sustenance from the trees just as they looked to their surroundings to provide shelter and protection. Alencastro, "História geral," 83–85; Schwartz, *Slaves*, 127; Thornton, "Angola," 55.

104 Miller, "Central Africa," 50. One version of the *Relação* registers the battlefield death of a "captain" described as the "brother of the Bangala," perhaps indicating an Imbangala presence among the Palmares leadership. Lara and Fachin, *Guerra*, 143.

105 Miller, *Kings*, 232.

106 Miller, *Kings*, 176.

107 Miller, *Kings*, 240.

108 Thornton, "Central Africa," 94.

109 Thornton, "Angola," 54. Njinga called her fortified capital a kilombo. Heywood and Thornton, *Central Africans*, 134.

110 Heywood, *Njinga*, 122.

111 Staller, *Converging*, 13.

112 The bishop called the Imbangala "jagas." Miller, "The Imbangala," 566; "Relação [. . .]," September 9, 1619, in Brásio, *Monumenta*, 6:378.

113 Thornton, "The African Experience," 426.

114 Thornton, "The African Experience," 426.

115 Heywood, *Njinga*, 191–92, 255. Also see Alencastro, *The Trade*, 276–77.

116 The Imbangala incorporated the practices so thoroughly that scholars misunderstood nganga a nzumbi as a distinctively Imbangala position, though they had likely adapted it from the Mbundu. Miller, *Kings*, 255.

117 Miller, *Kings*, 257.

118 Staller, *Converging*, 114.

119 As early as the fifteenth century, Thornton writes, West Central Africans developed a "distinctly African variant of Christianity, one that included the spiritual power to protect and deliver humans to a new group of Otherworld beings such as saints, angels, the Virgin Mary, and Jesus." Thornton, "Afro-Christian," 77. This is just one example of what Selma Pantoja calls "the enormous capacity of traditional African cosmologies to respond creatively to the unprecedented challenge" of European invasions. Pantoja, "Inquisição," 132. Candido cautions against overemphasizing the significance of Christianity in West Central Africa, where "most people . . . deliberately or not, ignored" it. Candido, *An African*, 12. Also see Fromont, *The Art*.

120 R. Ferreira, *Cross-Cultural*, 182.

121 "Diário da viagem [. . .]," 1645, in Gomes, *Mocambos*, 170.

122 Staller, *Converging*, 11.

123 On the difference between West Central African and European definitions of witchcraft, see Thornton, "Afro-Christian," 65–67; Thornton, *A History*, 167–69; and Thornton, "Religious," 81–82. In Brazil, Laura de Mello e Souza argues, witchcraft, or sorcery, "mimicked the process of colonization," defined first in mainly European terms and evolving over time to eventually encompass Indigenous and African concepts. L. Souza, "Sorcery," 41. Also see Geschiere, *The Modernity*, 11, 13; Gordon, *Invisible*, 10; L. Souza, *The Devil*; Sweet, *Recreating*, 161–90; and White, *Speaking*, 19–22.

124 "Diário da viagem," 170. Thornton, who consulted the original Dutch version, translates this part to read that those who escaped were "beaten to death," which Hoogbergen seems to confirm as well. Hoogbergen, "Palmares," 36; Thornton, "Les États," 780.

125 Thornton, *A History*, 161.

126 McKnight, "Confronted Rituals."

127 McKnight, "Confronted Rituals," n. p.

128 Miller, *Kings*, 13.

129 Piersen, "White Cannibals"; Thornton, "Cannibals."

4. FLYING HOME?

1 Lara, *Palmares*, 324.

2 Lara, *Palmares*, 407.

3 Alves, *Dicionário*, s.v. "lenga." For her translations, Lara uses J. Nascimento, *Diccionario*. More elaborate linguistic work will likely yield definitions not captured in either dictionary.

4 I thank James Sweet for this insight. On nkisi, see MacGaffey, "The Personhood."

5 Translated in Sweet, "Calundu," 42.

6 Laman, *The Kongo*, 41–42; Thornton, *The Kongolese*, 12.

7 Though not a causal relationship, it is nonetheless significant that, as they did elsewhere in Brazil, letters guaranteeing legal freedom in late seventeenth- and early eighteenth-century Pernambuco often described the newly freed person as the same as anyone "born free from the belly [barriga] of their mother," a precursor to what well over a century later would become the so-called Free Womb Law, which granted legal freedom to children born to enslaved mothers. See numerous documents in Instituto Arqueológico Histórico e Geográfico Pernambucano (hereafter, IAHGP), códice 292: Garanhuns, 1713–1724.

8 "Flying Africans" and the idea of transcending death (or enslavement) through flight gained increased visibility in the United States thanks to the Federal Writers' Project, popular folk tales, and novels by the likes of Toni Morrison. See Gomez, *Exchanging*, 117–18; Gomez, "A Quality," 86–89; V. Hamilton, *The People*; Morrison, *Song*; Powell, "Summoning"; Smallwood, *Saltwater*, 186; Snyder, *The Power*, 57–58, 157–66; and Snyder, "Suicide," 39–40, 43. In some traditions, Igbo Landing is located elsewhere in the Low Country of South Carolina. Brown, *African-Atlantic*, 139–42. For a compelling discussion of flight (oriented toward Africa) as a multifaceted way to transcend bondage and racism, and to seize freedom, see Commander, *Afro-Atlantic Flight*.

9 Kea, "'When I Die,'" 159–60. Ordinarily, death by suicide would prohibit Akan people from entering the place "where the ancestors dwell," but an exception would have been made in this case because the rebels took their lives in battle. Konadu, *The Akan*, 99.

10 Hertzman, "Fatal Differences."

11 Rucker, *Gold Coast*, 183.

12 Barnet, *Biography*, 43. The English-language version of the biography translates "brujas isleñas" (island witches) as "Canary Island witches," but I have employed a more literal interpretation to indicate that the original phrase may refer to a number of islands, perhaps even Cuba. Barnet, *Cimarrón*, 46. Also see Pérez, *To Die*, 39.

13 T. J. Desch-Obi suggests an even more widespread phenomenon. As long as the deceased possessed spiritual strength and received proper burial, he writes, "Any African was believed to have the potential for flight." Desch-Obi, *Fighting*, 138. Almost always drawing on examples from the Caribbean and North America and involving men and women from West Africa, other scholars have drawn conclusions similar to Desch-Obi's. V. Brown, *The Reaper's*, 132–33; Piersen, "White Cannibals," 158.

14 The contested boundaries of Igbo identity further illustrate the limits of a purely demographic explanation. See Chambers, "'My Own Nation'"; Chambers, "Tracing Igbo"; Chambers, "Rejoinder"; Falola and Njoku, *Igbo*; and Northrup, "Igbo."

15 Translated in Grinberg, *A Black Jurist*, 80. Also see A. Brown, "'A Black Mark.'"

16 For example, Bastide, *The African*, 82.

17   For initial starting points, see J. Queiroz, "Entre"; and Sweet, *Domingos Álvares*, 53–72.
18   Thornton, "Religious," 75.
19   Staller, *Converging*, 117.
20   Miller, "Retention," 97.
21   Thornton, "Religious," 80.
22   Pantoja, "Inquisição," 124.
23   R. Ferreira, *Cross-Cultural*, 1–5.
24   Klieman, "'The Pygmies,'" 146. Also see MacGaffey, *Religion*, 132–33.
25   Staller, *Converging*, 101.
26   Marcussi, "Utopias," 28.
27   Miller, *Kings*, 254.
28   We may also think here of Christina Sharpe's poignant meditation on what it means to "defend the dead" today. Sharpe, *In the Wake*, 10.
29   Thornton, "Religious," 79.
30   Staller, *Converging*, 101.
31   For example, TSO-CP, April 24, 1743, caderno 102, fol. 110r, ANTT; TSO-CP, February 3, 1743, caderno 109, fol. 21r, ANTT; TSO-CP, November 6, 1760, caderno 125, fol. 3r, ANTT.
32   TSO-CP, March 14, 1714, caderno 79, fols. 379r–v.
33   I did not include accusations of sodomy, polygamy, or blasphemy. On the Pernambuco cadernos, also see Machado, "Classificação"; Wadsworth, "In the Name"; and Wadsworth, "Jurema."
34   Sweet, *Recreating*, 128.
35   There is substantial literature on the cases from Bahia and Minas Gerais. Kananoja, "Infected"; Marcussi, "Cativeiro"; Marcussi, "Utopias"; L. Souza, *The Devil*; Sweet, "Calundu." For Pernambuco, see TSO-CP, September 23, 1716, caderno 86, fol. 232r, ANTT; TSO-CP, n.d., caderno 108, fol. 240v, ANTT.
36   Marcussi, "Utopias," 25.
37   "Cópia [. . .]," June 25, 1687, in Gomes, *Mocambos*, 281–83.
38   TSO-CP, October 6, 1692, caderno 69, fol. 267r, ANTT.
39   TSO-CP, June 26, 1716, caderno 84, fol. 148r, ANTT.
40   "Registo Geral de Mercê, Joaquim de Almeida," January 28, 1697, Registo Geral de Mercês, Mercês de D. Pedro II, liv. 11, fol. 155r, ANTT.
41   Calainho, "Mandingueiros"; Calainho, "Metrópole"; C. Cruz, *A escola*, 184–90; Hawthorne, *From Africa*, 241–43; Rarey, *Insignificant Things*; V. Santos, "As bolsas"; Sweet, *Recreating*, 179–87.
42   TSO-CP, June 2, 1692, caderno 66, fol. 256b, ANTT; TSO-CP, n.d., caderno 77, fols. 327r–327v, ANTT.
43   TSO-CP, July 12, 1712, caderno 84, fols. 297r–8r, ANTT.
44   TSO-CP, July 16 and 17, 1692, caderno 66, fols. 256ar–256av, ANTT.
45   Domingos Álvares, a powerful healer from Benin, spent time in Pernambuco during the 1730s and had an outsized impact while there. So did Joseph Francisco

Pereira, a Mina man. Calainho, "Mandingueiros," 19; Sweet, *Domingos Álvares.* Also instructive by way of comparison is Rucker, *Gold Coast,* 189.

46 G. Lopes, "Negócio," 191–92; F. Melo, "'Que negros,'" 59–60; TST, http://www
.slavevoyages.org/estimates/BVh1VpZW, accessed June 28, 2023; Sweet, *Domingos Álvares,* 57.

47 TSO-CP, December 19, 1705, caderno 76, quote on fol. 86r, ANTT; TSO-IL, processo de Antónia Maria, August 12, 1712, to July 13, 1713, processo 1377–1, ANTT.

48 TSO-CP, June 10, 1779, caderno 130, fol. 166r, ANTT.

49 Marcussi, "Cativeiro," 37.

50 TSO-CP, October 3, 1712, fol. 376r, ANTT.

51 On rain and insects, see Kananoja, *Central African,* 201–2. Goats could be thought of to represent human beings on account of their ability to stand on two feet and to kneel. MacGaffey, *Kongo,* 245.

52 "Ritos Gentilicos de Angolla," 1720?, TSO, Conselho Geral, livro 272, fol. 123r, ANTT.

53 Sweet, *Domingos Álvares,* 61.

54 Cavazzi da Montecuccolo, *Istorica,* 231.

55 Translated in Fromont, "Collecting," 153.

56 For some reason, the author who translated Cavazzi's text into Portuguese omitted "Ganga-n-zumbi" from this passage. This may explain why, even while suggesting that (n)zumbi could have held importance in Palmares, Schwartz seems to foreclose a potential link between (n)zumbi and Zumbi, writing, "The Ganga Zumba of Palmares was probably the holder of this office [nganga a nzumbi]." Cavazzi da Montecuccolo, *Descrição,* 1:210; Schwartz, *Slaves,* 127.

57 Linguistic work may take us further in this line of thought. According to Marcos Leitão Almeida, the proto-Bantu root *-zumba* meant "adultery" and in Kisikongo (a language in the Kikongo cluster) was also "fornication, criminal intercourse." Did this root correspond to Palmares's Gan(g)a Zumba? M. Almeida, "Speaking," 403.

58 TSO-IL, processo de João Pereira da Cunha, September 18, 1749, to February 4, 1766, processo 9691, ANTT. The case is discussed in Kananoja, "Healers."

59 Processo de João Pereira da Cunha, fol. 13v, 14r.

60 TSO-CP, October 26, 1722, caderno 92, fols. 250r–278r, ANTT.

61 TSO-CP, October 26, 1722, fol. 268v. The testimonies differ about whom the animal belonged to. Marcussi analyzes the same case and treats zumbi and the goat as more distinct entities, suggesting that the goat was used for one form of curing—Caçuto—and that when that did not work, treatments focused on zumbi were used instead. Marcussi, "O zumbi," 166.

62 TSO-CP, October 26, 1722, fol. 253r.

63 TSO-CP, September 12, 1718, caderno 87, fol. 331r, ANTT.

64 TSO-CP, April 27, 1709, caderno 89, fols. 69r (quotation), 70r, 75r, ANTT. Also see TSO-CP, May 31, 1717, caderno 86, fol. 252r, ANTT; TSO-CP, April 27, 1719, caderno 89, fol. 68v, ANTT.

65   TSO-CP, June 5, 1753, caderno 114, fol. 95r, ANTT.

66   TSO-CP, February 8, 1753, caderno 114, fols. 96r, 96v, ANTT. Also see TSO-CP, February 16, 1761, caderno 124, fol. 430r, ANTT.

67   C. Cruz, *A escola*, 195–226; Grünewald, Savoldi, and Collins, "*Jurema*"; M. Nascimento, "'O tronco'"; Wadsworth, "Jurema."

68   C. Cruz, *A escola*, 137.

69   Sweet, *Domingos Álvares*, 248. Also see Wadsworth, "Jurema," 148.

70   C. Cruz, *A escola*, 205, 219.

71   "Danças Negras," Ordens Régias, liv. 17, doc. 23, fol. 39r, Arquivo Público Estadual Jordão Emerenciano (hereafter, APEJE).

72   Lara, *Legislação*, 37, 282.

73   M. Almeida, "Speaking," 293–99. Also see Sweet, "Research Note," 90–92.

74   Kiddy, "Ethnic," 229.

75   See, for example, Palacios, *Campesinato*, 44, 51.

76   For example, Vallejos, "Slave Control," 2.

77   In 1728, the Overseas Council approved a request to send enslaved people "from all the [African] nations" to Minas Gerais in order to prevent the kind of communication, unity, and rebellion that they believed mass importation from one region could foster. Lara, "Do singular," 88. Also see Aguiar, "Negras," 13, 38; Bergad, *Slavery*, 150–52; Brügger and Oliveira, "Os Benguelas"; Kiddy, "Ethnic," 235, 236, 243; Luna and Costa, "Algumas"; Luna and Costa, *Minas*, 47–50; and Senna, *Chorographia*, 214–17.

78   There is a sizable literature on Brazil's internal trade, though most of it focuses on the post-1850 era, when slave ships from Africa nearly ceased to arrive on Brazilian shores. See, among others, Butler, "Slavery"; Conrad, *The Destruction*, 47–69; Graham, "Another Middle Passage?"; Neves, "Sampauleiros"; and Slenes, "The Brazilian."

79   "Sobre [. . .]," July 13, 1718, in "Cartas do Conde de Assumar," 252. Also see "Carta [. . .]," November 21, 1719, in "Bello Horizonte"; C. Guimarães, "Mineração," 158; Higgins, "*Licentious Liberty*," 175–76; and Schwartz, *Slaves*, 122.

80   "1746, Expedição mandada fazer," 619. This document is also discussed in C. Guimarães, "Mineração," 159–60. On quilombos in Minas Gerais, also see W. Barbosa, *Negros*; Gomes, *A hidra*, 368–95; C. Guimarães, *Uma negação*; Higgins, "*Licentious Liberty*," 175–208; D. Ramos, "O quilombo"; and L. Souza, "Violência."

81   C. Guimarães, "Mineração," 141.

82   D. Ramos, "O quilombo," 165, 174 (quote on 165); Vallejos, "Slave Control," 23–25. Also see Mariana L.R. Dantas, "'For the Benefit.'"

83   C. Guimarães, "Mineração," 156.

84   I am deeply grateful to Kalle Kananoja for lending me his transcription of this case, which he discusses in Kananoja, *Central African*, 133. Due to archive closures and the global pandemic, I was unable to visit the collection where this document is held, but in addition to using Kananoja's notes, I commissioned Estevam Martins to complete a second transcription of the case in order to

confirm spellings and details. Depositions for the case are located in Devassas Eclesiásticas, z-8, fols. 96r–100r, Arquivo Eclesiástico da Arquidiocese de Mariana (hereafter, AEAM).

85 For more on the slave trade through Benguela, see Candido, *An African*, 154–75.

86 Devassas Eclesiásticas, fol. 96r, AEAM. The "dolls" that witnesses mentioned evoke objects from a famous case several decades later in Minas Gerais involving an Angolan man known as Pai Caetano as well as objects (including shrines) that in West and West Central Africa could become possessed by spirits. Kananoja, "Pai Caetano," 29; Nogueira, "Relações," 142–43; Thornton, *Africa*, 244.

87 Devassas Eclesiásticas, fol. 97r, AEAM.

88 Devassas Eclesiásticas, fol. 97v, AEAM.

89 Devassas Eclesiásticas, fols. 97v–98r, AEAM.

90 C. Guimarães, "Mineração," 157; L. Souza, "Violência," 193.

91 Lara, "Do singular," 90.

92 Brewer-García, "Hierarchy"; Rowe, *Black Saints*; Thornton, *The Kongolese*. I am grateful to Brewer-García for her incredibly helpful comments about Benedict.

93 Brewer-García, "Hierarchy," 493; Reginaldo, "Rosário dos Pretos," 137; Rowe, *Black Saints*, 3–4.

94 Rowe, *Black Saints*, 73–74; Karasch, *Slave Life*, 282–83. Soares, "O Império," 62.

95 Delfino, "O culto," 11–12. Also see Delfino, "O Rosário"; Mulvey, "Black Brothers," 277; and D. Souza, "Devoção."

96 Paula, *Montes Claros*, 611. Saint Benedict retained fascinating meanings in Minas Gerais in the twentieth century. See Vogt and Fry, *Cafundó*, 216–17, 221–22.

97 M. Assunção, "Quilombos," 448–53; Gomes, *A hidra*, 161. Saint Benedict was among several quilombos in Maranhão named for Catholic saints and with "chapels" and "saint's houses." Members of the Saint Sebastian quilombo also commemorated Saint Benedict's Day. Gomes, "Africanos," 84. In Maranhão, Benedict also became associated with the West African deity Verequete (also Verekete). Eduardo, *The Negro*, 79; Ferretti, "Sincretismo," 191.

98 Reginaldo, "Rosário dos Pretos."

99 Cadornega, *História* (1972), 3:27–8; Heywood and Thornton, *Central Africans*, 188; Reginaldo, "Rosário dos Pretos," 145.

100 Livro e Capítulo do Compromisso da Irmandade de N. Senhora do Rosário da Vila de Iguarassu, fol. 5r (quotation), 9v, APEJE. There was also diversity in Black brotherhoods dedicated to Benedict in Bahia and Minas Gerais. Mariana L.R. Dantas, "Humble Slaves," 130; Parés, *The Formation*, 57; D. Souza, "Devoção," 115–16.

101 Anderson Oliveira, *Devoção*, 289.

102 Thornton, *The Kongolese*; Thornton, "Afro-Christian." In Kongo, Cécile Fromont describes "spaces of correlation," where Africans "recast heterogeneous local and foreign ideas and forms into newly interrelated parts of [an] evolving worldview." Fromont, *The Art*, 1.

103　Bastide, *The African*, 60. On Zambi "saints," also see H. Carvalho, *Ethnographia*, 519; and A. Ramos, *O negro*, 104–5.

104　Bastide, *The African*, 60.

105　Cascudo, *Dicionário*, 108.

106　TSO-CP, August 4, 1716, caderno 86, fol. 42v, ANTT; TSO-CP, August 8, 1716, caderno 88, fols. 53v–54v, ANTT.

107　"Consulta [. . .]," February 12, 1701, Pernambuco, caixa 19, doc. 1867, fols. 1r–2r, AHU; "Requerimento [. . .]," before February 17, 1727, Pernambuco, caixa 35, doc. 3197, AHU.

108　"Carta Patente de Domingos Simões Jordão," August 7, 1730, Registo Geral de Mercês, Mercês de D. João V., liv. 17, fol. 110r, ANTT; "Consulta [. . .]," February 17, 1734, Ceará, caixa 3, doc. 153, fols. 1v–2v, AHU; "Registo Geral de Mercê, Domingos Simões Jordão," October 11, 1718, Registo Geral de Mercês, Mercês de D. João V, liv. 10, fol. 213r, ANTT.

109　"Ordenou [. . .]," December 8, 1679, CCA, *Disposições*, VI-III-I-1-31, doc. 94, fol. 362r, AUC.

110　Scott, *The Common Wind*.

111　TSO-CP, June 2, 1774, caderno 129, fol. 135r, ANTT; Mott, "Feiticeiros," 20.

112　The refusal of voice also resonates in a discomfiting way with an incident from West Africa in 1694, when an English captain attacked a talking shrine. He was then told that the shrine itself did not talk and rather gave voice to a deity, who would not speak to Europeans. Thornton, *Africa*, 244.

113　TSO-CP, September 1, 1716, caderno 84, fol. 168r, ANTT.

114　TSO-CP, December 1742, caderno 109, fol. 20r, ANTT.

115　TSO-CP, September 16, 1716, caderno 86, fol. 219v, ANTT. Similar ceremonies were at the center of a denunciation made decades later against the "Blacks of Angola" for causing great "disorder" in Pernambuco. Rodrigues, "Malungos," 89.

116　I thank James Sweet for his insights about this example.

5. PEDRO, PAULA, AND THE REFUGEES

1　"Requerimento [. . .]," before March 12, 1724, Pernambuco, caixa 30, doc. 2723, fol. 1r, AHU.

2　"Mandou [. . .]," March 9, 1712, CCA, *Disposições*, VI-III-I-1-32, doc. 12, fol. 118v, AUC.

3　"Informação geral," 199.

4　Lara, *Palmares*, 347–48.

5　J. Mello, *Tempo*, 186; R. Nascimento, "Palmares," 40–42.

6　J. Mello, *Tempo*, 187, 194.

7　Price, "Refiguring," 217. Some scholars reject this hypothesis. The debates are summarized in Carlin and Arends, *Atlas*, 137–38, and detailed in Huber and Parkall, *Spreading*, 177–240, 251–98.

8　Translated in Baerle, *The History*, 236, quote on 275.

9　Baerle, *The History*, 297.

10   Slave Voyages website, https://www.slavevoyages.org/american
      /database#results, accessed June 29, 2023.

11   Inter-American Slave Trade database Voyage No. 107985, sourced from Hey-
      wood and Thornton, *Central Africans*, 45.

12   Barreto, *Fortificações*, 156–57. According to Eduardo de Almeida Navarro,
      Tamandaré comes from Tamandûaré, the name of a "great shaman" in Tupi
      "mythology." Navarro, *Dicionário*, 599.

13   Morgan, *Reckoning*, 46. Also see, among others, Bennett, *African*, 156–57; Can-
      dido, *An African*, 147; and McKittrick, "Mathematics," 17.

14   F. Freire, *Nova Lusitania*, 281; Lara, "Diferentes," 2.

15   "Carta [. . .]," April 18, 1662, CCA, *Disposições*, VI-III-1-1-31, doc. 106, fol. 81r, AUC.

16   "Escreveo [. . .]," March 23, 1661, CCA, *Disposições*, VI-III-1-1-31, doc. 16, fol. 49r, AUC.

17   "Requerimento [. . .]," 1698, in Gomes, *Mocambos*, 396.

18   "Consulta [. . .]," January 18, 1708, Pernambuco, caixa 22, doc. 2061, fol. 7r, AHU.

19   "Registo Geral de Mercê, Agostinho Moreira Guterres," November 19, 1709,
      Registo Geral de Mercês, Mercês de D. João V, liv. 3, fol. 175v, ANTT.

20   "Informação [. . .]," after February 28, 1729, Pernambuco, caixa 38, doc. 3398,
      anexo 18 (April 26, 1695), AHU.

21   Documenta Palmares, accessed January 25, 2022. Lara locates the Campos
      do Ipanema within the boundaries of Palmares during the 1680s but outside
      the smaller area she uses to demarcate the mocambos of the late 1690s. Lara,
      Palmares, 358.

22   For example, "Bando [. . .]," April 17, 1739, CCA, *Disposições*, VI-III-1-1-32, doc. 83,
      fol. 620v, AUC; "Carta [. . .]," May 25, 1757, Pernambuco, caixa 84, doc. 6978, AHU.

23   Higgins, *"Licentious Liberty,"* 33–36.

24   See, for example, "Escreveo [. . .]," October 19, 1709, CCA, *Disposições*, VI-III-
      1-1-32, doc. 44, fols. 61r–61v, AUC.

25   "Bando [. . .]," September 20, 1708, CCA, *Disposições*, VI-III-1-1-32, doc. 63, fol.
      69v, AUC.

26   "Carta [. . .]," November 6, 1704, Conselho Ultramarino: Registo de cartas
      régias (1698–1713) (hereafter, Registo), cod. 257, fols. 166r–166v, AHU.

27   "Mandou [. . .]," May 1, 1714, CCA, *Disposições*, VI-III-1-1-32, doc. 362, fol. 178v, AUC.

28   Quoted in K. Silva, *Nas solidões*, 186. Also see, for example, "Nomeou [. . .],"
      October 7, 1735, CCA, *Disposições*, VI-III-1-1-32, doc. 351, fol. 512v, AUC.

29   "Carta [. . .]," January 10, 1749, Pernambuco, caixa 68, doc. 5782, anexo 13 (Feb-
      ruary 7, 1743), AHU.

30   For a vivid illustration, see Lara, *Palmares*, 358.

31   Documenta Palmares, accessed January 25, 2022.

32   "Registo Geral de Mercê, Domingos João de Carvalho," December 12, 1718,
      Registo Geral de Mercês, Mercês de D. João V., liv. 10, fol. 389v, ANTT.

33   "Carta [. . .]," June 24, 1700, Pernambuco, caixa 18, doc. 1826, anexo 1, AHU;
      Damasceno, "A ocupação," 125.

34   Lisbon, May 6, 1709, Registo, cod. 257, fol. 225v, AHU; Lara, *Palmares*, 353.

35   Damasceno, "A ocupação," 127.

36 "Auto [. . .]," July 23, 1715, Pernambuco, caixa 27, doc. 2442, anexo 3, AHU.

37 Damasceno, "A ocupação," 127. Quotes in "Portaria [. . .]," Manuscriptos Coleção Pombalina, PBA-115, fol. 355r, Biblioteca Nacional de Portugal (hereafter, BNP).

38 Lara, *Palmares*, 350–51.

39 "Carta régia [. . .]," January 23, 1697, Pernambuco, caixa 17, doc. 1714, fol. 1r, AHU.

40 Mário Martins de Freitas suggests, exaggeratedly it seems certain, that some of the men who bankrolled expeditions against Palmares made so much money from selling prisoners that they wanted the wars to continue indefinitely. M. Freitas, *Reino negro*, 2:592.

41 Lara, "Diferentes," 10–11.

42 Lara, *Palmares*, 346–54.

43 Gomes, *A hidra*, 132. Also see M. Assunção, "Quilombos."

44 Gomes, *A hidra*, 136.

45 See, for example, Gomes, "A 'Safe Haven.'" There is also a chance that Maranhão served as a temporary stopping point on a longer journey to more populated regions of Brazil or perhaps the Caribbean. New research is revealing more connections between colonial Brazil and the Caribbean than previously thought, including slave voyages that either passed through or began in Maranhão. Wheat, "Brasil."

46 Gomes, *A hidra*, 325–48 (quotes on 326 and 327). Also see Lara, *Campos*, esp. 237–48.

47 Gomes, *A hidra*, 331.

48 On either side of that gap, there are suggestive hints: records of ships carrying enslaved people purchased in Pernambuco to Buenos Aires. See the Slave Voyages website, https://www.slavevoyages.org/american/database#results, accessed June 29, 2023.

49 Prado, *Edge of Empire*, 13. Also see Kühn, "Clandestino"; and Schultz, "'The Kingdom,'" 150. By the early nineteenth century, and perhaps earlier, the word "quilombo" (or "qilombo") made its way into the Spanish lexicon in Buenos Aires and surrounding areas, where escape from slavery was a "pervasive" action. Borucki, *From Shipmates*, quote on 10; Portilla Manfredini, "Diffusion."

50 Lara, *Palmares*, 345–46.

51 Read, "'A Change," 97.

52 "Consulta [. . .]," December 2, 1681, Pernambuco, caixa 12, doc. 1209, fol. 1r, AHU.

53 "Consulta [. . .]," February 28, 1682, Pernambuco, caixa 12, doc. 1220, fol. 1r, AHU. I am grateful to Carmen Alveal for her insights about this document.

54 "Consulta [. . .]," June 19, 1693, Conselho Ultramarino: Secretaria do Conselho Ultramarino (hereafter, SCU), caixa 1, doc. 80, fol. 1r, AHU.

55 "Consulta [. . .]," December 9, 1681, Pernambuco, caixa 12, doc. 1210, fol. 1r, AHU.

56 Nardi, "Retrato"; Salvado, "O Estanco," 137.

57 "Consulta [. . .]," December 9, 1681, fol. 1r.

58 Junta da Administração do Tabaco, livros de ponto dos operários 719 and 721, ANTT.

59 Nardi, "Retrato," 327.

60 J. Fonseca, *Escravos*, 140.

61 "Portaria [. . .]," March 31, 1713, Seção de Reservados, Coleção Pombalina, Código 115, Livro dos Acentos da Juntas de Micões, Cartas Ordinarias, Ordens e Bando que se Escreverão em Pernambuco no *Tempo do Governador Felix Jose Machado de Mendonça Eça Castro e Vasconcellos* (hereafter, Livro dos Acentos), fol. 134, BNP.

62 "Portaria que foi ao Capitão André Furtado [. . .]," April 18, 1713, Livro dos Acentos, fol. 139, BNP.

63 "Portaria que foi ao [. . .] Ouvidor [. . .] das Alagoas [. . .]," April 18, 1713, Livro dos Acentos, fols. 139–40, BNP.

64 See Lara, "Diferentes."

65 Quoted in Lara, *Palmares*, 352.

66 "Para o Governador de Pernambuco," October 26, 1706, Registo, cod. 257, fols. 199v–200r, AHU.

67 It is unclear how often Palmaristas came to serve the colonial army as guides, soldiers, and other capacities. See "Consulta [. . .]," May 16, 1703, Pernambuco, caixa 20, doc. 1923, fol. 4v, AHU; Lara and Fachin, *Guerra*, 47; and Mattos, "'Black Troops,'" 12.

68 "Requerimento de Lázaro Coelho de Eça [. . .]," before October 26, 1754, Conselho Ultramarino: Brasil-Alagoas (hereafter, Alagoas), caixa 2, doc. 145, fols. 17r–17v, AHU.

69 Space limitations prevent me from doing any justice to the literature on pawnship in Africa, but a useful guide is found in Lovejoy, "Pawnship." On how transatlantic slavery transformed and blurred old lines separating the free and enslaved in West Central Africa, see Candido, *An African*, 191–236; R. Ferreira, *Cross-Cultural*, 52–87; and R. Ferreira, "Slaving," 122–23.

70 Lovejoy, "Pawnship," 78.

71 Lovejoy, "Pawnship," 72–74; Candido, *An African*, 191–236; R. Ferreira, *Cross-Cultural*, 52–87; R. Ferreira, "Slaving," 122–23. Marcos Abreu Leitão de Almeida challenges this chronology, tracing in West Central Africa evidence of pawnship, or at least early forms that preceded pawnship, to much earlier. M. Almeida, "Speaking," 151–90.

72 In this sense, the refugees also suggest how we may revisit with new eyes the "insurgent geographies" that Yuko Miki lucidly charts during the late nineteenth century in Espírito Santo, where quilombo members "sought to live as free agents while deeply enmeshed in that society's midst." Perhaps the complex relationships that they forged there may be understood not only as "a political practice to stake their own claims on Brazil's postcolonial terrain," but also as a localized expression of a longer series of contestations and negotiations. An open question that I hope this book continues to propel forward is how to understand and reimagine the more well-documented nineteenth century in closer conversation with the seventeenth and eighteenth. Miki, "Fleeing," 496, 499.

73   "Carta de Caetano de Melo [d]e Castro [. . .]," August 4, 1694, in Gomes, *Mocambos*, 344.

74   Pearson, *The Portuguese*, xiv; "Registo Geral de Mercê, Caetano de Melo de Castro," January 29, 1716, Registo Geral de Mercês, Registo Geral de Mercês do Reinado de João V, liv. 7, fol. 419r, ANTT.

75   "Consulta [. . .]," May 28, 1691, Conselho Ultramarino: Brasil-Rio de Janeiro (hereafter, BRJ), caixa 9, doc. 1.770, fol. 1r, AHU; "Consulta [. . .]," November 28, 1706, Lisbon, BRJ, caixa 14, doc. 2.934, anexo (January 28, 1707), AHU; "Informação [. . .]," after April 4, 1696, Pernambuco, caixa 17, doc. 1698, AHU.

76   At least two Palmares veterans received sesmarias outside of Pernambuco (in Ceará and Piauí). Damasceno, "A ocupação," 185.

77   In a sample of twenty combatants, Dimas Bezerra Marques identified five who later went to Ceará. Dimas Marques, "Pelo bem," 109–10.

78   "Carta de Padrão, Feliciano Prudente," July 22, 1709, Registo Geral de Mercês, Mercês, de D. João V, liv. 7, fol. 515r, ANTT.

79   Dimas Bezerra Marques, "Pelo bem," 107.

80   "Consulta [. . .]," May 10, 1703, Pernambuco, caixa 20, doc. 1921, fol. 8r, AHU.

81   "Consulta [. . .]," February 27, 1705, Pernambuco, caixa 21, doc. 1992, fols. 3r–3v, AHU. Also see L. Oliveira, "Capitães-mores," 129–32. Lelou and his son were accused of falsifying some of Lelou's records. While they avoided punishment, an officer (also a Palmares veteran) who helped them did not. C. Albuquerque, *A remuneração*, 114–16. "Como parece [. . .]," November 15, 1697, Consultas de Pernambuco, códice 265, fol. 123r, AHU.

82   "Consulta [. . .]," after August 25, 1705, Pernambuco, caixa 21, doc. 1998, fol. 1r, AHU.

83   "Consulta [. . .]," May 16, 1703, Pernambuco, caixa 20, doc. 1923, fols. 4r–5r, AHU.

84   "Aviso [. . .]," January 19, 1684, Pernambuco, caixa 13, doc. 1272, anexo 1, AHU. This was the officer found guilty of helping Lelou and his son falsify records.

85   "Consulta [. . .]," July 29, 1704, Pernambuco, caixa 21, doc. 1974, fol. 1v, AHU.

86   Candido, *An African*, 76.

87   Thornton, *A History*, 260.

88   "Consulta [. . .]," May 25, 1686, Pernambuco, caixa 14, doc. 1366, fols. 4r–4v, AHU.

89   Livro do lançamento dos direitos dos escravos vindos do Brasil, 1720, Provedoria e Junta da Real Fazenda do Funchal, Escravos do Brasil (1718–1721), fol. 2v, ANTT.

90   The original report, from 1697, left the total number vague: "a hundred some." The figure of 130 was stated in 1698. "Carta [. . .]," May 12, 1697, Pernambuco, caixa 17, doc. 1720, fol. 1r; "Consulta [. . .]," January 13, 1698, in Gomes, *Mocambos*, 400.

91   Mendonça, "As facetas," 113–14; "Requerimento de Lázaro Coelho de Eça [. . .]," anexo 11 (January 8, 1737); "Requerimento do capitão Luís Mendes da Silva [. . .]," before December 14, 1759, Pernambuco, caixa 92, doc. 7367, AHU.

92   "Requerimento de Lázaro Coelho de Eça [. . .]," anexo 14 (December 22, 1733).

93   This and the remaining quotes in this paragraph are from "Requerimento de Lázaro Coelho de Eça [. . .]," anexo 11.

94   Lara, "Diferentes," 11.

95   "Carta [. . .]," March 10, 1682, in Gomes, *Mocambos*, 253. Also see chapter 1.

96   "Requerimento de Lázaro Coelho de Eça [. . .]," anexo 11.

97   In the following years, the age limit for those who could remain in Pernambuco would alternate between seven and twelve. "Alvará [. . .]," April 7, 1693, in Gomes, *Mocambos*, 329; "Condições [. . .]," March 3, 1687, in Gomes, *Mocambos*, 277; "Condições [. . .]" December 3, 1691, in Gomes, *Mocambos*, 290.

98   "Condições [. . .]," March 3, 1687, 278; "Condições [. . .]" December 3, 1691, 291; Lara, "Diferentes," 15.

99   "Condições [. . .]," 1694, in Gomes, *Mocambos*, 336.

100   "Condições [. . .]," 1694, 336.

101   "Consulta [. . .]," December 1700, caixa 19, doc. 1859, anexo 4, AHU.

102   Ferreira, "O Brasil," 5.

103   "Carta [. . .]," August 4, 1694, 345.

104   "Carta [. . .]," August 4, 1694, 345.

105   "Carta [. . .]," August 4, 1694, 344.

106   "Pareceres [. . .]," n.d., in Gomes, *Mocambos*, 348, 349.

107   "Alvará [. . .]," March 12, 1695, in Gomes, *Mocambos*, 363.

108   "Consulta [. . .]," January 27, 1695, in Gomes, *Mocambos*, 357.

109   Alvará [. . .]," March 12, 1695, 363; "Consulta [. . .]," January 27, 1695, 358.

110   "Parecer [. . .]," 1695, in Gomes, *Mocambos*, 360–61.

111   "Alvará [. . .]," March 12, 1695, 363.

112   Lara, *Legislação*, 41–47.

113   "Alvará [. . .]," in Lara, *Legislação*, 333; Miller, *Way of Death*, 348.

114   "Alvará [. . .]," in Lara, *Legislação*, 333.

115   "Informação [. . .]," after February 28, 1729, Pernambuco, caixa 38, doc. 3398, anexo 44 (February 9, 1694), AHU.

6. THE POWERFUL AND ALMOST POWERFUL

1   According to Loreto Couto, one of the sons was Arda, another but fleeting suggestion of a non-Angolan presence in Palmares. Loreto Couto, *Desagravos*, 459.

2   "Ordenou [. . .]," February 18, 1696, CCA, *Disposições*, VI-III-I-1-31, doc. 76, fol. 578r, AUC; Lara, *Palmares*, 323, 341.

3   On the challenges that Black soldiers faced across the northeast, see K. Silva, *Nas solidões*, 79–108.

4   J. Mello, *Henrique Dias*, 71.

5   "Registo [. . .]," December 20, 1707, in DH, vol. 59 (Rio de Janeiro: Typ. Baptista de Souza, 1943), 31–32.

6   "Registo [. . .]," March 16, 1694, in DH, vol. 57 (Rio de Janeiro: Typ. Baptista de Souza, 1942), 44.

7   Mendes, "O serviço," 106.

8 "Ordenou [. . .]," March 4, 1696, CCA, *Disposições*, VI-III-I-I-31, fol. 579v, doc. 83, AUC; "Ordenou [. . .]," March 6, 1696, CCA, *Disposições*, VI-III-I-I-31, doc. 80, fols. 578v–579r, AUC; "Parecer [. . .]," August 21, 1697, Consultas de Pernambuco, códice 265, fols. 117r–117v, AHU; K. Silva, *Nas solidões*, 198–99.

9 *Documentação*, 1:315–17; Dimas Bezerra Marques, "Pelo bem," 98; A. Mendonça, "As facetas," 105–6.

10 He was later denied entrance to other orders. Raminelli, "Privilegios"; Vicira, "Entre perdas," 76.

11 F. Costa, *Anais*, 4:408.

12 F. Lopes, *Índios*, 144. On the challenges and limited success of Indigenous petitions, also see Raminelli, "Nobreza."

13 "Requerimento de Lázaro Coelho de Eça [. . .]," anexo 7 (December 24, 1738).

14 A. Mendonça, "As facetas," 108.

15 "Requerimento de Lázaro Coelho de Eça [. . .]," anexo 17 (July 30, 1755).

16 Raminelli, "Privilegios," 7. Arco Verde was Tabajara, while Pinheiro Camarão was Potiguar. On the power wielded by elites in both groups in Pernambuco, see Vieira, "Entre perdas."

17 Mendes, "O serviço," 105; "Requerimento [. . .]," before December 15, 1691, Pernambuco, caixa 15, doc. 1559, anexo 1, AHU.

18 F. Lopes, *Índios*, 146.

19 F. Costa, *Anais*, 4:408.

20 For an overview of the literature, see Kidd, "Neither Peddlers."

21 E. Mello, *A fronda*, 332.

22 F. Costa, *Anais*, 4:409; Raminelli, "Privilegios," 7–8.

23 "Requerimento [. . .]," n.d., in Gomes, *Mocambos*, 412, 422.

24 Damasceno, "Direitos"; K. Silva, *Nas solidões*, 203.

25 "Condições [. . .]," 1694, in Gomes, *Mocambos*, 337.

26 Damasceno, "Direitos," 109–10.

27 Damasceno, "Direitos," 99, 104.

28 See "Diligência de Habilitação [. . .] de Francisco Álvares Camelo," September 6, 1684, Mesa da Consciência e Ordens, Habilitações para a Ordem de Cristo, Letra F, maço. 34, no. 19, ANTT. Camelo also had business dealings with the Dutch. Dimas Bezerra Marques, "Pelo bem," 112.

29 Dimas Bezerra Marques, "Pelo bem," 111.

30 "Carta de [. . .] António Álvares Bezerra," October 18, 1700, Registo Geral de Mercês, Mercê de D. Pedro II, liv. 13, fol. 395v, ANTT. Also see, for example, "Diligência de Habilitação [. . .] de António Álvares Bezerra," October 19, 1700, Mesa da Consciência e Ordens, Habilitações para a Ordem de Cristo, Letra A, mç. 41, no. 13, ANTT; "Diligência de Habilitação [. . .] de Francisco Álvares Camelo," September 6, 1684, Mesa da Consciência e Ordens, Habilitações para a Ordem de Cristo, Letra F, mç. 34, no. 19, ANTT.

31 "Alvará de António Álvares Bezerra," January 3, 1702, Registo Geral de Mercês, Mercê de D. Pedro II, liv. 13, 3, fol. 396r, ANTT.

32 Damasceno, "Direitos," 107.

33 "Consulta [. . .]," January 13, 1698, in Gomes, *Mocambos*, 401.

34 Damasceno, "Direitos," 113.

35 Damasceno, "Direitos," 114.

36 Damasceno, "Direitos," 111–12; K. Silva, *Nas solidões*, 205.

37 Damasceno, "Direitos," 112; *Documentação*, 1:261–65.

38 "Consulta [. . .]," January 18, 1708, Pernambuco, caixa 22, doc. 2061, fol. 7r, AHU.

39 "Consulta [. . .]," January 18, 1708, fol. 7r; Lara, "Diferentes," 20.

40 "Carta [. . .] de Agostinho Moreira Guterres," November 19, 1709, Registo Geral de Mercês, Mercês de D. João V., liv. 3, fol. 175v, ANTT.

41 "Alvará [. . .] de Agostinho Moreira Guterres," May 23, 1715, Registo Geral de Mercês, Mercês de D. João V., liv. 7, fol. 242r, ANTT.

42 Damasceno, "Direitos," 112. Also see "Carta [. . .] de Domingos João de Carvalho," December 12, 1718, Registo Geral de Mercês, Mercês de D. João V., liv. 10, fols. 389r–389v, ANTT; Sesmaria Pernambuco (hereafter, PE) 0093, August 18, 1724, Plataforma SILB (Sesmarias do Império Luso-Brasileiro) (hereafter, SILB).

43 "Certidão [. . .]," November 2, 1739, Pernambuco, caixa 55, doc. 4751, fol. 1r, AHU.

44 "Certidão [. . .]," June 10, 1752, Pernambuco, caixa 73, doc. 6115, fol. 1r, ahu.

45 "Certidão [. . .]," May 9, 1742, Pernambuco, caixa 57, doc. 4940, fol. 1r, AHU.

46 *Documentação histórica*, 2:121–25 (quote on 123); "Requerimento [. . .]," before January 11, 1760, Pernambuco, caixa 93, doc. 7376, anexo 1, AHU.

47 "Consulta [. . .]," December 20, 1697, doc. 44, in Ennes, *As guerras*, 270; Carvalho Franco, *Dicionário*, 298.

48 See, for example, "Bando [. . .]," November 16, 1711, CCA, *Disposições*, VI-III-I-I-32, doc. 78, fols. 110r–111r, AUC; "Mandou [. . .]," September 24, 1715, CCA, *Disposições*, VI-III-I-I-32, doc. 68, fols. 228v–229r, AUC; "Bando [. . .]," August 8, 1722, CCA, *Disposições*, VI-III-I-I-32, doc. 33, fols. 305r–305v, AUC.

49 "Bando [. . .]," November 30, 1740, CCA, *Disposições*, VI-III-I-I-32, doc. 109, fols. 630v–631r, AUC; "Ordem [. . .]," n.d. (likely late 1740), CCA, *Disposições*, VI-III-I-I-32, doc. 112, fols. 631v–632v, AUC.

50 V. Brown, *Tacky's Revolt*, 45.

51 Kalina Vanderlei Silva writes, "Every free man in Portuguese America was a military element" and participant in a colonial project of asserting domination that was especially pronounced in Pernambuco. K. Silva, *O miserável*, 141.

52 V. Brown, *Tacky's Revolt*, 59.

53 TSO-CP, 1702, caderno 74, fols. 338r–338v, ANTT. Some enslavers and clergy members raped enslaved boys and men with the intention "to feminize [the victim] — to conquer him both physically and psychologically." Sweet, *Recreating*, 74. Also see, for example, Mott, *O sexo*, 43–45.

54 "Requerimento de Luís de Mendonça Cabral [. . .]," before September 30, 1705, Pernambuco, caixa 22, doc. 1999, anexos 2 (March 20, 1699, marked as folha 1) and 15 (July 20, 1694, marked as folha 9), AHU.

55 Apipucos was one of Pernambuco's most productive plantations and eventually gave name to the neighborhood in Recife, where Gilberto Freyre, the famed Mestre de Apipucos (the Master of Apipucos), was born and raised.

56 "Requerimento de Luís de Mendonça Cabral [. . .]," fol. 1r.

57 "Requerimento de Luís de Mendonça Cabral [. . .]," fol. 1r.

58 "Requerimento de Luís de Mendonça Cabral [. . .]," anexo 4 (November 18, 1694).

59 "Carta [. . .] de Luís de Mendonça Cabral," August 4, 1706, Registo Geral de Mercês, Mercês de D. Pedro II, liv. 2, fols. 129r–129v, ANTT.

60 "Diligência de Habilitação Para a Ordem de Cristo de Salvador Curado Vidal," February 15, 1669, Mesa da Consciência e Ordens, Habilitações para a Ordem de Cristo, letra S, maço 64, no. 6, ANTT. In 2012, Negreiros (along with Henrique Dias and Antônio Filipe Camarão) joined Zumbi (who was included in 1996) in Brazil's *Livro dos heróis e heroínas da pátria* (*Book of Heroes and Heroines of the Fatherland*), a monument dedicated to a select group of national heroes. "Panteão da Pátria: Os 43 heróis e heroínas do Brasil," *Brasil Online*, July 4, 2018, https://www.bol.uol.com.br/listas/panteao-da-patria-os-43-herois-e-heroinas -do-brasil.htm.

61 Alencastro, *The Trade*, 291. Suspicion about Antônio's role in their disappearance hardly dented his power or standing, and for years he trumpeted the fact that he brought the objects to Brazil, using the story to leverage favor and wealth, even as others in Pernambuco leveled additional accusations against him. "Consulta [. . .]," May 31, 1688, Pernambuco, caixa 14, doc. 1447, AHU; "Diligência de Habilitação Para a Ordem de Cristo de Salvador Curado Vidal"; "Carta [. . .] de António Curado Vidal," May 30, 1667, Registo Geral de Mercês, Mercês (Chancelaria) de D. Afonso VI, liv. 10, fol. 123r, ANTT.

62 "Consulta [. . .]," November 26, 1676, Pernambuco, caixa 11, doc. 1064, AHU.

63 "Consulta [. . .]," January 21, 1689, Pernambuco, caixa 15, doc. 1470, fol. 1r, AHU.

64 See, for example, Sesmaria Paraíba (hereafter, PB) 0027, SILB.

65 "Alvará de 3 de março de 1741," in Lara, *Legislação*, 297.

66 "Ofício [. . .]," August 30, 1787, Pernambuco, caixa 160, doc. 11530, fol. 1r, AHU.

67 "Ofício [. . .]," October 2, 1784, caixa 153, doc. 11031, AHU; "Requerimento [. . .]," before May 28, 1802, Pernambuco, caixa 234, doc. 15812, AHU.

68 "Ofício [. . .]," September 4, 1761, Pernambuco, caixa 96, doc. 7571, AHU. The file comprises two documents, the first of which is unnumbered. I have assigned numbers to those pages.

69 The case is also discussed in Alveal, "From Colonial"; and in Damasceno, "A ocupação," 212–15, 244–63. On the Vieira de Melo family dynasty, see Morais, "Em busca," 153–58, 445.

70 "Ofício [. . .]," September 4, 1761, fols. 15r, 26r.

71 "Ofício [. . .]," September 4, 1761, fol. 5r.

72 "Ofício [. . .]," September 4, 1761, fol. 3v.

73 Carmen Alveal calls his domain a de facto "colonial lordship." Alveal, "From Colonial."

74 Alfredo Cavalcanti, *História*, 38.

75 Alfredo Cavalcanti, *História*, 46.

76 Quoted in A. Marques, "Entre lajedos," 80.

77 Alfredo Cavalcanti, *História*, 47–48.

78 Alveal, "From Colonial," 50; "Ofício [. . .]," September 4, 1761, fol. 10v.

79 "Ofício [. . .]," September 4, 1761, fol. 1v.

80 "Ofício [. . .]," September 4, 1761, unnumbered fol. 4r.

81 "Ofício [. . .]," September 4, 1761, fol. 7v.

82 Alfredo Cavalcanti, *História*, 49.

83 Alveal, "From Colonial," 55.

84 J. Dias, *A terra*, 105.

85 Rêgo, *Os aldeões*, 75.

86 Alfredo Cavalcanti, *História*, 98.

87 "Municipios Pernambucanos em Revista: Garanhuns," *Lavoura e Criação* (São Paulo) 9, nos. 1–3 (March 1950): 49.

88 Rêgo, *Os aldeões*, 291–311.

89 Alfredo Cavalcanti, *História*, 54.

90 Alfredo Cavalcanti, *História*, 190; J. Dias, *A terra*, 109.

91 The letters discussed in this paragraph are found in códice 292, Garanhuns (1713–1724), n.p., IAHGP.

92 Some of those who granted (or otherwise ceded) legalized freedom to the enslaved were military veterans. One, who was married to a woman he had enslaved, freed three young men, at least two of whom were the couple's children. At least four of the thirty-one who secured cartas de alforria were born in Africa, six were Indigenous or mixed race (with one Indigenous and one white parent), and the rest either were born in Brazil or were simply referred to as "slave," with no indication of birthplace. In all, females outnumbered males nearly three to two.

93 "Carta [. . .]," March 22, 1732, Pernambuco, caixa 42, doc. 3819, anexo 1, AHU.

94 "Consulta [. . .]," November 18, 1699, in Gomes, *Mocambos*, 439.

95 "Ordenou [. . .]," October 27, 1712, CCA, *Disposições*, VI-III-I-1-32, doc. 166, fol. 130r, AUC.

96 "Requerimento [. . .]," before January 8, 1725, Pernambuco, caixa 31, doc. 2789, AHU.

7. THE "INDIANS OF PALMARES"

1 A longer version of this chapter, including more extensive secondary citations, appears in Hertzman, "The 'Indians.'"

2 "Carta [. . .]," August 2, 1746. Alagoas, caixa 2, doc. 116, fol. 1r, 1v, AHU.

3 Whitehead, "Carib."

4 Because the phrase "Indians of Palmares" has a complicated, contested lineage—explored below—I place it in quotation marks each time that I use it.

5 In the 1990s, archaeologists excavated Serra da Barriga and concluded that Indigenous people played a large role in Palmares. Historians are skeptical of the claims, and it is, as Silvia Lara points out, curious that the archaeologists seem to have overlooked the fact that Indigenous and paulista soldiers were present

in the area after 1695, which may explain the evidence that archaeologists have (perhaps mistakenly) dated to the seventeenth century. For citations and further discussion, see the introduction as well as Hertzman, "The 'Indians,'" 429; Lara, *Palmares*, 135.

6   See Miki, *Frontiers*; Paraíso, *O tempo*.

7   Herzog, *Frontiers*, 110–11.

8   "Carta [. . .]," November 27, 1733, in *DH*, vol. 100 (Rio de Janeiro: Biblioteca Nacional, 1953), 122. See also "Carta [. . .]," April 25, 1747, Alagoas, caixa 2, doc. 119, fol. 1r, AHU; and "Carta [. . .]," December 10, 1739, Pernambuco, caixa 55, doc. 4767, AHU.

9   "Carta [. . .]," August 2, 1746, Alagoas, caixa 2, doc. 116, fol. 1r, AHU.

10   "Ofício [. . .]," December 9, 1775, Pernambuco, caixa 121, doc. 9238, fol. 9r, AHU.

11   "Carta [. . .]," August 2, 1746, Alagoas, caixa 2, doc. 116, fol. 1v, ahu. Also see "Bando [. . .]," May 5, 1705, CCA, *Disposições*, VI-III-1-1-32, doc. 6, fols. 9v–10r, AUC.

12   "Carta [. . .]," August 2, 1746, Alagoas, caixa 2, doc. 116, fol. 2r, AHU.

13   "Informação geral," 384, 387, 393–94. Concern with Indigenous flight and movement between aldeias persisted for years. See, for example, "Carta [. . .]," June 26, 1725, Pernambuco, caixa 31, doc. 2821, AHU; and "Provisão [. . .]," October 11, 1745, Pernambuco, caixa 62, doc. 5290, AHU.

14   Indigenous people appear to have sought to leverage the desire to situate aldeias as shields to separate coastal cities from Palmares. For example, see Vieira, "Entre perdas," 74.

15   "Requerimento [. . .]," December 14, 1759, Pernambuco, caixa 92, doc. 7367, anexo 1, AHU.

16   Mariana Albuquerque Dantas, *Dimensões*, 44.

17   See, for example, "Consulta [. . .]," December 1700, Pernambuco, caixa 19, doc. 1859, AHU; and Vieira, "Entre perdas," 82. On the practice of placing aldeias near forts and sending missionaries to both, see "Carta [. . .]," April 25, 1747, Alagoas, caixa 2, doc. 119, AHU.

18   During the second half of the eighteenth century, the Diretório dos Índios governed the aldeias and their land claims. During the nineteenth century, after the diretório was dissolved, state policy toward Indigenous people became decentralized, though the 1850 Land Law (discussed later) played a pivotal role in shaping land policy throughout Brazil. See R. Almeida, *O Diretório*; Langfur, *The Forbidden*, 61–67; Miki, *Frontiers*, 106–7; P. Sampaio, "Política," 181–88; and Aldemir Barros da Silva Jr., "A construção."

19   *Documentação*, 1:316.

20   For more details about Urucu, see L. Almeida, "Índio."

21   J. Cabral, "Vestigios," 15.

22   Duarte, "Tribos," 114.

23   "Relatório [. . .]," April 4, 1640, in J. Mello, *Fontes*, 1:184–85.

24   "Relatório [. . .]," April 4, 1640, 1:174.

25   "Sobre [. . .]," November 26, 1643, in J. Mello, *Fontes*, 2:130.

26 Other aldeias, especially in Pernambuco, were similarly created to protect colonial settlements. See Damasceno, "A ocupação," 51, 122; and Lara, *Palmares*, 210, 308, 341.

27 "Memorial," 97.

28 "Aldeia de Santo Amaro do Palmar," Documenta Palmares, https://palmares .ifch.unicamp.br/ifch_maps/7, accessed December 26, 2021.

29 "Carta [. . .]," July 19, 1726, Alagoas, caixa 1, doc. 38, fol. 6r, AHU.

30 "Consulta [. . .]," January 25, 1700, Conselho Ultramarino: Brasil–Baía (hereafter, Bahia), caixa 34, doc. 4269, fol. 4v, AHU; "Memorial," 97.

31 "Consulta [. . .]," January 25, 1700, Bahia, caixa 34, doc. 4269, fol. 4v, AHU. See also "Carta [. . .]," June 21, 1700, Pernambuco, caixa 18, doc. 1821, AHU.

32 "Memorial," 98.

33 "Memorial," 98.

34 "Carta [. . .]," December 30, 1699, Bahia, caixa 34, doc. 4270, AHU.

35 "Carta [. . .]," July 19, 1726, Alagoas, caixa 1, doc. 38, fol. 8v, AHU.

36 "Requerimento [. . .]," March 26, 1726, Alagoas, caixa. 1, doc. 34, anexo, AHU.

37 *Almanak*, 233.

38 "Requerimento [. . .]," September 18, 1772, Pernambuco, caixa 113, doc. 8698, AHU.

39 O. Galvão, "Ligeira," 287–88.

40 *Falla dirigida*, supplement 1, p. 9. This and other provincial reports are available at CRL Digital Delivery System, Center for Research Libraries, http://ddsnext.crl .edu/, accessed November 21, 2022.

41 "Extrato [. . .]," May 1761, Pernambuco, caixa 95, doc. 7527, no. 26, AHU; *Relatorio Lido*, 56.

42 G. Rodrigues, "A tentativa," 3.

43 "Carta [. . .]," August 30, 1730, Pernambuco, caixa 40, doc. 3666, fol. 3r, AHU.

44 G. Rodrigues, "A tentativa," 3.

45 F. Costa, *Anais*, 4:408–9.

46 G. Rodrigues, "A tentativa," 7.

47 "Carta [. . .]," August 30, 1730, Pernambuco, caixa 40, doc. 3666, fol. 3r, AHU.

48 The conspiracy also conjures images of the insurrection jointly planned by Black and Indigenous people in Bahia in 1814. Schwartz, "Tapanhuns," 13–14.

49 "Ofício [. . .]," December 26, 1731, Pernambuco, caixa 42, doc. 3781, AHU. Five years later, another conspiracy in Paraíba intended to unite aldeias from across the region, inspire "Blacks to kill their masters," and attack whites with a combination of poison, "witchcraft," and arms. "Consulta [. . .]," February 8, 1735, Conselho Ultramarino: Brasil–Paraíba (hereafter, Paraíba), caixa 9, doc. 769, AHU. In 1751 a Portuguese military commander sent twenty soldiers "into Palmar" to apprehend a group of "Indian thieves and witch doctors [who were] harming residents." "Requerimento [. . .]," August 1, 1768, Pernambuco, caixa 106, doc. 8195, anexo 7, AHU.

50 "Carta [. . .]," April 28, 1786, caixa 29, doc. 2149, fol. 3r, AHU. See also "Ofício [. . .]," August 14, 1784, Paraíba, caixa 28, doc. 2133, AHU; and "Ofício [. . .]," April 29, 1786, caixa 29, doc. 2153, AHU.

51   For other references to Indigenous uprisings in Pernambuco, see "Mandou
      [. . .]," July 1, 1722, CCA, *Disposições*, VI-III-I-1-32, doc. 7, fols. 295r–v, AUC.

52   R. Rodrigues, *Os africanos*, 78.

53   Frescarolo, "Informações," 105.

54   For suggestive ideas about the long-term, if indirect, relationship between
      nineteenth-century insurrections and Palmares, see L. Almeida, *Memorial*; Marcus
      Carvalho and França, "Palmares"; Lindoso, *A utopia*; and Palacios, *Campesinato*.

55   "Ofício [. . .]," October 13, 1815, caixa 21, pacote 03, doc. 04, Instituto Histórico e
      Geográfico de Alagoas (hereafter, IHGA).

56   Marcus Carvalho, "Os índios," 67.

57   Joaquim José de Costa to Rodrigo de Sousa da Silva Pontes, October 18, 1837,
      caixa 1539, Arquivo Público de Alagoas (hereafter, APA).

58   The Indigenous people of Alagoas and Pernambuco also likely shared the
      "repertoire of creative strategies" deployed across several centuries, as Heather
      Roller shows, by Indigenous people in the Amazon and Paraguay River basins
      against predatory Iberian and Brazilian states. Roller, *Contact Strategies*, 189. See
      also Mariana Albuquerque Dantas, "Do aldeamento"; and E. Silva, *Aldeia*.

59   See, among others, Devine Guzmán, *Native*; and Miki, *Frontiers*.

60   "Carta de José Caetano Moreira e outros," 1821, in Antunes, *Índios*, 80. This
      book contains transcriptions of a number of important nineteenth-century
      documents.

61   The petition's fate may be traced in Antunes, *Índios*, 80–86.

62   A representative document from 1823 describes "frequent" "uprisings and
      disorders" in Palmeira dos Índios. Letter from Manoel Cavalcante de Albu-
      querque, August 15, 1823, caixa 1259, APA. The armed mobilizations around
      independence are especially notable, given the often-evoked contrast between
      the violent independence wars of Spanish America and Brazil's ostensibly
      more passive independence process. Also see the provocative work of Mariana
      Albuquerque Dantas: for example, *Dimensões*.

63   E. Costa, *The Brazilian*, 82.

64   Motta, "Terra," 83, 86–89. For more on the Land Law (including additional cita-
      tions of relevant scholarship), see E. Costa, *The Brazilian*, 78–93; Miki, *Frontiers*,
      115–18; and V. Moreira, "Terras," 158–63.

65   V. Moreira, "Nem selvagens," 156.

66   Letter from José Rodrigues Leite Pitanga, December 11, 1850, caixa 0320, APA.

67   Indigenous petitioners also situated Brazil's emperor as the latest in an unbro-
      ken line of distinguished royal leaders; for example, petitions noted that Indig-
      enous people had originally received their land from the "august predecessors
      of Your Majesty" and the "noble kings, predecessors of His Imperial Majesty."
      "Requerimento [. . .]," ca. 1860–65, caixa 21, pacote 01, doc. 38, p. 3, IHGA; "Ofício
      [. . .]," July 12, 1830, caixa 23, pacote 03, doc. 29, p. 1, IHGA. See also Mariana
      Albuquerque Dantas, *Dimensões*, esp. 111.

68   "Documentos sobre a historia: Indios da provincial das Alagoas; Questão dos
      Paulistas e Palmares," caixa 0006, pasta Títulos e Terras Indígenas, p. 1, APA.

69 "Documentos," p. 2 (emphasis in original). The handwriting suggests that the unsigned page was also written in the nineteenth century, likely by a member of the IHGA, which produced similar accounts of Palmares. For an overview of the IHGA's writings on Palmares, see Danilo Marques, "Sob a 'sombra,'" 121–39.

70 On Silveira, see "Lista de Verbetes," ABC das Alagoas, http://abcdasalagoas.com .br/verbetes.php, accessed June 27, 2022.

71 "Processo [. . .]," February 4, 1812, Acervo Arthur Ramos, doc. 25, I-36,25,024, fol. 1r, BN.

72 "Processo," February 4, 1812, fol. 43r.

73 "Ofício [. . .]," July 12, 1830, caixa 23, pacote 03, doc. 29, fol. 5r, IHGA.

74 "Relatório [. . .]," April 29, 1851, in Antunes, Índios, 92–96.

75 José Rodrigues Leite Pitanga to Antonio Coelho de Sá e Albuquerque, April 22, 1854, caixa 0006, pasta Títulos e Terras Indígenas, APA. The diretor's ambiguous relationship with the aldeias—as both their ally and exploiter—is discussed in Aldemir Silva, "A construção."

76 "Mappa [. . .]," December 12, 1861, caixa 0006, pasta Títulos e Terras Indígenas, APA.

77 Falla dirigida, supplement 1, p. 10.

78 "Atestado [. . .]," June 6, 1862, in Antunes, Índios, 108.

79 Joaquim José da Costa to João Lins Vieira Cansanção do Sinimbu, May 2, 1840, APA, caixa 1539.

80 Paraíso, O tempo.

81 Falla dirigida, supplement 1, p. 3; "Carta [. . .]," March 5, 1840, in Antunes, Índios, 150–51.

82 E. Silva, "O nosso direito," 268.

83 E. Silva, "O nosso direito," 270.

84 E. Silva, "Manuel Valentim," 172, 193 (quote).

85 Letter from Jozé Prudente Telles da Costa to King Pedro II with appendixes, February 22, 1858, caixa 1252, APA. See also Jozé Prudente Telles da Costa to Augusto Thomas do Amaral, n.d., caixa 1252, APA. Additional documents in caixa 1252 suggest that antagonism from the Church, via land grabs or abusive priests, was common.

86 Marcus Carvalho, "Os índios," 93.

87 Farias, "Xucuru-Kariri," 110.

88 For a concise overview, see M. Cunha, Legislação, 21–23.

89 "Planta da Extincta Aldeia do Riacho do Matto," Seção de Mapas, 1403, APEJE.

90 E. Silva, "Manuel Valentim," 196–97. See also Mariana Albuquerque Dantas, "Do aldeamento"; and E. Silva, Aldeia, 69–108.

91 "Requerimento [. . .]," ca. 1860–65, caixa 21, pacote 01, doc. 38, IHGA. The same argument of continuous occupation, substantiated in extant laws, was often used against Indigenous communities, whom white settlers regularly accused of deserting their land.

92   Letter from José Fernandes da Costa Pereira Jr., Rio de Janeiro, October 4, 1874, caixa 0320, APA.

93   "Guerra dos Palmares," *O Constitucional* (Maceió), July 23, 1851, p. 4.

94   I discuss the dance in much more detail that I can here in Hertzman, "Quem." Quilombo attracted significant attention from twentieth-century folklorists but little critical analysis since then. For a critical balance of the twentieth-century work, see D. Reis, "Dança"; and D. Reis, "Quilombo."

95   J. Rocha, *Folguedos*, 121.

96   See, for example, Matthew, *Memories*, 200.

97   "Guerra dos Palmares," 4.

8. GREATER PALMARES

1   Marquez, "Witnesses." Christine M. DeLucia's treatment of place as a way to access histories that are "oftentimes unseen and unheard" is instructive. DeLucia, *Memory*, 3. Also see, among others, K. Basso, *Wisdom*; Cronon, "A Place"; and LaPier, "Land."

2   Guerra, *Velhas*.

3   Mario Behring, "A morte do Zumby," *Kosmos*, September 1906, n.p.

4   "Registo [. . .]," December 20, 1707, in DH, vol. 59 (Rio de Janeiro: Typ. Baptista de Souza, 1943), 31–32.

5   Damasceno, "A ocupação," 126. A search for "Hainam" on Documenta Palmares yields Santos's petition with a summary that places a question mark following the word. See https://palmares.ifch.unicamp.br/fichas/busca-avancada?filter=Hainam&search_type=simple-search, accessed May 31, 2023.

6   "Registo da Carta [. . .]"; "Registro da Carta do Padrão [. . .]," December 20, 1707, in Gomes, *Mocambos*, 462–63; Registo Geral de Mercê, Páscoa dos Santos, December 20, 1707, Registo Geral de Mercês, Registo Geral de Mercês do reinado de João V, liv.2, fol. 151r, ANTT.

7   I am indebted to Ikuko Asaka and John Marquez for deciphering the phrase.

8   A. Marques, "A travessia," 71–73; A. Oliveira, "Os Kariri"; K. Silva, *Nas solidões*, 19, 26–27.

9   "Consulta [. . .]," May 10, 1703, Pernambuco, caixa 20, doc. 1921, fol. 9r, AHU. Also see "Requerimento [. . .]," before March 24, 1695, Pernambuco, caixa 17, doc. 1676, anexo 1 (November 21, 1694), AHU.

10 "Nomeou [. . .]," December 11, 1705, CCA, *Disposições*, VI-III-I-1-32, doc. 50, fol. 20r, AUC.

11 "Carta [. . .]," January 2, 1706, Pernambuco, caixa 22, doc. 2009, fol. 1r, AHU.

12 "Carta [. . .]," January 2, 1706, fol. 1v.

13 "Escreveo [. . .]," September 2, 1711, CCA, *Disposições*, VI-III-I-1-32, doc. 26, fol. 94r, AUC.

14 Instead of "town" or "city," Kalina Vanderlei Silva prefers "urban center" (núcleo urbano), while Gilberto Freyre used "rurbano," a mash-up of "rural" and "urban." Freyre, *Rurbanização*; K. Silva, *Nas solidões*, 235.

15 TSO-CP, August 24, 1718, caderno 87, fol. 317r, ANTT.

16 "Bando [. . .]," May 5, 1705, CCA, *Disposições*, VI-III-I-I-32, doc. 6, fol. 9v, AUC.

17 "Escreveo [. . .]," December 5, 1711, CCA, *Disposições*, VI-III-I-I-32, doc. 36, fol. 96v, AUC.

18 "Consulta [. . .]," October 29, 1729, doc. 74, anexo 2 (May 24, 1729), in Ennes, *Os primeiros*, 487.

19 "Carta [. . .]," December 10, 1730, Alagoas, caixa 1, doc. 65, fol. 1r, AHU. At the time, "continent" (continente) referred to "dry land" (terra firme). Antonio Silva and Bluteau, *Diccionario*, s.v. "continente."

20 "Consulta [. . .]," December 19, 1741, Lisbon, Pernambuco, caixa 57, doc. 4906, fol. 1r, AHU.

21 "Carta [. . .]," September 26, 1744, Pernambuco, caixa 60, doc. 5174, AHU.

22 "Ofício [. . .]," December 9, 1775, Pernambuco, caixa 121, doc. 9238, anexos 3 (quote) and 4, AHU. Also see "Ofício [. . .]," January 1761, Pernambuco, caixa 94, doc. 7448, AHU.

23 Some forts remained through at least 1780. "Consulta [. . .]," September 4, 1780, Pernambuco, caixa 137, doc. 10241, AHU.

24 "Requerimento do capitão Luís Mendes da Silva [. . .]," before December 14, 1759, Pernambuco, caixa 92, doc. 7367, anexo 1, AHU.

25 A. Marques, "A travessia," 66.

26 The king's decree is reproduced in Instituto Archeologico e Geographico Alagoano, *O centenario*, 76. (The Instituto later changed its name to Instituto Histórico e Geográfico de Alagoas.)

27 "Informação geral," 476. "Tapamondé" may be an Indigenous word, though I have not been able to find a clear definition.

28 Lara, *Palmares*, 399–401.

29 Lara and Fachin, *Guerra*, 42.

30 Lara and Fachin, *Guerra*, 49.

31 Damasceno, "Direitos," 106; *Documentação*, 4:102–3.

32 *Documentação*, 4:107.

33 "Requerimento [. . .]," before February 26, 1757, Pernambuco, caixa 82, doc. 6878, anexo 2 (August 13, 1755), AHU.

34 See, for example, Gomes, *A hidra*, 346.

35 A. Pinto, *Apontamentos*, 2:396.

36 Lara and Fachin, *Guerra*, 19.

37 De Luna, *The Long*. On macaco's many meanings in contemporary Brazilian Portuguese, see Schneider, *Dictionary*, 177–83.

38 "Circumstancias," 95; *Documentação*, 4:118.

39 Marcuzzo, Romero, and Cardoso, "Detalhamento," 12.

40 Noting that the river was also utilized by colonial forces and that settlements atop Serra da Barriga faced the river and therefore provided sight lines to spot

enemy convoys, two archaeologists write, "Resistance, is . . . written in the settlement pattern itself." Orser and Funari, "Archaeology," 68.

41 See Bordoni, *A língua*, 417; Navarro, *Dicionário*, 302–3, 513; Tibiriçá, *Dicionário tupi*, 137, 141, 190; Tibiriçá, *Dicionário de topônimos*, 88.

42 Parsing what Africans may have heard in the word will require deeper linguistic work. The proto-Bantu root *-ndá* means garden, and the more widespread *-gùndà* denotes a forest or "luxuriant vegetation." Tempting as these meanings are, there is no obvious sound change or agglutination that would have formed "Mundaú" from either root. ID 1509 (and VAR 777), BLR 3.

43 Espindola, *Geografia*, 33–36; Ivan Lima, *Ocupação*, 80.

44 Lara and Fachin, *Guerra*, 17.

45 Espindola, *Geografia*, 34, 65.

46 Alencastro, *The Trade*, illustration 11 between pages 252 and 253; Alves, *Dicionário*, s.v. "lunga."

47 Cadornega, *História* (1680), Azul 645, tomo 3, fol. 200.

48 Vansina, *How Societies*, 192.

49 Desch-Obi, "Combat," 354. Redinha, *Subsídios*, 164. Deep in the Brazilian interior, in a mountainous area of Goiás, Kalunga became the name of a quilombo. Karasch, *Before Brasília*, 206–12; Karasch, "Central Africans," 118. For an intriguing case study in Minas Gerais, see Vogt and Fry, *Cafundó*, 243–55. On the many meanings that priests and ethnographers recorded for (and perhaps assigned to) kalunga in West Central Africa, see, for example, Baião, *Elementos*, 121, Quadro Comparativo; Chatelain, *Folk-Tales*, 294; and Laman, *The Kongo*, 3:60.

50 Miller, *Kings*, 59–60 (quote on 59).

51 See, for example, Diégues, *O bangüê*, 160, and the "Engenho Mucambo" next to the "Engenho Banguella" in José da Silva Pinto, *Carta topographica da capitania das Alagoas*, Maceyó (Maceió), 1820, BN Digital, http://objdigital.bn .br/objdigital2/acervo_digital/div_cartografia/cart526824/cart526824.jpg, accessed July 3, 2023.

52 *Documentação*, 2:266.

53 Gilberto Freyre considered the practice evidence of the land "recreating the names of its owners in its own image and likeness." Freyre, *The Masters*, 457.

54 Though the municipality was officially created in 1873, an 1862 law established a comarca (a judicial and religious district) called Palmares. J. Ferreira, *Enciclopédia*, 18:189.

55 S. Galvão, *Diccionario*, s.v. "Cumbe," "Cumbe de Baixo," and "Cumbe de Cima."

56 For example, Saignes, "Life."

57 M. Andrade, *Dicionário*, 167; Michaelis, s.v. "cumbé," https://michaelis.uol.com .br/palavra/aVnj/cumb%C3%A9/, accessed July 3, 2023. Also see Vogt and Fry, *Cafundó*, 300.

58 One Tupi dictionary translates Cumbe as "ugly" or "muzzle," Cumbé as a name for sluggish or weak animals, and Cumbi as the roof of a mouth. Bordoni, *A língua*, 178.

59 ID 2034, 2035, 4309, and 4311, BLR 3. Albino Alves provides several meanings of kumbi, including "place of pasture preferred by cattle." Alves, *Dicionário*, s.v. "kumbi."

60 Guthrie, *Comparative*, vol. 3, s.v. "*-kúmb-*" (C.S. 1266). There is one language zone (K42: Ikuhane and Subiya, Central Africa) in which /ku/ sounds changed to /zu/, opening the possibility of a Cumbi-to-Zumbi link. A great deal more work and evidence would be required to substantiate such a link. Janson, "Bantu," appendix 1. For more Brazilian examples, see Angenot, Angenot, and Maniacky, *Glossário*, 104.

61 Alfredo Cavalcanti, *História*, 27–28; J. Dias, *A terra*, 52.

62 Bordoni, *A língua*, 199; M. Melo, *Onomástica*, 19; M. Melo, *Toponymia*, 29.

63 "Registro [. . .]," June 4, 1660, in Gomes, *Mocambos*, 179.

64 Alveal, "From Colonial," 16–17; Alfredo Cavalcanti, *História*, 31.

65 Colonial documents call the mocambo's leader "Andola Quitugi," which Lara suspects is an alternate colonial rendering of Andalaquituche. Documenta Palmares; Lara, *Palmares*, 198.

66 Alfredo Cavalcanti, *História*, 36; Damasceno, "A ocupação," 127.

67 I am grateful to Silvia Lara, who suggested this possibility to me.

68 Alfredo Cavalcanti, *História*, 37.

69 Alfredo Cavalcanti, *História*, 42.

70 Alfredo Cavalcanti, *História*, 36.

71 Alfredo Cavalcanti, *História*, 57–58.

72 Alfredo Cavalcanti, *História*, 88–89.

73 Alfredo Cavalcanti, *História*, 53.

74 Alfredo Cavalcanti, *História*, 45. A different transcription of the 1712 record of sale excludes the name Maria, making it instead "Mocambo da Negra," a name that would appear on subsequent maps. Torres, *A terra*, 42.

75 Damasceno, "Direitos," 100; *Documentação*, 4:92.

76 Alfredo Cavalcanti, *História*, 44.

77 Alfredo Cavalcanti, *História*, 36, 52.

78 Gonzaga Patriota, address to the Câmara dos Deputados (Brasília), September 11, 2013, https://www.camara.leg.br/internet/sitaqweb/TextoHTML.asp ?etapa=3&nuSessao=272.3.54.O&nuQuarto=19&nuOrador=1&nuInsercao =0&dtHorarioQuarto=14:06&sgFaseSessao=BC%20%20%20%20%20%20 %20%20&Data=11/09/2013&txApelido=GONZAGA%20PATRIOTA&txEtapa =Com%20reda%C3%A7%C3%A3o%20final.

79 Alfredo Cavalcanti, *História*, 41, 62–63.

80 Loreto Couto, *Desagravos*, 459.

81 Loreto Couto, *Desagravos*, 460.

82 Antonio Silva and Bluteau, *Diccionario*, s.v. "quilombo."

83 This map and several others referenced in this chapter could not be reproduced in a way that would be visually coherent and engaging for the reader. José da Silva Pinto, *Mapa topográfico em que se mostrão as terras [. . .]*, 1813, BN

Digital, http://objdigital.bn.br/objdigital2/acervo_digital/div_cartografia
/cart515170/cart515170.jpg, accessed May 26, 2023.

84 "Certidão," *Diário de Pernambuco*, August 12, 1870, 3; *Folhinha*, 400; *Mensagem*, 42.

85 Slave Voyages website, http://www.slavevoyages.org/estimates/OoBbl3lX, accessed July 3, 2023.

86 Marcus Carvalho, *Liberdade*, 51.

87 Marcus Carvalho, *Liberdade*, 86.

88 Quoted in F. Costa, *Arredores*, 17. Valérie Loichot's description of bodies of water that claimed great numbers of Black lives seems apt here: "Whether forsaken swamp, sea abyss, or riverbed, unspecified places of dying or repose render all ground ambiguous: the dead are both nowhere to be found and potentially everywhere." Loichot, *Water Graves*, 13. Also see de la Torre, "The Well."

89 Honorato, *Diccionario*, 1–2.

90 Marcus Carvalho, *Liberdade*, 85.

91 V. Costa, "Trajetórias," 104.

92 Quoted in Marcus Carvalho, *Liberdade*, 86.

93 S. Galvão, *Diccionario*, s.v. "Afogados."

94 S. Galvão, *Diccionario.* s.v. "Afogados."

95 "Escravos Fugidos," *Diário de Pernambuco*, February 6, 1835, 4.

96 "Escravos Fugidos," *Diário de Pernambuco*, February 9, 1836, 4.

97 Borborema, Andrade, and Sá, "Da cartografia," 12; M. Marques, "Homens," 53.

98 Watkins, *Palm Oil*, loc. 50, 97 of 348.

99 "Correspondencia," *Diário de Pernambuco*, March 17, 1854, 3; "Editaes," *Diário de Pernambuco*, November 19, 1852, 2; "Editaes," *Diário de Pernambuco*, July 17, 1860, 3.

100 Sir Douglas Fox and Associates and H. Michell Whitley, "Planta da Cidade do Recife," 1906, Museu da Cidade do Recife (hereafter, MCR).

101 "Correspondencia," 3.

102 S. Galvão, *Diccionario*, s.v. "Boa Vista."

103 *Diário de Pernambuco*, March 11, 1829, 222.

104 Marcus Carvalho, "O Quilombo do Catucá," 10. Also see Marcus Carvalho, "O Quilombo de Malunguinho"; and J. Melo, "Quilombos."

105 Marcus Carvalho, "O Quilombo do Catucá," 6. Kimbundu (katuka, to shake or make tremble), Kikongo (kàtúka, to leave, and kâtúká, to stretch), and Portuguese (catucar, to nudge) dictionaries suggest several possible meanings, and agglutination may also be instructive, especially the West Central African proto-Bantu *-túká* ("banana") and *ka-*, a prefix commonly attached to Class 12 nouns (augmentatives, derogatives, diminutives, and amelioratives). ID 5455, BLR 3; Katamba, "Bantu," 104, 115; N. Lopes, *Novo dicionário*, 85; Swartenbroeckx, *Dictionnaire*, 123–24.

106 Quoted in I. Santos, *A caverna*, 54–55.

107 Quoted in I. Santos, *A caverna*, 113.

108 Lara, "O território," 18.

109 Brandão, *Os negros*, 39.

110 *Almanak*, 236.

111 "Notícias do día," *Diário da Manhã* (Maceió), August 18, 1882, 2; "Assassinato," *Jornal do Pilar*, February 3, 1876, 2; "Quilombos," *Jornal do Pilar*, January 26, 1876, 2.

112 L. Almeida, *Memorial*.

113 Michaelis, s.v. "macuca," https://michaelis.uol.com.br/palavra/A85bq/macuca-2/, accessed December 10, 2023.

114 Bordoni, *A língua*, 334.

115 M. Almeida, "Speaking," 278; ID 5467, BLR 3.

116 De Luna, "Sounding," 598. Also see Katamba, "Bantu," 109, 115; and appendix A of this book.

117 Coleção Instituto Arqueológico, doc. 0380, IAHGP.

118 Espindola, *Geografia*, 249. "Valhacouto" may be translated as "hideout" with the implication that it was a place of refuge for evildoers, including and perhaps especially those who escaped slavery. In other contexts, the word has more positive connotations: "refuge." Bluteau, *Vocabulario*, s.v. "valhacouto."

119 Leoncio José Pereira de Farias, "Exploração e traçado da linha telegráfica entre Rio Formoso e Tamandaré," BR RJANRIO 4Q.0.MAP.103, Arquivo Nacional (hereafter, AN), https://sian.an.gov.br/sianex/Consulta/Pesquisa_Livre_Painel_Resultado.asp?v_CodReferencia_id=93427&v_aba=, accessed May 26, 2023; E. Pinto, *Etnologia*, 68.

120 Great Britain Parliament House of Commons, *Accounts*, 48; Victor Fournié, "Sciencias," *Diário de Pernambuco*, September 5, 1881, 8.

121 Macedo, *Brazilian*, 143–46; Oliveira Filho and Messias, "Da circum-navegação." The War of the Triple Alliance pitted Brazil, Argentina, and Uruguay against Paraguay, resulting in catastrophic loss of human life, especially in Paraguay.

122 Vital de Oliveira, *Roteiro*, 161.

9. FARTHER NORTH

1 J. Carvalho, "Formação," 49. Paraíba has received little attention in the historical literature on Brazil, slavery, and quilombos. A small but growing historiography on slavery and the African Diaspora in Paraíba has been pioneered almost entirely by scholars based there. See Galliza, "Análise"; M. Guimarães, "Diáspora"; M. Lima, "Liberdade"; H. Mello, "Datas"; Octávio, *A escravidão*; S. Rocha, *Gente*; S. Rocha and Fonseca, *População*; S. Rocha and Guimarães, *Travessias*; and Sousa, "Nas veredas." This literature is shaped by the foundational work of Ademar Vidal: "Tres seculos."

2 The city was renamed João Pessoa in September 1930 in honor of the former state president who had just been elected vice president of Brazil and then assassinated days later. The assassination paved the way for Getúlio Vargas to seize the presidency, launching one of the most consequential political careers in Brazilian history. Leitão, "Uma cidade," 145–49.

3 J. Carvalho, "Formação," 48, 50.

4 Baerle, *The History*, 214.

5 J. Carvalho, "Formação," 76.

6 K. Silva, *Nas solidões*, 74–75.

7 "Ofício [. . .]," July 20, 1768, Pernambuco, caixa 105, doc. 8186, fol. 1r, AHU.

8 The TST does not include Paraíba as a searchable point of disembarkation. I have used information pieced together by Matheus Silveira Guimarães, who notes that even his careful work cannot account for enslaved people who ended up in Paraíba via overland routes. M. Guimarães, "Diáspora." Also see Klein and Luna, *Slavery*, 76.

9 M. Guimarães, "Diáspora," 152; L. Lima, "Cativos," 133–47.

10 Vidal Filho, "Nossa," 135.

11 In 1811, pretos and pardos composed as much as 60 percent of the province's total population. S. Rocha, *Gente*, 111. Also see M. Medeiros and Sá, *O trabalho*, 49–60.

12 Irenêo Joffily, "Um episodio da Secca de 1793 (Continuação)," *Gazeta do Sertão*, February 22, 1889, 2. Also see Aquino, "Quilombos," 255. There is some debate about the extent of Jorge Velho's time in Paraíba. See E. Almeida, *História*, 32–34.

13 "Carta Patente, Pascoal Coelho Freitas," January 30, 1723, Registo Geral de Mercês, Mercês de D. João V, liv. 14, fol. 365r, ANTT; Dimas Marques, "Pelo bem," 109; "Relação [. . .]," 1733, Ceará, caixa 2, doc. 151, AHU.

14 M. Lima, "Liberdade," 236–38. On Cumbi, also see Aquino, "Quilombos," 256–57; L. Pinto, *Síntese*, 57; and Vidal, "Tres seculos," 109.

15 "Requerimento [. . .]," before June 9, 1701, Paraíba, caixa 3, doc. 243, fol. 5r, AHU; "Requerimento [. . .]," before March 12, 1724, Pernambuco, caixa 30, doc. 2723, anexo 1, AHU. This may have been the same mocambo that, according to a 1697 account, had stood in the "Serra da Capaiba" since the early 1680s. "Carta Patente de Manuel Frazão de Figueiroa," 1697, Registo Geral de Mercês, Mercês de D. Pedro II, liv. 9, fol. 127v, ANTT.

16 The 1731 report is transcribed in several sources, including Porto, *Paraíba*, 91.

17 Instituto Brasileiro de Geografia e Estatística, https://www.ibge.gov.br/cidades -e-estados/pb/alagoa-grande.html, accessed July 5, 2023.

18 Serviço de Regularização de Territórios Quilombolas do Instituto Nacional de Colonização e Reforma Agrária (hereafter, INCRA), Superintendência Regional No. 18 (Paraíba), *Relatório*, 8. For more on the community, see Aires, *Comunidade*; H. Lima, "'Já veio'"; Luiz, "Das ressignificações"; and A. Moreira, "A luta." On Alagoa Grande, see J. Freire, *Alagoa Grande*.

19 Paiva and Souza, *Relatório*, 124. Also see Aires, *Comunidade*, 40–41.

20 "Zumbi, 1728 — Registro d'uma Carta de Sesmaria de Terras [. . .]," December 12, 1728, liv. 3, Sesmarias, 1722–1727, Acervo Digital Neabi, Universidade Federal da Paraíba (hereafter, ADN-UFPB). A summary of the sesmaria is found in Tavares, *Apontamentos*, 1:130.

21 "O Alferes Izidro Pereita Gondim e Agostinho Pereira Pinto," May 4, 1757, liv. 7, Sesmarias, 1757–1764, ADN-UFPB, summarized in Tavares, *Apontamentos*, 1:246–47.

22   In addition to the two previously cited, see "José da Costa Gondim," May 3, 1795, liv. 10, Sesmarias, 1780–1808, ADN-UFPB; J. Leal, *Itinerário*, 163; and Tavares, *Apontamentos*, 1:373, 441–42, 480.

23   See, for example, "Carta [. . .]," April 22, 1729, Paraíba, caixa 7, doc. 565, fol. 1r, AHU; "Carta [. . .]," July 6, 1729, Paraíba, caixa 7, doc. 593, AHU; and Menezes, "Negros," 50.

24   Luig and Von Oppen, "Landscape," 22. A twentieth-century Kimbundu definition of "kilombo" is also interesting in this respect: a place with water believed to be inhabited by a supernatural being and "with a more-or-less mysterious history, where one should not go alone." Neto, "Kilombo," 6.

25   Colson, "Places," 51.

26   Luig and Von Oppen, "Landscape," 22.

27   See, for example, K. Basso, *Wisdom*, 12.

28   R. Brown, "'Walk,'" 307.

29   For an overview, see Slenes, "The Great," especially 191–96. Also see Colson, "Places," 54; Harms, *River*, 134; Klieman, "The Pygmies," 149; and Schuler, "Enslavement," 194–95. Zumbi nature spirits in the Brazilian northeast by name alone seem to be distinct from Kongolese simbi spirits found in multiple sites in the diaspora, though there are some intriguing points of comparison, including that simbi are often imbricated in questions of life and death and that some transform from nature spirits to water spirits. See R. Brown, *African-Atlantic*, 4–6, 111–14; Janzen, *Lemba*, 282–84; Klieman, "The Pygmies," 146, 200; and MacGaffey, *Religion*, 132–33.

30   Thornton, *The Kongolese*, 12.

31   Schuler, "Enslavement." Oscar de la Torre shows that in select Amazonian waterscapes, African and diasporic beliefs about water and spirituality interacted with Indigenous and European ideas. Future research may indicate the extent to which the same was true for Zumbi aquatic spaces. De la Torre, "The Well." Also see Diegues, "Água," 21–26.

32   "Governo da Provincia," *O Publicador*, October 15, 1864, 2.

33   C. Almeida, *Atlas*, ix.

34   C. Medeiros, *Diccionário*, 112. Also see Ehret, *An African*, 166–68. A full exegesis of mulungú in Brazil awaits.

35   Prefeitura de Alagoa Grande, "História," http://www.alagoagrande.pb.gov.br /historia/, accessed July 5, 2023.

36   M. Guimarães, "Diáspora," 148; "Idéa da população," 16; L. Silva, "'Esperança,'" 127–28.

37   M. Guimarães, "Diáspora," 151.

38   M. Guimarães, "Diáspora," 145.

39   Moura Filha, *De Filipéia*.

40   Archimedes Cavalcanti, *A cidade*, 33; M. Guimarães, "Diáspora," 139.

41   M. Guimarães, "A população"; I. Pinto, *Datas*, 1:106.

42   Barcia, *West African*, 65, 144–45; M. Guimarães, "A população," 3; Slave Voyages website, https://www.slavevoyages.org/past/database, accessed July 31, 2023.

43 "Repartição da Polícia," *O Publicador*, February 14, 1867, 1.

44 Koster, *Travels*, 51.

45 M. Lima, "Liberdade," 249–53; S. Rocha, *Gente*, 77–78.

46 Koster, *Travels*, 52. Witnesses leveled accusations against enslaved Blacks in the port area for practicing "witchcraft" and some of the same rituals denounced in Pernambuco. For example, TSO-CP, April 29, 1749, caderno 108, fol. 128r, ANTT; TSO-CP, July 12, 1745, August 19, 1745, and November 21, 1745, caderno 109, fols. 113r–14r, ANTT.

47 Koster, *Travels*, 51.

48 "Editaes," *A Regeneração*, March 7, 1862, 4.

49 "Leilão de um engenho," *O Publicador*, July 27, 1864, 3.

50 *Diario da Parahiba*, August 29, 1884, 3; "Editaes," *O Publicador*, November 24, 1865, 4.

51 "Editaes," *O Publicador*, August 25, 1866.

52 Rodriguez, *Roteiro*, 97.

53 "Comunidades Remanescentes de Quilombos (CRQ's)," Fundação Cultural Palmares, http://www.palmares.gov.br/?page_id=37551, accessed July 5, 2023. Norte-rio-grandense refers to a person or thing from Rio Grande do Norte.

54 "Tabela 3175: População residente, por cor ou raça, segundo a situação do domicílio, o sexo e a idade," https://sidra.ibge.gov.br/Tabela/3175, accessed November 30, 2019.

55 D. Araújo, *Dinâmica*, 38; Lira, *História*, 153.

56 See R. Araújo, "A invisibilidade"; L. Assunção, *Jatobá*; L. Assunção, *Os negros*; Maria Carvalho, Reesink, and Cavignac, *Negros*; Cavignac et al., *Relatório*; Cavignac, Macêdo, and Nascimento, *Guia*; and A. Souza, *Liberdades*.

57 Hajstrup, *Viagem*, 84 of 152.

58 Jesus, "Abrindo," 15; "Requerimento [. . .]," before September 20, 1732, Pernambuco, caixa 43, doc. 3895, AHU.

59 Patrícia Dias, "Onde fica," 62, 74–75. Rio Grande do Norte's current borders crystalized during the late nineteenth and early twentieth centuries. See Fernandes, *O (in)imaginável*.

60 Cascudo, *História*, 52–53; Cavignac et al., *Relatório*, 42.

61 "Cópia [. . .]," July 14, 1722, doc. 155, in Porto Alegre, Mariz, and Dantas, *Documentos*, 159; Cavignac et al., *Relatório*, 64.

62 Patrícia Dias, "Onde fica"; T. Silva, "A ribeira."

63 Dias and Alveal, "Um estudo," 491, 502.

64 Quoted in Cascudo, *História*, 46.

65 See, for example, Cascudo, *História*, 47.

66 Cascudo, *História*, 44.

67 Cascudo, *Nomes*.

68 Cavignac et al., *Relatório*, 35.

69 Cascudo, *Nomes*, 106–7.

70 Cascudo, *Nomes*, 118.

71 Cascudo, *Nomes*, 85. Açu and Assú are not always applied consistently, though "Açu" is generally used to the river and "Assú" the larger sertão, with the notable (and confusing) exception being the regular references to the Guerra do Açu. There is also a city that is spelled both "Açu" and "Assú." Patrícia Dias, "Onde fica," 17n3, 62, 74–75; T. Silva, "A ribeira," 16.

72 *Falla Que o Ilm. e Exm. Snr. Doutor*, Mappa 37.

73 "Sesmaria Francisco Teixeira de Seixas," August 14, 1733, Ch. de D. João V, liv. 99, Fundo Sesmarias do Instituto Histórico Geográfico do Rio Grande do Norte (hereafter, Fundo Sesmarias IHGRN), Laboratório de Experimentação em História Social-Universidade Federal do Rio Grande do Norte (hereafter, LEHS-UFRN). Also see "Sesmaria D. Anna Fonseca Gondim," April 13, 1745, liv. 4, Fundo Sesmarias IHGRN, LEHS-UFRN; and "Sesmaria Bento Fernandes de Lima," May 14, 1748, liv. 5, Fundo Sesmarias IHGRN, LEHS-UFRN.

74 "Sesmaria Bento Fernandes de Lima," January 24, 1754, liv. 5, fol. 67r, Fundo Sesmarias IHGRN, LEHS-UFRN.

75 "Sesmaria Bento Fernandes de Lima," May 14, 1748. This may be the same stream referenced in Lyra, *O Rio Grande do Norte*, 31.

76 Vieyra, *A Dictionary*, s.v. "couto."

77 Bluteau, *Vocabulario*, s.v. "couto."

78 Cascudo, *Nomes*, 84.

79 Cascudo, *Nomes*, 29; "Requerimento [. . .]," before May 31, 1738, Rio Grande do Norte, caixa 4, doc. 245, fol. 1r, AHU; "Requerimento [. . .]," before August 22, 1738, caixa 4, doc. 250, anexo 1, AHU; "Sesmaria Lourenço Mendes de Andrade," March 27, 1804, liv. 7, Fundo Sesmarias IHGRN, LEH-UFRN. Paulo Pereira dos Santos describes the Rio Grande–Ceará borderlands as a refuge for people who escaped slavery. P. Santos, *Evolução*, 126.

80 "The Wealth They Carried" is adopted from O'Brien, *The Things*.

81 "Sesmaria Francisco Teixeira de Seixas," fol. 335v.

82 Joffily, *Notas*, 118; Pinho, *História*, 94; Schwartz, *Sovereignty*, 347–48; J. M. Silva, "Biographia," 258.

83 On the Black soldiers who moved to Rio Grande do Norte, see K. Silva, *Nas solidões*, 198–99.

84 "Sesmaria, Luís da Silveira Pimentel," August 28, 1692, CE 0566, Plataforma SILB http://www.silb.cchla.ufrn.br/, accessed June 15, 2019.

85 "Documento 44," in Ennes, *As guerras*, 270; Carvalho Franco, *Dicionário*, 298.

86 Lemos, *Capitães-móres*, doc. 14, 2:96; T. Silva, "A ribeira," 61–62, 95, 142. Among these were paulistas who received land grants for their service. See, for example, Monteiro, *Blacks*, 80.

87 Alveal, "Converting," 172; T. Silva, "A ribeira," 144–45; K. Silva, *Nas solidões*, 185–214. Tyego Franklim da Silva suggests that at least one power broker in Rio Grande may have manipulated a royal order granting land to paulistas who fought in Palmares to secure land for himself and those close to him, despite not actually fighting in Palmares. T. Silva, "A ribeira," 145–46.

88 See, for example, TSO-CP, caderno 105, fols. 30r–v, ANTT; TSO-CP, caderno 108, fols. 135, 239r–245r, ANTT; TSO-CP, caderno 109, fols. 92r–v, ANTT; AND TSO-CP, caderno 118, fol. 64r, ANTT.

89 V. Barbosa, "Bernardo Vieira de Melo"; Carvalho Franco, *Dicionário*, 242; Puntoni, *A guerra*, 172–73.

90 Júlio Alencar, "Para que enfim," 142; Carvalho Franco, *Dicionário*, 242; Jesus, "Abrindo," 93.

91 One of Vieira de Melo's brothers married the second daughter of the same man. Patrícia Dias, "Onde fica," 64; Carvalho Franco, *Dicionário*, 242.

92 Júlio Alencar, "Para que enfim," 144.

93 Patrícia Dias, "Onde fica," 118–20, 169, 172–75, 190–91.

94 T. Silva, "A ribeira," 81–85.

95 See, for example, "Consulta [. . .]," December 20, 1697, Pernambuco, caixa 17, doc. 1741, fols. 4v–6r, AHU; Mendes, "O serviço," 137–38; Puntoni, *A guerra*, 178; and "Registo [. . .]," January 16, 1692, in *DH*, vol. 30 (Rio de Janeiro: Typ. Arch. de Hist. Brasileira, 1935), 339–41.

96 "Consulta [. . .]," May 22, 1698, Pernambuco, caixa 18, doc. 1754, fol. 2r, AHU.

97 "Consulta [. . .]," December 11, 1699, doc. 70, in Ennes, *As guerras*, 411–12.

98 M. Freitas, *Reino negro*, 2:604; Dimas Marques, "Pelo bem," 118.

99 Mendes, "O serviço," 145–46.

100 H. Galvão, *Velhas*, 20–24.

101 Augusto, "Famílias," 196; Manoel Dantas, *Denominação*, 15–16.

102 Cavignac et al., *Relatório*, 56.

103 Cascudo, *Nomes*, 133; T. Medeiros, *Aspectos*, 216.

104 Lyra, *O Rio Grande do Norte*, 34.

105 When I delivered a lecture in 2019 at the Universidade Federal do Rio Grande do Norte (UFRN), in Natal, many of the students in attendance were surprised to learn that there was a place named Zumbi up the coast.

106 "Relação das povoações, fogos, e almas q. contem a divisão concernente a capela do porto dos Touros, em 15 de Abril de 1832," Fundo Touros RN, Série Criação da Freguesia, IHGRN. By 1919, the population had grown to 568. Vicente, "Diccionario," 97. For more details on the area, see P. Araújo, "'Não é terra'"; and Tenório Filho, *Porto*.

107 Cascudo, *Nomes*, 133. According to Cascudo, "Punahu" (also spelled Punaú) means "River of Butterflies," and today the beach by that name is a short distance from Praia Zumbi. Cascudo left behind no additional details about the 1777 Zumbi sesmaria, and an exhaustive search at archives in Natal, including the documents maintained by Carmen Alveal and other researchers at UFRN, who created Plataforma SILB, an online database of sesmarias cited in the notes here and in chapter 6, yielded little further information. See the project's website (http://www.silb.cchla.ufrn.br/) and Pereira, "Geoprocessamento."

108 Vital de Oliveira, *Roteiro*, 29.

109 Vital de Oliveira, *Roteiro*, 29.

110 "Consulta [. . .]," August 8, 1684, Pernambuco, caixa 13, doc. 1297, fol. 2v, AHU.

111 Posadillo y Posadillo, *Derrotero*, 150. On shipwrecks in the area, also see *Diario do Rio de Janeiro*, December 11, 1864, 1; *Diario do Rio de Janeiro*, December 20, 1864, 1; Medeiros Filho, *Naufrágios*; and A. Pinto, *Apontamentos*, s.v. "Zumbi."

112 The story of the ship is recounted in Medeiros Filho, *Naufrágios*, 24–31. Much of the text there comprises transcriptions of original documents, which were lost years ago when the IGHRN reorganized its archive.

113 Medeiros Filho, *Naufrágios*, 26.

114 Medeiros Filho, *Naufrágios*, 28. The second-hand language here is ambiguous; the women are described as *negrinhas*, which suggests they were young, perhaps children.

115 Lee and Newfont, *The Land*.

10. KILLING ZUMBI (AGAIN)

1 See França and Ferreira, *Três vezes*, 58–83; and Reis, "Zumbi," 43–96. For an extended treatment of local and regional history being articulated onto national history in Mexico and Peru, see Mallon, *Peasant*, 137–244.

2 On one of the earliest rejections of the story, in the 1880s, see Reis, "Zumbi," 67. For a longer treatment of the suicide story, see Hertzman, "Fatal."

3 Chapman, "Palmares," 31–32.

4 E. Carneiro, *O Quilombo*, 12–14; Herskovits, *The Myth* (1941), 91; Herskovits, *The Myth* (1967), 91. The later printings of *The Myth* also came after the pioneering Black anthropologist Irene Diggs published an article in 1953 about Palmares that also dispelled the legend of Zumbi taking his own life. In 1983, Cedric Robinson's landmark book, *Black Marxism*, reproduced much of Diggs's account, but he edited it to suggest that Zumbi died at Serra da Barriga (though not by suicide). Diggs, "Zumbi," 67; Robinson, *Black Marxism*, 134–35.

5 Bethell, *Brazil*, 157, 161.

6 My use of "dense" here draws on Robyn D. G. Kelley's discussion of "the density of Black being," as well as the application of his concept in Native American studies. Kelley, "On the Density." Also see Andersen, "Critical"; and Pexa, *Translated*, 13.

7 O Liberal Genuíno, "Communicado," *Diário de Pernambuco*, January 27, 1857, 1.

8 O Liberal Genuíno, "Communicado," 1.

9 Y. Castro, *Falares*, 49; J. Ribeiro, *Diccionario*, 216–22; Romero, *Estudos*, 35.

10 Alfredo do Valle Cabral, "Achegas ao estudo do folklore brazileiro," *Gazeta Litteraria*, September 20, 1884, 348.

11 Cabral, "Achegas," 348–49. I quote most of the definitions but also shorten and synthesize some of the longer entries.

12 Cabral, "Achegas," 349.

13 The text referenced is Capelo and Ivens, *De Benguella*.

14　Antonio Joaquim de Macedo Soares, "Estudos lexicographicos do dialecto bra-zileiro," *Revista Brazileira*, terceiro tomo, 1° anno (March 1880), 269, https://hdl.handle.net/2027/umn.31951002791431y, accessed July 6, 2023.

15　Cabral, "Achegas," 349.

16　Cabral, "Achegas," 349.

17　Cannecattim, *Diccionario*; Cannecattim, *Collecção*. Also see Vieira-Martinez, "Building," 92–99.

18　See chapter 3 and I. G. H., "Dei Progressi," 78; Luca, *Nuovi elementi*, 207; and Douville, "Voyage," 185, 198.

19　Cabral, "Achegas," 349.

20　Cabral, "Achegas," 349.

21　Pedro Dias, *Arte*; Cannecattim, *Diccionario*.

22　Capelo and Ivens, *De Benguella*, 1:103.

23　Batulukisi, "Framed Figure," 117.

24　Capelo and Ivens, *De Benguella*, 1:103.

25　Heintze, "Hidden," 24.

26　It is unclear whether this ambaquista was from Ambaca. No place in Angola, Vansina writes, "was more important in the slave trade" than Ambaca. But by the late nineteenth century, "ambaquista" could refer to Luso-Africans from other parts of Angola. Vansina, "Ambaca," 1. Also see Fleisch, "Angola"; Heintze, "Hidden"; Kukanda, "A personalidade"; Medina and Henriques, *A rota*, 149–50; and Miller, *Way of Death*, 644.

27　Capelo and Ivens, *De Benguella*, 1:103.

28　Batulukisi, "Framed Figure," 116–17.

29　Capelo and Ivens, *De Benguella*, 1:104. A few years earlier, a traveler reported that in the hinterlands of Libolo and Kisama, locals refrained from attacking him because they took him to be "a benevolent sent by *n'gana Zambi* ('God Almighty')." But on a separate trip along the Cuanza River, he "caused fright among men, women, children," who took him to be a Cazumbi, "small" spirits (or gods) "that only enter into questions of minor importance within homes." Batalha, *Costumes*, 21, 34.

30　Cabral, "Achegas," 350.

31　Cabral, "Achegas," 350.

32　Cabral, "Achegas," 350.

33　M. S., "Correspondencia: Notas ao folklore brasileiro do Sr. Valle Cabral," *Gazeta Litteraria*, December 2, 1884, 401.

34　I have not found a good reference for acauran, but caburê and variations that others have linked to it (including kaburé, caburé, and caboré) present intrigu-ing paths. An ornithologist noted a "mimetic" quality in Austral pygmy owls (*Glaucidium nana*, King) in Argentina known as caburé for the dark tufts of hair on the back of their heads, which make them look as if they have two sets of eyes. Similar birds and tales of their mystic powers circulated in Paraguay and Brazil, where caburé was also a racial label for Indigenous and mixed-race people. In Paraíba, the word could mean "person who only goes out at night," which was also another definition of little-z zumbi. Cascudo, *Dicionário*, 150; Koslowsky, "'El Caburé'"; Navarro, *Dicionário*, 211.

35 M. S., "Correspondencia," 401.

36 M. S., "Correspondencia," 401.

37 Cannecattim, *Collecção*, 175, 176; Cannecattim, *Diccionario*, 266.

38 See, for example, L. Guimarães, "Francisco," 59.

39 L. Guimarães, "Francisco Adolpho de Varnhagen," 57; Varnhagen, *História*.

40 Varnhagen, *História*, 2:785.

41 For example, Battel et al., *The Strange*; Bentley, *Dictionary*; Bentley, *Life*; Dennett, *Notes*; Merolla da Sorrento, "A Voyage." For an interesting reference to "Zombi" in Spanish that then circulated in Brazil, see Eugenia F. O. A., "Appendice: O Zombi pintor, ou o mulato de Murillo," *O Chronista*, March 15, 1838; and Muñoz Maldonado, *Los Pintores*, 5–22. Also see (in Portuguese) Marecos, *Juca*, 6.

42 Chatelain, *Folk-Tales*.

43 João Silva, *Entertaining Lisbon*, 44.

44 Academia Brasileira de Letras, https://www.academia.org.br/academicos/rocha-pombo/biografia, accessed March 30, 2022.

45 Rocha Pombo, *História*.

46 J. Martins, *O Brazil*, 64; Rocha Pombo, *História*, 2:566.

47 J. Martins, *O Brazil*, 66; Rocha Pombo, *História*, 2:566–67.

48 Sarmento, *Os sertões*.

49 Sarmento, *Os sertões*, 15.

50 Sarmento, *Os sertões*, 71–73.

51 Sarmento, *Os sertões*, 96.

52 Sarmento, *Os sertões*, 98–99.

53 Rocha Pombo, *História*, 2:418.

54 Miller, *Kings*, 13.

55 Brandão, "Documentos"; Brandão, *Os negros*; Brandão, "Os negros," 60–77.

56 Emphasis in original. Brandão, *Os negros*, 32.

57 Sarmento, *Os sertões*, 139.

58 R. Rodrigues, *Os africanos*, 78.

59 See Weinstein, *The Color*, 37, 75, 355–56.

60 Cascudo, *Dicionário*, 740.

61 Cascudo, *Geografia*, 19.

62 Cascudo, *Dicionário*, 740.

63 The collection was republished in 2008 in Monteiro Lobato, *O Saci-Pererê*.

64 Cascudo, *Dicionário*, 159–61.

65 Cascudo, *Geografia*, 123.

66 Cascudo, *Geografia*, 26.

67 Cascudo, *Geografia*, 354.

68 Bastide, "L'Islam," 214.

69 Octavio da Costa Eduardo also describes a "Gunoco" of Nupe origin in Maranhão. Eduardo, *The Negro*, 82, 85.

70 Emphasis in original. Querino, *A raça*, 47. Gunocô, which could change shape and form, remained mysterious to the ethnographers who studied it. According to Eduardo, Xangô, the powerful Candomblé thunder deity, or orixá, disguised himself as Gunocô to evade the wrath of another powerful orixá, Yemanja, whom he abandoned after fathering her children. Eduardo, *The Negro*, 82. Also see Bastide, *O candomblé*, 139; Bastide, *Diálogo*, 371, 374; Antônio Carneiro, *Os mitos*, 242–51, 461–64; and J. Castro, *Miguel Santana*, 24–26, 39, 43.

71 Frikel, "Traços," 69. Frikel attributes the quotation to multiple (unnamed) informants.

72 TSO-CP, June 2, 1774, caderno 129, fol. 135r.

73 The fact that Islam also likely played a role in this trajectory (especially in West Africa and possibly also in Bahia) adds yet another layer of richness.

74 Monteiro Lobato, *O Saci-Pererê*, 45–46.

75 Monteiro Lobato, *O Saci-Pererê*, 120. If West Central African zumbi helped shape the tradition that became known as Saci, other indications of Z/zumbi's presence in Minas Gerais are also found once again in the land, in places such as the Zumbi Forest (Matta do Zumbi), a little-known place near the colonial mining center Diamantina that appears fleetingly in writing toward the end of the nineteenth century. Diamantina is also known for its vissungos, songs sung by enslaved people who labored in the mines. Mário de Andrade described vissungos as "work songs of Blacks from Benguela" in Minas Gerais, but at some point, the songs also took on religious meaning, with special connection to death and burials, and Zambi appears in multiple forms in the songs, which were shaped by a diverse collection of Africans and their descendants, who came from not only West Central Africa but also West Africa and beyond. M. Andrade, *Dicionário*, 566; Broadus, "*Vissungo*"; Camara, "Vissungo"; Machado Filho, *O negro*, 69–112; S. Queiroz, *Vissungos*. Reference to the Matta do Zumbi is in "Secção Official," *Liberal Mineiro*, January 22, 1884, 3.

76 P. Fonseca, "Memoria dos feitos"; Lara and Fachin, *Guerra*, 80–84; Lara, *Palmares*, 388–89; Reis, "Zumbi," 54–55.

77 This and the remaining quotes from the story are in P. (Pedro) Fonseca, "Variedade: Um baptismo posthumo," *Pharol* (Juiz de Fora), May 29, 1885, 2.

78 Cascudo, *Made*.

79 Ribas lost his sight at the age of twenty-one; nonetheless, he became a prolific writer and folklorist, whom one author calls "the Homeric figure of African literature." Burness, "From the Boundaries," 15 (quotation); Hamilton, *Voices*, 45.

80 Much of their correspondence is housed at the Instituto Câmara Cascudo (hereafter, ICC). On Ribas's influence on *Made in Africa*, see A. Neves, "Câmara Cascudo."

81 Ribas, *Ilundo*.

82 Cascudo, *Made*, 117–18; Ribas, *Ilundo*, 42–43. Ribas also defined "dele (êlê)" as a bird, whose name was an "alteration" of the Kimbundu ndêle, which had been

previously translated by Chatelain as "white bird." Chatelain, *Kimbundu*, 125; Ribas, *Dicionário*, 76.

83 Cascudo, *Made*, 113.

84 Emphasis in the original. Cascudo, *Made*, 114.

85 Cascudo, *Made*, 113, 118.

86 Cascudo, *Made*, 118.

87 Though, as we have seen, not in Candomblé. Cascudo, *Made*, 165–66.

88 Cascudo, *Lendas*, 64.

89 TST, African Origins Database, African ID 70104.

90 For example, TST, African Origins Database, African IDs 54159, 178045, 178129, and 183117. Followed out even further in time, we find Gullah speakers naming their children Zumbi and Zambi and Rastafarians in 1930s Jamaica hailing Ethiopia's Haile Selassie as "King Zambi." Megenney, "Words," 9; Schuler, "Liberated," 348–49.

91 Bastide, *The African*, 427; Neiva, *Guia*, 2:1011–12, 1320–22, 1848–49.

11. CONNECTED AND BEYOND

1 While a full account of the Left's engagement with Palmares and Z/zumbi is yet to be written, useful surveys are found in França and Ferreira, *Três vezes*, 84–147; and A. Reis, "Zumbi," 99–112.

2 E. Mello, *A fronda*, 455–62.

3 Southey, *History*, 3:98. Also see "Narração historica," 65, 291.

4 J. Martins, *Os martires*; E. Mello, *A fronda*, 273–74, 457.

5 J. Martins, *Os martires*, 273 (the page is mistakenly numbered 275 but falls between 272 and 274).

6 José Alencar, *Guerra*, 137–38.

7 José Alencar, *Guerra*, 137.

8 Alencastro, *The Trade*, 297; Bluteau, *Vocabulario*, s.v. "mazombo"; Monte Carmelo, *Compendio*, 208; A. Silva and Bluteau, *Diccionario*, s.v. "mazombo."

9 Kaoma, *God's Family*, 41. We would need to know more about the local evolution of the term in Southeast Africa to take this conclusion further.

10 See chapter 8.

11 M. Almeida, "African Voices," 180.

12 Thornton, *A History*, 287. Also see R. Brown, *African-Atlantic*, 67.

13 Alpers, "'Mozambiques'," 44.

14 De Luna, "Sounding."

15 De Luna, "Sounding," 598.

16 "Requerimento [. . .]," before September 4, 1753, Pernambuco, caixa 75, doc. 6240, fol. 36v, AHU.

17 "Continuaçam da Carta de Pitia a Damam," *Correio do Rio de Janeiro*, November 18, 1823, 363.

18 "Despachos de exportação nos dias 18 a 19," *Jornal do Commercio* (Rio de Janeiro), July 20, 1839, 4.

19 Serviço Geográfico Militar, *Ilha do Governador* (Rio de Janeiro: Serviço Geográfico Militar, 1922), http://objdigital.bn.br/objdigital2/acervo_digital/div_cartografia/cart544907/cart544907.html, accessed July 7, 2023. The island was named for Salvador Correia de Sá, governor of Rio de Janeiro twice during the sixteenth century. Cultivation of sugar on the island began on a plantation that he owned. Ipanema, *História*, 19, 63.

20 The concoction included whale fat, which was also used in Zumbi Soap. Ipanema, *História*, 129.

21 Ipanema, *História*, 81.

22 "Annuncios," *O Despertador*, August 12, 1841, 4; "Escravos Fugidos," *Diário do Rio de Janeiro*, November 15, 1845.

23 "Noticiario," *O Fluminense* (Niterói), October 2, 1881, 2; "Parte forense," *O Fluminense*, October 6, 1882, 2; *Relatorio apresentado*, A-8.

24 "Historia de um casamento," *Diário do Rio de Janeiro*, November 17, 1858, 3.

25 "Juca Rosa," *Diario de Noticias* (Rio de Janeiro), November 30, 1870, 4. On Rosa, see P. Johnson, *Automatic Religion*, 79–106; G. Sampaio, "Juca Rosa"; and G. Sampaio, *Juca Rosa*.

26 He also wrote, "In respect to *Zambi*, in Rio de Janeiro, they [Blacks] only knew that it is the 'greatest of saints,' but they don't know what it is like or how to worship it." A. Ramos, *O negro*, 105, 107.

27 See Dimas Marques, "Pelo bem," 109.

28 Brasil, "Cucumbis," 303.

29 Brasil, "Cucumbis," 307; Moraes Filho, *Festas*, 109–16.

30 Translated in Heywood, "The Making," 257.

31 Heywood, "The Making," 257. Also see Karasch, *Slave Life*, 248. As we have seen, some Kongolese were also familiar with (n)zumbi.

32 The fact that the revelers evoke "Mother" and "Father" suggests an additional line of inquiry about gender that echoes several other examples discussed in previous chapters.

33 Quote in Arora, "Brasil acucareiro," 21; Griz, "O Zumbi."

34 Vidal, *Lendas*, 279.

35 J. Cruz, "Frei Damião," 42.

36 M. Silva et al., "O Distrito," 10.

37 Interview conducted by the author and Damiana de Oliveira Silva with Antonio de Paiva Fagundes at his home, on October 19, 2019, Praia de Pititinga, Rio Grande do Norte.

38 Interview conducted by the author and Damiana de Oliveira Silva with Valdete Gomes da Silva Ferreira at her home, on October 19, 2019, Zumbi, Rio Grande do Norte.

39 Vidal, *Guia*, 20.

40 Brandão, *Viçosa*, 22; J. Ferreira, *Enciclopédia*, 19:190–91.

41   J. Ferreira, *Enciclopédia*, 19:191.

42   Brandão, *Viçosa*, 40.

43   Interview conducted by Julie Cavignac, on October 30, 2019.

44   Talvani Guedes da Fonseca, "Os herdeiros de Zumbi," *Realidade*, April 1969, 112–24.

45   Studart, "Dezenove documentos." The remaining quotations in this paragraph are found on page 254.

46   Augusto, "Famílias."

47   Augusto, "Famílias," 204.

48   Ennes, *As guerras*.

49   Augusto, "Famílias," 189.

50   Augusto, "Famílias," 190; A. Mello, *Biografias*, 171.

51   According to the 2010 census, Canguaretama had a population that was 34 percent white, 4 percent Black, and 61 percent pardo/a. Instituto Brasileiro de Geografia e Estatística, https://sidra.ibge.gov.br/Tabela/3175#resultado, accessed December 11, 2019.

52   "FAMÍLIA GALVÃO: A família Galvão presente na história de Zumbi dos Palmares," FAMÍLIA GALVÃO (blog), January 23, 2013, http://galvaodorn.blogspot.com/2013/01/a-familia-galvao-presente-na-historia.html.

53   V. Andrade, "A questão."

54   Interview conducted by the author with Sérgio Marques Caetano in his home, on October 21, 2019, Sibaúma, Rio Grande do Norte. Cavignac, who has worked with residents of Sibaúma for years, introduced me to Caetano.

55   Cavignac et al., *Uma Sibaúma só!*, 39.

56   Fonseca, "Os herdeiros."

57   Cascudo, *História*, 44; Fonseca, "Os herdeiros," 120.

58   Cavignac et al., *Uma Sibaúma Só!*, 65.

59   *Falla que o Illm. e Exm. Senhor Dr.*, 4.

60   Bertha Nivack, letter to the editor, *Realidade*, May 1969, 11.

61   Fonseca, "Os herdeiros," 117.

62   Carlos Alberto Nóia, letter to the editor, *Realidade*, June 1969, 8.

63   Edward Robinson de Barros Cavalcanti, letter to the editor, *Realidade*, June 1969, 8.

64   "A bem da verdade," *Realidade*, June 1969, 8–9.

65   Cavignac, "Índios," 195.

66   "Parque Quilombo dos Palmares," https://www.uol/estilo/especiais/parque-memorial-quilombo-dos-palmares.htm, accessed July 10, 2023.

67   Lara and Fachin, *Guerra*, 34, 79.

68   See A. Araujo, "Dandara"; and Hertzman, "Fake News."

69   In a similar vein, not related directly to Palmares, see Hertzman and Xavier, "Let's Build."

70   Silveira, "A evocação"; Silveira, "Vinte de Novembro." Despite the name, the day is not exactly "national"; its observation varies by town, state, and region.

71   Stevens and Floy, "Southey's Letters," 547.

1   Guerra, *Velhas*, 132.
2   See, for example, Reesink, "Raízes," 87;
3   M. Rodrigues and Campos, "Caminhos," 283.
4   Price, "Refiguring," 212.
5   Fundação Cultural Palmares, "Quadro Geral de Comunidades Remanescentes de Quilombos," June 30, 2022, https://www.palmares.gov.br/?page_id=37551.
6   On the many ways that contemporary quilombos have formed, see, for example, Hoffman French, *Legalizing*; Mattos, "Novos"; and Mattos and Abreu, "'Remanescentes.'"
7   Compelling here too are the "little diaspora[s]" of free people of color that Carlos A. M. Lima shows to have emanated from Rio de Janeiro during the eighteenth and nineteenth centuries. C. Lima, "Pequena."
8   Aires, *Comunidade*, 107–17.
9   I elaborate this point more fully in Hertzman, "The 'Indians.'"
10   DeLucia, *Memory*, 3.
11   DeLucia, *Memory*, 325.
12   Amado, *Jubiabá*, 63.
13   This act of flight, like the ones taken by the characters in Toni Morrison's *Song of Solomon*, may be read not to "imply triumph" but instead as "ambiguous, disturbing." Quote on p. xiii.
14   C. Diegues, *Ganga Zumba*; C. Diegues, *Quilombo*.
15   A useful account is found in Stam, *Tropical*, 226–31.
16   Fusco, "Choosing," 13.
17   Quoted and translated in Stam, *Tropical*, 231.
18   Fusco, "Choosing," 13.
19   Fusco, "Choosing," 12.
20   C. Diegues, *Quilombo*, at 1 hr., 54 mins., and 39 sec.
21   D. Freitas, *Palmares*, 125–27.
22   See Pascoal Gomes, "Negros e homossexuais 'disputam' Zumbi," *Folha de São Paulo*, May 19, 1995, section 3, p. 5; Luiz Mott, "Debate: Era zumbi homosexual?," *EAVirtual: Revista del Grupo de Estudios Afroamericanos de Barcelona*, no. 3 (2005): 85–93. I am grateful to Silvia Lara for sending me these articles.
23   Arruti, "A emergência," 7.
24   "Passeio virtual," Parque Memorial Quilombo dos Palmares, https://serradabarriga.palmares.gov.br/, accessed June 19, 2023; Law No. 12.519, November 10, 2011, http://www.planalto.gov.br/ccivil_03/_Ato2011-2014/2011/Lei/L12519.htm.
25   Correia, "Como."
26   Hertzman, "Fake News."
27   Pedro Borges, Nataly Simões, and Gustavo Fioratti, "Fundação Palmares censura biografias de lideranças negras históricas em seu site," *Folha de São Paulo*, June 15, 2020, https://www1.folha.uol.com.br/ilustrada/2020/06/fundacao

-palmares-censura-biografias-de-liderancas-negras-historicas-em-seu-site
.shtml; Márcio Falcão and Fernanda Vivas, "MPF aponta improbidade em
post de Sérgio Camargo, da Fundação Palmares, com 'repúdio' a Zumbi," *G1*,
May 14, 2020, https://g1.globo.com/politica/noticia/2020/05/14/mpf-aponta
-improbidade-em-post-de-sergio-camargo-da-fundacao-palmares-com
-repudio-a-zumbi.ghtml. Also see J. Lopes and Neves, "Quando."

28   Fundação Cultural Palmares. "João Jorge Rodrigues é empossado como Presidente da Fundação Palmares." April 28, 2023, https://www.gov.br/palmares/pt
-br/assuntos/noticias/joao-jorge-rodrigues-e-empossado-como-presidente-da
-fundacao-palmares.

29   Farfán-Santos, *Black Bodies*, 34–38.

30   Curvelo, "O direito," 22–23.

31   A. Carneiro and Nichols, "Demarcação," 151. Also see A. Ferreira, "Extensão," 31.

32   C. Melo, "Memórias," 100.

33   Some residents of Muquém, a quilombo near Serra da Barriga, also identify 1695 as the moment when their community came into being. The importance of water in Palmares took a tragic turn in 2010, when the Rio Mundaú flooded, devastating Muquém. L. Ribeiro, "Território," 84–108.

34   This process is discussed in Amorim, "MNU representa"; Conselho Deliberativo do Memorial Zumbi, "Memorial Zumbi"; Correia, "Como"; I. Leite, "The Transhistorical"; Danilo Marques and Correia, "O Movimento," 30–33; J. Santos, "Memorial"; Serra, "Monumentos," 173–74; Ana Silva and Gomes, "A Lei"; and Silveira, "A evocação." For interesting discussions of how these mobilizations could inform movements elsewhere, see Bledsoe, "Marronage"; and Price, "Scrapping."

35   J. Santos, "Memorial," 231 of 389.

36   Conselho Deliberativo do Memorial Zumbi, "Memorial," 227 of 389.

37   J. Santos, "Memorial," 241–42 of 389.

38   *Abdias Nascimento e Lélia Gonzalez na Serra da Barriga, em Alagoas*, n.d., https://www.youtube.com/watch?v=x9OBwUoFpIE, accessed May 28, 2023.

39   Prefeitura de Marechal Deodoro, https://www.marechaldeodoro.al.gov.br/a
-cidade/historia/, accessed June 22, 2022.

40   Magalhães, Ferrare, and Silva, *O Convento*, 190.

APPENDIX A

1   De Luna, "Sounding," 589–90.

2   M. Almeida, "African," 187.

3   See Nurse, "The Contributions," 380; and Schoenbrun, "Words," 969.

4   For another helpful guide for thinking about this, see Berry, "Poisoned," 300–306.

5   Crowley and Bowern, *An Introduction*, 78–79. Words are deemed to be cognates "if (a) they are of similar or relatable meaning and phonetic shape, and (b) they

can be demonstrated to have derived by direct oral transmission from a single item in a proto-language." Nurse, "The Contributions," 362.

6 De Luna and Fleisher, *Speaking*, 139.

7 For those whose eyes glaze over at the sight of asterisks and other odd symbols, Africanists have been working on reconstructions for a long time and there is no shortage of useful texts. See, among others, M. Almeida, "Speaking"; de Luna, "Bantu Expansion"; de Luna, "Sounding"; de Luna and Fleisher, *Speaking*; Guthrie, *Comparative*; Nurse, "The Contributions"; and Vansina, *Paths*.

8 Stockwell and Minkova, *English*, 56.

9 Katamba, "Bantu," 115–16.

10 De Luna and Fleisher, *Speaking*, 13.

11 See chapter 3 as well as De Luna and Fleisher, *Speaking*, 104; Bostoen, "Bantu"; Janson, "Bantu."

12 A useful overview map is available at Wikipedia, s.v. "Guthrie classification of Bantu languages," last modified June 7, 2023, 7:33 (UTC), https://en.wikipedia .org/wiki/Guthrie_classification_of_Bantu_languages. Scholars have updated and revised the classification system, whose broad geographic outlines none-theless remain in place. The most recent revision is Maho, NUGL *Online*.

13 ID 1259 and 1261, BLR 3.

14 Crowley and Bowern, *An Introduction*. For annotated bibliographies, see Rob-beets, "Comparative"; and Salmons, "Comparative-Historical Linguistics."

15 De Luna and Fleisher, *Speaking*; Nurse and Philippson, *The Bantu Languages*. A concise overview of the field is found in Fourshey, Gonzales, and Saidi, "Leza," 107–12.

16 Royal Museum for Central Africa, Bantu Lexical Reconstructions 3 database, https://www.africamuseum.be/en/research/discover/human_sciences/culture _society/blr. There are also two websites still under construction at the time this book went to press: https://africanmatrilinealhistories.blogs.bucknell.edu/ and https://atlanticlanguagearchive.georgetown.edu/.

17 Basso and Gonçalves, *História*; Teyssier, *História*; Wetzels, Menuzzi, and Costa, *The Handbook*.

18 Cabral, Rodrigues, and Duarte, *Línguas e culturas Tupí*; Navarro, *Dicionário*; Navarro, *Método*; Aryon Rodrigues and Cabral, *Novos*.

BIBLIOGRAPHY

PRINCIPAL ARCHIVES CONSULTED IN PERSON

Acervo da Comissão Permanente de Desenvolvimento do Centro Histórico de
João Pessoa (ACPD-CHJP)
Acervo Digital Neabi, Universidade Federal da Paraíba (ADN-UFPB)
Arquivo Histórico Waldemar Bispo Duarte (Paraíba, AHWBD)
Arquivo Metropolitano da Arquidiocese de Natal (Rio Grande do Norte,
AMAN)
Arquivo Público de Alagoas (APA)
Arquivo Público Estadual Jordão Emereciano (Pernambuco, APEJE)
Arquivo Público Estadual do Rio Grande do Norte (APERN)
Biblioteca Nacional (Rio de Janeiro, BN)
Biblioteca Pública do Estado da Bahia (BPEB)
Biblioteca Pública Juarez de Gama Batista (Paraíba, BPJGB)
Fundação Casa de José Américo (Paraíba, FCJA)
Instituto Arqueológico Histórico e Geográfico Pernambucano (IAHGP)
Instituto Câmara Cascudo (Rio Grande do Norte, ICC)
Instituto Geográfico e Histórico da Bahia (IGHB)
Instituto Histórico e Geográfico de Alagoas (IHGA)
Instituto Histórico e Geográfico Paraibano (IHGP)
Instituto Histórico e Geográfico do Rio Grande do Norte (IGHRN)
Instituto do Patrimônio Histórico e Artístico Nacional-Paraíba (IPHANP)
Laboratório de Experimentação em História Social, Universidade Federal do
Rio Grande do Norte (LEHS-UFRN)
Museu da Cidade de Recife (MCR)
Museu Théo Brandão (Alagoas, MTB)
Núcleo de Estudos Afro-Brasileiros e Indígenas, Universidade Federal de
Alagoas (NEABI-UFAL)
Prefeitura Municipal de João Pessoa (PMJP)

PRINCIPAL ARCHIVES CONSULTED ONLINE OR VIA REMOTE RESEARCH ASSISTANCE

Arquivo Eclesiástico da Arquidiocese de Mariana (Brazil, AEAM)
Arquivo Histórico Ultramarino AHU
Arquivo Nacional Torre do Tombo (Portugal, ANTT), https://digitarq.arquivos.pt/
Arquivo da Universidade de Coimbra (Portugal, AUC)
Biblioteca Nacional Digital (Brazil, BN Digital), https://bndigital.bn.gov.br/
Coleção Conde dos Arcos (CCA)
Documentos Históricos (Brazil, DH), https://memoria.bn.br/DocReader
    /DocReader.aspx?bib=094536&pagfis=1
Hemeroteca Digital (Brazil, BN Hemeroteca), http://memoria.bn.br/hdb
    /periodico.aspx
Instituto Histórico, Geográfico e Antropológico do Ceará (Brazil, IHGAC)
Projeto Resgate (Brazil, BN Resgate), http://resgate.bn.br/docreader/docmulti
    .aspx?bib=resgate

OTHER ONLINE TOOLS AND COLLECTIONS

Academia das Ciências de Lisboa (Portugal, ACL), https://www.acad
    -ciencias.pt/
Arquivo Nacional (Brazil, AN), https://www.gov.br/arquivonacional/pt-br
Bantu Lexical Reconstructions (Belgium, BLR 3), https://www.africamuseum.be
    /en/research/discover/human_sciences/culture_society/blr/any_lexicon
    _dictionary
Biblioteca Brasiliana Guita e José Mindlin (Brazil, BBM), https://www.bbm
    .usp.br/en/
Biblioteca Digital do Exército (Portugal, BDE), https://www.exercito.pt/pt
    /biblioteca-digital-do-ex%C3%A9rcito
Biblioteca Nacional de Portugal (Portugal, BNP), https://www.bnportugal
    .gov.pt/
British Library (United Kingdom, BL), https://www.bl.uk/
Center for Research Libraries (United States, CRL), http://ddsnext.crl.edu
Documenta Palmares (Brazil, DP), https://www.palmares.ifch.unicamp.br/
Hathi Trust Digital Library (United States, HTDL), https://www.hathitrust.org/
Instituto Brasileiro de Geografia e Estatística (Brazil, IBGE), https://www.ibge
    .gov.br/
Instituto Histórico e Geográfico Brasileiro (Brazil, IHGB), https://ihgb.org.br/
Internet Archive (United States, IA), https://archive.org/
John Thornton's African Texts (United States, JTAT), http://www.bu.edu/afam
    /faculty/john-thornton/john-thorntons-african-texts/.
Plataforma Sesmarias do Império Luso-Brasileiro (Brazil, SILB), http://www.silb
    .cchla.ufrn.br/

Trans-Atlantic Slave Trade (United States, TST) database, https://www
.slavevoyages.org/

PRINTED SOURCES AND WORKS CITED

Abreu, João Capistrano de. *Capítulos da história colonial*. Rio de Janeiro: Centro
Edelstein de Pesquisas Sociais, 2009. Accessed July 29, 2023. https://
www.google.com/books/edition/Cap%C3%ADtulos_da_hist%C3%B3ria
_colonial/olFiBAAAQBAJ?hl=en&gbpv=1.
Aguiar, Marcos Magalhães de. "Negras Minas Gerais: Uma história da diáspora
africana no Brasil colonial." PhD diss., Universidade de São Paulo, 1999.
Aires, José Luciano de Queiroz, ed. *Comunidade quilombola Caiana dos Crioulos:
Alagoa Grande — PB*. João Pessoa: Editora do Centro de Comunicação,
Turismo e Artes, Universidade Federal da Paraíba, 2022.
Alberto, Paulina L. *Black Legend: The Many Lives of Raúl Grigera and the Power of
Racial Storytelling in Argentina*. New York: Cambridge University Press, 2022.
Albuquerque, Cleonir Xavier de. *A remuneração de serviços da guerra holandesa
(A propósito de um sermão do Padre Vieira)*. Recife: Universidade Federal de
Pernambuco, Instituto de Ciências do Homem, 1968.
Albuquerque, Durval Muniz de, Jr. *The Invention of the Brazilian Northeast*. Trans-
lated by Jerry Dennis Metz. Durham, NC: Duke University Press, 2014.
Alencar, José Martiniano de. *Guerra dos Mascates: Chronica dos tempos coloniaes*.
2nd ed., 2 vols. Rio de Janeiro: H. Garnier, 1896. http://hdl.handle.net/2027
/mdp.39015063033693.
Alencar, Júlio César Vieira de. "Para que enfim se colonizem estes sertões: A
câmara de Natal e a Guerra dos Bárbaros (1681–1722)." Master's thesis,
Universidade Federal do Rio Grande do Norte, 2017.
Alencastro, Luiz Felipe de. "Os africanos e as falas africanas no Brasil." In
África-Brasil: Caminhos da língua portuguesa, edited by Charlotte Galves,
Helder Garmes, and Fernando Rosa Ribeiro, 15–26. Campinas: Editora da
Universidade Estadual de Campinas, 2009.
Alencastro, Luiz Felipe de. "História geral das guerras sul-atlânticas: O episódio
de Palmares." In *Mocambos de Palmares: Histórias e fontes (séc. XVI–XIX)*,
edited by Flávio dos Santos Gomes, 61–89. Rio de Janeiro: 7Letras, 2010.
Alencastro, Luiz Felipe de. "Palmares: Batalhas da guerra seiscentista sul-
atlântica." In *Revoltas escravas no Brasil*, edited by João José Reis and Flávio
dos Santos Gomes, 30–72. São Paulo: Companhia das Letras, 2019.
Alencastro, Luiz Felipe de. *The Trade in the Living: The Formation of Brazil in the
South Atlantic, Sixteenth to Seventeenth Centuries*. Edited by Michael Wolfers
and Dale Tomich. Translated by Gavin Adams and Luiz Felipe de Alencas-
tro. Albany: State University of New York Press, 2018.
Allen, Scott Joseph. "'A Cultural Mosaic' at Palmares? Grappling with the
Historical Archaeology of a Seventeenth-Century Brazilian Quilombo."

In *Cultura material e arqueologia histórica*, edited by Pedro Paulo de Abreu Funari, 141–78. Campinas: Instituto de Filosofia e Ciências Humanas, Universidade Estadual de Campinas, 1998.

Allen, Scott Joseph. "Os desafios da arqueologia de Palmares." In *Mocambos de Palmares: Histórias e fontes (séc. XVI–XIX)*, edited by Flávio dos Santos Gomes, 119–30. Rio de Janeiro: 7Letras, 2010.

Allen, Scott Joseph. "'Zumbi Nunca Vai Morrer': History, the Practice of Archaeology, and Race Politics in Brazil." PhD diss., Brown University, 2001.

Allewaert, Monique. "Super Fly: François Makandal's Colonial Semiotics." *American Literature* 91, no. 3 (September 2019): 459–90.

Almanak do Estado das Alagoas para 1891. Maceió: Typographia da Empreza Gutenberg, 1892.

Almeida, Candido Mendes de. *Atlas do Imperio do Brazil comprehendendo as resepectivas divisões administrativas, ecclesiasticas, eleitoraes e judiciarias*. Rio de Janeiro: Lithographia do Instituto Philomathico, 1868.

Almeida, Elpídio de. *História de Campina Grande*. 2nd ed. João Pessoa: Editora Universitária, Universidade Federal da Paraíba, 1979.

Almeida, Luiz Sávio de. "Índio, capital e terra: O aldeamento do Urucu." In *Terra em Alagoas: Temas e problemas*, edited by Luiz Sávio de Almeida, José Carlos da Silva Lima, and Josival dos Santos Oliveira, 207–31. Maceió: Editora da Universidade Federal de Alagoas, 2013.

Almeida, Luiz Sávio de. *Memorial biográfico de Vicente de Paula, o capitão de todas as matas: Guerrilha e sociedade alternativa na mata alagoana*. Maceió: Editora da Universidade Federal de Alagoas, 2008.

Almeida, Marcos Abreu Leitão de. "African Voices from the Congo Coast: Languages and the Politics of Identification in the Slave Ship Jovem Maria (1850)." *Journal of African History* 60, no. 2 (2019): 167–89.

Almeida, Marcos Abreu Leitão de. "Speaking of Slavery: Slaving Strategies and Moral Imaginations in the Lower Congo (Early Times to the Late 19th Century)." PhD diss., Northwestern University, 2020.

Almeida, Rita Heloisa de. *O Diretório dos Índios: Um projeto de "civilização" no Brasil do século XVIII*. Brasília: Editora da Universidade de Brasília, 1997.

Almeida, Suely Cordeiro de. "Rotas atlânticas: O comércio de escravos entre Pernambuco e a Costa da Mina (c. 1724–c. 1752)." *História* (São Paulo) 37 (2018): 1–31.

Alpers, Edward A. "'Mozambiques' in Brazil: Another Dimension of the African Diaspora in the Atlantic World." In *Africa and the Americas*, edited by José C. Curto and Renée Soulodre-La France, 43–68. Trenton, NJ: Africa World Press, 2005.

Alveal, Carmen Margarida Oliveira. "Converting Land into Property in the Portuguese Atlantic World, 16th–18th Century." PhD diss., Johns Hopkins University, 2007.

Alveal, Carmen Margarida Oliveira. "From Colonial Lordship to Territorial Authority: The Pursuit of Antônio Vieira de Melo in Ararobá Sertão

(Pernambuco, 18th Century)." *Revista Brasileira de História* 35, no. 70 (December 2015): 1–24.

Alves, P. João Albino. *Dicionário etimológico Bundo-Português: Ilustrado com muitos milhares de exemplos, entre os quais 2.000 provérbios indígenas.* 2 vols. Lisboa: Tipografia Silvas, 1951.

Amado, Jorge. *Jubiabá.* 15th ed. São Paulo: Livraria Martins, 1965.

Amorim, Alessandro Moura de. "MNU representa Zumbi (1970–2005): Cultura histórica, movimento negro e ensino de história." Master's thesis, Universidade Federal da Paraíba, 2011.

Andersen, Chris. "Critical Indigenous Studies: From Difference to Density." *Cultural Studies Review* 15, no. 2 (September 2009): 80–100. Accessed July 6, 2023. https://search-ebscohost-com.proxy2.library.illinois.edu /login.aspx?direct=true&db=sih&AN=45149757&site=ehost-live&scope =site.

Anderson, Robert Nelson. "The Quilombo of Palmares: A New Overview of a Maroon State in Seventeenth-Century Brazil." *Journal of Latin American Studies* 28, no. 3 (1996): 545–66.

Andrade, Mário de. *Dicionário musical brasileiro.* Edited by Oneyda Alvarenga and Flávia Camargo Toni. Belo Horizonte: Editora Itatiaia, 1999.

Andrade, Vanessa de Cássia. "A questão fundiária da comunidade de Sibaúma/ RN," *Mercator* (Fortaleza) 14, no. 1 (April 2015): 61–76. Accessed July 10, 2023. http://www.mercator.ufc.br/mercator/article/view/975.

Andrews, George Reid. *Afro-Latin America, 1800–2000.* Oxford: Oxford University Press, 2004.

Angenot, Geralda de Lima V., Jeane-Pierre Angenot, and Jacky Maniacky. *Glossário de bantuismos brasileiros presumidos.* Revista Eletrônica Língua Viva, number 2 (2013). Accessed June 20, 2023. http://www.revistalinguaviva.unir.br.

Angenot, Jean-Pierre, Catherine Barbara Kempf, and Vatomene Kukanda. "*Arte da Língua de Angola* de Pedro Dias (1697) sob o prisma da dialetologia Kimbundu." *Papia* 21, no. 2 (2011): 231–52.

Antunes, Clovis. *Índios de Alagoas: Documentário.* Maceió: N.p., 1984.

Aquino, Aécio Villar de. "Quilombos e remanescentes de quilombos na Paraíba." In *Os quilombos na dinâmica social do Brasil,* edited by Clóvis Moura, 255–70. Maceió: Editora da Universidade Federal de Alagoas, 2001.

Araujo, Ana Lucia. "Dandara e Luísa Mahin não são reais." *Intercept Brasil,* June 3, 2019.

Araujo, Ana Lucia. *Reparations for Slavery and the Slave Trade: A Transnational and Comparative History.* London: Bloomsbury Academic, 2017.

Araújo, Denílson da Silva. *Dinâmica econômica, urbanização e metropolização no Rio Grande do Norte (1940–2006).* Recife: Fundação Joaquim Nabuco, Editora Massangana, 2010.

Araújo, Pedro Pinheiro de, Júnior. "'Não é terra de préstimo e nunca foi povoada': A territorialização dos sertões do Cabo de São Roque (1500–1719)." Master's thesis, Universidade Federal do Rio Grande do Norte, 2019.

Araújo, Rodrigo Wantuir Alves de. "A invisibilidade africana na historiografia do Rio Grande do Norte." Paper presented at the XVIII Semana de Humanidades, Natal (Brazil), June 7–9, 2010. Accessed July 5, 2023. http://www.cchla.ufrn.br/shXVIII/artigos/GT17/Rodrigo%20Wantuir%20GT%2017.pdf.

Arora, Shirley L. "Brasil acucareiro [sic]." *Abstracts of Folklore Studies* 12, no. 1 (Spring 1974): 17–23. https://catalog.hathitrust.org/Record/004354212.

Arruti, José Maurício Andion. "A emergência dos 'remanescentes': Notas para o diálogo entre indígenas e quilombolas." *Mana* 3, no. 2 (1997): 7–38.

Assunção, Luiz. *Jatobá: Ancestralidade negra e identidade*. Natal: Editora da Universidade Federal do Rio Grande do Norte, 2009.

Assunção, Luiz. *Os negros do Riacho: Estratégias de sobrevivência e identidade social*. Natal: Editora da Universidade Federal do Rio Grande do Norteu, 2009.

Assunção, Matthias Röhrig. "Quilombos maranhenses." In *Liberdade por um fio*, edited by João José Reis and Flávio dos Santos Gomes, 433–66. São Paulo: Companhia das Letras, 2019.

Augusto, José. "Famílias nordestinas." *Revista do Instituto do Ceará* 55 (1941): 189–204.

Baerle, Caspar van. *The History of Brazil under the Governorship of Count Johan Maurits of Nassau, 1636-1644*. Translated by Blanche T. van Berckel-Ebeling Koning. Gainesville: University Press of Florida, 2011.

Baião, Domingos Vieira. *Elementos de gramática Ganguela: Idioma falada na região do Cubango, província de Angola*. Lisbon: Centro dos Estudos Filológicos, 1938.

Ball, Erica, Melina Pappademos, and Michelle Stephens, eds. "Reconceptualizations of the African Diaspora." Special issue, *Radical History Review* 9, no. 103 (Winter 2003).

Barbosa, Virgínia. "Bernardo Vieira de Melo." *Pesquisa Escolar Online, Fundação Joaquim Nabuco*. Accessed July 6, 2023. http://basilio.fundaj.gov.br/pesquisaescolar/index.php?option=com_content&id=494.

Barbosa, Waldemar de Almeida. *Negros e quilombos em Minas Gerais*. Belo Horizonte: N.p., 1972.

Barcia, Manuel. *West African Warfare in Bahia and Cuba: Soldier Slaves in the Atlantic World, 1807-1844*. New York: Oxford University Press, 2016.

Barnet, Miguel. *Biography of a Runaway Slave*. Revised edition. Edited by Miguel Barnet and translated by W. Nick Hill. Willimantic, CT: Curbstone Press, 1994.

Barnet, Miguel. *Cimarrón: Historia de un esclavo*. Madrid: Ediciones Siruela, 2002.

Barragan, Yesenia. *Freedom's Captives: Slavery and Gradual Emancipation on the Colombian Black Pacific*. Cambridge: Cambridge University Press, 2021.

Barreto, Annibal. *Fortificações do Brasil: Resumo histórico*. Rio de Janeiro: Biblioteca do Exército, 1958.

Basso, Keith H. *Wisdom Sits in Places: Landscape and Language among the Western Apache*. Albuquerque: University of New Mexico Press, 1996.

Basso, Renato Miguel, and Rodrigo Tadeu Gonçalves. *História concisa da língua portuguesa*. Petrópolis Brazil: Editora Vozes, 2014.

Bastide, Roger. *The African Religions of Brazil: Toward a Sociology of the Interpenetration of Civilizations.* Translated by Helen Sebba. Baltimore: Johns Hopkins University Press, 2007.

Bastide, Roger. *O candomblé da Bahia: Rito nagô.* São Paulo: Companhia das Letras, 2001.

Bastide, Roger. *Diálogo entre filhos de Xangô: Correspondência 1947-1974.* São Paulo: EDUSP, 2017.

Bastide, Roger. "L'Islam Noir à Bahia d'après les Travaux de l'école Ethnologique Brèsilienne." *Revista de História* (Universidade de São Paulo) 2, no. 5 (1951): 212-15.

Batalha, Ladislau. *Costumes angolenses.* Lisbon: Companhia Nacional Editora, 1890. http://hdl.handle.net/2027/wu.89012189338.

Battel, Andrew, Ernest George Ravenstein, Samuel Purchas, and Anthony Knivet. *The Strange Adventures of Andrew Battell of Leigh, in Angola and the Adjoining Regions.* London: Hakluyt Society, 1901. Accessed June 27, 2023. https://archive.org/details/strangeadventureoobattrich.

Batulukisi, Niangi. "Framed Figure, Holo, Zaire." In *Visions of Africa: The Jerome L. Joss Collection of African Art at UCLA,* edited by Doran H. Ross, 116-17. Los Angeles: Fowler Museum of Cultural History, University of California, Los Angeles, 1994.

Beaurepaire-Rohan, Henrique de Visconde. *Diccionario de vocabulos brazileiros pelo tenente-general Visconde de Beaurepaire-Rohan [. . .]* Rio de Janeiro: Imprensa Nacional, 1889.

"Bello Horizonte: Memoria historica e descriptiva—documentos." *Revista do Arquivo Público Mineiro* 23 (1929): 215-305. Accessed June 28, 2023. http://www.siaapm.cultura.mg.gov.br/modules/rapm/brtacervo.php?cid=669.

Bennett, Herman L. *African Kings and Black Slaves: Sovereignty and Dispossession in the Early Modern Atlantic.* Philadelphia: University of Pennsylvania Press, 2018.

Bentley, W. Holman (William Holman). *Dictionary and Grammar of the Kongo Language: As Spoken at San Salvador, the Ancient Capital of the Old Kongo Empire, West Africa.* Baptist Missionary Society, 1887.

Bentley, W. Holman (William Holman). *Life on the Congo.* London: Religious Tract Society, 1887. http://archive.org/details/lifeoncongooobentiala.

Bergad, Laird W. *Slavery and the Demographic and Economic History of Minas Gerais, 1720-1888.* New York: Cambridge University Press, 1999.

Berry, Chelsea L. "Poisoned Relations: Medicine, Sorcery, and Poison Trials in the Contested Atlantic, 1680-1850." PhD diss., Georgetown University, 2019.

Bethell, Leslie. *Brazil: Essays on History and Politics.* London: Institute of Latin American Studies, School of Advanced Study, University of London, 2018. Accessed May 18, 2023.

Beyer, Klaus. "Morphology." In *The Oxford Handbook of African Languages,* edited by Rainer Vossen and Gerrit Jan Dimmendaal, 48-65. New York: Oxford University Press, 2020.

Bezerra Neto, José Maia. "Fugindo, sempre fugindo: Escravidão, fugas escravas e fugitivos no Grão-Pará (1840–1888)." Master's thesis, Universidade Estadual de Campinas, 2000.

Birmingham, David. "The Date and Significance of the Imbangala Invasion of Angola." *Journal of African History* 6, no. 2 (1965): 143–52.

Blakely, Allison. *Blacks in the Dutch World: The Evolution of Racial Imagery in a Modern Society.* Bloomington: Indiana University Press, 1993.

Blanchard, Peter. *Under the Flags of Freedom: Slave Soldiers and the Wars of Independence in Spanish South America.* Pittsburgh: University of Pittsburgh Press, 2008.

Bledsoe, Adam. "Marronage as a Past and Present Geography in the Americas." *Southeastern Geographer* 57, no. 1 (Spring 2017): 30–50.

Bluteau, Rafael. *Vocabulario portuguez, e latino,* [. . .] *autorizado com exemplos dos melhores escritores portuguezes, e latinos* [. . .] *pelo padre D. Raphael Bluteau* [. . .], 8 vols. Coimbra: Collegio das Artes da Companhia de Jesus, 1712–21. Accessed May 15, 2023. https://catalog.hathitrust.org/Record /010823632.

Bogues, Anthony. *Empire of Liberty: Power, Desire, and Freedom.* Hanover, NH: Dartmouth College Press, 2010.

Bonvini, Emilio. "Os vocábulos de origem africana na constituição do português falado no Brasil." In *África no Brasil: A formação da língua portuguesa,* edited by José Luiz Fiorin and Margarida Petter, 101–44. São Paulo: Editora Contexto, 2008.

Borborema, Ana Cláudia Bezerra de Albuquerque, Henrique José Lins Ferreira de Andrade, and Lucilene Antunes Correia Marques de Sá. "Da cartografia dos antigos engenhos à cartografia holandesa e portuguesa." Paper presented at the 1º Simpósio Brasileiro de Cartografia Histórica, Paraty, May 10–14, 2011.

Bordoni, Orlando. *A língua tupi na geografia do Brasil.* Campinas, SP: S.N., 1983.

Borucki, Alex. *From Shipmates to Soldiers: Emerging Black Identities in the Río de La Plata.* Albuquerque: University of New Mexico Press, 2015.

Bostoen, Koen. "Bantu Spirantization: Morphologization, Lexicalization and Historical Classification." *Diachronica* 25, no. 3 (2008): 299–356.

Bostoen, Koen A. G., and Inge Brinkman. *The Kongo Kingdom: The Origins, Dynamics and Cosmopolitan Culture of an African Polity.* Cambridge: Cambridge University Press, 2018.

Bostoen, Koen, and Gilles-Maurice de Schryver. "Seventeenth-Century Kikongo Is Not the Ancestor of Present-Day Kikongo." In *The Kongo Kingdom,* edited by Koen A. G. Bostoen and Inge Brinkman, 60–102. Cambridge: Cambridge University Press, 2018.

Bostoen, Koen, Odjas Ndonda Tshiyayi, and Gilles-Maurice de Schryver. "On the Origin of the Royal Kongo Title Ngangula." *Africana Linguistica,* no. 19 (2013): 53–83. Accessed June 27, 2023. https://www.persee.fr/doc/aflin _2033-8732_2013_num_19_1_1017.

Bowen, Merle. *For Land and Liberty: Black Struggles in Rural Brazil.* Cambridge: Cambridge University Press, 2021.

Boxer, Charles Ralph. *The Dutch in Brazil, 1624–1654.* Oxford: Clarendon Press, 1957.

Boxer, Charles Ralph. *The Golden Age of Brazil, 1695–1750: Growing Pains of a Colonial Society.* Berkeley: University of California Press, 1962.

Brandão, Alfredo. "Documentos antigos sobre a guerra dos negros palmarinos." In *O negro no Brasil: Trabalhos apresentados ao 2º Congresso Afro-Brasileiro (Bahia)*, 275–89. Rio de Janeiro: Civilização Brasileira, 1940.

Brandão, Alfredo. *Os negros na história de Alagoas.* Maceió: EDICULTE, 1988.

Brandão, Alfredo. "Os negros na historia de Alagôas." In *Estudos afro-brasileiros: Trabalhos apresentados ao 1º Congresso Afro-Brasileiro reunido no Recife em 1934*, 55–92. Rio de Janeiro: Ariel, 1935.

Brandão, Alfredo. *Viçosa de Alagoas: O municipio e a cidade (notas historicas, geographicas e archeologicas).* Recife: Imprensa Industrial, 1914.

Brasil, Eric. "Cucumbis carnavalescos: Áfricas, carnaval e abolição (Rio de Janeiro, Década de 1880)." *Afro-Ásia* 49 (2014): 273–312.

Brásio, António, ed. *Monumenta missionária africana.* 15 vols. Lisbon: Agência-Geral do Ultramar, 1952–68. Accessed June 27, 2023. https://archive.org/details/monumentamissionariaafricana/MonumentaMission%C3%A1ria Africana-01.001/.

Brewer-García, Larissa. *Beyond Babel: Translations of Blackness in Colonial Peru and New Granada.* Cambridge: Cambridge University Press, 2020.

Brewer-García, Larissa. "Hierarchy and Holiness in the Earliest Colonial Black Hagiographies: Alonso de Sandoval and His Sources." *William and Mary Quarterly* 76, no. 3 (July 2019): 477–508.

Brienen, Rebecca Parker. *Visions of Savage Paradise: Albert Eckhout, Court Painter in Colonial Dutch Brazil.* Amsterdam: Amsterdam University Press, 2006. Accessed May 18, 2023.

Broadus, Victoria R. "*Vissungo*: The Afro-Descended Culture of Miners and Maroons in Brazil's Diamond District." PhD diss., Georgetown University, 2023.

Brown, Alexandra K. "'A Black Mark on Our Legislation': Slavery, Punishment, and the Politics of Death in Nineteenth-Century Brazil." *Luso-Brazilian Review* 37, no. 2 (2000): 95–121.

Brown, Ras Michael. *African-Atlantic Cultures and the South Carolina Lowcountry.* New York: Cambridge University Press, 2012.

Brown, Ras Michael. "'Walk in the Feenda': West-Central Africans and the Forest in the South Carolina-Georgia Lowcountry." In *Central Africans and Cultural Transformations in the American Diaspora*, edited by Linda M. Heywood, 289–317. Cambridge: Cambridge University Press, 2002.

Brown, Vincent. *The Reaper's Garden: Death and Power in the World of Atlantic Slavery.* Cambridge, MA: Harvard University Press, 2007.

Brown, Vincent. "Spiritual Terror and Sacred Authority in Jamaican Slave Society." *Slavery and Abolition* 24, no. 1 (April 2003): 24–53.

Brown, Vincent. *Tacky's Revolt: The Story of an Atlantic Slave War*. Cambridge, MA: Belknap Press, 2020.

Brügger, Silvia, and Anderson de Oliveira. "Os Benguelas de São João del Rei: Tráfico atlântico, religiosidade e identidades étnicas (séculos XVII e XIX)." *Tempo (Niterói)* 26 (2009): 177–204.

Brusciotto, Giacinto. *Grammar of the Congo Language as Spoken Two Hundred Years Ago*. Translated by James Mew. Hodder and Stoughton, 1882. Accessed June 27, 2023. https://www.google.co.jp/books/edition/Grammar _of_the_Congo_Language_as_Spoken/KIoCAAAAQAAJ?hl=en&gbpv =1&pg=PR1&printsec=frontcover.

Burness, Don. "From the Boundaries of Storytelling to the History of a People." In *Celebrating the 60th Anniversary of "Things Fall Apart*," edited by Désiré Baloubi and Christina R. Pinkston, 11–20. Cham, Switzerland: Palgrave Macmillan, 2021.

Butler, Kim D. "Defining Diaspora, Refining a Discourse." *Diaspora* 10, no. 2 (2001): 189–219.

Butler, Kim D. "Multilayered Politics in the African Diaspora: The Metadiaspora Concept and Minidiaspora Realities." In *Opportunity Structures in Diaspora Relations: Comparisons in Contemporary Multilevel Politics of Diaspora and Transnational Identity*, edited by Gloria P. Totoricaguena, 19–51. Reno: Center for Basque Studies, University of Nevada, 2007.

Butler, Kim D. "Slavery in the Age of Emancipation: Victims and Rebels in Brazil's Late 19th-Century Domestic Trade." *Journal of Black Studies* 42, no. 6 (September 2011): 968–92.

Cabral, Ana Suelly A. C., Aryon Dall'Igna Rodrigues, and Fábio Bonfim Duarte, eds. *Línguas e culturas Tupí*. Campinas: Editora Curt Nimuendajú, 2007.

Cabral, João Francisco Dias. "Narração de alguns successos relativos a Guerra dos Palmares de 1668 a 1680." *Revista do Instituto Archeológico e Geographico Alagoano* 1, no. 7 (December 1875): 165–71.

Cabral, João Francisco Dias. "Vestigios de uma antiga familia estabelecida no territorio de Santa Maria Magdalena da Lagoa do Sul." *Revista do Instituto Archeológico e Geographico Alagoano* 2, no. 11 (December 1879): 14–18.

Cadornega, António de Oliveira de. *História geral das guerras angolanas, 1680*. Edited by José Matias Delgado. 3 vols. Lisboa: Agência-Geral do Ultramar, 1972.

Cadornega, António de Oliveira de. *História das guerras de Angola*. 3 vols. Manuscrito. Academia das Ciências de Lisboa, 1680.

Calainho, Daniela Buono. "Mandingueiros negros no mundo atlântico moderno." *Transhumante* 16 (2020): 10–32. Accessed June 28, 2023. https://revistas.udea .edu.co/index.php/trashumante/article/view/342692/20803908.

Calainho, Daniela Buono. *Metrópole das mandingas: Religiosidade negra e Inquisição Portuguesa no Antigo Regime*. Rio de Janeiro: Garamond, 2008.

Camara, Andréa Albuquerque Adour da. "Vissungo: O cantar banto nas Américas." PhD diss., Universidade Federal de Minas Gerais, 2013.

Camp, Stephanie H. M. *Closer to Freedom: Enslaved Women and Everyday Resistance in the Plantation South*. Chapel Hill: University of North Carolina Press, 2004. Accessed May 18, 2023. http://ebookcentral.proquest.com/lib /uiuc/detail.action?docID=413243.

Candido, Mariana. *An African Slaving Port and the Atlantic World: Benguela and Its Hinterland*. Cambridge: Cambridge University Press, 2013.

Candido, Mariana P. "South Atlantic Exchanges: The Role of Brazilian-Born Agents in Benguela, 1650–1850." *Luso-Brazilian Review* 50, no. 1 (2013): 53–82.

Cannecattim, Bernardo Maria de. *Collecção de observações grammaticaes sobre a lingua bunda, ou angolense*. Lisboa, 1805. Accessed July 7, 2023. https://hdl .handle.net/2027/nyp.33433069249138.

Cannecattim, Bernardo Maria de. *Diccionario da lingua bunda ou angolense, explicada na portugueza e latina*. Lisboa, 1804. Accessed July 7, 2023. https://hdl .handle.net/2027/hvd.hxj4az.

Capela, José. "Mozambique and Brazil: Cultural and Political Interferences through the Slave Trade." In *Africa and the Americas*, edited by José C. Curto and Renée Soulodre-La France, 243–58. Trenton, NJ: Africa World Press, 2005.

Capelo, H., and R. Ivens. *De Benguella ás terras de Iácca: Descripção de uma viagem na Africa Central e Occidental*. 2 vols. Lisbon: Imprensa Nacional, 1881. Accessed July 6, 2023. http://library.si.edu/digital-library/book /debenguellasterro1cape.

Carlin, Eithne B., and Jacques Arends, eds. *Atlas of the Languages of Suriname*. Leiden: KITLV Press, 2002.

Carneiro, Andrea Flávia Tenório, and Sue Nichols. "Demarcação de territórios quilombolas: A questão técnica e seus impactos sociais." In *O Incra e os desafios para a regularização dos territórios quilombolas: Algumas experiências*, edited by Rui Leandro da Silva Santos and Renata Leite, 143–58. Brasília: Instituto Nacional de Colonização e Reforma Agrária, 2006.

Carneiro, Antônio Joaquim de Souza. *Os mitos africanos no Brasil: Ciencia do folklore*. São Paulo: Companhia Editora Nacional, 1937.

Carneiro, Edison. *O Quilombo dos Palmares*. 5th ed. São Paulo: W. M. F. Martins Fonte, 2011.

"Cartas do Conde de Assumar ao Rei de Portugal." *Revista do Arquivo Público Mineiro* 3 (1898): 251–56. Accessed June 28, 2023. http://www.siaapm.cultura .mg.gov.br/modules/rapm/brtacervo.php?cid=117.

Carvalho, Henrique Augusto Dias de. *Ethnographia e historia tradicional dos povos da Lunda*. Lisbon: Imprensa Nacional, 1890. http://archive.org/details /ethnographiaehisoodias.

Carvalho, Juliano Loureiro de. "Formação territorial da mata paraibana, 1750–1808." Master's thesis, Universidade Federal da Bahia, 2008.

Carvalho, Marcus J. M. de. "Os índios e o ciclo das insurreições liberais em Pernambuco (1817–1848): Ideologias e resistência." In *Indios do Nordeste: Temas e problemas*, Vol. 3, edited by Luiz Sávio de Almeida and Marcos Galindo, 67–96. Maceió: Editora da Universidade Federal de Alagoas, 2002.

Carvalho, Marcus J. M. de. *Liberdade: Rotinas e rupturas do escravismo no Recife, 1822–1850*. 2nd ed. Recife: Editora Universitária da Universidade Federal de Pernambuco, 2010.

Carvalho, Marcus J. M. de. "Negros da terra e negros da Guiné: Os termos de uma troca, 1535–1630." *Revista do Instituto Histórico e Geográfico Brasilero* 161, no. 408 (September 2000): 329–42.

Carvalho, Marcus J. M. de. "O Quilombo do Catucá em Pernambuco." *Caderno CRH*, 4, no. 15 (December 1991): 5–28.

Carvalho, Marcus J. M. de. "O Quilombo de Malunguinho, o rei das matas de Pernambuco." In *Liberdade por um fio: História dos quilombos no Brasil*, edited by João José Reis and Flávio dos Santos Gomes, 407–33. São Paulo: Companhia das Letras, 1996.

Carvalho, Marcus J. M. de, and Anna Laura Teixeira de França. "Palmares, a Cabanada, a 'gente das matas.'" In *Mocambos de Palmares: Histórias e fontes (séc. XVI–XIX)*, edited by Flávio dos Santos Gomes, 131–48. Rio de Janeiro: 7Letras, 2010.

Carvalho, Maria Rosário de, Edwin Reesink, and Julie Cavignac, eds. *Negros no mundo dos índios: Imagens, reflexos, alteridades*. Natal: Editora da Universidade Federal de Rio Grande do Norte, 2011.

Carvalho Franco, Francisco de Assis. *Dicionário de bandeirantes e sertanistas do Brasil: Séculos XVI–XVII–XVIII*. São Paulo: Comissão do IV Centenário da Cidade de São Paulo, Serviço de Comemorações Culturais, 1954.

Cascudo, Luís da Câmara. *Dicionário do folclore brasileiro*. 12th ed. São Paulo: Global, 2012.

Cascudo, Luís da Câmara. *Geografia dos mitos brasileiros*. 3rd ed. São Paulo: Global Editora, 2010.

Cascudo, Luís da Câmara. *História do Rio Grande do Norte*. Rio de Janeiro: Ministério da Educação e Cultura, Serviço de Documentação, 1955.

Cascudo, Luís da Câmara. *Lendas brasileiras*. 5th ed. Rio de Janeiro: Edições de Ouro, 2002.

Cascudo, Luís da Câmara. *Made in Africa (pesquisas e notas)*. 5th ed. São Paulo: Global Editora, 2001.

Cascudo, Luís da Câmara. *Nomes da terra: Geografia, história e toponímia do Rio Grande do Norte*. Coleção Cultura. Natal: Fundação José Augusto, 1968.

Casimir, Jean. *The Haitians: A Decolonial History*. Translated by Laurent DuBois. Chapel Hill: University of North Carolina Press, 2020.

Castro, Eugenio de. *Ensaios de geographia linguistica*. 2nd ed. São Paulo: Companhia Editora Nacional, 1941.

Castro, José Guilherme da Cunha. *Miguel Santana*. Salvador: Editora da Universidade Federal da Bahia, 1996.

Castro, Yeda Pessoa de. *Falares africanos na Bahia: Um vocabulário afro-brasileiro.* Rio de Janeiro: Academia Brasileira de Letras, 2001.

Cavalcanti, Alfredo Leite. *História de Garanhuns.* 2nd ed. Recife: Centro de Estudos de História Municipal, 1983.

Cavalcanti, Archimedes. *A cidade de Parahyba na época da Independência: Aspectos sócio-econômicos, culturais e urbanísticos em volta de 1822.* João Pessoa: Imprensa Universitária, 1972.

Cavazzi da Montecuccolo, Giovanni Antonio. *Descrição histórica dos três reinos do Congo, Matamba e Angola.* Translated by Graciano Maria de Leguzzano. 2 vols. Lisbon: Junta de Investigações do Ultramar, 1965.

Cavazzi da Montecuccolo, Giovanni Antonio. *Istorica descrizione de' tre' regni Congo, Matamba et Angola: Situati nell'Etiopia inferiore occidentale e delle missioni apostoliche esercitatevi da religiosi Capuccini.* Bologna: Giacomo Monti, 1687. Accessed May 24, 2023. http://archive.org/details/istoricadescrizioocava.

Cavazzi da Montecuccolo, Giovanni Antonio. *Missione Evangelica al Regno de Congo* (1668). Translated by John Thornton, n.d. Accessed May 24, 2023. http://www.bu.edu/afam/faculty/john-thornton/john-thorntons-african-texts/.

Cavignac, Julie. "Índios, negros e caboclos: Identidades e fronteiras étnicas em perspectiva. O caso do Rio Grande do Norte." In *Negros no mundo dos índios: Imagens, reflexos, alteridades,* edited by Franco Carvalho, Edwin Reesink, and Julir Cavignac, 195–244. Natal: Editora da Universidade Federal de Rio Grande do Norte, 2011.

Cavignac, Julie, Cyro Holando de Almeida Lins, Stéphanie Campos Paiva Moreira, and Augusto Carlos de Oliveira Maux. *Uma Sibaúma só! Relatório antropológico da Comunidade Quilombola de Sibaúma (RN).* Natal: Instituto Nacional de Colonização e Reforma Agrária, Departamento de Antropologia da Universidade Federal do Rio Grande do Norte, 2016.

Cavignac, Julie, Muirakytan K. de Macêdo, and José Clewton do Nascimento. *Guia cultural afro do Seridó.* Natal: Troncos, Ramos e Raízes, 2018.

Cavignac, Julie Antoinette, José Antônio Fernandes de Melo, Gilson José Rodrigues Junior, and Sebastião Genicarlos dos Santos. *Relatório Antropológico da Comunidade Quilombola de Boa Vista (RN).* Natal: Convênio Universidade Federal do Rio Grande do Norte/Instituto Nacional de Colonização e Reforma Agrária-RN, 2007.

Chambers, Douglas B. "'My Own Nation': Igbo Exiles in the Diaspora." In *Routes to Slavery: Direction, Ethnicity and Mortality in the Atlantic Slave Trade,* edited by David Eltis and David Richardson, 72–97. London: Frank Cass, 1997.

Chambers, Douglas B. "Rejoinder—The Significance of Igbo in the Bight of Biafra Slave-Trade: A Rejoinder to Northrup's 'Myth Igbo.'" *Slavery and Abolition* 23, no. 1 (2002): 101–20.

Chambers, Douglas B. "Tracing Igbo into the African Diaspora." In *Identity in the Shadow of Slavery,* edited by Paul E. Lovejoy, 55–71. New York: Continuum, 2000.

Chapman, C. E. "Palmares: The Negro Numantia." *Journal of Negro History* 3 (1918): 29–32.

Chatelain, Héli. *Folk-Tales of Angola: Fifty Tales, with Ki-Mbundu Text, Literal English Translation [. . .].* Published for the American Folk-lore Society by Houghton Mifflin and Company, 1894. http://archive.org/details /folktalesangolaoochatgoog.

Chatelain, Héli. *Kimbundu Grammar: Grammatica elementar do Kimbundu ou lingua de Angola.* Genebra, Typ. de C. Schuchardt, 1888. http://archive.org /details/kimbundugrammaroochatgoog.

Cheney, Glenn Alan. *Quilombo dos Palmares: Brazil's Lost Nation of Fugitive Slaves.* Hanover, CT: New London Librarium, 2014.

"Circumstancias sobre diversas aldeias e missões de Indios, que desde annos remotos existem na provincia das Alagoas." *Revista do Instituto Archeológico e Geographico Alagoano* 1, no. 4 (June 1874): 93–96.

Colson, Elizabeth. "Places of Power and Shrines of the Land." *Paideuma* 43 (1997): 47–57.

Commander, Michelle D. *Afro-Atlantic Flight: Speculative Returns and the Black Fantastic.* Durham, NC: Duke University Press, 2017.

Conrad, Robert Edgar. *The Destruction of Brazilian Slavery, 1850–1888.* Berkeley: University of California Press, 1972.

Conselho Deliberativo do Memorial Zumbi. "Memorial Zumbi: Um informe à sociedade brasileira para o progresso da ciência (SBPC)." In *Cultura em movimento: Matrizes africanas e ativismo negro no Brasil,* edited by Elisa Larkin Nascimento, 217–228 (of 389). São Paulo: Selo Negro, 2014. Kindle edition.

Correia, Rosa Lucia Lima da Silva. "Como os nêgos dos Palmares: Uma nova história de resistência na Serra da Barriga-AL." PhD diss., Universidade Federal do Pará, 2016.

Costa, Emilia Viotti da. *The Brazilian Empire: Myths and Histories.* Revised ed. Chapel Hill: University of North Carolina Press, 2000.

Costa, Francisco Augusto Pereira da. *Anais pernambucanos.* 2nd ed. 11 vols. Recife: Governo de Pernambuco, 1983.

Costa, Francisco Augusto Pereira da. *Arredores do Recife.* 2nd ed. Recife: Funda-ção Joaquim Nabuco/Editora Massangana, 2001.

Costa, Francisco Augusto Pereira da. *Vocabulário pernambucano.* 2nd ed. Recife: Governo do Estado de Pernambuco, Secretaria de Educação e Cultura, 1976.

Costa, Valéria Gomes. "Trajetórias negras: Os libertos da Costa d'África no Recife (1846–1890)." PhD diss., Universidade Federal da Bahia, 2013.

Couto, Antonio do. *Gentio de Angola svfficientemente instruido nos mysterios de nossa Sancta Fé [. . .].* Lisbon: D. Lopes Rosa, 1642. Accessed May 30, 2023. http://hdl.handle.net/2027/chi.16997936.

Cronon, William. "A Place for Stories: Nature, History, and Narrative." *Journal of American History* 79, no. 3 (March 1992): 1347–76.

Crowley, Terry, and Claire Bowern. *An Introduction to Historical Linguistics.* 4th ed. Oxford: Oxford University Press, 2010.

Cruz, Carlos Henrique. *A escola do diabo: Indígenas e capuchinhos italianos nos sertões da América (1680-1761).* Florence: Firenze University Press, 2019.

Cruz, João Everton da. "Frei Damião: A figura do conselheiro no catolicismo popular do Nordeste brasileiro." Master's thesis, Pontifícia Universidade Católica de Minas Gerais, 2010.

Cunha, Manuela Carneiro da, ed. *Legislação indigenista no século XIX: Uma compilação (1808-1889).* São Paulo: Comissão Pró-índio de São Paulo, 1992.

Cunha, Olívia Maria Gomes da. *The Things of Others: Ethnographies, Histories, and Other Artefacts.* Leiden: Brill, 2020.

Curto, José C., and Renée Soulodre-La France, eds. *Africa and the Americas: Interconnections during the Slave Trade.* Trenton, NJ: Africa World Press, 2005.

Curvelo, Maely Carlos da Silva. "O direito à educação quilombola: Quilombolas, escolas e projetos políticos pedagógicos em Bom Conselho-PE." Undergraduate thesis, Universidade Federal Rural de Pernambuco, 2018.

Damasceno, Felipe Aguiar. "Direitos de propriedade em terras rebeldes: As sesmarias dos Palmares de Pernambuco, 1678-1775." *Ler História*, no. 70 (September 15, 2017): 95-119.

Damasceno, Felipe Aguiar. "A ocupação das terras dos Palmares de Pernambuco (séculos XVII e XVIII)." PhD diss., Universidade Federal do Rio de Janeiro, 2018.

Dantas, Manoel. *Denominação dos municipios (Rio Grande do Norte).* 2nd ed. Natal: Sebo Vermelho Edições, 2008.

Dantas, Mariana Albuquerque. "Do aldeamento do Riacho do Mato à Colônia Socorro: Defesa de terras e aprendizado político dos indígenas de Pernambuco (1860-1880)." *Revista Brasileira de História* 38, no. 77 (2018): 81-102.

Dantas, Mariana Albuquerque. *Dimensões da participação política indígena: Estado nacional e revoltas em Pernambuco e Alagoas (1817-1848).* Rio de Janeiro: Arquivo Nacional, 2018.

Dantas, Mariana L. R. "'For the Benefit of the Common Good': Regiments of Cacadores do Mato in Minas Gerais, Brazil." *Journal of Colonialism and Colonial History* 5, no. 2 (2004).

Dantas, Mariana L. R. "Humble Slaves and Loyal Vassals: Free Africans and Their Descendants in Eighteenth-Century Minas Gerais, Brazil." In *Imperial Subjects: Race and Identity in Colonial Latin America,* edited by Andrew B. Fischer and Matthew D. O'Hara, 115-40. Durham, NC: Duke University Press, 2009.

Dawson, Kevin. *Undercurrents of Power: Aquatic Culture in the African Diaspora.* Philadelphia: University of Pennsylvania Press, 2018. Kindle edition.

de la Fuente, Alejandro, and George Reid Andrews, eds. *Afro-Latin American Studies: An Introduction.* Cambridge: Cambridge University Press, 2018.

de la Torre, Oscar. *The People of the River: Nature and Identity in Black Amazonia, 1835-1945.* Chapel Hill: University of North Carolina Press, 2018.

de la Torre, Oscar. "The Well That Wept Blood: Ghostlore, Haunted Water-scapes, and the Politics of *Quilombo* Blackness in Amazonia (Brazil)." *American Historical Review* 127, no. 4 (December 2022): 1635–58.

Delfino, Leonara Lacerda. "O culto dos mortos da nobre nação de Benguela na experiência devocional do Rosário dos Homens Pretos São João Del-Rei, MG (1793–1850)." *Afro-Ásia* 58 (2018): 9–49.

Delfino, Leonara Lacerda. "O Rosário dos Irmãos Escravos e Libertos: Fronteiras, identidades e representações do viver e morrer na diáspora atlântica, freguesia do Pilar-São João Del-Rei (1782–1850)." PhD diss., Universidade Federal de Juiz de Fora, 2015.

DeLucia, Christine M. *Memory Lands: King Philip's War and the Place of Violence in the Northeast*. New Haven, CT: Yale University Press, 2018.

de Luna, Kathryn M. "Bantu Expansion." In *Oxford Bibliographies: African Studies* (online), November 25, 2014.

de Luna, Kathryn M. *The Long African Atlantic*. Forthcoming.

de Luna, Kathryn M. "Sounding the African Atlantic." *William and Mary Quarterly* 78, no. 4 (October 2021): 581–616.

de Luna, Kathryn M., and Jeffrey B. Fleisher. *Speaking with Substance: Methods of Language and Materials in African History*. Cham, Switzerland: Springer, 2018.

Dennett, R. E. (Richard Edward). *Notes on the Folklore of the Fjort (French Congo)*. London: Published for the Folk-lore Society, 1898. http://archive.org /details/cu31924006487999.

Derby, Robin. "Zemis and Zombies: Amerindian Healing Legacies on Hispaniola." In *Medicine and Healing in the Age of Slavery*, edited by Sean Morey Smith and Christopher Willoughby, 21–44. Baton Rouge: Louisiana State University Press, 2021.

Desch-Obi, T. J. "Combat and the Crossing of the Kalunga." In *Central Africans and Cultural Transformations in the American Diaspora*, edited by Linda M. Heyward, 353–70. Cambridge: Cambridge University Press, 2002.

Desch-Obi, T. J. *Fighting for Honor: The History of African Martial Art Traditions in the Atlantic World*. Columbia: University of South Carolina Press, 2008.

Devine Guzmán, Tracy. *Native and National in Brazil: Indigeneity after Independence*. Chapel Hill: University of North Carolina Press, 2013.

Dias, Alfredo Gomes, and Augusto do Nascimento Diniz. "Os Angolares: Da autonomia à inserção na sociedade colonial (segunda metade do século XIX)." *Ler História*, no. 13 (1988): 53–75. Accessed June 22, 2023. https:// journals.openedition.org/lerhistoria/1794.

Dias, Dayane Julia Carvalho, and Carmen Margarida Oliveira Alveal. "Um estudo preliminar da demografia do Rio Grande do Norte colonial: Fontes, métodos e resultados." *Revista Brasileira de Estudos de População* 34, no. 3 (2017): 485–507.

Dias, João de Deus de Oliveira. *A terra dos Garanhuns*. Garanhuns, 1954.

Dias, Patrícia de Oliveira. "Onde fica o sertão rompem-se as águas: Processo de territorialização da Ribeira do Apodi-Mossoró (1676–1725)." Master's thesis, Universidade Federal do Rio Grande do Norte, 2015.

Dias, Pedro. *Arte da lingua de Angola: Oeferecida a virgem Senhora N. do Rosario, mãy 4, Senhora dos mesmos pretos.* Lisbon: Officina de Miguel Deslandes, 1697. https://archive.org/details/artedalinguadeanoodias.

Diegues, Antonio. "Água e cultura nas populações tradicionais brasileiras." In *Governança da água no Brasil: Uma visão interdisciplinar,* edited by Wagner Costa Ribeiro and Ana Paula Fracalanza, 13–34. São Paulo: Annablume and FAPESP, 2009.

Diegues, Carlos, dir. *Ganga Zumba: Rei dos Palmares.* DVD. Rio de Janeiro: Globo Video, 1980.

Diegues, Carlos, dir. *Quilombo.* DVD. New York: New Yorker Video, 2005.

Diégues, Manuel, Júnior. *O bangüê nas Alagoas: Traços da influência do sistema econômico do engenho de açúcar na vida e na cultura regional.* Maceió: Editora da Universidade Federal de Alagoas, 1980.

Diggs, Irene. "Zumbi and the Republic of Os Palmares." *Phylon,* 14, no. 1 (1953): 62–70.

Diouf, Sylviane A. *Slavery's Exiles: The Story of the American Maroons.* New York: New York University Press, 2014.

Documentação histórica pernambucana (sesmarias). 4 vols. Recife: Secretaria de Educação e Cultura, 1959.

Douville, J. B. "Voyage au Congo et dans l'interieur de l'Afrique Enquinnoxiale, Fait dans les Années 1828, 1829 et 1830." *Foreign Quarterly Review* 10 (August and October 1832): 163–206. Accessed May 28, 2023. https://catalog .hathitrust.org/Record/006057547.

D'Salete, Marcelo. *Angola Janga: Kingdom of Runaway Slaves.* Translated by Andrea Rosenberg. Seattle, WA: Fantagraphics, 2019.

Duarte, Abelardo. "Tribos, aldeias e missões de índios nas Alagoas." *Revista do Instituto Histórico de Alagoas* 28 (1969): 83–153.

Dutra, Francis A. "African Heritage and the Portuguese Military Orders in Seventeenth- and Early Eighteenth-Century Brazil: The Case of Mestre de Campo Domingos Rodrigues Carneiro." *Colonial Latin American Historical Review* 15, no. 2 (1992): 112–41. https://digitalrepository.unm.edu/clahr /vol15/iss2/1.

Dutra, Francis A. "Blacks and the Search for Rewards and Status in Seventeenth-Century Brazil." *Proceedings of the Pacific Coast Council on Latin American Studies* 6 (1979): 25–35.

Earle, Rebecca. *The Return of the Native: Indians and Myth-Making in Spanish America, 1810–1930.* Durham, NC: Duke University Press, 2007.

Eduardo, Octavio da Costa. *The Negro in Northern Brazil: A Study in Acculturation.* Seattle: University of Washington Press, 1948.

Edwards, Brent Hayes. *The Practice of Diaspora: Literature, Translation, and the Rise of Black Internationalism.* Cambridge, MA: Harvard University Press, 2003.

Edwards, Brent Hayes. "The Uses of Diaspora." *Social Text* 19, no. 1 (Spring 2001): 45–73. muse.jhu.edu/article/31891.

Ehret, Christopher. *An African Classical Age: Eastern and Southern Africa in World History, 1000 B.C. to A.D. 400.* Charlottesville: University Press of Virginia, 1998.

Ehret, Christopher. *The Civilizations of Africa: A History to 1800.* Charlottesville: University Press of Virginia, 2002.

Eltis, David, Stanley L. Engerman, Seymour Drescher, and David Richardson, eds. *The Cambridge World History of Slavery*, Vol. 3, AD 1420–AD 1804. Cambridge: Cambridge University Press, 2011.

Ennes, Ernesto, ed. *As guerras nos Palmares (subsidios para a sua história).* Brasiliana, v. 127. São Paulo: Companhia Editora Nacional, 1938.

Ennes, Ernesto, ed. *Os primeiros quilombos.* Unpublished manuscript, Biblioteca Helio Viana. Instituto de Filosofia e Ciências Humanas, Universidade Estadual de Campinas.

Espindola, Thomaz do Bomfim. *Geografia alagoana: Ou, descripção fysica, política e historica da provincia das Alagoas.* Maceió: Typographia do Liberal, 1871. Accessed July 3, 2023. https://digital.bbm.usp.br/handle/bbm/6731.

Falla dirigida á Assembléa Legislativa das Alagoas, pelo Presidente da Provincia Antonio Alves de Souza Carvalho [. . .]. Maceió: Typographia do Diario do Commercio, 1862.

Falla que o Illm. e Exm. Senhor Dr. Antonio Bernardo de Passos, Presidente da Provincia do Rio Grande do Norte, dirigio à Assemblea Legislativa Provincial no acto da abertura de sua sessão ordinaria em o 10 do Julho de 1855. Recife: Typographia de M. F. de Faria, 1855.

Falla que o Ilm. e Exm. Snr. Doutor Antonio Bernardo de Passos, Presidente da Provincia do Rio Grande do Norte, dirigio à Assembléa Legislativa Provincial, no acto da abertura de sua sessão ordinaria em 4 de Julho de 1854. Pernambuco: Typographia de M. F. de Faria, 1854.

Falola, Toyin, and Raphael Chijioke Njoku, eds. *Igbo in the Atlantic World: African Origins and Diasporic Destinations.* Bloomington: Indiana University Press, 2016.

Farfán-Santos, Elizabeth. *Black Bodies, Black Rights: The Politics of Quilombismo in Contemporary Brazil.* Austin: University of Texas Press, 2016.

Farias, Ivan Soares. "Xucuru-Kariri: Memórias, identidade e estratégias socio-culturais para reaver o território tradicional." In *Índios de Alagoas: Cotidiano, terra e poder,* edited by Luiz Sávio de Almeida and Amaro Hélio Leite da Silva, 103–16. Maceió: Editora da Universidade Federal de Alagoas, 2009.

Fernandes, Saul Estevam. *O (in)imaginável elefante mal-ajambrado: A retomada da questão de limites entre o Ceará e o Rio Grande do Norte e a formação espacial e identiária Norte-Rio-Grandense (1894–1920).* Natal: Instituto Federal Rio Grande do Norte, 2016.

Ferreira, Antonio Carlos de Santana. "Extensão rural e desenvolvimento local em comunidades quilombolas: Um estudo junto a agricultores e agricultoras, de comunidades quilombolas, nos municípios de Bom Conselho e Garanhuns, no Estado de Pernambuco." Master's thesis, Universidade Federal Rural de Pernambuco, 2008.

Ferreira, Jurandyr Pires, ed. *Enciclopédia dos municípios brasileiros*. 36 vols. Rio de Janeiro: Instituto Brasileiro de Geografia e Estatística, 1957–64.

Ferreira, Roquinaldo. "Central Africa and the Atlantic World." In *Oxford Research Encyclopedia of African History*, edited by Thomas T. Spear. Oxford: Oxford University Press, October 30, 2019. https://doi-org.proxy2.library .illinois.edu/10.1093/acrefore/9780190277734.013.53.

Ferreira, Roquinaldo. *Cross-Cultural Exchange in the Atlantic World: Angola and Brazil during the Era of the Slave Trade*. Cambridge: Cambridge University Press, 2012.

Ferreira, Roquinaldo. "O Brasil e a arte da guerra em Angola (sécs. xvii e xviii)." *Revista Estudos Históricos* 39 (2007): 1–23. Accessed June 22, 2023. https:// bibliotecadigital.fgv.br/ojs/index.php/reh/article/view/1400.

Ferreira, Roquinaldo. "Slaving and Resistance to Slaving in West Central Africa." In *The Cambridge World History of Slavery*, Vol. 3, AD 1420–AD 1804, edited by David Eltis, Stanley L. Engerman, Seymour Drescher, and David Richardson, 111–31. Cambridge: Cambridge University Press, 2011.

Ferretti, Sérgio E. "Sincretismo afro-brasileiro e resistência cultural." *Horizontes Antropológicos* 4, no. 8 (June 1998): 182–98.

Figueiredo, Manoel. *Hidrographia, exame de pilotos no qual se contem as regras que todo piloto deue guardar em suas nauegaço[n]es [. . .]*. (Lisbon, 1625). Accessed June 22, 2023. http://hdl.handle.net/2027/ucm.5316517468.

Finch, Aisha K. *Rethinking Slave Rebellion in Cuba: La Escalera and the Insurgencies of 1841-1844*. Chapel Hill: University of North Carolina Press, 2015.

Fleisch, Axel. "Angola: Ambaquista, Imbangala, and Long-Distance Trade." In *Encyclopedia of African History*, edited by Kevin Shillington. New York: Routledge, 2004. Accessed July 6, 2023. http://proxy2.library .illinois.edu/login?url=http://search.credoreference.com/content/entry /routafricanhistory/angola_ambaquista_imbangala_and_long_distance _trade/0.

Florentino, Manolo, and Márcia Amantino. "Runaways and Quilombolas in the Americas." In *The Cambridge World History of Slavery*, vol. 3, AD 1420–AD 1804, edited by David Eltis, Stanley L. Engerman, Seymour Drescher, and David Richardson, 111–31. Cambridge: Cambridge University Press, 2011.

Folhinha de Almanak: Ou diario ecclesiastico e civil para as provincias de Pernambuco, Parahiba, Rio Grande do Norte, Ceará e Alagoas para o ano de 1859. Pernambuco: Typographia de M. F. de Faria, 1858.

Fonseca, Antônio José Victoriano Borges. *Nobiliarchia pernambucana*. 2 vols. Rio de Janeiro: Biblioteca Nacional, 1925. Accessed May 31, 2023. https:// archive.org/details/nobiliarchia-pernambucana-vol-1/page/163/ mode/2up.

Fonseca, Jorge. *Escravos no sul de Portugal: Séculos XVI–XVII.* Lisbon: Editora Vulgata, 2002.

Fonseca, Pedro Paulino da. "Memoria dos feitos que se deram durante os primeiros annos de guerra com os negros quilombolas dos Palmares, seu destroço e paz aceita em junho de 1678." *Revista do Instituto Histórico e Geográfico Brasilero* 39 (1876): 293–322.

Fonseca, Pedro Paulino da. "Variedade: Um baptismo posthumo," *Pharol* (Juiz de Fora), May 29, 1885, 2.

Foreman, P. Gabrielle, et al. "Writing about Slavery? Teaching about Slavery? This Might Help." Community-sourced document. Accessed May 18, 2023. https://www.pgabrielleforeman.com/writing-about-slavery-guide.

Fourshey, Catherine Cymone, Rhonda M. Gonzales, and Christine Saidi. "Leza, Sungu, and Samba: Digital Humanities and Early Bantu History." *History in Africa* 48 (2021): 103–31.

França, Jean Marcel Carvalho, and Ricardo Alexandre Ferreira. *Três vezes Zumbi: A construção de um herói brasileiro.* São Paulo: Três Estrelas, 2012.

Freeburg, Christopher. *Counterlife: Slavery after Resistance and Social Death.* Durham, NC: Duke University Press, 2021.

Freehafer, Virginia. "Domingos Jorge Velho: Conqueror of Brazilian Backlands." *Americas* 27, no. 2 (October 1970): 161–84.

Freire, Francisco de Brito. *Nova Lusitania, historia da guerra brasilica, a purissima alma e savdosa memoria do serenissimo Principe dom Theodosio, Principe de Portvgal, e Principe do Brasil.* Lisboa: J. Gabram, 1675. Accessed May 30, 2023. http://link.gale.com/apps/doc/CY0104065084/SABN?sid=bookmark-SABN&xid=ec68601d&pg=1.

Freire, José Avelar. *Alagoa Grande — Sua história: De 1625 a 2000.* 2nd ed. João Pessoa, Paraíba, Brasil: A União, 2002.

Freitas, Décio. *Palmares: A guerra dos escravos.* 4th ed. Rio de Janeiro: Edições Graal, 1982.

Freitas, Décio, ed. *República de Palmares: Pesquisa e comentários em documentos históricos do século XVII.* Maceió: Editora da Universidade Federal de Alagoas, 2004.

Freitas, Mário Martins de. *Reino negro de Palmares.* 2 vols. Rio de Janeiro: Companhia Editóra Americana, 1954.

Frescarolo, Frei Vital de. "Informações sobre os indios barbaros dos certões de Pernambuco: Oficio do Bispo de Olinda aconpanhado de varias cartas [1802–4]." *Revista do Instituto Histórico e Geográfico Brasilero* XLVI, Parte Primeira, no. 1 (1883): 103–19.

Freyre, Gilberto. *The Masters and the Slaves (Casa-Grande and Senzala): A Study in the Development of Brazilian Civilization.* Translated by Samuel Putnam. New York: Knopf, 1946.

Freyre, Gilberto. *Rurbanização: Que é?* Recife: Editora Massangana, 1982.

Frikel, Protásio. "Traços da doutrina gêge e nagôu sôbre a crença na alma." *Revista de Antropologia* 12, nos. 1–2 (1964): 51–81.

Fromont, Cécile. *The Art of Conversion: Christian Visual Culture in the Kingdom of Kongo*. Chapel Hill: University of North Carolina Press, 2014.

Fromont, Cécile. "Collecting and Translating Knowledge across Cultures: Capuchin Missionary Images of Early Modern Central Africa, 1650–1750." In *Collecting across Cultures: Material Exchanges in the Early Modern Atlantic World*, edited by Daniela Bleichmar and Peter C. Mancall, 134–54. Philadelphia: University of Pennsylvania Press, 2011.

Fuentes, Marisa J. *Dispossessed Lives: Enslaved Women, Violence, and the Archive*. Philadelphia: University of Pennsylvania Press, 2016.

Funari, Pedro Paulo de Abreu. "A arqueologia de Palmares: Sua contribuição para o conhecimento da história da cultura afro-americana." In *Liberdade por um fio: História dos quilombos no Brasil*, edited by João José Reis and Flávio dos Santos Gomes, 26–51. São Paulo: Companhia das Letras, 1996.

Funari, Pedro Paulo de Abreu, and Aline Vieira de Carvalho. "Interações étnicas e culturais em Palmares." In *Objetos da escravidão: Abordagens sobre a cultura material da escravidão e seu legado*, edited by Camilla Agostini, 149–66. Rio de Janeiro: 7Letras, 2013.

Fusco, Coco. "Choosing between Legend and History: An Interview with Carlos Diegues." *Cinéaste* 15, no. 1 (1986): 12–14.

Galliza, Diana Soares de. "Análise das fontes para o estudo da escravidão na Paraíba." *Acervo: Revista do Arquivo Nacional* 3, no. 1 (January/June 1988): 83–89.

Galvão, Hélio. *Velhas heranças*. Natal: Sebo Vermelho Edições, 2012.

Galvão, Olympio E. de Arroxella. "Ligeira notícia sobre a Villa e Comarca de Porto-Calvo actualmente." *Revista do Instituto Archeológico e Geographico Alagoano* 1, no. 10 (December 1877): 283–88.

Galvão, Sebastião de Vasconcellos. *Diccionario chorographico, historico e estatistico de Pernambuco [. . .]*. 2nd ed. 4 vols. Rio de Janeiro: Imprensa Nacional, 1908–21.

García Márquez, Gabriel. *Chronicle of a Death Foretold*. Translated by Gregory Rabassa. 1981. Reprint, New York: Vintage, 2003.

Garfield, Robert. *A History of São Tomé Island, 1470–1655: The Key to Guinea*. San Francisco: Mellen Research University Press, 1992.

Genealogical Department of the Church of Jesus Christ of Latter-Day Saints. *Basic Portuguese Paleography*. Research Papers Series H, No. 20, Salt Lake City, Utah, 1978.

Geschiere, Peter. *The Modernity of Witchcraft: Politics and the Occult in Postcolonial Africa*. Translated by Janet L. Roitman. Charlottesville: University Press of Virginia, 1997.

Gomes, Flávio dos Santos. "Africanos e crioulos no campesinato negro do Maranhão oitocentista." *Outros Tempos* 8, no. 11 (2011): 63–88.

Gomes, Flávio dos Santos. *De olho em Zumbi dos Palmares: Histórias, símbolos e memória social*. São Paulo: Claro Enigma, 2011.

Gomes, Flávio dos Santos. *A hidra e os pântanos: Mocambos, quilombos e comuni-dades de fugitivos no Brasil (séculos XVII–XIX)*. São Paulo: Editora da Universidade Estadual Paulista, 2005.

Gomes, Flávio dos Santos, ed. *Mocambos de Palmares: Histórias e fontes (séc. XVI–XIX)*. Rio de Janeiro: 7Letras, 2010.

Gomes, Flávio dos Santos. *Palmares: Escravidão e liberdade no Atlântico Sul*. São Paulo: Contexto, 2005.

Gomes, Flávio dos Santos. "Review of Marcelo D'Salete's Cumbe and Angola Janga: Uma história de Palmares." *American Historical Review* 125, no. 1 (February 2020): 160–64.

Gomes, Flávio dos Santos. "A 'Safe Haven': Runaway Slaves, *Mocambos*, and Borders in Colonial Amazonia, Brazil." Translated by Sabrina Gledhill. *Hispanic American Historical Review* 82, no. 3 (August 2002): 469–98.

Gomez, Michael A. *Exchanging Our Country Marks: The Transformation of African Identities in the Colonial and Antebellum South*. Chapel Hill: University of North Carolina Press, 1998.

Gomez, Michael A. "A Quality of Anguish: The Igbo Response to Enslavement in North America." In *Trans-Atlantic Dimensions of Ethnicity in the African Diaspora*, edited by Paul E. Lovejoy and David V. Trotman, 82–95. London: Continuum, 2003.

Gordon, David M. *Invisible Agents: Spirits in a Central African History*. New African Histories. Athens: Ohio University Press, 2012.

Graham, Richard. "Another Middle Passage? The Internal Slave Trade in Brazil." In *The Chattel Principle: Internal Slave Trades in the Americas*, edited by Walter Johnson, 291–324. New Haven, CT: Yale University Press, 2004.

Great Britain Parliament House of Commons. *Accounts and Papers of the House of Commons (Session 17 January–16 August 1878)*, vol. 73, 1878. Accessed July 3, 2023. https://books.google.co.jp/books?id=MCxcAAAAQAAJ&printsec=frontcover&hl=ja&source=gbs_ge_summary_r&cad=0#v=onepage&q&f=false.

Green, Toby. "Beyond an Imperial Atlantic: Trajectories of Africans from Upper Guinea and West-Central Africa in the Early Atlantic World." *Past and Present* 230, no. 1 (February 2016): 91–122.

Grinberg, Keila. *A Black Jurist in a Slave Society: Antonio Pereira Rebouças and the Trials of Brazilian Citizenship*. Translated by Kristin McGuire. Chapel Hill: University of North Carolina Press, 2019.

Griz, Jayme. "O Zumbi de 'mansinha.'" *Brasil Açucareiro* 80 (August 1972): 61–64.

Groesen, Michiel van, ed. *The Legacy of Dutch Brazil*. New York: Cambridge University Press, 2014.

Grünewald, Rodrigo de A., Robson Savoldi, and Mark I. Collins. "*Jurema* in Contemporary Brazil: Ritual Re-Actualizations, Mysticism, Consciousness, and Healing." *Anthropology of Consciousness* 33, no. 2 (2022): 307–32. doi:10.1111/anoc.12150.

Guattini, Michelangelo, and Dionigi Carli. *Viaggio nel regno del Congo [. . .].* Presso Iseppo Prodocimo, 1679. Accessed June 26, 2023. https://archive .org/details/bub_gb_QZbunKU1YcsC.

Guerra, Flávio. *Velhas igrejas e subúrbios históricos.* Recife: Departamento de Documentação e Cultura, Prefeitura Municipal do Recife, 1960.

Guimarães, Carlos Magno. "Mineração, quilombos e Palmares: Minas Gerais no século XVIII." In *Liberdade por um fio: História dos quilombos no Brasil,* edited by João José Reis and Flávio dos Santos Gomes, 139–63. São Paulo: Companhia das Letras, 1996.

Guimarães, Carlos Magno. *Uma negação da ordem escravista: Quilombos em Minas Gerais no século XVIII.* São Paulo: Icone, 1988.

Guimarães, Lucia Maria Paschoal. "Francisco Adolpho de Varnhagen (1816–1878)." In *Os historiadores: Clássicos da história do Brasil,* edited by Maurício Parada and Henrique Estrada Rodrigues, 47–65. Petrópolis: Editora Vozes, 2018.

Guimarães, Matheus Silveira. "Diáspora africana na Paraíba do Norte: Trabalho, tráfico e sociabilidade na primeira metade do século XIX." Master's thesis, Universidade Federal da Paraíba, 2015.

Guimarães, Matheus Silveira. "A população africana na Irmandade de Nossa Senhora do Rosário: A Cidade da Paraíba e o mundo atlântico." *Revista Crítica Histórica* 7, no. 13 (June 2016): 1–19. https://doi.org/10.28998 /rchvl7n13.2016.0005.

Guthrie, Malcolm. *Comparative Bantu: An Introduction to the Comparative Linguistics and Prehistory of the Bantu Languages.* 4 vols. Farnborough: Gregg International Publishers, 1967.

Hajstrup, Peter Hansen. *Viagem ao Brasil (1644-1654).* Edited and translated by Benjamin Micolaas Teensma, and edited by Bruno Romero Ferreira Miranda and Lucia Furquim Werneck Xavier. Recife: Companhia Editora de Pernambuco, 2016. Kindle edition.

Hamilton, Russell G. *Voices from an Empire: A History of Afro-Portuguese Literature.* Minneapolis: University of Minnesota Press, 1975.

Hamilton, Virginia. *The People Could Fly.* Illustrated by Leon and Diane Dillon. New York: Alfred A. Knopf, 2004.

Harms, Robert W. *River of Wealth, River of Sorrow: The Central Zaire Basin in the Era of the Slave and Ivory Trade, 1500-1891.* New Haven, CT: Yale University Press, 1981.

Hartman, Saidiya. "Venus in Two Acts." *Small Axe* 12, no. 2 (2008): 1–14.

Hartman, Saidiya. *Wayward Lives, Beautiful Experiments.* New York: W. W. Norton, 2019.

Hawthorne, Walter. *From Africa to Brazil: Culture, Identity, and an Atlantic Slave Trade, 1600-1830.* Cambridge: Cambridge University Press, 2010.

Heintze, Beatrix. "Hidden Transfers: Luso-Africans as European Explorers' Experts in Nineteenth-Century West-Central Africa." In *The Power of*

Doubt: Essays in Honor of David Henige, edited by Paul Stuart Landau,
19–40. Madison, WI: Parallel Press, 2011.

Helg, Aline. *Slave No More: Self-Liberation before Abolitionism in the Americas.*
Translated by Lara Vergnaud. Chapel Hill: University of North Carolina
Press, 2019.

Helton, Laura, Justin Leroy, Max A. Mishler, Samantha Seeley, and Shauna
Sweeney, eds. "The Question of Recovery: Slavery, Freedom, and the
Archive." Special issue, *Social Text* 33, no. 4 (December 2015). Accessed
June 22, 2023.

Henderson, James. *A History of the Brazil; Comprising Its Geography, Commerce,
Colonization, Aboriginal Inhabitants, &c. &c. &c.* London: Longman, Hurts,
Rees, Orme, and Brown, 1821. Accessed May 15, 2023. http://www2.senado
.leg.br/bdsf/handle/id/518715.

Herskovits, Melville J. *The Myth of the Negro Past.* 1st ed. New York: Harper, 1941.
Accessed May 27, 2023.

Herskovits, Melville J. *The Myth of the Negro Past.* 4th ed. Boston: Beacon Press,
1967.

Hertzman, Marc A. "A Brazilian Counterweight: Music, Intellectual Property
and the African Diaspora in Rio de Janeiro (1910s–1930s)." *Journal of Latin
American Studies* 41, no. 4 (2009): 695–722.

Hertzman, Marc A. "Fake News, Fake History? A Racist Judge Takes on
Zumbi." *Revista Z Cultural,* August 7, 2019. Accessed May 18, 2023. http://
revistazcultural.pacc.ufrj.br/fake-news-fake-history-a-racist-judge-takes
-on-zumbi/.

Hertzman, Marc A. "Fatal Differences: Suicide, Race, and Forced Labor in the
Americas." *American Historical Review* 122, no. 2 (April 2017): 316–45.

Hertzman, Marc A. "The 'Indians of Palmares': Conquest, Insurrection, and
Land in Northeast Brazil." *Hispanic American Historical Review* 103, no. 3
(August 2023): 424–60.

Hertzman, Marc A. "Quem dançou Quilombo?: Caminhos menos trilhados
nos Estudos Afro Latino-americanos." In *Estudos Afro Latino-americanos:
Histórias, memórias e culturas,* edited by Denise Barata, Roberto Augusto A. Pereira, and Denilson Araújo de Oliveira, 1–21. Rio de Janeiro:
Editora, Multifoco, 2024 (forthcoming).

Hertzman, Marc A., and Giovana Xavier. "Let's Build a Monument to Anas-
tácia." *Public Seminar,* July 30, 2020. Accessed August 12, 2023. https://
publicseminar.org/essays/lets-build-a-monument-to-anastacia/.

Herzog, Tamar. *Frontiers of Possession: Spain and Portugal in Europe and the Americas.* Cambridge, MA: Harvard University Press, 2015.

Heywood, Linda M., ed. *Central Africans and Cultural Transformations in the
American Diaspora.* Cambridge: Cambridge University Press, 2002.

Heywood, Linda M. "The Making of Kongo Identity in the American Diaspora: A Case Study from Brazil." In *The Kongo Kingdom: The Origins,
Dynamics and Cosmopolitan Culture of an African Polity,* edited by Koen A. G.

Bostoen and Inge Brinkman, 254–74. Cambridge: Cambridge University Press, 2018.

Heywood, Linda M. *Njinga of Angola: Africa's Warrior Queen*. Cambridge, MA: Harvard University Press, 2017.

Heywood, Linda M. "Portuguese into African: The Eighteenth-Century Central African Background to Atlantic Creole Cultures." In *Central Africans and Cultural Transformations in the American Diaspora*, edited by Linda M. Heyward, 91–113. Cambridge: Cambridge University Press, 2002.

Heywood, Linda M., and John K. Thornton. *Central Africans, Atlantic Creoles, and the Foundation of the Americas, 1585–1660*. New York: Cambridge University Press, 2007.

Higgins, Kathleen J. *"Licentious Liberty" in a Brazilian Gold-Mining Region: Slavery, Gender, and Social Control in Eighteenth-Century Sabará, Minas Gerais*. University Park: Pennsylvania State University Press, 1999.

Hilton, Anne. *The Kingdom of Kong*. Oxford: Clarendon Press, 1985.

Hoffman French, Jan. *Legalizing Identities: Becoming Black or Indian in Brazil's Northeast*. Chapel Hill: University of North Carolina Press, 2009.

Holden, Vanessa M. *Surviving Southampton: African American Women and Resistance in Nat Turner's Community*. Urbana: University of Illinois Press, 2021.

Honorato, Manoel da Costa. *Diccionario topographico, estatistico e historico da provincia de Pernambuco*. Recife: Typographia Universal, 1863.

Hoogbergen, Wim. "Palmares: A Critical View on Its Sources." In *History and Histories in the Caribbean*, edited by Thomas Bremer and Ulrich Fleischmann, 23–55. Madrid: Vervuert and Bibliotheca Ibero-Americana, 2001. Accessed August 12, 2023. https://publications.iai.spk-berlin.de/receive/riai_mods_00001741.

Hooghe, Sr. Romein de, *Les Indes Orientales et Occidentales, et autres lieux [. . .]*. Ca. 1685. Accessed May 28, 2023. https://hdl.handle.net/2027/gri.ark:/13960/t6b35bz05?urlappend=%3Bseq=65.

Huber, Magnus, and Mikael Parkvall, eds. *Spreading the Word: The Issue of Diffusion among the Atlantic Creoles*. London: University of Westminster Press, 1999.

"Idéa da população da capitania de Pernambuco, e das suas annexas, extenção de suas costas, rios, e povoações notaveis, agricultura, numero dos engenhos, contractos, e rendimentos reaes, augmente que estes tem tido &ª &ª desde o anno de 1774 em que tomou posse do governo das mesmas capitanias o Governador e Capitam General Jozé Cezar de Menezes." *Annaes da Bibliotheca Nacional do Rio de Janeiro* 40 (1918): 1–112.

I. G. H. "Dei Progressi della Geografia e della sua Letteratura nel Triennia Finito Coll'Anno 1831 (Parte Terza)." *Antologia: Giornale di scienze, lettere e arti* 7 (July–September 1832): 58–83. Accessed July 6, 2023. https://www.google.com/books/edition/Antologia/5-xFAAAAcAAJ.

"Informação geral da capitania de Pernambuco." *Annaes da Bibliotheca Nacional do Rio de Janeiro* 28 (1906): 117–496.

Instituto Archeologico e Geographico Alagoano. *O centenario da emancipação de Alagoas*. Maceió: Officinas a vapor da Casa Ramalho, 1919. Accessed May 30, 2023. http://hdl.handle.net/2027/uc1.l0064581762.

Ipanema, Cybelle de. *História da Ilha do Governador*. Rio de Janeiro: Mauad X, 2013.

Janiga, Constance Gabrielle. "Sebastião da Rocha Pita's 'História da América Portuguesa': Literariness and the Imaginative Reconstruction of the Past." *South Atlantic Review* 55, no. 1 (January 1990): 35–45.

Janson, Tore. "Bantu Spirantisation as an Areal Change." *Africana Linguistica* 13 (2007): 79–116.

Janzen, John M. *Lemba, 1650–1930: A Drum of Afflication in Africa and the New World*. New York: Garland, 1982.

Jesus, Mirian Silva de. "Abrindo espaços: Os 'paulistas' na formação da capitania do Rio Grande." Master's thesis, Universidade Federal do Rio Grande do Norte, 2007.

Joffily, Irenêo. *Notas sobre a Parahyba: Fac-símile da primeira edição publicada no Rio de Janeiro, em 1892, com prefácio de Capistrano de Abreu*. Edited by Geraldo Irenêo Joffily. Brasília: Thesaurus Editora, 1977.

Johnson, Jessica Marie. *Wicked Flesh: Black Women, Intimacy, and Freedom in the Atlantic World*. Philadelphia: University of Pennsylvania Press, 2020.

Johnson, Paul Christopher. *Automatic Religion: Nearhuman Agents of Brazil and France*. Chicago: University of Chicago Press, 2021.

Johnston, Harry Hamilton. *A Comparative Study of the Bantu and Semi-Bantu Languages*. 2 vols. Oxford: Clarendon Press, 1919.

Jones, Gayl. *Palmares*. Boston: Beacon Press, 2021.

Jorge, Marcos. *Doutrina Christãa . . . acrescentado pelo Padre I. Martinz . . . De novo traduzida na lingoa do Reyno de Congo, etc.* Lisbon: Geraldo da Vinha, 1624. British Library. Accessed May 30, 2023. https://access.bl.uk/item /viewer/ark:/81055/vdc_100031235839.0x000001#?c=0&m=0&s=0&cv =0&xywh=-1190%2C-97%2C3530%2C1912.

Kananoja, Kalle. *Central African Identities and Religiosity in Colonial Minas Gerais*. Abo, Finland: Abo Akademi University, 2012.

Kananoja, Kalle. "Healers, Idolaters, and Good Christians: A Case Study of Creolization and Popular Religion in Mid-Eighteenth Century Angola." *International Journal of African Historical Studies* 43, no. 3 (2010): 443–65.

Kananoja, Kalle. *Healing Knowledge in Atlantic Africa: Medical Encounters, 1500–1850*. New York: Cambridge University Press, 2021.

Kananoja, Kalle. "Infected by the Devil, Cured by Calundu: African Healers in Eighteenth-Century Minas Gerais, Brazil." *Social History of Medicine* 29, no. 3 (2016): 490–511.

Kananoja, Kalle. "Pai Caetano Angola, Afro-Brazilian Magico-Religious Practices, and Cultural Resistance in Minas Gerais in the Lat Eighteenth Century." *Journal of African Diaspora Archaeology and Heritage* 2, no. 1 (May 2013): 18–37.

Kaoma, Kapya J. *God's Family, God's Earth: Christian Ecological Ethics of Ubuntu.* Zomba, Malawi: Kachere Series, 2014.

Karasch, Mary C. *Before Brasília: Frontier Life in Central Brazil.* Albuquerque: University of New Mexico Press, 2016.

Karasch, Mary C. "Central Africans in Central Brazil, 1780–1835." In *Central Africans and Cultural Transformations in the American Diaspora,* edited by Linda M. Heyward, 117–51. Cambridge: Cambridge University Press, 2002.

Karasch, Mary C. *Slave Life in Rio de Janeiro, 1808–1850.* Princeton, NJ: Princeton University Press, 1987.

Kars, Marjoleine. *Blood on the River: A Chronicle of Mutiny and Freedom on the Wild Coast.* New York: New Press, 2020.

Kars, Marjoleine. "Dodging Rebellion: Politics and Gender in the Berbice Slave Uprising of 1763." *American Historical Review* 121, no. 1 (February 2016): 39–69.

Katamba, Francis. "Bantu Nominal Morphology." In *The Bantu Languages,* edited by Erik Nurse and Gérard Philippson, 103–20. London: Routledge, 2003.

Kea, Ray A. "'When I Die, I Shall Return to My Own Land': An 'Amina' Slave Rebellion in the Danish West Indies, 1733–1734." In *The Cloth of Many Colored Silks: Papers on History and Society, Ghanaian and Islamic in Honor of Ivor Wilks,* edited by John Hunwick and Nancy Lawler, 159–93. Evanston, IL: Northwestern University Press, 1996.

Kelley, Robyn D. G. "On the Density of (Black) Being." In *Scratch,* edited by Christine Kim, 9–10. New York: Studio Museum in Harlem, 2005.

Kent, R. K. "Palmares: An African State in Brazil." *Journal of African History* 6, no. 2 (1965): 161–75.

Kidd, Gray F. "Neither Peddlers nor War: Unraveling 180 Years of Historical Literature on Pernambuco's 'Peddlers' War,' 1710–1711." *CLIO: Revista de Pesquisa Histórica* 37 (December 2019): 300–325.

Kiddy, Elizabeth W. "Ethnic and Racial Identity in the Brotherhoods of the Rosary of Minas Gerais, 1700–1830." *Americas* 56, no. 2 (1999): 221–52.

Klein, Herbert, and Francisco Vidal Luna. *Slavery in Brazil.* Cambridge: Cambridge University Press, 2009.

Klieman, Kairn A. *"The Pygmies Were Our Compass": Bantu and Batwa in the History of West Central Africa, Early Times to c. 1900 C.E.* Portsmouth, NH: Heinemann, 2003.

Kodesh, Neil. *Beyond the Royal Gaze: Clanship and Public Healing in Buganda.* Charlottesville: University of Virginia Press, 2010.

Kodesh, Neil. "History from the Healer's Shrine: Genre, Historical Imagination, and Early Ganda History." *Comparative Studies in Society and History* 49, no. 3 (2007): 527–52.

Konadu, Kwasi. *The Akan Diaspora in the Americas.* Oxford: Oxford University Press, 2010.

Koslowsky, Julio. "'El Caburé' *Glaucidium Nanum* (King): Raro Caso de Mimetismo." *El Hornero* 1, no. 4 (September 1919): 229–35. Accessed May 27,

2023. https://hdl.handle.net/2027/uiug.30112111968563?urlappend
=%3Bseq=241%3Bownerid=13510798902364617-245.

Koster, Henry. *Travels in Brazil by Henry Koster in the Years from 1809 to 1815*.
Philadelphia: M. Carey and Son, 1817.

Kraay, Hendrik. "Arming Slaves in Brazil from the Seventeenth Century to
the Nineteenth Century." In *Arming Slaves*, edited by Christopher Leslie
Brown and Phillip D. Morgan, 146–79. New Haven, CT: Yale University
Press, 2006.

Kraay, Hendrik. *Race, State, and Armed Forces in Independence-Era Brazil: Bahia,
1790s–1840s*. Stanford, CA: Stanford University Press, 2001.

Kühn, Fábio. "Clandestino e ilegal: O contrabando de escravos na Colônia
do Sacramento (1740–1777)." In *Escravidão e liberdade: Temas, problemas e
perspectivas de análise*, edited by Encontro Escravidão e Liberdade no Brasil
Meridional, 179–206. São Paulo: Alameda, 2012.

Kukanda, Vatomene. "A personalidade luso-bantu: Cristalização e ambivalência
(o caso do Ambaquista)." Paper presented at the Segundas Jornadas Luso-
Bantu, São Tomé, 1999.

Lahon, Didier. "Inquisição, pacto com o demônio e 'magia' africana em Lisboa
no século XVIII." *Topoi* 5, no. 8 (June 2004): 9–70. https://doi.org/10.1590
/2237-101X005008001.

Laman, K. E. *The Kongo*. 4 vols. Lund: Upsala, 1953–68.

Landers, Jane. "Leadership and Authority in Maroon Settlements in Spanish
America and Brazil." In *Africa and the Americas: Interconnections during the
Slave Trade*, edited by José C. Curto and Renée Soulodre-la France, 173–84.
Trenton, NJ: Africa World Press, 2005.

Langfur, Hal. *Adrift on an Inland Sea: Misinformation and the Limits of Empire in
the Brazilian Backlands*. Stanford, CA: Stanford University Press, 2023.

Langfur, Hal. *The Forbidden Lands: Colonial Identity, Frontier Violence, and the
Persistence of Brazil's Eastern Indians, 1750–1830*. Stanford, CA: Stanford
University Press, 2006.

LaPier, Rosalyn. "Land as Text: Reading the Land." *Environmental History* 28,
no. 1 (2023): 40–46.

Lara, Silvia Hunold. *Campos da violência: Escravos e senhores na capitania do Rio de
Janeiro, 1750–1808*. Rio de Janeiro: Paz e Terra, 1988.

Lara, Silvia Hunold. "Depois da Batalha de Pungo Andongo (1671): O destino
atlântico dos príncipes do Ndongo." *Revista de História* 175 (July 2016):
205–25.

Lara, Silvia Hunold. "Diferentes ou iguais? O destino dos prisioneiros das
guerras contra os Palmares." Presented at the 8° Encontro Escravidão e
Liberdade no Brasil Meridional, Porto Alegre, 2017.

Lara, Silvia Hunold. "Do singular ao plural: Palmares, capitães-do-mato e o
governo dos escravos." In *Liberdade por um fio: História dos quilombos no
Brasil*, edited by João José Reis and Flávio dos Santos Gomes, 81–109.
São Paulo: Companhia das Letras, 1996.

Lara, Silvia Hunold, ed. *Legislação sobre escravos africanos na América Portuguesa.* Madrid: Fundación Histórica Tavera/Digibis/Fundación Hernando de Larramendi, 2000.

Lara, Silvia Hunold. "O território dos Palmares: Cartografia, história e política." *Afro-Ásia* 64 (2021): 12–50.

Lara, Silvia Hunold. *Palmares e Cucaú: O aprendizado da dominação.* São Paulo: EDUSP, 2021.

Lara, Silvia Hunold. "Palmares and Cucaú: Political Dimensions of a Maroon Community in Late Seventeenth-Century Brazil." Paper presented at the 12th Annual Gilder Lehrman Center International Conference, New Haven, CT, October 29–30, 2010.

Lara, Silvia Hunold. "Quem eram os 'Negros do Palmar'?" In *Escravidão e cultura afro-brasileira: Temas e problemas em torno da obra de Robert Slenes,* edited by Gladys Sabina Ribeiro, Jonis Freire, Martha Campos Abreu, and Sidney Chalhoub, 57–86. Campinas: Editora da Universidade Estadual de Campinas, 2016.

Lara, Silvia Hunold, and Phablo Fachin, eds. *Guerra contra Palmares: O manuscrito de 1678.* São Paulo: Chão Editora, 2021.

Leal, Claudia. *Landscapes of Freedom: Building a Postemancipation Society in the Rainforests of Western Colombia.* Tucson: University of Arizona Press, 2018.

Leal, José. *Itinerário da história (Imagem da Paraíba entre 1518 e 1965).* João Pessoa: Gráfica Comercial Ltda., 1965.

Lee, Debbie, and Kathryn Newfont, eds. *The Land Speaks: New Voices at the Intersection of Oral and Environmental History.* New York: Oxford University Press, 2017.

Leitão, Deusdedith. "Uma cidade revolucionária e a atual denominação." In *Uma cidade de quatro séculos: Evolução e roteiro,* edited by Wellington Augiar and José Octávio, 145–49. João Pessoa: Governo do Estado da Paraíba, 1985.

Leite, Ilka Boaventura. "The Transhistorical, Juridical-Formal, and Post-Utopian Quilombo." In *New Approaches to Resistance in Brazil and Mexico,* edited by John Gledhill and Patience A. Schell, 250–68. Durham, NC: Duke University Press, 2012. Accessed November 6, 2020.

Leite, Serafim. *História da Companhia de Jesus no Brasil.* 10 vols. Lisbon: Livraria Portugália, 1938–1950.

Lemos, Vicente de. *Capitães-móres e governadores do Rio Grande do Norte.* 2 vols. Rio de Janeiro: Typ. do Jornal do Commercio, 1912.

Lienhard, Martin. "Milonga: The 'Dialogues' between Portuguese and Africans in the Congo and the Angola Wars (Sixteenth and Seventeenth Centuries)." Translated by Ineke Phaf-Rheinberger. In *AfricAmericas: Itineraries, Dialogues, and Sounds,* edited by Ineke Phaf-Rheinberger and Tiago de Oliveira Pinto, 91–123. Madrid: Iberoamericana/Vervuert, 2008.

Lima, Carlos A. M. "Pequena diaspora: Migrações de libertos e de livres de cor (Rio de Janeiro, 1765–1844)." *Locus* 6, no. 2 (July 2000): 99–110. https://periodicos.ufjf.br/index.php/locus/article/view/20517.

Lima, Hezrom Vieira Costa. "'Já veio tudo dos antepassados': História, memória e identidade étnica em Caiana dos Crioulos." Master's thesis, Universidade Federal da Paraíba, 2015.

Lima, Ivan Fernandes. *Ocupação espacial do Estado de Alagoas*. Maceió: N.p., 1992.

Lima, Ivana Stolze. "Escravidão e comunicação no mundo atlântico: Em torno da 'língua de Angola,' século XVII." *História Unisinos* 21, no. 1 (January–April 2017): 109–21. Accessed June 26, 2023. https://revistas.unisinos.br/index.php/historia/article/view/htu.2017.211.09/5952.

Lima, Luciano Mendonça de. "Cativos da 'Rainha da Borborema': Uma história social da escravidão em Campina Grande-século XIX." PhD diss, Universidade Federal de Pernambuco, 2008.

Lima, Maria da Vitória Barbosa. "Liberdade interditada, liberdade reavida: Escravos e libertos na Paraíba escravista (século XIX)." PhD diss., Universidade Federal de Pernambuco, 2010.

Lindoso, Dirceu. *A utopia armada: Rebeliões de pobres nas matas do Tombo Real (1832–1850)*. 2nd ed. Maceió: Editora da Universidade Federal de Alagoas, 2005.

Lira, Augusto Tavares de. *História do Rio Grande do Norte*. Brasília: Senado Federal, 2012.

Lockley, Tim. "Runaway Slave Colonies in the Atlantic World." In *Oxford Research Encyclopedia of Latin American History*. April 2, 2015. Accessed June 21, 2023. https://oxfordre.com/latinamericanhistory/view/10.1093/acrefore/9780199366439.001.0001/acrefore-9780199366439-e-5.

Loichot, Valérie. *Water Graves: The Art of the Unritual in the Greater Caribbean*. Charlottesville: University Press of Virginia, 2020.

Lopes, Fátima Martins. *Índios, colonos e missionários na colonização da capitania do Rio Grande do Norte*. Special edition for the Acervo Virtual Oswaldo Lamartine de Faria. Natal: Instituto Histórico e Geográfico do Rio Grande do Norte, 1998. Accessed May 15, 2021. https://colecaomossoroense.org.br/site/acervo-oswaldo-lamartine/.

Lopes, Gustavo Acioli. "Negócio da Costa da Mina e comércio atlântico: Tabaco, açúcar, ouro e tráfico de escravos: Pernambuco (1654–1760)." PhD diss., Universidade de São Paulo, 2008.

Lopes, Juliana. "A visibilidade do primeiro Camarão no processo de militarização indígena na capitania de Pernambuco no século XVII." *Revista Anthropológicas* 16, no. 2 (2005): 133–52.

Lopes, Juliana Serzedello Crespim, and Paulo Sérgio da Costa Neves. "Quando a memória é o pomo da discórdia: O 13 de maio de 2020 e a Fundação Palmares." *Revista de História*, no. 181 (2022): 1–30.

Lopes, Nei. *Novo dicionário banto do Brasil: Contendo mais de 250 propostas etmológicas acolhidas pelo Dicionário Houaiss*. 2nd ed. Rio de Janeiro: Pallas, 2012.

Lorenzino, Gerardo A. "Linguistic, Historical and Ethnographic Evidence on the Formation of the Angolares, a Maroon-Descendant Community in São Tomé (West Africa)." *Portuguese Studies Review* 15 (2007): 193–226.

Loreto Couto, D. Domingos do. *Desagravos do Brazil e glorias de Pernambuco.* Rio de Janeiro: Officina Typographica da Bibliotheca Nacional, 1904.

Lovejoy, Paul E. "The African Diaspora: Revisionist Interpretations of Ethnicity, Culture and Religion under Slavery." *Studies in the World History of Slavery, Abolition and Emancipation* 2, no. 1 (1997): 1–21.

Lovejoy, Paul E. "Pawnship, Debt, and 'Freedom' in Atlantic Africa during the Era of the Slave Trade: A Reassessment." *Journal of African History* 55, no. 1 (2014): 55–78. doi:10.1017/S0021853714000073.

Luca, Ferdinando de. *Nuovi elementi di geografia [. . .] secondo l'ordine dell-insegnamento.* Naples: Soc. Filomatica, 1833. Accessed May 28, 2023. https://www.google.com/books/edition/Nuovi_elementi_di_geografia /f7dm_1BP4XoC.

Luig, Ute, and Achim Von Oppen. "Landscape in Africa: Process and Vision." *Paideuma* 43 (1997): 7–45.

Luiz, Janailson Macêdo. "Das ressignificações do passado: As artes da memória e a escrita da história da Comunidade Remanescente de Quilombos Caiana dos Crioulos, Alagoa Grande-PB." Master's thesis, Universidade Federal de Campina Grande, 2013.

Luna, Francisco Vidal, and Iraci del Nero da Costa. "Algumas características do contingente de cativos em Minas Gerais." In *Escravismo em São Paulo e Minas Gerais*, edited by Francisco Vidal Luna, Iraci del Nero da Costa, and Herbert S. Klein, 17–32. São Paulo: EdUSP, 2009.

Luna, Francisco Vidal, and Iraci del Nero da Costa. *Minas colonial: Economia e sociedade.* São Paulo: Enio Matheus Guazzelli, 1973.

Lyra, Augusto Tavares de. *O Rio Grande do Norte, 1911.* Rio de Janeiro: Typ. do Jornal do Commercio, 1912. Accessed May 30, 2023. http://hdl.handle.net /2027/uc1.$b23524.

Macedo, Joaquim Manoel de. *Brazilian Biographical Annual*, vol. 1. Rio de Janeiro: Typ. e lith. do Imperial Instituto Artistico, 1876. Accessed July 3, 2023. https://books.google.co.jp/books?id=-MAzAQAAIAAJ&redir _esc=y.

MacGaffey, Wyatt. "A Central African Kingdom: Kongo in 1480." In *The Kongo Kingdom: The Origins, Dynamics and Cosmopolitan Culture of an African Polity*, edited by Koen A. G. Bostoen and Inge Brinkman, 42–60. Cambridge: Cambridge University Press, 2018.

MacGaffey, Wyatt. "Dialogues of the Deaf: Europeans on the Atlantic Coast of Africa." In *Implicit Understandings: Observing, Reporting, and Reflecting on the Encounters between Europeans and Other Peoples in the Early Modern Era*, edited by Stuart B. Schwartz, 249–67. Cambridge: Cambridge University Press, 1994.

MacGaffey, Wyatt. *Kongo Political Culture: The Conceptual Challenge of the Particular.* Bloomington: Indiana University Press, 2000.

MacGaffey, Wyatt. "The Personhood of Ritual Objects: Kongo 'Minkisi.'" *Etno-foor* 3, no. 1 (1990): 45–61.

MacGaffey, Wyatt. *Religion and Society in Central Africa: The BaKongo of Lower Zaire*. Chicago: University of Chicago Press, 1986.

Machado, Alex Rolim. "Classificação e perseguição: Os agentes da Inquisição, os negros, pardos e mulatos em uma sociedade escravista (Alagoas colonial, 1674–1820)." *Sankofa: Revista de História da África e de Estudos da Diáspora Africana* 7, no. 14 (December 2014): 23–61.

Machado Filho, Aires da Mata. *O negro e o garimpo em Minas Gerais*. Rio de Janeiro: Livraria José Olympio, 1943.

Maddieson, Francis. "The Sounds of the Bantu Languages." In *The Bantu Languages*, edited by Erik Nurse and Gérard Philippson, 15–41. London: Routledge, 2003.

Magalhães, Ana Cláudia, Josemary Ferrare, and Maria Angélica da Silva, eds. *O Convento Franciscano de Marechal Deodoro—Santa Maria Madalena*. Brasília: Instituto do Patrimônio Histórico e Artístico, 2012.

Maho, Jouni Filip. NUGL *Online: The Online Version of the New Updated Guthrie List, a Referential Classification of the Bantu Languages*. 2009. Accessed June 1, 2023. https://brill.com/fileasset/downloads_products/35125_Bantu -New-updated-Guthrie-List.pdf.

Maia, Antonio da Silva. *Dicionário complementar: Português-Kimbundu-Kikongo (línguas nativas do centro e norte de Angola)*. Cucujães: Depositária Editorial Missoes, 1964.

Maiden, Martin. *A Linguistic History of Italian*. London: Longman, 1995.

Malacco, Felipe Silveira de, and Ivan Sicca Gonçalves. "Entre Senegâmbia e Angola: Comércio atlântico, protagonismo africano e dinâmicas regionais (séculos XVII e XIX)." *Afro-Ásia* 62 (2020): 46–97.

Mallon, Florencia E. *Peasant and Nation: The Making of Postcolonial Mexico and Peru*. Berkeley: University of California Press, 1995.

Mamiani della Rovere, Lodovico Vincenzo. *Arte de grammatica da lingua brasilica da naçam Kiriri*. Lisbon: Officina de Miguel Deslandes, 1699. Accessed August 2, 2023. https://archive.org/details/artedegrammaticaoomami/page/ n1/mode/2up.

Mantero, Francisco. *Manual Labour in S. Thomé and Principe*. Translated by John Alfred Wyllie. Lisbon: Annuario Commercial, 1910.

Marcgrave, Jorge (Georg Marggraf). *História natural do Brasil*. Edited by Afonso de E. Taunay. Translated by José Procopio de Magalhães. São Paulo: Imprensa Oficial do Estado, 1942.

Marcussi, Alexandre A. "Cativeiro e cura: Experiências religiosas da escravidão atlântica nos calundus de Luzia Pinta, séculos XVII–XVIII." PhD diss., Universidade de São Paulo, 2015.

Marcussi, Alexandre A. "Utopias centro-africanas: Ressignificações da ancestralidade nos calundus da América Portuguesa nos séculos XVII e XVIII." *Revista Brasileira de História* 39, no. 79 (2018): 19–40.

Marcussi, Alexandre A. "O zumbi e o bode diabólico: Disputas em torno de uma cerimônia religiosa africana em Benguela no século XVIII." In *Heresias em perspectiva*, edited by Thereza Baumann and Yllan de Mattos, 149–68. Lisbon: Cátedra de Estudos Sefarditas, 2022.

Marcuzzo, Francisco F. N., Vanessa Romero, and Murilo R. D. Cardoso. "Detalhamento hidromorfológico da Bacia do Rio Mundaú." Paper presented at the XIX Simpósio Brasileiros de Recursos Hídricos, Maceió, Alagoas, November 27, 2011. Accessed July 3, 2023. https://rigeo.cprm.gov.br/jspui /bitstream/doc/17403/4/artigo_rio_mundau.pdf.

Marecos, Ernesto. *Juca, a matumbolla: Lenda africana*. Lisbon: Typ. do Panorama, 1865.

Marggraf, Georg, and Willem Piso. *Guilielmi Pisonis, M. D. Lugduno-Batavi, De medicina Brasiliensi libri quatuor*. Lugdun, Batavorum: Amsterdam, 1648. Accessed May 30, 2023. https://www.scribd.com/doc/30980521/marcgrave -1648-historia?secret_password=dmouy4lt7dxwdcomdh6#.

Marques, Alexandre Bittencourt Leite. "Entre lajedos e lagoas: Formação territorial, habitações e bens culturais no povoado de Alagoinhas nos sertões de Pernambuco (1775–1835)." Master's thesis, Universidade Federal Rural de Pernambuco, 2012.

Marques, Alexandre Bittencourt Leite. "A travessia de escravos dos sertões de Angola para os sertões de Pernambuco (1750–1810)." *CLIO: Revista de Pesquisa Histórica* 37, no. 2 (December 2019): 58–81. https://periodicos.ufpe .br/revistas/index.php/revistaclio/article/view/242172, Accessed October 10, 2023.

Marques, Danilo Luiz. "Sob a 'sombra' de Palmares: Escravidão, memória e resistência na Alagoas oitocentista." PhD diss., Pontifícia Universidade Católica de São Paulo, 2018.

Marques, Danilo Luiz, and Rosa Lúcia Lima da Silva Correia. "O Movimento Negro, o NEABI/UFAL e a implementação do programa de políticas de ações afirmativas da Universidade Federal de Alagoas (2003–2022)." *Revista Escritas do Tempo* 4, no. 10 (April 2022): 23–45.

Marques, Dimas Bezerra. "Pelo bem de meus serviços, rogo-lhe está mercê: A influência da guerra de Palmares na distribuição de mercês (Capitania de Pernambuco, 1660–1778)." Master's thesis, Universidade Federal de Alagoas, 2014.

Marques, Maria Eduarda Castro Magalhães. "Homens de negócio, de fé e de poder político: A ordem terceira de São Francisco do Recife, 1695–1711." PhD diss., Pontifícia Universidade Católica do Rio de Janeiro, 2010.

Marquez, John C. "Witnesses to Freedom: Paula's Enslavement, Her Family's Freedom Suit, and the Making of a Counterarchive in the South Atlantic World." *Hispanic American Historical Review* 101, no. 2 (May 2021): 231–63.

Martin, Bonnie. "Slavery's Invisible Engine: Mortgaging Human Property." *Journal of Southern History* 76, no. 4 (2010): 817–66.

Martins, Joaquim Dias. *Os martires pernambucanos (victimas da liberdade nas duas revoluções ensaiadas em 1710 e 1817)*. Recife: Typografia de F. C. de Lemos e

Silva, 1853. Accessed July 7, 2023. http://www2.senado.leg.br/bdsf/handle /id/221682.

Martins, Joaquim Pedro Oliveira. *O Brazil e as colonias portuguezas*. 3rd ed. Lisbon: A. M. Pereira, 1888. http://archive.org/details/obrazileascolonioooliv.

Martins, Roberto Borges. "A obsessão com o tráfico, a legislação escravista e os códigos negreiros portugueses." Paper presented at the XII Congresso de História Econômica/13ª Conferência Internacional de História de Empresas, Niterói, Brazil, August 28–30, 2017. Accessed June 23, 2023. https:// abphe.org.br/arquivos/roberto-borges-martins.pdf.

Matthew, Laura E. *Memories of Conquest: Becoming Mexicano in Colonial Guatemala*. Chapel Hill: University of North Carolina Press, 2012.

Mattos, Hebe. "'Black Troops' and Hierarchies of Color in the Portuguese Atlantic World: The Case of Henrique Dias and His Black Regiment." *Luso-Brazilian Review* 45, no. 1 (2008): 6–29.

Mattos, Hebe. "Henrique Dias e a guerra preta: Algumas considerações sobre a polissemia das categorias de cor no mundo atlântico português dos seiscentos." In *África-Brasil: Caminhos da língua portuguesa*, edited by Charlotte Galves, Hélder Garmes, and Fernando Rosa Ribeiro, 15–26. Campinas: Editora UNICAMP, 2009.

Mattos, Hebe. "Novos quilombos: Re-significações da memória do cativeiro entre descendentes da última geração de escravos." In *Memórias do cativeiro: Família, trabalho e cidadania no pós-abolição*, edited by Ana Lugão e Hebe Mattos, 255–301. Rio de Janeiro: Civilização Brasileira, 2005.

Mattos, Hebe, and Martha Abreu. "'Remanescentes das comunidades dos quilombos': Memória do cativeiro, patrimônio cultural e direito à reparação." *Iberoamericana* 11, no. 42 (June 2011): 145–58.

McKittrick, Katherine. *Demonic Grounds: Black Women and the Cartographies of Struggle*. Minneapolis: University of Minnesota Press, 2006.

McKittrick, Katherine. "Mathematics Black Life." *Black Scholar* 44, no. 2 (Summer 2014): 16–26.

McKnight, Kathryn Joy. "Confronted Rituals: Spanish Colonial and Angolan 'Maroon' Executions in Cartagena de Indias (1634)." *Journal of Colonialism and Colonial History* 5, no. 3 (2004).

Medeiros, Coriolano de. *Diccionario chorographico do Estado da Parahyba*. Parahyba: Imprensa Oficial, 1914.

Medeiros, Maria do Céu, and Ariane Norma de Menezes Sá. *O trabalho na Paraíba: Das origens à transição para o trabalho livre*. João Pessoa: Editora Universitária, Universidade Federal da Paraíba, 1999.

Medeiros, Tarcísio. *Aspectos geopolíticos e antropológicos da história do Rio Grande do Norte*. Natal: Imprensa Universitária, 1973.

Medeiros Filho, Olavo de. *Naufrágios no litoral potiguar*. Natal: Instituto Histórico e Geográfico do Rio Grande do Norte, 1988.

Medina, João, and Isabel Castro Henriques. *A rota dos escravos: Angola e a rede do comércio negreiro*. Lisbon: Cegia, 1996.

Meeussen, A. E. "Bantu Grammatical Reconstructions." *Africana Linguistica* 3 (1967): 79–121.

Megenney, William W. "Words of African Origin Used in Latin America." *Hispania* 66, no. 1 (March 1983): 1–10.

Mello, Antonio Joaquim de. *Biografias de alguns poetas, e homens illustres da provincia de Pernambuco.* Typographia Universal, 1858.

Mello, Evaldo Cabral de. *A fronda dos Mazombos: Nobres contra mascates, Pernambuco, 1666–1715.* São Paulo: Companhia das Letras, 1995.

Mello, Evaldo Cabral de. *Olinda restaurada: Guerra e açúcar no Nordeste, 1630–1654.* Rio de Janeiro: Editora Forense-Universitária, 1975.

Mello, Humberto. "Datas e notas para a história do negro na Paraíba." *Revista do Instituto Histórico e Geográfico Paraíbano* 82, no. 25 (December 1991): 113–22.

Mello, José Antônio Gonsalves de. *D. Antonio Filipe Camarão: Capitão-mor dos indios da costa do Nordeste do Brasil.* Recife: Universidade do Recife, 1954.

Mello, José Antônio Gonsalves de, ed. *Fontes para a história do Brasil holandês.* 2 vols. Recife: MinC-Secretaria da Cultura, 1985.

Mello, José Antonio Gonsalves de. *Henrique Dias: Governador dos Pretos, Crioulos e Mulatos do Estado do Brasil.* Recife: Universidade de Recife, 1954.

Mello, José Antônio Gonsalves de. *Tempo dos flamengos: Influência da ocupação holandesa na vida e na cultura do norte do Brasil.* 3rd ed. Recife: Fundação Joaquim Nabuco/Editora Massangana, 1987.

Melo, Cláudia Fernanda Teixeira de. "Memórias e sentidos de natureza nas práticas educativas da Comunidade Quilombola Castainho/PE." PhD diss., Universidade Federal de Sergipe, 2018.

Melo, Filipe Matheus Marinho de. "'Que negros somos nós?': Africanos no Recife, século XVIII." Master's thesis, Universidade Federal Rural do Pernambuco, 2021.

Melo, Josemir Camilo de. "Quilombos do Catucá: Uma herança dos Palmares no Pernambuco oitocentista." In *Os quilombos na dinâmica social do Brasil,* edited by Clóvis Moura, 189–216. Maceió: Editora da Universidade Federal de Alagoas, 2001.

Melo, Mário. *Onomástica pernambucana; nomes antigos e correspondantes modernas das vilas, cidades e comarcas, dos distritos e municípios, de acôrdo com o decreto-lei estadual n.o 952 de 31 dezembro de 1943.* Recife: Livraria Universal, 1944.

Melo, Mário. *Toponymia pernambucana.* Recife: Imprensa Official, 1931.

"Memorial." *Revista do Instituto Archeológico e Geographico Alagoano* 1, no. 4 (June 1874): 96–98. Accessed May 28, 2023. https://hdl.handle.net /2027/hvd.32044092679117?urlappend=%3Bseq=146%3Bownerid =27021597764376491-162.

Mendes, Laura Peraza. "O serviço de armas nas guerras contra Palmares: Expedições, soldados e mercês (Pernambuco, segunda metade do século XVII)." Master's thesis, Universidade Estadual de Campinas, 2013.

Mendonça, Anne Karolline Campos. "As facetas jurídicas de um homem subalternizado (Alagoas colonial, 1755)." *Revista Crítica Histórica* 7, no. 16 (December 2017): 102–26.

Mendonça, Renato. *A influência africana no português do Brasil.* 3rd ed. Porto: Livraria Figueirinhas, 1948.

Menezes, Mozart Vergetti de. "Negros e indígenas na economia da Paraíba (1654–1755)." In *População negra na Paraíba: Educação, história e política,* edited by Solange P. Rocha and Ivonildes da Fonesca, 1:41–54. 2 vols. Campina Grande: Editora da Universidade Federal de Campina Grande, 2010.

Mensagem apresentada ao congresso legislativo do estado em 6 de Março de 1899 pelo Governador Dr. Joaquim Corrêa de Araujo. Pernambuco: Typ. de Manoel Figueiroa de Faria and Filhos, 1899.

Merolla da Sorrento, Jerom. "A Voyage to Congo and Several Other Countries, Chiefly in Southern Africk." In *A General Collection of the Best and Most Interesting Voyages and Travels in All Parts of the World; Many of Which Are Now First Translated into English. Digested on a New Plan,* edited by John Pinkerton, 16:195–316. London: Longman, Hurst, Rees, and Orme [etc.], 1814. Accessed May 30, 2023. https://archive.org/details/ageneralcollecto2pink goog/mode/2up.

Metcalf, Alida C. "Millenarian Slaves? The Santidade de Jaguaripe and Slave Resistance in the Americas." *American Historical Review* 104, no. 5 (December 1999): 1531–59.

Miki, Yuko. "Fleeing into Slavery: The Insurgent Geographies of Brazilian Quilombolas (Maroons), 1880–1881." *Americas* 68, no. 4 (April 2012): 495–528.

Miki, Yuko. *Frontiers of Citizenship: A Black and Indigenous History of Postcolonial Brazil.* Cambridge: Cambridge University Press, 2019.

Miles, Tiya. *Ties That Bind: The Story of an Afro-Cherokee Family in Slavery and Freedom.* Berkeley: University of California Press, 2015.

Miller, Joseph C. "Central Africa during the Era of the Slave Trade, c. 1490s–1850s." In *Central Africans and Cultural Transformations in the American Diaspora,* edited by Linda M. Heyward, 21–70. Cambridge: Cambridge University Press, 2002.

Miller, Joseph C. "The Imbangala and the Chronology of Early Central African History." *Journal of African History* 13, no. 4 (1972): 549–74.

Miller, Joseph C. *Kings and Kinsmen: Early Mbundu States in Angola.* Oxford: Oxford University Press, 1976.

Miller, Joseph C. "Retention, Reinvention, and Remembering: Restoring Identities through Enslavement in Africa and under Slavery in Brazil." In *Enslaving Connections: Changing Cultures of Africa and Brazil during the Era of Slavery,* edited by José C. Curto and Paul E. Lovejoy, 81–121. Amherst, NY: Humanity Books, 2004.

Miller, Joseph C. *Way of Death: Merchant Capitalism and the Angolan Slave Trade, 1730–1830*. Madison: University of Wisconsin Press, 1988.

Mitchell, Elise A. "Black and African American." *Journal of the Early Republic* 43, no. 1 (Spring 2023): 85–100.

Mobley, Christina Frances. "The Kongolese Atlantic: Central African Slavery and Culture from Mayombe to Haiti." PhD diss., Duke University, 2015.

Monte Carmelo, Luís de. *Compendio de orthografia, com sufficientes catologos, e novas regras [. . .]*. Lisbon: Antonio Rodrigues Galhardo, 1767. Accessed July 7, 2023. https://purl.pt/9.

Monteiro, John M. *Blacks of the Land: Indian Slavery, Settler Society, and the Portuguese Colonial Enterprise in South America*. Translated by James Woodard and Barbara Weinstein. Cambridge: Cambridge University Press, 2018.

Monteiro Lobato, José Bento. *O Saci-Pererê: Resultado de um inquérito*. Edited by Arlete Alonso, Cecília Bassarini, and Luciane Ortiz de Castro. São Paulo: Editora Globo, 2008.

Moraes Filho, Mello. *Festas e tradições populares do Brasil*. Belo Horizonte: Livraria Itatiaia Editora, 1979.

Morais, Ana Lunara da. "Em busca da perpetuação: Reprodução social e poder económico da nobreza da terra nas capitanias do norte, sécs. XVI–XVIII." PhD diss., Universidade de Évora, 2021.

Moreira, Alecsandra Pereira da Costa. "A luta pela terra e a construção do território remanescente de Quilombo de Caiana dos Crioulos, Alagoa Grande — PB." Master's thesis, Universidade Federal da Paraíba, 2009.

Moreira, Vânia Maria Losada. "Nem selvagens, nem cidadãos: Os índios da Vila de Nova Almeida e a usurpação de suas terras durante o século XIX." *Dimensões* 14 (2002): 151–67.

Moreira, Vânia Maria Losada. "Terras indígenas do Espírito Santo sob o regime territorial de 1850." *Revista Brasileira de História* 22, no. 43 (2002): 153–69. https://doi.org/10.1590/S0102-01882002000100009.

Morgan, Jennifer L. *Laboring Women: Reproduction and Gender in New World Slavery*. Philadelphia: University of Pennsylvania Press, 2004.

Morgan, Jennifer L. *Reckoning with Slavery: Gender, Kinship, and Capitalism in the Early Black Atlantic*. Durham, NC: Duke University Press, 2021.

Morrison, Toni. *Song of Solomon*. New York: Vintage International, 2004.

Mott, Luiz R. B. "Feiticeiros de Angola na Inquisição Portuguesa." *Mneme* 11, no. 29 (July 2011): 1–21.

Mott, Luiz R. B. *O sexo proibido: Virgens, gays e escravos nas garras da Inquisição*. Campinas: Papirus Editora, 1988.

Motta, Márcia Maria Menendes. "Terra, nação e tradições inventadas (uma outra abordagem sobre a Lei de Terras de 1850)." In *Nação e poder: As dimensões da história*, edited by Sonia Regina de Mendonça and Márcia Maria Mendes Motta, 81–92. Niterói: Editora da Universidade Federal Fluminense, 1998.

Moura Filha, Maria Berthilde. *De Filipéia à Paraíba: Uma cidade na estratégia de colonização do Brasil: Séculos XVI–XVIII*. Brasília, DF: Instituto do Patrimônio Histórico e Artístico Nacional, Superintendência do Iphan na Paraíba, 2010.

Mulvey, Patricia A. "Black Brothers and Sisters: Membership in the Black Lay Brotherhoods of Colonial Brazil." *Luso-Brazilian Review* 17, no. 2 (Winter 1980): 253–79.

Munanga, Kabengele. "Origem e histórico do quilombo na África." *Revista USP* 28 (December 1995–February 1996): 56–63.

Muñoz Maldonado, José. *Los Pintores de antaño*. N.p.: Juan de Gasso, sucesor de Gassó Hermanos, (n.d.). Accessed July 7, 2023. https://www.google.co .jp/books/edition/Los_Pintores_de_anta%C3%B1o/aI_7U7ySQXgC?hl =en&gbpv=0.

Nafafé, José Lingna. *Lourenço da Silva Mendonça and the Black Atlantic Abolitionist Movement in the Seventeenth Century*. Cambridge: Cambridge University Press, 2022.

Nardi, Jean-Baptiste. "Retrato de uma indústria no antigo regime: O Estanco Real do Tabaco em Portugal (1675–1830)." *Arquivos do Centro Cultural Português* 28 (1990): 321–39.

"Narração historica das calamidades de Pernambuco." *Revista do Instituto Histórico e Geográfico Brasilero* 53, no. 2 (1890): 1–308.

Nascimento, Abdias do. *O quilombismo: Documentos de uma militância pan-africanista*. Petróplois: Vozes, 1980.

Nascimento, Elisa Larkin, ed. *Cultura em movimento: Matrizes africanas e ativismo negro no Brasil*. São Paulo: Selo Negro, 2014. Kindle edition.

Nascimento, José Pereira do. *Diccionario Portuguez-Kimbundu*. Typographia da Missão, 1907.

Nascimento, Marco Tromboni de S. "'O tronco da Jurema': Ritual e etnicidade entre os povos indígenas do Nordeste—O caso Kiriri." Master's thesis, Universidade Federal da Bahia, 1994.

Nascimento, Rômulo. "Palmares em fontes holandesas: Sobre os *boschnegers* entre a guerrilha e a ordem." In *Mocambos de Palmares: Histórias e fontes (séc. XVI–XIX)*, edited by Flávio dos Santos Gomes, 39–47. Rio de Janeiro: 7Letras, 2010.

Nascimento, Rômulo Luiz Xavier. *Palmares: Os escravos contra o poder colonial*. São Paulo: Editora Terceiro Nome, 2014.

Nascimento, Rômulo Xavier. "'E agora Nassau'? Discussão sobre abastecimento e o sistema escravista no centro da estratégia sul-atlântica batava." In *História da escravidão em Pernambuco*, edited by Flavio José Gomes Cabral and Robson Costa, 241–66. Recife: Editora Universitária da Universidade Federal de Pernambuco, 2012.

Navarro, Eduardo de Almeida. *Dicionário tupi antigo: A língua indígena clássica do Brasil: Vocabulário português-tupi e dicionário tupi-português, tupinismos no português do Brasil, etimologias de topônimos e antropônimos de origem tupi*. São Paulo: Global, 2013.

Navarro, Eduardo de Almeida. *Método moderno de Tupi antigo*. São Paulo: Global Editora, 2006.

Neiva, Severino Henrique de Lucena, ed. *Guia Postal (geográphico) da República dos Estados Unidos do Brasil*. 2 vols. Rio de Janeiro: Typographia da Directora Geral dos Correios, 1931.

Neruda, Pablo. "Keeping Quiet." In *Extravagaria*, translated by Alastair Reid, 26–29. New York: Farrar, Straus and Giroux, 1974.

Neto, Maria Conceição. "Kilombo, quilombos, ocilombo . . ." *Mensagem: Revista Angolana de Cultura* 4 (1989): 5–19.

Neves, Alexandre Gomes. "Câmara Cascudo e Oscar Ribas: Diálogos no Atlântico." *Revista Crioula* 4 (November 2008). Accessed May 30, 2023. https://doi.org/10.11606/issn.1981-7169.crioula.2008.54047.

Neves, Erivaldo Fagundes. "Sampauleiros traficantes: Comércio de escravos do Alto Sertão da Bahia para o oeste cafeeiro paulista." *Afro-Ásia* 24 (2000): 97–128.

Nieuhof, Joan (Johan). *Memorável viagem marítima e terrestre ao Brasil*. Edited by José Honório Rodrigues. Translated by Moacir N. Vasconcelos. São Paulo: Livraria Martins, 1942.

Nieuhof, Johannes (Johan). *Joan Nieuhofs Gedekwaerdige Zee en Lantreize. Door de voornaemste Landschappen van West en Oostindien*. Amsterdam: By de Weduwe van Iacob van Meurs, 1682. Accessed June 27, 2023. https://archive.org/details/johannieuhofsgedoonieu.

Nogueira, André. "Relações sociais e práticas mágicas na capitania do ouro: O caso do Negro Angola Pai Caetano (Vila Rica—1791)." *Revista Científica da Faminas* 1, no. 3 (December 2005): 125–47.

Northrup, David. "Igbo and Myth Igbo: Culture and Ethnicity in the Atlantic World, 1600–1850." *Slavery and Abolition* 21, no. 3 (2000): 1–20.

Nurse, Derek. "The Contributions of Linguistics to the Study of History in Africa." *Journal of African History* 38, no. 3 (1997): 359–91.

Nurse, Derek, and Gérard Philippson, eds. *The Bantu Languages*. London: Routledge, 2003.

O'Brien, Tim. *The Things They Carried*. New York: Broadway Books, 1998.

Octávio, José. *A escravidão na Paraíba: Historiografia e história: Preconceitos e racismo numa produção cultural*. João Pessoa: União Superintendência de Imprensa e Editora, 1988.

Offen, Karl. "Environment, Space, and Place: Cultural Geographies of Colonial Afro-Latin America." In *Afro-Latin American Studies: An Introduction*, edited by Alejandro de la Fuente and George Reid Andrews, 486–533. Cambridge: Cambridge University Pres, 2018.

Olival, Fernanda. "Mercados de hábitos e serviços em Portugal (séculos XVII–XVIII)." *Análise Social* 38, no. 168 (2003): 743–69.

Olival, Fernanda. "Mercês, serviços e circuitos documentais no Império Português." In *Domínio da distância: Comunicação e cartografia*, edited by Maria Emília Madeira Santos and Manuel Lobato, 59–70. Lisbon: História e

Cartografia, Departamento de Ciências Humanas, Instituto de Investigação Científica Tropical, 2006.

Olival, Fernanda. *As ordens militares e o estado moderno: Honra, mercê e venalidade em Portugal (1641–1789)*. Lisboa: Estar Editoria, 2001.

Oliveira, Anderson José Machado de. *Devoção negra: Santos pretos e catequese no Brasil colonial*. Rio de Janeiro: Quartet, 2008.

Oliveira, Antonio José de. "Os Kariri: Resistências à ocupação dos sertões dos Cariris Novos no século XVIII." PhD diss., Universidade Federal do Ceará, 2017.

Oliveira, Leonardo Paiva de. "Capitães-mores das capitanias do norte: Perfis, trajetórias e hierarquias espaciais no Rio Grande e Ceará (1656–1755)." Master's thesis, Universidade Federal do Rio Grande do Norte, 2018.

Oliveira, Maria da Glória de. "Fazer história, escrever a história: Sobre as figurações do historiador no Brasil oitocentista." *Revista Brasileira de História* 30, no. 59 (2010): 37–52.

Oliveira, Maria Inês Côrtes de. "Quem eram os 'Negros da Guiné'? A origem dos africanos na Bahia." *Afro-Ásia*, nos. 19–20 (1997): 37–73. Accessed December 11, 2023, https://periodicos.ufba.br/index.php/afroasia/article/view/20947.

Oliveira, Maria Lêda, ed. *A "Historia do Brazil" de Frei Vicente do Salvador: História e política no Império Português do século XVII*. Rio de Janeiro: Versal, 2008.

Oliveira, Maria Lêda. "A primeira *rellação* do último assalto a Palmares." *Afro-Ásia* 33 (2005): 251–324.

Oliveira Filho, João Pacheco. *A presença indígena no Nordeste: Processoes de territorialização, modos de reconhecimento e regimes de memória*. Rio de Janeiro: Contra Capa, 2011.

Oliveira Filho, Sergio Willian de Castro, and Luana Costa Pierre de Messias. "Da circum-navegação da Vital de Oliveira às novas tabelas de rações: Alimentação e saúde a bordo dos navios da Marinha Imperial Brasileira, 1879–1886." *História, Ciências, Saúde-Manguinhos* 27, no. 4 (October–December 2020): 1285–1308.

Orser, Charles E., Jr., and Pedro Paulo de Abreu Funari. "Archaeology and Slave Resistance and Rebellion." *World Archaeology* 33, no. 1 (June 2001): 61–72.

O'Toole, Rachel Sarah. "As Historical Subjects: The African Diaspora in Colonial Latin American History." *History Compass* 11, no. 12 (December 2013): 1094–110.

Paiva, Ricardo de, and Vânia R. Fialho de Paiva e Souza. *Relatório de identificação: Caiana dos Crioulos*, 1998. Appended to Serviço de Regularização de Territórios Quilombolas do Instituto Nacional de Colonização e Reforma Agrária, Superintendência Regional No. 18 (Paraíba), *Relatório técnico*.

Palacios, Guillermo. *Campesinato e escravidão no Brasil: Agricultores livres e pobres na Capitania Geral de Pernambuco (1700–1817)*. Translated by Walter Sotomayor. Brasília: Editora da Universidade de Brasília, 2004.

Palmer, Colin A. "Defining and Studying the Modern African Diaspora." *Journal of African American History* 85, nos. 1–2 (2000): 27–32.

Palmié, Stephan. "African States in the New World? Remarks on the Tradition of Transatlantic Resistance." In *Alternative Cultures in the Caribbean: First International Conference of the Society of Caribbean Research, Berlin 1988*, edited by Thomas Brenner and Ulrich Fleischmann, 55–68. Frankfurt: Vervuert, 1993.

Palmié, Stephan. *Wizards and Scientists: Explorations in Afro-Cuban Modernity and Tradition*. Durham, NC: Duke University Press, 2002.

Pantoja, Selma. "Inquisição, degredo e mestiçagem em Angola no século XVIII." *Revista Lusófona de Ciência das Religiões* 3, nos. 5–6 (2004): 117–36. Accessed June 27, 2023. https://revistas.ulusofona.pt/index.php/cienciareligioes /article/view/4582.

Paraíso, Maria Hilda Baqueiro. *O tempo da dor e do trabalho: A conquista dos territórios indígenas nos sertões do leste*. Salvador: Editora da Universidade Federal da Bahia, 2014.

Parés, Luis Nicolau. *The Formation of Candomblé: Vodun History and Ritual in Brazil*. Translated by Richard Vernon. Chapel Hill: University of North Carolina Press, 2013.

Paschel, Tianna S. *Becoming Black Political Subjects: Movements and Ethno-Racial Rights in Colombia and Brazil*. Princeton, NJ: Princeton University Press, 2016.

Patterson, Orlando. *Freedom, Volume I: Freedom in the Making of Western Culture*. New York: Basic Books, 1992.

Paula, Hermes Augusto de. *Montes Claros: Sua história, sua gente e seus costumes*. Rio de Janeiro: N.p., 1957.

Pearson, M. N. *The Portuguese in India*. Cambridge: Cambridge University Press, 1987.

Pedreira, Pedro Tomás. "Os quilombos dos Palmares e o Senado da Câmara da Cidade do Salvador." *Mensario do Arquivo Nacional* 11, no. 3 (March 1980): 14–17. Accessed June 26, 2023. http://memoria.bn.br/docreader/005959/4466.

Pereira, Elenize Trindade. "Geoprocessamento das sesmarias das capitanias do norte do Estado do Brasil, Plataforma Sesmarias do Império Luso Brasileiro (1650–1750)." In *O retorno dos mapas: sistemas de informação geográfica em história*, edited by Carlos Valencia and Tiago Gil, 114–37. Porto Alegre: Ladeira Livros, 2016.

Pérez, Louis A. *To Die in Cuba: Suicide and Society*. Chapel Hill: University of North Carolina Press, 2005.

Perlman, Merrill. "Black and White: Why Capitalization Matters." *Columbia Journalism Review*. Accessed October 16, 2022. https://www.cjr.org/analysis /language_corner_1.php.

Perry, Keisha-Khan Y. *Black Women against the Lab Grab: The Fight for Racial Justice in Brazil*. Minneapolis: University of Minnesota Press, 2013.

Pexa, Christopher J. *Translated Nation: Rewriting the Dakhóta Oyáte*. Minneapolis: University of Minnesota Press, 2019.

Piersen, William D. "White Cannibals, Black Martyrs: Fear, Depression, and Religious Faith as Causes of Suicide among New Slaves." *Journal of Negro History* 62, no. 2 (April 1977): 147–59.

Pinho, Wanderley. *História de um engenho do Reconcavo, Matoim Novo-Caboto— Freguezia, 1552–1944.* Rio de Janeiro: Z. Valverde, 1946.

Pinto, Alfredo Moreira. *Apontamentos para o diccionario geographico do Brazil.* 3 vols. Rio de Janeiro: Imprensa Nacional, 1894. Accessed July 3, 2023. https://nrs.lib.harvard.edu/urn-3:fhcl:10837347.

Pinto, Estevão. *Etnologia brasileira: Fulniô, os últimos Tapuias.* São Paulo: Companhia Editora Nacional, 1956.

Pinto, Irineu Ferreira. *Datas e notas para a historia da Parahyba.* 2 vols. Parahyba do Norte: Imprensa Official, 1908.

Pinto, Luiz. *Síntese histórica da Paraíba, 1501–1960.* Rio de Janeiro: Gráfica Ouvidor, 1960.

Pires, Maria Idalina da Cruz. *Guerra dos bárbaros: Resistência indígena e conflitos no Nordeste colonial.* Recife: Governo do Estado de Pernambuco, 1990.

Portilla Manfredini, Jorge. "Diffusion and Semiosis of the Word 'Qilombo': From Bantu to Rio Platense Spanish." *Academia Letters,* 2021.

Porto, Waldice Mendonça. *Paraíba em preto e branco.* João Pessoa: União Companhia Editorial, 1976.

Porto Alegre, Maria Sylvia, Marlene da Silva Mariz, and Beatriz Góis Dantas, eds. *Documentos para a história indígena no Nordeste (Ceará, Rio Grande do Norte e Sergipe).* São Paulo: Núcleo de História Indígena e do Indigenismo and Fundação de Amparo à Pesquisa do Estado de São Paulo, 1994.

Posadillo y Posadillo, Isidro. *Derrotero de Las Costas del Brasil.* Madrid: Depósito Hidrográfico, 1872. Accessed May 30, 2023. https://catalog.hathitrust.org /Record/011260793.

Powell, Timothy. "Summoning the Ancestors: The Flying Africans' Story and Its Enduring Legacy." In *African American Life in the Georgia Lowcountry: The Atlantic World and the Gullah Geechee,* edited by Phillip Morgan, 253–80. Athens: University of Georgia Press, 2010.

Prado, Fabrício. *Edge of Empire: Atlantic Networks and Revolution in Bourbon Río de La Plata.* Berkeley: University of California Press, 2015.

Price, Richard, ed. *Maroon Societies: Rebel Slave Communities in the Americas.* 3rd ed. Baltimore: Johns Hopkins University Press, 1996.

Price, Richard. "Refiguring Palmares." *Tipití: Journal of the Society for the Anthropology of Lowland South America* 1, no. 2 (2003): 211–19. https:// digitalcommons.trinity.edu/tipiti/vol1/iss2/3/.

Price, Richard. "Reinventando a história dos quilombos: Rasuras e confabulações." *Afro-Ásia* no. 23 (2000).

Price, Richard. "Scrapping Maroon History: Brazil's Promise, Suriname's Shame." *New West Indian Guide* 72, nos. 3–4 (1998): 233–55.

Puntoni, Pedro. *A guerra dos bárbaros: Povos indígenas e a colonização do sertão nordeste do Brasil, 1650–1720.* São Paulo: Hucitec, 2002.

Putnam, Lara. "The Transnational and the Text-Searchable: Digitized Sources and the Shadows They Cast." *American Historical Review* 121, no. 2 (April 2016): 377–402.

Queiroz, Josinaldo Sousa de. "Entre a permissão e a proibição: Conflitos entre africanos, capuchinos italianos e a administração secular na capitania de Pernambuco (1778–1797)." Master's thesis, Universidade Federal de Pernambuco, 2018.

Queiroz, Sônia. *Vissungos: Cantos afrodescendentes em Minas Gerais*. Edited by Neide Freitas and Sônia Queiroz. 3rd ed. Belo Horizonte: Viva Voz, 2015.

Querino, Manuel. *A raça africana e os seus costumes*. 2nd ed. Salvador: Progresso Editora, 1955. Accessed May 30, 2023. http://archive.org/details /aracaafricana.

Raminelli, Ronald. "Impedimentos da cor: Mulatos no Brasil e em Portugal, c. 1640–1750." *Varia Historia* 28, no. 48 (December 2012): 699–723.

Raminelli, Ronald. "Nobreza indígena: Os chefes potiguares, 1633–1695." In *A presença indígena no Nordeste: Processoes de territorialização, modos de reconhecimento e regimes de memória*, edited by João Pacheco Oliveira Filho, 47–68. Rio de Janeiro: Contra Capa, 2011.

Raminelli, Ronald. "Privilegios y malogros de la familia Camarão." *Nuevo Mundo Mundos Nuevos* (online), March 17, 2008. Accessed May 30, 2023. http:// journals.openedition.org/nuevomundo/27802.

Ramos, Arthur. *O negro brasileiro*. 2nd ed. São Paulo: Companhia Editora Nacional, 1940.

Ramos, Donald. "O quilombo e o sistema escravista em Minas Gerais do século XVIII." In *Liberdade por um fio: História dos quilombos no Brasil*, edited by João José Reis and Flávio dos Santos Gomes, 164–92. São Paulo: Companhia das Letras, 1996.

Rarey, Matthew Francis. *Insignificant Things: Amulets and the Art of Survival in the Early Black Atlantic*. Durham, NC: Duke University Press, 2023.

Read, Ian. "'A Change Very Perceptible and Very Oppressive': Climate, Epidemics, and Race in Brazil." *Luso-Brazilian Review* 58, no. 2 (2021): 81–117. Accessed June 28, 2023. muse.jhu.edu/article/851139.

Redinha, José. *Subsídios para a história, arqueologia e etnografia dos povos da Lunda: Campanha etnografica ao Tchiboco (Alto-Tchicapa)*. Lisbon: Museu do Dundo, 1953.

Reesink, Edwin. "Raízes históricas: A Jurema, enteógeno e ritual na história dos povos indígenas no Nordeste." In *As muitas faces da Jurema: De espécie botânica à divindade afro-indígena*, edited by Clarice Novaes da Mota and Ulysses Paulino de Albuquerque, 61–96. Recife: Edições Bagaço, 2002.

Reginaldo, Lucilene. "Rosário dos pretos, 'São Benedito de Quissama': Irmandades e devoções negras no mundo atlântico (Portugal e Angola, século XVIII)." *Studia Historica. Historia Moderna* 38 (2016): 123–51.

Rêgo, Alberto da Silva. *Os aldeões de Garanhuns: Sua gente, seus jornais, suas associações, o mundo literário, os "players," os poetas e árvores genealógicas*. Recife: Centro de Estudos de História Municipal, 1987.

Reis, Andressa Mercês Barbosa dos. "Zumbi: Historiografia e imagens." Master's thesis, Universidade Estadual de São Paulo-Franca, 2004.

Reis, Demian Moreira. "Dança do Quilombo: Os significados de uma tradição." *Afro-Ásia* 17 (1996): 159–71.

Reis, Demian Moreira. "Quilombo: Uma dança de luta entre índios guerreiros e negros quilombolas." *Palmares em Revista* 1 (1996): 153–74.

Reis, João José. "Quilombos e revoltas escravas no Brasil." *Revista USP* 28 (February 1995): 14–39.

Reis, João José, and Flávio dos Santos Gomes, eds. *Liberdade por um fio: História dos quilombos no Brasil*. São Paulo: Companhia das Letras, 1996.

Reis, João José, and Flávio dos Santos Gomes, eds. *Revoltas escravas no Brasil*. São Paulo: Companhia das Letras, 2019.

Reiter, Bernd, and Jhon Antón Sánchez. *Routledge Handbook of Afro-Latin American Studies*. New York: Routledge, 2023.

Relatorio apresentado à Assembléa Legislativa Provincial do Rio de Janeiro [. . .] 8 de Agosto de 1881 pelo presidente, Dr. Marinho Alvares da Silva Campos. Rio de Janeiro: Imprensa Industrial de João Paulo Ferreira Dias, 1881.

Relatorio Lido Perante a Assembléa Legislativa da Provincia das Alagoas [. . .]16 de março de 1870 pelo presidente [. . .] Dr. José Bento da Cunha Figueiredo Junior. Maceió: Typographia Commercial de A. J. da Costa, 1870.

Restall, Matthew. "Black Conquistadors: Armed Africans in Early Spanish America." *Americas* 57, no. 2 (October 2000): 171–205.

Restall, Matthew. "A History of the New Philology and the New Philology in History." *Latin American Research Review* 38, no. 1 (February 2003): 113–34.

Restall, Matthew. *Maya Conquistador*. Boston: Beacon Press, 1999.

Restall, Matthew. *Seven Myths of the Spanish Conquest*. Oxford: Oxford University Press, 2004.

Ribas, Óscar. *Dicionário de regionalismos angolanos*. Matosinhos, Portugal: Contemporânea, 1997.

Ribas, Óscar. *Ilundo: Divindades e ritos angolanos*. Publicações do Museu de Angola. Luanda: Museu de Angola, 1958.

Ribeiro, João. *Diccionario grammatical*. 3rd ed. Rio de Janeiro: Livraria Francisco Alves, 1906.

Ribeiro, Levy Felix. "Território e memória: Uma etnografia na comunidade remanescente quilombola do Muquém em União dos Palmares— Alagoas." Master's thesis, Universidade Federal de Alagoas, 2018.

Robbeets, Martine. "Comparative Reconstruction in Linguistics." In *Oxford Bibliographies: Linguistics* (online). March 28, 2018.

Roberts, Andrew. *A History of the Bemba: Political Growth and Change in North-Eastern Zambia before 1900*. Madison: University of Wisconsin Press, 1973.

Roberts, Neil. *Freedom as Marronage*. Chicago: University of Chicago Press, 2015.

Robertson, William Spence. *History of the Latin-American Nations*. New York: D. Appleton, 1922.

Robinson, Cedric J. *Black Marxism: The Making of the Black Radical Tradition*. 2nd ed. Chapel Hill: University of North Carolina Press, 2000.

Rocha, Aurélio. "Contribuição para o estudos das relações entre Moçambique e o Brasil no séc. XIX (tráfico de escravos e relações políticas e culturais)." *Estudos Afro-Asiáticos*, no. 21 (December 1991): 199–233.

Rocha, Gabriel de Avilez. "Maroons in the Montes: Toward a Political Ecology of Marronage in the Sixteenth-Century Caribbean." In *Early Modern Black Diaspora Studies: An Anthology*, edited by C. L. Smith, 15–35. New York: Palgrave Macmillan, 2018.

Rocha, José Maria Tenório. *Folguedos e danças de Alagoas: Sistematização e classificação*. Maceió: Secretaria de Educação e Cultura de Alagoas, Departamento de Assuntos Culturais, Comissão Alagoana de Folclore, 1984.

Rocha, Solange P. *Gente negra na Paraíba oitocentista: População, família e parentesco espiritual*. São Paulo: Editora da Universidade Estadual Paulista, 2009.

Rocha, Solange P., and Ivonildes da Silva Fonseca, eds. *População negra na Paraíba: Educação, história e política*. 2 vols. Campina Grande: Editora da Universidade Federal de Campina Grande, 2010.

Rocha, Solange P., and Matheus Silveira Guimarães, eds. *Travessias atlânticas e a Paraíba afro-diaspórica*. Recife: Editora da Universidade Federal de Pernambuco, 2018.

Rocha Pita, Sebastião da. *Historia da America Portugueza, Desde o Anno de Mil e Quinhentos do seu descobrimento, até o de mil e setecentos e vinte e quatro*. Lisbon: Joseph Antonio da Sylva, 1730. Accessed June 26, 2023. https://digital.bbm.usp.br/handle/bbm/4714.

Rocha Pombo, José Francisco da. *Historia do Brazil*. 10 vols. Rio de Janeiro: B. de Aguila, 1905. Accessed May 30, 2023. https://catalog.hathitrust.org/Record/000318687.

Rodrigues, Aldair. "Malungos e parentes: 'Sumário contra os Pretos de Angola do Continente de Pernambuco' (1779)." *Sankofa: Revista de História da África e de Estudos da Diáspora Africana* 12, no. 22 (May 2019): 63–92.

Rodrigues, Aryon Dall'Igna. "O artigo definido e os numerais na língua Kirirí: Vocabulários Português-Kirirí e Kirirí-Português." *Revista Brasileira de Linguística Antropológica* 4, no. 2 (December 2012): 169–235.

Rodrigues, Aryon Dall'Igna, and Ana Suelly A. C. Cabral, eds., *Novos estudos sobre línguas indígenas*. Brasília: Editora da Universidade de Brasília, 2005.

Rodrigues, Gefferson. "A tentativa de sublevação do Índio Antônio Domingos Camarão em Pernambuco (1730)." *Acervo: Revista do Arquivo Nacional* 34, no. 2 (August 2021): 1–13. Accessed July 1, 2023. https://revista.an.gov.br/index.php/revistaacervo/article/view/1701.

Rodrigues, Michelle Gonçalves, and Roberta Bivar Carneiro Campos. "Caminhos da visibilidade: A ascensão do culto da Jurema no campo religioso de Recife." *Afro-Ásia* 47 (2013): 269–91.

Rodrigues, Pero. "Copia de uma carta do Padre Pero Rodrigues, Provincial da Provincia do Brazil da Companhia de Jesus, para o Padre João Alvares da mesma Companhia: Assistente do Padre Geral." *Annaes da Bibliotheca Nacional do Rio de Janeiro* 20 (1898): 255–65.

Rodrigues, Raimundo Nina. "A Troya Negra: Erros e lacunas da história de Palmares." *Revista do Instituto Archeológico, Histórico, e Geográphico Pernambucano*, September 1904, 645–72.

Rodrigues, Raimundo Nina. *Os africanos no Brasil*. 7th ed. Brasília: Editora Nacional, 1988.

Rodriguez, Walfredo. *Roteiro sentimental de uma cidade*. São Paulo: Editôra Brasiliense, 1962.

Rogers, Thomas D. *The Deepest Wounds: A Labor and Environmental History of Sugar in Northeast Brazil*. Chapel Hill: University of North Carolina Press, 2010.

Roller, Heather F. *Contact Strategies: Histories of Native Autonomy in Brazil*. Stanford, CA: Stanford University Press, 2021.

Romero, Sílvio. *Estudos sobre a poesia popular do Brasil*. 2nd ed. Petrópolis: Editora Vozes, 1977.

Rowe, Erin Kathleen. *Black Saints in Early Modern Global Catholicism*. Cambridge: Cambridge University Press, 2020.

Rucker, Walter C. *Gold Coast Diasporas: Identity, Culture, and Power*. Bloomington: Indiana University Press, 2015.

Saignes, Miguel Acosta. "Life in a Venezuelan Cumbe." In *Maroon Societies: Rebel Slave Communities in the Americas*, edited by Richard Price, 64–73. Baltimore: Johns Hopkins University Press, 1996.

Saillant, Francine, and Ana Lucia Araujo. "Zumbi: Mort, Mémoire et Résistance." *Frontières* 19, no. 1 (n.d.): 37–42.

Salgado, Graça Azevedo, ed. *Fiscais e meirinhos: A administração no Brasil colonial*. Rio de Janeiro: Editora Nova Fronteira, 1985.

Salmons, Joseph. "Comparative-Historical Linguistics." In *Oxford Bibliographies: Linguistics* (online). November 8, 2016.

Salvado, João Paulo. "O Estanco do Tabaco em Portugal: Contrato-Geral e consórcios mercantis (1702–1755)." In *Política y Hacienda del Tabaco en los Impérios Ibéricos (Siglos XVII–XIX)*, edited by Santiago de Luxán, 133–54. Madrid: Centro de Estudios Políticos y Constitucionales, 2014.

Sampaio, Gabriela dos Reis. "Juca Rosa: Spiritual Leader and Healer." In *The Human Tradition in Modern Brazil*, edited by Peter M. Beattie, 53–68. Wilmington, DE: Rowman and Littlefield, 2003.

Sampaio, Gabriela dos Reis. *Juca Rosa: Um pai-de-santo na corte imperial*. Rio de Janeiro: Arquivo Nacional, 2009.

Sampaio, Patrícia Melo. "Política indigenista no Brasil imperial." In *O Brasil imperial, Vol. 1*, edited by Keila Grinberg and Ricardo Salles, 175–206. Rio de Janeiro: Civilização Brasileira, 2009.

Santos, Irinéia Maria Franco Dos. *A caverna do diabo e outras histórias: Ensaios de história social das religiões (Alagoas, séculos XIX e XX)*. Maceió: Editora da Universidade Federal de Alagoas, 2016.

Santos, Joel Rufino dos. "Memorial Zumbi: Conquista do movimento negro." In Nascimento, *Cultura em movimento*, 229–242 (of 389).

Santos, Paulo Pereira dos. *Evolução econômica do Rio Grande do Norte: (século XVI ao XXI)*. 3rd ed. Natal: Departamento Estadual de Imprensa, 2010.

Santos, Vanicléia Silva. "As bolsas de mandinga no espaço atlântico: Século XVIII." PhD diss., Universidade de São Paulo, 2008.

Sarmento, Alfredo de. *Os sertões d'África (apontamentos de viagem)*. Lisbon: F. A. da Silva, 1880. Accessed May 30, 2023. http://archive.org/details /ossertesdafricaa00sarm.

Schneider, John T. *Dictionary of African Borrowings in Brazilian Portuguese*. Hamburg: Helmut Buske Verlag, 1991.

Schoenbrun, David L. "Words, Things, and Meaning: Linguistics as a Tool for Historical Reconstruction." In *The Oxford Handbook of African Languages*, edited by Rainer Vossen and Gerrit J. Dimmendaal. New York: Oxford University Press, 2020.

Schryver, Gilles-Maurice de, Rebecca Grollemund, Simon Branford, and Koen Bostoen. "Introducing a State-of-the-Art Phylogenetic Classification of the Kikongo Language Cluster." *Africana Linguistica* 21 (2015): 87–162.

Schuler, Monica. "Enslavement, the Slave Voyage, and Astral and Aquatic Journeys in African Diaspora Discourse." In *Africa and the Americas*, edited by José C. Curto and Renée Soulodre-La France, 186–213. Trenton, NJ: Africa World Press, 2005.

Schuler, Monica. "Liberated Central Africans in Nineteenth-Century Guyana." In *Central Africans and Cultural Transformations in the American Diaspora*, edited by Linda M. Heyward, 319–52. Cambridge: Cambridge University Press, 2002.

Schultz, Kara Danielle. "'The Kingdom of Angola Is Not Very Far from Here': The Río de La Plata, Brazil, and Angola, 1580–1680." PhD diss., Vanderbilt University, 2016.

Schultz, Kirsten. *From Conquest to Colony: Empire, Wealth, and Difference in Eighteenth-Century Brazil*. New Haven, CT: Yale University Press, 2023.

Schwartz, Stuart B. "Looking for a New Brazil: Crisis and Rebirth in the Atlantic World after the Fall of Pernambuco." In *The Legacy of Dutch Brazil*, edited by Michiel van Groesen, 41–58. New York: Cambridge University Press, 2014.

Schwartz, Stuart B. "Mocambos, quilombos e Palmares." *Estudos Econômicos* 17 (1987): 61–88.

Schwartz, Stuart B. *Slaves, Peasants, and Rebels: Reconsidering Brazilian Slavery*. Champaign: University of Illinois Press, 1996.

Schwartz, Stuart B. *Sovereignty and Society in Colonial Brazil: The High Court of Bahia and Its Judges, 1609–1751.* Berkeley: University of California Press, 1973.

Schwartz, Stuart B. "Tapanhuns, negros da terra e curibocas: Causas comuns e confrontos entre negros e indígenas." *Afro-Ásia* nos. 29–30 (2003): 13–40.

Scott, Julius S. *The Common Wind: Afro-American Organization in the Revolution against Slavery.* London: Verso, 2018.

Senna, Nelson de. *Chorographia de Minas Geraes.* Rio de Janeiro: Typ. Lith. P. de Mello and Company, 1922.

Serra, Ordep. "Monumentos negros: Uma experiência." *Afro-Ásia* 33 (2005): 169–205.

Serviço de Regularização de Territórios Quilombolas do Instituto Nacional de Colonização e Reforma Agrária, Superintendência Regional No. 18 (Paraíba). *Relatório técnico de delimitação do território da communidade Quilombola de Caiana dos Crioulos.* October 2015.

"1746, Expedição mandada fazer por Gomes Freire de Andrada para bater os quilombos." *Revista do Arquivo Público Mineiro* 8, no. 1 (1903): 619–21. Accessed June 28, 2023. http://www.siaapm.cultura.mg.gov.br/modules /brtexport/index.php?cid=406&mid=31&full_pdf=1.

Sharpe, Christina. *In the Wake: On Blackness and Being.* Durham, NC: Duke University Press, 2016.

Silva, Aldemir Barros da, Jr. "A construção do campo de ação indigenista na província de Alagoas." In *Olhares sobre a província de Alagoas,* edited by Aldemir Barros da Silva Júnior and Moisés Sebastião da Silva, 75–118. Arapiraca: Eduneal, 2018.

Silva, Ana Carolina Lourenço Santos da, and Flávio Gomes. "A Lei 10.639 e a patrimonialização da cultura: Quilombos, Serra da Barriga e Palmares — Primeiros percursos." *Revista Teias* 14, no. 34 (2013): 92–101. Accessed July 10, 2023. https://www.e-publicacoes.uerj.br/index.php/revistateias /article/view/24349.

Silva, Antônio da. "Sermão . . . no Collegio do Arr[ecif]e de Pern[ambu]co pello P.e Antonio da Sylva [. . .]." (n.d.), COD.6751, Manuscritos Reservado, Biblioteca Nacional de Portugal. Accessed May 24, 2023. http://purl.pt /16671.

Silva, Antonio de Moraes, and Rafael Bluteau. *Diccionario da lingua portugueza composto pelo padre D. Rafael Bluteau, reformado, e accrescentado por Antonio de Moraes Silva natural do Rio de Janeiro.* 2 vols. Lisboa: Simão Tadeu Ferreira, 1789. Accessed June 21, 2023. https://digital.bbm.usp.br/handle/bbm/5412.

Silva, Daniel Barros Domingues da, and David Eltis. "The Slave Trade to Pernambuco, 1561–1851." In *Extending the Frontiers: Essays on the New Transatlantic Slave Trade Database,* edited by David Eltis and David Richardson, 95–129. New Haven, CT: Yale University Press, 2008.

Silva, Edson. *Aldeia de Escada: Conflitos, esbulhos de terras e resistências indígena em Pernambuco no século XIX.* Maceió: Editora Olyver, 2021.

Silva, Edson. "Manuel Valentim: 'Uma Guerra Civil de 12 Anos': Mobilizações indígenas na Zona da Mata Sul de Pernambuco, na segunda metade do século XIX." *Outros Tempos* 19, no. 34 (2022): 170–207.

Silva, Edson. "O nosso direito: Conflitos e resistência indígena em Pernambuco no século XIX." In *Indios do Nordeste: Temas e problemas: 500 anos*, edited by Luiz Sávio de Almeida, Marcos Galindo, and Edson Silva, 265–80. Maceió: Editora da Universidade Federal de Alagoas, 1999.

Silva, J. M. Pereira da. "Biographia dos brazileiros distinctos por lettras, armas, virtudes, etc. — Sebastião da Rocha Pitta." *Revista do Instituto Histórico e Geográfico Brasilero* 12 (1849): 258–76.

Silva, João. *Entertaining Lisbon: Music, Theater, and Modern Life in the Late 19th Century*. New York: Oxford University Press, 2016.

Silva, Kalina Vanderlei. *O miserável soldo e a boa ordem da sociedade colonial: Militarização e marginalidade na capitania de Pernambuco dos séculos XVIIE e XVIII*. Recife: Prefeitura do Recife, 2001.

Silva, Kalina Vanderlei. *Nas solidões vastas e assustadoras: A conquista do sertão de Pernambuco pelas vilas açucareiras nos séculos XVII e XVIII*. Recife: Companhia Editora de Pernambuco, 2010.

Silva, Luiz Geraldo. "'Esperança de liberdade': Interpretações populares da abolição ilustrada (1773-1774)." *Revista de História*, no. 144 (June 2001): 107–49.

Silva, Luiz Geraldo. "Gênese das milícias de pardos e pretos na América Portuguesa: Pernambuco e Minas Gerais, séculos XVII e XVIII." *Revista de História* 169 (December 2013): 111–44.

Silva, Luiz Geraldo. "Palmares and Zumbi: Quilombo Resistance to Colonial Slavery." In *Oxford Research Encyclopedia of Latin American History* (online). Accessed October 16, 2020. http://oxfordre.com/latinamericanhistory.

Silva, Maria de Fátima de Sales, Rogério Chaves da Silva, and Severino Ramos Santana da Silva. "O Distrito de Zumbi." Unpublished manuscript. Last modified May 15, 2019.

Silva, Tyego Franklim da. "A ribeira da discórdia: Terras, homens e relações de poder na territorialização do Assu colonial (1680–1720)." Master's thesis, Universidade Federal do Rio Grande do Norte, 2015.

Silveira, Oliveira. "A evocação do 20 de Novembro: Origens." In *Mocambos de Palmares: Histórias e fontes (séc. XVI-XIX)*, edited by Flávio dos Santos Gomes, 149–54. Rio de Janeiro: 7Letras, 2010.

Silveira, Oliveira. "Vinte de Novembro: História e conteúdo." In *Educação e ações afirmativas: Entre a injustiça simbólica e a injustiça econômica*, edited by Petronilha Beatriz Gonçalves and Valter Roberto Silvério, 23–42. Brasília: Instituto Nacional de Estudos e Pesquisas, 2003.

Slenes, Robert W. "The Brazilian Internal Slave Trade, 1850–1888: Regional Economies, Slave Experience, and the Politics of a Peculiar Market." In *The Chattel Principle: Internal Slave Trades in the Americas*, edited by Walter Johnson, 291–324. New Haven, CT: Yale University Press, 2004.

Slenes, Robert W. "The Great Porpoise-Skull Strike: Central African Water Spirits and Slave Identity in Early-Nineteenth-Century Rio de Janeiro." In *Central Africans and Cultural Transformations in the American Diaspora*, edited by Linda M. Heyward, 183–208. Cambridge: Cambridge University Press, 2002.

Slenes, Robert W. "'*Malungu, ngoma vem!*' África coberta e descoberta do Brasil." *Revista* USP 12 (1992): 48–67.

Smallwood, Stephanie E. *Saltwater Slavery: A Middle Passage from Africa to American Diaspora*. Cambridge, MA: Harvard University Press, 2009.

Snyder, Terri L. *The Power to Die: Slavery and Suicide in British North America*. Chicago: University of Chicago Press, 2015.

Snyder, Terri L. "Suicide, Slavery, and Memory in North America." *Journal of American History* 97, no. 1 (June 2010): 39–62.

Soares, Mariza de Carvalho. "Descobrindo a Guiné no Brasil colonial." *Revista do Instituto Histórico e Geográfico Brasilero* 161, no. 407 (June 2000): 71–94.

Soares, Mariza de Carvalho. "Mina, Angola e Guiné: Nomes d'África no Rio de Janeiro setecentista." *Tempo* 3, no. 6 (December 1998): 71–94. Accessed June 21, 2023. https://app.uff.br/riuff/handle/1/157.

Soares, Mariza de Carvalho. "O Império de Santo Elesbão na cidade do Rio de Janeiro, no século XVIII." *Topoi*, March 2002, 59–83.

Sousa, Anicleide de. "Nas veredas negras do sertão: Histórias de vida familiar de escravizados no sertão brasileiro (Vila de Catolé do Rocha/Paraíba, 1836–1866)." Master's thesis, Universidade Federal da Paraíba, 2018.

Southey, Robert. *History of Brazil*. 3 vols. London: Longman, Hurst, Rees, and Orme [etc.], 1819. Accessed July 7, 2023. https://hdl.handle.net/2027/ucm.5311135710.

Souza, Aldinízia de Medeiros. *Liberdades possíveis em espaços periféricos: Escravidão e alforria no Termo da Vila de Arez (séculos XVIII e XIX)*. Natal: Editora da Universidade Federal de Rio Grande do Norte, 2018.

Souza, Daniela dos Santos. "Devoção e identidade: O culto de Nossa Senhora dos Remédios na Irmandade do Rosário de São João del-Rei—Séculos XXVIIIe XIX." Master's thesis, Universidade Federal de São João del-Rei, 2010.

Souza, Laura de Mello e. *The Devil and the Land of the Holy Cross: Witchcraft, Slavery, and Popular Religion in Colonial Brazil*. Translated by Diane Grosklaus Whitty. Austin: University of Texas Press, 2004.

Souza, Laura de Mello e. "Sorcery in Brazil: History and Historiography." In *Sorcery in the Black Atlantic*, edited by Luis Nicolau Parés and Roger Sansi, 41–54. Chicago: University of Chicago Press, 2011.

Souza, Laura de Mello e. "Violência e práticas culturais no cotidiano de uma expedição contra quilombolas: Minas Gerais, 1769." In *Liberdade por um fio: História dos quilombos no Brasil*, edited by João José Reis and Flávio dos Santos Gomes, 193–212. São Paulo: Companhia das Letras, 1996.

Souza, Thyago Ruzemberg Gonzaga de. "De Nina Rodrigues a Arthur Ramos: A reinvenção de Palmares nos 'estudos do negro.'" *Temporalidades: Revista de História* 5, no. 2 (May–August 2013): 161–80. Accessed June 26, 2023. https://periodicos.ufmg.br/index.php/temporalidades/article/view/5481.

Souza, Thyago Ruzemberg Gonzaga de. "A Troya Negra de Nina Rodrigues: O Quilombo dos Palmares, um espaço do racismo científico." *Quipus* 2, no. 2 (November 2013): 93–109.

Spacca (João Spacca de Oliveira), and Jorge Amado. *Jubiabá de Jorge Amado*. São Paulo: Companhia das Letras, 2009.

Spiegel, Gabrielle M. "The Task of the Historian." *American Historical Review* 114, no. 1 (February 2009): 1–15.

Staller, Jared. *Converging on Cannibals: Terrors of Slaving in Atlantic Africa, 1509–1670*. Athens: Ohio University Press, 2019.

Stam, Robert. *Tropical Multiculturalism: A Comparative History of Race in Brazilian Cinema and Culture*. Durham, NC: Duke University Press, 1997.

Stern, Steve J. "Paradigms of Conquest: History, Historiography, and Politics." In "The Colonial and Post-Colonial Experience: Five Centuries of Spanish and Portuguese America," edited by Tulio Halperín Donghi. Supplement, *Journal of Latin American Studies* 24 (1992): 1–34.

Stevens, Abel, and James Floy. "Southey's Letters." *National Magazine: Devoted to Literature, Art, and Religion*. December 1856. Sabin Americana: History of the Americas, 1500–1926. Accessed August 1, 2023. https://link.gale.com /apps/doc/CY0105133637/SABN?u=uiuc_uc&sid=bookmark-SABN&xid =1919a82a&pg=550.

Stewart, Whitney Nell. "White/white and/or the Absence of the Modifier." *Journal of the Early Republic* 43, no. 1 (Spring 2023): 101–8.

Stockwell, Robert P., and Donka Minkova. *English Words: History and Structure*. Cambridge: Cambridge University Press, 2001.

Studart, Guilherme (Barão de Studart), ed. "Dezenove documentos sobre os Palmares pertencentes á collecção Studart." *Revista do Instituto do Ceará* 20 (1906): 254–89.

Sutton, Elizabeth A. *Early Modern Dutch Prints of Africa*. Burlington, VT: Ashgate, 2012.

Sutton, Elizabeth A. "Possessing Brazil in Print, 1630–1654." *Journal of Historians of Netherlandish Art* 5, no. 1 (Winter 2013): 1–28.

Swartenbroeckx, Pierre. *Dictionnaire Kikongo et Kituba-Français*. Bandundu, Zaire: Centre d'Etudes Ethnologiques-Bandundu, 1973.

Sweeney, Shauna J. "Market Marronage: Fugitive Women and the Internal Marketing System in Jamaica, 1781–1834." *William and Mary Quarterly* 1, no. 2 (2009): 197–222.

Sweet, James H. "African Identity and Slave Resistance in the Portuguese Atlantic." In *The Atlantic World and Virginia, 1550–1624*, edited by Peter C. Mancall, 225–47. Williamsburg, VA: Omohundro Institute; Chapel Hill: University of North Carolina Press, 2007.

Sweet, James H. "Calundu: A Collective Biography of Spirit Possession in Bahia, 1618–Present." In *The Gray Zones of Medicine: Healers and History in Latin*

America, edited by Diego Armus and Pablo F. Gómez, 40–54. Pittsburgh: University of Pittsburgh Press, 2021.

Sweet, James H. *Domingos Álvares, African Healing, and the Intellectual History of the Atlantic World.* Chapel Hill: University of North Carolina Press, 2011.

Sweet, James H. "The Hidden Histories of African Lisbon." In *The Black Urban Atlantic in the Age of the Slave Trade*, edited by Jorge Cañizares-Esguerra, Matt D. Childs, and James Sidbury, 233–47. Philadelphia: University of Pennsylvania Press, 2013.

Sweet, James H. *Recreating Africa: Culture, Kinship, and Religion in the African-Portuguese World, 1441–1770.* Chapel Hill: University of North Carolina Press, 2003.

Sweet, James H. "Research Note: New Perspectives on Kongo in Revolutionary Haiti." *Americas* 74, no. 1 (January 2017): 83–97.

Tavares, João de Lyra. *Apontamentos para a historia territorial da Parahyba.* Edição Fac-Similar. 2 vols. João Pessoa[?]: Coleção Mossoroense, 1982.

Tenório Filho, Antonio. *Porto dos Touros: Freguesia e villa.* Natal: Sebo Vermelho, 2020.

Teyssier, Paul. *História da língua portuguesa.* Translated by Celso Cunha. Lisboa: Livraria Sá da Costa, 2001.

Thompson, Alvin O. *Flight to Freedom: African Runaways and Maroons in the Americas.* Kingston, Jamaica: University of the West Indies Press, 2006.

Thompson, Alvin O. "Gender and Marronage in the Caribbean." *Journal of Caribbean History* 39, no. 2 (2005): 262–89.

Thornton, John K. *Africa and Africans in the Making of the Atlantic World, 1400–1800.* 2nd ed. Cambridge: Cambridge University Press, 1998.

Thornton, John K. "The African Experience of the '20. and Odd Negroes' Arriving in Virginia in 1619." *William and Mary Quarterly* 55, no. 3 (July 1998): 421–34.

Thornton, John K. "Afro-Christian Syncretism in the Kingdom of Kongo." *Journal of African History* 54, no. 1 (2013): 53–77.

Thornton, John K. "Angola e as origens de Palmares." In *Mocambos de Palmares: Histórias e fontes (séc. XVI–XIX)*, edited by Flávio dos Santos Gomes, 48–60. Rio de Janeiro: 7Letras, 2010.

Thornton, John K. "Cannibals, Witches, and Slave Traders in the Atlantic World." *William and Mary Quarterly* 60, no. 2 (April 2003): 273–94.

Thornton, John K. "Central Africa in the Era of the Slave Trade." In *Slaves, Subjects, and Subversives: Blacks in Colonial Latin America*, edited by Jane Landers, 83–110. Albuquerque: University of New Mexico Press, 2006.

Thornton, John K. *A Cultural History of the Atlantic World, 1250–1820.* Cambridge: Cambridge University Press, 2012.

Thornton, John K. "Les États de l'Angola et la formation de Palmares (Brésil)." *Annales: Histoire, Sciences Sociales* 63, no. 4 (2008): 769–97.

Thornton, John K. *A History of West Central Africa to 1850.* Cambridge: Cambridge University Press, 2020.

Thornton, John K. *The Kingdom of Kongo: Civil War and Transition, 1641–1718.* Madison: University of Wisconsin Press, 1983.

Thornton, John K. *The Kongolese Saint Anthony: Dona Beatriz Kimpa Vita and the Antonian Movement, 1684–1706.* Cambridge: Cambridge University Press, 1998.

Thornton, John K. "New Light on Cavazzi's Seventeenth-Century Description of Kongo." *History in Africa* 6 (1979): 253–64.

Thornton, John K. "Religious and Ceremonial Life in the Kongo and Mbundu Areas, 1500–1700." In *Central Africans and Cultural Transformations in the American Diaspora,* edited by Linda M. Heyward, 70–90. Cambridge: Cambridge University Press, 2002.

Tibiriçá, Luiz Caldas. *Dicionário de topônimos brasileiros de origem tupi: Significação dos nomes geográficos de origem tupi.* São Paulo: Traço Editora, 1985.

Tibiriçá, Luiz Caldas. *Dicionário tupi português: Com esboço gramática de tupi antigo.* São Paulo: Traço Editora, 1984.

Torres, Luiz B. *A terra de Tilixi e Txiliá: Palmeira dos Índios dos séculos XVIII e XIX.* Maceió[?]: Serviços Gráficos de Alagoas, 1975.

Trouillot, Michel-Rolph. "Anthropology and the Savage Slot: The Poetics and Politics and Otherness." In *Recapturing Anthropology,* edited by Richard G. Fox, 17–44. Santa Fe, NM: School of American Research, 1991.

Uring, Nathaniel. *A History of the Voyages and Travels of Capt. Nathaniel Uring: With New Draughts of the Bay of Honduras and the Caribbee Islands: And Particularly of St. Lucia, and the Harbour of Petite Carenage, into Which Ships May Run in Bad Wheather, and Be Safe from All Winds and Storms: Very Useful for Masters of Ships That Use the Leeward Island Trade, or Jamaica.* London: Printed by W. Wilkins for J. Peele, 1726. Accessed May 30, 2023. http://link.gale.com/apps/doc/CY0102708023/SABN?sid=bookmark-SABN&xid=7dff9d25&pg=82.

Vainfas, Ronaldo. "Deus contra Palmares: Representações senhoriais e idéias jesuíticas." In *Liberdade por um fio: História dos quilombos no Brasil,* edited by João José Reis and Flávio dos Santos Gomes, 60–80. São Paulo: Companhia das Letras, 1996.

Vainfas, Ronaldo, ed. *Dicionário do Brasil colonial, 1500–1808.* Rio de Janeiro: Editora Objetiva, 2000.

Vallejos, Julio Pinto. "Slave Control and Slave Resistance in Colonial Minas Gerais, 1700–1750." *Journal of Latin American Studies* 17, no. 1 (May 1985): 1–34.

Vansina, Jan. "Ambaca Society and the Slave Trade, c. 1760–1845." *Journal of African History* 46, no. 1 (2005): 1–27.

Vansina, Jan. "The Foundation of the Kingdom of Kasanje." *Journal of African History* 4, no. 3 (1963): 355–74.

Vansina, Jan. "The History of God among the Kuba." *Africa: Rivista trimestrale di studi e documentazione dell'Instituto italiano por l'Africa e l'Oriente* 38, no. 1 (March 1983): 17–40.

Vansina, Jan. *How Societies Are Born: Governance in West Central Africa before 1600.* Charlottesville: University of Virginia Press, 2004.

Vansina, Jan. "On Ravenstein's Edition of Battell's Adventures in Angola and Loango." *History in Africa* 34 (2007): 321–47.

Vansina, Jan. *Paths in the Rainforests: Toward a History of Political Tradition in Equatorial Africa.* Madison: University of Wisconsin Press, 1990.

Vansina, Jan. "Portuguese vs. Kimbundu: Language Use in the Colony of Angola (1575–c. 1845)." *Académie Royale des Sciences d'Outre-Mer* 3 (2001): 267–81.

Vansina, Jan. "Quilombos on São Tomé, or in Search of Original Sources." *History in Africa: A Journal of Method* 23 (1996): 453–59.

Varnhagen, Francisco Adolfo de (Visconde de Porto Seguro). *Historia geral do Brazil: Antes de sua separação e independencia de Portugal.* 2 vols. 2nd ed. Rio de Janeiro: E. and H. Laemmert, 1877. Accessed June 2, 2023. https://archive.org/details/historia-geral-do-brazil-antes-da-sua-separacao-e-independencia-de-portugal-vol-2/page/786/mode/2up.

Vicente, Pe. Antonio. "Diccionario historico, geographico e ethnographico do Brasil: Touros (respostas ao questionario de historia)." *Revista do Instituto Histórico e Geográfico do Rio Grande do Norte* 18–19 (1920–21): 91–100.

Vidal, Ademar. *Guia da Paraíba: Roteiro das condições históricas, econômicas, geográficas e sociais do estado.* Rio de Janeiro: Indústria do Livro, 1943.

Vidal, Ademar. *Lendas e superstições: Contos populares brasileiros.* 2nd ed. Rio de Janeiro: Emprêsa Gráfica O Cruzeiro, 1950.

Vidal, Ademar. "Tres seculos de escravidão na Parahyba." In *Estudos afro-brasileiros: Trabalhos apresentados ao 1º Congresso Afro-Brasileiro reunido no Recife em 1934,* 105–52. Rio de Janeiro: Ariel, 1935.

Vidal Filho, F. "Nossa capital em 1850." *Revista do Instituto Histórico e Geográfico Parahybano* 13 (1958): 133–38.

Vieira, Geyza Kelly Alves. "Entre perdas, feitos e barganhas: A elite indígena na capitania de Pernambuco, 1669–1732." In *A presença indígena no Nordeste: Processoes de territorialização, modos de reconhecimento e regimes de memória,* ed. João Pacheco Oliveira Filho, 69–90. Rio de Janeiro: Contra Capa, 2011.

Vieira-Martinez, Carolyn E. "Building Kimbundu: Language Community Reconsidered in West Central Africa, c. 1500–1750." PhD diss., University of California, Los Angeles, 2006.

Vieyra, Antonio. *A Dictionary of the Portuguese and English Languages.* 2 vols. London: J. Nourse, 1773. Accessed July 6, 2023. https://books.google.com/books?id=MTZAAAAAYAAJ.

Vinson, Ben, III. *Bearing Arms for His Majesty: The Free-Colored Militia in Colonial Mexico.* Stanford, CA: Stanford University Press, 2001.

Vinson, Ben, III. "Introduction: African (Black) Diaspora History, Latin American History." *Americas* 63, no. 1 (2006): 1–18.

Viotti, Ana Carolina de Carvalho. "As proposições de Antonio de Saldanha da Gama para a melhoria do tráfico de escravos 'Por questões humanitárias e econômicas', Rio de Janeiro, 1810." *História, Ciências, Saúde-Manguinhos* 23, no. 4 (December 2016): 1169–89.

Vital de Oliveira, M. A. (Manuel Antonio). *Roteiro da costa do Brasil do Rio Mossoro ao Rio de S. Francisco do Norte*. Rio de Janeiro: Perseverança, 1864. http://archive.org/details/roteirodacostadooovita.

Vogt, Carlos, and Peter Fry. *Cafundó: A África no Brasil, linguagem e sociedade*. São Paulo: Companhia das Letras, 1996.

Wadsworth, James E. "In the Name of the Inquisition: The Portuguese Inquisition and Delegated Authority in Colonial Pernambuco, Brazil." *Americas* 61, no. 1 (July 2004): 19–54.

Wadsworth, James E. "Jurema and Batuque: Indians, Africans, and the Inquisition in Colonial Northeastern Brazil." *History of Religions* 46, no. 2 (November 2006): 140–62.

Warner-Lewis, Maureen. "The African Diaspora and Language: Movement, Borrowing, and Return." In *Tracing Language Movement in Africa*, ed. Ericka A. Albaugh and Kathryn Michelle de Luna, 321–41. New York: Oxford University Press, 2018.

Watkins, Case. *Palm Oil Diaspora: Afro-Brazilian Landscapes and Economies of Bahia's Dendê Coast*. New York: Cambridge University Press, 2021. Kindle edition.

Weinstein, Barbara. *The Color of Modernity: São Paulo and the Making of Race and Nation in Brazil*. Durham, NC: Duke University Press, 2015.

Wetzels, Leo, Sergio Menuzzi, and João Costa, eds. *The Handbook of Portuguese Linguistics*. Blackwell Handbooks in Linguistics. Malden, MA: Wiley-Blackwell, 2016.

Wheat, David. *Atlantic Africa and the Spanish Caribbean, 1570–1640*. Chapel Hill: University of North Carolina Press, 2015.

Wheat, David. "Brasil en el Tráfico de Esclavos Havia Las Antillas, Venezuela y Cartagena de Indias, Siglos XVI–XVII." In *Congresso Latinoamericano de História Económica*. Lima, 2022.

White, Luise. *Speaking with Vampires: Rumor and History in Colonial Africa*. Berkeley: University of California Press, 2000.

Whitehead, Neil Lancelot. "Carib Ethnic Soldiering in Venezuela, the Guianas, and the Antilles, 1492–1820." *Ethnohistory* 37, no. 4 (Autumn 1990): 357–85.

Williamson, Kay, Roger Blench, Bernd Heine, and Derek Nurse. "Niger-Congo." In *African Languages: An Introduction*, ed. Bernd Heine and Derek Nurse, 11–42. Cambridge: Cambridge University Press, 2000.

Wright, Willie Jamaal. "The Morphology of Marronage." *Annals of the American Association of Geographers* 110, no. 4 (2020): 1134–49.

Zandvliet, Kees. "Mapping the Dutch World Overseas in the Seventeenth Century." In *Cartography in the European Renaissance*, vol. 3, part II, ed. David Woodward, 1433–61. Chicago: University of Chicago Press, 2007.

Zeleza, Paul Tiyambe. "Rewriting the African Diaspora: Beyond the Black Atlantic." *African Affairs* 104, no. 414 (January 2005): 35–68.

Zwartjes, Otto. *Portuguese Missionary Grammars in Asia, Africa and Brazil, 1550–1800*. Amsterdam: John Benjamins, 2011.

INDEX

abandoned settlements, 26, 203–4; burning of, 318n14; mythical absence and, 226–27; Tapera d'Angola and, 38–40

Abreu, João Capistrano de, 26–27

Aca Inene Fort, 43

Acioli, Zenóbio, 160–61

Afogados, 207–10

Afonso I (King), 104

Africa: Afro-Latin American Studies, language, and, 15–20; Christianity and, 247–49, 256–57; language in, 15–20, 86–103; map of African coast, xxix; prisoners in, 45. *See also* West Central Africa; *specific locations*

African diaspora, 13–14, 215, 269, 279; Butler on, 319n38; engenhos and, 287; language and, 16–20; memoryscapes and, 287–88; toponyms and, 228

Africanist comparative historical linguistics, 16–20, 299

Afro-Latin American Studies, 15–20

afterlives, 4, 11, 210–11, 261

agriculture, 56–58, 175–76, 186; environment and, 32–34. *See also* engenhos

Alagoa Grande, 221–22

"Alagoan Legend," 255–56

Alagoas, 56, 156, 176–78; Indigenous uprisings and, 179–84; place and, 197–98

aldeias, 177–80, 184–86, 354n49

Alencar, José de, 15, 264

Alencastro, Luiz Felipe de, 17, 317n55

Almeida, Joaquim de, 114

Almeida, Marcos Abreu Leitão de, 265, 330n21, 331n23

Almeida, Pedro de, 59, 136; Early Wars and, 42–45; peace treaty and, 41, 45–48; return to Portugal, 46; successor to, 45–46

Almodôvar genealogy forum, 325n36

Amado, Jorge, 290–91

Amaro, 46, 48

Amas (Black women caregivers), 85–86, 88, 93, 106, 240, 244–45, 289, 292

Ambaca, 116–17

ambaquistas, 247

ancestors, 111–12, 126, 220–21; family lineages and, 230–32. *See also* family; spirits

Anderson, Robert, 37

Andrade, Gaspar de, 126

Angoij, 92–93

Angola, 5; Colombia and, 104–5; Dutch occupation of, 27–28; language in, 87, 91–93, 98–99; "Pagan Rites from Angola," 116; Saint Benedict and, 122–23, 268–69; slavery and, 29; Tapera d'Angola, 38–40, 282, 284

Angola janga, 37–40

Angolan wave, 29

Apodi River, 228

Ararobá, 134

archives, 4–6, 136; archival silence and, 191–92; counter-archives, 191; historical narratives and, 272–79; language and, 16; on Rio Grande do Norte, 235–36; Zumbi's death and, 273–78

Arte da lingua de Angola (Dias, P.), 87–88

Article 68, 3, 292

Aztec empire, 24

calhambolas, 35, 321n68

calundu, 113, 115–16, 121, 230

Camarão, Dom Antônio Domingos, 177–78

Camarão, Dom Antônio Filipe, 66, 351n60

Camargo, Sérgio, 293

Camelo, Belchior Álvares, 156, 182–83

Camelo clan, 182–83

Camilio, Bento Surrel, 37, 155

Campos de Garanhuns, 134, 161

Camuanga, 73–76, 135, 157

Candido, Mariana, 315n20, 333n65

Candomblé, 123–24, 255, 280, 291, 294, 371n70

Cannecatim (monk), 249–50

cannibalism, 100, 112

Capelo, Hermenegildo, 243–50, 257–58, 369n29

Capibaribe River, 208

caregivers, 85

Cariri, 201–2, 216, 320n50

Carnaval, 268

Carneiro, Domingos Rodrigues, 64–67, 77, 240–41

Carneiro, Edison, 11, 240, 261, 277, 318n14

Carrilho, Fernão: conquests of, 43–45, 49–50, 59, 76, 113–14, 137; "cruel war" and, 49–50, 52; Gan(g)a Zumba and, 43–44; in Porto Calvo, 44; rebel Blacks and, 43, 52; spirits and, 113–14

Carvalho, Domingos João de, 135, 157–58

Carvalho, Marcus J. M. de, 12, 32, 36

Cascudo, Luís da Câmara, 227–29, 232, 252–54, 257–59

Casimir, Jean, 18

castration, 160

Castro, Aires de Sousa de, 45–48, 91–92, 124

Castro, Bras de Sousa, 151

Castro, Caetano de Melo de, 54, 68–69, 72, 142, 159–60, 280; spiritual terror and, 84

Castro, Yeda Pessoa de, 242

Castro Ganasona, Dom Pedro de Sousa, 151

Catholicism, 125; Catholic baptisms, 46, 151, 322n109; in Cidade da Parahyba, 223

Catucá, 210

Catumbi, 267

Cavalcanti, Alfredo Leite, 202–3

Cavignac, Julie, 271–76

Ceará-Mirim, 228

Chapman, Charles E., 240

Chatelain, Héli, 250

children, 10, 85, 93, 126, 134–35; infanticide and, 100; kidnapping of, 144–49. See also filhos dos Palmares

Christianity, 337n119; Africa and, 247–49, 256–57; Christian symbols, 91, 245–47; in mocambos, 24; witchcraft and, 103–4

Cidade Alta (in Cidade da Parahyba), 223

Cidade Baixa (in Cidade da Parahyba), 223

Cidade da Parahyba, 215, 222–26. See also João Pessoa

Cocal, 184–85

Colombia, 104–5

Comissão História Zumbi (Zumbi History Commission), 217, 270

comparative historical linguistics: Africanist, 16–20, 299; guideposts and importance of further inquiry of, 299–300; key terms, symbols, tools, and concepts of, 301–2; linguistic labels and, 86–93; multiple meanings in, 34–37; "orthographic error" and, 84–86, 105–6; reading linguistic "fossils" and, 94–98; resources, 303–6; term meanings and, 34–37; Z/zumbi case study and, 302–3; Z/zumbi meaning and, 242–55

conquest: by Carneiro, D. R., 64–67; by Carrilho, 43–45, 49–50, 59, 76, 113–14, 137; chronology of Early Wars and, 40–50; famous conquerors and, 42–43; Indigenous uprising and, 50–53; by Inojosa, 60–63, 67; by Jorge Velho, 37, 51, 59, 67–71, 76, 133–34, 144–48, 215–16; by Lopes Galvão, M., 55–60, 66–67, 77–79, 114; rumors about, 329n114; Serra da Barriga and, 54, 67–74; war and, 6–9, 40–53, 262–63, 271–79

Conselho Ultramarino (Portuguese Overseas Council), 28, 42, 50, 55, 57–60, 64–65, 71, 73, 75, 138, 147–48, 156, 160, 170, 341n77; council of Penedo and, 170–72

Convento São Francisco, 295–96

Correa, Francisca and partner "Manuel," 120–25

Correia, Luís, 263

cosmology of flight, 109–12

Printed and bound by CPI Group (UK) Ltd, Croydon, CR0 4YY

21/10/2024

14577348-0001